Like a Song, Like a Dream

LIKE A SONG,
LIKE A DREAM

A Soviet Girl's Quest for Freedom

Alla Rusinek

With an afterword by Ezra Rusinek

Charles Scribner's Sons   New York

Acknowledgments

I would like to acknowledge the help of Jesse Z. Lurie who played such an important part in the writing of this book; of Norbert Slepyan, my editor for his continual guidance; and of my father-in-law, E. Rusinek, for his valuable contributions.

46413

1

According to my papers, on the 28th of May 1949, I was born in Moscow.

My mother did not know the date of her birth, but she used to say that she remembered she had been born in winter. If I had not known my birthdate, I probably would have established it by means of a similar memory. When I was still small enough to be carried on my father's shoulders, I was taken to Red Square. I remember riding my father above an endless crowd of people, shouting, singing, laughing happily, carrying paper flowers and portraits. And far away on the brown marble of Lenin's mausoleum, there stood the man in the portraits, waving his right hand to the crowd. In his usual military uniform and thick moustache, Stalin could not be mistaken. So I could always say that I was happy enough to be born in time to see Stalin alive.

When we think about our childhood, it comes to us in episodes that have found their places deep in our memory. They quietly sleep there in nests until some train of thought disturbs them and they awake. And pictures, old family pictures, show you a child who lived her own life, but who can give you through memories we all share in common some of her impressions.

I was a plump child with an extraordinarily big, bald head and unbelievably large cheeks, as if I kept something in store for a rainy day. My mother and aunts later told me in secret that I was a very ugly child and that they didn't like to show me in public. It was no secret to me though. My older sister Myra, with her wonderful curly hair and beautiful face, was the "film star" in the family, and next to her I looked even more ugly.

Yet I did not entirely accept the world's verdict of me. I thought everybody was wicked, and I constantly bore a grudge against them. Why didn't they say anything about my big dark eyes? I liked my eyes and, since no one else did, I admired them myself.

When I was four years old, I dreamt that all our relations came to visit us. They were beautifully dressed and noisy. Gathering around my sister, they praised her with exclamations of delight. Everyone forgot about me, and I sat under the bed next to a night pot, a huge lump in my throat. One of my aunts noticed me and took me in her arms, smiling mockingly, as though understanding my feelings. The lump melted and I began to cry. I awoke from the dream with a feeling of wetness all around and under me. Mother looked at me with surprise and smiled knowingly.

That was a time of short silk dresses and small straw hats, and my father's ambition was to dress his daughters in silk and velvet. I still remember two of those dresses — my sister's, white with green flowers, and mine, dark brown with free designs in yellow. Mother never got rid of old clothes, and we could always find neatly tied in bundles our baby caps or mama's jacket, red with white spots, which she wore when she was pregnant. Much later, I would take that jacket with me to a new world.

My sister was eight and I was six when something strange happened. We were then going to the kindergarten. Mother and father were both working and had their own life of adult people which we knew nothing about. We couldn't follow their talks, but one day we just noticed that they had begun to shout at each other more often. The air in our room suddenly grew stuffy, the darkness more gloomy. And then everything changed. I remember mother running back and forth holding both of us by the hand.

There was a place in Moscow which used to be a symbol of our short happy childhood. It was a port on the Moscow River where father worked as an accountant on a ship. He often took us with him on journeys in summer, and we felt as though we were queens on that ship that looked so rich with its carved wooden staircases, mirrors, and carpets.

The port had a beautiful park with rows of bushes and trees and bright flowers. A huge stone woman, a happy and strong

Soviet woman with a small model of a ship in her hands, welcomed us at the entrance. Soviet working people liked to come to this park on Sundays to renew their feelings of richness and strength which had been weakened by exhausting work.

One day that summer of 1955—I was then six—mother took both of us there, but again it was all different. She was running angrily, deeply unhappy. Frightened, we tried to keep up with her. But father's ship had already left. It would come back in a month, but father would never return to our home, to our dark room with the big wardrobe that divided it into two parts, one for children and the other for parents. There was a young woman on his ship, who worked in the barber shop. She was much younger and prettier than my mother, and my father, who was handsome and sexy, didn't need anything else. He was fifty-four years old and his new—third—wife was twenty-four.

For many years I couldn't understand what mother and father had found in common with each other that had caused them to marry. The answer came to me much later when I myself understood that love is too wicked to give people an ability to really understand each other. "Love is so cruel that you can fall in love with a goat," a Russian proverb says. Neither of them was a goat, yet love played a cruel trick on them.

❖   ❖   ❖

The year 1913 was one of prosperity for the great Russian Empire. The shops and marketplaces were full of goods. The country was rich. But poor people everywhere are always poor. If you don't have money, you can only stand aside and watch. Sometimes it's worthwhile to run away from poverty.

Abram, a house painter from Dvinsk, a small Latvian town, decided to move. *"Meshane makom, meshane mazel"*—"Change of place, change of luck," Jews say.

Poverty haunted this quiet, pious man and his family. He couldn't look into his wife's eyes. When he had proposed to her eight years before, he had brought her parents from Germany to Dvinsk to show them his house full of good furniture. Only then did they give consent to the marriage. After the wedding, when the parents left for Germany, the furniture also left. Abram had borrowed it from his neighbor. The young bride wept for three days, and Abram, trying to console her, promised to work hard and to buy her even better furniture.

Eight years passed and things got worse. They already had four children. One day Abram said to his wife, "Listen to me, Sheinele, a good man gave me a piece of good advice. It is easier to live in Russia. Life is cheaper there. There is a good town of Vologda there. Good Jews also live there and they are rich and they need painters."

Sheina shrugged her shoulders and they moved.

Abram moved to save his children from hunger, but he himself was doomed to die of starvation. Thirty years later, after Leningrad had been blockaded for a year by the Germans, he died. His son took his skeleton covered with skin to the place where thousands were being buried, and later could not even find the place.

Still, the children of Abram Glazman were not among the Jews of Dvinsk, Riga, Germany, and Holland—among tens of thousands of them—who were shot and burned in Rumbula, the forest near Riga. They were not there because "a good man gave a piece of good advice" to Abram Glazman: move.

"And Abram took his wife Sarah and they went forth to go into the land of Canaan, and into the land of Canaan they came," says the Bible. But. . . .

"Out of the frying pan into the fire," the Russian saying goes. Soon after coming to Vologda, Sheina died of consumption, slowly and quietly, without complaint. Abram stopped working and did nothing but pray. His four children—Moishe, Musja, Pesja, and Basja—had to earn their living and feed their pious father. One by one, their mother's beautiful German dresses disappeared into the bazaar. Together with them, the spirit of a proud and beautiful woman began to sift out of the house. The two oldest sisters, Musja and Pesja, went to the bazaar to sell *papirossen.** Musja, the eldest, with long figure and long face, adjusted to the new profession very quickly. Pesja, a short girl with a round figure and a mass of curly hair, stood near her

---

* Cigarettes.

quietly, looking down. She was the only one in the family to inherit Sheina's proud spirit and it prevented her from doing the low business of selling. In the evening they both went to the house of rich relatives to get their portion of two hot potatoes for dinner.

One day, when they were as usual selling their papirossen, a strict man in a military uniform came up to them and told them to leave the bazaar and never come back. It was the Great October Revolution of 1917, which shook the world and forbade Musja and Pesja to sell *papirossen* in the bazaar. All private business was forbidden—and praying also. Abram had to work. His children went to school.

Well, it was a good thing to study. Abram didn't have anything against it. Musja still did everything about the house. Moishe was also working. Two of the girls were carried away by their studies. Pesja couldn't tear herself from books, and whenever Musja asked her to help with the housework, Pesja began to cry. Pesja became very quiet and reserved. Nobody could understand her new world, nobody could enter it.

"But *kinderlach*," Abram would say, "today is Shabbat, you can't go to school. Our God blessed Shabbat, the seventh day. You are Jews and have to keep it. I forbid you to go to school today."

Next Saturday the children left the house as if to go for a walk. The books had already been hidden in the yard under the fence and covered with straw. Soon they were at school. It didn't take long after this incident for Moishe to become Michail; for Musja, Maria; Pesja, Polina; and Basja, Berta.

And it was so that one day Polina took a big basket, put in it her dress, a warm scarf, two sheets and some money, and left for the railway station on her way to the new world. She went to Moscow.

2

Father was gone and everything changed in our family. In fact, there was no family any more. I loved my father more than my mother, although he was very strict and I was often afraid of him. But sometimes he was very affectionate. I loved his smell and his unshaven cheeks when he used to take me on his lap in the evenings (many, many years later, when I touched unshaven cheeks which were not those of my father, I remembered him).

I knew that he was disappointed in me. He had only wanted a second baby in the hope of having a son, but I turned out to be a girl and he could not even look at me for some time. I knew this, but hoped by my strong attachment to win his love, and had nearly achieved it when he left.

I believed that he would come back some time. And he did. I was not yet seven then and Myra was eight. She had already finished the first year of school and was learning to play the violin. I didn't do anything but attend a kindergarten.

One day our kindergarten group went out for a walk. It was March and rather cold. I was dressed in very shabby shoes and an old coat which was tight on me. Everything had changed since father had gone.

We were walking in pairs when I noticed a man staring at me. He was very dark: his clothes, hair, sad eyes, and unshaven cheeks, all dark. His face seemed so familiar to me that I stopped. But it was several minutes before I realized that this was my father.

"Father!" I screamed and rushed to him crying. I embraced his legs and buried my face in his coat. He stood, stroking my head.

"You didn't recognize me, did you?" I cried and thought that his face had changed very much. Only later I learned that the right side of his face was paralyzed. Crying, but happy with his coming, I felt that I loved him more than ever. I think it was because I began to feel sorry for him, though without understanding why.

Father had come to Moscow to arrange his affairs and was leaving soon for Krasnodar, a small town near the Black Sea, where he lived with his young wife. He wanted to take both of us with him to spend spring and summer at the sea, but as Myra had to study I went alone without feeling much sorrow about leaving everything and everyone behind. I was with my father and very happy. When the summer was over, I flatly refused to go back. I don't remember the reaction of the two sides, but somehow I stayed.

I spent my first year at school with the other children of the town, typical village children who were often dull. I felt far ahead of them and none of them seemed to challenge me. I had come from "the capital." I was elected monitor of the class and was the teacher's favorite. That was when my vanity triumphed. I was brilliant and snobbish, generously helpful and strict with my classmates. They didn't object, but dully accepted me. Russian village people are often like that. Soon I completely forgot my life in the capital, adopted my classmates' village language, and became suntanned and skinny—in other words, provincial.

We lived in a big wooden house with a garden surrounded by a wooden fence. We had ducklings, chickens, and a dog. In the summer I spent most of the day in the yard. My father and his wife, Marina, whom I gradually began to call "mama," were at work or went together to the sea. I was left alone and walked around our garden or stood at the gate looking at the street. But I was not bored. It was hot and dusty in summer. Our street, deeply rutted from the carriage wheels and the horses' legs, was covered with thick layers of gray, warm dust. I buried my feet in it or drew lines with a wet finger on my dirty naked body. I could be happy alone for many hours, as I had so many things to think about. I thought and patiently waited for my father.

One day they didn't come back for a long time and I began to feel terribly hungry. There was nothing in the house that I could eat, so I wandered about the yard thinking about my hun-

ger and suffering from it. Suddenly, while passing our dog, I
noticed a dry slice of brown bread in the dust. My mouth began
to water. I squatted and stared at it. It looked very good, but
could I take bread from a dog? Of course, she wouldn't eat it. It
was too dry. But it is just not good taste to take food from a dog.
And then, the bread was dirty. But I could shake it well and the
dust would come off. But could I take it if it was already lying in
the dust near a dog?

I squatted and thought for a long time. At last I took the
bread. When my father and Marina returned, I didn't say a word.
I couldn't tell my father about my degradation. I loved him and
wanted to be loved. In fact, I was jealous, but I didn't show it,
realizing that Marina had more right to him than I had. So I
loved him silently. Sometimes he asked me to scratch his back
when it itched. I sat behind his pale back with its tiny freckles
and thought it was not beautiful or manlike. And to ask a girl to
scratch your back was also not in good taste. My fingers ached
from the effort, but my father was rarely satisfied. Each time, I
finished this ceremony exhausted and offended deep within
me.

However, this didn't happen often and didn't make me love
my father less—or be less proud of him. He was a big, important
man, an accountant on a sovkhoz (Soviet collective farm). And
he often told me that an accountant was more important than the
director. I didn't doubt him and proudly told my classmates this
and made them believe it.

*   *   *

My father came from a very well-to-do family of Ashkenazic
Jews who had lived in Turkmenia, in the little Oriental town of
Tchardjow. Oh, these eternally wandering Jews! How did they
find their way there? Sephardic or Bokharan Jews living in
Turkmenia came from the south. But what brought families of
Eastern European Ashkenazic Jews to this distant and hot corner
of the Russian Empire?

The family legend is that one of the great-grandfathers,
Milchen by name, was drafted into the Czarist Army. According
to the law of 1827 issued by Czar Nicholas I, Jewish boys of

twelve were to be taken into the army for twenty-five years. This was one of the attempts of the Czars to convert Jews to Christianity by force. The first six years of this service were called "cantonment," and the soldiers were called "cantonists." My paternal great-grandfather was a cantonist.

The regiments of the Russian Army were based in Central Asia and, when the time of their service was over, the soldiers rarely went back to the places from which they were taken as little boys and where they were already forgotten. They preferred to remain in warm Turkmenia. With his name changed to Milkin (his Russian fellow soldiers couldn't pronounce Milchen), my great-grandfather, still true to the Jewish religion in his soul (as were most of these cantonists), settled in Tchardjow.

The next generation, my father's parents, were the owners of several hatshops and belonged to the upper middle class of the Jewish community in Turkmenia. Their four beautiful children, Rosa, Tsal, Esther, and Michael, enjoyed a happy and carefree childhood until. . . .

Again the Great October Socialist Revolution. . . . But who then cared about all these words. It was just a big disorder. No more shops, no hats, no family. Just as on a sinking ship everyone seizes his life preserver and the indifferent ocean carries each in a different direction, families were broken and dispersed.

And Tsalik, a handsome, heedless boy, suddenly found himself in the Red Army and in exile on a terrible island, Solovki, in the White Sea. He never meant to be bad and always thought only about women and an easy life. His parents had hoped to marry him into a well-to-do family and to give him half the business, to keep him within bounds.

Then everything was changed. In exile he married a Russian woman who couldn't bear him children. One day they found a baby girl crying on their porch and adopted her. With the passing years, she began to look more and more like Tsalik.

In the thirties they went to live in Moscow. Tsalik became an accountant. He loved to count money, dreaming that one day he would count his own capital. But then he was also artistic, loved music, and played the violin. He went through World War

II in the ranks of the millions of soldiers, was wounded, and came back like other millions, exhausted, penniless, ragged. Vague ambitions still lived in his tired mind and he was ready to begin again.

He worked as an accountant in a public dining room and there he met Polina. She was obviously unmarried, for she used to come there to have dinner every day. She was a vivid, busy woman far into her thirties. But there was something about her that attracted Tsalik. He began to talk to her. Polina was an important person. She worked as a Manager of the buildings of a whole district, and was very active in the Party. She enjoyed the respect and attention of all around her. Before the war she had been a teacher of history, but when the war broke out the Party had sent her to this job and she always accepted the place where the Party needed her. Dark-haired, with a mass of Jewish curls and green eyes, she was good-looking, but beginning to fade. She had never married. She was too busy.

There was something in this woman that Tsalik needed. Her strength, her activity, practical mind, contacts. He was definitely attracted to her; perhaps he even loved her. And her name was a touchstone. His mother had been Polina, his first wife had been Polina, and now this woman. . . .

Polina fell in love with the good-looking, sexy, ambitious, and definitely irresponsible man. She loved him with the love of an aging, busy woman; her whole being demanded him. She thought she could find a place for him in her hectic life and could even have children with him. At any rate, she wouldn't be lonely at night.

She brought him to her room and they began to live together. He never went back to his first family. His first wife did not give him a divorce, so he and Polina lived together unmarried. When their first daughter was born, they called her Miriam. Polina was against this symbol of nationalism, but he insisted. The choice of the second daughter's name then belonged to Polina and she called her a then popular Russian name—Alla.

The birth of the second child made the first wife surrender.

She divorced Tsalik and even came to his home to help with the babies, bringing with her their adopted first daughter.

On the 17th of June 1949, three weeks after the birth of their second daughter, Polina and Tsalik married; she was thirty-nine, he forty-eight. He felt young, and was filled with ambitious ideas. Of course, he had not thought of having two daughters, but he decided to make the best of it. "Polina," he used to say, "I could leave you, but I shall never leave my two daughters. They will be the happiest of children and I shall dress them in silk and velvet."

He left his job in the dining room and went to the north with a geological expedition because in the north the same professions received higher pay. He planned to stay there two years to make money, but within a year Polina had difficulty saving him from prison, for he was already in deep trouble for some illegal transaction.

When he came back home, she found in his pocket a letter from a Siberian woman who begged him to come back to her and their newborn daughter.

He was impossible, she thought. Such an old man! But she was mistaken. He was not old even in 1955 when, already fifty-four, he left her with two daughters and a pair of silk and velvet dresses for them.

A new daughter was soon born to him and his third wife. Only his tragic death stopped this hard and unhappy race after youth, women, and an easy life.

*   *   *

I had been living with my father and his wife for a year and a half when I began to notice some strange attention constantly being paid to me. My mother's sister came to our small town with presents for me and spent several fruitless hours with me, trying to get me to go back with her. I couldn't even understand her and thought the idea crazy.

After she left, father was constantly being called to some office or other and, by his sad and tired look, I understood that again it concerned me. Several times he knelt beside me and said,

"Maybe it would be better for you to go to your mother, dear. You will live in the capital. You will learn to play the piano." I was sure father himself didn't think this way, but wanted to give me a free choice. I appreciated this and hastened to assure him of my love and loyalty. He would stand up with a deep sigh, even sadder. Poor womanish heart! How could I understand then that if a man gives you a free choice, he already wants you to leave deep in his heart? Even when older, how often do we give credit to men for being gentlemen when they have already betrayed us.

Soon I myself was called to the mysterious place. It turned out to be a local court which was looking into the conditions of my life, my development, and the attitude toward me in the family. Mother was trying to get me back and had appealed to the Supreme Court which transferred the case to the local authorities. It proved to be a long and complicated process.

I made a very bad impression on the court. They wondered at the amount of hatred in the child's eyes and voice. I hated all of them and often didn't answer their questions, fearing traps. One thing I knew and said for sure: "I don't want to go back there." The judges tried to be kind and reassuring to me, an apparently downtrodden, underdeveloped child, but their kindness soon turned me to hysterics during the examination and I was left alone "lest a psychiatric trauma be caused to the child," so the documents read.

Yet the process continued and, like a loyal and silent dog, I used to wait for my father to come out of the court building. When he came out, I usually began to cry.

"Why are you crying, Alla?"

"I am sorry for you."

"Why? Nobody does me any harm, you silly girl. They are all polite and fair."

I didn't answer and continued to cry as we went slowly home, he holding me by the hand. I couldn't explain to him that I hated anybody humiliating him and this process was just that. I didn't want anyone asking him provocative questions. And I was sure that only I by my loyalty and love to him supported him at this difficult moment. But I kept these thoughts to myself, being afraid he would not understand and would treat me like a small child.

The verdict was reached. I learned about it only at the moment of its execution.

*   *   *

On a rainy day—or maybe it was a sunny day, but it seemed to me gray and threatening—I sat in the kitchen at a wooden table, looking at the plate before me. There was a feeling of alarm in me. I couldn't understand why I suddenly found myself alone in the house, while everybody went outside. To exorcise the fear which I could not explain, I swung my legs back and forth under the table, backward and forward, quicker, quicker, quicker. . . . Suddenly the door opened and my mother rushed into the room. She lifted me from the stool, crying, "My daughter!" and, carrying me under her arm, rushed back to the yard. I understood immediately that I was being taken away by force. I began screaming for help in a loud voice. My sister Myra followed behind us holding me by my feet. I bit my mother on her arm as hard as I could, but she didn't notice it until much later. Everybody was standing in the street—father, Marina, and, of course, the neighbors. All stood like statues, not moving and silent. A militiaman stood near my father. A truck was waiting in the street and in seconds I found myself pushed into it. Then, as if catching on at the last moment, everybody began to shout.

"My God, the child doesn't want to go to her mother," a woman in an apron with her arms crossed on her breast exclaimed.

"Alochka! We'll soon be together again!" father cried. The motor began to rattle, the truck shook and then moved forward, leaving everything and everybody behind. I sobbed and screamed for hours. "Papa will die without me!" I repeated hundreds of times, between sobs. I was sure he would not be able to live through our parting. I would not be able to help and comfort him. He would die of sorrow. I was so tortured at my helplessness that I couldn't stop crying. Finally, tired and exhausted, I fell asleep and awoke to find myself far away from my home and father.

Mother took us, reunited sisters, to the Black Sea where I enjoyed myself as much as I could, still hoping and thinking I would return to my father. Little by little, I began to appreciate the advantages of my new life, feeling clean and nourished, being taken care of and noticed by somebody.

When we returned to Moscow, I was carried away by the wonders of the life in the capital—a bathroom, a toilet in the flat, a telephone, and the whole big city seen out of the window. Mother immediately enrolled me in the musical school, which I left after two years of suffering. The two years in the village had passed not without their consequences. It was difficult for me to adapt. Yet in the elementary school I was an excellent pupil. After two short postcards, I stopped writing to my father and soon forgot him.

When he came to Moscow a year later, I hardly recognized him, avoided his eyes, and was terribly confused when he reminded me of my promise to come back to him. He held me by the elbows between his knees and I turned aside. I felt myself a traitor, but was powerless. I couldn't bear any more changes in my life. I wanted to be left alone and felt relieved when father left.

A year later in May of 1960, we learned that he had been killed by a drunken Georgian on the holiday of the 1st of May. We were excited and frightened for one day, but he had not been part of our lives and we didn't feel sorrow when he died. "A dog deserves a dog's death," mother commented and the incident seemed closed, at least for us.

But mother became more reserved and silent. She began to complain of inner sorrow and often cried, which we couldn't stand, for this was so strange for our strict, strong mother. She was afraid to stay at home alone and kept us from going to school. Often her scenes turned to hysterics. Finally, six months after the May accident, in December 1960, mother was taken to a mental clinic "in a deep manic-depressive state after a strong psychic trauma."

I couldn't understand all this and just tried to escape from my home life. My new life at school helped. I liked to study, enjoyed the feeling of belonging to a collective, to the Soviet people, to the country, to the world. When, about two years later, I heard about the assassination in the United States of President Kennedy, I was more upset about that than I had been about my own father's death.

I was concerned about the destiny of the world.

On my way to school, I like to push a little stone before me all the way from home to school. I find one somewhere near the entrance of our house and try to keep it with me. Then I have the feeling that I am not going alone but with a friend. I don't have to talk to him; on the contrary he helps me to think. Almost all of my classmates meet one another on the way to school and go together, but I don't have friends. And really it's better to go with a little stone in front of you. He doesn't speak and I don't have to listen to him. Whenever I meet my classmates by chance, I suffer because I don't understand what they are talking about. I listen to them silently or try to keep up a conversation which does not interest me. They talk about teachers, classmates, studies, and I like to think about something else. One day I asked my classmate whether she ever talks to herself. She did not understand and thought I was crazy. It is really better to walk with a little stone.

I never manage to get it to the school building. It is very difficult. Lessons begin at 8:30 and I leave my house at 8:20. I have only ten minutes and it is rather a long way. First I have to cross a very wide road heavy with traffic. I kick my stone very hard so that it will reach the opposite side and I run after it. Sometimes it strikes someone's feet and he looks at me as though I were mad. So I look back at him. What can I do? I don't say, "Sorry." It won't help. I *am* sorry, but I don't like saying useless words.

Then I have to pass through a big park. In the morning it is empty and I can walk freely with my companion. We pass a big fountain and enter a sidewalk with even rows of bushes. Here I always begin to think and, as I think very slowly, I begin to walk very slowly. At the end of the park, I suddenly realize I am late and I leave my companion and begin to run. In vain. I am always late. The pupils and the teachers on duty stand at the entrance and take my daybook to put a note in it. I promise, not them, but myself, not to be late anymore and to stop thinking on the way. But the same thing happens every day and I can't do anything with myself. I hate this word "can't" and myself for being so weak-willed.

It is no use trying to leave my home earlier. I am very sleepy in the morning and can hardly get my head off the pillow. Then I have to make something for my breakfast and wait until everyone finishes with the bathroom. We have two other families in our apartment, and everyone leaves at the same time. So we all run along the corridor half-dressed, hurrying to school or to work.

There are eleven people in our big three-room apartment. The largest room is occupied by the family of a Deputy Minister, the smallest by a shopcleaner and her two children. All the adults hate each other secretly, but we six children get on together fine.

I always forget to collect my books and notebooks the evening before and that takes time. Myra is also in a hurry. Her school is even farther and we irritate and bother each other. Mother leaves for her work. She is an economist in a housekeeping office. We all leave without saying good-by to each other as other families do. I don't think we like it at home.

Mother is always tired and Myra and I are irritable. Myra plays the piano and I can't do my homework, so we quarrel often. Mother doesn't pay any attention to us. She lies on the sofa, exhausted and sad. We don't ask her anything. We know that she is ill. And we don't help her very much because we don't like it at home. It is not good. I would rather think about something else.

I like my school very much. It is very interesting. I am already a sixth-year pupil and a member of a Pioneer organization.

I like to study, but more than that I like our social work at school. We have a lot of circles this year and I am a member of nearly all of them. I play in a drama circle and sing. I work in a geographical and botanical corner and I am a member of a group that makes the wall newspaper. Then this year we have a special task—to study the activities of the people's volunteer corps of our district during World War II and the general history of our district since the eighteenth century.

There is a beautiful eighteenth-century church in our district. It is the main object of my study. It is one of the few churches in Moscow still open to worshipers. These are all mainly old women. I hate standing there among the dreadful revivals of the past, but I have to do it because it is my task. I have found out that there are old inscriptions on the walls which I must find. I have already visited the church twice, but every time I fear to come up to the priest and ask him about them. I feel sick in that darkness among those bowing and mumbling people, candles, open coffins, and icon eyes looking straight at you wherever you move. Last time I suddenly saw a young woman with a boy standing quietly near the wall. They were both praying. My Pioneer conscience could not remain still. I decided to stare at them steadily. Maybe they would think I knew the boy and would report him to his school. He was probably a Pioneer and yet was doing such a terrible thing. I decided to make them leave the church through the shaming power of my stare.

The woman noticed my unwavering glance. She obviously became frightened and screened the boy as if protecting him from me. I felt uneasy and looked aside and hurriedly left the church.

All the way home I scolded myself for again being so weak-willed. I was not yet a Leninist Pioneer. But that frightened look of hers. . . .

I like to do social work because it gives me a feeling of being useful and it is interesting. Of course it takes a lot of time, but I don't hurry to go home after lessons. I don't like it at home.

I also don't like the first moment of entering the classroom.

It seems that everyone is staring at me and sees that something is not in order about me. Maybe it is my crumpled red necktie or my old disheveled dress with a shining big spot on my behind or on my elbows, or maybe there is a hole in my stockings. There shouldn't be, but I don't really remember. I never look into a mirror. I am afraid. Whenever I pass a big mirror in the lobby and happen to see myself, I think, how ugly I look. This terribly straight hair that is always in disorder and my bad complexion and thick brows. And the wrinkles in my stockings. I know all the other girls look prettier, but they must have grandmothers or perhaps even housemaids to help them in the morning. I can't do it for myself. No, that's not right. I can, but I have no time. I must try to be better. But their dresses are new and mine is very old and I can't do anything about it.

Poverty is not a vice and I never feel ashamed of it. It is just that I don't like that first moment of entering the classroom. I walk across the room quickly, trying to look as indifferent as possible, and take my seat, which I don't leave for the whole day. Then I begin to feel confident and even superior as I witness my classmates' failures in their studies.

During the breaks, the teachers usually don't allow us to stay in the classroom. We must walk in the hall, so all the pupils walk in couples in a big circle and the teachers on duty stand in the middle of it. This is law and order and I understand it, but I don't like it because I have no one to walk with me and I feel very awkward walking alone. Again there is that feeling of everybody staring at me. So I try to stay in the classroom if possible.

There are thirty-nine pupils in our class. Each desk has seats for two pupils, so there is one empty seat at one of the desks. This is my desk. I occupy it alone. On the first day I enter the classroom and take the desk I like, usually one of the first. All the others fight for the back seats and I don't like to do what everybody else does. Besides, I am not afraid of a teacher.

I enjoy being alone. This is my little world. If it were possible I would put a fence around it. I like to draw my world. It is a little wooden house with one window on a little hill. There is a winding path down to a river. There is no fence around my little

house because it is surrounded by high mountains. I draw my
world when I am bored by a lesson.

It isn't that I don't like my classmates. I do like them because I know that I must be kind to people. This is one of the
main qualities that I want to achieve in my drive for self-
perfection. But they seem to have something against me. I like to
study and they all think that I value myself too highly. On the
contrary, I feel I am full of shortcomings and try to work harder,
but they don't seem to understand. They never elect me to the
leading Pioneer posts, although every year I am so active. They
all seem to think that I am snobbish, but I just don't want to
show that I feel inferior because I am from a poor family and not
the daughter of a diplomat or an army general, as some of them
are.

But do I really feel that way? I know that in our country the
poor have become the important people, so in fact I am better
than they are. Our teachers say I am brilliant and something
extraordinary as a person. I am assiduous, modest, and very responsible. The other day they learned that I washed the bedding
at home and couldn't believe that we do it ourselves. Mother
never gives it to the laundry. I like washing, but it does take a lot
of time. When I am finished, I always call Myra to help me wring
out the sheets and covers. We take it by the two ends and begin
to twist it in different directions. We make a big sausage out of it.
Last time Myra let it slip and it struck me on the head. It didn't
hurt, but I was all wet and a little offended because it seemed
like a slap in the face.

I like to make things clean. It is another part of my process
of self-improvement. I must learn how to do everything. But
frankly speaking I do not think poverty is such a nice thing,
especially when mother takes free food from a public dining
room and it turns out to be rotten stuff.

All my classmates seem to have something against me. Every
year I feel it the first day I come to school. First, I sit alone
when everyone else has his friend to sit with. Then they begin
the registration and the teacher calls everybody one after another to her table to get the details about himself and his

parents. The rest of us are supposed to do something else while this is going on, but we usually listen with fascination to the answers. It is interesting to know the background of everyone, beyond the walls of the school, what peculiarities and differences are behind the gray and brown uniforms, and the equality of the five-mark system of estimating our capacity. So we listen. "An army general." "A professor." "An actor." "A member of the USSR delegation to the United Nations." "An expert of a Department of the Foreign Ministry." "An international correspondent." And so on. My turn comes about in the middle. My name begins with "M." "Mother—an engineer of economics, father—dead, no father." It is all right, but I am already feeling ill because the beginning of my registration has been unpleasant. It bothers me every year and I cannot understand it.

First the teacher asks my name, "Milkina Alla Tsalevna." I always spell my father's name because no one can understand it. Then she asks my nationality and it begins. The whole class suddenly becomes very quiet. Some look at me steadily. Others avoid my eyes. I have to say this word. All the rest say, "Russian, Ukrainian." I have to say this word, which sounds so unpleasant. Why? There is really nothing wrong with its sound, *"Yev-rei-ka."* But I never hear the word except when people are cursing somebody or I never see it unless it is written on the walls like an insult. Maybe it is just that people make it sound so unpleasant and there is really nothing wrong with the word. But I cannot solve the problem at the moment when I stand at the teacher's table and she looks at me impatiently. Every time I try to overcome my feelings, but each year the word comes out in a whisper: "Yev-rei-ka." It seems to me that all the faces of the pupils merge into one grinning mass. Having answered several other questions, I go to my seat, exhausted and upset.

Maybe all my problems have something to do with this. I heard one girl say that I was a typical Jew and an upstart and that Stalin hadn't killed enough of us. I didn't understand. I had never heard about Stalin having something to do with the Jews. I must find out about it. And I heard boys calling each other Jews when they were fighting. Why should this bother me? I live in the most progressive country in the world where there are many nationalities and all are brothers. Soon we shall all be simply Soviet citizens—national differences will remain with our parents. They are not important, I am sure, but there are some things I cannot understand.

A year ago my mother heard about this school and she was determined to enroll me in it. It is a special school where pupils study English and other subjects in English. My sister studies music and my mother wanted me to get some special education.

I didn't want to come. I dread all kinds of changes, especially when they involve competition. I am always afraid I will fail and it is very humiliating. But mother made me try and I passed all the examinations. But then I didn't find my name on the list. I had not been accepted. I called my mother at her job and told her about it. "It is all right, Mum," I tried to console her, "I am not upset, I can go to my old school." But she didn't listen to me. She already had something else on her mind. All the following week she was busy, visiting, telephoning. In the talks with her friends, she always said: "anti-Semites."

"Mum, what are anti-Semites?"

"Those who are against Jews."

"But why aren't they called anti-Jews?"

"I don't know. Maybe they think it sounds nicer. But it is all the same."

"And who are anti-Semites?"

"Those who didn't take you into the school."

"But why are they anti-Semites?"

"Leave me alone. I am tired. But don't be afraid. You shall study there. Children ought to be accepted when they have passed the examinations."

"You're right. But I don't like to push when someone doesn't want me. And I don't want you to beg."

"I am not begging yet. Right now I am demanding. And we have to do that. Otherwise we shall never achieve anything."

I became frightened. Mother talked as though we were surrounded by enemies. On the 1st of September, I didn't go to any school. Mother didn't surrender. Next day in the morning she took me by the hand and we went to the English school. In the lobby she met the Director, a tall, bony woman with a long, pale face. Instead of eyes, she had two gray little buttons, one pale pink button for her mouth, and you could see her nose only by looking at her from the side. All three buttons showed irritation at our appearance, but mother didn't even give her a chance to open her mouth.

"This is my daughter. I am hurrying to my job and she is staying here. She shall study here. And don't look so. . . . Soon you will be proud of having her at your school."

And she left. I felt a lump in my throat, but I was so frightened I couldn't even cry. The woman looked at me with disgust and told me to follow her. I followed and thought that I seemed to have been born to be humiliated at every step of my life.

I began to study and they soon acknowledged that mother was right. They talked about me at the parents' meeting as an example of diligence, excellent behavior, and loyalty. I liked being praised because it made me feel how good I could have been had I really worked hard. I begged my mother to go to one of these meetings and to listen, but she said: "It is not interesting. They always say the same things about you."

She never asked me about my studies. She was tired and sick.

❋   ❋   ❋

I don't think they are anti-Semites. Maybe they were, but now they like me. And as far as Stalin is concerned, if he really did kill Jews, he is being condemned now.

When I first began to study, I liked him very much, even more than Lenin because he dressed in a military uniform, wore a moustache, and looked like my father. I used to fight with Myra about this. She said Lenin was a greater man. And I struck Lenin's portrait in our ABC book with my fist and she struck Stalin's. But then at school we were told that Stalin was not good and now nobody mentions him. But I understood how great Lenin was and that he was the only one forever.

I am happy that I was born in our wonderful country. I

might have been born in that dark and cruel America and lived, starving, in slums. Here I can take part in creating and building communism for the happiness of mankind. I, a young Pioneer, by my small deeds, help that great work of the Soviet people.

I wish I could talk now to Lenin and ask him: "Vladimir Ilyich, what do you think about our life, about our people? Do you think I am working enough and acting in accordance with your behests?"

I am sure he would have been happy to see what progress we have made in our industry, agriculture, and the way people live. I always feel that he is watching me and I try to do everything better. I recently learned a new song which says: "Lenin is always alive, Lenin is always with you, Lenin is in you and in me!" Yes, Lenin was so great that a part of him is in every Soviet citizen and in me also.

A month ago I visited Lenin's mausoleum. I like to visit Red Square and the Kremlin. It inspires me. But this was a special visit—I wanted to talk to Lenin. The weather was not very good, but I like gray days—this time it suited my mood. The line of people waiting at Lenin's mausoleum is always about 1,500 meters long and I had difficulty finding the end of it somewhere in Alexandrovsky Garden. The line moves constantly, but it usually takes three hours to reach the mausoleum. This was my first visit and it seemed to me of great importance.

I kept looking around, examining the people in the line, trying to get some clue to their thoughts. But they were all so different that I could get no response or understand them. I preferred to look at the Kremlin Wall, the dark red building of the Historical Museum, the Kremlin Red Stars.

The line kept moving and I found myself in the middle of Red Square. The square was empty except for the line, for it is closed from all other sides when the mausoleum is open. Militiamen around the square and all along the line kept order.

When I was only three hundred meters from the mausoleum, I noticed some uneasiness in the line and soon understood the reason. A heavy drop of water struck my nose. I looked up and saw that the sky had become dark gray with low swollen clouds which moved slowly and threateningly. One gust of wind and all the heaviness came down on the square.

I covered my head in terror. Heavy drops struck like bullets. The impact was so sharp it was unbearable. Floods of water beating on my face, shoulders, legs, going through my clothes, cold, wet, painful. I looked around desperately for escape.

But nobody in the line moved. It turned into a line of huddled shoulders and bent heads. It was as if they did not dare move. The square was empty and the Kremlin Walls and the Red stars in the towers and the militiamen—all were looking at the line to see if anyone would move. Maybe even Lenin himself was peeping through a secret window. What would they all do if we moved? Fear was more powerful than execution by rain. Nobody moved.

The next day the newspapers reported that this had been the heaviest storm in many years and the power in the city had been off for half an hour. But there had been one line in the whole of the city—out of hundreds of other lines—that didn't break up. And that was the line to Lenin. A picture in the newspaper showed the line of huddled shoulders and bent heads in the dark square. I had not been mistaken. Somebody had been watching and even taking pictures. Everyone was delighted at this story. We hadn't moved. . . .

When I reached the mausoleum, the storm had stopped. I was gradually recovering and doing my best to get my breath back. I was approaching the two famous Lenin guards. These are two soldiers with rifles who stand on both sides of the entrance. They stand, I think, for an hour or two without moving until two others come to relieve them. The changing of the guards is very beautiful. Now, while I was passing them, I saw with disappointment that both of them were blinking.

I remembered my last visit to Red Square the month before. It was the fortieth anniversary of the All-Union Pioneer Organization and I was elected as one of the best Pioneers of one of the best schools of Moscow to stand on the guest platform next to the mausoleum and watch the Pioneer parade. I was standing there

among foreign guests and other Pioneers together with the director of my school. Suddenly all the Pioneers began to push and
stretch their hands forward. The first cosmonaut, Yuri Gagarin,
was passing us and all of them crying out his name were trying to
touch him. He was smiling his famous shy smile. I started back
with horror and disgust. It always made me shudder to see my
ideals from portraits and books alive and so very close. The reaction of the crowd strengthened my disgust. The great first cosmonaut was as disappointingly alive as these two Lenin guards.

I entered the mausoleum and began to go down the staircase. Everything was of dark red marble. Then we all turned to
the right and continued to go down. I was expecting to see Lenin
after each turn, but instead, I found myself again and again at
the beginning of a staircase going down. I became nervous. I had
always thought that Lenin was lying in the marble cube that is
seen on the square. But that, it seemed, is only a big gravestone.
Lenin was like everyone else, lying in a grave. But I didn't want
to go down to the grave. I didn't like it. It seemed to me like a
trap.

We made one more turn and I realized that we had entered
a big, dark hall with light coming from the center of it. I peered
through the bodies surrounding me and saw a large glass box
and, lying in it, a little man in a black suit. He looked like Lenin,
but he seemed too small. Small head, small fist lying on his chest,
small feet. . . . I felt sick. "Comrades, pass! Comrades, don't stop!"
I heard many low voices mumbling. It came from men in military
uniforms standing along the walls. I again felt surprised that
Lenin's grave-mates were alive and even could talk. In a few
seconds more I found myself climbing the endless marble steps
and soon bright sunlight from the clear, wet sky blinded me. I
turned my face to it with relief, screwing up my eyes against the
sun's bright rays. It was all over so quickly.

I hurried past the marble blocks with the names of the
Soviet great that were buried in the Kremlin walls and hastened
to leave. I was hungry and wanted to go home.

On my way home I decided I would never go again. Of
course, Lenin was alive and sacred, but it was his teaching and

not this small body in the glass box. And that terrible storm had spoiled everything. It seemed to me like a personal offense, as though someone were mocking me. I remembered that I had heard someone's terrible screams of laughter coming through the noise of the storm. And the merlons of the Kremlin wall were like teeth bared in a terrible grin.

Laughter. . . . Do I deserve laughter? It is not often that I suffer from it, but I fear it because it means humiliation. And I hate humiliation. It is like when I am late for my classes and the teacher on duty looks at me. . . .

Yes, in the very same way that she is looking at me now. I am again late for the first lesson.

Anguish. . . . I can't get out of this state. It is always with me, it has become a part of me. What am I yearning for? I don't know what I want. I feel an emptiness in my mind, in my life. And I despise myself. This anguish is without end. I feel it like a snake somewhere near my heart or in my lungs.

All is rotten. All this: school, Komsomol, the institute, my job, people. All this social work, socialist competition, red flags—all is nonsense and lies. It is like a large billboard which I look at from a distance, but when I approach I realize it is only a canvas daubed with slogans and fat faces.

I alone am foolish enough to believe all this. All the others mock me and they are quite right. One must live only for oneself. There is no such thing as collective mutual love and respect, responsibility. There is only you and, maybe, your family. If you take good care of yourself and mind your own business, you will do better in and for this society.

But I cannot live for myself and I have no family. It is all my own fault. Now there is only this emptiness, this terrible anguish. I have lost my way. I feel like a robot who was suddenly left without a program or one whose program turned out to be all wrong.

Maybe if I read, educate myself, learn more about literature, music, art, the world, improve myself, I'll find the way—or someone will find me useful. But who?

⁕   ⁕   ⁕

I graduated from the school I used to love so much and never went back to visit. In the last years I understood it was all lies and grew to hate it. After I finished school, I felt so tired that I didn't dare go to the Technical Institute, as I had always dreamed. I went to the Foreign Languages Institute because it seemed easier. But the four examinations turned out to be four executions by humiliation. There were no human examiners there —just pigs sitting at the tables with their cloven hooves holding documents, grinning.

English: They entrapped me very quickly. I made some mistake and they smiled in satisfaction. *Four* (good). You may go.
Russian: I spoke on Turgenev. The pig interrupted me. "You don't speak good Russian. Where are you from?" She looked at my registration card. *Four* (good). You may go. (I don't speak good Russian! I always received very good grades in composition. And am I not Russian? Russian? I have to repeat it to myself in order to understand the meaning. Of course not. I am not Russian, I am Jewish. How could I forget?)
History—Composition: both *fours*. I was not accepted. I received only a sixteen instead of an eighteen.

It was all done so quickly. I decided to smile and went to work as a secretary at a research institute.

A few weeks later I learned that I had been accepted in the Correspondence Department of the Institute. That meant I could study by myself or attend evening classes and come to the Institute for my examinations. The authorities had taken into consideration the recommendation of my school, which couldn't bear the fact that I hadn't been accepted into any institution of higher learning, and they also considered the fact that I was an orphan.

An orphan? I am not an orphan. My mother is in a hospital. But they consider me as being an orphan.

It happened during my final examinations. My sister and I were sitting in a room and mother was standing on the balcony. She always stood there for hours looking down into the yard from our third-floor apartment. We thought it all right because at least she was in the fresh air. She hadn't been able to go out for she was very weak. After the terrible winter of 1961 when she was in a mental clinic, she began to develop a dreadful sickness. Her hands and then her legs refused to move and her face became like that of a statue. Her whole body gradually became paralyzed. She shrunk and her hair turned gray. It was Parkinson's disease.

That afternoon she was standing on the balcony when we heard her call us. We rushed to the balcony door and stopped short. Mother stood on the other side of the balcony railing on a narrow cornice, holding on to the balcony with her weak, white hands. It took us a few seconds to realize the situation and we rushed to her and seized her by the hands. How had she gotten there? Then I noticed a chair standing on the balcony. We tried to raise her, but she was too heavy and cried with pain. The railing of the balcony was sharp and cut her breast. We didn't know what to do. I thought of her age, her weight, and the yard down there. The houses in the yard were all seven-storied and gray. Now they looked like children's bricks with daubed windows, and every window had a man or a woman in it. One with hands in his pockets, another with his arms crossed on his chest, all silent, without expressions on their faces. So we stood—the world, indifferent and curious, and we three, embracing. Two of us were standing on the balcony and the third was outside over an abyss. In desperation, groaning, not paying any attention to her pain, we raised her once more and she fell over into our arms. Once back in the room, we couldn't talk. The next day I took her to the hospital.

I could never believe that mother was insane. She was so reasonable even when she talked of suicide. She couldn't accept

her dreadful disease, she would say, she didn't want to be a
burden to us, she hated this life, all her past, the Party which left
her without help. . . . We never thought she really meant suicide.
But the doctors said that an attempt at suicide meant that a
person was insane. Maybe they thought there just couldn't be
unhappy people in our country.

On the way home from the hospital, I felt relieved. Mother's
illness was always a reproach to our youth and health. She would
sit completely motionless, only her large green eyes moving, following us around the room. And when she walked, she moved
like some slow, awkward insect, turning slowly, the movement of
her eyes outstripping all her body movements. She rarely smiled,
but when she did—I would gladly give anything just to see her
smile once more. Her smile was wide and light, like the sunrise
over a lifeless desert, innocent as the smile of a baby. She often
reminded me of a baby by her awkward movements and that
wonderful smile which only babies and old people have. Her
head was beautifully shaped with long, straight silver hair—it
once had been curly. She looked old and still so beautiful in her
disease. Yet she was only fifty-six. In her younger years she had
enjoyed waltzing and we often took her by the hands and danced
a waltz around her, she turning around with us. Then she would
smile.

This happened all too seldom. The rest was pain, suffering,
talk of suicide, and eternal reproach in her big eyes. And now it
had happened. She was in the hospital and I was going home
exhausted, but relieved, after a sleepless night. It was shameful
to feel relief, but I had to be honest. I needed a bit of rest.

The sun was gentle and caressing as in early spring. It had
been raining during the night and the whole world was wet and
clean. And the sun was also wet and smiled at me as through
happy tears. I liked the streets with their puddles and wet trees,
weeping clean shop windows, and the smell of damp, breathing
earth in the air. I felt myself a part of it.

Seventeen, sun, spring. . . . I am slender and my arms are
long and thin. I am like one of those young trees. I have big
brown eyes and my smile is mysterious. This young man is fol-

lowing me. Yes, he smiles at me. He likes me. Yes, I also like myself. Am I not a beautiful little part of this wonderful world? Well, then there must be some place for me in it. I shall find it. I must wait a little.

*   *   *

Anguish. . . . Eighteen is a terrible age. I am so sick and tired of this work—eight long hours, working like a dog. And yet I like to work, whatever or for whomever I do it. If I begin, I can't stop, and work until the last moment and come home exhausted.

And, of course, they like me very much there. Everybody. So what? My teachers also liked me, and they were lying to me.

I cannot understand this world. I am in complete discord with it. Perhaps *I* am insane.

"Alla, what do you want to be when you finish at the Institute?"

"I don't know for certain, Chief, but I like the work here. I like active work, dealing with information."

"Oh, yes, you're a capable girl. Even now you could do the work as well or better than most of these dozens of graduates. You could have made a wonderful career here."

"But?"

"But your documents are not good. You know, I want to be frank with you. Is it written in your passport—Jewish?"

"Yes, of course."

"And can't you change it?"

"Why should I? I was born with it."

"Well, of course, it is your right to think that way. But it will always handicap you."

*   *   *

"Dina, tell me, please. We are both Jewish. You are my friend. Was it difficult for you to find a job?"

"I can't call it difficult. I am used to it and take it for granted."

"What?"

"That I am a second-class person."

"But why?"

"Because I am Jewish."

"I can't believe you. Aren't we all citizens of the Soviet Union? I can understand that there are some anti-Semites, but we don't depend on them. We are governed by a just and progressive State. I cannot be anti-Semitic. We should be able to achieve what we want."

"You think so? Well, I don't believe in what is taught. I believe in what I experience. But you'll see for yourself."

"No, no, no! I can't believe you."

       ✿   ✿   ✿

"Well, Chief, what is going on here? The personnel department has fired so many useful engineers from our department. Does the fact that they're Jewish have something to do with it or am I mistaken?"

"Maybe not. But look. There are thirty percent Jews working in the whole Institute. And among the fired employees there were thirty percent Jews. It seems to be just."

"What kind of justice is this? You know you can't afford to lose these people. You need them."

"Well, if we keep those whom we need, we shall make a Jewish bazaar out of our Institute."

"Are the Jews to blame that they are the most capable and diligent here? Where should they go?"

"I never told you I could solve the Jewish problem, so don't ask me. You know I'm not an anti-Semite. Although I don't usually like Jews. There is something about them, I don't know. what it is . . . well, typically Jewish. Please, don't be offended. I don't mean you. You are not like them. I am sorry you are registered Jewish."

"I am not sorry. I belong to them."

       ✿   ✿   ✿

"Dina, I still can't believe there is no way out. I can see that many of the Party people are narrow-minded, undeveloped, and often cruel."

"Oh, don't exaggerate. They are just simple, good-natured people who come from the village and treat people as if they were cattle. They are just not in the right place."

"That is the point. And that is why I think there is still hope. Our duty is to get into the Party and change it from the inside, change its ways and methods. But the idea itself is right and we must try to realize it."

"What idea?"

"The idea of socialism and a Communist future, equality."

"And dictatorship?"

"But this is a dictatorship of the proletariat!"

"Words, words, words, and nonsense. The main thing is that it is a dictatorship and of one party only."

"What is wrong with that. There cannot be other parties in our country. Everybody thinks the same."

"Are you sure?"

"If somebody doesn't, then he is wrong."

"Oh, God! Alla, are you sure you know what is right and what is wrong?"

"I don't know . . . any longer. Forgive me, Dina. I always ask you such stupid questions. You must consider me a complete fool. People at my age have usually formed their points of view, whatever they are, and I am still groping."

"It is good you have begun to ask questions."

"You know, Dina, I am afraid I don't want to come to the conclusions you have come to."

                    *   *   *

"Chief, I can't believe this. You've applied for membership in the Communist Party! You! You, who have always been so cynical about it and talked about the corruption in it."

"I have no way out. I am Chief of a Department. If I want to advance in my career or go abroad on business, I have to be a member of the Party."

"So you will take part in the corruption. Those old fools are gradually dying out and soon the Party will consist of career-makers like yourself. And this is the Party that rules over hundreds of millions of people. Don't you understand that by our indifference and conformism we add to the crimes?"

"I don't think I shall add to the general corruption by my deed or change anything if I don't do it. I don't think anything can be changed in the near future. I have ceased believing in all these 'justices,' 'freedoms,' 'equalities.' "

"What do you believe in, then?"

"In nothing. I just don't waste time in thinking about it. Or, maybe . . . I do believe in something—in my two children, in my apartment, comfort, salary. I want to keep them."

"What will you say to your children when they grow old enough to ask questions?"

"I shall see. Why should I think about it now? I want them to have a happy childhood and then . . . maybe . . . they can live through their lives like me—without problems."

※   ※   ※

"Dina, I want to ask you a very strange question. But, please, don't take it as the question of a girl at her 'awkward' age. I just want to know your opinion. What is the sense, the purpose of life? Why do we go on living if we don't believe in anything, if we consider ourselves powerless? Can you answer that?"

"I think so. It's only my opinion and I'm not sure you'll accept it. We live for the sake of our children."

"I was amazed."

"Yes, to give birth to children, to keep the generations going, to keep life in this world and, if possible, to make it better. But in general we are born to live and to continue life."

"You know, it is so terriby simple that I cannot but believe in it. It is fantastic, but you've made me feel better."

※   ※   ※

Anguish. . . . There is no end to it. Yesterday Dina told me that the meaning of life is in children. At first I thought it a revelation but then. . . . It doesn't solve my problems now. I still don't know what to do. I feel I must read, read, read, but I don't know by what system to go, where to begin. And I have no strength, no will. I am so weak, I despise myself.

Just to go to some other place, to see new cities, historical places, people. Maybe the truth is hiding from me there. At least I shall have some fun. Why not accept this invitation from our second cousin in Riga? This family gathering is, of course, non-sense, but Riga must be an interesting little place.

It will be awfully expensive. But it might be worth trying. Myra also wants to go. It will be easier to go together and then we shall discuss what other places are worth visiting. One a year, at least. And during the year, we shall save our money. I think we can make it. Meanwhile, Riga in August. It feels good to come to a decision and to have a plan.

I am going on a long trip in search of happiness, like a young son of a Czar in search of a bride. First stop, Riga.

The train arrived in Riga in the afternoon. We were already late for the ceremony and we hurried. It was exciting to come to a new place.

We entered an old apartment—two rooms and a kitchen —on the second floor of a shabby house. Every room and the corridor was filled with people, about eighty of them.

The religious ceremony was just over and the young couple met us at the door. I kissed my second cousin, a girl with huge black eyes and short curly hair. We congratulated the bride and groom and entered the crowd. I was sorry to have missed the marriage ceremony with its canopy, the *chuppah*, held over the wedding couple. But the noisy crowd was so interesting that I soon forgot my loss. Entering the first room, I glanced at a strange thing standing in the corner of the corridor. Four tall, thin sticks were wrapped in dark red velvet inscribed with some yellow figures or letters, which had been golden many years before. An old man with a black beard and a little black cap on his head was taking his leave at the door. It occurred to me that the scrolls and the old man had something to do with the cere-mony, but this thought was lost in all the new impressions crowd-ing in on me.

There were some relatives known to me and I joined them, wanting to feel at ease in this strange crowd. I was struck by the number of Jewish faces. In fact, there was not a Russian male at this wedding. The black and red curly hair, big dark eyes, large noses, and delicate features of the small vivid women made me smile joyfully. I really felt something for these people who were so bright and original and yet the pitiful remains of something great which was never to be revived. And I belonged to these people.

Yiddish was heard from all sides. Why do they talk so loudly? A real Jewish bazaar!

Everybody was invited to sit down at the tables. Two rows of tables covered with picturesque Jewish dishes occupied the whole room. There were hardly enough places for everybody, but it was fun. At last all the guests found their places and the host called for attention.

He asked the oldest man present to be the toastmaster of the evening. Everyone joined in his request by applauding. The man sitting near the young couple smiled and slowly stood up. "He has been in Israel for three months as a guest," one of my cousins whispered.

In a hoarse, low voice, the old man began: "My dear friends! I am happy to be given the opportunity to be the first to congratulate the beautiful young couple upon their wedding, to wish them happiness and love for the years to come. I am happy to congratulate all of you, my people, on the birth of a new Jewish family that has been united according to the laws of our people, of our Torah. This fact is even more important now when our brothers defend our State thousands of kilometers from this place. And though we are so far from them, we feel our shoulders and elbows together with theirs."

I didn't hear the continuation. Lightning had struck my world. It swayed and turned upside down. A red transparent shroud stood before my eyes and behind it I saw those whom the old man was talking about. "Pitiful remains?" a voice inside me asked. "Impossible to revive?"

And I remembered. On the 6th of June on my way to work in the Underground, my glance fell on the opening pages of the morning issue of *Pravda* in the hands of the man standing next to me. "Israeli aggression." "The clouds of war over the Middle East." Oh, God! That country with such a Jewish name. It must have something to do with Jews. Then why did they do this? How did they dare? Is it not enough that everybody dislikes them all the same? Annoyed and frightened, I had turned aside from the burning words and made myself forget the whole thing. It was not difficult. I never read newspapers. I was tired and busy and had no time to think.

How could I fail to understand? Aggressors, capitalists, agents of American imperialism—all the junk the government had said about them had blinded me. My Jewish people was actually defending itself, and for the first time in thousands of years in its own State! My own people struggling there for life! I needed only this small word "brothers" to realize it. I began to feel how an indefinite "they" was turning into a strong definite "we" in my mind.

I clenched my teeth in order not to scream with the emotion that filled me. I managed to gain control when the second speaker stood up. He was a young man with red curly hair, blue eyes, and an aquiline nose. When he began, I couldn't understand a word he said. "What language is he speaking?" I asked my cousin in a whisper. "It is Hebrew!"

Hebrew—the ancient language. It is so different from Yiddish, the language of "pitiful remains." Strong and distinct sounds and syllables struck my heart like a hammer. This is the language of a proud and strong people. Proud and strong. Yes, we are. I feel it now. I bent my head, unable to look into the faces of the others. I was ashamed, but I was happy too.

The wishes of happiness and love continued. The guests demanded that the young couple kiss each other again and again to the shouts of "Bitter!" demanding that they sweeten the party with their kiss. (These Jews couldn't avoid this typical Russian custom which gives everyone such pleasure.) The room was filled with the clatter of glasses and forks, the fizzing of champagne, and laughter. I didn't take my eyes off my red-headed Messiah, trying to imbibe his energy and his inner fire.

When the table ceremony was over, the guests gathered in groups, their hands flying up and down, to the left and to the right. The Jews were talking: women gossiping, young people telling anecdotes, men noisily discussing something. I joined the group of men gathered around the red-headed one. He was speaking:

"This is a wonderful book. By an American Jew. Listen to just only one episode from it. There was a pogrom in a small Russian town. Many Jews were killed and among them a pious old man, a father of two sons. He was killed with a Torah in his hands which he had saved from the burning synagogue. One of the sons came at night to the house of the gymnasium director, the organizer of the pogrom, and killed him. The same night the two boys, Yossi and Yaakov, escaped the town and decided to go to Palestine.

"The police were already searching for them and they walked only at night, hiding days in the forest or in the houses of Jews. They went from one Jewish settlement to another, from one rabbi to another, maintaining only one direction—to the south. More than three years passed before they reached the Holy Land.

"Grown and tempered, they were standing on a hill and a beautiful valley was spread beneath them. 'We shall build our state here!' they swore. And they did it."

The men around me were listening silently with some kind of nervousness in their eyes. I shamelessly stared at the speaker with delight and eagerness. He noticed it and, having found a convenient moment, came up to me. "Let's get acquainted! We must be relatives." Having found out that we were ridiculously distant relatives, we came to the point. "Are you interested in what I was telling everybody about?"

"You can't imagine how much I am. I don't know anything, but I want to learn everything, everything. What can I do? I came here only for five days."

"There are Jews in Moscow."

"But I don't know anybody."

"I'll help you, don't be afraid. The main thing is that you want to learn."

"Yes, yes, of course!" I assured him once more.

"Look here. I have a friend. She is a girl of approximately your age and she is very interesting. She knows what to tell you. More than that, in a month she is going to study in Moscow and she will help you in everything. I'll arrange your meeting tomorrow."

Everything was happening as if by magic. Some force was pushing me onto a new road. I was nervous, but eager to undergo this change.

Next day I met Ruth in the street and she took me to her home. She was only two years older than I, but I felt myself a little girl compared to her. And she treated me as if I were much younger, but there was nothing humiliating about it. I felt as though I were being caressed and led along the new path with care and consideration. She didn't have to talk much in her house. I could see everything on the shelves, in the bookcase, among the records. I looked through everything, and touched everything. All of this had come from Israel. I handled every picture postcard, trying to penetrate into the world of each one. The names Yaffa Yarkoni and Simon Dubnow, the blue sky and yellow sand on the pictures—everything was a revelation. I was horrified by the thought that I might have missed all of this and was reassured by the knowledge that I had found it.

Ruth was one of the divine discoveries—her mass of curly hair and her deep serious eyes, even her name, which came from Israel, all had a special meaning for me.

We arranged to meet in Moscow.

She gave me the book about which the red-headed Messiah had been speaking. It was in English. I didn't see anything of the city I had come to visit or any of my relatives. I didn't see my new friends. The whole of that week, I lay on a bed, reading Leon Uris's *Exodus*.

6

I returned to Moscow and to myself as if from a fascinating and frightening dream. I felt as though I had sinned against. . . . Against what? Against whom? My former point of view, those who taught it to me, the State? I began to feel the State all around me and above me like a huge, tight box. "But I haven't done anything," I told myself. "It is just in my mind." But the system had so strongly possessed my mind that I felt any change in me must be noticed. I felt watched and trapped. I sat at home, biting my knuckles, thinking.

By daring even to think "against," I had become an enemy, and all the Communist irreconcilability to enemies, which I had been taught and with which I had agreed, would be directed against me.

I was afraid and yet I felt confident there was no way back. I couldn't forget about that tiny piece of land or about the small street in the center of Moscow where there stood a building with a six-pointed star on it holding my newly discovered identity. All this was fact and I could only be ashamed for being a coward. What will be, will be.

I returned to my work and began my second year in the Institute for Foreign Languages.

On Saturdays my apartment was filled with new acquaintances, young Jewish boys and girls, a noisy and gay company. The Jewish holiday of Simhat Torah was approaching and I felt it would be my first step on the new path and waited for it with excitement. I wanted to give to my new life everything I possessed. I could sing—I would sing Jewish songs. I knew English—I would read and translate literature on Jewish subjects. I was energetic—I would give my energy to these new activities.

Ruth brought us the words of the Israeli songs known in

Riga: *"David—melech Israel"* ("David—the King of Israel"),
"Eretz Zavat Halav u Dvash" ("The Land of Milk and Honey"),
"Havah Nagila" ("Let Us Rejoice"), and we learned them. My
sister played the piano for us and the learning seemed easier.
With her accompaniment we also learned to dance the *hora*, our
whole house trembling under the feet of ten to fifteen leaping
young people. Every day the company gathered.

I reveled in these noisy meetings and in the fact that
four KGB men were watching my house. And, just as in my
Komsomol past, I wanted the meetings to be effective and productive. I begged my guests not to waste time on chattering and
the telling of anecdotes, but to thoroughly prepare for the coming holiday. It seemed as though the change in the objective of
my pursuits did not matter provided my thirst for activity that
would express my vanity was satisfied.

One day Ruth introduced me to her close friend, a man who
was to play a very important role in the strengthening of my
point of view. At that time I was not yet sure of my opinions and
had many unanswered questions; the accusations against Israel
in the press and on the radio affected me. I was feeling rather
than thinking during this period.

When I met this man, I understood that he would answer
my questions. "David," he introduced himself, looking at me with
interest and welcome. Ruth looked proud, as if she were showing
him some special kind of gift.

David was a short, thickset man over thirty. His heavy eyelids, which made the shape of his deeply set dark eyes very
irregular, his prominent aquiline nose and his small mouth radi-
ated strength and confidence. He reminded me of the leaders of
the Judean war in a book by Feuchtwanger that I was reading.
And I was not mistaken. He was really a very strong and devoted
man with years of Soviet camps in his past for his Zionist point of
view. I became attached to him very quickly and he responded
with a warm, paternal attitude.

He used to come to our weekly meetings, bringing his recorder with Jewish tapes, and he would sing and dance with us. I

appreciated his selflessness and felt that he was giving up his time and efforts to help us, the kids, because he thought the youth the most important ingredient for Jewish rebirth in Moscow. When everybody left, he used to sit in our huge old armchair and I sat at his feet on a small stool, asking my endless questions. This position seemed most suitable considering my attitude toward him.

"Please, David," I begged. "Don't think I have any doubts. No, I am sure because I feel we are right. But I would like to have some factual proofs for myself and perhaps for those to whom I may want to prove something. What is this all about, this problem with the Arabs, the refugees? Do we have the right to be in Israel?"

And he would tell me the background of the problem, the history, and the facts about the Six-Day War.

"Don't worry," he would comfort me after that. "Israel is strong enough now to defend herself. All this fuss in the United Nations about the Middle East problem is nothing but the fighting of politicians over spheres of influence. You can't judge by this who is a friend and who is an enemy, and you can't rely on anyone. We had to become strong enough to defend ourselves. Just imagine! Our people, those eternally unhappy Jews now have their own state and army, and they win victories. If the fighters of the Warsaw ghetto had foreseen this, they would have known they were not dying in vain.

"What should really worry us here is that we are not in Israel and cannot take part in defending and building it. We must be as strong as Israel to withstand everything and to live until the moment when we shall be able to realize our dream."

"Yes, I understand, to withstand everything. . . . I haven't done anything yet, David. But I want to and will do everything I can. But if some day I am called by the KGB, what shall I say?"

"Tell the truth."

"What do you mean?"

"Yes, tell them that you want to emigrate to Israel. And always remember that it is your right, recognized both by the

Soviet Constitution and international law. Try once and forever
to get rid of the feeling that you are committing a crime by that
wish. No, you have the right and you are right."

He was more than a friend and a teacher, he was the embodiment of everything he taught. Every Jewish hero I learned
about, every Israeli leader, Israel herself, had for me the image of
David.

The KGB never took their eyes off David, and were doing
their best to entrap him again. But he seemed to know the limits
of what he could do and was keeping within them. If he was
working with the youth, then he made sure that it looked like
harmless meetings over a bottle of wine and sandwiches; if he
received and passed on materials, no one could ever suspect they
had come to or from David. The KGB understood everything,
but they could never catch him. At last in 1969 they decided to
get rid of him in another way. They let him go to Israel.

For three days hundreds of people from different parts of the
Soviet Union came to say good-by to David. His house trembled
with songs, dances, loud talking, joyful laughter. I understood
then that what he gave to me was only a tiny part of himself.
There was enough soul, heart, and strength in him for all these
hundreds of people. And they all came to thank him and share
his happiness. But he was not very happy. He felt as a soldier
feels, leaving the battlefield at the beginning of a great battle,
leaving his friends, leaving the whole of still blind Soviet Jewry
behind.

And at such a moment: when activities were for the first
time beginning to be organized; after the first meeting in Moscow
of representatives of different groups from various cities, in
which he himself took part; after his proposal about writing collective petitions was at last accepted. No, David was not happy
then. He ran from one person to another, introducing them, distributing tasks and materials that had been his, trying to fill the
gap he was leaving. No, he would never forget them, he would
keep in contact with them from Israel, he would try to help as
much as he could, he would try to be useful to them even there.

He repeated all this dozens of times. He talked to everybody about his love, and then rushed into the circle to dance. He was completely drunk, but the famous kosher wine which his loving friends from Georgia brought in a small tun didn't help him to get rid of his sorrow, his feeling of guilt.

This was in 1969, but in the autumn of 1967 I had only just come to know David.

Together with David, Josephus Flavius, Judas Maccabaeus, and Bar Kokba entered my life. I began with *The Jewish War* by Feuchtwanger. I read it with frenzy and despair, imbibing the new sounding names, visiting the newly discovered places, acquiring the new spirit. When the scene of the destruction of Jerusalem came, I lay on my bed, covered myself with a blanket, and read the chapter slowly and attentively. When everything was over, I covered my head with the blanket and began to cry. It was a long, ritual-like weeping of relief. Suddenly I realized that I was crying about myself.

On the day of Simhat Torah that autumn, I put on a white scarf with a blue six-pointed star embroidered on it, which I had made specially, and went to my classes at the Institute. Before the end of the lessons, I went up to the teacher and asked for permission to leave.

It was our national holiday, I explained, and I had to go to the public celebration. She looked at me as if I were mad and allowed me to go, having understood nothing. Since when did Jews begin to have national holidays and, more than that, celebrate them publicly, I saw in her astonished look.

That scarf and the frank declaration were typical of the young people who had just become aware of their Jewishness. We always began by overdoing and exaggerating and had to learn gradually to be cautious. The older people who joined the movement had, on the contrary, to learn to be more free.

The day was cool and rainy, but I didn't wear my coat for it would prevent me from dancing and, in general, from feeling free. I was not late, but could not help quickening my steps; my heart beat violently.

I took the direct train in the Underground from Sokolniki to Dzerdzhinskaya, the center. Each stop marked an increase in my excitement and by the time we reached Dzerdzhinskaya I could hardly control the trembling of my knees. The train stopped, the automatic doors opened, and I saw Ruth waiting for me on the platform. We looked at each other silently and walked toward the exit.

On the escalator I felt joy and relief. I saw people singly, in couples, and in small groups with the signs of holiday on their faces. They were all silent, but their eyes were like a password for me. Once somebody had compared those eyes to the eyes of a cow—big, warm, brown, and sad. It was true, but only partially. Those eyes were not slow like those of a cow, but were easily frightened and quick to sense danger. The eyes of a gazelle.

We reached the top of the stairway and went out into the huge, dark square. All those going in our direction avoided each others' eyes, but quickened their steps as if drawn by some great magnet.

The square was one of the biggest in Moscow, with a high monument in the center of it. The stone leader of the Soviet Tche-ka, the secret police under Lenin's government, fearful and fearless Felix Dzerdzhinsky, one of the ideals of my Pioneer childhood, gave me a strange look from his pedestal. It suddenly occurred to me that his hand in the pocket of his long military coat was holding a revolver. Ruth didn't pay any attention to him. Maybe she was on different terms with this guard of the Soviet system.

We passed the huge building of the KGB headquarters, then the building of the Central Committee of the Young Communist League. All this had acquired a different meaning for me, but I tried to shake off those thoughts. Only those lighted windows in the KGB building didn't leave my mind. What could possibly be going on there at this hour? Interrogation, discussing the destinies of people, gray anonymous men preparing their punishment for me? Nonsense, it has nothing to do with me. Nothing! Not yet. . . .

After we crossed Dzerdzhinsky Square, we went along side

streets. No, not went—ran. And people near us also ran until we all at last reached a narrow street on the right. We turned into it and the sight took my breath away. The street went downhill and all along it as far as the eye could see there was a sea of dark heads. Thousands of people. A hollow hum rose from that moving mass, reminding me of boiling lava. "Too many Jews together," I thought with horror. The fatal figures flashed through my mind: six million, tens of thousands at Babi Yar, tens of thousands in Rumbula. . . . I stopped, but Ruth pushed me slightly, and I plunged into the boiling sea.

We found it hard to move in that crowd, but Ruth wanted to find our friends down near the synagogue. The weak light from the street lamps fell on the faces and they stayed in my memory like snapshots. Where had I seen all these faces? Again hazel eyes, pale skin. I remembered thumbing the pages of a book of pictures taken in the ghettos. The faces behind the barbed wire, in a long line of people going to—I had closed the book immediately, feeling sick. And now they appeared before me again—alive.

The expressions were different, laughing, delighted—and frightened, inspired—and attentively listening. It was hard to move. I saw faces and faces and felt that I was walking on them.

At last Ruth found our friends and we joined a group of young people singing Hebrew songs. David was among them. I was introduced to those whom I hadn't met before. Their names delighted me: Mordechai, Yoseph, Dan, Moshe. . . . The names themselves sounded to me like a challenge.

"And what about you?"

"My name is quite Russian—Alla."

"Choose for yourself a Hebrew one."

"I shall be delighted to. What names do you know that sound like mine?"

"Ayala."

"Ella."

"No, no, this is all nonsense." Ruth interrupted. "I have a brilliant idea. How do you like Aliya?"

"Aliya. . . ." I remembered *Exodus*. Aliya "Alef," aliya "Bet."

Aliyah means rising, *aliyah* means returning to our motherland Israel. Aliya is my new name and I shall have to live up to it.

We formed a large circle. Most of the boys and girls came from the institutes, so the bags with books were piled in the center. We embraced each other at the shoulders and began to dance a *hora*, singing "*Hava Nagila.*" The circle grew and grew. Other people broke in and joined the line. And with every new-comer, joy grew in my heart. I wanted to leap up to the sky, to sing as well and as loud as I could, and my voice didn't fail me. My new friends began to leave the circle one by one and to form circles in other places. Soon I found myself alone among strange people. I hesitated, but seeing their longing looks, continued to sing. They clapped their hands and repeated the words after me. I finished all the songs I knew and began from the beginning. It was hard to stand. People were pressing from behind. I didn't notice how I became the center of the circle without stopping my song. The chorus around me grew and grew. I couldn't see the end of the crowd surrounding me. I was frightened, but I couldn't stop, and sang and sang and explained the words to the strange people around me and sang again with them. When it became impossible to sing, I began to dance.

Freilachs! The dance of wild joy, just be happy and dance, forget everything and dance, dance as well as you can. No one ever taught me this dance. My heart prompted me. The people around me clapped and sang the melody. Suddenly David rushed into the circle and joined me in the dance. Oh, David, I shall never forget how we danced *freilachs!* Leaping high, his arms flying up, he danced as if striving toward the heavens. His burning eyes came out of their deep sockets and fixed on the heavens. He begged, he demanded something from the heavens, he danced the dance of praise to the heavens. Cries of joy bellowed out from his chest. I couldn't check my own cries of happiness and whirled and whirled endlessly. One by one people began to join us and the circle was filled with dancing Jews. Exhausted, I stepped aside. Some one suddenly seized my hand and kissed it.

"I shall never forget you. Thank you." I saw a middle-aged man with tears in his eyes. He immediately disappeared into the crowd, but other people surrounded me, touching my scarf, wanting something from me.

I heard Ruth's voice and made my way through the crowd. She was standing in a tight circle, leading a chorus of voices.

"*Mi ata?* (Who are you?)"

"Israel!"

"*Mi im'cha?* (Who is your mother?)"

"Israel!"

"*Mi avicha?* (Who is your father?)"

"Israel! Israel! Israel!"

The answering voices roared, screamed as if they wanted the whole world to hear them. They were not satisfied that the stone guardian on the square certainly heard them through his hundreds of ears moving here and there through the crowd.

Why are they not afraid? Why am I not afraid? Because it is dark? Because we are together? Because we are near the synagogue? Or . . . because no one yet has been punished? Do they come here after they have been called to the KGB? Shall I come here if I am called and threatened?

No, enough questions. Not on this night, which in recollection seems to be happening again.

The circle becomes narrower. Everyone stands shoulder to shoulder showing each other by finger to lips that the next song will be without words. Hand in hand, with clenched lips, swinging, boys and girls start to sing. The melody begins very quietly, then grows louder and louder as if there is not enough room for it in our throats. Slow and solemn, it becomes aggressive and demanding, threatening and promising. It tears Jewish hearts, flows through our burning eyes, makes our hands clench tighter. The melody without words drowns everything around and swells into a hymn over the city. "Hatikva"* . . .

Now the crowd turns the world upside down. This narrow street is the world. It is without size. The noise and tension have reached such a point that they threaten to break through the sky. The crowd cannot bear even this limit above it. No limits! Freedom! Freedom!

* The Zionist hymn and the national anthem of Israel.

We are trying to make our way through the mass of bodies. This group is dancing a *hora*, that one is singing "*Shalom Aleichem*," this one is screaming with laughter at a joke.

"Kids, go home, it is late," the cautious voice of an old man mumbles.

"Home? Ech, *papasha*, it is a long way home!"

The crowd is applauding.

This group is singing Yiddish songs. It is not very large. The young people do not know Yiddish and do not want to return to it. Hebrew and the spirit of Israel are reigning on this planet, the term of life of which is six hours—from 6 P.M. to midnight.

Again we find ourselves in the middle of a circle. There is no end of strength and will. Only *hora* can express what is burning inside, trying to escape. And the dancing circle is growing. Soon a big square is formed in the crowd. People rush inside it and form a second circle, then a third. The whole world is whirling in *hora*. "*Hava nagila v' nismecha-ah-ah-ah!!!*" "Let's be glad and rejoice!"

What a feeling it is to dance *hora* on this night. Your hands are on the shoulders of strange young people. Strange? No, on this night there are no strangers. Dear, beautiful faces are passing you in the whirling dance. Where shall I meet you next? In the Hebrew study group? In prison? In Israel?

And again I sing: "It is so simple. Repeat after me, '*Le shana habah b'yerushalaim* . . .'—'Next year in Jerusalem.'"

And more: "*Yerushalaim shel zahav*" ("Jerusalem of Gold") "*Sharm-el-Sheikh*."

"Where did you learn it? Do you know Hebrew? Do you have a textbook? I want to meet you. Please call me."

A hand bearing a paper with a number on it reaches above the heads.

"And me! Let's all get together."

But some people stand silent looking at you with devouring eyes. What possesses them? Shyness? Fear?

Several times my sister tried to get me to go home, but I didn't even hear her. Then she found a way of bringing me to my senses. She, together with her friend, seized me by the hands and

shoulders and made me stand still for a few moments. After half
a minute, I felt a terrible giddiness and a weakness in my knees
and almost fell. Six hours without stop!

They took me home. I was silent, able to produce only
coarse, inarticulate sounds. The silence all around pressed in on
me. I was half dead, but really happy after so many years. There
was again something to live for.

Dina dear,

*I am so sorry I failed to find time to visit you, but I really
couldn't. Almost every day after my work is over, I go to my
classes in the Institute and they are not finished until 11 P.M. As I
travel home, I struggle to keep my eyes open. I'm afraid that if I
close them I won't be able to open them again. And when I enter
the subway I feel terrified; I know that I will not be able to resist
and will fall asleep in the car. But due to some kind of instinct, I
always awaken at my stop, but feel terrible.*

*My life seems to me then so black and unhappy. I damn ev-
erything—the Institute, the subway, myself—and go swinging,
struggling again to keep my eyes open, to my house. The street is
always completely dark and empty. It is already after midnight
and I think with irritation that even drunkards and dogs are
asleep at such a time. And what is it all for? No sense at all in
anything—in my work, in my studies, in the whole of my life. To
work in order to have money, to study in order to have a diploma, to live—in order to live.*

*But enough of complaining. I should stop torturing you with
it, at least in written form. I should remember the advice of all
clever and experienced people—wait.*

*I feel very lonely in our department since they fired you.
Berman has also been "relieved" of his position "due to reorgani-
zation." Gurvitz was advised to look for another job the same
week and Aronson decided to leave himself. The snob decided to
make a fine gesture—to leave, being sure he would be sacked
soon.*

*I never told you that I spoke to him once. I could not resist
the temptation to stir up a Jew. You know what he told me? That
he is a man of the Universe, he does not classify himself as Jew*

or Russian. He was born here and therefore he is a citizen of the Soviet. Well, now he is gone like other good Soviet citizens who just happened to be Jews. I am sorry for him now. There had been a real pogrom. The next week they began to hire Russian engineers.

And only I am left—alone—like a chinchbug that stays in a house no matter what happens to it—fire, flood, earthquake. I know the reason I am left. My chief said: "You are lucky to be almost an orphan. They cannot fire you, according to the law. I know they would like to."

So you see, I am lucky. Why should I complain? By the way, mother is very bad now, worse than ever. We hope to get her into a hospital, but until now they have all refused us. Her disease is incurable and they don't keep people in the hospitals who are considered hopeless. I don't know what we shall do. Last time, she was taken to the hospital from the subway station. It is terrible to think about, but it is on my mind all the time.

We had left her sitting on a bench in the yard. When we came to take her home, she wasn't there. Hours passed and she didn't come home. We ran our feet off looking for her, but couldn't find her. You cannot imagine the feeling of losing your mother in the street. Children can be lost—they are helpless. But your mother? The evening came, the night passed—I was obsessed with the thought that she was wandering somewhere in the night, not far from us.

Neither the militia nor the Central Ambulance Service knew anything. At last in the morning when we re-called all the hospitals, she turned out to be again in that mental hospital. She had been taken from our subway station where she was standing on the edge of the platform looking down on the rails.

We rushed to the hospital. She was lying on a bed in a corridor of the overcrowded hosptial, her face as white as the pillow, her hair completely gray. She looked at us silently and we could find no words to ask, to scold, to beg. Her eyes moved from Myra's crying face to mine and there was such suffering and despair in them.

Why is it so? I constantly seek for an answer. Why is she suffering so much? What for? And then I cannot get away from the fear that this may turn out to be hereditary. No! No! No! I shall resist it. Just be calm and avoid nerve-wracking situations. Of course, I shall overcome it. The main thing is that I know about it and it won't come unexpectedly.

On weekends I sleep late and then do my homework for the Institute or something about the house, though, as I told you, I don't see any sense in all the routine I continue to go through. I feel that I must do it or I will be completely lost.

I'm sure you didn't expect to get a letter like this from me *and you're probably wondering where all my new friends are; whether I'm disappointed in everything I found out about my national identity. No, I'm not disappointed and everything is in its place, except perhaps for the friends. I'll try to explain it to you and maybe it will help me understand what has happened.*

I had never met so many people as of late and I had never known they could be so different and interesting. And, speaking frankly, I would have preferred they be more simple, but good, than so many-sided in their human faults. I understand that I am just one of this menagerie, but the contact with them turned out to be too difficult for me.

The young people who used to gather at my place seemed to be interested only in dancing, singing, and just getting together for the sake of fun. I became tired of learning Hebrew songs in Russian transcription without understanding a single word; of looking at beautiful picture postcards without knowing what was on them; of talking about Israel without learning about it. I know it is possible to learn a lot, but they didn't seem to be interested.

You know, since my school years, I have always tried to choose for my friends people who were better than I—better in everything: in character, in intellect, and especially in erudition. I always preferred to take rather than to give. I have always thought and do think I do not possess enough to share with anybody. I wanted and do want first to accumulate knowledge and learn human virtues and then maybe I shall be able to give something. You will probably object to the possibility of borrowing virtues. But I really think that if one feels imperfect and wishes to become better, one can learn to be kind by rubbing shoulders with kind people and by studying their relationships to the world.

You showed me a lot in this respect, but I learned much more of the virtue of kindness after meeting a really wicked human being. He was among those who interested me most among my new acquaintances. He was the most interesting specimen in this large menagerie of human beings. He is a middle-aged man, a husband, a father, a Jew, and a good doctor. But all this is not as important as that he is a collection of several traits which are expressed in him in their highest possible degree.

I met him first at one of our Jewish gatherings. David introduced us and from that moment, our many months' long conversation didn't stop. I was highly flattered by his attention to me, which was probably due to my talent as a good listener, and I listened eagerly for all those months. In his book-lined study he introduced me to the worlds of Freud, Kafka, Joyce, and Proust, Chagall, and Mann, Greek mythology and the Bible, Aznavour, and Joan Baez.

*In his home I discovered a whole world and in him—human
nature. Because to know and understand him meant to know one
half of humanity. While listening to him, I was learning logical
thinking and self-expression, emotional perception of the world
around me, of art, literature, and music. I was learning to understand and to see through human nature—and I was learning to
hate and despise people. Yes, because that is what he preaches,
not by direct words, but through his whole expression of himself.*

*Oh, if you could only have listened to him talking scandal
about people. His whole logical thinking, wit, erudition, knowledge of human nature and the psychiatric vocabulary were
summoned for his talking which he usually did after meals while
wearing a pleasant smile under his bristled moustache. It was
one of his numerous vocations. One would probably call it mere
gossiping, but he did it with such skill that you could not help
being delighted by it and learning it subconsciously. And I could
not deprecate anything about this great Lilliputian with such a
simple human word as "gossiping."*

*Why Lilliputian? He existed for and in a tiny Lilliputian
world that he created for himself. This world was limited by the
walls of his apartment and consisted of himself, his wife, and his
two children. All his acquaintances, his patients, his relatives,
including his only brother, an old and sick man, belonged to the
other world which he hated and despised.*

*And side by side with the qualities of a great intellectual, he
possessed also the features of a man in the street, a fussy little
Jew. He was delighted and jumped like a schoolboy with every
new success in his psychiatric practice which any other talented
doctor would have taken for granted. He did not like to give help
free of charge to his patients whether they sought it at his home
or at his place of work—a state district dispensary—and like a
diligent ant he took everything he got from his patients in kind
or cash to his home, to his two Jewish children—his creation, his
sense of life. It was for their sake that he built that closed world
in the center of Moscow, a world inhabited only by his dear ones
and art, literature, philosophy, the Muses, and a spirit of intellectual meditation.*

*I took delight in this expression of parental love. Everything
for his children. For his children he would step over dead bodies.
I saw that he read, listened to music, enjoyed art with the
thought that he would immediately pass his riches on to his son
and daughter. Everything he had acquired in forty years he
wanted to put into the heads of his seventeen-year-old son and
his beautiful twelve-year-old daughter. And he did. When he first
told me about his son, he exclaimed passionately: "My son is a
refined intellectual." Those words produced a tremendous impression on me. They shocked me. I did not really understand*

*the word "refined," though I knew about refined sugar or oil.
"Refined intellectual" was something quite new to me. But I
believed it must be something great.*

*The two offsprings' heads were filled with a tremendous
amount of the world's intellectual treasury. They spent all their
days reading, with the sounds of music in their ears, or talking
with the only clever persons in the world, themselves and their
father. All the rest of the world, these little sages hated.*

*Well, that is not completely true. There was one thing in the
world the doctor, and accordingly his children, loved. And that
was Israel. They listened to the broadcasts of "Kol Tzion" five
times a day, five broadcasts of one and the same program. They
dreamed of this wonderland where people must walk along the
streets emanating rays of intellect. And they were all so thirsty
for intellect in others. They were sure that Israel was that lost
world, that lost planet of supermen to which they belonged. And
if it had not been for their Lilliputian quality of "cautiousness,"
their great love for Israel would have made them heroes in the
movement which is being born now. During our more than a
year's acquaintance he was extremely kind to me and even interested in me. At the same time, though, everything that was behind me—my family, my former friends, my job and studies—was
entirely dismissed. I did not resist, but on the contrary gladly
submitted to this.*

*I just silently worshiped the doctor. One would probably
expect some romantic side of the story and would not be mistaken. It was there, with the doctor's son, and it was as great and
as disgusting as everything else about this time.*

*At last, one day, I was banished, very quietly and simply, by
telephone, just a moment before I was going to leave my house
and fly to them as I had every day during these long months.
These months had been like a whole life to me, but the lifetime
was over and the unexpected death came. I died there by the
telephone and I spent a whole day and night in another world.*

*During this day and night, I didn't think about the death or
how unexpected and cruel it was. I was just trying my best to be
born again, to return to the world, to life. And to this end I used
all the methods of psychiatric analysis I had learned in the doctor's school; I summoned the effort of a drowning person. And,
indeed, I was like a person who had just been taught to swim
and then thrown into the sea without help. And I knew there was
no one to save me if I failed to save myself.*

*That night I spent sitting on the sofa with my legs crossed,
looking at the white wall opposite me. I didn't dare move for fear
of pushing myself into a deeper abyss from which return would
be impossible. I clasped myself in my arms to keep myself from
moving and sat so all through the night. In the morning I went*

out and walked along the streets. Then I bought an airflight ticket to a distant town and continued wandering about the city waiting for the flight. Finally, I made the first successful effort—I returned the ticket and slowly went home. I had no more strength to struggle and when I reached home, I lay down on the floor. But when I returned to myself, I knew that I had returned to life. Yet I ate almost nothing for several days and felt terribly sick and weak. But I was alive.

So much for the story. It can be as long as a lifetime. I haven't given you the doctor's name, for the Jewish name he bears does not suit such a person. Let him stay in your mind as "Homo sapiens" wicked. Yet I admit that he taught me to see and appreciate the richness of the world and he taught me—in the end—to love people. He also taught me never to stand with both of my feet on one board, but always on two, so that if one breaks under me, there will be a second one to support me—and the second one should be myself—never to give myself completely to someone or something, so that if he or it betrays or leaves me, I shall still have something left.

The lesson was very difficult and dangerous, but I passed the final exam and now I can safely re-enter the world.

I did not really tell you about my relations with other people, but this story is already too much for one letter. I shall write about others some other time.

Yours sincerely,
Alla

Dear Dina,

How are you? Did you find a new job? Please, come to visit us some day.

Mother is at last in the hospital. Now she will be thoroughly examined, as her intestines do not digest food well. I think her primary disease has now begun to paralyze her internal organs. Anyway it is better when she is in a hospital, especially now that an epidemic of grippe has spread through the city. At least she will be isolated from that. And, of course, we shall both be freer and calmer, although it is like covering your head with a blanket and imagining that the world has ceased to exist. I know that we do not help her enough and this feeling of relief when she is not at home is shameful. But what is the use of knowing it and shaming myself if I continue to behave in the same way?

How do you like this weather? Every day is like a fairy-tale New Year's holiday. I just love it. The soft white carpet muffles me up and protects me from the whole world. It is like the heavy rains of autumn which I also love because they put a protective wall between me and the world. I like to be at home alone in such weather. Yes, I am again alone. And I like it, as always. I think loneliness is the most productive state for a person. I hate anybody interfering with my studies or with my being face to face with myself.

I use my loneliness to the fullest. I use every free minute for reading and studying Hebrew. Every Saturday and Sunday, I go to the Foreign Languages Library where I discovered a large collection of literature on Israel and Hebrew textbooks. That is what should be done instead of wasting time in aimless dancing and singing in the streets and holding forth that Hebrew is forbidden for studies and there are no books on Jewish history. This is all true, but at least the first steps can be taken—to find old Russian and foreign books in the two central libraries. And this I do now. I found a dozen American Hebrew grammar books which I compare and extract from them everything I need on a certain question, and little by little the Hebrew grammar becomes clearer and clearer to me. The hours that I spend in the library make me happy for the first half of the next week. The second half I feel happy looking forward to the coming weekend.

Frankly, sitting in the library over the Hebrew file, I hoped I might meet somebody who was also working with this catalog. The meeting came very quickly and turned out to be more important for me than I had expected.

One Saturday I did not find the file in its usual place. With a rapidly beating heart, I began to look around the room. At last I saw an old man looking through my file. (By this time I was already calling it "my" to myself.)

"Will you please give me the file for just a moment?"

"Yes, here you are." He moved the box to me without taking his eyes off my face. I kept on looking for the necessary card as long as I could until the man broke the silence. "Do you know Hebrew?"

"No, but I am studying it now."

"What books do you use?"

I explained my system to him.

"Who helps you?" he asked.

"Nobody. I do it myself," I answered proudly and didactically. "Do you know Hebrew?"

He smiled sadly and answered, "Hebrew is one of my professions. I have just finished a textbook on Hebrew."

I jumped and could hardly keep my eyes from popping out. "Will it be published?"

"Well, that is a question. If you need any help in Hebrew, I shall be delighted to help you. My book will never be published, but you can use it."

We made an appointment for the next week.

My Hebrew teacher (what a wonderful thing to be able to

write these words!) is a soft-spoken old man with big dark eyes. Never before have I seen an old person with such large, open eyes, but Morduch Lazarevitch Roodshtein has a big, open heart also, and you feel you have an access to it through his eyes.

During the entire week, I wondered how I was going to pay for the lessons and, as I could not find any possible solution, I went to my first lesson with the determination that I would pay any price he asked and just give up one of my meals. But the problem was solved much more easily. When he heard my question, my teacher looked at me with sad surprise. I understood immediately and felt ashamed. Lessons in Hebrew in the Soviet Union are free, at least with such people as Morduch Lazarevitch.

My teacher gives me lessons in Hebrew grammar and tells me to enlarge my vocabulary by myself. At home I work on the grammar exercises from his textbook.

He has worked on this textbook for many years. It consists of grammar paragraphs, exercises, and short texts. Many texts are on the theme of life in the Soviet Union, but this has not helped in getting it published. The Council of the Institute of Asia and Africa gave it a very high appraisal, but the question of publishing it remains open. The teacher understands that this policy of delay means that the authorities have decided that the publishing of such a book is inexpedient. He does not hope any more. He teaches. Besides me he has several other pupils, but he works with everyone individually. It can be explained both by pedagogical principles and by cautiousness.

The textbook is accompanied by a supplementary book called The Destiny of the Language. *It tells about the history of Hebrew from the biblical period up to its miraculous rebirth in the State of Israel. He has given the manuscript to me to read at home and has asked me for my comments. I shall have the book for a week. Perhaps you'll drop in one day and look through it.*

I sit enchanted at his lessons. Very often he takes out the Bible or a book of poetry containing the expressions we have just learned. This makes me feel at the beginning of a long, unknown, and wonderful road. I am anxious to continue along the road as swiftly as possible.

The teacher lives very far from me, at the opposite end of Moscow, but I do not notice the cold, the crowd in the subway, or the hour and a half for the trip.

I am terribly happy now and hope this lasts longer.

Yours,
Alla

The teacher never talked to me about Israel or about applying for an exit visa. I knew nothing about his private life and never dared ask him. But in 1971 he arrived in Israel during the mass emigration from the Soviet Union. It had been the dream of his whole life, and it was now coming true. He went to Israel with his wife, leaving behind his only son and beloved granddaughter. When his son was small, this Hebrew scholar did not talk about Jewish problems or anti-Semitism in his presence in order to protect him. When the son grew up, he didn't want to hear about it.

This teacher of a new generation of young Hebrew scholars in Moscow spent three wonderful months in Israel, reading to the public his Hebrew poetry and meeting Israeli poets and writers. He died of a heart attack on the stage in front of his Israeli listeners at one of his performances. God bless his sacred memory!

Dina dear,

I have just learned that the KGB is concerned with my person and has been for quite a long time. No, I am not at all frightened and even feel intrigued and a little proud. But I have to tell you everything from the beginning.

One evening when I was already in bed, Myra came home and, without taking off her coat, sat down on the bed near me. Her look seemed very strange.

"I was there," she said.

"Where?"

"There."

I understood. I suddenly grew cold and felt a terrible headache. Myra was smiling. You know she always smiles that stupid smile when she is excited. But the corners of her lips were trembling. I didn't say anything, but waited for her to begin.

"It happened yesterday. After I had finished my lesson in the sixth class, I left the classroom and saw a man standing near the door. He said he was waiting for me and asked me to go out with him to the staircase where we could talk quietly. At first I thought that he was a parent of one of my pupils, but his bold manner surprised me. When we reached the staircase, he showed me his identity card—KGB. Can you imagine what I felt? I knew immediately it had something to do with you."

"Stop, Myra. What did he look like?"

"Well, nothing special. Very ordinary, colorless face, middle-aged, green hat and gray raincoat. Very polite, soft-spoken."

(Dina! Remember this description. This is he who follows you, who stands near you in the synagogue, who watches near your house for hours. Dina, if you see a man who seems very much an ordinary man-in-the-street, without anything special about him, take care! He is the KGB.)

"What did he ask you?"

"Better ask what he didn't ask. From the very beginning. About parents, school, friends. And he knew everything about our family: that father had died, that mother is ill and that she is a veteran member of the Party—everything. You know, it's a terrible feeling when you meet a strange man and he knows everything about you. There was nothing special in this talk at the school, but at the end he said that he had more questions, but did not want to interfere with my work. So he invited me to come today to his office in Lubianka Street. When I heard this name and remembered that building on Dzerdzhinskaya Square, I nearly fell from the stairs.

"So now I have just come from there. At five I went to Lubianka Street and went in through the side door. You know— those huge black doors. There was a pass for me at the entrance and a man took me to the room which was indicated on the pass. We walked along long, narrow corridors, then turned and walked again, and again turned, until I couldn't orientate myself. There were doors on both sides of the corridors; some were open and the rooms were empty. Others were closed. The building seemed completely empty, but somewhere at the end of those endless corridors my visitor of yesterday was waiting for me. When I was finally shown into a room, the man who brought me left immediately.

"My visitor of yesterday seemed happy to see me. He greeted me and invited me to sit down. In the room there was just a table with a chair on each side of it. He began again to ask the same questions, but this time he put down my answers on paper. At last he began to ask about you. What are your interests? Who are your friends? Who influences you? I answered who else can influence you but I, your elder sister. Then he asked who used to come to our place during the young peoples' parties. I said I didn't know the surnames. He asked me the first names. I began to think of all the Jewish and popular names I knew, except of those who came to us, and gave him some. He asked if there was anyone by the name of David. I said I couldn't remember everybody who used to come and maybe there had been a David among them.

"He showed me several pictures and asked if I could identify anybody. There was nobody I knew on them. He asked whether you were going to the synagogue on Passover. I said that as far as I knew you were not going. At the end of the conversation, he asked me for permission to bother me once more if they needed more information. He said they did not call you because you are so young and they did not want to frighten you. He was very polite. Then he showed me out."

We sat silently for awhile. I wanted to say that I was sorry that she had become so involved in this. She has nothing to do with my activities. But I saw she did not need my apology.

I have never understood my sister completely, nor my mother. We, three women, have lived all our lives together, but have never come to know one another deeply. Mother had her own life, and her way of thinking is completely strange to me. We two daughters are also going different ways in our lives.

In the summer of 1967 when we were both in Riga, she became more interested in Israel than I. But when we returned to Moscow, she forgot everything, resumed her usual way of life, and did not want to be bothered. My noisy company antagonized her. She saw people's faults, but refused to see the important idea that was behind them. Nothing could reawaken her interest in Israel.

But she never disapproved of my point of view. She agreed that I was right and was proud of me and, in some way, even envied me my obsession. But she herself was bound by a love for the country in which she was born, and to give up her life to go to a country she didn't know was strange to her. And a hypocrite she could not be.

During the telling of her story, my fright had subsided. I was able to consider everything quietly. It had been several months since I was in the synagogue or a large group of Jews had come to my place. The KGB definitely wanted to intimidate me. Well, to a certain degree, they did. I am afraid, but just a little. I was not going to be in the synagogue on Passover. But now two feelings struggle inside me. One is fear and the second is the wish to go there to spite them, to show that I am not afraid.

But, in fact, I do not want to go to the synagogue. I do not feel like dancing or singing now. And I have an unpleasant aftertaste from my meetings with some people.

I shall try to explain this to you as I have already promised to do, and you judge me, please. After that trip to Riga, I became acquainted with a lot of people, all very different and interesting. I thought they belonged to a heroic movement for the rebirth of our nation, and they must be courageous and idealistic if they dared to defy our system and give up their lives to their historic motherland. So they were heroes to me and I was proud to belong with them. But after a certain period of rubbing shoulders with my new friends, I realized that they were all human beings and were not strangers to human vices. One shocked me as an outrageous liar, a second was full of jealousy, and a third was a fool. But what made me completely unhappy was the discovery that grown-up men, heroes in the Jewish movement,

married and fathers, were very unreserved in their relations with
women and young girls, behavior from which I myself suffered
more than once.

I began to feel uneasy, to put it mildly. I had always thought
that people who are involved in one holy cause cannot be immoral or dishonest in other things. Or, if they had not been
perfect before their involvement in the holy cause, it made them
better in all things. I never thought people could be heroes in
one regard and immoral in another. And maybe there are no
heroes at all but only heroic situations which make people behave in a certain way. So these people whom I had thought to be
heroes are no better than I am. So why, therefore, should I feel
uneasy if people turn out to be only human and not monuments
of heroism? Because I must have somebody to look up to? Have I
the right to demand that other people be better than I? And, if
they are no better, to reject them?

So, you see, you don't have to tell me anything. I answer all
my questions and reason with myself. But still I cannot get rid of
the unpleasant aftertaste of the discovery and prefer again to be
alone.

I am happy that this disappointment has not influenced my
belief in Israel as it did Myra's. She saw Israel through the people who brought her the idea and, having been disappointed, lost
it—maybe forever. I have remained face to face with Israel
without mediators. And I shall keep this bond.

And yet I sometimes wonder whether this, too, may not be
another of my mistakes, a new food for my boundless idealism. I
really think idealists are dangerous people. Since people have not
found absolutely true ideals, they find something else and are
eager to serve their idols. Idealists are active, tireless, selfless.
They are ready for heroic deeds and crimes. They will step over
anyone in the implementation of their ideals. Richness, glory,
individual power—are they not ideals? But there are ideals
which can be more dangerous—social justice, communism, equality, internationalism, racial purity—for their sakes idealists step
over millions of dead bodies, over whole nations.

I myself very nearly became an accomplice to the crime that
is being committed here. So I am afraid of making a second
mistake and am trying to understand what is happening to me.

There are variables and constants in this world. Variables
are political points of view, social orders, opinions, and those still
undefined concepts of ideals. They are all subject to change in
the course of life.

The constant is that which is given you by birth, belonging
to a family, a nation. You can be proud of it or you can be
ashamed of it, but you can never change it. And you must be
responsible for your belonging. That is my point.

I belong to the Jewish nation. And this is a constant. Israel has been reborn for the sake of our nation and someone must go there. And who is that someone if not I. It is simple and, I think, true. I admit again that there is some kind of idealism in this: I want to give up my life to the country, to the nation. But besides that I feel that Israel needs me. I also feel that I need Israel much more than she needs me. And that makes me think that I am beginning to depart from that class of dangerous people.

Yours,
Alla

Mama!!! I wanted to scream in pain and despair. If I could give one long scream, maybe I would feel better. But the scream was only inside. It tore my head and chest apart but would not come out. Ma-ma-a!!!

It happened on the morning of January 16, 1969. Myra and I were at home and both in a very good mood. The sun shone brightly over the soft snow and we told each other something very funny. I remember Myra was jumping with laughter on the sofa when the telephone ring interrupted her. She took up the receiver, listened for a few seconds, and burst into sobs.

Mother had been in the hospital for a month. For the last week we had not been allowed to visit her, since no one was allowed to visit the hospital because of an epidemic of grippe. Mother also had a cold.

Myra put down the receiver and I could hardly hear her through the sobs: "Mother died. . . ."

The sun went out, the snow turned yellow. The floor was swinging under me. I had no tears. I was too terrified to cry. But Myra was crying and I did not want to see it. We had never known how to comfort each other. I went to mother's room, knelt in front of her bed, and put my head on it.

There is no more mother. The world remained as it was, life

goes on and there is no "mama" in it. How can it be? How stupid
and unimportant everything that has occupied me is now. All
those ideas, plans, people—everything. How stupid and unimportant if there is no more mama. What shall we do now, how do
we live now, if there is no mama? How can it *be* that there is no
mama?

She had died the night before at 9:00 P.M. and nobody had
noticed it. She was as quiet as always, but dead. They saw her
only in the morning. There was nobody beside her at the moment
of death. She was alone, as always. What did she think? Or did
the fever that wracked her weak body not permit her to think?
Nobody had been beside her for a whole week and perhaps she
had wanted to say something to us. How could she leave us
without saying anything? We must have had a talk, we must
have understood each other at last. I am sure she had something
very important to say.

She must be very calm now. She is at rest at last. I am happy
for her. There will be no more pain in her eyes. She is sleeping
quietly now for the first time during all those years. There are
some people who cannot be ill, who can never accept illness.
Mother could not and, after she became a complete invalid, did
not want to live. But she didn't want to die. . . . Death came.
Mama, was it painful? Is it painful to die of pneumonia? However it was, she is better now.

But what shall we do now? How could you go without forgiving us our sins against you? Our relatives have always warned
me that after your passing away I would never forgive myself for
being rude to you. Maybe they were right. But I shall not think
of my behavior now. What is the use of it if you cannot forgive
me? And God will not forgive me.

But there is one thing I shall never forget. And I do not ask
God to forgive me for it, for I shall never forgive myself.

That terrible night. I sat on the sofa, half insane, and you
did not sleep in the next room. You felt something had happened
to me and you wanted to help. You felt I was suffering and you
forgot about your sufferings. You called me many times, "Alla . . .
Alla. . . ." And I was silent. I was afraid to move. And you called

to me. You wanted so much to help me, to talk to me. And I rejected your help. I forced myself to say only: "Please, mama, don't." All the next day your nervous glance followed me, but I avoided it. I should have come to you and cried out everything. You would have told me how to be heedful of people and I would have been myself again. Instead I rejected your help, struggled alone, and came out cold-hearted and strong. But I missed that moment when you wanted to talk to me and I lost you forever.

Who were you? What did you think? Did you really mean it when you used to say, "Don't trust people"? Were you serious when you told me, "Try Israel. Maybe you will find happiness there. Here I did not find it." But then you denied your words and demanded that I stop my activities. And there was so much fear in your eyes then. What made you—who was so strong and proud—be afraid? What would you say if I decided to leave Russia now?

But I do not want anything now. I just want you back, to try to understand, to feel each other. Please come back!

I passed my hand over the bed. It was empty. No. . . . And you are right. You are better off there. You will have a new bed now. Not yet. We shall have to buy it. How much does it cost? Where shall we buy it? Ah, the relatives must decide it. Let it just be as quickly as possible. You must already have been taken to the morgue. It is so cold there. You must be freezing there, lying naked on a cold marble table. I do not want you to lie there, I hate even to think about it. Wood is warmer. And we shall bring you your favorite blue dress. . . .

I have a headache. I shall go to sleep. Mama. . . .

*   *   *

In three days everything was ready for the funeral. We went to the morgue. There was a round hall with a long table in the center. We sat on chairs near the door. Soon the side door opened. I closed my eyes. When I opened them, the coffin was already on the table. I looked at mother from where I sat. Very pale, her facial bones covered with white skin, gray hair, very unnatural. We did not move.

"Shall we take the deceased to the bus?" the huge Russian

attendant asked. "The deceased." The words struck me. There was something old-church Slavonic in it. They do not use the phrase much now. But what could be better than these quiet comforting words? The coffin was covered and taken to the bus. It was a very small wooden coffin, the cheapest. I did not mind. I knew that there were coffins lined with black and red silk or with white silk inside and tassels on the ends. No, I would not have insulted mother with tassels. Death is superior to all this.

The bus moved quietly along the Moscow streets. There were Myra and I, a few relatives absorbed probably in thinking about their own ends, and mother lying at our feet. I suddenly felt a strong feeling of tenderness toward the coffin and wanted to stroke it. But the relatives watched our reactions to the death intently during the intervals between their philosophizing, and I did not move.

We arrived exactly on time. Coffins were entering the crematorium—relieved mourners coming out. The crematorium is a dark gray building with a tall tower breathing out black smoke. It must have been built by sadists to spoil the life of the whole neighborhood and all the passers-by. There was no more space in the ground and urns were put into specially constructed cement walls. Some of these walls were inside buildings and looked like incubators. I once saw there a young woman whose mother's urn had been put on the very top of such a wall. She was crying bitterly and I understood her.

We were lucky. We had got a place in the ground for mama, the old grave of a second cousin.

Our turn came and we all entered the hall. The coffin, which had been placed on a black velvet platform, was opened and musicians began in a businesslike way to play something sad to help people weep. Mama's hands were covered by a white sheet.

For the first time I began to cry. I cried and cried. The tears washed my tired thoughts and wet the fur collar of my coat. Myra was sobbing beside me. Trying to catch a trembling of her eyelids, I did not take my eyes off mother's face. My relatives insisted that I kiss her, but my face was very wet and I didn't want to let my tears fall on her, lest she raise her hand to wipe them away.

A woman attendant came in and said, "Your time is up!" She closed the coffin, turned some invisible lever, the coffin went down like an elevator, and two black velvet doors closed. The music stopped. The end. As we went to the exit, the next coffin was coming in.

⁕ ⁕ ⁕

Several months later we got a small white urn in the shape of a flower pot. I held it without fear, feeling the same tenderness toward it that I had felt toward the coffin. A worker took the stone off the grave, we put the urn in there, and arranged the ground again.

I seldom found time to go to mother's grave, but when I did, I never felt sad. I was quiet and comfortable and talked a lot to mother, telling her all my news.

And in 1969 I had more news than I had ever had in my life.

Today, September 22, 1969, I was expelled from Komsomol. Yes, I have to write these words and try to believe them. The girl who wrote my diary for 1962–63 could never have believed them. But they are true.

After what happened today, I rushed to a bookshop, bought a pen and a little notebook. I could not wait to get home. I am afraid I shall lose what I feel now, this feeling which makes my head burn and my heart beat violently. In two hours perhaps this will not seem so awful and in two days perhaps I shall forget it, just as Anne Frank got used to her life as a prisoner and the inhabitants of the Warsaw ghetto passed corpses in the streets without paying any attention.

Not that I compare my situation to theirs. I just want to remain clearly aware of what is happening to me. Let me recall everything from the beginning.

After mother's death, I could see no reason to delay applying for an exit visa to Israel. There was nothing to keep me in this country. I had lost everything that tied me to it. I saw my future life as being in Israel. I knew the struggle to get there would be long and I had to begin it as soon as possible. One of my distant relatives in Riga had been allowed to leave Russia and I had asked him to arrange an invitation from a relative for me. In two months the invitation arrived. I took it from the postman and just sat looking at the envelope without opening it. Until that moment my plans had never seemed real, but now this document with the red seal of the Israeli Foreign Ministry was a signal for me to begin. With the invitation in my hands, I realized for the first time that there was no way back.

Next day I went to the Department of Visas of the Interior Ministry and was instructed on the procedure for making application. I had to provide: two photographs, a document from the housing authorities, two copies of a filled-in questionnaire, stamps of state taxes for four rubles, and a character reference from my place of work. That was it! I had already heard that the last item would cause all the trouble. It would be a signal for all your colleagues to bait you and finally to throw you out. Does the Interior Ministry really want to know whether you are good enough at your work to go to Israel? No, this is just one of the more refined methods of torture. In my case it took them five months to give me the character reference.

I asked for it one day at the end of April. My Chief said, "I know, you want to catch a millionaire there and become rich. But look at yourself. Don't you think there are enough really pretty, sweet-scented girls there?" I didn't argue. People think in different ways and if I had begun to tell him of my ideals, he would have made fun of them. He was witty enough to do it rather cruelly.

Two days later a member of the Party Committee of the Institute, a handsome middle-aged man, a Jew, invited me for a talk. He began to tell me a lot about his travels abroad in Western Europe, how side by side with wealth he saw terrible poverty there, how strongly he missed his motherland during these trips. I listened silently and very attentively. When he finished two hours later, I said: "Will you please try to hasten the giving of my character reference? I want to leave as soon as possible." He shrugged his shoulders and let me go.

A week later the secretary of the Committee of Komsomol, a young handsome Jew, came to talk to me. He began to tell me about his numerous trips abroad, how people of a Communist point of view were persecuted, how members of Communist parties could exist and publish their newspapers only with the help of the Soviet Union. I listened to him silently and with understanding. When he finished, I asked: "When will my character reference be ready?" He shrugged his shoulders and said: "You cannot be given this document without being expelled from Komsomol." I had expected this but wanted to resist to see what would happen. "I cannot agree with this, but as you will have to convene a Komsomol meeting I shall explain my point of view on this question at the meeting."

The meeting was not convened for three months. In the meantime I was on leave for two weeks and when I returned I found the whole of my department changed. The moment I arrived at the Institute, I was called to my Chief for a talk. He preferred to talk to me in the corridor.

"Do you take the salaries of our workers from the cashier?"

"Yes, I usually do it and give them out according to a register."

"Did you ever take money from the salaries of some people?"

"What do you mean?"

"No, please, do understand me correctly. Look here, last week someone reported to the Director that you used to take a ruble from the salaries of all Jews in the department and gather them for Israel."

"Do you believe it?"

"Of course not. I just wanted to make sure."

"Did they ask the Jews themselves?"

"Yes, all of them were called to the Special Department and they all denied it."

"Thank them for nothing."

"I think it would be better if you didn't sit in that room any more. Your presence will make their imaginations work harder. Move to my room. You will be alone and no one will bother you."

He hurried to his room, worried that he had already stayed too long with me in the corridor. I remained alone, people passing me by. I felt terribly tired though the working day had just begun. I thought:

"It is only the beginning. What else will they invent against me? Dozens of grown-up people against me. Have they forgotten everything for which they used to love me and take care of me? That I am young and an orphan, that I have been kind and am a good worker? Now they consider me a traitor. No, they are afraid themselves. Well, if you are afraid, I shall not be; if you try to destroy me to save yourselves, I shall despise you."

I entered the room. Everyone immediately became silent and absorbed in his work. I gathered my things, looked around the room with a sunny smile, and left it. I wanted to cry.

People passed me looking down at the floor or up at the ceiling or just aside, each to his own liking. But a few people who had never greeted me before began to utter a short "Hello" while passing me quickly, looking aside. This was enough to make me strong.

Time passed. I reminded them every day about the character reference, but they postponed it from week to week. They seemed to be consulting someone in higher echelons. Mine was one of the few cases in Moscow and the Party authorities were not yet experienced in handling such situations.

At last the date of the first meeting was set. On that day I worked as usual at my files, trying to avoid thinking about the meeting. But when I was at last invited to come down to the Party Committee's room, I felt I had never for a moment stopped thinking about it. Yet I also felt as if I were going to an exam unprepared. I couldn't even imagine what kind of questions would be asked. I went downstairs slowly, trying to overcome my nervousness. I succeeded only as I opened the door. It was just like an examination where my nervousness disappears the moment I take the examination ticket.

There were about ten people in the room, the members of Komsomol, and two Party members. Everyone seemed to be feeling uneasy and I thought to myself that at least one person should be at ease, and it might as well be I.

I sat down in a chair in the center of the room. They were all sitting along the walls. The necessity of turning my head to answer each question made me feel peculiar. I knew only one thing for certain. I would not be aggressive or give them any possibility of accusing me of anti-Soviet convictions.

"You want to apply for an exit visa to Israel. What is the reason for it?"

"You know I am an orphan and in Israel I have relatives."

"But do you know what kind of a state Israel is?"

"That doesn't change anything. Whatever Israel is, my relatives happen to live there and I want to be reunited with them."

"You have a good job, you study here, the State took care of you, and at last you are a grown-up person. Whom are you trying to deceive with your story about relatives?"

"I want to be reunited with my relatives," I repeated distinctly and loudly.

"But do you know that this desire of yours does not conform to the principles of Komsomol?"

"No. I do not see any connection between these two things."

"Read the Rules of Komsomol. In the first paragraph it states: 'The member of Komsomol must be loyal to his Soviet motherland.'"

"Who says I am not?"

"But you want to leave it."

"That does not mean I am not loyal. I can even remain loyal to it after I leave it."

"How can you if you want to leave for Israel, an aggressive, nationalistic, imperialist state, the enemy of the Soviet Union?"

"There are Communists all over the world. All of them are

loyal to the Soviet Union. Israel has two Communist parties. Maybe I shall work for communism there." (God forbid!—I could not help saying to myself.)

"But you are leaving the Soviet Union, so you cannot remain a member of Komsomol. It is simply unnatural."

"Of course it is. As soon as I am allowed to leave the country, I shall resign. But I am not leaving yet and who knows when I shall be allowed to go. And just for having the desire to leave, you cannot expel me."

"Who said we cannot? We shall." This was said by one of the Party members, the Deputy Secretary of the Institute's Party Committee, a middle-aged Jew.

The questions were pouring in from all sides. It was like a game where one person stands in a circle and the other players throw him a ball and he returns it. I enjoyed it and tried to behave according to my understanding of the game—to be logical and not aggressive.

"But do you know that our state supports the Arab countries with armaments?" the pretty Secretary of the Komsomol Committee, who used to travel a lot, asked.

This was a blow below the belt and I couldn't help throwing the ball back with hatred, "Unfortunately, I do." Now they had caught me.

The Party member jumped up. "What do you mean by 'unfortunately'?"

I looked at him with disgust and didn't answer. "I think, comrades, the case is clear," the Deputy Secretary pushed forward. "All this argument is useless. A member of Komsomol dares to apply to leave the Soviet motherland to go to a capitalist and, I would even say, fascist state."

"I'm sorry," a voice behind me interrupted. I turned around. It was my colleague, a young Jewish boy who had never seemed enthusiastic about my ideas and was one of those who had assured me that he belonged to no national group but to the whole world of people. I listened to him with surprise. His voice trembled with his inner struggle. "I am sorry, comrades, but I do not think we can say this. All of us know very well that there are some really fascist states like Greece, for example, and the imperialist United States that is waging war in Vietnam. And yet our country still has diplomatic relations with them, though none with Israel."

("Thank you for nothing," I thought.)

"Our state," the Party man answered in an irritated voice, "defines its diplomatic relations according to its interests and current policy."

Everybody was dumfounded at such idiotic frankness. Silence fell in the room.

"Let's start the voting," the Komsomol Secretary hurried to break it. "Who is in favor of expelling Alla Milkina from the ranks of Komsomol for behavior not in accordance with the Rules of Komsomol?"

The hands began slowly to rise. One, two, three . . . nine. My unexpected supporter was last. He hesitated, but having looked convulsively around, he slowly raised his hand. Unanimous!

"The resolution will be confirmed at the Institute's Party Committee meeting and then at the District Komsomol Committee. Only then will you be given the character reference."

I stood up and left the room.

✻   ✻   ✻

I left the Research Institute and went out into the street. It was late summer: stuffy, dusty Moscow. I looked to the left, then to the right. Where should I go? How I wished there was somebody to whom I could tell all this. But I have nobody. So why are you standing here indecisively? Go home, enjoy your loneliness. Talk to yourself. You chose to be alone. You neglected friends. But if I had them now, would it be any better? Don't they have the same troubles? Would they be interested in listening to the same story? Who really needs me? Nobody. And why should I mix with them just to make myself believe I am not alone? No, I'd better go home, cook a good dinner for myself, wash something, and just be by myself.

✻   ✻   ✻

The second meeting didn't differ from the first. After it I was deprived of my quarterly premium which I needed to help make ends meet. The atmosphere around me grew more and more tense. Two Jewish engineers left after they had been called to the Special Department and asked about their contacts with me. Someone had reported to the Department that one of them was the leader of the underground Zionist organization and I was his assistant. Poor men! And they had nothing to do with me!

Though I was not afraid, the baiting made me more and more exhausted. I returned home half-dead with fatigue, tension, and hunger. I stopped taking care of myself, didn't arrange my long hair, dressed slovenly. In one month I began to look like an old hag.

Finally the day of the "complete solution of the Jewish question" arrived. And it was today, the 22nd of September 1969.

In the morning I began to feel very nervous and could do nothing. I was certain this meeting would be more businesslike and less terrifying than the previous ones. This time I would be meeting with professional Communists who are more careful in dealing with people than are those Party members who feel they must constantly prove their loyalty.

Our Secretary of Komsomol accompanied me to the District Komsomol Committee. Walking beside him, I thought that I could never have gone out with him socially although he was rather good-looking. He was a terrible fool and a coward. He was afraid not only of his chiefs, but of me. When he was alone with me, he was very polite.

We had to wait in the reception room, for there was a long line of young boys and girls who were being accepted into Komsomol. I sat there remembering the day in 1965 when I had been accepted into Komsomol. I was not yet fourteen, but because of my good grades and behavior and my activities in social work, I had been recommended for membership in Komsomol. I remember how disappointed I was when we were accepted not individually but in large groups and when all the pupils without exception, including those who did not deserve it to my mind, were accepted. I had thought membership in Komsomol a great honor, but it had been given to everyone. I remembered how I had looked every minute at my Komsomol badge—a red banner with a golden profile of Lenin—and how I took my Komsomol card everywhere with me.

Now, a little more than five years later, I am again in the office of the District Komsomol Committee.

When my turn came, we entered the big hall of the meetings of the Bureau of the Committee. There was a large portrait of Lenin and a tall, thin, neatly dressed man sitting under it at the head of a long table, covered with a green velvet tablecloth. There were three other members of the Bureau, the representatives of the larger enterprises of the District: a man who resembled the pictures of workers on placards and two women who looked like weavers, those old women of about thirty who do their hair only in buns and wear neat white blouses—anything else would be considered "imitation of the capitalist West."

They met me with a broad smile as though I were the next candidate for Komsomol and invited me to sit down at the end of the table. My Secretary hastened to dispel their illusion. The mask of welcome left their faces, to be replaced with a very real expression of dislike. My illusion, of having to deal with business-like professional Communists, was dispelled.

Then I suddenly became deaf. I saw their shouting mouths, but could not make out one word from the flood. I sat with my hands on my lap under the table, trying to hide the short and threadbare sleeves of my old sweater. But as soon as I understood that they were insulting me, I forgot about that. I lifted both hands and stretched them forward with coupled fingers on the table. My back straightened. I raised my head and looked directly at them. Scraps of their words began to reach my mind.

"You have eaten Russian bread. We gave you an education."

"Who is that aunt of yours, a capitalist?"

"You hid your real face for five years, you deceived Komsomol!"

"Your parents are buried in this land." (I remembered the death of my mother, the Party veteran. This made me open my mouth.)

"I want to reunite with my family."

"We, the Soviet people, are your family."

"Please, let me choose my family myself."

"Shut up, don't you dare speak in such a tone or we shall arrange things so that you never go to your Israel."

I was silent.

"Ah, let her go to the devil himself. Give me her card." My Secretary ran up to him and handed in my Komsomol card. The Secretary of the Bureau looked at it with disgust.

"I don't understand," cackled one of the weavers, "How can *they* do it?"

"Don't you know," the worker explained, "that *they* always betrayed us and will always betray. Who do you think betrayed us during the war?"

I am silent! How happy I am to hear this. For all of my twenty years I have waited to hear these words and now they have been said. Never before could I really understand what anti-Semitism was and here it is. Now I have no more doubts. I know that I am right because I have seen what is wrong, what is evil.

I clenched my teeth and forbade myself to open my mouth. The shouts continued until the Secretary said at last: "Go away. We hope to see you no more."

"Thank you," I smiled at him, stood up, and went to the door.

"You've already prepared an anti-Soviet article, haven't you?" the worker sent the last shot at my back. My back answered him with silence and disappeared behind the door.

I neither noticed how my Secretary took leave of me nor how I passed the big park in front of the Committee's building. Even the drizzling rain could not put out the flame which was burning inside me and in my face. I wanted to do something. I was almost running, although I didn't know where to go. Then I decided that in spite of what had happened or rather because of it, I must go to my classes at the Institute. I would continue to study, I would continue to live in spite of them. I bought the notebook and a pen in a bookshop, went down into the subway, and began to write in the subway car. How right I was to begin then. Now, as I am finishing, I feel much quieter. I have already lost the shock at feeling the hatred directed against me. My holy indignation has combined with a feeling of happiness that I am on the right path. But I shall never forget the hatred.

❋   ❋   ❋

A week later when I had gathered all the necessary documents, I went to the Interior Ministry to hand in my application. The official, a red-headed dried-up woman, was not very welcoming. She looked through my documents and, having found nothing wrong, she provided me with "discouraging" information about military service for girls in Israel. When I did not respond, she concluded: "I accept your documents, but I assure you that you will be refused."

"Why?"

"Because you haven't any close relatives there."

"What if I haven't any close relatives at all?"

"Then you should stay here."

I stood up and left the room. I had finally gone through the seven circles of Hades, and felt terribly relieved. But I shall be alone no more. There are people doing the same thing I'm doing and thinking the same way. I must be with them.

At David's "going away" party I saw many new people of different ages, professions. They are all together and I shall join them. I'll find friends my own age, I'll be young again. And I'll start the same way I came to Zionism two years ago—at the celebration of Simhat Torah in the synagogue. Next year in Jerusalem.

❋   ❋   ❋

On the 4th of October, I approached the synagogue with mixed feelings of happiness and the remorse of a prodigal daughter. The narrow street had become even more crowded than two years before. I passed through the dancing, singing, shouting, and laughing crowd without seeing a single familiar face. But I hoped to meet my old acquaintances in front of the synagogue.

That day in the morning a man had called me on the telephone: "This is Yosif speaking."

"What Yosif?"

"I came from Riga."

I searched back in my memory and fortunately it didn't fail me. "Oh, yes, how are you and when did you come?"

He was one of the boys whom I met in Riga. I hadn't known him well, but I remembered him as a tall, very handsome boy with curly black hair. We arranged to meet in the evening in front of the synagogue.

And now I ran into him there. We turned aside. At twenty years old he only slightly resembled that teen-ager of 1967. He gave me regards from my Riga acquaintances and asked about me. I suddenly felt that I wanted to tell him everything. All that had happened in the last two years poured out of me. There was something of Riga in him and he looked at me with the eyes of Riga. And those eyes were sad. Yes, Yosif, I know that I look awful. Yes, Riga, I know that I have changed a lot. But I have come back and that is the most important thing.

We joined one of the circles and soon lost each other in the crowd. I met some of my old acquaintances. They greeted me and asked no questions. I was grateful to them for this. New dances, new songs, new boys and girls dancing their ritual dances of the reborn Jew in circles. How much I had missed!

A foreign-looking but clearly Jewish man was standing in the center of one of the most active circles. There was a tape recorder in his bag and he spoke constantly into a microphone, translating the meanings of the songs. I prompted him with the translation of one of the lines in order to show that I knew English. I was not mistaken. He seized me by the hand: "Do you know English?"

"Yes."

"Would you consent to answer some of my questions in English?"

"Yes, with pleasure."

We stepped aside and I told him my story. One of his questions was: "Why are you all not afraid to be here?"

The question was difficult and I replied with a joke: "We fear nothing near the synagogue."

I don't know whether he was satisfied with the answer, but I was not. It was not true. People can be afraid in any place. I was not afraid then because I had never yet been punished, because I did not realize the real danger of it. I think the majority of those who were there were in the same position. When I came to realize the danger, I became very much afraid, but I still came to the synagogue.

A week later my aunt told us with excitement and fear that her friends had heard on a Yiddish broadcast from Israel an interview with a Moscow Jewish girl who had been expelled from Komsomol and had applied for an exit visa to Israel. Myra looked at me then with a smile.

I left the synagogue alone and went home. I was full of excitement after my interview with a foreign correspondent, joy about my return, and dreams of new friends, parties, activities. The long way home in the subway passed very quickly. I did not even notice how I reached my house in the darkness that usually frightened me.

Suddenly I saw that a man in a gray raincoat had entered my house before me. When I entered, I noticed him standing in the doorway. He stepped aside and let me pass. I began to climb the steps and it immediately occurred to me that he wanted to see which apartment I lived in. I climbed slowly trying to think of something, but the safest thing was to enter my apartment and be at home. I opened the door, closed it behind me, and stood near it holding my breath. The steps came up and then approached my door. The moment was so tense that I stopped being afraid and became all ears. The man lit a match and was probably looking at the number of the apartment. Then he hurried down the stairs. As soon as he reached the ground floor, I opened my door and ran up to the window in the staircase from which I could see the street. Three men in gray raincoats came out of our entrance. I followed them with my eyes, smiling: "You haven't forgotten me, have you? O.K. I shall try my best to live up to your suspicions."

∽10∽

What a marvelous idea. We are going to Riga in December. Natasha, Basja, Olja, Bettie, and three boys. We decided to go at one of the last parties—just decided and that was that. None of us has any idea of how we will make it, but we all know we'll manage somehow.

It sometimes happens that an idea takes you so strongly that you feel if you don't carry through with it, you will not forgive yourself. For example, I cannot imagine now where I shall get the money for the trip. Then I think that by the end of the month I shall get my two weeks' salary and this will be just enough for the tickets to Riga and back. What shall I do when I come back to Moscow? I don't know. It will have to work out one way or another.

Maybe I shouldn't go. Oh, no. I must get away for a time. I must see something new. I am sure it will mean a lot to me. And then think of the fun with the friends. Cannot I give myself this pleasure? Just to dream about the trip makes me happy.

I shall go in my red velveteen suit and take Myra's black and white dress. She doesn't wear it any more and it is so becoming on me. All the girls are wonderful. Bettie is going with her husband, Zeyev. Two years ago when he used to come to my place he was Vladimir. Now he has become very religious and has learned a lot of Hebrew. She does not know what to do with him. He refuses to eat meat because it is not kosher. Where can she get kosher meat in Moscow? A funny couple.

Pretty, plump Basja will make us laugh all the way. She is so funny with her typically Jewish mannerisms. Olja has not changed much since 1967 when David first brought her to one of my parties. She has remained very bashful. Natasha is new. She is the youngest among us, only eighteen, but she is quite mature.

It is pleasant to have these friends. I think about them and it helps me not to pay attention to the situation at my job. And now the trip to Riga completely possesses my thoughts.

We are going for four days—December 4, 5, 6, and 7. The 5th of December is the holiday of the Soviet Constitution, so there will be no work. And the 6th and 7th are the weekend. But the most important thing is that these days are the Jewish holiday of Hanukkah. That is what really made us think about going to Riga. In Moscow almost nobody really knows how to celebrate Jewish holidays. And if they do celebrate, then they do it very symbolically in a Zionist way. But in Latvia all the rituals are carefully observed, and young people of our age know them as well as their parents. The whole of Jewish Riga will celebrate Hanukkah in families or in groups, but certainly according to all religious rules. And we want very much to see and to join in this celebration.

So we are going. We have decided and at least nothing can prevent me. All the others have to ask permission from parents, to ask them for money. I go when I want and where I want. I am free and independent. Is it good? I don't know. When I see problems between fathers and sons or when I watch a family quarrel, I want to close my eyes and ears and run away. But sometimes I feel I want someone to say "stop" or to advise me. But would I obey? I doubt it.

Are we really going to Riga? I cannot believe it! How happy I am!

*   *   *

The trip is over. We are flying back to Moscow. Every minute of those four days was happiness. Every moment was full of meaning. But I am not sorry it is over; such concentrated joy could not and should not last too long. Moreover, I feel that there will be a continuation of everything we found there. I saw it in the faces of our friends who saw us off at the airport.

We arrived in Riga just in time for the lighting of the first Hanukkah candle. (Now I know something about it.) We went to beautiful Ruth's apartment where the party was going to take place. Ruth has changed a lot since 1967, but she is still the same hospitable and easygoing girl. We are both a little reticent. It is so difficult to get rid of the unpleasant aftertaste of what separated us two years ago and was one of the reasons for my retiring. But we shall try our best, shall we not, Ruth? Isn't the idea that unites people more important than all the trifles that occasionally separate them? And I shall never forget that you were the first to tell me about Israel and what it meant to be Jewish. You brought me salvation in your beautiful hands saying: "Look . . . Listen . . . Read!" I remember your hands holding picture postcards with a blue sky and orange trees or thumbing a volume of Dubnov's *History of the Jews* or showing me a record of Yaffa Yarkoni. You gave me part of your great love for Israel and for this I shall always be grateful.

Ruth's mother rushed to us with questions in Hebrew. I hastened to escape. Her Hebrew, learned in a prewar Hebrew high school, was too good and too fluent for me to understand it. Zeyev would have to uphold the honor of the young Moscow Zionists.

The apartment was already full of people and many more were expected. They all knew we were coming and came earlier specially to meet us here. My dear friend since 1967, Tsvisha, everybody's pet; serious and mature Lev and his younger brother Yehoshua; Yosif, whom I had met in Moscow on Simhat Torah. I didn't expect to see him, for he had not been sociable in 1967. I felt very free with everybody else, but he made me nervous. He was too handsome and every time he spoke to me I began to talk very quickly and stupidly, avoiding his eyes. I certainly didn't want any emotional involvement now and there must be many girls in Riga who were interested in him. But he was so handsome, that I involuntarily sought him in the crowd.

Natasha was already talking to the brothers, Lev and Yehoshua. Lev was very clever and erudite. I wondered what they were talking about. Probably the eternal problem of Russian Jews, whether it was more important to revive Jewish culture in the Soviet Union or go to Israel. It seemed so stupid to argue, when everyone had already applied for visas to Israel. Anyway, what would be the use of reviving the culture when it had been deliberately and cruelly destroyed over and over again through-

out the centuries? Well, Jews love to discuss. I could imagine the
flood of facts, quotations, and Hebrew sayings Lev was throwing
at Natasha.

The group in the corner seemed to be on the brink of a
quarrel. Of course, Yiddishists and Hebraists. The Hebraists
seemed self-composed and calm, confident of their victory. The
Yiddishists were very aggressive, but Yiddish has no importance
among the new generation of Russian Zionists.

The evening had not yet begun. We discussed the new songs
we had learned. For us songs were a main source of inspiration.

"Let's have a contest—one song from Riga, then one from
Moscow. Then we'll see who knows more."

"O.K." Riga began with a Hasidic song: *"Yossis alayich
Elochayich, kimsos hosn al kalo"* ("The Lord will rejoice over
you [O Israel] as a groom rejoices over his bride"). A wonderful
song! But I winked at Natasha; we answered with one of our best
"Lo yisa goy el goy herev, lo yilmedu od milhama" ("Nation shall
not lift up sword against nation, neither shall they learn war any
more"). They were delighted. The contest continued. Riga won.
Many more songs, nearly all of them in Hebrew or in Yiddish,
while most of ours were in Russian. But *"Lo yisa goy"* was recognized as the best song of the evening. And we knew something
else that nobody, I was sure, knew in the Soviet Union—three
Israeli folk dances. We had learned them from American tourists
on the night of Simhat Torah. We danced and Riga admitted
defeat.

Then someone spoke. A middle-aged man told us the story of
Hanukkah. He was excited, looking at something far away. He
was there then, fighting together with Judah Maccabee, cleans-
ing the Holy Temple, lighting the oil in the small jug. He had
quite forgotten that he was in the twentieth century, thousands
of miles away from his Holy Land, among young people born in
Galut, and that he was telling the story of their ancestors—a
story some of them had never heard before.

A thoughtful silence fell in the room full of standing people.
And then one of Ruth's family began to recite the benedictions
and lit the first candle. I could not follow his biblical Hebrew, so

I looked around. I looked at the Jewish faces in the light of the candles. Their eyes reflected the glimmering flame, or perhaps it was their inner flame, aroused by the story of Hanukkah. Every time I see Jewish faces around me, I feel happy and safe. I touched Natasha's hand, "Look, aren't they wonderful, these people? They look like Israelis." But how could I know, having never been there? They were beautiful and that was why they looked like Israelis.

And Jewish eyes—eyes that can tell you everything, eyes that reveal, eyes that beg, demand, but seldom laugh. Eyes that live their own lives separate from their faces. Eyes that make me strong and sad, proud and frightened.

The boy, Leib Khnokh, could be described in two words—eyes and beard. Huge, black, sad eyes and a curly black beard. I wondered if Mary, his pretty girl friend, was not afraid of his eyes. There was one boy who was always laughing and couldn't stand still for a minute. He was full of energy, joy, and youth. His name was Izja Zalmanson. He was very young, good-looking, strong. Why shouldn't he be happy and gay? Why should we always carry the burden of our history? We might be the first generation of Happy Jews. (*Leib Khnokh, aged twenty-six, an electrician, was arrested on June 15, 1970. Sentenced to ten years of imprisonment in a hard labor camp. Mary Khnokh (neé Mendelevitch), twenty, student, arrested on June 15, 1970, pregnant. Released at the end of 1971. Arrived in Israel with her newly born son. Israel Zalmanson, age twenty-two, student. Arrested on June 15, 1970. Sentenced to eight years in a hard labor camp.*)

I looked at the Jewish faces. My dear people, I love you, I love my distant motherland. I wish that all of you will soon be in Israel and we will celebrate Jewish holidays at home. All of you are struggling for emigration to Israel, but I don't want you to become heroes because heroes appear when the people are in trouble. Pharaoh, let my people go without making them heroes!

The benedictions were over and I finished my prayer. Wine, cookies, jokes, conversation. The Riga boys helped us to learn the words of a new song. They wrote them down easily in Hebrew. Unbelievable!

It was already late at night when one of Ruth's best friends arrived. Always late, always busy, and tired, he was completely unaware of and uninterested in his good looks. He came to gatherings like this and sat in an armchair half-asleep. But at least he spent an hour among friends. I greeted him. I had met Misha in 1967. *Michael Shepshelovich, age twenty-seven, engineer, arrested in November 1970. Sentenced to two years in a hard labor camp.*

Pinchas, Leib's brother, with a deep bass voice, sang "Let My People Go." This song, by an unknown author, is so moving that we in Moscow could not help but sing it aloud at the synagogue. And now in Riga everybody joined in his singing with an aggressive readiness—bearded boys and slender girls, sad men, and vivid Jewish women.

> *I say to Pharaoh*
> *Let My People go;*
> *Let the Jewish People go*
> *To their homeland.*
>
> *Never shall I tire of repeating:*
> *Let My People go!*
>
> *Into God's way*
> *Let My People go!*
>
> *For your own safety*
> *Don't keep My People*
> *Let My People go home.*

Ruth introduced us to a boy from Minsk. She said he was famous for his wonderful Russian, Yiddish, and Hebrew songs about Israel and about us, the Russian Jews. I had noticed him but would never have thought he was a composer and a poet. I would have characterized him as a mixture of Odessan Jewish hooligan and a *yeshiva* student. He was thickset with a wide neck and short beard, which set off his wide face. His sharp eyes were sometimes indifferent and often mocking. He looked out through round glasses which constantly drooped on his nose and which he automatically straightened with his middle finger. His rapid speech was interspersed with Jewish *hochmas* and his jokes could make even statues blush.

But how he changed when he sang his songs about Israel, beating the tempo with his right foot and swinging his right hand. Then he looked like a praying Hasid.

"*Nu*, Isroel, did you bring something new?"

"You know, I never come to Riga without new songs. This time I have two. One in Russian and one in Hebrew. I have called the first song 'The Nearest East of Mine.' Listen to it:

> *I live so far from you*
> *In a distant and strange land*
> *But in my heart I am from my birth with you*
> *The Nearest East of mine.*
> *The land calls me*
> *In which I never have been*
> *My land—my star*
> *The Nearest East of mine.*

> *When war came to your land*
> *I suffered together with you*
> *And together with you I burned in its flame*
> *The Nearest East of mine.*
> *And together with you after all troubles*
> *I was happy with the victory*
> *I am your soldier and I am the same age**
> *The Nearest East of mine.*

> *There the air is mine and the sand is mine*
> *And all the people are my friends*
> *My land, my country*
> *The Nearest East of mine.*

> *I believe I shall cover all these thousands of kilometers*
> *And I shall come to you*
> *And I shall come down to your land*
> *The Nearest East of mine.*

> *My dear fatherland,*
> *It is lost in strange sands*
> *My shield with six points*
> *The Nearest East of mine.*

No one moved or uttered a word. Nothing could express better the thoughts of everyone than this song. And these thoughts were sad. I had felt a lump in my throat at the words, "I

* Isroel was born on the 14th of May 1948, the Independence Day of Israel.

shall come down to your land." How could young people be so
sentimental? But we are young only in age; in mind we are all
two thousand years old.

Isroel broke the silence with his second song which was in
Hebrew. It was called: *"Kahol velavan"* ("The Blue and the
White").

> *The blue and the white*
> *These are my colors*
> *The blue and the white*
> *The colors of my land*
> *The blue and the white*
> *These are my colors*
> *For all my days, forever.*
>
> *The blue and the white*
> *There are no other colors.*
> *The blue and the white*
> *I repeat and repeat*
> *The blue and the white*
> *Like a song, like a dream,*
> *The blue and the white*
> *A hope and peace.*
> *The blue and the white*
> *Hermon and Kinnereth*
> *The blue and the white*
> *My heart sings.*
> *The blue and the white*
> *The sky and the snow*
> *The blue and the white*
> *This is so wonderful!*
> *The blue and the white*
> *These are my colors*
> *For all my days—forever.*

By the second couplet we had all joined in singing the magic
line "The blue and the white." The chorus grew and grew and the
song sounded like a hymn. We had been waiting for this song for
years, the song of our faith and hope, our oath of allegiance and
love for our motherland. Now it came and in the language of our
distant past and near future—Hebrew.

✿   ✿   ✿

Next morning we went to the Riga suburb of Rumbula. Thirty-six thousand Jews from the Riga Jewish ghetto had been shot and burned there. Until the sixties the bones had lain unburied. Then the Jews of Riga came with their children, made several huge graves, and put the bones in them. One grave was for the children. Each season the Jewish youth of Riga go there to clean the graves and to plant new flowers. On the anniversary of the destruction of the ghetto, thousands of Jews come there to pray for the memory of those slain.

In 1967 Ruth had brought me there and I took part in the summer maintenance of the graves. During heavy rains, little white bits of bones appear again and again on the ground—there is no end to them. The earth itself seems to remind people of the tragedy. At that time I had gathered some of these little pieces with black traces of fire and brought them to Moscow. Every time I felt fear, tiredness, or despair, I looked at those bones. They helped me to gain strength. The fire that had burned them nurtured the flame that had been lit in me.

And I remembered. One day at my friend's house I happened to see an album of photos from the Warsaw Jewish ghetto. The book was published in Poland and was a very rare thing in Russia. In fact such literature was "unadvisable" for a Soviet citizen. I had never seen it since that time. But every picture stamped itself upon my memory forever. During the whole week after I saw the book, I could think about nothing but those pictures. I was frightened, deadly frightened.

What if it comes again? They will take me. No, I shall escape. I do not look Jewish. They will not recognize me as a Jew. But Myra? They will catch her immediately. Then that will be the end. I shall go wherever they take her.

Stop it! I am going mad. This will never come again. Never. And then I have nothing to do with this. I was even born long after this. I am just imposing these thoughts on myself. They are unnatural.

Unnatural? But do not I belong to them? Do not even fingertips feel when the whole body is suffering? If they don't, then they are sick, their main senses are atrophied. But the fact is that

they will die if the whole organism dies whether they feel it or
not. But I feel and this is natural. This was my pain, my fear, my
Holocaust. Can I forget all this?

This time we all went to Rumbula. The Jews from Moscow,
far from all Jewish mass graves, went to swear that we also
would not forget.

The remaining days passed in careless happiness. We went
to the seashore and danced a sunny *hora* on the snow-covered
shore of the northern sea. We retold Jewish jokes and fell into
snowdrifts with screams of laughter. We threw snowballs and
drank coffee with whipped cream in empty seaside coffeehouses.

The stars shone in the black sky and the moon threw its
silver light over the snow carpet and the fairy-tale fir trees especially for us. And for us beautiful medieval Riga became more
majestic.

Tsvisha, Lev, and Yehoshua were with us all the time.
Yehoshua, with his silent girl friend, Rochl, and Lev with
Natasha, continuing their endless conversation and he looking
attentively into her serious eyes.

But Yosif surprised me more than anyone. He seized every
free minute to join us and went with us on our trip to the seashore. Every time I saw him joining our evening Hanukkah parties or running to us along the shore, joy swept over me, but I
showed it to no one and hardly to myself.

Generally we were all in love with each other and could
hardly imagine parting. We promised that we would use the New
Year holiday to meet. It was beyond all reason in respect to
money and time, but they promised to come to Moscow.

On the 7th of December, they saw us off at the airport. We
had paid our last silent visit to the Rumbula graves near the Riga
airport and went slowly to the terminal. Until the last moment
we could not imagine that we were parting, but the moment
came. We shook hands with all the boys except Tsvisha to whom
we could not help giving a kiss. Yosif was the last to whom I
came to say good-by. I put on the most careless air I could and
smiled:

"Please, Yosif, come to us on the New Year."

"I doubt it, but who knows."

We all ran to the plane, waving good-by. I looked back at Yosif and stood dumfounded. I could barely see his face, but his glance pierced me. There was such sorrow in his eyes that I was ready to rush back. "How could you not understand?" his eyes seemed to say. But I could not believe it and ran to the plane.

When we were airborne, everyone was sad. Then someone said, "Do you remember that joke about...."

"Leave us alone."

11

The New Year was coming and we decided to welcome it in a circle of young people no older than twenty-five. The Zionist community had grown greatly during the past two years and we could afford to divide into two groups for the New Year's night.

It had long been our dream to form a youth group and to feel that we were not only Zionists, but young people as well. Later on we would be able to develop different kinds of activities for this group, different from those of the older people. We wanted generally to get together, go on trips, dance, drink, make new friends, and fall in love. If we were to live under such conditions for many years, we should develop and live naturally, according to the laws of Nature and social life.

The celebration of the New Year was the first step in this plan. Forty boys and girls wanted to come and we had a problem about a lack of space and food. We were not acquainted with the majority of our guests, who had all been invited through a chain of acquaintances. It would be interesting to see new people, but our happiness on that night depended on the coming of the boys from Riga. We were waiting for their call with bated breath. The boys had only three or four days of holidays before their examinations. They had to spend two nights on a train or pay a lot of money for airplane tickets. Therefore, we felt, their decision to come or not come would show their real interest in us: Lev's in Natasha, Tsvisha's in all of us, and Yosif's in . . . me.

No, I can't believe it. It is all nonsense. I am not a little girl to get myself involved in this childish game. But who is talking about love? I am waiting for all of them. I am interested only in useful and interesting friendships and further "business" ties. Do you understand this, you big fool? In order to make the suggestion more effective, I knocked three times at my forehead.

The call came very unexpectedly. All four of us—Natasha, Basja, Olja, and I—were at my place discussing the problems of the coming party. After I lifted the receiver and heard the words, "Riga is calling you," my hands began trembling, something jumped in my stomach, and I turned to the wall to conceal from the others the color of my face, which I was certain must have been green or even purple.

It was Tsvisha on the phone, as usual. He had only three minutes to talk, so, after the usual first "Hi, how are you?" he immediately said that they were all coming. "Who? You?" I asked, stammering. "What do you mean 'Who'? We. I, of course. Then, Lev and . . ." he was mumbling for at least half a minute "and Yosif."

The girls couldn't hear all this so they were sitting like runners on their marks with their mouths open. I discussed in short the date and the hour of the boys' arrival, the weather, and the three minutes were over.

"Nu?" the girls breathed out.

"They are all coming."

"Who, 'they'?" they shouted at me.

"All three."

"And Lev?"

"And Tsvisha?"

"And Yosif?" they all asked at once. We laughed, we danced, and then suddenly we all rushed to do something for the party.

There were only three days left.

❋   ❋   ❋

On the 31st of December, we were on our feet from early in the morning, cooking, washing, and decorating the apartment of our friends, Bettie and Zeyev. They were one of the first Zionist couples to be married in the synagogue. I was not present at their *chuppah*, but they say that Rabbi Levin was unpleasantly surprised to see the newcomers, carried out the ceremony very quickly, and, when all the guests began to sing Israeli songs, hurriedly stood up to show that the ceremony was over.

Bettie was still having terrible problems with his *kashrut* (kosher diet) and Zeyev was wasting away. He was stubborn, like all mathematicians, and no less stubborn in Hebrew than in *kashrut*. During the two years since I had last seen him, he had turned into a walking encyclopedia of Hebrew.

So we were preparing for the evening, and our friends from Riga, who had already arrived in the morning, were walking around the capital. At last, when they couldn't stand the frost of — 30° C, they came. All three of them with black curly hair, tall and slender in black suits, white shirts, and black neckties. With beating hearts, we all pretended as much indifference as we could and extended all our affection to Tsvisha.

One by one, by couples and groups, the guests began to arrive and we were soon packed in like sardines. I was rushing from the kitchen to the room with dishes and bottles, having no time to talk to anybody or to take part in the general discussion— which was already flaring up.

"Have you heard about the universal census in January?"

"Sure. We have already discussed it."

"Are you really going to write that your mother tongue is Hebrew?"

"Of course, I am."

"But it's a lie, it is not true."

"Are you afraid to lie to them? Didn't they lie to you all of your life?"

"But we can't use their methods. And besides the census is statistics, not politics."

"No, now it has become politics. They'll show the results to the whole world and say that we forgot our language. We don't need it."

"That's why we have to learn it, but not lie in the official documents."

"One doesn't interfere with the other. We have to declare that we do exist."

"Ah-ah-ah-ah . . . !"

"What are you shouting?"

"I want you all to shut up. You are shouting like crazy."

"Excuse me for interrupting all of you. I have heard that you don't want to lie. Wonderful! But first we have to define what a mother tongue is and then see whether it is a lie to say that Hebrew is our mother tongue."

"As far as I am concerned, Hebrew has nothing to do with me. My mother tongue is Yiddish."

"How do you do! Where did you come from?"

"Why not? I also consider Yiddish my mother tongue."

"But Yiddish is a dying language!"

"Yiddish is the language of European Jewry and American Jewry. The whole of Jewish literature of the last centuries was created in Yiddish. Six million people were speaking Yiddish."

"But they will never return. And Yiddish in fact died together with them. Our reborn people speak Hebrew, our real language, the language of the Bible, not a jargon of German."

"I see that you talk according to Lenin."

"Hey, you, this is not a place to mention the classics of Marxism-Leninism."

"Jews! I heard a very interesting suggestion. It will surely put an end to all this argument. We will write neither Hebrew nor Yiddish. We shall write—Jewish language."

"That's fine!"

"No, I don't like compromises. I shall write Yiddish."

"You are all crazy! It is three minutes to midnight."

"Where is my glass?"

"There are plenty of them on the table."

"What is that in the bottle? It smells nice."

"Stop shouting. We must hear the striking of the clock over the radio."

"But don't forget to switch off when the hymn begins."

"Be sure I won't."

"Listen, it is already five. . . ."

"Six, seven, eight. . . ."

"Eleven, twelve!!!"

"L'chayim, l'chayim, l'chayim!!!"

We all—Natasha, Basja, Olja, I, and the boys from Riga—found ourselves, as if not intentionally, in one place. At that moment we wanted to be together. Though not yet daring to say anything aloud, our glances at that moment were clear enough. "I love you all! And I really wish you great happiness and that it come very soon . . . this year in Jerusalem!"

There was a hidden irony in our saying it, but we could not know it. We said it with a bitter smile and without the slightest hope.

Behind us were the echoes of *"L'chayim."* "To life!"

The argument was beginning again when we heard somebody's sad voice from the window:

"Look here, people are already having a good time and we are still arguing."

We all looked out of the window. A Russian man was trying to walk, swinging from one side of the road to the other. At last he met with a telegraph pole, embraced it, kissed it, and sat down in a snowdrift. "Their" New Year was already in full swing.

We decided to put on some music in order to avoid another argument. We had gathered Israeli records from all of our friends. A modern Western record would have offended most of the young people and they would have begun discussing our acceptance of other cultures.

The soft velvety voice of Yaffa Yarkoni filled the room. She sang *"K'she haynu yeladim"*—"When we were children." Everything of this kind, as for example, *"Hayu zmanim"*—"Those were the times"—strongly appealed to us. We felt it had something to do with us. We dreamt about the time when we would be able to say these words about ourselves in a different world.

Yaffa Yarkoni helped us not to go beyond the Israeli culture and to feel young. She helped us to fall in love. The boys embraced the girls' waists and the dancing couples began to mark time in the semidarkness. Nobody could really dance well and there was no mood to shake the floor with modern dances. We were all "serious people."

In my rushing from the kitchen to the room, in joining different groups for singing or discussion, I didn't lose sight of Yosif. I could not help admiring him. Tall and very broad-shouldered, though not unreasonably huge, he seemed too big for this small apartment. When it became very hot, Riga's boys shocked us by asking permission to take off their jackets. This was unheard of among young people in Moscow. So now Yosif was sitting in his white shirt and I suffered from the desire to touch his shoulders which emanated strength that seemed almost tangible under the delicate fabric. He rarely spoke and when he did, his face and lips scarcely moved, which added some special charm to his manners. His dark serious eyes would say a lot. He was unquestionably handsome, but what was more important was that he was not aware of it. Usually such an awareness spoils a man's manners, gives him some stupid superficial self-confidence. There was nothing of this kind in Yosif. He was perhaps even too modest, which made him sometimes seem awkward.

I had to admit that he was fascinating to such a degree that girls were afraid to build any hopes about him and left him without attention. Late at night, terribly tired and hardly moving, I found him sitting alone near a wall. Having explained to myself that I ought to be polite and engage him in conversation, I sat down next to him. He seemed glad to see me, which I immediately interpreted as being caused by boredom.

"Why are you not dancing?" I asked—the most stupid question I could think of.

"I am not a good dancer."

Silence.

"I didn't expect to see so many people here," he said with a note of disappointment.

"This was a very good opportunity to gather all of them to make friends and then to act together." (I hated myself for being so terribly businesslike at that moment.)

"I see you are eager to do something."

"And you are not?"

"We have always been doing something," he said evasively.

"I am not going to lose time. Two months ago I applied for the visa. The refusal will come in January. Time passes and, if we have to vegetate here, we must use this time for a good purpose. When I get this damned refusal, I am not going to sit idle."

"What are you going to do?" he asked sadly.

"I don't know yet, but something."

"How many times have you applied?"

"This is the first time."

"Ah-ah. We have applied for eight years."

I felt ashamed. "Did you try to do something else? Did you write to somebody in the government?"

"Better ask to whom we didn't write."

"Well, tell me, what can be done? Can we live like this through our young years? To wait is not the best form of living."

"Last year when some of the families in Riga got permission to leave, we were sure that our turn also had come. Everybody congratulated us beforehand. And when we were again refused, I was sure I would collapse, I would not live through it. But, I did, you see that I am still alive. And now I am more ready to wait than ever. This year I can't apply at all because now they expel us from the university for applying. Then, the Army, and after that there will be no hope at all. There can be no end to it, but still we have to remain alive."

I was terrified by his words, which sounded like a verdict. I could not accept it. I needed some hope. And I felt this hope. So I was quite serious and sincere when I predicted something great would take place in the coming year:

"Still I have a definite presentiment that this year of 1970 will be special. Something great, bad or good, I don't know, is going to happen. I am sure. You will see."

"Maybe, but don't expect too much," he said. "You can be easily disappointed."

There was tenderness in his tone. I felt that he cared about what I felt, but I immediately attributed it to the general kindness of his nature. To end this difficult conversation, I asked, "Whom do you have in Israel?"

"My father's mother and sister are there and also my mother's brother."

I felt stupid. He had not only political or national feelings, but must be yearning for close relatives, the more so since his grandmother was nearly ninety years old, as I learned afterward.

"And whom do you have in Israel?" he asked.

"An aunt from Tel Aviv!"

"What do you mean?"

"Don't you know the song? It's a new joke song in Moscow. A Jew from Moscow says that he loves his Tel Aviv aunt most of all and he can't live without her. In answer to a strict lady's question in the OVIR he answers that he wants to go to his beloved aunt. And he tries to prove to everybody that he must go to his Tel Aviv aunt and that she is impatiently waiting for him on the Mediterranean shore. So now we call all these second cousins twice removed who send us invitations Tel Aviv aunts. I have something of this kind."

I didn't want to interrupt our talk and was ready to sit with him all through the night, but the evening seemed to be over and I had to say good-by to the departing guests.

For the first time since we had started our long talk, I dared to look straight into his eyes. I looked and drowned. So deep they were, so much they wanted to say. They were like open gates to the soul, calling, calling. . . .

I felt my heart beating in my throat. No, I can't believe it! Does he really mean it? And why? Who are you? Where did you come from? Who or what created you and brought you here to me?

⟨∽12∽⟩

The 20th of November 1938 was a wonderful sunny day, untypical for Liepaja in late autumn. Everyone said that it was a good sign for a happy marriage. The wedding that was to take place that day was on everybody's lips. One of the wealthiest and most respected men of the Jewish community of Liepaja, Yosif Rusinek, was marrying off his twenty-four-year-old son Ezra. The bride was the twenty-three-year-old beautiful daughter of Yeshiahu Baron-Rosa. The match seemed perfect on all counts— bride and groom were young, handsome, well-to-do, and the object of envy and delight of the whole community.

Ezra had recently returned from France where he had studied at a technical school for watchmakers and he was now working in his father's watch factory. A true Zionist, Ezra was one of the founders of the "Herzlia" Zionist organization in Liepaja and after his return from France he became the leader of the local "Beitar" Zionist group. Calm and effective, he won everybody's respect, managing the camp for training youth for settlement in Palestine, getting certificates to Palestine, and gathering money for those who were emigrating. Certificates were valid for two persons, so those who were ready to go had to marry. Thus many artificial couples were able to enter British-ruled Palestine, some of them remaining together afterward, others parting as soon as they reached the Promised Land.

To go to Palestine was Ezra's dream, but he thought he could do it more easily than those from poor families and he was needed in Liepaja. Besides Yosif Rusinek was not very interested in leaving all his developing business to emigrate to Palestine. His wife, Rachel, businesslike and strong in character, had been trying to persuade him to go, since she felt the approaching danger from Germany, but when Rusinek bought new equipment for his factory and started to build his fourth house, she realized that further effort was useless.

Rumors of the Nazi threat became more frequent and threatening, but the Jews of Liepaja thought that if such people as Rusinek did not leave, there was no need for them to hurry. Many of them preferred to stay for the time being.

The brilliant and handsome Ezra had been the object of the hopes of many girls and their parents in the town and it was unexpected when quiet, modest Roza Baron became his choice. She had been living for three years in Palestine, studying at the Hebrew University in Jerusalem. The summer of 1938 she came to Liepaja on vacation with her friend and roommate Miriam, Ezra's younger sister.

They had both come especially to be present at the wedding of Ezra's second sister, the town's beauty, Hadassah. Before anyone realized it, Ezra, who was generally free with girls, was courting Roza and in November the town was taken by surprise by the announcement of the marriage. The young couple asked their parents not to make a large celebration, but just a small dinner for the family circle. They preferred to have the money go for arranging their move to Palestine.

The night before the wedding, Roza could not sleep. She had no doubts about her marriage. No, everything pointed to a happy life—they loved each other passionately, they were both from well-to-do families, and they both wanted to move to Palestine. There was nothing to worry her, but she had to follow the eternal custom of all young brides and spend a sleepless night in exciting dreams over the coming day and approaching happiness. Then the 20th of November 1938 dawned as a wonderful sunny day, which seemed one more sign that the marriage would be happy and unclouded.

The ceremony took place in the morning at the Barons' home and the two families contributed all the magnificence that was possible for such a small wedding. In the semi-darkness of the hall, the beautiful women in long, elegant silk and velvet dresses with high shoulders and men in tail coats and top hats discussed admiringly the slender bride and handsome groom. The glimmering candles, the sparkling silver of candelabras, and the women's diamonds were the only light in the hall. Tall, old Mr. Rusinek, with a large candelabrum in his hand, led his son to the *chuppah* as a father confident and proud of his heir. An aged, bearded rabbi recited the benedictions to a respectful silence. Everything—the beauty and love of the young couple, the elegance, the solemnity of the religious ceremony—added to the greatness and symbolism of the moment.

The young husband and wife left the same evening for Estonia to spend their honeymoon and to send from there one thousand English pounds to the British bank in Palestine.

This money, as proof of capital, would provide them with the right to obtain a special bourgeois entrance visa to Palestine. But soon Great Britain issued the "White Paper" which limited the number of entrance visas even for capitalists. So the young Rusineks had to wait for a regular certificate, which was delayed from month to month. Meanwhile Roza became pregnant and gave birth to a baby daughter whom they called Ilana. At last in June 1940, the long-awaited visa was received.

But it was fated that the moving be delayed once more, and this time not for months, but for tens of years. The second time the problem came from another quarter. On the 17th of June 1940, several days before they received their visa certificate, the Red Army occupied Latvia, and the people there found themselves in a large prison called the Soviet Union. Now the problem of an exit visa arose, but this proved insoluble. The Russians had their own plans with respect to the population and these plans were put into operation very quickly. One day the workers came to Rusinek and took the keys of the factory. Now it belonged to them. Everything was done quietly and quickly. Factories, shops, buildings were taken over and the owners did not resist. An iron fist bound everybody's hearts, wills, and minds.

Old Mr. Rusinek was appointed director of his own factory and Ezra worked there as an engineer. They still lived in their well-furnished, comfortable apartment and, watching little Ilana growing rapidly, the whole family forgot their troubles. But then a terrible rumor began to spread among the former propertied people. No one spoke of it aloud, but everyone grew fearful at the thought of it. No one could run away. Before long the rumor became a reality.

On Saturday, the 14th of June 1941, at four o'clock in the morning, a long ringing sound awoke the family. Ezra jumped out of bed, but everyone else seemed paralyzed with the one frightening question in their minds. Ezra stroked Roza gently, asked her to be quiet, and went to open the door. When he returned, he was terribly pale and told Roza to dress quickly. In a minute the house was full of policemen who began to search in all the drawers, wardrobes, kitchen. The family was ordered to pack in an hour, taking only the most necessary things. What was necessary? The women began to take everything that was at hand and throw it into suitcases.

The hour passed. They took the small, sleepy baby, the suitcases packed every which way, and left their home for good.

They were taken to a distant railway station with long rows of freight cars standing in it. The men were separated from the women and children and all were loaded into the cars. There were already many other people there—all pale, tired, and frightened. The torturing questions were in everyone's eyes: "Where are we going? What will be the end of this?" But there were no answers and it was better that way.

The train with the men in it soon left. The women and children were kept until nightfall and only then did their train also begin to move slowly. After several hours, it stopped. The women had been sitting silent, afraid to say a word. Tired children were sleeping.

Suddenly one of the cars was opened and Ezra entered. The door behind him was immediately locked and all found themselves again in darkness. Nobody could understand what was happening, least of all Ezra. All of the men were in the other train. None of them knew in what direction they were headed. At that particular stop Ezra had suddenly been called out of his car by a soldier. It seemed to be a railway station in an unknown suburb. The soldier led him along the rails to the women's train.

Years later, they learned that a Soviet secret police officer who used to buy watches in Rusinek's shop saw Ezra in the first train. That train, with former capitalist and bourgeois political leaders, was headed for forced labor camps. Ezra was there not as the son of his father but as a Zionist leader. The unexpected savior sent a soldier to take Ezra to the second train with the members of the families of the former capitalists, which was bound for Siberian exile. Thus Ezra was reunited with his wife, mother, and daughter.

In a month they reached the Yenisei River and were loaded onto a steamship. The families were being distributed among different kolkhozy (collective farms) on the banks of the river. No one wanted to take a family with an old woman and a baby, so the Rusineks were left until last and sent to the distant village of Yefremovka. While standing on the ship and looking at the wild forests and empty villages on the banks of the river, old Frau Rusinek said, "They brought us here not to live but to die."

But the Rusineks and thousands of other Jewish and Latvian families were brought there to struggle for life. Some of them won—others perished.

The Rusineks were at first lodged in an old stable. There was no work and no one knew what to do with them. They exchanged the clothes they had with them for food. The peasants, who were dressed in rags, were glad to give bread, potatoes, milk, and even meat for dresses, jackets, and trousers. Once a week the family was obliged to register with the authorities so that the latter should know that their "exiles" had not run away. But where could they run to? The Taiga? After several weeks, their living conditions improved. They were settled in a room with another Jewish family. They even had a Russian stove. But no stove could cope with the Siberian winter and icicles grew in the upper corners of the room. Little Ilana would lie in bed watching these icy monsters. There were beds in the room and a table which served as a bed for one of them at night. Life went on.

The Siberian women neighbors were intrigued by Roza. "They say you studied at the University. What did they teach you there? You don't know how to do anything. You cannot even wash the floors or milk a cow." When they heard that in big cities the toilet was in the house, they threw up their hands: "My God, what a stink must be in the house!"

And the Rusineks lived there, learned to wash floors made of boards, to milk their cow, Zorka, to bring water in two big pails from a distant well, to use the wooden toilet several tens of meters from the house.

At last they discovered that somebody in the village had a clock and the commandant of the district owned a watch. Ezra repaired them and got food for the family. Then Miriam, who was living in Palestine, discovered where they were and began to send parcels. Someone advised Miriam to send them an invitation to come to Palestine, which by a miracle reached the family. Ezra took it to his commandant. The man proved to be very kind.

"Take it away immediately," he said, "or I shall have to report you. I have not seen this. Forget about it."

Ezra asked permission to move to a city where he could earn more by his work. And after a while they were loaded onto a steamship and went to Krasnoyarsk.

Years passed. Life in Krasnoyarsk was better. In 1943 old Yosif Rusinek was released from the labor camp as unfit for work. Though he had seldom been employed in hard labor but had repaired watches for the authorities of the camp, the harsh regime of the life had undermined his health. He went back to his family with a serious heart condition.

Still he was anxious to return his family to life and to their home. In 1947, when the time of their exile expired, he went to Riga, registered himself in its suburb (the capital of the Union Republic was closed to former exiles then), and began to arrange things for the return. Meanwhile, the family still lived in Krasnoyarsk, waiting for news from him.

One day while Ezra and old Frau Rusinek were out, a postman brought a telegram from Riga. Roza was at home and at that moment was teaching the seven-year-old Ilana how to wash the floors. The little one felt very important and was upset when the postman interrupted them. Roza took the telegram, read it, and with a scream dropped into a chair: "Father suddenly died of heart attack," said the telegram.

When Ezra came home, they both had only one thought over-riding their own grief and despair—to protect their mother. They ran to the post office and begged the telegrapher to type another message that should simply speak about father's illness. Several days later they showed Frau Rusinek the real telegram. Rachel lay in bed and did not talk or eat for several days. Meanwhile an old family friend buried Yosif Rusinek in the Riga cemetery.

That same year the Rusineks were finally able to return to Riga. What happiness to come back, to see old friends, all of whom offered their help, their rooms. This time the tears were of joy.

But Hadassah did not come to meet her mother and brother. She, her husband, and their two-year-old son had perished in the ghetto. Roza found none of her large family. All were gone. Only brother Mulja was living in Israel. And there were not even graves over which to cry and pray for them. Roza shuddered as she remembered having considered leaving little Ilana with her family.

But they had come back to live and again to hope. They had many friends; they had Miriam and Mulja in Israel. They now had their long-dreamed-of motherland, the State of Israel. For this it was worth coming back to life. Roza found that she was pregnant, and when the baby arrived in its due time, it was a beautiful strong crying son, demanding a happy life. He was given his grandfather's name and became a symbol of the family's rebirth.

Yosif was only nine months old when the family again had to escape. In 1950 the Soviet authorities began sending to Siberia all the families that had returned from exile. This time the Rusineks did not wait for the night guests, but packed the necessary things and left Riga. After a few months of wandering, they settled in an old southern Russian town on the Azov Sea— Taganrog. The first years were difficult, but they passed. Ezra began to earn more by his work, the family was gradually adjusting to the environment. They now had peace and safety. Riga friends did not forget them and came almost every summer to see them. Friends of their Zionist youth, who had returned from exile or from the ghetto's half life, came, aged and quiet. How much can a human being endure? A lot, if they are all still alive. They came now with their late little ones, big-headed, big-eyed, big-eared Jewish children, and for their sakes' their parents would not lose hope.

Every year Ezra and Roza quietly celebrated the Jewish holidays and their clever Ilana and little Yossi knew that there were things that should not be mentioned at school.

Miriam was the first to learn that old people in Latvia were being allowed to reunite with their children and immediately sent an invitation to her mother, but the Russian authorities of the Taganrog District refused the application. Then Ezra thought of another way. He registered his mother in Riga in his friend's home and the application was sent to the Riga Department of Visas. It worked.

The entire family went to Moscow to see off their eighty-year-old mother and grandmother, who was making her long-awaited *aliyah*. All were silently crying. Rachel held her beloved grandson by the hand and didn't let him go until an airport servicewoman separated them at the barrier. From there she went alone. Miriam met her in Vienna. It was 1961.

And in 1963 the entire family moved back to Riga.

They immediately began to apply for exit visas with Miriam's invitations. All were refused. After the first application, Ilana was expelled from the fifth year of the Medical Institute and began to work as a nurse. That blow was unexpected, but it strengthened all of them. They would not give up now. In 1964 Ilana married and in 1965 little Hadassah opened her large dark eyes to the world. Yes, they would live. Live . . . and struggle.

❦*13*❦

The first days of the New Year, 1970, passed with a carelessness and joy which we were all trying hard to hold on to. We went skiing and tobogganing and just walking along the streets. In the evenings we went to the fanciest cafes and spent much money. We could not deny ourselves this pleasure which added to the happiness of being together.

We tried not to get involved in any of the Zionist activities because of the visiting boys from Riga; we just wanted to have a rest from everything. But suddenly on the 3rd of January, we got a note saying that an American rabbi was visiting Moscow and that night he was having dinner in the synagogue. We immediately rushed there.

The dinner had already begun. A gray car was standing near the entrance of the synagogue and two gray civil men were idling about. We entered the synagogue, hoping to see the rabbi coming out. One of the synagogue men, in black rags, a mumbling hunchback, rushed to turn us out, but a second one, black-bearded, but no better dressed, shouted at him: "Don't dare, you spy! They came to see the rabbi. It is their right. Didn't they come to their home?"

The scene amused us. We felt stronger. But when the hunchback retreated hastily, we understood that we could easily be fooled. There were other exits to the synagogue. One by one we penetrated into the backyard and stood near the window and door of the dining room. We could hear the clatter of crockery and low voices.

"They are eating," we said to each other.

"Yes," we answered each other.

We knocked at the door and excused ourselves for interrupting the dinner. Another hunchback appeared. It seemed that the rabbi, being himself a tall and handsome man, liked to surround himself with dwarfs.

"What do you want?" the hunchback asked rather inhospitably.

"We want to see the rabbi."

"What rabbi?"

"The American one."

"Go away!" he suddenly said rather illogically. "Go away or I will call the militia. You are hooligans."

The door closed. We looked at each other and then knocked again.

The hunchback appeared again. This time he was supported by a long, bony old woman who shouted at us in a whisper through the hole in the window.

"We are not hooligans. We only want to talk to the rabbi. We are also Jews."

"You are not Jews, you are hooligans. I told you that once already. So don't bother us." He pulled the door, but this time it didn't close. The strong foot of one of the boys was holding it.

The hunchback became furious. He thought we were going to rush into the room, but we were very careful not to make noise, lest we find ourselves in the hands of the militia.

"We want to speak to the rabbi!" we repeated three times loudly, once in Russian, once in Yiddish, once in English. The rabbi didn't come out. We let the hunchback close the door.

We again looked at each other and suddenly a brilliant idea struck one of us. We began to sing. "Let my people go," "*Artsa Alinu*" ("We went up to our country"), "*Shalom Aleichem*," "*Palmach*"—anything that came into our heads.

The rabbi did not come out.

We continued our concert until we got a signal that the hunchback was calling the KGB. We divided into couples and dispersed through the nearby backyards.

The rabbi did not come out. . . .

A few days later an article appeared in *Izvestia* that an American Rabbi so-and-so had visited the Moscow Choral Synagogue. His visit took place in a friendly and cordial atmosphere. The Chief Rabbi of Moscow told Rabbi so-and-so about the happy life of Jews in the Soviet Union. Rabbi so-and-so left for the United States with a feeling of satisfaction at having received a full and exhaustive picture of Jewish life in the Soviet Union.

The rabbi did not come out to the Jews. . . .

*   *   *

All four days passed under a constant dread of parting. We tried our best to forget it, but the end of every wonderful evening reminded us of the end to come.

On the second day of January when we went tobogganing I hit my foot violently. It became terribly swollen and I could hardly step on it, but nothing could prevent me from taking part in all our gatherings, and I spent the rest of our days leaning on Yosif's arm. Every evening he took me home and in the morning he came to pick me up. We usually walked in silence or talked quietly on general subjects. When, in the evenings, we reached the door of my apartment, I hastened to say "good night" and disappeared behind the door. He was left noticeably disappointed and upset, but I made certain not to be responsible for what had to happen sooner or later anyway.

On the evening of the 3rd of January we went to one of the best Moscow restaurants, Pekin. Its Chinese waiters had long since left Russia, but the menu was still Chinese. We were not acquainted with the dishes and decided to order those that had the funniest names. Thus, trepangs that didn't want to be chewed but slipped immediately inside appeared on the table; then followed a pork ball and the seed of a lotus tree and other different "mao-tze-tungs." We all helped to spoil each other's appetites by suggesting other dishes like "gefilte" snakes or cocktail of flies.

At last, having nourished ourselves with Homeric laughter, we all went to dance. While everybody else was dancing, Yosif and I sat at the table, but at the end of the evening I asked him to dance with me. He was surprised but game. He was really a bad dancer, but I enjoyed feeling myself in his arms. On my part I did my best to move gracefully on my one good leg.

We couldn't all part just like that. We had to promise something to each other. And we promised to go together in four months to Tallinn, the capital of Estonia, a small but very beautiful city which has managed to preserve its Middle Ages character and looks like the scenery for a knight's ballad.

The next day we saw off our boys. Tsvisha and Lev were leaving by train in the morning. We stood on the platform, not knowing how to express how much we would miss each other. We sang our favorite song "*Lo yisah goy el goy herev.*" The girls tried to keep back their tears. I didn't cry but I was ready to hang myself.

The train began to move. Tsvisha began to kiss all of us on our cheeks. We all turned our backs on Natasha and Lev to give them time to say their own good-by to each other.

The train left. Yosif was to leave in a few hours by plane. We went to our friend's house to spend these hours. Time mercilessly passed. When we got to the friend's house, I retired to a small room to lie on a bed and to give Yosif an opportunity to come to me. He came immediately and asked about my leg.

I was very excited. I stood up, tried to walk, and looked for something on the table. He asked me to sit down. I did. There were pictures scattered all over the floor. We had used them for decorating our New Year's party. One showed dancing Hasidim, the second dancing young Indians, and the third seemed made especially to depict our friendship. A girl and a boy are sitting on a swinging rope, kissing. One end of the rope holds the Kremlin tower with a red star and the other the tower of the Dome Cathedral of Riga with a rooster on it. Both towers are bent to each other under the heaviness of friendship and love of the boy and the girl.

"I shall take it with me to Riga," Yosif said, showing me the picture.

"What for?" I asked and shrugged my shoulders.

His face fell at such lack of understanding or unwillingness to understand.

"It was all childish, and not serious. This picture is not true." I did my best to worsen the situation. "I wish it were you who had hurt your leg, not me."

"Why?"

"Then you could stay longer in Moscow."

"What for if everything was childish?"

"Just so. It is very nice to be all together."

"Didn't you understand that I didn't come to be all together?"

It was already too much. I didn't answer.

The talk continued like that all during our trip to the airport until, seeing the lights of the terminal in front of me, I understood that I was playing games with my own destiny.

"Don't pay attention to me, Yosif, I am just trying to sound very clever."

"What for?"

"I don't know. Perhaps to keep myself safe."

"Safe from what?"

"Safe from disappointment."

He did not understand. He was to learn many things before he would be able to understand what I say. But at that moment he was patient enough not to ask any more questions.

I just added, "Everything will be O.K. Tallinn will solve everything, I promise you."

Standing aside, I gave him time to say "good-by" to everybody. Then he ran toward the boarding bus, embraced and kissed me on his way, and climbed aboard the bus. I found a small piece of paper in my hand with his address. I looked at it. I liked his handwriting, but his second name, which I saw for the first time, sounded very strange and out of place: Rusinek.

And Yosif Rusinek was sitting in the bus which hadn't yet moved and looking at me with his torturing gaze. There was a big question in his look. I couldn't answer it yet, so I avoided his eyes.

*   *   *

We were left alone with our thoughts. Natasha couldn't understand herself, and Lev's "attack" frightened her and put her completely at a loss. Lev, it seemed, was not going to lose time and was as swift as a tank. He was going to write frequent letters and in March he planned to spend three weeks of his annual vacation in Moscow. At the end of March, he wanted to go back to

Riga with Natasha's love ensured and definite plans in mind. I was delighted with his purposefulness and swiftness and wished him success.

For me, the four months that I had to wait until our Tallinn meeting seemed more than an eternity. I was happy and proud to have deserved attention from such a boy as Yosif and yet sad that I had let myself become involved in a love story which was such a good nutrient for my bacilli of craziness. We were each to wait alone for the great thing that I had predicted had to happen this year and for Tallinn. But deep in our hearts, we prayed that the second would take place before the first.

The day after they left, we counted and told each other that we had 116 days to wait and each day we counted again and informed each other of the number of days left. We thought and talked only about Tallinn. We saved every kopeck to gather money for May. We all had new clothes made that were as fancy as possible. We were crazy. Natasha and Olja, who worked together in a Research Medical Institute as laboratory assistants, would be standing at the dissection of a corpse looking somewhere ahead. Then they would nudge each other and whisper, "Stop thinking about Tallinn." I was sitting at my table over papers for hours, thinking, then scolding myself, and again thinking. We were all crazy.

I gave myself and Yosif two weeks before I wrote him the first letter. In the meanwhile we all took our exams in the Institutes, but we cared nothing about our marks. We felt our studies in Russia were purposeless and useless, yet we continued because you don't simply leave a university.

*   *   *

On the 13th of January, I, like all of us, received my long-awaited refusal. It came, as to all of us, in the form of a postcard saying, "Please call us at Tel. No. so-and-so." Like all of us, I called the given number and, like all of us, I heard the words, "Your application to leave for permanent residence in Israel has been refused." Like all of us, I asked: "When can I apply again?" Like all of us, I heard, "In a year." Not like all of us, I said, "Thank you" because I am usually polite over the telephone. To make the conversation more amusing, I answered myself before the woman-automaton and proved to be always exact. But it seemed to me that I heard in her tone something special concerning only me. She seemed to be saying: "You crazy girl! We don't even pay any attention to your application. You think we don't know what kind of an aunt you have in Israel. Stop interfering with our serious work! You will never be allowed to leave, but you will be punished, like all of you Jews!"

But maybe it only seemed that way to me. Not like all of us, I was quite alone after this telephone call. I couldn't describe it to anyone, so "like" it was and I didn't expect any special reaction in myself to this "news."

I finished my long working day and dragged myself home. I felt exhausted as never before. On reaching home, I threw my bag somewhere, didn't wash, didn't go to the kitchen to make something to eat, but sat down dully on the sofa. My whole body was tired. Every finger, every bone was aching. I leaned my head against the wall and turned it left and right, right and left. The electric light bothered me. I felt sick to my stomach.

And my eternal companion, who had been silent since "the doctor's lesson," my inner Satan, the author of all my bad thoughts, was immediately there: "What have you done? You have made your bed, now lie in it. People who were fond of you now hate you and are afraid of you. You could have made such a brilliant career there and now you are nothing. Your life is senseless, it is nothing but emptiness. Israel?!!! It is your imagination. What do you know about it? A few postcards and a number of songs. Is it worth sacrificing your whole life? And if it is something, you will never get there!!!

"What have you got instead? Loneliness. Yes, yes, complete loneliness. You try to play games with your new friends, try to feel young and don't really get any satisfaction from it. Don't deceive yourself. And from me you can't conceal anything."

"Shut up!!!" I cried to him. "Don't you know there is no way back and there's no use in such talk?" But this was all I could tell him, as he was not the kind of person to accept fine words. He was the other part of me.

And suddenly a feeling of terrible guilt swept over me. I thought about those good comfortable Jewish people whom I had been "stirring up" all those years. Besides having deprived them of their equanimity, I may have pushed them to the same abyss of hopelessness and baiting. Did I have the right to do it? Is it in my power to judge people, to decide what is bad and what is good for them, to change their destiny?

But I was bringing truth to them. And by no means do I blame those who had once brought it to me. I am grateful. If there was somebody to blame, it was only myself. I had free choice and I had chosen my own destiny.

But those people on whom I was trying to impose my new truth. . . . Yes, that was it. New truth, old truth, my truth, his truth, their truth. What is more important—all these truths or happiness and peace of mind?

My glance passed along the shelves of my bookcase: the box with the bones from Rumbula, a textbook on the history of the Communist Party, an album of pictures of the State of Israel, a typed brochure from the Underground democratic movement in the Soviet Union. I closed my eyes. I was dizzy. I shall answer no more questions. New answers—new truths.

I looked at the clock. It was 11 P.M. I had been sitting in thought for four hours. All the Russian programs of the "Voice of Israel" were over, but I switched on the radio. I heard Israeli music and then a low, strong, man's voice speaking in Hebrew. I smiled, seeing my poor devil, Satan, flying away through the window as devils are supposed to escape at the sound of a cock at dawn.

I stood up, stretched myself, and went to the kitchen. I had been unexpectedly and easily saved.

ᏬᏬ*14*ᏬᏬ

Natasha suddenly had a great many troubles.

I had met her mother at one of the Jewish parties in September 1969, the first one I had visited after my "voluntary retirement" for two years. I hardly remembered her face, but when I suddenly ran into her at the Committee for Standards which I often visited on business, I recognized her immediately. At that party she was playing the piano and her father, a hale and hearty man, was dancing *freilachs*. She was very happy to see me and was eager to introduce me to her eighteen-year-old daughter, Natasha. At that time young Jews had begun to have very specific problems and badly needed the friendship of their own people. I was pleased to learn that they lived only three minutes' walk from my office and I should be able to visit them even during my lunch hours. Soon I became their frequent visitor, as well as a very good friend to Natasha.

Natasha and Inna, her mother, who was thirty-seven and looked very young, were more like two sisters than mother and daughter. And they treated each other as sisters, with all the shortcomings and advantages of such a relationship. They lived in a big room in an apartment of several other rooms, each being occupied by another family. The apartment didn't have a bathroom and the house seemed to be falling apart. It was one of those beautiful houses in the center of old Moscow with a view of the Kremlin, a house which once had been owned by the Russian bourgeoisie and every apartment had been rented by a respectable family. After 1917 the apartments were each crowded with several proletarian families and since then left almost uncared for.

The room now occupied by the Slepyan-Kamzel family was divided by a large cupboard into three parts: entrance, a corner for a bed, and "the hall." The grandfather slept on the bed, Natasha and Inna on a sofa, and the grandmother made for herself a folding bed at night.

I liked the family very much for their intelligence, vividness, and hospitality. They compressed in themselves Jewish and Soviet history.

Abram Kamzel came from a well-to-do Jewish family, with all the children following different paths in life. One son was an Anarchist, the daughter was a Socialist Revolutionary, and Abram became a Bolshevik. In the saddle on a fiery horse, he had galloped through World War I, the Revolution, and the Civil War, fighting for communism, defending his young state, and brandishing his saber against the revivals of the old order, among them religion in the Jewish *shtetl*. And just so, in the saddle, swinging his saber, he had burst into a Jewish *shtetl*, fallen in love with sixteen-year-old Ronja, stood for a few minutes with her under the *chuppah*, then lifted her into his saddle, and galloped off.

Keeping pace with the breakneck course of history, he had been in the diplomatic service and various Party posts, always active, indefatigable.

Then in 1938 he fell out of his saddle, was expelled from the Communist Party, and sentenced to be shot. He was "an enemy of the people," "a traitor against the course of communism." Some miracle saved him. He jumped again into his saddle and rushed to fight against fascism, but this time his horse was lame in one leg.

In 1952 he again fell, was expelled from the Party, and lost his job. He was reduced simply to being a Jew. Soon he again saddled his Communist horse, but this time it was lame in both legs. It limped for some additional kilometers of time and then fell down and died.

Abram had a son and a daughter. His son had his own life with his family and, in addition, was a good Communist. His daughter, Inna, with a mass of curly red hair and burning eyes, inherited his idealism and activity, and viewed life as her parents saw it. Together with her father's horse, her fiery foal had been gradually becoming lame, but she was not afraid to look truth in the face.

When she was nineteen, she married a young Communist, Leonid Slepyan, a promising scientist, but in five years they parted, for his horse galloped through life without a single slip. He couldn't see deeply into things and in general they were quite different. Four-year-old Natasha had never since seen her father.

So three generations were lost in an open field when the idea of Israel found its way to them in 1967. Together they abandoned their dead Communist horses and went their new way, but this time on foot.

In 1969 the Party Organization of the Krasnopresnensky District of Moscow celebrated the 50th anniversary of the Party service of eighty-year-old Abram Kamzel, a recipient of a special Party pension. With a bitter smile, Abram received his golden diploma and sat down to write an application for a Party reference, the document which was demanded by the OVIR—the Department of Visas—for an application for Israel. In some months Abram Kamzel was for the third and last time expelled from the Communist Party.

At the same time Natasha was expelled from Komsomol at her Institute of Electronic Machine-building and was given sick leave for a year under the condition that she never come back to the Institute. Inna had gone through her own seven circles of hell in the Committee for Standards and had obtained her employer's reference.

They needed only one more document to be able to apply for the exit visa to Israel. Among other numerous documents, the OVIR demands a written and legalized permission from the parents of those who want to leave for Israel without them, irrespective of the former age or family status. This permission is required to indicate that the parents have no objection to their children leaving them without material support and, in general, that they are aware of the children's desire.

The OVIR didn't really pay any attention to this useless

scrap of paper and was ready to accept not only written permission, but also written prohibition. But without this paper, one could not apply.

And this was Natasha's problem. She had to find the man, unknown to her, somewhere in the Soviet Union, who was her father and ask for something he would not understand. The Jewish circle of acquaintances helped to find Leonid Slepyan in Novosibirsk and spoke to her father. He was very polite and largest universities, a respected Communist of a high military rank. He had a second wife and a young son.

On January 2, 1970, in the presence of Lev, Natasha called Novosibirsk and spoke to her father. He was very polite and surprised, at first could not understand anything but then, having grasped the character of the matter, interrupted and said that he was flying out immediately to Moscow and would speak to her personally. One step had been made successfully.

In a week he arrived and turned out to be a plump man and, by his face, definitely Natasha's father. This fact filled Natasha with disgust more than anything else.

The talks took place during three days in a hotel with Inna present. She did not interfere, but just looked at him victoriously. "Did you expect your daughter to be so strong, beautiful, and clever?" her stare was saying.

At first, of course, he refused definitely to give any documents of the kind and began holding forth about loyalty, Communist ideals, and the like. Natasha was ready for this kind of talk, but she was not going to argue with him on his terms. From requests she turned to demands, providing him with very clear explanations. She suggested that he should write that he had not seen his daughter for fifteen years and that he had not been responsible for her upbringing.

He could not do it and flatly refused. How could he, a Communist, confess that he had not seen his own child for so many years and didn't even take any interest in her. All kind methods having been exhausted, Natasha turned to the last one—threats. She told him that if he didn't give her this paper, she would certainly continue her struggle for the exit visa and write an official application through his Party organization, as well as write about the case abroad. Then he would hear his own name over the foreign radio program for the Soviet Union.

The stubbornness of the Communist was shaken. He made the last weak attempt. "And if I need your material help when I am old?" he asked.

"What did you say?" Natasha asked, horrified. Inna choked with anger. Her burning eyes reminded him of everything; that he counted with his own hands exactly fifty-two rubles and twenty-eight kopecks without adding a kopeck when she per-mitted him to send the allowance due his daughter on divorce instead of having it come through his place of work; that he never during these fifteen years had congratulated his daughter on her birthday.

The "father" was sorry to have said it.

At the end of the third day, he surrendered and wrote a paper with these words: "I have no financial claims on my daughter, but personally I do not approve of her decision." The same day he left Moscow.

During the entire three days, Natasha had been outwardly quiet but extremely nervous. On the third day in the evening I was sitting at home waiting for her call. She called and I heard her weak voice: "I am not well."

"What has happened?"

I did not receive any answer.

"Do you want me to come?"

"Yes, yes, immediately," I heard her sobs.

I put down the receiver and left at once to go to her. In half an hour I was at her place. She was lying on the bed like a little old woman, covered with an old warm scarf. She had already stopped crying, but she shivered and constantly rubbed her left cheek. She said that in taking leave he had kissed her on the cheek and she felt it was dirty.

I sat near her stroking her hand and said quietly, "You are a strong girl. You did something that not everybody would be able to do. It was a big victory. You should be proud of yourself. Now we shall be strong and persistent like you and we shall achieve everything that we want. And in 107 days we shall go to Tallinn. . . ."

Natasha smiled and soon fell asleep.

✻   ✻   ✻

In March, Lev again came to Moscow. Natasha was very much excited and frightened. She was afraid of the big question because she could only answer it negatively or not at all. I advised her not to torture herself beforehand and assured her that the answer would come of itself in time. Two weeks after his coming, she was deeply in love.

They spent all of her free time together, he meeting her every day after work. They sat quietly in the dark corner of her room, whispering, telling each other many important things about themselves, getting to know each other.

Often I invited them to my quiet place, treated them to something tasty, and gave them good music to listen to. We sat together in the light of candles, dreaming of Tallinn. I had heard that Lev loved Mendelssohn's First Concerto for Violin and bought the record especially. We listened to it every day and we came to love it. The tension and excitement of the first part of the concerto reminded us of "the great thing" that was to come, and we became silent and thoughtful with its opening sounds.

One such evening was suddenly spoiled by a strange visit. A young blond, but Jewish-looking, man came and asked for me. I was astonished as I had never seen him before. And such a person could hardly have any relationship to me. He was dressed in foreign clothes in a pretentious kind of carelessness typical of those who care a great deal for their clothes. I was shocked by his Russian-style sheepskin coat of which we had only just begun to hear rumors from abroad. He was good-looking and I smiled to myself that such a visitor should come to see me, but soon everything became clear.

He said that he had heard about me from this one and that one (he mentioned some Jewish names which I had never heard before). I tried to tell him that I didn't know these people, but he answered quickly that it was not important and continued. He wanted me to join his company and also take my friends there. He was an artist and worked for the "Mosfilm" studio. He could introduce me to the cream of society, all of whom were interested in . . . Israel. They could get and exchange information and then, together with me, develop some activities. "We need your activity and energy!" he added. "If you help us, we can arrange later your escape to Israel, but only if you give your consent to work there for us."

"For whom?"

"For us." Poor boy! He got completely mixed up, I thought.

I looked at him with a smile, giving him time to say his say. I was really disappointed. I didn't expect the KGB to work so crudely.

My two guests were sitting in the second room as quietly as two mice. I was glad that they understood the situation and that this fellow would not see them in my apartment. I very politely saw the man out, took his telephone number, and closed the door behind him. I was not going to get myself involved in this provocation, even with my full understanding, but a week later I took one of our friends to the artist's place to show him the man and to remember him, just in case.

On the eve of Lev's departure, Natasha said to me, "You know, I love him. I really love him."

"Congratulations."

"No, I am very serious. It is so hard. You know, I can't tell you everything, but he is in danger. He can even be taken prisoner. It is so awful—I am so afraid for him."

At that time we hardly knew each other's part in the activities, but surely any of us could at any moment be arrested. I could easily believe her.

Lev was a typical Latvian Jew, as we understood these two words. He inherited from his parents an unusual delicateness of manners, politeness, love of his home and family. We attached these qualities to Latvian Jews because the Soviet morality, which ruins the family and coarsens outward relations among people, hadn't succeeded in doing there in twenty-five years what it had been doing in Russia for fifty years.

He was a chemist, not only by profession, but by nature

also. We always admired the way he set a table, when he took crystal or silver liqueur glasses and mixed cocktails like a new compound in a laboratory. He was outwardly reserved and exact and accurate in everything, including his relations with other people. He did not make friends easily, but when he did, he gave all his heart to the friendship. That was why, when I earned his friendship after three years of acquaintance, I valued it highly and was proud of it.

In 1969 he was expelled from the sixth year of the University for a "desire to leave for permanent residence in the State of Israel." Those who were not engaged in studies were taken into the army. In autumn 1970, during the draft, Lev's fate would be decided. He was very short-sighted, tall, slender, but strong. His being drafted depended only on the decision of the medical commission—or so we then thought, naïvely.

We could not imagine that our delicate, neat, brilliant Lev would go into the Soviet Army, which is a czardom of dirtiness, drunkenness, immorality, and humiliation.

When Natasha went to see Lev off at the railway station, I followed them at a short distance. I knew that she would be in distress after his departure and didn't want to leave her alone. I was afraid for her.

I was standing in a square in front of the railway station waiting for Natasha to come out, when I suddenly heard her voice calling me from behind. She was approaching from another side, deathly pale and walking as if she could hardly move. I ran toward her and had scarcely approached her when she began screaming. The passers-by stopped to look at her. I seized her head and pressed it to my shoulder to make her screams less loud. She choked and calmed down. Her hot tears mixed with the ice drops on my fur collar. It bothered her and she raised her head sobbing.

"I can't live like this any more. I am afraid for him. I want to be with him. I don't want to lose him. He is in such danger."

I was embarrassed and confused in the face of such suffering. In such cases I never know what to say or how to comfort a person.

"What do they want from her?" I thought. "She is so innocent, she can't have done them any harm yet. She doesn't deserve
it."

Who "they" were, I didn't know. Maybe it was God himself
or Fate, but we preferred "they" in thinking about our political
enemies who were, of course, not responsible for our loves. But I
had to say something to her and I began:

"Natulik, we are not at war. Nothing threatens his life. I am
sure everything will settle itself one way or another. But if something happens, you must feel sure that you will always wait for
him, however long it is. This confidence will help." I would have
cut out my tongue if I had known then that I could evoke evil by
making those evil prophecies. "By the way, do you know when
Lev first became interested in you?"

"No," she said, suddenly becoming animated.

"He told me this. It was on Hanukkah in Riga on the evening of the first candle. He was reciting the benedictions over
the candles when you suddenly raised your eyes and looked at
him. He saw your deep serious eyes and immediately understood, 'This is she!' "

Natasha smiled and said, "You know how to comfort me."

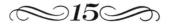

15

I took Natasha with me that evening, as I had to pick up a
typewriter and bring it to my house. At that time I had begun to
type a lot—everything I was given and everything I myself
wanted to type.

According to our main principle, "If you dance, you don't
sing." I, having begun to type, should have stopped all my active
outward involvements. But I could both sing and dance and I
could talk to people and, moreover, I knew English. So I couldn't
stop appearing at the synagogue every Jewish holiday where we

gave our famous performances of Israeli songs and dances. Violating all the laws of conspiracy, I continued to do everything I found it possible to do.

Having decided to involve the girls in the typing, I arranged with them that they come to my place whenever they had free time and type as much as they could. We had quite a number of things to do. We typed collective petitions of Jews, historical selections, articles about modern Israel, as well as explanations for the Hebrew textbook *Elef Milim*. At the same time I was translating a guidebook of Israel by Zeev Vilnay into Russian and was preparing a picture album from 250 Israeli picture postcards, with explanations taken from the backs of the cards. Having discussed and then checked the translations with our own "specialist" on Israel from Riga, I typed it.

This all helped us to feel that we were doing something useful and, if we had to wait, we were not wasting our lives doing nothing.

One day we were to meet a young American student who, according to his words, had something to say to the Jews. Natasha and I met him in the center of Moscow and we all went to a cafe. He proved to be unaware of anything and really wanted to listen more than to speak. He could hardly explain to which Jewish organizations he belonged and the only thing that we could get from him were two books on religion, several Jewish skullcaps, and prayer books. At that time we appreciated everything, but needed something else. At the end of the talk, he suddenly handed out ten rubles. He wanted to make his contribution to the cause and tried to prove that we could buy many important things with it. We laughed and said that we didn't need it, we had money and, in general, we didn't take money just like that. But he could not be dissuaded and at last forcefully put the money into one of our pockets. We were then in the street and didn't want to attract attention. He took his leave and we were left with his ten rubles, embarrassed and confused. We didn't yet know that this was the American way.

On our way back home, we suddenly found ourselves discussing not the talk, but the boy himself, his manners and clothes. Three things shocked us: he didn't help with our coats when we were leaving the cafe; he didn't pick up the coin which one of us had dropped; and, in saying good-by, he shook hands with us with his gloves on. We wondered whether it was generally like that in America.

Having discussed all this, we laughed—so unnatural it seemed to us. We were going down the escalator into the subway. I turned to face Natasha, who was standing behind me:

"Why not? Why should we always be clever and business-like? Why is it not natural to discuss boys and clothes? Why should we go with a boy to a cafe only when we have to hide from the KGB? How old are you?"

"I am eighteen," she sighed.

"And I am twenty. And we are two old maids."

"But, Alka, some time, many years from now, we shall say '*Hayu zmanim* . . .' ("Those were the times") and people will say, 'Those are the women who were in prison in Russia.' "

"Yes, exactly. I don't know why, but we are sure that we shall have to go through prison."

"Because all this can't end well. We've turned your apartment into a real typing factory; we talk just like that with foreigners."

"But I didn't see any followers this time."

"Not this time, then next time. By the way, what about the article from Samizdat I brought you the other day, by Esenin-Volpin?"

"I've read it already, but he writes about what we should say when we get caught. I wish somebody would write about what we must do not to get caught."

"So do I. But let's forget about it. Let us dream instead."

"Of what?"

"Let's imagine that at this very moment we are told to leave."

"Just now, in the Underground?"

"Yes, what will you do?"

"I shall rush to the airport."

"Me also. But I shall call home and tell the folks first."

"O.K. And then we shall rush to the airport, just as we are."

"Without suitcases?"

"Of course. What do they matter then? Do we need them at such moment? We shall throw away our fur coats also and fly and fly. Isn't it great?"

"Fantastic. Take care, it is the end of the escalator."

Next day was Saturday. Natasha came early in the morning because we wanted to start typing as soon as we could. But, having adjusted our typewriters, we both suddenly felt that it was difficult to work without breakfast.

It was the end of the month and I had neither a penny nor a piece of bread at home. Having realized that we were both hungry, we could not forget about it and suffered terribly. The work didn't go well.

At the same time we couldn't look in one another's eyes, trying hard not to think about the American's rubles that were in my bag. They had already been allocated for two big albums that we had to order for our guidebook. But hunger soon proved to us that the work suffered from our stupid stubbornness and we began to think aloud:

"Isn't it better to have a good breakfast now and then do a really good piece of work?"

"But this isn't our money!"

"But what is the problem? In a couple of days, we'll get our salaries and buy the albums."

"And then we shall run out of money, not at the end, but in the middle of the month."

"Then we shall not buy them. Maybe this damned American gave us money to buy food, so that we could work. That would also be a contribution to the cause."

"You know, I am sick to my stomach and I have a headache."

"That always happens two hours before death."

"Thank you. O.K., there's no use wasting time. The money is

in the bag. Go buy something and I'll put some water on the stove."

In ten minutes Natasha returned with her hands full of packages.

"Anything left?"

"No."

"Fine."

We began preparing the food and soon were enjoying hot potatoes with herring, eggs, tea, and bread with butter. We noticed nothing until the food disappeared from the table and then we sat down immediately to type. Again we were avoiding one another's eyes, this time with shame. But the American fellow had made a good contribution to the Jewish cause in Russia.

I was corresponding regularly with Yosif, writing about everything except our "work." He was not only a bad dancer, but an awful pen pal. His letters were very short; everything in his life seemed boring to him and he had difficulty finding things to write about. But I could understand the main thought from his half-page notes. He missed me greatly, was dreaming about our Tallinn trip, and was thinking only of me. With every letter, I admired him more and more. He had already passed two of my three tests for a boyfriend: he was Jewish and he wanted to go to Israel. But did he take part in "the work," was he courageous enough to face the danger? Did he think about and want to help those who also wanted to go?

The answer came to me quite unexpectedly and filled me with joy and pride. One day I was approached by one of my friends and told that I might soon have a call from a man in another city.

"He will begin to tell you something which you will not understand. Don't be surprised. Just try to remember every word and then tell me. The contents will seem strange to you, but just try to remember everything. O.K.?"

I nodded. No questions asked. Two weeks passed and nobody called. Soon I forgot about it. Then one day Yosif called me from Riga, as we usually called each other every week, not

being satisfied with just letters. "The work" played a very important part in our lives and it was extremely difficult to talk about
anything else. We exchanged greetings, asked about our moods,
studies, friends, and relatives. This time the talk was as usual.
When all the subjects had been exhausted and I expected Yosif
to say good-by, he suddenly began to tell me some nonsense. I
asked him what it was. He was a little bit embarrassed, but
repeated it. This time I caught the words and understood.

I was so happy to learn that "the man" was Yosif himself
that I could not conceal my joy over the telephone. Yosif then
for many hours cudgeled his brains to understand my extreme
joy over the contents of his information. And I immediately
rushed to my friend, passed the information on to him, and
thanked him for the call, "the man," and the nonsense.

"Why?" he couldn't understand.

"Just so. You made me happy."

*   *   *

On the eighth of April, I was as usual working in my office.
Twice when I was absent from the office, a man with a foreign
accent had called me, my colleagues had said. I didn't want to
miss the call the third time and was sitting in the room waiting.
It came very soon. It was Yosif, with his Latvian-Jewish accent.
I was surprised that he should call me at my job and that his
voice was so near. He asked his usual questions, but I could hear
a smile in his voice. Then he suddenly asked when I would finish
work. A wild thought struck me.

"Where are you?"

"I am here, two minutes' walk from you."

I gave a cry of joy and jumped almost up to the ceiling.

"When? Why? For how long?" I asked wildly, not waiting
for the answers.

Soon I was running to him. I ran into him and hid my face
on his chest. He bent forward awkwardly, trying to find my
cheek, and kissed me in the hair. I became frightened. We had
seemed so close in our letters and now I felt shy before him.

He had to leave the same night and no one was to know

about his coming. We took a taxi to get home as quickly as we could. At home I changed my clothes and started to prepare supper. He became angry.

"Don't do anything! I didn't come to eat. Sit down for a little while. I'll have to go very soon."

I was in distress. Just a few hours and then again so far from each other. I sat down, but almost immediately stood up and began to walk to and fro in my tiny room. Yosif was sitting on the sofa with his feet set against the opposite wall. We were in a cage, in a cage of my room, in a cage of shyness and fear.

Something had to be done. We began to talk. Somehow we began to discuss the threat of the army for the Jewish boys and I said that if they escaped the Russian Army and went to Israel, there would be the army again, this time our army, but with danger to their lives.

"But don't you see it is something different? And why should you think about it now when we are still here?" The necessity for him to comfort me made both of us freer. He drew me to him and embraced me. I was so thin that he seemed to embrace emptiness. I raised my head and smiled at him and then he was kissing my hands, my face, my neck, and then suddenly stopped and began to smell my hair.

"What do you smell there?"

"Just so. It smells so good. So different. You are quite different."

All too soon we had to rush to the airport. His plane was leaving at midnight. We arrived on time and even had a few minutes to kiss each other shamelessly in front of people. At the last moment he rushed to the plane.

Suddenly a dark figure approached from somewhere at the side and stopped Yosif. I stood frozen with terror. But in a minute Yosif ran to the plane and it soon took off. It was a mistake. The man had just asked him for his ticket. But I understood it as a sign of everything that was awaiting us in our common future and that would not always turn out to be a mistake.

ALLA, 1972.

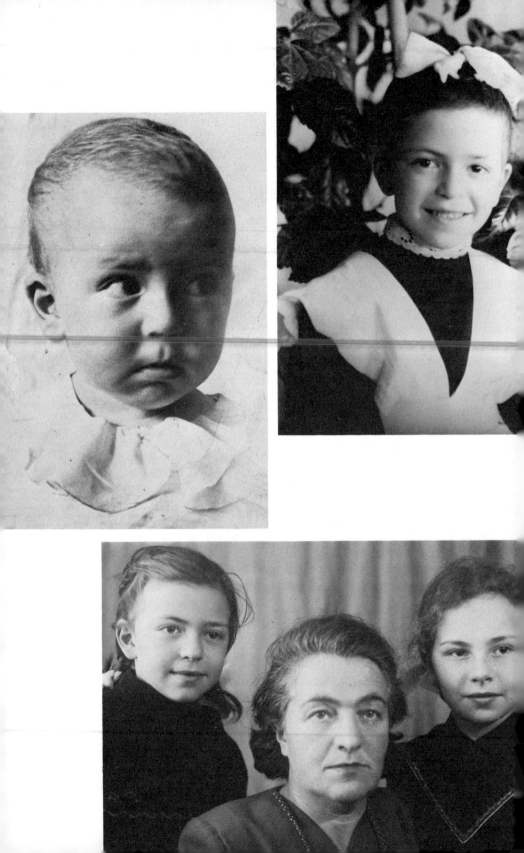

Far left: 1949. "I WAS A PLUMP CHILD WITH AN EXTRAORDINARY BIG AND BALD HEAD . . ."

Top left: 1956. "THAT YEAR I WENT TO SCHOOL . . ."

Lower left: FROM LEFT TO RIGHT: ALLA, HER MOTHER AND SISTER MYRA. "WE THREE WOMEN LIVED ALL OUR LIVES TOGETHER BUT NEVER CAME TO KNOW EACH OTHER DEEPLY."

Below: 1962. "I AM NOW IN THE SIXTH FORM . . . AND I AM A MEMBER OF THE EDITORIAL BOARD OF OUR CLASS NEWSPAPER."

Far left: 1966. "IN THE SUMMER I FINISHED SCHOOL . . ."

Top left: DANCING A HORA ON THE BALTIC SEASHORE, 1967.

Lower left: ALLA (TO THE LEFT) AND MYRA (TO THE RIGHT) AT A COUSIN'S WEDDING IN RIGA, 1967.

Above: ALLA WITH AN AMERICAN JEWISH TOURIST GIRL IN RED SQUARE, MOSCOW, 1969.

Above: THE WEDDING CEREMONY, OCTOBER 1970.

Left: "I LOOK AT YOSSI AND WE BOTH CANNOT BUT LAUGH OF HAPPINESS AND JOY."

Right: THE WEDDING CAKE.

Above: JANUARY 1971, AMSTERDAM. "I TRY TO EXPLAIN TO THEM WHAT A SOVIET JEW IS, WHAT HIS IDEALIZING ZIONISM IS, WHAT HIS HEROISM IS."

Right: ISRAEL, LOD AIRPORT, MARCH 1971.

WELCOMING THE SABBATH
DURING THE EIGHT-DAY HUN-
GER STRIKE NEAR THE WAILING
WALL IN SOLIDARITY WITH
THE PRISONERS OF THE LEN-
INGRAD TRIAL, DECEMBER
1970.

MAY 1972. "IT IS SO WONDERFUL THAT WE ARE THREE NOW."

The official reaction in the press to the growth of Zionism was developing in proportion to the number of applications for exit visas to the OVIR. The officials could easily ignore us, but our mood was being reflected abroad in the speeches of Golda Meir, in numerous special meetings of the Knesset, and in the activities of American Jewry.

Not a single day passed without a long article against Zionism appearing in *Pravda* or *Izvestia*, which called the activities abroad political provocation aimed at the Soviet State. "Zionism, a Poisoned Weapon of Imperialism," "To Whose Tune Do the Zionists Dance," "The Provocateurs at Work," etc., etc. And new books appeared, published in "best-seller" editions—*Take Care, Zionism!, Judaism in Its True Colors*—both with a black cover showing a Jew with a large nose and burning, rapacious eyes. We, the young Jews, who didn't remember Stalin's anti-Semitic campaigns, realized that our turn had come. And we had to face it, to read it, and to swallow it. Our futile fury grew when similar articles appeared with Jewish names under them. The procedure of the 1952 campaign was being repeated.

Jews were beating their breasts trying to prove they were loyal, happy, satisfied. They hated Zionism and Israel and all imperialists of the world. "I have this and that, I don't need Golda Meir's protection," "I don't know what is Jewish in me except the word on my identity card," "Our Soviet Motherland has protected us from fascists. We live among brothers." And so on.

We were burning with a desire to run somewhere, to find those Jews, to spit in their servile faces, to prove our point to somebody. But what was the use? Everyone has a right to his own point of view and, if they were compelled to sign those articles, what can you do with people who are afraid? Whatever the number of signatures on those articles, we knew the number of applications for exit visas to Israel was incomparably larger. Some of the Jews wrote open individual or collective letters to *Pravda*. We read and reread them. They were open only to us Jews who thought differently and to the world as they reached it. In the Soviet Union there was no reaction to them.

OPEN LETTER

To: L. Berenshtein and M. Fridel—authors of the article, "To Whose Tune Do The Zionists Dance" (Izvestia–No. 292, December 14, 1969).

Lately, in the newspapers Pravda *and* Izvestia *there have appeared articles devoted to the attitude of Jews living in the USSR toward the State of Israel. The authors of these articles—G. Plotkin, L. Berenshtein, and M. Fridel—are Jews, and they have evidently taken upon themselves the mission of speaking in the name of the entire Jewish population of the USSR.*

As we, the signatories to this letter, are also Jews living in the USSR, the questions mentioned in the articles directly concern each of us—and this is why we consider it necessary to answer the authors of the article, "To Whose Tune Do The Zionists Dance."

And so you, L. Berenshtein and M. Fridel, write that the Parliament of Israel has adopted a resolution in which it demands "respect" for the indubitable right of every Jew to live on the soil of his historical motherland—that is to say, Israel.

It is here to the point to ask: do you know of any other historical motherland of the Jews that is not "so-called"? Perhaps you wish to say that the Jews—unlike other peoples—have no historical motherland, or, at least, should not have one? Or, as you are trying to convince the reader, that the Jewish national question can be solved only in the field of class struggle? What it comes to is that it is not historical continuity, not the ancestral spiritual heritage, not the history of the country and its people, that shape the soul of a person, but the class struggle and only the class struggle. Moreover, you consider that the Jewish problem can be only political, social, and even religious, but by no means national (in the sense of their own statehood).

But how much more human, after your awkward lines, appear to us other words about the Fatherland, patriotism, and internationalism, expressed by I. Vuzylev and A. Kraminov in this same Izvestia *(December 15, 1969), in the article, "Love and*

*a Ring": ". . . We feel ourselves citizens and workers of the huge,
proudly expansive, global territory that is called the Union of the
Soviet Socialist Republics. And we feel that it is our Fatherland.
. . . This is a personal attitude as well. And it is precisely this that,
sooner or later, had to impel us and did impel us to visit that
corner of the earth, small in comparison with the vast areas of
the country, that is situated to the north of Moscow and is called
'Rus,' around which Russian statehood was constructed, around
which the Russian people confirmed itself and felt itself to be
one. All of us are children of our parents. Our existence, everything that we are, we owe to them first and foremost. And this
gratitude toward an endless number of generations surely makes
up part of the lofty concept of patriotism. And another part of it
is the consciousness of the fact that each of us is a link in this
chain of generations and bears full responsibility toward those
that follow us. After all, it is doubtful whether true internationalism is within the reach of a person who lacks the feeling of
national dignity. Because how can the soul and the beauty of
another nation be understood by one who is capable of scorning
his own spiritual heritage?"*

Do you hear, L. Berenshtein and M. Fridel? What can you
say to this? What source nourishes your feelings of national dignity? To what endless row of generations are you grateful? You
who come out in the name of the "Jewish population of our
country," will you be able to read P. Markish, S. Halkin,
L. Kvitko, I. Fefer, and Bergelson in your own, Jewish, language?
Do you know even one Jewish letter? Are you proud of the
spiritual heritage of your people—even of the Bible, if only in its
literary and historical aspect? Do you, your children, and your
grandchildren know about the heroic national uprisings of the
Maccabees and of Bar Kochba against foreign rulers? What do
such names as Yehuda Halevi, Maimonides, Moses Mendelssohn,
Ch. N. Bialik, and S. Frug say to you? Or is all this not your
history, not your spiritual heritage? If so, then what is yours?
And where is it? Is it only the "field" . . . the bare field of class
struggle? And on the basis of what national spiritual heritage do
you dress up as internationalists?

On April 1, 1964, in the newspaper Izvestia it was written:
"The constant striving for unity, for life on the land of the ancestors has preserved the Armenian nation." Then why don't you see
that it is precisely these forces—the striving for unity and for life
on the land of the ancestors—which have preserved the Jewish
nation as well through centuries of even greater trials? By what
right do you—the pathetic product of assimilation!—come out in
the name of the "Jewish population"? And don't try to convince
the readers that the decision of the Israel Knesset demanding
respect for "the indubitable right of each Jew to live on the soil

of his historical motherland," is an anti-Soviet campaign. Don't follow the path of blackmail, don't hark back to those times when violation of laws was a habitual matter. And don't hasten to stick the label of "traitors" and "betrayers of the Homeland" on the Soviet Jews who have so far only expressed their desire to unite with their kin on the land of Israel.

Neither the French, nor the English, nor the Russian peoples had to prove to the entire world their right to a national existence. The history of the Jews was different. The Jewish people had to prove this right. And it was proved in 1947. And the world recognized this right. And the Soviet Union was one of the first to recognize the State of Israel. Doesn't this mean that from now on every Jew HAS THE RIGHT to take part in the building of HIS STATE and in the formation of a JEWISH national culture on the land of HIS ancestors? And you, the so-called "representatives of the Jewish nationality," are not ashamed to make police threats and describe this right and the open expression of the will of the people to return to the land of its ancestors as "treachery" and "betrayal"!

As for the class struggle, it is successfully carried out by the Communist Party of Israel (even two of them!), which is, incidentally, the only legal Communist Party in the entire Near East, the representatives of which even sit in the same Knesset whose resolution inspired you with the idea for your article.

It is clear that your aim is to prove to readers both in the Soviet Union and abroad that the idea of settling in the "land of the ancestors" in Israel is alien to the Jews of the Soviet Union. You should take a look into the Visas and Registration Section attached to the Ministry of Interior of the USSR and ask, how many tens of thousands of Jews come there in the vain hope of getting a permit to leave the USSR and to reunite with their relatives in Israel? Although the lawfulness of their strivings is not refuted, these people are nevertheless deprived of the possibility of achieving their lawful aim. This open violation of human rights becomes more and more obvious and acquires greater and greater publicity before public opinion.

And this is in spite of the fact that, under the Universal Declaration of the Rights of Man, "all of whose provisions"—according to Izvestia no. 289—"have long since become a habitual norm of life," states, in article 13: "Every person has the right to leave any country, including his own, and to return to his country."

Try to understand, L. Berenshtein and M. Fridel, that the right to leave any country is the lawful right of every person and is nowhere in the world regarded as "treachery" and "betrayal of the Fatherland."

Therefore the recent appeal to the UN on the part of the eighteen Jewish families from Georgia, complaining against the

Soviet organs that arbitrarily impede their departure, is also fully understandable. It was precisely this appeal that was the basis for the resolution of the Israel Parliament, something that you have preferred not to mention in your article.

Persons who desire to go to Israel do exist. There are thousands and thousands of them. This is not "a fabrication on the part of bourgeois slanderers." These people exist and openly protest against the infringement of their human rights.

And we add our voices to this protest.

As for you, L. Berenshtein and M. Fridel, like every one "who knows the laws of social development," you must be aware that the wheels of history cannot only not be turned back, they cannot be stopped either. And today, when the Jewish State has been revived and has existed for twenty-two years, "the striving for unity, for life in the land of the ancestors," is natural and incontestable.

Therefore all the Soviet Jews who wish to reunite with their people in the land of Israel would certainly welcome respect for their indubitable right "to live in the land of their historical motherland."

And to the great Power which gave shelter to many generations of Jews, we repeat the words of our distant ancestors who demanded the right of Exodus from Egypt: "LET MY PEOPLE GO!"

> *Vitaly Svechinsky*
> *Dora Kolyaditskaya*
> *Mark Elbaum*
> *Tina Brodetskaya*
> *Lev Freidin*
> *Bliuma Diskina*

Moscow, December 1969

OPEN LETTER

To: The Editorial Office of the newspaper Pravda

In Pravda *of 13/1/70 were published letters to the editorial office under the general heading "Exposure of the Provocateurs."*

All the letters are founded on your paper's assertion, which does not correspond with fact, that the appeal of the Government of Israel had been directed to all the Jews of the USSR. In fact the call for emigration was addressed only to those Jews who wish to emigrate to Israel within the framework of family reunification or for other reasons.

I do not doubt for a minute the genuineness of the published

*letters and the sincerity of their authors. But, with some varia-
tions in the answers published (from coarse, foul insults to the
Government of Israel in the letters of persons that do not contain
the authors' social position, to the restrained expression in the
letters of the more intellectual economists and the librarian), all
these letters have one thing in common: they are written by
citizens of Jewish origin, who do not wish to regard themselves
as Jews.*

*This idea is expressed in all the letters, but it is particularly
frankly stated in the letter of G. Tsypin. This, so to say Jew,
writes: "I don't know what has remained in me of Jewishness,
perhaps only the nationality paragraph in my passport, but as
long as I am considered (!) a Jew. . . ."*

*Here it is, the fruit of assimilation, when a man lacks na-
tional pride and national dignity, he turns into a person without
kin and without a tribe.*

*As long as the writer does not consider himself a Jew, the
question arises whether he and others like him have the right to
appear publicly in the name of the Jews on a matter that concerns Jews exclusively (Jews not only by origin) and no one
else.*

The editorial office of Pravda *has made an obvious miscal-
culation in publishing letters like the one quoted, because it follows from them that there is no national life for Jews in the
USSR. Not a single one of the authors mentions (and they have
no grounds for it) any national, cultural, or spiritual life of the
Jews in the USSR, a life without which the normal existence of
any nation is unthinkable.*

*Can you find among the Russians, Ukrainians, Bielorussians,
Georgians, Armenians, and other peoples of the USSR any persons asserting that all that has remained in them of their nationality is but a paragraph in the passport? Such a statement on the
part of the Jews testifies to the pitiful situation of their national
culture and their national life! There are no Jewish schools,
newspapers, magazines, theaters, or textbooks for learning the
Jewish language! . .*

*A policy that is directed toward assimilation does bear some
fruit, but as a whole it is doomed to failure. Nobody has yet
succeeded in assimilating the Jews throughout the 2,000 years of
their homeless history, when there was no Jewish State. This will
still less succeed now, when the Jewish State exists and is a
center of attraction for all Jews who have kept their national
pride and dignity.*

V. Polsky

In April the authorities surpassed themselves. They organized a press conference for foreign journalists with prominent

Jews—one minister, military general, scientists, actors, government officials. The press conference was broadcast on television and then repeated three times during the week. The newspapers gave the full text of the conference.

Of course, the press conference was not announced beforehand as the organizers had feared that other Jews would come "to greet their compatriots," so we could only grind our teeth ex post facto watching the television, the mocking faces of the American correspondents, and the pale faces with nervous tics of the speaking Jews.

And the whole of Russia was splitting its sides with laughter over the "new performance of the Soviet Circus with tame Jews." "It serves them right," the anti-Semites said. More intelligent people would shrug their shoulders with disgust. And only the gray Soviet masses, the basis of power, would believe, agree, and approve.

"Other" Jews answered the press conference with a letter which became known to the world as "the letter of the 39" and was to become one of the first great rallying points of the now open struggle of Soviet Jewry for exodus. Only since then, we have added to our appeals the awkward phrase, "for those who want it."

To USSR Ministry of Foreign Affairs
The Chief of the Press Department
L. M. Zamyatin

We are those Jews who insist on their desire to leave for Israel and who are being constantly refused by the Soviet authorities.

We are those Jews who have more than once addressed open statements to the Soviet press but whose letters were never published.

We are those Jews who were not invited to the press conference on the 4th of March and were not invited to express their point of view.

We suppose that you must feel uneasy about the one-sidedness of the press conference organized by you, more so, that you certainly know, at least from the press, that since 1968 when the Soviet authorities began accepting applications of Jews who want to leave for Israel, till November 1969 more than 80,000 applications were handed in. (See the well-known Soviet press weekly Newsweek, *November 24, 1969.) And this happened in the atmosphere when the desire of a Soviet Jew to live in the land of his forefathers is not encouraged, to put it mildly.*

If we suppose that every application was handed in by a family even if not large, even if of three persons, this already means that more than 240,000 Jews in the Soviet Union are unsuccessfully seeking permission to leave.

Proceeding from the elementary understanding of justice formulated already in ancient Rome as "Let the other side be also heard!" you, of course, will like to remedy that disappointing situation which was created by the one-sidedness of the press conference organized by you on the 4th of March.

That is why we Jews, unlike "the citizens of Jewish origin," we, who are ready any moment, leaving everything behind, as we are, even to make our way on foot to the State of Israel, request you to give us also the opportunity to appear at a news conference before Soviet and foreign journalists and to make a declaration.

Please inform us through the press on the place and time of this news conference.

The text of our open declaration is as follows.

DECLARATION

The Anti-Israel campaign in the Soviet press has reached its culmination in the recent press conference of a number of prominent persons of Jewish origin.

The participants of the press conference expressed the opinion of only a certain, even if numerous, part of Soviet Jewry. We do not belong to that part and think that our opinion is characteristic of many of our fellow Jews, although we admit that indecision is preventing many of them from openly expressing their views.

We declare:

The military events in the Middle East have once more been used for anti-Israeli propaganda. This is shameful propaganda, for war is a great disaster and, if Arabs perish in this war, this does not please Jews.

The emotional heat of anti-Israel propaganda is now very great, and we consider it necessary to clarify that the myth of the imperialist character of Israel is nothing more [than] a method of political propaganda. The accusations that Israel desires to move all the Jews to its territory irrespective of their will are unfounded. Only the help in moving those who want it is Israel's humane task.

The idea of Jewish statehood has nothing to do with preach-

ing of racism and national exclusiveness. Internationalism is peculiar to the Jewish national character and is consecrated by Jewish law. It is said: "Seventy bullocks were offered up by Israel for the seventy nations of the world." (Tanhuma 88, 3)

The attempt to criticize the idea of Jewish statehood from the "class" point of view, to substitute the class problem for the national one is groundless. Unification of people according to the national principles does not and is not supposed to exclude various contradictions among them, including the so-called "class" ones. In any case this is the internal affair of a nation.

The essential task of the press conference was to show that its participants had reached prominent positions in society, in spite of their Jewish origin. But this was all they could show, for their Jewish origins do not mean that they have preserved their spiritual link with the national Jewish culture. Every Jew has of course a right to any degree of assimilation. We, however, do not want to forfeit our national identity and our spiritual link with our people.

We worship those sons of the Jewish people who accepted torture and death to preserve their national identity, for, thanks to them, the Jewish nation was preserved. We are proud of our people who have carried their religion, language, culture and national traits through thousands of years of suffering and are proud that this people has now found in itself the will to revive the State of Israel and to defend it.

And it is the very preservation of the national identity of Jews that is the problem in the Soviet Union. No references to completely equal and joyful labor with Russians and no examples of a brilliant military or social career can divert our attention from the problem, for in this, Russians remain Russians, and Jews cease to be Jews. Forcible assimilation in this case does not mean, for example, prohibition of reading Jewish books. It means that young Jews do not know how to read Jewish books as there are no schools in the Soviet Union where the Jewish language is taught.

But we are in our right to remain Jews and to educate our children in the spirit of Jewish culture, and we believe that those who prefer or will be compelled to remain in this country can defend their right to be Jews not only by origin.

One of the basic issues of the Jewish question in the USSR is a guarantee of the right of repatriation. The Soviet Union does not recognize that right, and many thousands of Soviet Jews who want to leave for Israel are being refused. The reasons for this anti-repatriation policy given at the press conference do not even deserve to be argued against.

We shall insist on our right to decide our own destiny, including the choice of citizenship and country of living. We are

*able ourselves to estimate all the possible difficulties awaiting us
concerning military events, change of climate, or of social order.*

*The present state of our citizenship includes the right for the
State to demand from us no more than obeying the laws, and our
claims to freedom of repatriation are based on Soviet laws and
guarantees of international law.*

*The Jewish people has undergone many persecutions and
suffering, many malicious or well-intentioned assimilation campaigns and has succeeded in maintaining its identity.*

*We believe that now also Jews will respond to the anti-Israel
campaign not by abdicating, but that on the contrary, their pride
in their people will grow stronger and that they will declare:
"Next year in Jerusalem!"*

Moscow, March 8, 1970

No press conference for "other" Jews followed, but all those
who signed the letter were called for individual talks by the local
Party committees. The talks, with a representative from the KGB
present, were as usual and no repressions followed them. But
those who were members of the Communist Party were expelled
from the membership. However, that had long ago stopped
being a punishment. It had become one of the honorary awards
on the heroic road to Israel.

*   *   *

On the 22nd of April, the Soviet Union and "the whole of
the progressive world" celebrated the 100th anniversary of Lenin's
birth. We knew of its approach by the appearance of more and
more red color in the streets and a general fuss in our places of
work and Institutes. On the "Great Day" there was a meeting in
the Palace of Congresses with the representatives of all Communist and Working Class Parties of the world as guests of
honor. We had heard before that Meir Vilner, the leader of one
of the two Communist groups in Israel, would be present. It
didn't bother us, for we had long ago understood what Meir
Vilner was and felt he had no more to do with Israel than did a
Chinese peasant.

But in the afternoon, when we were at Natasha's place, her
grandfather suddenly decided to switch on the television to
watch the meeting, all the while wearing the sarcastic smile of a

former Communist. We immediately saw a good-looking, middle-aged man with gray hair approaching the speakers' platform, while the whole Palace resounded with applause. Before we could recognize him, he began his speech:

"*Haverim Yakarim!* Dear comrades!" and he followed with the usual Communist nonsense in brilliant Russian.

The fact that this fellow had used "our Hebrew" even for the greeting had irritated us terribly. We left the house and went to the synagogue. It was the third day of Passover and two nights of the "dark" Jewish holiday were over, but we still found a small group of young Jews there. We spent that evening in teaching them simple Hebrew songs on the staircase of the synagogue with red banners swinging threateningly over our heads.

I was on my way home late at night when I was suddenly terrified by a frightening sight in the sky. A huge portrait of Lenin was hanging high up against the stars and was lit by giant searchlights. When I came to myself after the first fright, I thought with disgust that they were already surpassing their Chinese brother-enemies in idolatry.

I stopped looking at it and began to think instead that there were only eight days left till Tallinn.

17

In April the time for our visit to Tallinn was quickly approaching. How long it had been! But the waiting was over, the eternity had passed, and we had to pack and think about tickets. Our fancy clothes were already finished and we filled our suitcases almost entirely with the new things. Natasha and I had dared to have pants suits made, which were still unheard of in Moscow but which we hoped would be accepted in Tallinn and Riga and appreciated by our boys.

The problem of tickets proved to be difficult. Many students

and working people traveled dring the vacation period beginning with the first of May. There were no tickets. At last, having
paid off somebody, we got tickets for a very strange train which
went to Tallinn in fifteen hours.

We boarded the train and easily found places for ourselves.
The carriage was almost empty. The seats were hard and we
began to arrange our bags under our heads. Everyone was in
good spirits and, soon exhausted, we fell asleep.

In our dreams the hard benches seemed to penetrate into
our bones and some hard object in the bag turned into a Turkish
execution device for the head, but our sleep was too sound and,
without awakening, we simply changed sides. In the middle of
the night, we all suddenly awoke and could not find each other.
Other people were sitting on our benches, blocking us from the
world; others were sitting on the floor; children were sleeping on
sacks. They were all wearing quilted jackets, warm worn ker-
chiefs, or fur caps. The air was filled with the smell of Russian
sweat, stale straw, and everything that means a Russian village.

After the first shudder, looking out through the fringe of
legs in tarpaulin boots from the upper benches, we began to call
each other weakly:

"Alla!"

"Natalik!"

"Basja!"

"Sanja, Olja?"

"Where are we? Who are they?"

"Just people."

The people were sleeping soundly or sitting still looking
steadily in front of them. As if they had been traveling like that
for an eternity, they didn't notice us or each other. No one was
talking.

We soon understood that they were not traveling for long.
At a certain moment, they began to waken their children and got
off at the next stop. At one of the stops, the carriage was filled
with soldiers. We shrank into dark corners, trying to hide ourselves. They were all huge and silent, with gloomy, exhausted

faces. Without words, they lay down quickly on the benches or on the floor and fell asleep. Two soldiers sat down on our bench and offered their coats to us. Not wanting to offend them, we accepted and answered their simple questions.

The soldiers on the next benches suddenly became drunk and, before we knew it, they began violently beating each other. The carriage began to shake. Basja stretched out her plump white little hand with pearl nails as if trying to defend herself from the heap of bodies that was ready to come down on us.

Suddenly Natasha began to laugh. I also couldn't stand the tension anymore and began to giggle. Then Natasha began to recite some stupid childrens' poem, swinging her arms, and overturned a bottle of milk on the people who lay on the floor. She began to giggle and said:

"It is only milk, don't worry!"

A woman with milk running down her head looked at Natasha as if she were mad and didn't utter a word. They were all dumb.

The people kept coming and going, coming and going. They were all alike and yet different. The smells depended on which village they came from. The whole of Russia seemed to be moving, the real Russia, which was concealed from the rest of the world.

This was not the first time we had seen these people. All of us had gone through the Komsomol work in kolkhozy (collective farms) and had seen and experienced that life. But on our way to Tallinn, this meeting with Russia seemed to be a terrible mistake.

As we approached Estonian territory, the people began to leave and soon we found ourselves alone in the carriage. We fell on the benches and were asleep immediately, having forgotten their hardness and the absence of pillows.

We awoke in the afternoon as the train was approaching Tallinn. The terrible night seemed to be a bad dream. We quickly put ourselves in order.

The boys were standing on the platform in the gray Tallinn rain. When the train stopped, they entered the carriage to help

us with our suitcases. Again I felt shy and didn't dare come up to
Yosif for a kiss. The moment of which we had dreamed all these
116 days and nights had come. Yosif and Lev immediately took
their places near me and Natasha like guards, and Tsvisha took
Basja, Olja, and Sanja under his care. Laughing and interrupting
each other, we told them about our night. But on approaching
the city, we decided to forget about everything that didn't concern Tallinn and entered it in silence.

On the way I asked Yosif not to separate us from the rest,
but he interrupted me with anger and despair:

"I have had enough of Moscow's New Year's holiday. Now I
want to have only you and don't care about the rest. If anybody
dares to interfere with us, I shall be direct and frank with
him."

His despair came from his already being aware of my club
born and independent character, and he feared my resistance.
His anger was at the whole world that parted us for such long
periods and at such long distances. He squeezed my arm above
the elbow as if trying to keep me from going away, but he
needn't have done it. I didn't want to be strong and independent
any more. I belonged to him.

We crossed some unseen border and found ourselves in the
medieval city. This was the sixteenth century in Western Europe. Two- and three-storied buildings with high red-tiled roofs
and small windows with iron shutters were bent over narrow
cobbles. Tall gray churches and towers pierced the sky with
their spires like bony old Don Quixotes with spears. Everything
was unnaturally clean and there was not a single man in the
street or a single face in the windows. On a corner we saw a huge
clock hanging over the road. I shuddered. It had two large hands
and no figures at all. I looked around, fearing that a horse with a
coffin would appear from behind the corner or a faceless man in
black would fall down and disappear.

"This is the world of Ingmar Bergman," Yosif said, as if
reading my thoughts.

In the central square we found at last some people who
passed us with stony faces. They were almost all pale of com-

plexion, with gray hair, thin, and dried-up. All the men were neatly dressed and the women wore all kinds of elegant little hats—something you rarely see in other republics.

To celebrate the First of May, the square was decorated with a huge portrait of Lenin and Soviet slogans on stripes of red material. But here it didn't irritate us. Lenin looked not like a guest or an invader, but more like a stranger who suddenly found himself in the wrong place. The famous turn of his head now made him look like a man who moves his head left and right to find out how to escape. The slogans looked like ribbons that someone had dropped by accident. Time had stopped here in the sixteenth century and the spears that hung over entrance doors and pierced the street reminded us that the unseen knights of Estonia were on guard and ready to repulse any invasion by the modern world.

But this was only scenery. And the "dropped ribbons" and "frightened" stranger enveloped half of a big building in the square on every Soviet holiday.

The German Teutonic style of Tallinn didn't appeal to me, but I admired the national pride and bright identity of the Estonians. Our walks in the city passed under a melodic fugue by Bach descending from a violin played by a little musician in black sitting on one of the clouds. His music was sometimes penetrated by the warning sounds of the Mendelssohn First Concerto.

We had four days to spend in Tallinn and more than ten famous restaurants to visit. Sleeping in a big room in a student's dormitory that we had rented, we tried to get up early to be ready for a short tour of the city and at least five visits to restaurants or small bars. In the morning, after a whole night of laughter, jokes, singing, and dancing in our room, we shouted through a thin wall to awaken each other.

The new world delighted us and the boys introduced us to it with the pride and confidence of habitués. They were not habitués in this world, but they had been born and brought up for it. The life which they lived working in factories with drunkards and immoral people, living in communal apartments with the same people for neighbors and all this after years of exile to distant regions of Russia—this life they considered temporary and strange and the world they lived in foreign.

We sat in semi-dark restaurants and the delicate sparkling crystal was reflected in lights in our burning eyes. The boys treated us to the tastiest food and most interesting cocktails.

In one of the restaurants we watched a variety show—one of the few existing in the Soviet Union. Young beautiful singers shook the room with the passion of their singing. Slender, half-naked girls danced among the tables. We clapped our hands with childish delight and couldn't tear our eyes from the play of the muscles of the strong and handsome male dancers. This small world with colored lights and beautiful music in the round hall of the restaurant filled us with passion and joy. It reflected our hidden inner feelings and encouraged us to live and feel.

After one such visit, Natasha and I went out into the street completely drunk, half with the strong cocktail, half with plea-sure and happiness. We walked in the streets and couldn't stop laughing loudly. We uttered some indistinct sounds, trying to say something to each other, but immediately split our sides in laughter. Yosif and Lev looked at each other seriously and said:

"What a shame! Let's walk at a distance as if we don't know them."

And they ostentatiously stepped back with stony faces, but with laughter in their eyes. We laughed all over the street, took each other by the hands, and ran forward. Suddenly Natasha stopped and put her finger to her mouth. "Sh-h-h." Then she minced on her tiptoes after a passing sailor. I ran after her and grabbed her.

"But I want to pull him by the ribbons on his cap," she protested.

We laughed and began to hold each other, having forgotten who wanted to run and who didn't.

"O.K.," she said at last seriously. "Then I want to kiss this militia man. Don't stop me."

We both walked decisively toward the man and suddenly were grabbed by our boys. They had been running after us, having guessed what we were up to, and had decided to separate us. We waved to each other laughing and clung to our lords.

At the entrance to our room, I whispered to Natasha not to tell the others anything about our state. She winked at me and we entered the room with serious indifferent faces.

"I am terribly drunk," announced Natasha in a loud voice.

    ✿   ✿   ✿

"I found you and I am not going to lose you. You are mine and I want to defend you from all the evil of this life. I want you to forget all the troubles that were, all the disappointments and all the people who have ever done you any harm. I just forbid you to remember. Do you understand? Do you promise me? Now I shall stand between you and all of them so that you can never meet them again. Because . . . I love you. I mean it. I have never in my life said these words and didn't want to say them to you before. I wanted to feel it to the full. And now I say: I love you. . . . And it means for me that you are the only, the closest, and the best in this world. My beloved . . . I love you."

Thus my bad dancer, my awful pen pal, and poor speaker, but the best human being in the world, brought to me our Song of Songs.

✿   ✿   ✿

On the 4th of May we all left for Riga to spend a week enjoying the city and the cold sea. Natasha and I came to be introduced to the families.

On our way to Yosif's house I stumbled about ten times, not seeing the way from fear. When we entered the doorway, I was ready to faint when Yossi said, "Not yet. This is not our entrance."

We crossed through the house and found ourselves in a backyard. At their doorway it was already no longer original to faint and I stood green with fear and dumb with shyness.

Yossi opened the door with his own key and I appeared before his mother.

✿   ✿   ✿

A week later I left Riga for Moscow with Yossi's love to support and defend me and with a heavy weight of uncertainty lying on my heart. We couldn't make any plans. We were both

not yet twenty-one, with our studies unfinished, without means
of support, without a place to live, both under the threat of
arrest, and in the middle of struggling for an exit visa. We were
both reasonable enough to realize all of this and not to decide
anything.

Natasha arrived in Moscow three days later, fat, pink, and
laughing with happiness all the time. She brought with her a full
suitcase with presents for the whole family, the announcement of
her engagement, and plans for the wedding in July.

But Moscow met her with the first shock of the many that
were to come—the beginning of "the great thing" that I had
predicted and that now became a reality.

18

The permission to leave for Israel that was granted to Natasha's family was so unexpected that it brought neither joy nor
the feeling of victory. They were the only family to receive this
permission and they were leaving all their friends behind. Natasha was leaving everything.

At the moment she heard the news she looked at everybody
around her with big astonished eyes. She understood all it meant
immediately. She began to cry, became weak, and could not
regain control during the three weeks before their departure.

Lev immediately came to Moscow. He was like a nurse with
a seriously ill patient and was full of love, caresses, and reason.
During this time Natasha was gripped by a wild idea—to stay
with him. But she knew that the family would not leave without
her. She was torn between two loves, with no way out. The
struggle broke her heart and her mind.

Only one thing would help a little, she thought. She begged
to be married to Lev and to be able to leave the Soviet Union
with the knowledge that they belonged to each other and were
bound by something more than their love. Under those condi-

tions and in such a short time, they could be married only in a religious ceremony. Most of their adult friends did not approve of this step, having already forgotten what love was or never having known it at all. But nobody could refuse her.

The wedding took place on the 24th of May, Lag b'Omer, in Sanja's apartment, and in the presence of only the closest friends, the rabbi of Malakhovka (a little settlement near Moscow), and ten witnesses.

The days passed agonizingly slowly, sinking in Natasha's tears. On the 24th of May, we dressed the bride in clothes that we had gathered from all over Moscow. With the most important representatives of the Jewish Zionist movement holding a big bedspread over their heads as a *chuppah*, the rabbi read his prayers, the young couple exchanged rings, and Lev broke the traditional glass with his foot. "*Mazel tov!*" And from under the *chuppah*, Natasha gave us her first smile in weeks, holding tightly a small piece of paper in her hand—a *k'tuba* (a Jewish religious marriage certificate).

On the 10th of June, the family left the Soviet Union.

*   *   *

Inna gave a last glance around her room, which was hard to recognize now. But the walls were still the same, her own dear walls with the traces of their life over the years. The corner near the window was covered with inkspots—there Natasha did her homework. There was another dark spot left by the back of her father's bald head. The big window and Hertzen Street down there and the Kremlin just down the street. . . .

But stop! There was no time for this. She looked over her family and took her sick mother by the hand. Natasha was supported by her friends as everyone went down the stairs.

Inna's three Russian friends, the young women with whom she studied in the Institute, came to say good-by.

The group went out into the street. Immediately about a dozen civilians in black surrounded them. They didn't interfere, but just stood and stared with their hands behind their backs and their legs apart. Inna felt her heart beating in her throat, but not a muscle moved on her face. Natasha saw nothing.

The family stood on the pavement waiting for a taxi. Half a minute hadn't passed when a black Volga came up. The driver looked out of the window and asked, "Who is for Sheremetyevo (the airport)?" Anxious to be on their way, Inna did not think a moment and ordered everyone into the car.

The black "guards" were left standing behind. "Scoundrels, scoundrels," the Russian women were exclaiming in whispers, seeing the real Soviet "freedom" for the first time. Inna hurriedly kissed her friends and said loudly, "Girls, stop being afraid!" And she entered the KGB black car where the whole family was already sitting.

The guards hurried to their cars and the column started on its way. The old Bolshevik and his romantic daughter were leaving Moscow with an escort of black governmental cars.

Inna leaned her head on the back of the seat and suddenly understood. The truth struck her like a flash of electric current. It came as soon as she tried to think over what had just happened, with the first glance at the driver's face. How could she fail to understand at once? A black Volga comes up in the center of the city and the driver asks for passengers just for Sheremetyevo. There was no doubt that a provocation was being arranged. Inna grew cold with terror, but knew what to do.

"Stop the car!" she ordered the driver. He did, suspecting nothing. "Everybody out of the car!" Inna said to the rest. Old Abram had also probably understood everything, but he was ready to fight. "No, we shall stay here. We shall go to the airport," he insisted. Inna was on the brink of hysterics. "Papa, go out immediately," she said quietly, but in an unnatural voice.

"Citizen! What happened?" they heard the driver's bawdy voice. "You said you wanted to go to Sheremetyevo!" he shouted threateningly.

"I have changed my plans. Here you are!" Inna said, handing out two rubles.

"Take your money back, you, mamochka," he roared, beginning to slip out of his role.

The "black" people were watching the scene from their cars with surprise, but did not move.

In three minutes the family was riding in a city taxi, not daring to discuss the situation in front of a strange man. The escort was still following the taxi.

They reached the airport after all their friends had arrived. They were all silent and cautious. A few days before, the KGB had called one of the happy Jews who had received permission after the Slepyans and told him to leave in silence without any noisy "Going-away party." The warning was serious and unambiguous and Jews didn't dare ignore it. Still, all the friends were there, though silent, with songs and cries of hope stuck in their throats. They all came to see off the first big family from Moscow to leave—to rejoice, to envy, to guess at the future.

Not knowing what to say, everyone tried to help with the numerous bags or sat silently or talked in whispers. Foreign tourists arriving in the capital of the Communist world cast curious glances at the silent but very uneasy crowd.

Natasha did nothing. She stood near her husband, holding his hand. They didn't talk. Her face was red and tears kept rolling down her cheeks. Some of the young people came up to her to say something and the corners of her lips twitched in a semblance of a smile. Everyone felt uneasy. Lev stood straight and tall with a stony face, not wanting to show his suffering. The ceremony with the tickets was soon over and it was time to say good-by and pass through the door in the glass wall, the wall that would separate them from the world they were leaving. The wall was thoroughly covered with thick curtains to prevent farewell looks; the curtains had appeared not long before, when the Jews began to leave.

Inna began hastily to kiss everyone around her. Later she wrote from Israel that she felt horrified that she might have kissed a KGB man in this crowd. Then we all came up to say good-by to the old people and Natasha. She was kissing everybody, leaving her tears on their cheeks and lips, looking for someone she had missed, trying to prolong the ceremony and delay the dreadful moment. At last she stopped, for no one was left, but Lev standing behind her. She stood for a moment, then turned around and walked toward him, swaying, ready to fall

into his arms. But his stony eyes stopped her. "Don't do it!" they
said. "Don't show!" And she understood. He kissed her cheeks as
if she was his child and pushed her slightly toward the door. "Go,
dear." And she went.

By that time the Jewish movement in the Soviet Union had
not only grown in quantity, but it had acquired some special
forms.

Our own theoreticians were writing: "Now we can call these
Jewish activities in the Soviet Union a national liberation movement. It has its own special aims, but its scale and methods are
similar to those of well-known liberation movements in world
history."

The main purpose of this movement was emigration to Israel by means of a legal, open struggle for an exit visa. But
everyone who took part in the movement remembered how he
had come to this idea and saw as his own important task the
bringing of this idea to those who were ready to accept it. It was
brought to them through information about Israel, distribution
of articles on Jewish history and religion, political and philosophical essays on the problem of Jewish revival, slides of historical places in Israel with accompanying explanations, Hebrew
textbooks, and everything that could possibly give people
knowledge and understanding of what Judaism and Israel meant.

Those who had at one time or another asked themselves
these questions: "What does Judaism mean? What is Israel?"
understood their unnatural and humiliating position in the Soviet Union and sought a solution. They greatly appreciated the
information we brought, longed for it, imbibed it, and soon
joined in the struggle for emigration. But there were still masses
of people whom the little Jewish "Samizdat," the circulation of

prohibited manuscript, could not reach, and this fact stimulated its growth. The Jewish "Samizdat" had appeared in two forms. One was a collection of articles on Israel, political and philosophical essays on the Jewish problem, and was duplicated by photographic methods and had the name, *Iton* (the Hebrew word for newspaper). The same and other articles also circulated separately in many copies.

The second was a periodical under the name of *Exodus* and reflected the struggle of the Soviet Jews for emigration. It was a collection of individual letters and collective petitions of Jews to the authorities and to the world organizations, as well as information about the trials, searches, and any other acts of the KGB against Jews. This publication was of great importance for those who had just begun the struggle for an exit visa and for world opinion.

We didn't know the sources of these publications, but we did our best to duplicate them and to distribute them among our circle of acquaintances.

Fully understanding the legal character of their struggle, the Jews made themselves acquainted with the numerous laws that concerned their problem. Twenty-year-old young people bombarded the officials of the OVIR and the Ministry of the Interior with juridical formulas and references to the laws.

At the end of May, Moscow was filled with red flags and placards and slogans. The country was preparing for the Sixteenth Congress of the Young Communist League of the USSR, which was going to take place on May 26 in the Kremlin Palace of Congresses.

I suddenly remembered that I had had something to do with this organization in the past and I decided to make some trouble for myself and the authorities. At that time we felt that we should be as bothersome as flies in summer and write as many letters to various organizations as we could. The record was held by one young person who wrote over one hundred letters in a few months. I was rather lazy in this regard and hated to write just for the sake of writing, but this opportunity seemed to me too good to miss and I wrote the following letter:

To the Presidium of the Sixteenth Congress of the Komsomol

I, Milkina Alla Tsalevna, born in 1949, former member of the USSR Young Communist League, ask for my appeal to the delegates of the Congress to be read out.

APPEAL

To the delegates of the Sixteenth Congress of the Komsomol and the representatives of progressive youth organizations of the whole world.

My whole life has been indissolubly linked with the Komsomol. The Komsomol was for me a symbol of justice and humanity, the personification of democracy, breadth of outlook and service to the ideals of internationalism.

The Komsomol appeared to be an organization capable of bringing us up as consistent and faithful soldiers in the struggle for freedom, equality, and brotherhood. This is why all my most intimate dreams and aspirations were always linked with the Komsomol. I felt that my actual work in the Komsomol organization formed precisely that meaning of life to which it is worth giving oneself fully.

These ideals are still dear to me and this gives me the right to appeal to the delegates of the Sixteenth Congress of the Komsomol.

In 1969 I lost my parents. As an orphan, I decided to reunite with my relatives who live in the State of Israel and who sent me an authorization to enter the country. My desire to go to Israel is explained not only by my wish for reunion with my relatives but also my long-standing aspiration to return to the country of my people.

I felt that my desire did not contradict the constitution of the Soviet Union or the statutes of the Komsomol, as I thought that the struggle for high ideals proclaimed by the Komsomol did not have any geographical frontiers.

But my request to Soviet organizations to grant me permission to leave for Israel provoked a tempest of indignation. I found myself surrounded by an atmosphere of hatred, of calumny, of blackmail, and of shadowings. Every minute somebody called me "traitor" to my face. The First Secretary of the Krasnaya Presnya Regional Committee of the Komsomol, L. L. Baidakov, stated openly that the Jewish people had always betrayed the Soviet Union and were still betraying it.

I was expelled from the Komsomol. All doors were closed to me. But this does not worry me now, I ask for only one door to be opened to me—the door to Israel.

I am twenty-one. I am a Jewess. Today I choose my path in

life. And today I understand that my fate is indissolubly linked with the fate of my people. I am desperate because I do not know my own language and the history and the culture of my people. Every participant of this Congress who lives on the terri-tory of his home country, amongst his own people, must under-stand me. I envy you, I envy you your fate and your possibilities, because a person deprived of his national identity, a person torn away from his homeland cannot have the feeling of being a fully valid personality.

I cannot imagine my future without returning home. But the answer I receive is always the same: YOUR APPLICATION IS REFUSED. The Assistant Head of the Moscow Department of Visas and Registration of Foreigners tells me cynically: "Not even in a year, not even in two years . . . not even in five years. . . ." This is the present-day policy of the Soviet Union and the government is not interested in the fact that for me these are years during which a person's character is formed and defined. The years when one acquires one's basic training, the years when one's direction and tasks in life are defined, will prove for me to be years of unending suffering, of extreme solitude far from my country and from the people who are close to me. They will be years of insecurity, of painful waiting and despair. Fighting against the terror that seizes my mind, I think: "If only I can survive. . . ."

Young people of the world, I appeal to you, my contem-poraries! I appeal to you and to all those who retain feelings of justice and humanity, to raise your voice against a gross violation of international law and elementary humanity.

Milkina Alla Tsalevna

25 May 1970

On the 26th of May at nine o'clock in the morning, I was at the Borovitsky Gate of the Kremlin—the main entrance to the Palace of Congresses—waiting for the delegates to arrive. There were a number of young civilians and middle-aged men loitering about and I had to keep my eye on them. I didn't expect to return home that day and I had asked Sanja to come and stand not too far from the palace to watch what happened to me.

I sent the first copy of the letter in through the reception room and I then waited for the foreign delegates to arrive. It was rather a long time before I noticed a French-looking young man and gave him my letter in an envelope. The second attempt failed. I had accosted a foreign-looking man in English, but he

didn't understand and asked in pure Russian, "What? What?" I
left him without answering, swearing to myself at the damned
Komsomol boys at the beck and call of the KGB who were so
successful in looking westernized.

Suddenly a black car approached the gate. Sleek, blond
young men jumped out of the back seat and rushed to open the
front door of the car. A smiling American Negro got out and
started for the entrance, accompanied by the fussy young men. I
blocked his way and handed out my last envelope. He jumped
back as if I held a grenade.

"It is a letter of solidarity," one of his guards explained and
obligingly stretched out his hand. "Give me the letter!"

"Take your hands away! It is not for you!" I muttered
through my clenched teeth in disgust and addressed the Negro
in English, "It is a letter to you personally. Please, read it."

He accepted the letter with trembling hands and thanked
me, and I stepped out of his way.

There were no other copies left, so I looked around and
slowly walked away. I was exhausted with tension. Several
blocks away from the gate, I met Sanja. He had not noticed
anyone following me and nobody seemed to be paying any attention to me, but he himself had gotten into a very stupid situation.

He had been standing among those "ordinary looking"
young men whom I feared most of all, when he suddenly realized that they were looking steadily at the lapel of his jacket. He
looked down and grew cold with terror. He had forgotten to take
off a badge which he had recently received from some American
Jewish tourists. On a blue circle, there was written in white:
"Israel needs peace."

When he raised his eyes, one of the men was approaching
him. His blood had already curdled with horror when he heard,
"Got a cigarette?"

Nothing happened. The men probably did not understand
English, but we decided not to tell anyone about the incident,
lest they consider us complete fools.

On my way home I began to think that the Soviet devil was

not as black as he had been painted. Our Jewish *chutzpa* (impudence) had already gone beyond all limits and we were still unmolested. Maybe there was no need for fear and caution, and we should understand that we could not only write letters, but openly demand and demonstrate. Perhaps the whole population of the country was afraid to lift its voices because of this imaginary fear and perhaps the authorities were supported by a terror which had been created before they came to power.

I remembered my first interview at the synagogue with an American correspondent. One of his questions had been, "Why are you all not afraid to be here, to sing these songs?" I couldn't answer then, but now I understood that the courage of thousands of people came only out of a feeling of impunity and that the fear had been gradually overcome because nobody had been punished for coming to the synagogue. Probably only particular individuals possessed the other kind of courage which would be tested if the authorities decided to punish.

A week later I was called for an interview at the Ministry of the Interior. The note was signed by Ovchinnikov, Chief of one of the departments of the Ministry. "Oho," I thought. "People wait for months to get an appointment with him and here he himself is calling me. I must have struck home."

I took some books with me, having decided to go after the interview to the library to read for my exams at the Institute. I didn't want to place any special significance on this talk and spent the day as usual. However impressive it might be, there might be many of them and I decided not to let them disturb the course of my everyday life.

The Chief made me wait for a while in his reception room, for which I forgave him—for once. At last I was invited to come in. A middle-aged, balding man in a military uniform greeted me without standing up. He was not short and had a slender, well-cared-for figure. He seemed to have no face because all his features and hair were the same pale blond color. Instead of eyes, he had a thin pince-nez with two sharp lights. I could easily imagine two well-polished boots under the table. "How banal," I thought. "They even look like the Gestapo." I sat down opposite him across the table, which was empty except for my personal card which he held constantly in his hand.

"You wrote to us, didn't you?"

"No."

"No?"

"I wrote to the Presidium of the Young Communist League. The address is a little different."

"Well . . . The Komsomol authorized us to answer you."

"So what is your answer?"

"Your request to leave for Israel is refused."

"Why?"

"Because Israel is waging an aggressive war against progressive Arab countries."

"Perhaps you think so, but I don't."

"Well, ours is an objective opinion. Yours is subjective."

"Again, that is what you think. In my opinion, my belief is objective."

"We shall not discuss it now. You are not allowed to leave. Is that clear?"

"No. I don't belong to you. You do not own me. I am a free person."

"It only seems that way to you."

"Well, then I shall have to struggle for my freedom."

"Ha-ha-ha-ha-ha."

I gave him time to finish his laughing performance which lasted for at least two minutes.

"Did you call me just to say this?"

"Yes."

"Then you have wasted my time." And I left the room without saying good-by. I had learned how to be impolite. When I came out into the street, I breathed in the fresh air, looked at the blue summer sky and the sun, and went on my way to the library.

In the summer my sister and brother-in-law rented a country house. Since they were both working, I spent the days practically alone, looking after my brother-in-law's twelve-year-old daughter, typing, and working at the album about Israel, which was almost ready.

Once a week I went to town to pick up some new portion of work and to get paper. Once when I had come to Moscow to pass along the typed materials and couldn't find anyone at home, I found myself far from home, late at night, with a storm about to break. I thought there was no use wasting time waiting for the storm to be over and stepped out into the street. Next day the papers were to write that it was the worst storm in many years, but that night I was on an empty street with rain pounding down. The heavy shower was especially unpleasant because I was wearing a woolen sweater and it was soon full of water. I walked in water up to my ankles. The wind swung the street lamps, and the shadows of the trees and telegraph poles danced a wild dance around me. My ears were deafened by thunder and my eyes began to ache at the bright lightning.

I did not react like King Lear, but accepted the terrible situation with some sense of humor. I considered the storm quite natural for my way of life and began to analyze the absence of fear in me.

First, I imagined what my feelings and thoughts would be if I were afraid of the storm. I immediately thought, what if a person was waiting for me, knowing I was out in this storm. Then I would probably feel uneasy. And, since there was nobody to wait for me and worry if I didn't come home that night, I was not afraid. It occurred to me that usually the greatest part of the fear that we experience in dangerous situations is the fear for those who are waiting and worrying. Having understood this, I smiled at the next flash of lightning and invited it to rage still more. There was not a single person waiting for me now and there was something comforting in feeling lonely.

That night I did not, as usual, connect the great storm with my "great" prediction.

⌒20⌒

On the 15th of June, I came to Moscow to pick up some things I needed for the country house. In the evening I packed them very awkwardly, having taken too much, and left my apartment. I planned on my way to drop in at my friend's place for a little chat and then take the bus to the village. I had two huge net bags with me and a big can, which I had filled with thirty eggs. I had put several pairs of shabby shoes to wear in the country in one net bag, and clean writing paper, carbon paper, and a lot of material from the "Samizdat" to read and to retype in the other.

The bags were terribly heavy and I stopped with relief on the third floor in front of my friend's apartment and rang the bell. The door was opened by some strange people and I saw that the apartment was full of men. "Oho," I thought, "the Jews have got together. I shall have a nice time now." But their strange silence and the expressions on their faces put me on guard. They were too tall for Jews, too blond, too ordinary looking.

"Search!!!" the thought pierced my mind. I saw my friend's desperate face in the back room. He had always been kind to me and didn't want me to get into trouble.

The men had already stretched out their hands. "Come in, you are welcome. Can I help you?" One took my bags away from me, the other took me into one of the rooms where women were sitting. My eggs, shabby shoes, and the papers were put carefully in the corner and I was politely warned. "Please, don't touch anything. Don't move. Sit quiet."

There were five people from the KGB, four men and one girl, whose role I understood later. We, the Jews, were three women and three men. The "visit" had struck pay dirt. The people who came to the house that evening were really important and had brought a lot of material with them, but I was not aware of this yet and thought my visit to be the most compromising for the host.

Fear, dreadful paralyzing fear, filled me. This was the first time in my life that I had felt real fear, fear for my life. Fear turned out to be red with yellow flaring candles. It blocked the whole world for me. I didn't see, didn't hear anything. I couldn't sit and stood leaning against the wall as if it were easier to meet the danger standing. A big hammer seemed to be striking me on the head, but I was numb and couldn't resist anything. It was bodily fear without understanding of what or why.

At last something deep in my mind began to function and told me I was terrified. I tried to shame myself out of it, but nothing helped. Fear was stronger, more vital, than any other feeling. I called to mind the image of Yossi and told myself he would be ashamed of me if he knew how I was reacting, but that didn't help either. On the contrary, it gave me more reason to fear. Yossi would suffer greatly if I disappeared that night. The thought almost made me cry, but I would not let them see me crying.

The man who was obviously the chief had finished with the materials of the others and turned to mine. He was working like a surgeon, taking every piece of paper carefully, examining it, and putting it to this or that side.

"Well, what is your name?" the man behind the red shroud asked.

"Why should I tell you my name when you didn't introduce yourself?" I stammered. Somewhere I had read that courageous people behaved like that.

He smiled and showed me his red identity card. Perhaps he had also read the same thing. There was nothing else to do but to give him my name, since he had my documents in front of him. Then he continued to examine my baggage.

"What is this?" he asked, pointing to the can.

"Eggs," I answered.

He lifted up the lid and looked into the can. I wished the eggs could explode out of there.

"And what is this?" he pointed to the first net bag.

"Shoes." This time he didn't open the bag.

"And this?"

"Paper. . . ."

He took the whole bag and put it on the table. His face lit up as one by one he began to put the typed sheets on one side and the clean paper on the other.

I looked at the table and images of the KGB headquarters, its chambers and tortures passed before my eyes. I thought, "If they go with me to the country house, they will find the typewriter and then I'm finished. How can I stand all this?"

The man stacked every sheet, dictating the name of it to his assistant.

"I typed translation from English, 'Modern Literature in Israel,' 52 pages; a typed translation from English, 'Education for the New Generation,' 48 pages; a typed translation from English, 'Massada,'; a typed collection of letters from Israel, 8 pages; and what is this?" he showed the sheets of paper to his assistant.

"It is Hebrew. Some poems, I think."

"Can you read it?"

"Not yet."

"Oh," I thought, "they prepare their own specialists in Hebrew. Idiot! He couldn't learn enough for such translation. But it really sounds respectable: a Department of Special Importance, Operative Group for Searches and Arrests, Preparatory Course in Hebrew for the staff."

"I am sorry, but we shall have to ask for your help," the man turned to me.

"You are welcome."

"Can you translate it?"

"Certainly." I began to recite in Russian without looking at the paper.

> *"When returns to me from the battlefield*
> *The man whom I love*
> *All the soldiers will embrace each other*
> *And the cannons become silent."*

"O.K. That's enough. And this one?"

"The air of mountains makes me drunk like wine
And the smell of pine trees,
And the wind in the twilight
Is full of ringing of bells.
My Jerusalem of gold
And of copper and of light
I am your violin to sing
Songs to you."

My voice quavered.

"Enough, thank you." And he put the song into the pile of Special Importance.

"Now, Alla Tsalevna Milkina, what an unfortunate visit for you," he began, with the smile of a boa constrictor. "Don't you have any sense of self-preservation?"

"No, you see, I was born only in 1949. If I had been born in 1937, I might have such a sense."

"No, Alla, it didn't help me either," said one of our women who had been born in 1937, the year of the Stalin purges.

"Then you would have had to be born in 1905," one of the KGB men said. That was the year of the first Bolshevik Revolution.

"Oh, that would not help me in all cases."

"If I were in your place now, I would not talk like that."

I shut up.

The man started to read my letters. I had two, one to my sister and one to my uncle that I had intended to mail the next day. And one letter was the last loving letter from Yossi. The man took a penknife and opened the two closed envelopes as if he were opening a living thing. He read all the letters thoroughly and then handed them to his assistant for a second reading.

"Now, you have a wonderful writing style."

"I don't need your compliments," I said, irritated especially by his reading Yossi's short letter.

"O.K.! Now, you begin, please, Tanja," he nodded to the girl and left the room.

Tanja came up to me, shy and confused, and asked me to

take off my clothes. I laughed. The length of the ceremony and all the talking had blown away the red shroud of fear and I had come to myself. This new act reminded me of a detective film and I unbuttoned my dress with a smile. The girl, following some strict instructions, looked into what seemed a dozen hidden places, thanked me, and turned to the other two women.

They looked at her with disgust.

"I am not going to show you what I have in my underpants."

"Neither am I."

The girl stepped back. By that time, the rest of the group had finished the same ceremonies with the men and brought their findings into our room, which had been turned into the headquarters. The table was piled with heaps of typed material, photocopies of Hebrew textbooks, films, and dozens of individual and collective letters from Jews to the General Secretary of the United Nations, U Thant, who was due to arrive in Moscow the next morning.

I realized that my papers were not the worst and didn't add much to the troubles of the family, at least. The whole procedure tired me and I lay down unceremoniously on the sofa. The whole KGB group began to examine the walls, the bedding, the cupboards, and so on.

Suddenly the doorbell rang. The KGB men looked at each other and one went to open the door. It was 12 o'clock at night.

"*Shalom, haverim!*" we heard the familiar voice of one of our friends and the cold answer, "How do you do! How do you do!"

They took him into our room and we saw with relief that he was without a single bag or book. We looked at his perplexed face and didn't show a sign of knowing him. Maybe some day we would have to prove that we were strangers and had met by accident.

They immediately searched him and took a small piece of paper from his jacket pocket. The little note said: "Grandma Ronja has unpleasant guests whom she did not expect." It meant that Sanja's apartment was being searched also. But our guests were also good readers and understood what it meant. The poor man who had brought the note was for a long time after called "*Shalom, haverim*" or "Grandma Ronja."

The search continued until three o'clock in the morning. At the end we were all sitting in a group discussing with our guests different items of the Criminal Code. They were polite and participated with frankness. At that time the KGB had put on a new mask. They assured us that they were only doing their job. They didn't have anything against us personally and treated us like common Soviet people. They acted only by order of the Prosecutor of Leningrad, who gave the orders to make the search in connection with an act of high treason committed that very morning in Leningrad.

We were at a loss and did not understand.

At three o'clock, the KGB left the house, leaving us behind in the apartment. We all had a cup of tea.

"Comrades!" one of the men exclaimed. "We are all witnesses of the greatest liberalization that Soviet Russia has ever known."

"You're crazy! What are you saying?" we all protested.

"Yes. If we are all sitting here and drinking tea after a night search, it means a real and great liberalization."

We all laughed and agreed.

21

The summer passed after the shock of June 15. Two more searches were made in other Jewish homes in Moscow and we all exchanged guesses and impressions of what they meant.

Both other homes had their own anecdotes about the terrible night. Sanja's father, in the full swing of the search, suddenly fell asleep sitting on a chair and began snoring terribly. His friends had often laughed at him for his snoring, but this time everybody envied him his unruffled calm. During the search, the

KGB men asked him, showing him the portrait of Theodor Herzl in his bookcase, "Who is this?"

"Grandfather," he answered.

He watched them writing down: "So-and-so claims that it is his grandfather."

"No, no!" he protested. "I didn't say 'my.' Just 'grandfather.' "

They crossed out the word "his" and "the portrait of a man with a black beard with his hands crossed on his chest" was registered as a portrait of "the grandfather." In each case it was perfectly true.

In the other Jewish home the KGB found a Hebrew lesson in full swing. The host, a man with a great deal of experience in dealing with the authorities, invited them in with a hospitable gesture and suggested to his pupils that the lesson go on. Somehow the pupils could not compose their thoughts after the coming of the "guests." The KGB men went about their search and the family cat watched, sitting on a small table in the room. Hours passed and the cat didn't move. After the search was over, the hostess picked the cat up and found under it their pocketbook with the names and addresses of all their friends. Just what the KGB wanted! Moved by the loyalty of the cat, the mother of the home treated it to a big steak and promised to take it to Israel.

But the whole business was not funny. We soon learned that fifty searches had been made all over the Soviet Union—in Leningrad, Riga, Kharkov, Kishinev, Sukhumi. Little by little we found out the reason for this campaign—or, to be more correct, the pretext.

On the 15th of June, in the morning, twelve young people (ten Jews and two Russians) had attempted to hijack a plane in a Leningrad airport to cross the border. The Jews who took part in this plot wanted to go to Israel. I was terrified when I learned their names: Israel Zalmanson and his brother and sister and her husband; Leib Khnokh and his young pregnant wife, Mary; Joseph Mendelevitch. I had met them all in Riga the previous year. Driven to despair, they had decided to challenge the Soviets and break through the tortuous bureaucracy by this courageous act.

Better such a risk than years of fruitless waiting. How I understood them and how I envied them their courage! Still. . . .

Most of them were leaving their parents behind and everyone knew that if you crossed the border you exposed your family to persecution. Could they have thought only of themselves at that moment? Maybe they wanted to be caught and draw the attention of the whole world to the plight of Soviet Jewry by their trial. But how could they take women—and one of them pregnant? And was the whole affair worth the breakup of all Jewish activities in the Soviet Union, mass searches, and arrests of many other people? Hadn't we already drawn the attention of the world by our open letters and legal activities? And besides, why choose this form of crossing the border at the very moment when our country, Israel, was suffering more than any other state from hijacking and world opinion was decisively against it?

No, they couldn't have failed to realize all this. We found it hard to believe the story because it was just unbelievable. And the events that followed it seemed typical and planned—all the searches carried out on the same day, the 15th of June, and all over the country. A short announcement of the attempt appeared in a Leningrad newspaper for that day. The KGB undoubtedly knew about the plan beforehand. Had it perhaps not only known, but instigated it? Was it a frame-up to find a pretext to search all important Jewish places, to arrest people, and to put an end to this Zionist "infection" inside their healthy body?

But these twelve people in fact went to the airport; they did plan to hijack the plane. They were arrested in the act of approaching the plane. The KGB sadists had been playing with them like a cat with a mouse. So what was it? A voluntary involvement in a provocation? Nonsense! There is no use in trying to guess. The future will show the truth.

In the meantime, we all curtailed our activities and I sat in my country house like a fool, waiting for the invitation from the KGB.

(Once a wife said to her husband: "Look here, Ivan. Guests will be coming soon. Go and wash your neck." Ivan sighed heavily and went to the washstand, but suddenly stopped on the way. "And if they don't come," he said, "I shall sit like a fool with a clean neck, hey?")

Such a fool was I, as I cleared my apartment of all compromising material and sat waiting.

⁕   ⁕   ⁕

In June I received a parcel through an English firm, Dinnerman and Company. These parcels came to Jews who had once signed a collective letter and we assumed that unknown friends or organizations wanted to help us. They themselves might not have realized what kind of help that was. These parcels often found us on the brink of starvation and despair. But even in such cases we sometimes could not help saving some of the things—so beautiful were they. Jewish wives, exhausted with economic problems at home, enjoyed wearing luxurious nylon fur coats over worn old dresses.

At that time I had left my job and was sitting in the country house as if in prison, dependent upon my sister's money. The decision to leave my job had come in April. I felt I could no longer stand the calls to the Special Department, the constant following, and the atmosphere of complete silence around me. I had to admit their success in making the place too "hot" for me to stay. The salary which I had been receiving could no longer save me from starvation anyway. I was leaving without sorrow and with confidence. The Chief, who had long before taken the other side, considered it his duty to warn me about the consequences.

"The authorities would not like you to be without a job."

"But why? According to the law, I have the right not to work as long as I am studying."

"I am not talking about the law. Your classes are only in the evenings and you will have a lot of spare time. Authorities do not like it when people have spare time."

"Why?"

"Because people begin to think, to read a lot, to ask themselves questions, meet many other people."

"A-ah, now it is clear."

It was a revelation. A lot about Soviet laws and ways of thinking became clear to me. But I was to make many more discoveries, which were no longer painful.

The Dinnerman parcel which arrived at the end of June saved me from the loneliness which had been choking me. I left my foolish country house and went by train to Riga, to Yossi.

At that moment, which was dangerous for both of us and full of unexpected visits and calls, I wanted to spend a few days with him. No letters or telephone calls could substitute for his single kiss, for a single look of his dark eyes. I rushed to Riga in spite of all the devils in the world.

I arrived in the morning, ran to his house, and rang the bell. Yossi opened the door and stood there dumfounded.

"You?"

"Me!"

"How?"

"So!"

He seized me without further questions and began to kiss my face and smell my hair, laughing with joy.

We spent three days just being together. Wherever we had to go, we were just two of us together, becoming irretrievably involved in a state where you feel you can't live your life without the other person, where you exist, move, think, create, only when he exists, moves, thinks, and creates somewhere near you—the feeling which is called love.

I returned to Moscow and sank back into emptiness. I entered the empty country house and sat heavily on a chair, looking at the paint on the wall without seeing anything or thinking. I sat like that for a long time until my emotion burst out. I lay on the bed, screaming, biting the pillow, and sinking in a flood of tears. This time reason didn't stop me or shame me. I understood myself and, deep in my heart, was glad that I had become a healthy person again. Yes, I was screaming and sobbing, but who wouldn't when she is in love and scores of obstacles stand in her way to marriage? To marry? No, even to be together. I shuddered at the thought of marriage. Marriage meant for us a terrible new obstacle on our way to exodus. How could we get ourselves involved in marriage when all of us were struggling for an exit? Both of our cases were a contribution to the general struggle and, if we stopped in the middle, wouldn't it be betrayal? But we could apply together! No, all these marriages had to wait until the border was crossed. Here—nothing, until we got out! But I wanted to be with him, I didn't want to lose him here or there! But he hadn't yet proposed. . . .

This train of thought went on and on, over and over, and no amount of reasoning could help me. I thought I would go crazy. I called Yossi and said, "I am dying."

"So am I," he said in a terrible voice.

"I can't live like this," I said evasively.

"I can't live without you. We must think of something. Maybe I shall come soon."

In a few days he came to spend a day in Moscow. We lay on the grass in the garden.

"I want you to be my wife," he said.

"So do I. When?" I knew what to ask.

"You know, with all these troubles around us and it is so difficult to find jobs and places to live, I think it is better to do it in a . . . year."

"O.K.," I said carelessly, jumping to my feet. "Then we shall talk about it again in a year."

I was not offended. I understood him perfectly, but at the same time I decided to find a new job in Moscow, to continue my studies, my regular life, and to cut off my head if it dared to think too much. I had again to be a good, reasonable girl, if there was a year to wait. But what kind of a period is a year? How long is it? I couldn't imagine.

            *   *   *

I still had half a year before I could again apply for an exit visa. Six endless months. It would be too easy for the OVIR if I left them in peace for this period. I had to do something, to go to someone to make a scandal, to write to someone somewhere. The third was the easiest for me. By that time the Israeli radio had announced the formation of the new Committee of Solidarity with the Jews of the Soviet Union. We felt that Israel had definitely heard our call and was trying to help. It had begun the previous year when Golda Meir for the first time put the Soviet Jewish question on the agenda of a Knesset meeting. Now we could feel that the second front was open. And the new committee was a new address to which we could send our letters and feel certain that someone would act on our behalf.

It was difficult for me to ask for something from anyone in Israel, but I knew that my letter, if received, would be read by different people all over the world and it would add to the general noise which we wanted to make about our problem. And I wrote this letter:

To the Israeli Public Committee of Solidarity with the Jews of the Soviet Union

From: Milkina Alla Tsalevna

Dear Sirs:

It is only extreme despair and a hopeless situation that force me, in this difficult moment for our Homeland, to appeal to the Israeli Government for help.

The establishment of the Israeli Public Committee of Solidarity with the Jews of the Soviet Union gives me hope and permits me to apply directly to you and to ask you to transmit my letter to those who can help me in any way to emigrate to the State of Israel.

I am twenty-one years old. I have no parents. My close relatives live in Israel. In 1969 I applied to the Soviet Government with the request to give me permission for emigration to Israel. However, all my appeals and complaints have been categorically denied.

From the time that I submitted documents for emigration to Israel, my life here has stopped. All the doors are closed to me, but I ask that only one be opened to me—the one to Israel. It is my Homeland, the land of my people, and I cannot imagine my life without my return to the land of my Homeland.

From my earliest childhood, I was isolated from any manifestations of the Jewish culture, even in those forms that are possible here in the Soviet Union. The Soviet educational system has done everything that it could to deprive me of my national face, to tear me away from Jewish culture and traditions, to force me to forget everything relating to my people. I heard the word "Jew" only as an insult, thrown about by those surrounding me. And, after leaving school and entering life, I found out that I had a "bad fifth point" in my form. But this was not the main thing.

There is in a human being something higher, something that is stronger than any educational systems and state apparatuses. And I have returned to my people. I am happy that I have acquired a Homeland and, together with it, a sense to my life. Everything that has now opened before me: the heroic history of my people, the literature, traditions, its great unbreakable spirit —all this has allowed me to say: "I am happy that I have been born a Jewess!" And the sense of my new life is in my return to my Homeland and in my service to my people, the people of Israel.

But even my first attempts to make use of my lawful rights, guaranteed to me by the Constitution of the USSR, have shown themselves unfruitful. The rights are not for me—because I am a Jewess, and a "traitress" to boot! I applied to the Ministry of the Interior of the USSR, to the Council of Ministers of the USSR, and to the Supreme Soviet of the USSR. The answer was the same. "No! Never!"

Finally, as a former Komsomol member, I appealed to the delegates of the Sixteenth Congress of the Leninist Young Communist League of the Soviet Union. An officer of the Committee of the State Security answered me in the name of the Leninist Komsomol. He invited me to the Ministry of the Interior and confirmed the refusal to my request. When I protested that I was a free person, he answered: "That's what it seems to you!"

Yes, I have already understood this. I am not a free person because I live in the Soviet Union and I am a Jewess. But—I want to be free. I want to return to my own country and, hand in hand with my brothers and sisters, to build it and to defend it.

Every new day that I spend far away from my Homeland brings me despair. Because each such day is a day lost in my life.

I beg you to do everything that is possible and to help me to get permission to emigrate to Israel—permission to live.

Respectfully yours,
Milkina

There was now the problem of smuggling the letter abroad. No special efficient ways were available then after the catastrophe of June 15. I had to do something myself.

So I went to the Sheremetyevo International Airport to hunt for foreign tourists. There were scores of them, for it was the summer tourist season. Singles, couples, and groups—they were all so bright, noisy, laughing. I could only choose one of them, so

I sat looking and listening. A terrible shyness and fear prevented me from acting quickly. I examined people around me. Was anyone watching me? No, but I couldn't move.

Suddenly an episode made me feel better. I saw a young French woman saying "good-by" to a man and crying bitterly. They must have been lovers and recent ones, and she didn't want to leave him. I looked at her with a smile. These beautiful, bright, noisy people from the other side also had sorrow and grief. They also could cry. At that particular moment I was happier than she was because I was not crying. I felt stronger. If there is sorrow all over the world, then we shall attack it together, so that there need no longer be partings or fear of parting anymore.

I looked around once more and saw the right one. He was a member of a French tourist group and spoke fluent Russian. I approached him quickly.

"Can you do me a favor and mail this letter from Paris?"

He looked at the letter. "I am sorry, but I can't. I am really very sorry. Please, excuse me," he said with a shy smile.

"It's O.K. Excuse yourself," I blurted out with disgust and turned away, ready to rush out of the terminal. But suddenly the failure made me stubborn. I had spent three hours in the terminal and I would not leave like that. "They are more afraid than we are," I thought bitterly about the Frenchman.

The right one proved to be a young French girl who looked at me with surprise and said, "Why not? Of course, I can take it. Give it to me. I shall put it deep in my pocketbook." Soon she was already in the plane.

I waved "good-by" and "thank you" to her and jumped gaily out of the terminal, sending my last smile at all suspicious-looking people in the hall. My letter was on its way.

*   *   *

On the 8th of August, Yossi and I went to Leningrad. Yes, just like that. I took a train from Moscow; he, a plane from Riga. We met in Leningrad, took each other by the hand, and ran along the streets, boulevards, and embankments of the city. It was a strange choice for a tour then, but Leningrad was not

only the place of the hijacking plot and the "cradle of the Great
October Revolution," it was also the most beautiful Russian city
of the eighteenth and nineteenth centuries, the city built by
Peter the Great, who had done his best to make it no less beautiful than the best capitals of Europe. Here Russian czars com-
peted with each other in luxury and magnificence. They were
neither intelligent nor liberal, but they loved to build. The mas-
terpieces of Petersburg are a monument to this.

We walked our feet off through the numerous and the best
picture galleries in the world, twisted our necks looking to the
right or to the left, up and down, at the huge cathedrals and
palaces. It was for all this that we came to Leningrad, to spend
ten days away from our world and together.

On the 9th of August, we went to a restaurant to celebrate
Yossi's twenty-first birthday. Before we left my uncle's apartment where we were staying, Yossi pulled me to him and said:
"Tallinn is Tallinn, Leningrad is Leningrad, but there always
comes an end."

"So what can be done?"

"I want to marry you."

"You told me that once. But when?"

"Whenever you want."

"Oh, you want me to decide?"

He stared at me with a desperate look. He wanted to get an
answer from me, but what answer did he want? And I decided to
be frank. This was no time to be shy or proud. My answer now
might decide my future.

"You know, with all that is going on around us, there is so
much danger that we can lose each other. I think we must marry
as soon as possible, so if anything happens, we will be together
and nobody can separate us. I understand that we don't know
each other very well, but, as for me, judging by what I do know
about you, I can expect only the best. And if I am running any
risk, I do it with confidence." Of course, I had to sound reasonable and clever, but the meaning of all this long speech was, "I
love you. I terribly want to marry you."

His face brightened and he smiled happily. "You know, I think so also."

"So when?"

"Now."

"How do you do!"

"No, I mean that after Leningrad we should go to Riga and register ourselves for marriage."

"Do you really mean this?"

"Why not?"

I was going to explode from the happiness that filled me and I began to laugh. I had never known before that happiness can be expressed in laughter. And he looked at me smiling.

In the restaurant we plunged into semi-darkness, low music, and the light clatter of crockery. We were certainly going to spend a huge sum of money there, but we didn't care. From that evening on, we would do everything together—saving, wasting —so nothing mattered then.

I looked at the handsome man opposite me who seemed so big across the small table. I could hardly believe that his beautiful hands with their long, straight fingers now also belonged to me. I could touch his shoulders whenever I wanted, put my fingers into his black curly hair. He is mine now. He is responsible for me and I for him, but the first is more important. From now on, I would not decide any large problem for myself. I would just stop thinking. My head would serve as a holder for face and hair, and I would be all body and nothing else. The silence bothered me. I wanted to shout, to jump, to beat the crystal, and I could hardly suppress wild sounds that were ready to escape me.

Yossi looked at me with his quiet smile. There were no more questions in his eyes. At last he was calm. He had achieved what he had wanted. He was taking me from that mad Moscow and, if I were to do stupid things or go crazy, at least I would do it under his care. He was like a parent watching his child playing with toys, but constantly on guard lest the child hurt herself.

We visited all the palaces of Petersburg with their luxurious halls—gold, silk, jewelry, silver, velvet, lace looked at us from under the glass covers. Now I felt stronger than all the czars. They had been overthrown and I was alive and happy; I was enthroned by my love. I jumped on the pedestals, overthrew the metal statues of the ex-emperors, and stood in their places. We stood silently in the house-museum of Pushkin over his deathbed and I felt pity for the greatest love poet of Russia, for he had not been as happy in love as I. I stuck out my tongue at the stony sphinxes on the bridges of the Neva. They stood opposite one another and would never be able to approach each other and they could not apply for exit visas. I was happy.

❖   ❖   ❖

On the eve of our leaving Leningrad for Riga, we came home late. My uncle and aunt were preparing to go to bed when suddenly the telephone rang at that late hour. I heard my uncle talking to someone, "Yes, Milkina, yes Alla—my niece." We looked at each other, surprised. My uncle finished his conversation and came into the room very pale.

"Switch on Kol Israel."

We did, but the program was already over and we heard only a phrase from "The News in Brief." "A letter of a young Jewish girl from Moscow to the Israel Committee of Solidarity with the Soviet Jews."

My uncle, an old Communist, who didn't know much about my plans, was angry and frightened. After several angry remarks, he left us alone, not being able to say much. Besides all the rest, he also felt sad because he was a good Jew.

I felt triumphant. I walked to and fro, feeling strong and impatient to act. Suddenly I felt irritated at being there far from Moscow, wasting time.

"You are so proud," Yossi said, looking at me with alarm.

"Yes, I am," I said shamelessly and rudely, and looked at him with challenge. I was not going to conceal my vanity from him. "Yes, I am very proud. I feel that it is my great victory."

"Yes, I congratulate you, but it is not your victory. You didn't do anything more than others in this case. It just worked out."

"Maybe you are right," but I could not stop. "But, you know, I want to be frank. I don't know what leads me in my way, real love for Israel or just a desire for anti-activities, heroism. There are certain kinds of people who can't live without idealism and struggling for something. Israel is just a dream for me, just my imagination. This dream hasn't the foundation it has for you. I created it myself and I don't know whether I did it for the sake of going to Israel or just for the sake of my own vanity."

Yossi looked at me with pain. "You, too, Brutus?"

"What do you mean?"

"I mean what I say. There are so many of this kind among us, but I didn't know you also belonged to them."

Everything I had said was not true. I knew I was not like that and had used this theory to check myself sometimes. I had said all this aloud, but I had not shown Yossi that it was my game with myself. But the fact that he had become so quickly disappointed in me and believed all this nonsense irritated and offended me terribly.

He found me late at night in the street and it was only his great love for me that helped us to overcome this misunderstanding. He accepted me with all that I was. Next day we left for Riga to announce our engagement and to discuss with the family the plans for our wedding.

That wonderful new feeling of becoming a wife! In the Leningrad-Riga train I felt for the first time a new capacity. Moving about our sleeper with unknown people around me, arranging our bags, or just sitting and looking out of the window at the passing forests, I had a very strange and pleasant sensation in my entire body which now seemed to become stronger and more elastic. In my entire being I felt the look of the man beside me and I knew that the look in those eyes would be with me all my life whatever I did and wherever I was. And all my acts would now take into account those eyes and their owner, his wishes and his needs. I would never more exist as a single human being—I was a half. And a half of something that was many times more than I ever was alone. If a few days ago I had felt myself in the middle of life, I was now at the very beginning.

I moved more quickly and more gracefully. I enjoyed my movements and that new sensation. What a wonderful new feeling it was to become a wife!

The night passed and we approached Riga. I felt confident in my future, yet I was very nervous. I did not know what the parents' reaction would be, but I was certain they would not be delighted and the thought of the impending serious talk made me tense. I hoped that the slow walk from the railway station to the Rusineks' home would calm me down.

Then—there was Ezra Rusinek approaching us . . . with a bunch of flowers. "Congratulations!" he said and smiled, looking into our startled frightened faces. "Go home, have breakfast and a rest. Mother is waiting for you. I'll be back home after two."

We ran home excited. Yossi's mother really was waiting for us with eggs in silver nests, cheese, and coffee ready on the table. We had a merry breakfast, a nice chat about Leningrad, and a short rest. When his father came home, we all became silent; his mother cleaned the table and they both sat down opposite us. The empty table between us seemed like a field of battle.

"Nu?" said father. "What do you have to tell us?"

My eyes fell and began to bore through the table.

"We want . . . uh—nu . . . uh this—I mean to marry," Yossi said.

"That is good," his father said. "Have you thought about everything? I mean, a place for living, your studies, work, a means of living?"

"I want to go home," I thought to myself.

"Oh yes, of course," Yossi hurried to assure the parents and began to set forth our plans. The thing did not prove to be too awful and the parents took a lively part in the discussion, but still when it was all over, I felt much relieved. And then, why should they not be happy with me? I am a fine girl and they would soon come to know me.

We did not have any problems with a means of living with both of us working and studying. On moving to Riga, I could change to the correspondence department and finish my fifth year of the Institute in Riga. The real problem was a place to live, which we did not have.

The Rusinek family lived in two rooms of a three-room apartment, with a young Russian couple for neighbors in the third room. Ilana, with her husband and little Hadassah, lived in one room, and the parents slept in the second room. Both rooms were very nice, although poorly furnished and sometimes re-minding one of a railroad station with all the inhabitants running about. Those inhabitants also included all the friends who never missed an evening to come for "a chat with Ezra," to sign a new collective letter, or just to sit and read a newspaper. With all of them gathered in the evening, the Rusineks' apartment could compete with the Moscow subway at rush hour.

Yossi, with his long legs, was out of place here in the full sense of the words. So, when by the age of seventeen, he had shamelessly reached six feet and the folding bed could no longer hold him, his parents had had to rent from their neighbors a closet adjacent to the kitchen and the bathroom. The closet was two square meters and in it they managed to put a small bed. Yossi was triumphant and in his letters to me he liked to men-tion: "I have retired to my room to write this letter to you." This delighted me and proved to me that he was a perfect match, but the real delight came when I became acquainted with "the room" personally.

Of course my room of eight square meters was a palace compared to the closet. There Yossi could at least stretch out his legs and rest them on the opposite wall, but the idea of his coming to live in Moscow had only arisen when we began to discuss the problem of applying for visas.

And then moving to Moscow turned out to be a wonderful way out. For the last two years, the Rusineks had not been able to apply, for the Riga Department of Visas (OVIR) began to ask for a reference from the school of a young applicant. This was in order to prove to them that the applicant was not due to be drafted. Thus an applicant had to inform his university about his wish and the authorities at the university then immediately expelled the student "for the desire to leave for Israel" or more evasively "for behavior unfitting a Soviet student." This trick of OVIR worked. Dozens of Jewish families were stymied by this and could not apply for years.

For a young man, being expelled from the university meant immediate draft into the army—two years of service and then five years prohibition from leaving the country for military reasons. Nobody had dared to risk this except Lev, who now was due to be drafted in November. He is quiet and strong, but poor Natasha! How she would suffer for him.

The Moscow OVIR did not do this and we could safely apply in Moscow. In this way was our living problem solved.

When all the problems had been discussed, we went to the City Registry office and registered our marriage for October 15, 1970. We could have been married in a month according to Soviet law, but we needed time for all the arrangements and so set it for the middle of October. In order to avoid a lot of gossip in Jewish circles, we decided that nobody should know about our plans.

That same day Lev came to visit us. We looked at him mysteriously, "You know, Lev, we want to keep it a secret, but you are our closest friend and so we are telling only you—we are getting married."

He looked at us with a complete lack of surprise and said, "If you think that it is not written on your happy faces, you're deeply mistaken." Then he smiled warmly and added: "Congratulations! Let it be happier with you than with me."

Next day we went to the seashore to soak up the last summer rays of the sun.

The Riga seashore . . . it is a whole world. If, in summer, you want to find some of your friends, go to the shore—it is a meeting place for the Jewish population of Riga, who own or rent country houses all along the shore. For us Russian-speaking Jews, the Latvian names of the railway stations always sounded strange and pleasant, reminding us of past times spent there: "Boulduri, Dzintari, Meluzhi. . . ." The Riga seashore is a special page in the life of Latvian Jews. Pictures: Miriam, Ezra, Hadassah on the shore; young Ilana and little Yossja, bespectacled Lev, and fat little Yehoshua, and finally little Hadaska, playing in the sand.

And now the whole Jewish seashore population seemed to be passing especially to see "the bride," the girl who had caught young Rusinek. We did not know whether our happy faces had given us away or rumor, which is stronger than all secrets.

One boy came up to me and politely invited me to come to Riga the following year. The whole shore resounded with laughter. He looked around confused, then understood, and grumbled in his bass voice: "Nu, what are you laughing at? I never know anything. No one tells me."

In a week I left for Moscow. Yossi's mother saw me off at the airport. In the terminal we ran into one of their acquaintances. Mother greeted him and introduced me: "Our daughter-in-law."

Daughter-in-law? Is it all real? I suddenly felt that I had a definite role in life. I was no longer a faceless actor in mass scenes, but had an important place in the performances of life. I felt very proud and entered the plane thinking of myself as a grown-up, independent woman.

When I reached Moscow, I found excitement among Zionist circles. People were being granted exit visas one after another. I went to the Department of Visas. At the entrance a young Jew, running out of the door, seized me in his arms, kissed me on the nose, and ran away shouting: "Permission, permission!"

With a rapidly beating heart, I entered the office. To my relief, the officer answered my inquiry to the effect that my refusal remained in force. Yet my nervousness did not leave me and when I learned that Basja was leaving I became panic-stricken. All kinds of feelings were mixed in me. I felt as if I were a small child and could do nothing alone. I was afraid I would be separated from Yossi; and I was ashamed of my feelings. I envied everyone who was leaving and I was afraid I would myself be given permission. And all these feelings were so jumbled together that I could do nothing but cry. When Yossi called from Riga, I couldn't utter a word and just sobbed into the receiver. Yossi kept shouting: "What has happened? Why are you crying? At least say something."

"Ba-a-sja is leaving," I sobbed into the receiver at last.

He sighed with relief. "So why are you crying? You must be happy for her."

"I am happy."

"So why are you crying?"

"I am afraid," and I started to cry again.

"Nu, stop it, please. Compose yourself. Everything will be all right," he assured me, but I felt he himself was not so sure.

He hung up the receiver and I was left crying, unable to do anything or to come to any decision. Next day Yossi suddenly called me again: "The registration will be on the 1st of October. I went to the registry office and this was the earliest that they could make the registration."

Oh, that Rusinek character. Why couldn't he have told me he was planning to do this? I would have hoped together with him, but to get a word out of a Rusinek is impossible.

The one month that I had to wait now until I went to Riga was a mere nothing compared to the month and a half. I discovered that I had to do so many things that I would hardly have enough time. And what a wonderful occupation it was to prepare one's own dowry.

We took out our huge old trunk, a dozen old bundles, and soon our room turned into a sea of *shmattes* (rags), which reached to our knees. Our Aunt Musja, who came to help us and to watch that justice be observed, stood in the middle of that sea like a general among defeated enemies. I screamed and begged them to throw all that away and Myra fell onto the bundles in convulsions of laughter.

But our general didn't pay any attention to us. She considered every *shmatte* with her experienced eye and expressed her thoughts aloud, "You can take this. This material you will divide in two. This dress hasn't served its time yet. It will do for a little longer. This to the bundle . . . this to the bundle . . . and this. . . ."

Soon all the *shmattes* were again packed into bundles and put into everlasting storage. I took some of the old pieces of fabric for sheets and tablecloths, the remains of father's practical mind and better times. And an old jacket of mother's, flannel, red with white spots. She had worn it when she was pregnant and when we grew up she put it on us when we had the flu. I washed and ironed it and put it deep among my things.

My aunt helped me sell some of the old furniture and bought for me a table and a double sofa. When the sofa was opened at night, it occupied the whole room from wall to wall. So we would have a real bedroom.

Then the day came when I waved everyone in Moscow my last maidenly good-by, invited the whole family for the wedding on the 17th of October, and went by train to Riga.

The day after I arrived in Riga, Yossi was urgently called to Moscow to meet one of our most active Zionists, at whose apartment I had visited on the 15th of June. The fellow had been called for interrogations several times and he felt he had to warn Yossi about the course of the questioning.

We were getting married during a terrible period. Person after person was being called for interrogation. Searches continued. Moscow and Riga, Leningrad and Charkov were in the clutches of the KGB, which tortured people with promises of exit and threats of prison. Everyone was torn between hope and fear. All Samizdat work was curtailed. As much as possible had to be concealed. Now the only way of struggle was caution.

And I was getting married. Father Rusinek constantly warned that if he were arrested, we should remain calm. And I wondered which one of the three of us would be arrested first or whether we should succeed in registering our marriage first.

I had brought from Moscow a pair of white shoes. And the wedding dress was supposed to come from Israel, from Miriam. Would it come in time? A wedding dress from Israel!

Newly married couples are given a pass to special shops for brides and bridegrooms. We decided to use the opportunity to buy gloves for Yossi. In the shop we ran into Ruth. She was also a bride and her wedding was set for the same day, October 17. We exchanged greetings, but I had little to say to her. She was so pale and tired. Every day there were hours of interrogations, threats of imprisonment—and all this before the wedding. The KGB kept their promise to give her a wedding gift. On the 7th of October, she was arrested and was not allowed to marry. Her fiancé, although he was granted an exit visa, remained to wait for her in Russia for the whole of her term of imprisonment—a year in a hard labor camp.

Nothing happened to us up to the day of our registration except that we overslept that morning. At 9:30 I jumped out of Yossi's bed closet and ran into a family friend with a camera, following me. I covered my face and ran into the bathroom.

The office was near the house and at five minutes to ten, a solemn procession of the Rusinek family directed its steps to this holy Soviet office, with the family friend's camera recording our every movement. We had asked for the registration at the earliest possible hour to avoid the music and the handshake of a deputy of the City Soviet, decorated with orders. We came very simply dressed, to the astonishment of the whole office staff. But there was one facility in the office I could not resist using—the photographer. And we were suitably punished: the picture was terrible.

The only thing we wanted to get from them was a seal and a notice in our passports saying we were married, meaning that we belonged to each other and no one could separate us.

The entire ceremony consisted of filling out forms and signing them. All was done in complete silence with the entire family standing around holding its collective breath and the family friend running around with his camera recording the historic moment for future generations. When the woman filling out the forms left the room for a moment, the friend passed his camera to Ezra, sat at her table shaking his head over the documents, looked through them and then shook our hands with a wide smile to the camera, and hastened to get away when the woman returned. That scene was the most impressive in the historic film.

At last the woman raised the seal and pressed it, first on Yossi's and then on my passport. The family let out a sigh of relief. Yossi and I winked at each other. *Mazel tov!*

The return trip passed in the same solemn manner. At home we all drank *"L'chayim"* and everyone returned to his usual occupation. Ezra, Yossi, and Ilana went to work. Mother and I sat at home chatting, discussing the wedding problems and waiting for our husbands.

The problems were usual. There were many close friends who could not be invited. By silent agreement, Jews avoided showing their acquaintance with each other in order not to reveal community ties. And at the same time a large party would not be expected at such a moment, especially one to which Jews from other towns would be invited.

But still about seventy guests had been invited, which was too many for the two rooms, even including the closet. So the parents had to rent a hall in the nearby Teachers' House.

Days passed. I was getting used to the family life, listening to stories, looking through the photograph albums, watching the home life of men with all their shirts, socks, jackets, and trousers, for my youth had been lived in feminine surroundings.

In consideration of the situation, we began our married life on the day of our civil registration without waiting for the religious ceremony. Our honeymoon began in the notorious bed closet.

Since it was adjacent to the bathroom, our sleep was accompanied by all the sound effects of such a neighborhood, which gave us rather romantic dreams of waterfalls, seas, rivers. Morning greeted us with the crash of pots and pans and the sizzling of frying eggs. Although the bed was very narrow, we were not concerned with falling out, for the walls on either side left us no room to fall. We awakened with the first visitor to the bathroom and listened with rage to the sounds of the waking house. The flushing of the toilet every fifteen minutes struck like a hammer on our heads. We both involuntarily became early birds, something we had never been.

When the last person left the bathroom, we put our heads out of our "bedroom" like partisans out of bushes and listened to hear whether anyone was approaching. When we had made certain the way was clear, we jumped directly out of bed into the kitchen and rushed into the bathroom.

We both looked terrible, but the parents surrendered first. They talked to some friends who immediately offered us a room in their apartment. In 1949 they had shared a room with Ezra, Roza, and baby Yossi. Now they were more than happy to invite Yossi and his wife to use one of their three rooms. The lady of the family, Frau Kil, liked to remember the times "when Yossi was not yet born," her good friend Frau Rusinek ("How is she there in Israel? She must be very old now."), and the years they had spent together in Siberia. She made us delicious cakes, "teiglach," and dreamed about our wedding party for which she would make a special kind of "teiglach."

On the 7th of October, Yossi as usual was leaving with his parents for his job after breakfast when the interurban interrupted telephone ring delayed him. Myra was calling from Moscow. I took the receiver.

"Alla?"

"Yes."

"Look here, I shall kill you." She always began with something pleasant. I tried to remember whether I had left a hot iron on the table or a teapot on the stove when I left, but then remembered that many days had already passed. And in her voice I heard that nervous smile that was so typical of her.

"What's happened?"

"There's a postcard for you here, from OVIR."

"What does it say?" I tried my best to keep my voice indifferent.

"It says: 'Please call us urgently. Telephone so-and-so.' "

"Urgently?" I raised my eyes to Yossi. He understood everything.

"O.K. Myra, thank you."

"What are you going to do?"

"I don't know. We shall see. I'll call you." The conversation was over.

It had happened. I went up to Yossi, put my hands on his chest, stroked him and said, "Don't worry. Everything will be all right. Go to work, dear. We'll call father. Don't be late for dinner."

When Ilana learned about the postcard, she ran home from her clinic and we went to father's place of work. The trolley-bus we took was as slow as if nothing had happened and I hated it for giving me time to think. I didn't want to think. I knew there were other people to think for me now and I was willing to leave it all to them. At last the trolley-bus came to our stop. Father was already standing there, quiet, but pale and tense. We walked silently to a nearby park. None of us doubted that it was the permission. Our long experience in dealing with the OVIR had taught us to understand every little thing in their behavior. And the word "urgently" meant a lot. We sat down on a cold bench. Father was silent. Ilana and I looked at him and waited. There was not a single thought in my mind. I was just waiting to be told what to do.

All my life I had really wanted someone to guide me. I had always thought there was someone stronger, cleverer, higher than I—the Party, the Komsomol, the school—and I was happy to serve them. In spite of the great change in my way of life, I was still ready to let my destiny rest in someone else's hands. But this time no one was willing to make a decision.

"You'll have to decide for yourself now," said father at last. "Only you and no one else."

Me decide? How could I? I didn't know what to decide. Yes, I really wanted to go to Israel. I wanted very much to go. But how could I leave Yossi and all of them behind? Would I be happy doing so? And it seemed to me a crime to leave one's husband and save oneself. Of course, I want to stay. But maybe they want me to go—to go and help him from Israel. It is a strong reason—to apply for an exit visa to rejoin your wife. No, it's nonsense. I'm just trying to justify my desire to go to Israel. Yes, at least let me be honest with myself. How will I feel if I lose this chance to leave for Israel? I have dreamed so much about it and now it is a reality. Israel . . . a dream . . . happiness. And Yossi . . . here in Russia, in danger. Doesn't he also want to go? A thousand times more than I. And what happiness could there be without him? The thought of him left behind in Russia. . . . No, I want to stay, I am sure. To be with him, to wait together, to struggle together. And if they want me to go? I am ready. It will be hard for me, but I shall go. The thought that I was doing it for them would help me.

Nu, say something. But father was silent. Oh, that Rusinek silence. But I saw now that the silence was deliberate. We all went to the chemical factory where Yossi worked. He came out and father and Ilana left us alone, my eyes following them with irritation. I was certain they would talk to each other. I looked at Yossi. This was the first time I had seen him in his overalls and I saw that he was sorry that I had. He had on a cotton suit, black with dust and chemicals, holes all over it, a white cap, and high rubber boots. And his divine pale face of a prophet looked out of all this. I felt ill and avoided looking at him. All of my irritation was turned on him.

"Are you going to tell me to decide for myself?"

"Don't be angry! If I knew what to do, I would have told you immediately. Calm yourself and let's think together."

I felt ashamed. Wasn't it harder for him than for me? If I go to Israel and he stays here without me? And if I stay, he will feel guilty.

We were standing in a wooden entrance gate with an indifferent man sitting behind a small window. I began to think aloud. "It is not yet certain that this is a permission," I said, hardly believing myself. "And if it is a permission, when they learn that I am already married, they will certainly annul it. But let's suppose they do allow me to go. Then I can leave only on one condition. You must be registered through the Moscow OVIR and apply there as we planned it before. Then, even if I leave, you will be able to apply safely and the rest of the family can then apply separately in Riga. I don't even want to go to call the OVIR before we get you registered as an inhabitant of Moscow. I am sure they will refuse me when they discover I'm married. I've heard about such cases. They think that such marriages are Jewish Zionist tricks, so they try to punish those who dare to make them. If they refuse, I'll be glad. But, to be on the safe side, we must register you in Moscow. Then, if they still tell me to leave, I shall go. I think it will be better if I am there. I feel you all think the same, but just don't want to say it."

Father and Ilana returned. Yossi kissed me on the forehead and we went home. In the evening we all discussed the plan and decided to put it into effect as soon as possible.

Next morning Yossi went to a doctor to get a certificate of sick-leave. He was successful. Any doctor would have believed his complaints, he looked so broken. That same afternoon we got tickets for an evening flight to Moscow.

Our plan was to spend one day in Moscow and take care of everything. If we didn't succeed, then I would stay in Moscow and Yossi would go back to Riga. On Saturday he had to go to the doctor again to reaffirm his sick-leave certificate. That Soviet red tape which had to be observed even at such a moment made me furious, but we were still living there and couldn't afford to make more trouble for ourselves.

At 12 P.M. on October 8, we arrived in Moscow. Next morning at eight o'clock, we left our house to begin our operation. Our plan involved several definite steps: militia, military registration and enlistment office, house-management office. The procedure of being discharged from the Riga military and house offices had been effected in one minute and I hoped that we could manage the Moscow business in one day. We were determined to try. It usually took people months, but I refused to consider failure and felt that if we didn't manage it, I would not be able to stand it.

All my nerves were taut. I felt as if I were walking on ice. I thought, "If the ice doesn't break, I shall be happy," and my hope grew as we approached the first step, but then there would be another step and another, each one to be taken in hope and fear.

The ice began to break immediately. We went to the militia and were informed that we must first go to the housing office. We took a bus back and ran into the office. The passport office is open after four o'clock and the secretary is not there. Can anybody give us the necessary form? No, her room is closed and she must fill it in herself. But try to go to the military office. She must be there now.

We took the subway and in half an hour were there. The woman had just left and gone to the militia. Can you enlist a newcomer now? No, a form from the passport office is needed and a document from the Institute. My God! We don't have one. O.K., we shall see about that later. Now to the militia.

We took the subway back and rushed into the militia. She was there. It's so wonderful we found you! You see, we are here only for a day, we must get him registered in my apartment. Can you give us the necessary form?—I work after four o'clock in the passport office.—But please, it is only noon now. We shall waste the whole day.—Leave me alone. I don't bother you at your work, so don't bother me. After four. She barked at us and left.

I could stand it no longer. Why did this have to happen at my happiest time? Why did I have to beg these people and run about to these dirty places? Why had I come back to this hateful Moscow? I was choking and sobbing on Yossi's chest and he didn't know what to do with me.

"Are you crazy? Stop immediately. People are staring at us. Pull yourself together. We still have time. Stop it. Where is your handkerchief? Here, take mine. And, Alochka, please, stop it."

We went out into the street. Stuffy, dusty. Where should we go? We had four hours of enforced idleness.

We took the subway to the airport terminal. Half an hour. There we bought Yossi a ticket back to Riga for the next morning. An hour, the line had not been so long. It was not the season for interurban flights. Only people on business and crazy people like us flew back and forth. Then we had dinner in the terminal restaurant. An hour. Only an hour and a half more. But let's not wait in the office. Better to be far from it, here in the terminal. No one must see me, no one must know I'm in Moscow. It might reach the OVIR. Better to be cautious, on the safe side. We could not even talk. Everything hung by a thread, and we were powerless to help each other. Better not to talk. How many people came to the airport even at such a season? Why are there always millions moving? Is there ever a single moment when everyone is at home, sleeping, resting, and no one is in terminals, on trains, planes, ships? Why do they go? They all have their reasons, but our reason is so special and so rare. Not many people can have such special reasons. And why are they sitting here? I always come just in time for a flight. I never sit in terminals. There are a lot of thieves in terminals. What a terrible thing is the militia. All together. Thieves, teen-agers getting their first passports, prostitutes. Like in the registry office.

When we had gone with Myra to register mother's death, we had been in line together with young parents registering their newborn baby. Myra began to cry when she turned in mother's passport. When we were children, we had liked to play with it. It was all torn. You can always tell a person's age by the look of his passport. Shall I turn in my passport when I get a visa? Certainly. Then it will be as though I have died and am turning in my own passport. Yossi's passport is quite different. There the writing is both in Lettish and Russian. Like in our marriage certificate. Could I ever have imagined my marriage certificate would be in Lettish? When she had registered us, Yossi couldn't find any place to put his legs; the chair was too small for him. He is sitting so motionless now. What is he thinking about?

"Alla, what are you thinking about?"

"Nothing."

"Really?"

"Yes. I don't remember."

Why was I thinking about our registration. Ah, yes. Our matriculation certificate—Lettish—passport—my death—mother—registration office—militia—thieves. Ah, yes. The terminal. What is the time? Half past three. We can go now.

Exactly at four o'clock, we were in the housing office. Slowly and indifferently, the woman took out the necessary form and began to fill it in. I couldn't sit, out of impatience. At last she finished. Militia works until five o'clock. We took a taxi to militia. Yossi rushed into the office and I stayed in the taxi in order not to waste time. I was jittery with nervousness. Suddenly Yossi ran out shouting, "My military document!" I rushed to him with it, he seized it, and disappeared again. In two minutes he reappeared, plunged into the taxi, and the car started on—"To the military office!"

"Made it," Yossi breathed out. "Idiot! He began to ask me all kinds of stupid questions. Why do I want to live in Moscow? Why doesn't my wife go to live with me in Riga? I gritted my teeth in order not to shout at him. Nudnik. He couldn't do anything. There is a law that a wife can register her husband in her apartment even in Moscow. But he wanted to get on my nerves. Can you imagine—short, fat, blond with tiny pig's eyes, filled with his own importance. Holds your papers in his hooves and asks you in a nasal twang all sorts of nonsense. Are we in time?"

"Don't know. Now it depends on the military office. If everything is O.K. there, we shall try to catch that woman in the housing office and hand in all the papers."

In the military office we rushed to the window and pushed in the form.

"And a reference from your Institute?"

"Er, you see, I don't have it with me. Maybe. . . ."

"O.K. It is not important. You can send it later. I'll register you without it now. Just don't forget to send it."

I nearly fainted with joy. Twenty-five minutes to six. We rushed to the subway. I was all out of breath, I'm not such a good runner. Yossi held me by the hand. At five minutes to six, we fell into the passport office.

"Oho," she raised her eyebrows at us, looked through all the papers and said: "Everything is correct. Next week you'll receive your passport with the seal of registration."

I was ready to kiss her. I loved this passport woman and her office, the militia and military office. We had made it!

"And you cried, silly little girl!"

Dead beat, we climbed the steps of my house and dragged ourselves to my apartment. It was nearly six. The OVIR worked until six o'clock. It would not be dangerous to call them then. They would not be able to tell me to come immediately. No, better not do it. Yossi would think I was very anxious to leave and would be upset.

"Yossi, let's call the OVIR."

"What for, it's already late."

"Just for fun."

"O.K."

I dialed the number.

"Good evening. This is Alla Milkina's sister calling. I have received a post card for her, but she is not in Moscow. What does the post card mean?"

"Yes, yes. This is very urgent. She is allowed to leave for Israel. Her visa is valid up until the 13th of this month (My eyes met over the bridge of my nose—four days!) Where is she? Can you find her immediately?"

"No, I don't know where she is exactly. She is traveling somewhere in the Baltic."

"That's bad. Please, tell her to come immediately when she appears."

"Certainly. Thank you. Good-by."

I put down the receiver and repeated the conversation to Yossi. I didn't give him time to react but hurried to add: "Like hell! If they are so anxious to throw me out, they can wait. I'm not going to leave now. Our wedding is planned for the 17th and on the 17th it will be. After that, we'll arrive at the OVIR as if nothing were the matter and announce that we are married. And then we'll see what they do. A week earlier, a week later doesn't matter. The important thing is that you are registered here. Ah, isn't it great? Don't you think I'm a wonderful girl?"

"You? Have you forgotten your hysterics in the militia? Weren't you ready to give up and lie down? If it weren't for me, you'd have sat there crying until now."

"Never. That was just for a moment."

"O.K., we're both great kids. I love you crying or not crying, but better not cry. You're not beautiful when you cry."

"Really? I shall try."

"By the way, now that everything is finished, why should you stay here? Myra can bring the passport when she comes to the wedding."

"You mean it? You really want me to come with you? Wonderful. Then why do we wait until morning? Let's fly tonight and get out of this hateful Moscow."

"O.K., it's a great idea."

In the central terminal we returned Yossi's ticket and bought two tickets for the midnight flight to Riga. We took a taxi to the distant Vnukovo airport and waited for the flight. Two sandwiches for me, a newspaper for Yossi, and the time passed quickly. But at 11:30, the flight had not been announced. We asked at the Information Desk. "Wait for the announcement," they said. In half an hour we heard: "The 12:00 o'clock flight to Riga is delayed eight hours because of bad weather."

We looked at each other with horror.

Then it struck us both simultaneously: this day had been the day of Yom Kippur of the new Jewish year of 5731.

I looked at a clock. Eight hours. The short hand had to move along more than half of the clock face. There was no question of returning to town. The return trip takes two hours and buses had already stopped running. Only taxis. No money for a taxi. Eight hours in the terminal. No place to sit. Hundreds of people sitting everywhere, lying on the floor with their bundles under their heads. Stink, stuffy air. And this—the central airport of the Soviet Union.

Eight hours. How can one endure it? Better not look at the clock. How badly I want to sit down—or at least to lean against a wall. But there doesn't seem to be a single piece of free wall. Better to walk, then the knees don't feel so tired. And if I try to look at the clock to watch every single move of the long hand in order to feel that time is passing—No, it doesn't help.

People couldn't stand the stuffy air and went out of the terminal to breathe. Then we grabbed a seat. I put my head in

Yossi's lap and tried to fall asleep. My legs were too heavy hanging down on the floor. I managed to put them on the bench. Dropped off for a minute. My whole body was aching. Yossi was groaning.

"Let's go out. There's no air here at all."

We went out and walked back and forth in front of the building. It was cold. We went back to our seat. It was occupied. The same cycle of ordeal was repeated. Within four hours, I completely lost all sense of myself. Time passed without my awareness. I walked, stood, sat—all unconsciously.

In the gray dawn of the next day, we stood for half an hour in the rain near the plane and at last boarded it. The shaking of the plane didn't allow me to fall asleep. I felt terribly ill and kept running to the toilet every half hour with fits of vomiting.

Two hours later, we entered our home in Riga. We couldn't even talk to tell the parents about our adventures. They put us in Ilana's room on two separate beds, covered us with warm blankets, and we fell into the abyss of deep sleep.

Several hours later, I awoke completely recovered and hungry and began to laugh at our night's adventure. Yossi was still sleeping and I felt bored. I wanted to awake him and ask, "How did you like it?" I went and sat down on his bed. Mother noticed my intention and hurried to stop me.

"Don't! Don't ever do it. He is always so angry when someone awakens him. They are such sleepyheads, these Rusinek men. Better not to touch them."

But I did want to wake him. He was sleeping on his stomach with his thick lips stretched out. I scratched his ear. He didn't move. Father came in to watch the reaction and to come to my help if trouble broke out. I scratched Yossi's nose. He frowned in his sleep, then opened his heavy eyelids, saw me, and smiled happily.

What a wonderful feeling to be a wife!

∽23∼

The last week before the wedding passed very quickly. No one had noticed our absence on the 9th of October and we decided to keep what had happened secret. The news would have disturbed everyone and spoiled the joy of the wedding.

All the friends of the family helped to prepare the wedding. Lev's and Yehoshua's mother, sweet Aunt* Milja, helped Roza to make *gefilte fish* and *gepeklte fleysh* (boiled spiced meat) beforehand. Ilana ran all over town to get the bedding and towels for our future married life (near or far future—all the same!). Others got together large tablecloths and plates and dishes for the wedding tables. All ran their feet off, using all sorts of influence to get good wedding gifts for us. The bearded family friend arranged to have a special *k'tuba* (marriage certificate) made for us. A month before I had gone to the Moscow synagogue to buy a *k'tuba*. One of the hunchbacks took five rubles from me and handed me a photocopy of something very indistinct with angels holding torches and not a single *Mogen David* on it. I threw it away as soon as I left the place. That Moscow synagogue is an embodiment of insult to all Russian Jews.

Two days before the wedding, the family friend brought and solemnly handed over the *k'tuba*. We all looked at it with delight. The usual handwritten text with blank spaces for names and dates was surrounded by a frame made with devotion and love. Rachel's tomb, David's tower, the monument of Trumpeldor, the emblem of Jerusalem, the scroll of the Torah, two Israelites carrying a huge bunch of grapes, a *Mogen David* at the bottom, and a transparent, hardly seen *menorah* as a background through the letters of the text. What could be a better symbol of our love and our union!

---

* In Russia grown-up women of close acquaintance, even if they are not relations, are called "Aunt" by younger people.

Lev sweated over a big placard with two words: "Mazel tov!" This reserved man said to us, "It is such a pleasure and comfort for me to do something for your wedding."

The long-awaited wedding dress and bridal veil arrived just in time, a week before the wedding. I had never seen anything so beautiful and at the same time so modest. A long, narrow dress with long, narrow sleeves—all made of white guipure. And an airy, light veil with two parts, one for covering the face. Everything for a Jewish bride.

We decided we would not let either Yossi or father see the dress and veil before the wedding, so their delight would be greater. October 17th came and we both forgot about the ill-timed permission. There were so many more important things to think about at the moment.

All the women began their busy day at a hairdresser. I went too, which was a stupid thing to do. To make my long hair curly, I would have had to wear curling pins for no less than all the hundred and twenty years of my life. But I had only one day at my disposal and for all of that day I looked like a Martian.

The rest of the time, I was occupied in making my own wedding cake. We had bought several round cakes, all of a different size. Then I began to decorate this tower with whipped cream, sweet butter cream, and all sorts of little sweet treats. When I had done this at home, Myra usually came along to make me nervous and to laugh at every crooked line of cream. This time Yossi came "to help me spiritually," but I threw him out of the kitchen and continued my work with my mouth open in zeal.

At four o'clock in the afternoon, the telephone rang and the whole family froze at the words: "Tel Aviv is calling." Miriam and grandmother were calling to congratulate the parents and Yossi, whom grandmother had last seen at the age of twelve and whom Miriam had never seen. By the way Father looked at me I knew he intended to pass the receiver to me. I ran away, but the family found me and dragged me to the telephone. I resisted and protested, "I don't want to, I don't know what to say, I'm afraid!" But the receiver was put into my hand and I heard the distant voice of an English-speaking lady. She spoke very warm words of congratulation without waiting for me to answer, so my function was limited to saying, "Yes, thank you . . . thank you . . . yes." For this I found enough English words in my vocabulary. The whole family was standing around me with tears in their eyes. Then I passed the receiver again to Ezra and Miriam at the other end handed it to eighty-nine-year-old grandmother. "Mama!" Ezra cried out. We all looked away.

The telephone talk was over and everyone in silence returned to his occupation. Father, mother, and Yossi to carrying the last plates and dishes to the hall, Ilana to drying her hair in the oven, and I to my "Tower of Pisa," thinking, "How much a part of this family I am, how much I feel all their griefs and joys. How wonderful that this time my ability to give myself completely to someone has not led me into trouble."

The time to get dressed came. The hairdresser came to arrange my curls. She assured me that they would certainly fall at my first movement. I accepted her verdict and retired to the second room to array myself in the wedding costume. I forgot all about the cooking and arrangement problems. Subconsciously putting a solemn expression on my face, I began to move slowly and carefully. I can't remember how I slipped into the cool, heavy dress, put on new elegant shoes, and arranged the veil on my hair. When the procedure was over, I looked in the mirror and sighed in pleasure. I looked very pretty even to me. Ilana came to make the last adjustments and opened the door. . . . Yossi began to blink helplessly, father hummed, and Ilana's imperturbable husband pronounced, "Not bad."

I stood in the doorway with my arms down along my sides and the ends of my lips trembling in a shy smile. It is nice to feel beautiful!

The whole family went to the synagogue. Myra, Yossi, and I took a taxi, stopped off at a photographer, and then went on to the synagogue.

On narrow, medieval Riga Street where the taxi stopped, a large crowd was already waiting for us. I trembled with cold and excitement. We all entered the synagogue and Yossi was imme-

diately separated from me. I stood in the cold entrance hall in a
circle of my sister, cousins, and girl friends. All the men gathered
in the main hall—father, Yossi, and witnesses discussing with the
men of the synagogue the filling in of the *k'tuba*. Lev and another
good friend of Yossi's, Elijahu, signed the *k'tuba* as witnesses. At
last when all that procedure was finished, I was led to a distant
corner of the hall and seated on a chair. Aunt Musja, Uncle
Misha, and his wife stood at my side ("If only poor Polina could
have seen all this" was in their eyes).

Suddenly I saw Yossi with two friends, a young couple, and
the parents beside him, approaching me. He came up and put
the veil down over my face. His solemn face nearly made me
laugh, but I controlled myself. I made my face as motionless as
his. I would allow no such mundane expression as laughter. Neither would I cry, although my nerves and deep emotions had me
on the brink of tears when I was told to stand up. I began to
move slowly to the music of a violin. The sounds of the violin—
mournful, complaining, sobbing, compelling—were touching my
soul. But I would not weep. Such music had always made me
cry, just as sad movies did, but this time I was the object of that
music, of that living movie, and I would not cry.

The silence in the synagogue seemed tangible. Everyone
had gathered near the *chuppah*. I moved past the empty rows of
synagogue seats, which would never more be filled with praying
men.

I reached the *chuppah* and began walking seven circles
around Yossi. I did not know their formal meaning, but for me
they were full of meaning. Those seven rounds were binding us
forever. They were giving me up to him at his full disposal, rule,
and responsibility. I was winding him seven times into my love
and care. Every round meant something new and something indispensable for our union: loyalty, care, tenderness, understanding, selflessness, passion—love. I was willing to go around more
and more.

Then we all stood under the *chuppah*, Yossi and I together.
There was no rabbi in the Riga synagogue, so the ceremony was

performed by the *gabbai* (manager) of the synagogue. He did not look nice, but we did not notice him. In this ceremony there were only Yossi and I.

"*Baruch atah adonai eloheinu, melech haolam. . . .*" We drank of the wine, we exchanged rings, the *gabbai* read the *k'tuba* and handed it to me. We drank of the wine again. "*Baruch atah adonai eloheinu. . . .*" A glass was put on the floor in front of Yossi. Everyone held his breath. Yossi raised his foot. . . . . Crash!

Mazel tov! Mazel tov! Mazel tov!

I started and came back to the world, so unexpected and loud was this cry of good luck by everyone. And the violin awoke also. Now it began to dance, jump, sing, transported by joy. I did not notice how the boys and girls formed a big circle and began to whirl in a *hora* around us: Lev, Yehoshua, Olja, Elijahu, Tsvisha.

The corners of my lips stretched wide and almost reached my ears. I could not make them return to a solemn position. Joy swept over me. Relatives, friends, even unknown people who happened to be in the synagogue, came up to congratulate us. I recognized no one and answered automatically: "Thank you, thank you. . . ." I did not notice when a huge bunch of flowers was thrust into my hands. I looked at Yossi and we both could not help laughing from joy.

On our way to the hall, we again took a taxi, made a circular route through the center of the town, and then went to the building. When we arrived, there was some fuss; we were asked to wait for awhile downstairs and at last the doors were opened. We climbed the stairs between two rows of people—women on the right and men on the left—to the music of the "*Hassene* song" sung by the Barry sisters. I nearly exploded with delight and self-importance.

In the big hall were two long rows of beautifully decorated tables. I thought with disappointment that again I would lose an opportunity to eat delicious food. I can never eat at a holiday table. And indeed everything, including the rare caviar, remained untouched on our table.

The two families sat down at the main table connecting the

two rows; all the rest of the guests found their places at other tables.

Father opened the evening celebration with the first toast. Other older people followed him in Russian, Yiddish, Hebrew: *"Kol hatan vekol kalah, kol Yosef vekol Alla!"* The whole table burst into laughter and applause every time some one included a Yiddish joke in his toast. Each time I nudged Yossi and demanded a translation, but he didn't have time to tell me between laughing and listening to the next joke. "And you know it is impossible to translate it into Russian." Toasts were given in the form of a joke or an anecdote, a poem, or a song. One man began to tell the whole story of how he had to marry his wife because he owed her parents forty rubles. His wife turned away from him with a smile which meant: "Talk, talk, talk—no one believes you." "But," he added, "according to the new regulations of the OVIR, I now owe them four hundred rubles."

The whole hall was filled with laughter and hand clapping. The point was that formerly a Jew had to pay forty rubles to get an exit visa if allowed to leave. But only a week before the entire Jewish Zionist population had been thrown into a panic by a new regulation. Everyone who was leaving for capitalist countries either as an emigrant or tourist had to pay four hundred rubles instead of forty. Since the Soviet Union is not a country which sends forth a lot of tourists or emigrants, the regulation was understood as a blow at the Jews. After the first shock, the Jews considered the situation, decided they would pay the fee whatever it was, and even began to be optimistic that it meant the government had decided to let them go and make money on them.

When I had heard about it, I also had gripped my head in despair. But then I thought of the last parcel from abroad which I had just received from an unknown source through Dinnerman and Co. in London. It was good to feel that we might manage even this with the help of Jews from all over the world.

Yes, Soviet Jews received news of the regulation with readiness and good humor, and the laughter at our wedding was the best proof of it.

Then our young friends followed the older generation. When their turn came, they bounded from their seats and ran to the far end of the hall where there was a piano. Gana sat at the piano and Elijahu, Yehoshua, Lev, Aviva, Tsvisha stood near her. Everybody in the hall began to smile in pleasant expectation.

The "kids" began with a well-known "*Hassene* song" in which they changed the words "*hatan vekalah*" (groom and bride) to Yosif and Alla.

And then came the words in Yiddish, "Even if this is a dream, it is a wonderful dream and we wish for the young couple that it become a reality as soon as possible."

Then the Yiddish song, "*Zol zain*,"

> *Let it be that I just build castles in the air*
> *And my God exists only in fairy tales.*
> *This helps me in grief and makes my dreams lighter.*
> *In dreams even the blue sky is more blue.*

And from a poem by Jabotinsky:

> *White as snow in this land of sorrow*
> *Blue as you, distant heaven attracting me*
> *Yellow as our shame. . . .*

Then the young people said: "But now we have only two colors —the blue and the white. *Kahol velavan*."

With the first words of the new favorite song, everyone smiled. Then they began to demand that I join them and I could not sit any longer. I loved this song and sang it better than any other, always being completely carried away by the melody and the words: "Like a song, like a dream." This time I flew to my friends in delight.

When the song was finished, Elijahu added in Hebrew in continuation of the last line of the song: "These are my colors forever. And forever since now the groom and the bride will be together. And this all began this way."

They began to sing in broken Hebrew:

> *Once a boy went to a party*
> *And met there a beautiful girl*
> *And this happened on the Baltic seashore.*

The second time the boy went to Moscow
And the girl was waiting for him there
And this was in the capital on the river of Moscow.

So the two came together in good luck
And we wish them liberation
May it come soon
And this will be happiness!

Next a joke was told by Lev: "Yesterday a citizen named Yosif Rusinek was arrested on Trolley-bus No. 5 for trying to get off through a closed door. He explained his strange wish by saying he felt sick in the trolley-bus and in general he felt bad there. The driver answered that if he felt bad he could open a window and that it was very easy to sit (here there was a play in Russian on the words "to sit down" and "to sit in prison") and that everyone in the trolley-bus was comfortable and had his own seat; and everyone was happy to go together to the stop of the Happy Future.

" 'But I don't want to go in the trolley-bus,' said citizen Rusinek. 'I want to get out. My grandmother is waiting for me.' He began again to try to force the closed door. The disturber was arrested and brought to this Teacher's House and you must decide what to do with him."

"Let him out! To grandmother!" Everybody cried.

Father laughed until he cried. Then there followed the reading of telegrams from Riga, Moscow, Jerusalem, and Tel Aviv.

What can be better for a Jew in the Diaspora than a dance! A strong, free *hora* or a merry *freilachs*. Everyone moved to the second part of the hall to join in or just to watch the dancing. *Freilachs* was for us and I pulled Yossi, who was resisting, into the circle and compelled him to dance with me. Fortunately, the strong old building stood the test. Yossi was embarrassed at the dance, sure that everybody was screaming in laughter watching his awkwardness. When the young people's *hora* ended, our elders formed a big circle for their *hora*.

After midnight, I put my veil on Olja's head as a sign for her to be married next. The serious ones remained at the tables and began their discussions, the merry ones continued dancing, and the most emotional sang. No one noticed when dawn came, but one by one guests began to take their leave.

And then we remembered. Tension filled our hearts. We had already decided that the evening after the wedding we should leave for Moscow. There was no use in delaying telling our friends about my permission.

We went up to each one separately and told them our story. Watching their shocked reactions, we were glad we had kept it secret until after the wedding. In the gray dawn we went slowly to our wonderful room to have our last quiet rest.

Next afternoon, the entire family was busy looking through and packing the wedding gifts and other useful things we would need for our life in Moscow. I was happy looking at these beautiful new plates and dishes and bedding that were now my own and that were for me a symbol of our new home. I remembered the broken dishes and torn bedding in my Moscow home.

In the evening a slow procession of the closest friends and the family saw us off at the station. It seemed as if all of us were just taking a walk in the city. We were all talking to each other, discussing everything except our departure. In this slow fashion we reached the railway station. Everybody stood silently by our train car. Mother began to cry. I suddenly realized for the first time that I was taking a son out of a large, united family. We entered the car and looked at them all through the window. They stood in the darkness of the night and only their black eyes sparkled in their pale faces. I could divine the message the eyes of Lev and his parents were sending to me: "How is Natasha? Stay near her." Others had in them envy that I might be leaving, but I was ready to exchange places with any of them.

24

On the morning of October 19, six days after my exit visa had expired, we arrived in Moscow. I had been able to play the game of indifference to the OVIR until after the wedding when, in fact, both of us could stand it no longer and rushed to Moscow. When we arrived in the city, I gathered all my resources to pull myself together and hold back that indecent impatience. We went to our Moscow apartment, put all our things in their places, sat for awhile, had breakfast, and then went quickly to the OVIR. I expected and hoped for a refusal.

"Good morning! I've just arrived from Riga and found this post card waiting for me."

"Milkina? At last you've turned up. You've had permission to leave long ago. You can get your visa now."

"Yes, thank you. But the fact is that I have married meanwhile."

"I don't think it is of any importance, but better go talk to Zolotukhin, the Deputy Chief of the Department."

Zolotukhin? What will he tell me now? Every time I had come to him during the past year, the purebred, neatly dressed official had talked to me lazily, hardly looking at me with his sleepy colorless eyes. His tone had seemed to say, "I don't want to waste my time on you, you mere nothingness." And each time he repeated monotonously, playing carelessly with a sharpened pencil. "Not in a year, not in two . . . not even in five years, probably never." I did not know how to talk to him. Not that I was afraid of him, but I felt that arguing with him would be like roaring at a dog sitting at a closed gate.

Others, however, didn't mind roaring at him. Basja used to stand in front of his table, strike her plump little fist on it, and shout, "You've fired all of us from our jobs! Who is going to feed my family? You?" Another Jew spoke more generally, "You must remember that fascism is not excusable. German fascism is being severely punished and your turn will come."

But really Zolotukhin was nothing—just a dog sitting at a gate. But as Jews could not see real guards of the gate, they poured out all their feelings on him. And when the first Moscow Jews began to leave, they laughed and said they would send him an invitation to come to Israel.

Only three months had passed since I had last visited him and listened to his monotonous prophecy about the chances of my getting exit permission. What would he tell me now?

Sleepy as usual, he looked through a list of names on his table (what Jews would not have given to be able to look through that list) and said with a drawl: "Yes, Milkina Alla Tsalevna, you are allowed to leave for Israel for permanent residence."

"Thank you. I have already heard this. I came to inform you that I have married meanwhile."

"So what? It does not matter." (Had I really expected anything else?)

"What about my husband?"

"I repeat: you, Milkina Alla Tsalevna, are allowed to leave —only you. Is that clear?"

"Clear." I stood up and left. There was no use talking to him, so I returned to the official handling my documents. "Zolotukhin has confirmed the permission, but you must take into consideration that I am now a member of a family. I shall expect my husband to be allowed to leave also."

"You had better leave now and your husband can apply for an exit permit on your invitation. Then we shall see."

"What about my passport? I was going to change it to my new surname."

"Please, don't do it. We've prepared your visa in your maiden name and it would take time to change it."

"All right. It really does not matter." I remembered the seal of marriage in my passport and that was the important thing. I went back to Yossi.

I didn't have to ask. Everything had already been decided. I was leaving.

"When shall I get the visa?" I had asked the official.

"It will be delayed a few days until a new regulation is issued. Meanwhile you can prepare all your documents and nine hundred rubles."

"Nine hundred rubles? Why?"

"That is the new regulation. Those who leave for capitalist countries pay four hundred rubles and those who leave for Greece, Spain, and Israel pay five hundred rubles more for denunciation of Soviet citizenship."

My God! Nine hundred rubles . . . What a sum! It was difficult even to imagine it. My mother, who had saved money all her life, had never managed to save a sum near this. It amounted to my yearly salary.

But Yossi comforted me, "If we had only this problem, you could consider that we had none. We'll sell some of your things and father will think of something."

And what a combination—Greece, Spain, Israel—the three countries which Soviet propaganda calls fascist. But why should we care what they call us? In fact, they lay their own fault at another's door.

And so I was leaving. What did I feel? Nothing. And it was better so. If I began to feel, I would feel too much.

We called the parents the same day and told them about my final permission. The news was received with sad acceptance.

That same evening I occupied myself with the most urgent task—looking through my goods and chattels and choosing the least torn and old clothes to take to the capitalist world. As it turned out, I could take nothing, or Yossi threw aside everything I was going to pack. "Shame on you," he kept exclaiming. "You'll never put it on there. Throw it away immediately." I did pack some of the things that were dear to me as a memory of our home: a large brown silk shawl and an embroidered Russian folk costume which were lying in our old trunk and which would probably continue to lie there even in the capitalist world.

I chose a few books which could be of use and interest to me in Israel. Four of them had been published before 1945 and so, according to a regulation, I had to get special permission from the State-Lenin Library to take them and had to pay for them.

The largest part of my luggage would be wedding gifts, which it was decided I should take with me to Israel. I also took records of Russian classical music and some elk's horns which my father had brought from an expedition to the North, and a few other souvenirs. And my mother's red and white jacket. There was really nothing to pack in a big trunk.

Next morning we began our rush. First to my Institute to get my matriculation certificate and a document on my studies for four years at the Institute—two different offices in different parts of the city. It took us a week to get it. I trembled in impatience and fury as I stood in lines, meeting with the usual procrastination and indifference.

We gave the list of those "valuable" four books to the library, but permission could only be given on showing them the exit visa. We had to leave it until the visa arrived.

Our k'tuba had to be copied, for I might need it in Israel. We found a good Jewish photographer who agreed to do it in two days. But the longest and most exhausting process was the copying and legalization of all the documents: my matrics, studies certificates, service record from my place of work, and our marriage certificate. All the documents had to be photocopied or retyped and then attested to first in the Central Moscow Notary office, then in the Supreme Court of Russia, then in the Foreign Ministry, and finally in the Dutch Embassy, which represented Israeli interests in the Soviet Union.

At last, on the 26th of October, I got the visa. I went for the last time to the Moscow OVIR. Never before had the procedure there been so businesslike and respectful. I was already a foreigner. At the door to the office, I took solemn leave of Yossi as a Soviet citizen, for on returning I would be a free person. I entered the room and sat down at a table. An official took my Soviet documents and stretched out her hand for something else.

I looked at her in wonder. "What else?" "A receipt from the bank." I grew cold. How could it have happened that we had forgotten to pay the money? I stood up and moved toward the door. "I'm sorry. I'll bring it now." She looked at me with a smile.

"Yossi," I rushed to my husband. "We're both big fools. Do you realize we forgot to pay the money?" He gripped his head in despair over our ability to forget everything even in such moments of our life.

Fortunately the bank was only two minutes walk from the office and in fifteen minutes I was again sitting at the official's table, having handed her a receipt for nine hundred rubles. Slowly and accurately, she began to fill in a long pink form with the magic words: to Israel for permanent residence.

At last with the long-awaited visa in my hand and no Soviet passport in my pocket, I left the room. Yossi smiled at me and shook my hand. I smiled back, but I was sad. The visa was valid until the 2nd of November. We had five more days.

The getting of the visa was followed by a new race—to the Dutch Embassy, the Austrian Embassy, Airflot booking office, again the library, the Foreign Currency Bank to get my hundred dollars which was the only money I was allowed to take out of the country, and finally to the custom house to send my luggage to Vienna.

All the days turned into a continuous chain of subways, buses, lines, running, sitting in offices. We were like hound dogs running about the city, hardly talking to each other.

Only at night did we turn to each other. We lay on our huge new sofa in the strong white light of the moon which looked directly in at us through our window. And we forgot about everything. Our bed was a magic carpet carrying us away from the earth into the quiet night of heaven. I wanted to become pregnant and we did our best, but failed. And when I realized that, I lost heart for the first time during all those days of pretending coolness.

We both avoided talking about our parting and only my careless stupid joke interrupted that mutually agreed-upon silence. "Nu, Yossi," I asked him once, meaning it as a joke, "Will you be true to me?"

He looked at me suddenly very seriously. There was again a question and pain in his eyes. "You know that you don't have to ask me that. It is I who should ask you."

Any other time I would have been offended by the emphasis of the difference in our natures. But this time there was no room for offense. I went up to him, raised my head, looked straight into his eyes, and said: "Look here, I think it is better if we don't promise anything to each other. The future will tell. Isn't it better if I don't promise but do wait for you, than vice versa? But just try to believe in me."

I don't think he was relieved by my words, but at least he was thankful for my frankness. And I was frank. I couldn't even promise myself anything. How could I know what was awaiting me in the future? But neither could I imagine that I wouldn't wait for him.

One evening we went to the Bolshoi Theater to hear *Eugene Onegin* by Tschaikovsky. It was one of the best productions of the theater, with its best cast. Sitting in one of the boxes, looking at the red velvet and gold bulwark of the great Russian culture, listening to Tschaikovsky's music in its true home, for the first time and the last time, I felt sorry and humbly ashamed that I was leaving.

In the afternoon of the 2nd of November, we took two taxis and went to the International Airport. Several times had I passed through that beautiful Russian suburb and had always tried to imagine my feelings, on my last trip, at the sight of those slender white birches standing along the road. This time I forgot to look at them. Nor did I look at the people around me. I just felt Yossi near me. I looked straight ahead all the way, seeing nothing. I didn't know how to behave, what to feel. And I felt nothing; I acted automatically. There were many friends, relatives, acquaintances, and unknown Jews who came to see me off and a second family which was also leaving. I did not notice who had come.

Two days before, even more had come to my place for the

usual going away party. I hardly remembered them. They sang, danced, talked loudly, gave me their names and addresses to send them invitations. I gave them sandwiches and coffee, and sometimes joined in the singing. But who they were, I hardly remembered.

And again they came to the airport. Newly reborn Jews with their aspirations, and readiness to struggle. And I was leaving. I was leaving my husband. What emptiness in my head. How many bags do I have? Where is the ticket? That woman going with me is with her sixteen-year-old son. I hardly know them. Her husband died a year ago and she is taking his ashes with her in a suitcase. Is it an analogy? No. Nonsense. How much time is left?

Yossi and I were walking hand in hand to and fro in the hall in silence. Nobody bothered us. Sometimes I thought they were casting glances at us waiting for the scene. But the scene would not be. I was not going to cry or tear my hair. I was determined not to. I doubt if I really wanted to.

I held his hand. He looked embarrassed, but I did not feel sorry for him. With his strength, he didn't need it. Nor did I deserve pity. So what was there to cry about? My head was empty. It was such heavy emptiness, and I tried my best to preserve it. I could not collapse then. I had a long way ahead. There was one person in that crowd who could make me cry—my sister. I avoided thinking about our parting. We talked very carelessly, pretending to be busy with the luggage, the ticket, and the like.

Suddenly Ezra came up to us: "It is time." My heart sank and at the same time the blood rushed to my head. I think I shook hands with everyone, kissed the relatives. And then there was Myra. My whole life, my broken family, my reproachful mother looked at me through her. My only sister, in her shabby fur coat, seemed so small there, standing alone and waiting for me to come to her. And I went and felt that my feelings would break me. I felt a choking lump in my throat and tears ready to flood. I knew that if I came closer to her, kissed her, said something, or even heard a word from her, I would collapse. I pressed her fur-coated sleeve. She turned away her eyes, clouded with tears, and I stepped away from her. She did not utter a sound.

I crossed the entrance through the glass wall. Yossi came with me to help me with the suitcases. We put them near one of the counters of the customs officials for a search. I had to show someone my ticket, to fill out some form. I moved very quickly, not looking at him, but holding him tightly by the sleeve.

"You are not allowed to be here," I suddenly heard someone addressing Yossi. It was a girl in the airport uniform.

"He must help me," I flung casually and held Yossi more tightly.

"It is not allowed." She did not leave us alone.

I felt a terrible fury rising in me. "Don't you see that I cannot manage all these bags alone?"

"My wife is leaving, can't you understand?" Yossi suddenly begged.

"But it is forbidden. You must go out, do you hear?" She began to be nervous.

I began to tremble with fury. "Yossi, don't talk to her. And you leave him alone," I was already shouting. "He will be with me here until I leave."

Yossi seized me and I turned away from her. She went away, but in a minute she returned with a woman official.

"It is not allowed that he be here. If you do not obey, you won't leave either."

I did not give her a glance, but I felt that more arguing would be useless and dangerous. "All right, Yossi. This is the end."

"Allochka," he said suddenly and his voice quavered.

"Don't you dare," I cried in despair and terror. "Go." He went away quickly.

I turned away and stood by the customs official. The last search in my life. The last Soviet official in my life. I stood and thought that I should never forgive myself for such a parting with Yossi. The man was not really interested in my things and looked only through the tops of the suitcases. When he took the four books, I handed him the permission. He told me to pay the twenty-nine rubles for them to the cashier and I suddenly remembered that I had no more Soviet money with me. I called for Yossi. He was again with me. We paid for the books, the woman official watching us fixedly.

I put my head on Yossi's chest. "Good-by, Yossi."

"Good-by, dear." He embraced me gently. I pressed my forehead against his chin, rubbed it against his prickly cheek. He kissed me softly, slowly turned around, and went away. I followed him with my eyes until he disappeared behind the curtained glass wall.

The customs official began the search again, feeling the clothes, boxes, pockets. At last he came across a package with letters. That was it! He began to look through them attentively, taking every single letter out of its envelope. Why do they like letters so much? Written material—the ideological arm. The man saw that all the letters were only love or everyday letters and began to just feel the envelopes. One of them, the thickest, attracted his attention. He opened it and took out many small pieces of paper covered with writing and folded in two. I glanced at them and blushed. It was a part of my diary which I had torn out of its notebook and put into one of the envelopes. The man settled down to reading. He seemed very interested. It was the part in which I had written about my being expelled from Komsomol and the way I had come to it. After he had read two pages, he understood that he needed nothing more from me.

"You can pack your things and shall leave this with us."

I felt very relieved. There was really nothing compromising for anyone in that part—only my feelings and thoughts. Were they afraid that I would show it to someone? I didn't need that, I remembered it by heart. Let them take it. Let them read it. Perhaps it would be enlightening for them. So in answer to his statement I just shrugged my shoulders and did not say anything. I went on to the last control pass post. On my way I passed the door in the glass wall. It was open. Yossi, Myra, Ezra, Ilana, and someone else all stood tightly pressed in the opening, looking at me.

"They took my diary," I cried to them.

"Scoundrels," Myra exclaimed loudly. She had come to herself and was aggressive as usual. I noticed Yossi's and Ezra's worried looks. "Don't worry. There is nothing important there."

I hurried to the control pass post. I was late. I stopped by a window in a glass box. A man in a military uniform checked all my documents, returned them, pressed a button, and an iron barrier separating me from a restricted area was moved aside. I took the first step and stood hesitating, not knowing where to go. There was a staircase in front of me. It must be there. I ran quickly up the stairs. Up, up, up! Suddenly I felt a sense of joy which gave me wings, and I flew up the stairs.

"Hello! What are you doing here? Where are you going?"

I looked in the direction of the voice. It was a girl who probably worked there. Her face seemed familiar to me, but I could not remember where I knew her from. Perhaps she was from the same Institute or I had worked together with her. A colorless face, one such as I can never remember. What does she want from me?

"I am going away from this country. Forever! Forever! Forever!"

I ran on, leaving the girl standing on the staircase dumfounded. I passed some large hall, then a glass corridor, then a small round hall. And here was the frontier guard and behind him—fresh air, a staircase down to the airfield, to the bus that would take me to the plane. From there, I knew I would see them all again, standing up on a big terrace for those who come to see their friends off. I ran down the stairs and looked up. There was no one there. The terrace was completely empty, all covered with thick snow. And far away there was the closed glass door with barely visible people pressing themselves against it. I waved my hand, just in case. . . .

In two minutes I was on board the airplane which was to take me to Vienna. "Only three hours of flight and there is my Homeland, my home," we used to sing.

What a terrible plane. It made much noise and trembled terribly.

It will be the last straw if I begin to feel sick, as I always do in planes. Just look at them. They serve caviar on foreign flights. I had better not look out of the window. I become dizzy. It is beautiful there. I am flying abroad? How does it sound? No, I am returning from abroad. I am making an *aliyah* to Israel. Doesn't that sound better? I must think this over. I must impress it on my mind in some way. No, I can't. What are *they* all doing now? Going home. By bus. Yossi is very quiet, I know. Are they talking about me?

By the end of the flight, I could not think at all. I was ill and dizzy and completely out of my senses. The plane landed safely and I went to the exit. There was a dark opening in front of me. I began to feel nervous as I approached that entrance to the world. I bent down, stepped out, and straightened up. A surge of feeling swept through me. A wild cry of joy, victory, and liberation escaped me. I breathed in the air. It was so rich, so warm. I felt I could swim in it. What was it? Was it true that the air of freedom had its special taste and smell? Or was the weather just warmer and milder in Vienna? Whatever it was, I felt happy. I had to feel happy. Whatever my fate might be, I was obliged to feel happy for the sake of the struggle behind me, for the sake of those who were left behind.

I ran happily down the steps. A bus took us to the terminal. I ran to the glass door and when I was half a meter from it it opened itself. I stood puzzled. Then stepped back. It closed. I stepped forward again. It opened again. What is this? Doors open themselves? Strange! Ah, this is one of the tricks of capitalism. I laughed, jumped back and forth on the black rubber spot, and at last ran into the hall looking around. Two curly-haired men immediately came up to me and said:

"*Shalom!* We are from the Jewish Agency."

"*Shalom!*"

∽25∽

In the Soviet Union
As Seen By Ezra Rusinek

It happened nine days after Alla left. By no means a surprise, but quite unpleasant.

On November 11, at 11 A.M., when I was as usual working in my watch department, I was suddenly called to the management office. At the entrance to the office, a young man with a pleasant appearance greeted me with a wide smile, as if he were an old friend: "I am from the KGB. We shall have to disturb you today. You won't work anymore today. Please go and turn your work over to someone else. I shall wait for you here."

He had no written order. That was not according to law, but there was no point in arguing. I used the opportunity to call home. Yossi had better disappear. Our number did not answer. I told a young Jew with whom I had been working that I was being taken to the KGB and asked him to keep calling our apartment and tell Yossi to leave immediately.

I checked my pockets, took out everything "unnecessary," and put on my coat. Then I dialed our number once more, but there was still no connection. The Chief was hurrying me, "You are being awaited. Don't delay."

I left the building with the young man. We got into a blue Volga. I was silent, but the young man began immediately, "Aren't you surprised that we trouble you?" What politeness! I answered, "No, I am not the first." Then he asked: "Did your daughter-in-law leave?"

"Yes, on the 2nd of November."

"And how is it with Yosif?"

"He will get an invitation from his wife and will leave also." I tensely waited for his answer.

"That will depend on you, on how you behave today."

I had been afraid of this all the time. For the last few months we had been waiting with tension for this call. I had expected it to come much earlier. So why had they not come to me until now? I had been watching the course of the investigation very attentively and there were not many people who knew as much about it as I did. I knew everything or almost everything about the activities in Riga concerned with the publishing of Samizdat. From the persons called to the KGB and the questions they had been asked, I knew what the KGB had already found out and what they had not, who of those called had confessed or confirmed facts and who had refused to give evidence or confirm the accusations. And I knew that the course of the investigation must lead them to me and that I would be called, but the question was at what stage of the investigation it would happen.

I was ready. For a long time I had hesitated in deciding how to behave at the interrogation—to say "no" to every accusation or to refuse to give evidence. Little by little, I had come to the conclusion that there was only one good way—to refuse to give evidence.

I was well aware that such a refusal was in itself a violation of the law. A witness was obliged to give evidence. And I realized also that at any moment I might myself be accused—I could not avoid that. Nevertheless, my decision was made not only from the point of view of expediency, but also on principle.

The blow the KGB struck at the Jewish movement in 1970 was aimed at intimidating the Jews. They were acting again according to Stalin's principles, although their methods had changed and had assumed a cloak of legality. But they had not succeeded in intimidating us, and the proof was in the following: In the summer of 1970, it was difficult to collect signatures to a letter and many Jews simply refused to sign. In autumn the situation changed completely. Despite the KGB pressure, Jews ceased to be afraid and exerted counterpressure through their collective letters.

Such conditions gave me the opportunity to behave as I had decided—to refuse to give evidence and not to talk to the interrogators at all. I knew I would have to give reasons for my refusal. They might be unfounded from a juridical point of view, but not from a moral one. I had them. The KGB had given the process of Samizdat the name "The Case of Anti-Soviet Activities." But what was anti-Soviet about it? Our activities were pro-Jewish, pro-Israel, pro-Zionist, if you like, but in no case anti-Soviet. Did we intend to overthrow the Soviet social order, to change something in the USSR? Nonsense! We wanted only one thing—reunification with our people in Israel, to share in its joys and difficulties, the whole of its fate. And no one was trying to settle scores with the Soviet Union, although we had enough reasons for that.

Only the abnormal imaginations of the KGB people, brought up by the "Father of Peoples," and thinking according to his logic, could bring them to the idea of "anti-Soviet activities." The old slogan, "He who is not with us is against us" was again being used.

My second reason for refusing to give evidence was Ilana's fate. It was already seven years since she had been expelled from the fifth year of the Riga Medical Institute. What had she done? Nothing. Together with us, she had applied for an exit visa to Israel. She did this in December 1963, and at the end of January, two young Jews who were in the same course, members of the Komsomol Committee, came to our house and told us—begging us not to tell anyone—that the KGB had called the Party Committee of the Institute and had ordered it to expel Ilana. At the same time the KGB had said the entire family had been refused exit visas.

And soon they convened a students' meeting, prepared several Russian students to condemn Ilana, and shut up those who wanted to express their incredulity. In a short time Ilana received an official notice of expulsion. She continued to attend lectures, but soon one of the lecturers ordered her to leave the auditorium and refused to continue in her presence.

How many letters had I written! How many times had I personally applied to ministers, prosecutors, and other high officials. Each time the same thing happened. The first reaction: "It is impossible. No one can be expelled for applying for an exit visa. If they did this, it was against the law." This would be the beginning. Then the minister or other official would call the rector of the Institute and as soon as he learned who had ordered them to expel Ilana, his attitude changed. He would spread his hands and say: "Nothing can be done."

And so in this way the KGB was following the tactics of the former General Prosecutor of the USSR, the theoretician of Stalin's legislation, Andrei Vishinsky: "For the sake of expediency, even the law can be ignored." This was his famous saying and though Vishinsky himself had been forgotten for a long time, his spirit and teachings were still alive.

Ilana's expulsion had a very simple purpose. The fact became immediately clear to the whole of Jewish Riga and frightened Jewish students from applying for exit visas. Nor could their parents apply.

All my complaints and protests brought no result. Each time Ilana heard, "Give up the idea of going to Israel and you will be studying again." To renounce Israel meant to spit in one's own face. Ilana would not agree to it. I suffered from the fact that she could not continue her studies, but I was and I am proud of my daughter. Not once did she reproach me. But my pain remained and now, facing the KGB, I was expected to tell them what they wanted to know. Like hell!

All this flashed through my mind during those minutes the blue Volga went along the streets of Riga in the direction of the center. So they are not satisfied with Ilana's spoiled life. Now they want to blackmail me with Yossi's destiny. And slowly, but persistently, the thought came to my mind, which had first occurred to me when Alla came and told me that she had been called to the OVIR. Then it struck me that her permission was not accidental, but the blackmail was being prepared. They had already decided to play upon the feelings of a father who wished for the happiness of his son and was ready to part with him so that he could go to his wife in Israel. For the sake of this, the father would also give the evidence which would be so useful for the investigation and the success of the process of intimidation.

Their reckoning was insidious and they had already created the necessary situation. I began to feel fury mounting in me,
something that had seldom happened to me.

We approached the KGB building. There is a gloomy joke
in Riga. They say that this building is the highest in the city.
Why? There are a lot taller than this one. The answer is because
even from its basement you can see Siberia. Now all the floors
were busy with the Jewish question as though the KGB had
nothing more to do. There were four of our friends already sitting in the basement now. What could the conditions there be?

Suddenly the young man said, "Wait in the car." I waited.
In two minutes he returned with two more men and they all sat
in the car. One of them had a long box and a probe. I wondered
what it could be. Then the young man said, "You've probably
understood that we are going to search your apartment, haven't
you?"

Of course, how could I not have understood immediately?
This box with the probe was a mine detector. But what were
they expecting to find? My apartment had long been "kosher."
Even for Passover, Jews do not clean their homes as well as they
did in the summer after all the searches that had started in June.
So what did they hope to find now in November?

We arrived at my house. The two new men went to find two
witnesses and the young man and I entered the apartment. Roza
met me at the door. I immediately warned her: "The comrades
have come to see what we have in our house." She understood
immediately.

But, oh God, what did I see! My Yossi was only just pulling
on his trousers! He probably had slept late as usual and the call
from my place of work, as I learned, had come through only a
minute ago. Of course, they switched on the connection only as
we left the KGB building for my place. They themselves would
need the telephone during the search. So what could be done
now? Yossi had been caught and the KGB had thought he was in
Moscow.

The other two entered with two witnesses. Everything according to the law. They showed me an order for the search "for

the purpose of finding typewriters, subjects, and typed materials that have relation to the case of anti-Soviet activities." All signatures were in their proper places and the order was confirmed by the Prosecutor of the Latvian Republic.

But one thing was very strange. This was the 11th of November and the order was signed and confirmed on the 28th of October. Almost two weeks had passed. Instead of coming on October 29, they were waiting—for what?

On October 28th I had left for Moscow to see Alla off, so they had been waiting for her to leave.

They began to search, but before they did, they suggested that I give them all the anti-Soviet materials I had, especially typewriters. Then they would cancel the search. So this was what they needed the mine detector for! I said I did not keep typewriters and offered them a Hebrew book that had just arrived that morning. But they didn't want it. Letters from Israel were not interesting to them. That was progress! A year before they had confiscated not only books and letters, but post cards, stamps, anything. Something had changed in their tactics.

The search was conducted very carefully. Nothing was spoiled, or torn; everything was handled carefully to avoid complaints of a violation of law. How times had changed!

The investigator looked for a long time at an engraving on the wall by the Riga Jewish painter Kuzkovsky, "The Step-mother." It shows an old termagant, who strokes a Jewish boy with one hand and with the other pinches him on the back. "And whom do you think this old woman symbolizes?" A provocative question.

"Decide for yourself," I answered.

All the books were thumbed through. All the old letters from Israel were looked at. Suddenly one showed the other a telegram from Miriam from Jerusalem in December of 1966. Neither could understand English. I took the telegram and read deliberately and distinctly: "In connection with Mr. Kosygin's statement that the Soviet Government will not prevent Jewish families from reuniting in Israel, I have sent such and such letters. . . ." They looked at each other and were obviously confused.

Then they looked through a file of typed applications for exit visas and took some of them. They obviously wanted to compare the type with that of Samizdat, but I was not disturbed. The Samizdat typewriters were never used for official letters.

Then our telephone notebook was put aside, but I still was not disturbed. The old notebook with important telephone numbers and addresses had been burned long ago.

One of the men opened the drawers of the table and looked through the old films. Suddenly a closed casket was in his hands, a metal one, and it wouldn't open. My polite Yossi took it and managed to remove the stained lid. Film fell out of the casket. The man took it and looked at it against the light. Yossi and I also looked at the film and then at each other. "What is this?" we asked each other with our eyes. "Samizdat? We are caught!"

The man happily showed the film to the witnesses. "Do you see? Film with a text," and he put it aside.

Suddenly there was a ring at the door. The interrogator went to the door and Mendel came in. Of course, he was supposed to come with a list of lawyers who could be approached in connection with the defense of the arrested. This was the third time he had walked in on a search.

"Who are you looking for?" the interrogator asked.

"The neighbor." Brilliant logic.

"What is his name?"

"Aljosha." (The neighbor's name was Volodja. At a previous time Mendel had said he came to see a Katja Ivanova.)

"His surname?"

"I don't know."

"His age?"

"I don't know."

"Your documents, please. . . . Ah, Mendel Gordin, how do you do? A familiar name." Mendel was searched and ordered to sit down on a chair and not to move.

It was already afternoon and the second room had not yet been searched. They sealed it up and left for the dinner hour interval. They seemed to realize that they would not find anything interesting. A car remained in the yard and the several men sitting in it did not take their eyes off our door.

At 4 P.M. the investigators came back with the Chief. The latter sat down at the table and looked through the confiscated material. He was obviously displeased.

"You will have to go with us," he said to me, although the search was not yet over.

The Chief, the young investigator, and I left for the KGB. We went to the investigation department on the sixth floor. A simple room, a telephone, a typewriter.

The Chief left. The young investigator, whose name was Amelkovitch, was to interrogate me. I took off my coat and lit a cigarette. The moment had come. Did they have an order for my arrest or not? I didn't know and they wouldn't tell me until the end of the interrogation. It depended on how many of the arrested had given evidence against me—one or two. If only one, it would not be enough for an arrest. If two, it would be quite another situation. I noticed that Amelkovitch was not hurrying, he was looking through some papers. He must be getting prepared for our talk. He would begin as though he were talking not for the record. His job was to bring the witness to a state of mind where he would answer the recorded questions in the way the interrogator wanted him to.

I knew what kind of an interrogator Amelkovitch was. Not the Stalinist who shouts, curses, and threatens. This man would talk with me as a friend, a well-wisher. He would offer me a cigarette, he would ask if I was hungry or wouldn't I like a drink or perhaps I was tired. He would not raise his voice. And occasionally he would say, "I understand you perfectly, believe me" or "I sympathize with you" or "I am very sorry," but at the same time he would persistently try to achieve his purpose. One of his most effective weapons was flattery. I knew of how two weeks before he had made a very clever man open his mouth with the help of flattery and patience.

Of course, to deal with such an interrogator is much less pleasant than dealing with a boor, and much more dangerous.

He began his talk with the heaviest weapon: "I must warn you
that a lot for you depends upon this talk. You son has a chance to
get an exit visa and you can hope to see your motherland in a
few years. But if you don't behave properly, you will have to
learn that no one gets an exit visa without our permission. Your
son will not see his wife very soon and you cannot imagine what
the consequences for you will be."

Again I felt fury rising in me and together with the fury,
contempt. That was good. It would help me to remain composed.
I didn't answer him but just looked straight into his eyes.

He continued: "Believe me, many of our people have considered whether to call you or not. Young people come to you,
listen to you, and then they are ready to commit any crime, as
for example, hijacking."

At that I could not be silent, and I interrupted him: "If I
had known about that hijacking plan. . . ."

Amelkovitch tried to catch me: "Wouldn't you have come to
us then?"

"No, of course not. But I would have done my best to talk
them out of this step, which I consider very wrong. I would have
tried to prove to them that it was the wrong way and that we
must follow the more difficult but right way of a mass struggle
for exit, an open and legal struggle, by appealing to world opinion, so that the entire world can know there are not just a dozen
but many Jews (I admit, not all of them) in the Soviet Union
who wish to leave, who feel their national ties with Israel, and
who are ready to demand persistently their right to live where
they wish.

"If I failed to persuade them, I would have found some
other way to prevent them from doing this. Because of this, they
have given you the opportunity to disrupt our activities by
searches and arrests.

"Your press conference with prominent Soviet Jews on
March 4 was aimed at intimidating Jews. You were already
planning this new attack, but just waited for a good pretext, for a
mistake on our part. And if there had not been 'the hijacker's
plot,' there would have been something else."

At this point Amelkovitch suddenly spoke with a strange intonation: "Yes, there would have been something else." I understood that I had hit the mark.

But Amelkovitch was just an interrogator. His task was to get information out of me, so he stopped "the general talk" and got down to business. For three hours he read me evidence in which my name was mentioned, for the entire three hours he tried to convince me that all the facts had been proved, tried to trap me in my own words, using all kinds of methods, such as "I shall ask you only about the typewriters, although we understand that you know much more. But I shan't ask you about everything."

The baby! Didn't I know that if in the KGB you confessed to one fact the tangle would keep unrolling and unrolling. At last at 8 P.M. he told me in a shrill voice that never had he had such an unpleasant interview and put a list of questions for the record into the typewriter.

The decisive moment had come. Everything so far had not been important. The important thing was what would be written on the record.

Always the threat of harm and suffering. In 1939 we had not managed to leave Russia. The certificate was delayed. The Second World War broke out. Then came the Siberian exile, returning to Riga, again exile and wandering all over Russia, returning to Riga in 1963 and beginning the struggle for exit. Then Ilana's expulsion. And now Yossi and Alla! Their happiness depended upon me. But all I was being offered was a KGB promise. Could I believe them? Could I believe the enemy? No, I shall believe only my children and care only for what they think about me. And the most important thing for me is that they not lose respect for me, their father. If I confess, I can hope for no respect from them. I knew my daughter and son and Alla. It was painful to think about their destroyed young lives, but nothing could be done. There was no other way.

I had taken leave of Roza long ago. I was delighted with her selflessness. Never once had I heard a word of reproach from her. I was sorry only for mother and Miriam. Still there was only one way—to refuse to give evidence and whatever would be, would be.

Amelkovitch was typing the first question: "Are you acquainted with the accused Shpilberg? Where and when did you become acquainted?" He looked at me and waited for the answer.

"I shall write the answer myself."

He took the list out of the typewriter and handed it to me. I wrote: "I refuse to give evidence." Amelkovitch had not expected this. All through our long discussion, I had not even given a hint of my refusal. He looked at me furiously: "When did you make this decision?"

"Just now, during our talk."

"You must give a motivation for the refusal."

"Just a minute." I took the record again and wrote: "because I am not involved in any anti-Soviet activities of any kind," and put my signature under it. He again put the list into the typewriter and repeated the question again about others of the accused. And each time I wrote the same.

And suddenly all my inner tension wore away and I became perfectly composed and cool. And it gave me great pleasure that Amelkovitch was evidently very nervous.

The telephone rang. I heard only Amelkovitch's desperate answer: "But can you understand that he just refuses to give evidence?" Aha, the Chief wanted to know if their labors had had results. Amelkovitch completed the interrogation, asked me to stand up, and took me into a tiny room at the other end of the corridor. I had to wait.

This room was familiar to me, for I had heard many stories about it. It serves as a place where a witness is taken "to think again." The room is rather gloomy—an old sofa with broken springs, a table, an ashtray. That is all. A lot of people had been taken here "to think again." It was not yet prison, just an "agitpunkt"—an agitation station.* The door was not closed, but

---

* "Agitpunkt" is a very important permanent agitation center in every district, village, settlement which serves for Party propaganda—especially before elections. Ezra uses this word ironically.

to try to leave would be useless. No one would let you out without a pass. Only the barred window reminded me of prison.

There are many funny anecdotes about this room. Many of our boys have been left here for "thinking," and sometimes the oppressive loneliness and feeling of doom and no way out led to a success for the KGB. But there were other cases which made the KGB shrug their shoulders and finally made them understand that they could not manage the Jews.

For example, Sasha was left there for quite a long time after an exhausting interrogation. The boy was tired, so he just fell into a peaceful sleep. *Chutzpa.* No pacing back and forth, three steps there, three steps here, wringing his hands in despair. Just sleep.

There was another case. Elijahu was left in this room many, many times. He had become religious, studied Hebrew, read prayers, and practiced it all very seriously. One day when he was left there, he remembered that the time of *Minchah* (the afternoon prayer) had come and he began to pray. When he was reading the eighteen benedictions (the *Shemoneh Esreh*), Amelkovitch entered the room, saw Elijahu standing and praying, swaying a little, and said, "Let's go!" Elijahu didn't pay any attention. He continued praying and just turned a little to the interrogator and mumbled "m-m-m-" which meant that it was forbidden to interrupt the *Shemoneh Esreh* prayer. Amelkovitch retreated, quietly closing the door behind him, and returned only minutes later, when Elijahu had finished the prayer.

So now it was my turn to sit there for half an hour while the chiefs were consulting. At last Amelkovitch came in and the first thing I saw in his hand was a summons to come the next day at 9 A.M. for a second interrogation. Together with it, Amelkovitch handed me a pass for leaving the building and then slowly, watching my reaction, handed me a second summons for Yossi, also for the following day at the same hour. So he was also to be involved. I didn't say a word and left.

It took only ten minutes to walk to our place, so there was no use calling the family. I entered the apartment and saw not only my folks, but several friends also. Everyone stared at me with a silent question in their eyes, but I asked first for a cup of tea.

I handed the summons to Yossi and he was silent. I told them about the interrogation, all the while watching Yossi's reaction. But both his and Ilana's reactions were the same, as I had expected. And when later I hinted that perhaps I should change my behavior the next day they all became indignant.

I wondered what was awaiting me tomorrow. Amelkovitch had promised me a confrontation with the arrested man. But would he really do it? I thought not. Though it is forbidden to talk during a confrontation to one arrested, Amelkovitch knew that I would do it anyway and this would spoil the course of their investigation.

And I was not mistaken. The confrontation did not take place. In the morning the two of us entered the building and were taken to different rooms. Amelkovitch warned me immediately: "Today the interrogation will take place in the presence of the Deputy Prosecutor of the Latvian SSR." Of course he meant the Deputy Prosecutor for supervision of the KGB, Chibisov. I had heard a lot about him already. His work was to provide the legal procedure during investigations, but I had heard from previous cases that he often interfered directly with the investigations and tried to pressure the accused.

Chibisov came in and sat down. "You have refused to give evidence. It is my duty to warn you of the consequences of your refusal. Comrade Amelkovitch, read to Rusinek the statute of the Criminal Code."

Amelkovitch took the Soviet *Talmud* and read ". . . six months of forced labor." I knew it without their reminding me.

"I've considered the matter," I answered and again became silent.

Chibisov tried again to explain to me that they were not going to accuse me, they just wanted to find out some facts. The search? Well, they wanted to locate the materials that had a connection with the criminal case. I might have in my house such materials even though I myself was not involved in anything. Wasn't it possible? I answered quietly, "Perhaps in your house it is, yes, possible. But there is not and never has been anything anti-Soviet in my house. And you have no right to demand that I observe the law. Laws are made not only to punish citizens, but to protect their rights also. If you divide citizens into two categories, one that has all rights and another without rights, then how can you ask me, whom your law does not protect, to observe the law?

"You, the prosecutors, did nothing when my daughter was expelled from her Institute against all Soviet law and against the UNESCO convention on the struggle against discrimination in education, which was ratified by the Soviet Union. Then you did nothing to restore law. Why do you expect me to respect the law? Let my daughter study, condemn those officials who expelled her, and then you may have the right to demand from me respect for your laws. But since you spit on Soviet law, I do the same."

I watched Chibisov growing red in fury and his lower jaw moving from side to side. As soon as I finished, he bellowed at me; "Israel is a hostile, capitalist, aggressive state and we are not going to train cadres for it."

"That happened in 1964 when the Soviet Union had normal diplomatic relations with Israel," I answered. "If you consider an application for an exit visa a violation of the law, then you should close all the OVIR's. And, by the way, your answer has nothing to do with the law."

Chibisov turned to Amelkovitch: "Begin the interrogation!" The latter began to type the questions from the day before as well as some new ones, and to each I answered in the same way I had before. This went on for a long time. Amelkovitch had not lied; they really asked only a small part of what I really knew. Perhaps they had understood any other way would be useless.

At last Chibisov stood up and said, "I will myself personally take care that you get the punishment you deserve." He left without saying good-by.

In accordance with ritual, Amelkovitch took me to the small

room, but returned very soon with the pass. "We shall call you
again and more than once." The expression on his face was not
very pleasant.

I stopped by my house and then went on to my job. Yossi
came to me later. His interrogation had been longer—two hours.
His summons had said that he was called to the Chief of the
Investigation Department, Brovadsky, which had made Yossi
nervous. Brovadsky was a Stalinist type of boor and Yossi hates
to have anyone shout at him. But when he reached the KGB, he
was taken to another investigator, one who had made the search
in our home, a dull official. The man automatically asked him
questions and automatically put the answers down on paper.
Yossi chose the tactic of "no." To every question, he gave a negative answer: "I don't know," "I am not acquainted," "I did not
give," and so on.

The first test had been passed, but the real fight was still
ahead.

✿   ✿   ✿

Meanwhile the Jewish struggle continued, a struggle with
still only one weapon—collective letters. But this weapon was a
strong one, and once we were able to make certain of this.

One day in the beginning of July 1970, an acquaintance of
mine, a sympathetic Jew, came and told me a story in secret. He
said: "The other day I went to Moscow on a business trip and
met in the Ministry an old friend of mine, Semyon by name. He
is far from Jewish activities, but his heart is very Jewish. In his
more favored times he was a 'court Jew' of one of the ministers of
the Government. The Minister was later promoted and became
Chairman of one of the State Committees. Semyon was on
friendly relations with the Minister and helped him deal with
his personal affairs, which he could not do himself because of
his post. In other words the Minister used Semyon's 'Jewish
head.'

"One day at the end of June 1970, the former Minister
called Semyon at his place of work and said, 'Come immediately
to Café Shokoladnitsa.' 'What has happened?' 'Come immediately!'

"Semyon left his work and rushed to the café. He saw his Minister in quite a gloomy state of mind.

" 'Semyon,' he said, 'We are old friends and I want to beg you for God's sake, if only in your dreams you think of Israel, throw it out of your head. If you want to live in peace to the end of your life, do it.'

"Semyon became frightened. Of course, he had never thought of Israel, but maybe the purges of 1953 were coming again? Then whether he had thought about Israel or not, nothing would help.

" 'Look here,' the Minister continued, 'At the last plenum the old man (that means Brezhnev) gathered some of the Central Committee members together and talked for the whole of an hour on the Jewish problem. He said that the abortive hijacking took place on the 15th of June not by chance and the immediate press release was also specially planned. On the 17th of June, U Thant was arriving in Moscow and it was convenient to show the Jews as criminals.

" 'Brezhnev said also that the fact that collective letters by Jews go abroad and are published there compromises the Soviet Union in international bodies. He ordered the KGB to nip in the bud even attempts at gathering signatures for such letters and the initiators should be revealed and punished. Every Jew who had connections with Israel or was simply interested in the country must be relieved of his position, if it is a post in which he has the right to make decisions.' "

The end of the story was not important. The fact that the authorities were concerned about our letters delighted us. We understood we were on the right track and should keep on.

I remembered Marx's saying: "If your enemy praises you, look back and think what was wrong in your actions." We could take the saying in reverse. If our enemy was concerned, we were doing the right thing. So even Marxism-Leninism helped us in our struggle. And we really utilized it more than once.

For example, after I refused to give evidence, a KGB man later reproached me. I answered: "I acted according to Lenin. When the Czarist police interrogated him, he answered: 'I refuse to give evidence, as my evidence can compromise my friends.'" The KGB man asked me no more questions.

By the middle of February 1971, we were in despair. Everything that had been done led to no results. The OVIR gave only fifteen to twenty exit visas a month and only to those Jews who had made no noise. It was a self-evident warning: sit quiet and you will be let out. But we could not agree to this. Meanwhile the newspapers were filled with articles in which Jews who applied for exit visas were called the enemies of the Soviet people. Could we remain silent?

A rumor spread that Vilna Jews had gone together to the Central Committee. Was it really so or not? We had no time to check on it. But suppose we try this weapon now? Is it legal? Every citizen has the right to approach any official body, must be received, and can leave a letter. Does this concern only an individual? What about a collective visit? Well, we can judge by collective letters. There is no law forbidding collective letters, but there is nothing the Soviet officials fear more. Why? Well, if a group of neighbors complain of a leaky roof in their house, it is all right. But if they complain they want more freedom, what can it not lead to? God forbid, tomorrow a group of workers will come asking for higher wages—what then? The only organizing force in the country is the Party and no one except it can organize the citizens in their acts. This is the law. And if someone else tries to do something, then instigators should be revealed and punished. Thus the masses will become frightened and be silenced.

This is the official Soviet logic and we must understand it. But we have nothing of which to be afraid. We long ago passed that border of fear where we could be easily intimidated. I, personally, was ready for everything. Only two days before, Yossi was refused an exit visa. So they had fulfilled their threat.

Well, what office will be receiving tomorrow? Thursday, February 19—the Soviet of Ministers of the Latvian SSR has a reception day. It is not very convenient in the morning. People are working and not everyone can leave his work. But the next evening reception will not be until the 24th, in the Ministry of the Interior. No, we cannot wait. Even if not many people come, this will be the beginning. We shall all go together to the reception room and demand a collective reception. What an unheard of plan for a Soviet State! But we have thrown aside caution. Despair gives us courage. Isn't it also unheard of that people are not allowed to rejoin their families for five, ten, and fifteen years?

During the preceding evening, there was a chain telephone set-up: "Tomorrow at 11 A.M. in the reception room of the Soviet of Ministers."

Next morning I arrived at the place and saw about twenty people. A narrow corridor, a table, benches along the walls. There was already a collective letter on the table. "Come up and put down your signature." The boys were wonderful! They'd thought of everything. The letter demanded a meeting with the Chairman of the Soviet of Ministers on the subject of leaving for Israel. And this was also a new phase of action. Until now signatures had been collected in secret. And now it was being done quite openly among strangers, Latvians, Russians, and quite probably KGB workers.

We waited a long time until all the visitors left. The order could not be violated. At last our turn came. We were already forty Jews. Six people entered the reception room. I remained in the corridor and tried to calm the others. Everyone could not enter the room. There was not enough space and what might it not have turned into if all forty people talked at once. After a few minutes the voices in the room became louder as people began to argue. When they started to shout, I knew we could fail. I opened the door and entered the room with several other people. At that moment the official at the table was shouting at one of the six: "And you I just refuse to talk to." I addressed everyone: "Comrades, please, let me talk to the representative of the Soviet of Ministers. Please, leave the room for five minutes." Everyone left and the door was closed behind them. David and I remained in the room. We sat down. Now we had to be calm.

"We did not come to make a scandal. We just ask that the Chairman of the Soviet of Ministers receive our petition. The earlier you allow us to go, the better it will be for you and the international reputation of the Soviet Union. Try to understand this."

He interrupted: "To whom am I speaking, permit me to ask." Of course, he had to report the names of the instigators, the disturbers of the peace. We told him our names and addresses.

"Who taught you to write collective letters?" he continued. "Who taught you to come to reception rooms in a crowd?"

"Lenin," I blurted out. "He always said that strength lay in the masses. Where an individual can achieve nothing, the masses will succeed."

If the official had asked where and when Lenin said this, I would have been in difficulty. But fortunately he did not, and the reference to the classic theoretician helped. The man changed his tone and promised that the Chairman would get to our business after the forthcoming Party Congress.

In fact, I was following Jabotinsky's teaching, not Lenin's. I always remembered his speech in Warsaw in 1938 where he warned against adventures, against a loss of a sense of reality. And taking this warning into consideration in the difficult times of February–March 1971 I was certain that there was some limit of action, a border we should not cross. If we had forgotten about this border, the results would have been bad for us. The same would have happened if we had not seriously considered our steps and avoided provocations.

The Soviet authorities' point of view on the problem of Jewish emigration changed from time to time. Different periods indicated this. In Riga, from April until June 5, 1967, a significant number of visas was issued. But people had to leave without their Soviet passports, with a piece of paper with a photograph on it and a place for all the seals, which was called an "exit visa." Everyone leaving for Israel was obliged to denounce his Soviet citizenship.

On the 8th of June 1967, three days after the beginning of the Six-Day War, emigration was stopped. It recommenced only in September of 1968 and continued until March 1969. A great many active Jews left during this period. After March 1969, the doors were again closed and only a few individual cases of emigration took place.

It was clear that there were two competing points of view in the Government concerning the Jews. One group was eager to get rid of "those troublemakers"; the second was decisively against the emigration. Our task was to reenforce the first opinion and not to give the second group an opportunity or pretext to make us knuckle down.

The border of what can and cannot be done is not unchangeable. What was impossible yesterday can be possible and necessary tomorrow. The important thing is to understand this border. We cannot afford to make mistakes.

On February 22 in the evening, we went to the reception room of the Ministry of the Interior. By this time we were about sixty Jews. The Deputy Minister received us. He waited for a long time until all other "non-Zionist" visitors had left and then we all entered his room. After we put a letter, just composed and signed, on his table, everyone began to attack him. The Jews were all talking at once. But can they do it any other way? Can a Jew allow another man to talk? Everybody told his own story, how many years he had been waiting: one was not allowed to go to his mother, another to his sister, a third to his second cousin, a fourth to his beloved mother-in-law, and so on and so forth.

The Deputy Minister was trying to remain calm, but did not always succeed. Eva jumped at him like a tigress. She had just received a refusal.

"You say that my daughter is staying here. That is why you refuse me. But where were you when my husband was sent to a forced labor camp and my daughter was left without a father? You—or others like you—killed my husband. Who thought then of my daughter?"

It was the first time in his experience that the Deputy Minister had seen or heard such a thing. It was all right. It would be a good lesson for him. We left after having demanded that next time the Minister himself should receive us.

Two days later on the 24th of February, Yossi, among twenty-four other Jews, began a sit-in strike in the Presidium of the Supreme Soviet of the USSR in Moscow. It was a memorable day for me. The struggle was spreading all over the Soviet Union. We all felt shoulder to shoulder with our Moscow comrades and I felt my son was with me in our common struggle.

On the eve of March 1, we gathered to discuss our behavior at the Minister's reception the next day. We must be organized. We should not all push together into the room. Six persons would enter at a time and each would tell about himself and his close friends. No one would speak on behalf of everybody. If the authorities decided to strike at us, each would be arrested as an instigator. Of course, they could arrest all six. Well, at least they would be six and not alone. We discussed the possible reaction for a long time. This visit might have important consequences. About seventy people might come.

But we were mistaken. One hundred Jews came. The reception room was too small, the air was stuffy. There were five or six other visitors. The Minister knew what was awaiting him and did not hurry. We waited patiently from 4 P.M. to 7 P.M. At 7 P.M. the militia closed the door. Now anyone could leave the building, but no one could enter it. So the people remained in the reception room.

At last all the "non-Zionist" visitors had left and only our large group remained in the building. Our boys stood by the doors to keep order and not to allow everyone to rush together into the Minister's room. Six of us entered the room and the door closed behind us. We handed the Minister our collective letter just signed by everyone in the reception room and began to speak in order, one after another. But he interrupted and did not allow us to speak. He received people only on individual problems, he said; everyone's question of emigration was considered separately. He refused to accept our collective letter or to talk to all of us together.

For fifteen minutes we argued, but the Minister was implacable and at last showed us to the door. We went out embarrassed. What could be done? Had we failed? The Minister argued on principle, but at the same time in accordance with policy. An individual can be refused easier than a group. Suddenly we saw that the Minister was leaving his room with his secretary. He considered the reception over. But no, we had not come to be turned back. If he would deal with individuals, then we would go one by one.

We settled the order and a wearisome waiting began. The Minister talked to every visitor, for several minutes, but to each one differently. For example, Yehoshua entered his room and asked "Am I a human being or not?" meaning he wanted his human rights. The Minister roared, "Get out!" Others had a longer conversation, but still the same result—a refusal. In other words the Minister had the longest reception day in his experience, from 4 P.M. to 12:30 A.M. But let someone else pity him.

That evening was most memorable for me. At 10 P.M. Ilana ran into the Ministry building and cried out in joy, "Yossi has permission!" Of course, I didn't stay in the building, but ran out together with her. "How? When?"

"He just called from Moscow. You know, after that strike on the 26th they were told to come today to the OVIR for an answer. Can you imagine how this nasty boy told us about his permission? 'Ten people are allowed to leave.' 'And you?' we asked. 'And I among them.' "

I felt great joy overwhelming me. Yossi was leaving. Half of my life was not in vain. I went home and although I was dead tired I could not go to bed. Every ten or fifteen minutes people came to report on the course of the reception. At 1 A.M. we summed up. In principle, this reception was a failure. The Minister had refused to receive a delegation and had given the usual negative answer to each one individually. There were no practical results, but still I thought our visit would have a certain impact on their future decisions.

At the same time the failure had some positive sides. What should we do now? The idea of a collective trip to Moscow had been discussed long before, but there were great differences of opinion. How many people could go? Who could go on a working day? To leave your work on a working day without permission could result in losing your job. And not everyone could afford a trip to Moscow. It was difficult to get tickets and where could we all spend a night in Moscow?

But the Minister had helped us with his refusals. No one would have gone to Moscow and the famous "hunger strike" that shook the world would not have taken place if on the 1st of March the Latvian Minister had promised at least some of the Jews that he would reconsider their applications for exit visas to Israel. But now, under the present circumstances, everyone was unanimous in the desire to go to Moscow, to the Presidium of the Supreme Soviet. We set the date—March 10. A lot of preparatory work had to be done before the trip. Everything had to remain secret: finding those who wanted to go, getting tickets, deciding who would go by plane, who by train—and all by different trains—and who would go by car; helping those who needed money for the trip. All this had to be done out of the reach of the KGB. If they had found out something or had we all gone by one train, they could have taken us off the train.

But they were feeling some sense of a coming explosion and decided to use the old tactic of divide and rule. Some of us were promised, "Sit quiet, do not take part in all these actions and you will be let out." And to our credit it should be pointed out that all who were promised exit visas to "sit quiet" did not believe the promises and took part in the Moscow "outing." We could already feel that there was a certain embarrassment in the KGB ranks and that our new actions might break them completely. Still we were not confident of victory. We looked forward to the forthcoming struggle with mixed feelings of hope and fear.

I could not take part in the preparatory work of the strike. I left earlier for Moscow to spend a few days with Yossi before his departure. Who could tell how long it would be before we would see each other again? In spite of that, I think no father ever took leave of his son as calmly as I did. What would happen with us was of no importance if Yossi could leave for freedom, could be together with his wife, could be happy. That was what I dreamed of. Packing, running back and forth, suitcases, documents, and at last on the morning of March 10 we left for the International Airport.

A small group of Jews had gathered in the terminal. Many of the most well-known Moscow Zionists were leaving. They were all in a deep depression. What would happen to those who remained? What would be the result of today's demonstration? The authorities might decide to strike a final blow and arrest everyone. Strange people! They had run a bigger risk, had won their victory, and now they were concerned about us. They didn't even seem happy to be leaving for Israel, but would rather have stayed to continue the struggle. I really could not understand them, but maybe if I were in their place. . . .

At 11:30 the first messenger arrived from the Supreme Soviet and happily reported, "Our numbers have increased. Quite unexpectedly, a large group came from Vilna with their wives and children, several families from Lvov, some from Tallinn and other cities."

"How many all together?"

"Don't know, had no time to count everybody."

Not only had the KGB not managed to find out about the increase, we ourselves knew nothing about it.

Noon. The second messenger came. "We have decided that every half hour until the departure, messengers shall come to the airport and tell about the course of the strike. Those leaving will be in Vienna in three hours and release the information to the world." The messenger told us, "The first statement to the Chairman of the Supreme Soviet was handed in. The Jews demanded to be received by him. If there is no answer to this, in the evening we shall declare a hunger strike."

A hunger strike? It was unheard of in the Soviet Union. Frankly, I was very uneasy. Maybe they are overdoing things, losing their heads. But perhaps this time they, the younger generation, were right.

Half past twelve o'clock. The next messenger came: "The foreign correspondents have appeared. The corridors are filled with men in civilian clothes. One of them came up to the UPI correspondent and said: 'Jackson, we are sick and tired of you, get out.' The large hall of the Reception Room of the Presidium is filled. There are not enough places to sit down. We have counted about 150 people all together. The authorities have not given any reaction until now."

*   *   *

The last minutes. Yossi was calm, even businesslike. We had always called him *kalte bauch* (cool headed). He took his leave of his friends and then of mother and me. "Please, no tears. Everything will be O.K." We watched him go through the customs check and waited until he appeared on the glass gallery. Now we could only see each other and talk by signs. He is already on another side of the world. I tried to memorize his face. This is my son. Not bad, I thought.

My Moscow friends called me to go to the Presidium and I myself felt that I must go. I waved to Yossi for the last time, asked Roza to stay until the end, and left.

We arrived at the Presidium. Several boys were waiting at the entrance. "The statement of the hunger strike has already been handed in. People are excited. None of the officials had come out, so we decided not to wait until night."

It had been done. There was no way back. Now we would have to stand by until the end.

I went into the hall. Everyone was sitting in complete silence. I sat down together with our boys and listened to them: "When the statement was handed in, we all sat down and became silent. Can you imagine, Ezra, 150 Jews silent for a whole hour? Wonderful discipline. In the beginning some began to make noise, so we threw them out and it became silent. Fifteen minutes later, Jackson came in, looked at the silent Jews, and said, 'I'm going to the telegraph.' "

Little by little the Jews began to talk. What can you do with them? But no one left.

Five o'clock. The reception hours were over. The doors were closed. The Director of the reception room came in and told everyone to leave. But we had not come to leave. We began to express our demands and spoke for quite a long time. Our demands were: reconsideration of all applications; in case of refusal, a reason. No answer. We were again told to clear the building. We refused. The Director left and immediately dark-

ness fell in the hall. They switched off the lights. Only thin rays
of daylight came through the closed curtains. What would follow? The corridor was lighted and filled with people in civilian
clothes and several militiamen.

The tension grew. People had to be distracted. Someone
remembered: Today is Purim. But where can we get *Megilloth
Esther*? Then someone said he has an *Haggadah shel Pesach*
(the Passover Seder text) with him and he began to read it
slowly and to translate it into Russian. I felt a holy fear. Maybe
we were also on the way of exodus from Russia.

The *Haggadah* was not finished. They suddenly switched on
the lights, but we saw that now the corridor was dark. Something was being prepared there. The dark corridor was full of
militiamen.

At eight o'clock the doors were flung open and a militia
detachment rushed into the hall. They stood along the walls and
among us, dividing us into squares. We were locked in.

We were informed: "You will be addressed by a militia
commissar." The Commissar of Militia was a general. He began
his speech in a hard voice and unambiguously: "Enough. You've
played these games enough. We are not going to endure them
any longer. Those who do not leave the hall in two minutes will
be detained as disturbers of the peace."

Two minutes. It was both a long time and a short time. It
was a short time for a discussion, but quite long enough for
making a decision. Several voices were heard: "Let's not leave.
Let them carry us out. We'll raise our feet and let them drag us
out."

But I was of another opinion. Fifteen days for disturbing
the peace is nothing. But such behavior could also be called
"resistance to militia" and this could have meant several years of
imprisonment. But this also was unimportant if we considered
what we had achieved so far. Nothing. And if we now gave them
this opportunity to provoke us, tomorrow they would consider
themselves winners. We exchanged a few words and the two
minutes were over. Several of us took our coats and said to
everyone, "Let's leave. Tomorrow at 11 A.M. here again."

Many people thought we were wrong, but the events of the second day showed that we were right. We left in small groups by different side streets all filled with militia. Neither we nor they had ever seen such a demonstration in the center of Moscow. In the reception room one of the militiamen asked a Jewish woman in a whisper: "Aren't you afraid to do this?" "We are afraid," she answered. "We are terribly afraid. That is why we are here." The man did not understand her.

On the 11th of March, we all came again. A delegation was received, but the answers were not definite. We were sent to the reception room of the Ministry of the Interior. Various high officials of the OVIR came out and talked to us there, but this was not what we had come for or what we had tried to achieve.

In the meantime the militia closed the doors. No one was allowed in; no one was allowed out. At four o'clock we suddenly felt that the ministry's staff was excited. In a minute a side door was flung open and the Minister of the Interior of the USSR, Schelokov, and several generals came in.

He talked to us for a long time. But the main thing he told us was that he had decided to send his representatives to all cities for reconsideration of all applications.

In that moment I felt that the hard work and struggle of all those years had not been in vain. We had won. I looked around and thought that I was proud of these people, the Soviet Jews. I was proud to belong to them.

⟲⟳ 26 ⟲⟳

In Freedom

Today I am in Flint, Michigan, somewhere in the North for a United Jewish Appeal dinner, a television interview. Tomorrow morning Harrisburg and then Pittsburgh, Pennsylvania. It is interesting how I've gotten used to all this flying. Tel Aviv, London, Amsterdam, and even that flight from Holland to New York. And now every day a flight and I feel at home. More than that, I even rest in planes, tired from all the speechmaking. I am no longer afraid to speak. I have learned. But I still feel very nervous meeting new people. I wonder whether they notice it. But when I begin to speak, I forget everything and feel very much at ease. In fact, I have come to like making speeches. When I see those interested faces in front of me, I feel very happy and want to tell them more and more. I try to explain to them what a Soviet Jew is, what his idealistic Zionism is, what his heroism is. I doubt that Americans can understand, but they listen attentively and this helps me.

Could I ever have imagined that I would be a speaker? In fact, I am not a speaker. I just like to talk to people who listen. I try to understand every new audience and talk to them accordingly—be it a UJA dinner or a meeting organized by the American Conference on Soviet Jewry, a university meeting, or a meeting of the clergy, be it an audience of fifty people or thousands of listeners.

My first speech in London, to a meeting of a thousand British Jews, was just terrible. I was so nervous and shy. I did not know what to say and spoke so slowly, so indecisively, that when I at last finished I wanted to hide under the table. But they did not give me the chance. They all suddenly stood up and applauded for several minutes. Then I wished the floor would open beneath my feet. But it was great. It gave me encouragement. I understood then what they wanted to hear. That's why the meetings in Holland afterward were so successful. And now I am flying to and fro in America, making speech after speech. A month and a half already, and it will go on until the end of March. And I came for only two weeks.

I don't feel bad here, I am just terribly tired. Especially when I am in New York. That strange stuffy air, even when you are outdoors, the constant piercing sounds of sirens, and the crackle of current whenever I touch something in the hotel rooms. It gets on my nerves terribly. When I am in New York, I feel ill. I can't eat anything. The food there seems as if from another planet. I dream constantly of hot boiled potatoes with herring and Russian brown bread with butter. Better not to think about it. In fact, New York is not to blame. It all began in London. It is just my nervousness. When I come back to New York and go into my room, I just fall on the bed and look steadily at the wall, unable to sleep or to think. Thank God, in the Barclay Hotel I can order food served in my room. In the Lexington I starved for days, nourishing myself only with that terrible crackle of current. Sometimes, looking out of the window at the city from my twenty-eighth floor room in the Hotel Lexington, I said to myself: "Well, you are in America. What do you think of it? You ought to think something." But I thought nothing. I just could not. All this is just too unbelievable to be able to comprehend it. I and America. America and I. Alla Milkina, a former young Pioneer-Leninist and a Komsomol member, comes to America. No, it sounds like a bad joke.

And yet people here are wonderful. Maybe it is typical for public relations or on the level where people really do not come to know each other well, but all the same I find delight in people. I have never seen so many smiles in all my life. They surround me everywhere, meet me in every city, caress me, and give me strength. Everyone is so easygoing that I do not really find it difficult to deal with strange people. They like to ask me whether or not I like America and I never know what to answer. On the one hand, I have no impressions at all; I am just afraid to have any. On the other hand, there are a lot of impressions which are all so different. And really this country is so big that it cannot leave one with only a single impression. It is all and it is everything. Sometimes it seems to me to be a world that had reached perfection in all its services and standard of living and has now started on the way back. But Americans on the contrary are very enthusiastic about great new challenges and think they have a lot to do. And in general they are very businesslike.

Even struggles here seem to be a matter of business. Every new struggle is immediately connected with an organization, an official hierarchy, money, fund-raising, competition, and so on. It seems to be a way of life. Civil rights, socialism, anti-smoking, Women's Lib (Oh, God!), Soviet Jewry, Jewish Defense League—everybody to his own liking. Those who don't like struggles struggle against struggles. Those who do not like to struggle through the establishment form their own establishment and think they are rebels.

It is good when good people are able to think something of themselves and it is good that people have that inner spiritual and physical activity to help others in need. I had never imagined that such readiness to help others was possible. American Jews are great. They deserve respect and gratitude from all of us. If it were not for them, we there would not be able to achieve anything. They are our second front. And whatever the psychological or political reasons for such activity, it helps us and we must be grateful.

I like to be here now with them—to travel, to speak. What is the use of going back? To whom? To what? This way time goes faster. And who knows how long I have to wait. It is nearly four months since I've seen Yossi. It is nothing. But I begin to forget his face. It is a terrible feeling. I close my eyes and try to imagine him. But his face does not come. Pictures don't say anything. They are not true. Only memory can bring his fullest image—his face, his mood, his body—all together. And it comes no more.

I know that it is because we have not had enough of each other. We did not have enough time to feel each other, to record each other on the tape of memory. These four months have felt like many years. I subconsciously add to them all the rest of the time which we have to wait and they grow into an eternity. But I am calm. Sometimes shamelessly calm. Why? All that has happened to us is too much like a tragedy, a plot for a film. And I am afraid to take part in a performance that is so banal. Even when I am alone, I cannot express my feelings with gestures or sounds—tearing the hair on my head, wringing my hands, groaning, wailing. My second self looks at me and mocks me. And in fear of it, I forbid myself to express the feelings. And after awhile, having been forbidden expression, the feelings them-

selves wear away. The other day I went to see *Love Story*. I
cried. I resisted, but in the end I burst into tears. But about Yossi
and myself, I do not cry. Yes, leukemia is terrible. You can't
foresee it, you can't resist it. It is so cruel. And if it is not leukemia, but the Soviet Union? What do you do then? Isn't it also
a tragedy?

Only once I collapsed, but it was only for a short time. On
the 19th of February, in the morning, I learned that Yossi's application for an exit visa had been refused. Was it unexpected? I
should have been ready for it, but I was not. The terrible news
came by telephone. Miriam received the telegram and called our
cousins in Brooklyn. It was a long time before they dared call
me. Our dear cousins in Brooklyn, they hoped together with me,
they cooked potatoes for me, on Saturdays they brought me half
dead to their home and put me to bed, they dressed me "like a
doll," they bought pots and pans for my new home, they read
and gathered every piece in the newspapers about me. I love
them so much and I am ashamed to be sad and suffer in their
presence. Can anything compare with their untold stories of
Bergen-Belsen, Maidanek, the stories of their neighbors and
friends with blue numbers on their well-cared-for white hands;
our dear cousins from Brooklyn, formerly of Poland.

And on February 19, they did not dare telephone me.
But they called at last and told me with tense, fearful voices.
And I put down the receiver. I was still in bed. The call had
awakened me. How much I wished that it had turned out to be a
nightmare, that nobody had called, or that I just hadn't understood. I sat in the bed, alone in the room, alone in the hotel,
alone in the world. I wanted to move, but I was afraid. I wanted
to cry, to shout, but it was only in my mind. I continued to sit
motionless in bed. My mind was quite reasonable. It even persuaded me: "Nothing has happened. You had to be ready for
this. It is only the beginning. You wanted to struggle for him.
Then why do you collapse at the first failure? Now this unties
your hands. Go on, speak, demand, beg, struggle for him! Didn't
you come here for this?" But all my motionless self answered
weakly: "No, I was not ready for this. I thought that I was at the

end of my strength, but now I see how much more is demanded of me. And I am terrified. I know I should be ashamed to be so weak. He is there. How much he has lived through, how much is in store for him. And all this without me. I know how much I mean to him. And it is my responsibility. I must be stronger for his sake. Russia has declared war on me. Shall I be frightened when I have the whole world on my side? I must get up and go. I have a big meeting today, a very important one—a thousand women activists of the UJA. I must stand up. Why am I not moving? Maybe I am paralyzed?"

I had completely lost command of my body and sat that way until the telephone rang again and roused me from my shock. I had to go to the meeting.

And I continue to go to the meetings and shall go until the end of March, maybe longer. I have my itinerary. It is like a crutch for me. People decide, plan, arrange meetings for me with important people. And I ask them, I beg them, but I do not believe them. U Thant said that he was not strong enough to influence the Soviet Union. Who is strong enough then? Yossi?

Yes, only he has the strength and everyone else who is there. And for them I hope. They are already on strike. They go together to the Supreme Soviet, to the Central Committee building and demand. This struggle will be victorious. I feel it. The newspapers say that the Jews were eating sandwiches while on strike yesterday, the 1st of March, in the reception room of the Presidium of the Supreme Soviet. What did Yossi eat? Did he bring it from home? Oh God, what will they do to them all?

We are landing. Snow everywhere—like in Russia. It must be warm now in Israel. This was my first winter out of Russia and I've spent it all outside of Israel.

Detroit. "You will be met on your arrival in Detroit by our representative and driven to Flint. Hotel reservations are at the Holiday Inn." O.K., I am waiting to be met and driven.

Myra is pregnant. Hard to imagine my sister having a baby. It is interesting. All through our lives, we developed physically with a difference in time of only a few months, although the difference in age is a year and ten months. It was the same with our first appointments. Then in March of 1970 she married and in November of the same year my wedding took place. And now she is pregnant. Nonsense. A stupid analogy.

At last I am met and driven to my destination. Soft, big American cars which take me to comfortable American hotels. I shall never remember them all. The Holiday Inn is as good as the others. I would love to have breakfast now and lie down for awhile, but they will certainly drag me immediately to a television station or to a newspaper office and forget to offer me something nourishing. It is interesting that the farther you get from New York, people become more and more tired, forgetful, haughty, less attentive. Why is this so—hard work or provincial haughtiness? If they do forget this time, I shall give them a hint or just ask for a sandwich. Do they have anything besides those terrible roast beef sandwiches which I hate? Meanwhile I shall check in.

"A room for Mrs. Rusinek? Yes, I have it reserved. Mrs. Rusinek, there is a note for you here from New York."

The Israeli Consulate—"Call urgently." These words sound so familiar. Urgently? Something has happened. They want me back? But why? There was that second strike in Moscow yesterday. Something must have happened to him. Oh God, I don't want to know anything.

"Where is a telephone?"

"This way, please, on the wall."

"Thank you . . . Israeli Consulate? *Simcha, shalom.* This is Alla calling."

"Alla? *Mazel tov.*"

Do you know what joy is? Joy is when a grown-up person in a midi-skirt begins to skip like a monkey; when you laugh like mad, embrace everyone, then seize your coat from a chair, then put it back and don't understand why you find yourself at this end of the world at such a moment; when you lose all sense of duty and call the UJA and cancel all the meetings; when you rush insanely back to New York, lie on your Barclay bed, and refuse to move all that damned week until his leaving Russia passes; when you take a dozen suitcases with pots and pans, clothes, and presents from the whole of America, and with your hands full run to the plane. New York—Vienna. Kissing good-by the sweet cousins and those great kids from the Student Struggle for Soviet Jewry; when you roll yourself up into a ball like a kitten in your seat and close your eyes tightly to fall asleep as quickly as possible so that the last night will pass unnoticed.

On the way the plane landed first in Brussels and I had to lounge about the terminal for half an hour. I found nothing better to do than to buy Chanel and imagine that I was the most elegant lady. The last hour of flight and I arrived in Vienna. I was so overloaded with luggage that I didn't have the time or the strength to philosophize on my coming back to Vienna in quite a new capacity. I was sure I would lose or leave something behind, so I watched myself very attentively. But it was already late. On leaving the plane, I could not find my ticket to Tel Aviv. Since I was the last person still on the plane, I decided to get off and continue the search in the terminal.

In the terminal I stood among my eight suitcases, bags, and packages and looked through them several times. Nothing helped. There was no ticket. I spat on all that business, thought that here was a subject for our first family scandal, registered my luggage, and left for the hotel where I had reservations for two.

I had two hours to rest and to think about my appearance. I knew I had to be as well-dressed as possible. This would not offend Yossi. On the contrary he would be happy to see his wife so elegant. But what should I wear? My black pants suit? It had been good enough for the $10,000 minimum dinner in New York with the Baron de Rothschild. I remembered that someone had called me especially to warn me that it was a black-tie affair and that I had to be dressed accordingly. I could not understand what he meant. Did he think I would appear in hot pants or a Russian sarafan? No, I had better leave this for our arrival in Israel. I could imagine how Miriam would laugh to see what America had done to me. Now I shall put on the blue pants suit. That had been good enough for both Mr. U Thant and Mayor Lindsay. So, I think, Yossi will also be satisfied. And my big black hat would be the last blow for him. He would certainly say, "What an elegant wife I have."

In the afternoon I went back to the airport. The two curly-headed men were already there, excited. For how many years had they met hardly a couple of Jews a month—old, sick invalids. Some of these had not even reached Israel alive. And now twenty people in one plane. A real exodus. And what people! Young, strong. Engineers, doctors, scientists. And they were bringing their children to Israel. The first large group in all these long years. And in this group there were those who took part in the Moscow sit-in strikes on the 24th of February and the 1st of March. The first Jewish *aliyah* from Russia achieved in struggle.

Time passed. The plane was late. I sat in the terminal and suffered from waiting. At last the two men jumped from their seats and ran away. The plane had landed. A drum inside me began to thump violently. I paced back and forth in the terminal, trembling with nervousness. Then I sat down. Why should I be nervous? He is already here. I have been so self-composed for all this time and now I'm suddenly trembling like a school girl. I squeezed myself to stop the trembling and forced myself to sit motionless. But this was beyond my strength. I bounced to my feet and went to the glass wall behind which they would appear. Every minute was a new torture. I began to feel sick to my stomach and wanted to cry. That was a bit too much. I raised my head to make the tears go away. There was nothing to cry over now. I pressed my forehead against the cold glass wall and again compelled myself not to move.

The passengers were already arriving, light, quick Western businessmen with bright suitcases, hurrying to their homes or hotels or offices. Slender gentlemen with good color in their faces and smiles for everyone. I continued not to move, looking steadily at the end of the long corridor behind the wall.

Suddenly my heart missed a beat. I saw something dark growing slowly in the far end of the corridor. It looked like a frightful crowd slowly approaching. "Refugees," flashed across my mind. Women in terrible Soviet hats with big black bags, men in dark, long, thick cloth coats with gray flabby faces. Chil-

dren holding their parents by the hands and no less frightened.
They were walking indecisively as though they were afraid the
floor would collapse under their feet. Little Russian Jews who
raised their hands in a great struggle and were frightened at the
victory they had achieved. Their first free steps were shy. They
did not know how to feel happy and they all looked sad. The two
men led them as carefully as a group of invalids or sick children.

I looked for Yossi in the crowd, but could not find him. At
last when the crowd came nearer, I saw someone trying to walk
more quickly but still afraid to pass ahead of the Jewish Agency
officials. I felt that it was he. They came nearer and nearer. Now
I could see him well. His appearance made me feel sick. Thin,
pale, long arms hanging helplessly out of that awful old gray
raincoat which was too tight for him. He had had his hair cut,
probably just before leaving, and his head seemed too big and
bony on his long neck. I felt ashamed of my own appearance.

He was looking for me with eyes like a helpless child, afraid
he would not find me. Once his look passed over me, but he did
not recognize me. I took off my stupid hat and then he saw me. A
shy, somewhat guilty smile appeared on his face. I felt the corners of my lips trembling and forced a smile.

We stood on either side of the glass wall and our eyes did
not know what to say. I showed him how to go to the door in the
wall. He went, but stopped in hesitation. Still a Soviet man,
afraid to violate discipline and order, to leave his group. I indicated to him that it was all right, but he did not know what to do.
The door was closed. How could he know that he had only to
step on that black rubber spot and it would open by itself? I
beckoned him and he took the step. The door opened and I ran
to him. The only thing I could do was put my head on his chest
and hide from him and myself. He kissed me on my head. We
were both afraid of each other. "It is all over," he said. "We shall
have to begin everything from the very beginning." I remembered that I had written that in one of my letters from America.
And it was so.

"Where are your suitcases?"

"Here they are." I saw three new small suitcases.

"What is there inside?"

"Your big pillow and a blanket from Aunt Musja in one, some plates and dishes in the second, and my clothes in the third."

"It is good that you brought a pillow. And I have eight pieces of luggage with me from America."

"Oho!"

"They are all presents from your cousins for us. They are so sweet. I'll tell you a lot about them. You know," I added happily, "I've lost my ticket to Tel Aviv."

"Really?" he answered no less happily. "You're still the same."

"Yes, I am quite the same."

The group was already leaving the terminal to board a bus to the Schoenau Transit Center of the Jewish Agency. "Let's go," I said. "I have a room for both of us in a hotel in the city, but first we'll go there to Schoenau to register you." I was explaining as I put on my hat and red midi-coat.

"What an elegant wife I have!"

We settled down in the bus. The Jews had already recovered and began to talk loudly, telling their usual jokes. The large, smoothly moving bus passed through the streets of Vienna, the clean small houses of the suburbs with their picturesque shops. All this—shop windows full of goods, signboards, clean streets, old people riding bicycles, the smells, colors, sounds—spoke of freedom and blessed capitalism.

Yossi leaned back with relief. "At last the Middle Ages are behind." He was very quiet. I didn't take my eyes off his face, watching his every reaction to that great event of exodus, expecting some unusual words from him.

"Why are you looking at me in such a manner?"

"I want to know what you feel, what you think. You must say something important."

"All right. I shall say—I love you."

✻   ✻   ✻

Hemda-leh! Wake up, dear. My little sleepyhead. It's time for your milk. Nu, open your eyes. Yes, yes, stretch yorself. Fine! Now, did you sleep well? Aren't you hungry? I see you are, but let me change you first. Now, here is your milk. Oho! You are really hungry. Don't hurry, your bottle isn't going to run away.

Be a good girl today. Your grandfather Ezra is coming to visit you tonight. And he is a rare guest. There are so many Jews still in the Soviet Union, so he has a lot of work again. So let him see you as a good, quiet girl. And in two weeks we shall go to visit your great-grandmother. She will be ninety-one then, and you must give her a good wide smile. Please, try to. You are always so serious.

Myra writes that your little cousin Ilana was smiling in the hospital, and you are already three months old and smile so rarely. Papa will come soon. Will you give him a smile? He has his Hebrew classes now on Mt. Scopus, so he won't be very late. It is not far from here. He will come in and say: "Where is my Lapa?" He calls you La-pa, a paw, or Laponka, a little paw. I call you Boosja. What does that mean? Nothing. Just Boosja or Boosenka, little Boosja. Our neighbors say that in Arabic it means "a kiss." So in Arabic you are a kiss. I have nothing against that.

But when you grow and are asked, "What is your name?" you will say, "Hemda." You will know how to pronounce it. For us it is so difficult. So we call you many other names. But we shall learn: "Hem-dah, Hem-dah." It sounds very beautiful when sabras (those born in Israel) pronounce it. That's why we called you Hemda. It is wonderful that now we are three. Life seems wonderful. It probably has some great sense. Do you know what it is?

Hemda, what have you done? Shame on you! Why do you always do it when you eat? I shall have to change you again. Now you are smiling. You feel good now? All right, then I forgive you. Finish your milk. Don't want it? Well, you've had quite enough. And now your bubble, please. I shall pat you on the back. Fine! God bless you! Now back to your bed, Boosenka. No, no, please don't cry. Here's your beautiful rattle. I shall come back soon. I shall go and finish my book now, and then I shall come back and play with you. O.K.? In fact, I have only to put a full stop and write—

THE END.

Afterword:
The Samizdat
BY
Ezra Rusinek

When does a Russian Jew learn for the first time that he is a Jew? Usually at school or even in kindergarten when he has been called by somebody with hatred or without it "Yid" or "Yidovka." Then he runs home crying, "Mama, I don't want to be a Jew!" And what does he hear from his parents? "Don't pay any attention." Can a small child understand? Never. But from that time on he does understand that his national origin is something shameful.

In 1955 we lived in deep Russia in the town of Taganrog after having escaped from exile. Sarah, our old friend from Riga, came to visit us.

"I have a book for you to read from Yasha. Read it quickly."

Yasha was a friend of my youth, a true Zionist, who had barely escaped prosecution but managed to live on in Riga under a constant threat.

To read quickly meant to read it in one night. The book was the articles and speeches of Jabotinsky, published in 1912. The first article was an address to Jewish teachers; in it Jabotinsky defines their task as bringing up Jewish youth in such a way that a downtrodden Srulik can become a proud Israel, that not a single Jewish boy or girl should be ashamed of his or her origin.

And this was said fifty years ago!

That made me remember a talk with a friend ten years previously in Siberia, when we were in exile. We were both fathers of children five or six years old. How should we bring them up?

He insisted, "When my son is sixteen, I shall tell him that he is a son of the Jewish people, that he has his motherland in Palestine. I'll explain to him who Herzl was, and Trumpeldor, Bar Kochba, and the Maccabees. But until then he should not be traumatized."

"You'll be too late," I answered him. "Your son won't understand you. We must begin now or we shall lose our children."

It seems to me that I was right.

That pamphlet of Jabotinsky was the beginning of *Samizdat* —self-publishing—in our family, though the Jewish spirit had always existed there. Quietly and cautiously we celebrated all Jewish holidays. Little silver stars of David were favorite precious things for our children. The words "shabbas," "bar-mitzvah," and "talis" were familiar to them. But Samizdat had to put into their minds and hearts something now and more important.

My daughter, Ilana, copied the text of the pamphlet and became interested. The manuscript was passed from one person to another among the few Jewish families in Taganrog. Some of them returned the pamphlet in an hour or two; others read and reread it several times and then came for a talk. And how long were those talks! There were a lot of things to discuss in those years: the Sinai campaign of 1956, the Youth Festival in Moscow in 1957 and the Israeli delegation which took part in it, and, of course, rare broadcasts in Russian and in Yiddish by "Kol Israel."

And again Yasha sent a book to read. This time it was *Exodus* by Leon Uris in German translation. And again—sleepless nights. What an explosive! But why don't they have this book in Russian? Why do they have it in English, German, Hebrew, French, and God knows what other languages, but no one has thought of publishing it in Russian for us here?

1963. We were able to move back at last to Riga. After settling down we immediately plunged into a Jewish atmosphere and became acquainted with the families that wanted to emigrate to Israel. Soon after that Yasha, my old dear friend, got permission to leave for Israel. Before this departure he begged that *Exodus* be translated into Russian and typed. "Do whatever you can," he said, and with these words he handed me the beginning of his translation.

But the book was so long. To abridge it would be to lose a great deal of the impact. What could be done? To whom could I speak? Who would translate? From what language? Where should we get a typewriter? Who would type?

One thing was clear: we must hurry. But equally clear was something else. If the KGB learned about it, prison awaited those who would be caught. Even if I could find someone among my acquaintances who could translate, he might become frightened or even report me to the KGB. And if someone did agree to do it, how could we pay for his work? My own salary was just enough to make ends meet. How could we buy a typewriter in a shop? The KGB registers all typewriters in shops as well as in offices and repair shops. There seemed no answers to all the questions. But we decided to try.

Cautiously, step by step, we looked for someone who might help. Finally we found a typewriter that had always been privately owned. The owner had left for Israel. I took the typewriter, changed the type a little, lubricated it, and headed for Sarah. "No one can do it but you. You also promised Yasha you'd do something. You can type, even if only with two fingers. Okay? Get on with it."

We asked Boris, one of our old Riga acquaintances, an expert in the history of Israel, a man with several languages at his fingertips, to translate the book. We didn't have to ask him twice.

And Sarah, after a long working day—living in one room with two daughters—typed evening after evening, two pages in two hours. The typewriter stood on a blanket to lessen the noise, so that neighbors passing her door would not hear her. Sarah chain-smoked and cursed indecently every time she heard a ring at her door. An acquaintance had dropped in for a chat and a cup of tea—these good-for-nothing people. Immediately the typewriter and the typed pages were covered with the blanket.

And what a typewriter it was! All my life I shall remember it. There was an "e" that would constantly stick, and after "n" the carriage would move twice. It was an ordeal, but what could we do? We didn't have our own typewriter repairman and taking it to a shop would be dangerous. There was nothing to do but bear it.

Every week the diligent Boris would call Sarah, "Come for a cup of tea, Sarochka," which meant that the next portion of the translation was ready.

Then there were problems with the paper. What kind should we use? If we used thin paper, we could make eight copies, if we used thick, only five copies. We decided "better fewer but better." These books would have to live and work among Soviet Jews for years, so the paper had to be good and thick. But good paper is not always in the stores and if we bought more than two packages at one time it would seem strange. So we waited for the paper to appear in the shops and then bought two packages in each of the shops, being careful that no acquaintances see us doing it.

The most difficult problem was with carbon paper. Soviet carbon paper is not good. The fifth copy is hardly readable. And good Polish carbon paper is on the market only once in an eternity. When it appeared, we declared a celebration, for the acquisition of a package of it meant that work could continue.

As each page was typed, the carbon paper was burned and the pages were taken to "the refrigerator," an incurious and true friend. And then I would be able to go home with a feeling of deep satisfaction at having done something useful that day.

Sometimes I committed the crime of stealing "state property" at my place of work. I took several sheets of carbon paper. But I did not feel guilty. The law that prohibits my people from learning their own language and history made this "crime" necessary. Nor were we concerned that we had violated Leon Uris's copyright by translating his work without his permission. We were sure he would not be bothered by it.

It took a whole exhausting year to translate and type the six hundred pages of the book. How many days of rest, movies, or theater performances were missed. Sarah sat at her work every evening and didn't leave the typewriter until two pages were ready. It was really the work of a "chalutz," a pioneer. Jabotinsky quotes Trumpeldor's explanation of the meaning of "chaltutz": "Ground must be dug? I dig. To shoot, to be a soldier? I go. Police? Doctors? Lawyers? Teachers? Water-carriers? Here you are, I do everything."

What a triumphant moment it was when on the last page Sarah could type "The End" in big letters. A great burden had been taken off our minds. The promise which we had given to Yasha and whose fulfillment had become our obligation toward the growing generation of proud Soviet Jews had been fulfilled.

But there were still problems. How should we bind our books? Giving them to a binding shop was out of the question. Again a friend helped. This time it was our pet crank; Tsipa. Few people knew his full name and it was hardly necessary. This middle-aged short man with the heart of a school-boy and the mind of a sage brought fun and laughter into every house. His asymmetrical eyes, like those of a kind Mephistopheles, twinkled with an always appropriate joke. But behind all this, his friends knew a devoted, selfless comrade who was to play an important role in the work.

This time Tsipa answered in his usual manner: "For a bottle of vodka? Okay." I promised to provide the bottle, and in a week the books were ready.

But the problems were not yet finished. Should the books remain in Riga or be sent to Russia? Who should read them first, young people or adults? How could we make certain that the KGB didn't find the books? And on and on.

After long discussions it was decided to keep two copies in Riga and to send the other three to true friends in Russia. The books should first of all be given to young people for reading. After each person read one, it had to be returned to the hands of the giver; there must be no passing from hand to hand. Every book must be kept under control.

A month passed. We were deluged by pleas from those who wanted to read the books. People came and begged: "For God's sake, put me on the list. My children must read it." Once in talking to a tourist from Israel I learned that many young tourists from the U.S.A. had begun to arrive in Israel and when they were asked why they chose to visit Israel rather than France, Italy, Spain, they answered that they had read *Exodus* by Uris.

But can this be compared with the book's effect on the Soviet Jews? The influence of *Exodus* on the national rebirth of Jewish youth in the Soviet Union can hardly be overestimated. May God give many years of happiness to Leon Uris!

The diligent Boris had received for his work a precious present—a book on the War of Liberation in 1948, and Sarah—a cigarette lighter which played incorrectly the melody of Hatikvah, the Israeli anthem. She was very proud of this little thing until the musical mechanism ceased to work.

The main thing was that nobody in the city knew who had made the books. The book began its life and successful work among hundreds of people, but the few who knew about its source never mentioned it, and it remained a secret for years.

One day suddenly Tsipa ran in very excited: "Congratulations! We are not alone! I have just seen an abridged *Exodus* in Russian—one hundred fifty pages." It had been made by another group. We were hiding from them and they from us. "Well," I said then, happy and proud. "Let them be fruitful and multiply."

                    *   *   *

One thing must be understood. This is a story of one little group in Riga, their rebirth and the beginning of their Samizdat. But there were scores of such small groups and individuals who were seeking their own ways, found them, and also began to be active. Some of them began earlier, some later. In different parts of the huge Soviet Empire Jewish eyes began to open, Jewish hearts began to beat. Only several years later were we to learn that in 1957, forgetting their fears, Jews in Moscow came in contact with the Israeli delegation to the Youth Festival.

The Sinai War and the Festival lit a tiny fire which was to flame into this big movement for liberation. The Festival brought to Moscow the children of those whom we had seen off to Palestine in the thirties. These youths came, and their Jewish brothers and sisters in Russia met them, youths whose parents could not leave for Palestine on time and had gone through Hitler's and Stalin's concentration camps. The Soviet Jews could not forget the young Israelis—their suntanned faces, their happy smiles, the songs and dances of a free people.

In 1958 small crowds of not more than two hundred people for the first time gathered in front of the Moscow synagogue to celebrate the holiday of Simhat Torah. In a few years this small crowd had turned into a sea of people, many thousands, a phenomenon that sends waves of emotion throughout the Jewish world now and rivets its attention to this small street in Moscow every year.

Who knows what has been going on in other cities: Vilna, Leningrad, Kiev, Odessa, Sverdlovsk. Their stories will also be told sometime. Gathered all together they will add one more page to the heroic history of our people. I am a bad teller of tales. This story deserves beautiful words, songs of praise and honor; it deserves its own Leon Uris.

Why is Jewish Samizdat necessary in Russia? Is it worth running such a risk? Aren't talks and "Kol Israel" broadcasts enough? Isn't the awkward Soviet anti-Israel and anti-Zionist propaganda enough in itself to arouse national self-consciousness in Russian Jews? What is the purpose of this Samizdat? Is it directed against the present social order in the country?

I think Jewish Samizdat is necessary so long as Soviet Jews are deprived of objective information about Israel and about their own past and present. The most important task of Samizdat until 1970 was to create a reserve of Jews interested in Israel and ready to come to it—in other words, the task of all Zionism.

One might ask the question: Weren't there in Riga and Vilna many people who were already potential emigrants? Yes, there were—several families—but the majority was completely ignorant about Jewish affairs. The younger generation was almost completely assimilated, dying in the national sense. Except for a narrow circle of intelligentsia in Moscow and Leningrad, the whole of Jewish Russia was sleeping. And in the Ukraine the Jews didn't even dare to dream about Israel. If asked about it, they waved their hands in fear and looked around to see who was watching.

No, talk alone couldn't help in this situation. Only written information could be decisive. Let's say a Jew read "Israel in Figures"; or Jabotinsky's 1910 pamphlet prophecying that the socialist revolution in Russia will not solve the Jewish problem; or the book about the Sinai campaign by Ben Gurion; or the book by Yaroslav Mniachko, *Aggressors**—and all this in Russian. The books would certainly inspire deep and long thinking, an inner struggle. Fifty years of Soviet power have played a role in the formation of the reader's mind. But the truth that falls like a seed into fertile soil wins out.

It was neither the fine words of talkers or tricks of adventurers that resulted in the explosion of 1970–71 but rather the systematic and tedious everyday labor of creating Samizdat. The notorious press conference of prominent Soviet Jews in the spring of 1970, aimed at intimidating Jews, opened the way to a huge force that had been hidden in Soviet Jewry and grew into a frightening and authoritative power. No tricks or blows of the KGB could stop it.

Jewish Samizdat is not directed against the existing social order. It is neither concerned with undermining Soviet power nor weakening it. Our interests are in Israel alone.

✻   ✻   ✻

1966. Tireless Boris succeeded in getting issues of the Israeli communist newspaper *Kol Ha'Am* and translated several articles from them. Fine! The communist paper—anti-Zionist, pro-Soviet, denying the wishes of Soviet Jews to leave for Israel, but the only Israeli paper that is allowed to come by mail to the Soviet Union—proved very useful. They published many articles about the economy and the policy of Israel. You just had to read between the lines and look for the necessary information behind them. In that way every month we could make a very interesting press bulletin of ten or fifteen pages. At first this was passed from hand to hand in written form, but we soon managed to type two bulletins. Of course, the news was at least a month late, but that did not matter if we had so many real facts from Israel. A closed,

---

* A book about Israel by the Slovak Communist writer Yaroslav Mniachko, in which the author condemns the Soviet and Czechoslovak attitude toward the Israel-Arab conflict.

strictly defined and not very large circle of readers was created. The bulletin was passed among those readers in a fixed order. It was our first periodical.

And for this I would like to express my gratitude to the Communist Party of Israel.

               ❊   ❊   ❊

Many times we got hints of other people who thought and probably already acted as we did. In 1962 Yasha had composed an anonymous "Letter to Brezhnev" in which he protested against the policy of forced assimilation of Jews in Latvia after World War II. "The Letter" was passed among friends in a manuscript of twelve pages. A year later it returned to Yasha as fifty pages. Some people had put in their notes on the same problem. These people were certainly going to meet each other one day.

May 1967. The atmosphere among Jews was growing tense; people were constantly talking about Nasser, the Canal, Eshkol, Dayan, Soviet policy, what the U.S. will say, what De Gaulle will do. Nervousness, fear—yet at the same time a deep confidence that Israel will stand. But who could even dream about the victory in six days? Jews lived next to their radios those days, dying for the news from Israel, the United States, Great Britain, Switzerland. Nothing was missed—neither the night discussions in the Security Council, nor the General Assembly news. There was no time to sleep.

But an exact systematic account of the events couldn't reach us. Israeli tourists stopped coming and with them we lost our only source of information. Then suddenly our Jewish luck helped us. A Jewish couple from Riga stayed in a hotel in Kiev in a room which had been previously occupied by tourists from France and on the table were two issues of *L'Express*, with a detailed description of the actions in the Middle East. The maid who had brought them up to the room became very confused. According to instructions she was supposed to take to the office every piece of printed information that foreigners left in their rooms. God forbid that Soviet citizens should read something from abroad! But a tip of ten roubles did its bit, and in a week the magazines were in Riga. Boris got to work immediately, and

Sarah, having opened her "monster," didn't get up until ten copies of the translation were ready.

But what were these ten copies for the whole of Riga, where everyone was now dying for a bit of information, where Jews who had not so long ago been indifferent to Israel now demanded news about it. This time Sarochka didn't have to overwork. Tens of former readers turned into typists or photographers, and scores of new copies spread through the city. So the Jews of Riga, and not only of Riga, learned the truth about the events before, during, and after the Six-Day War.

After that there was no stopping it. Translations from other foreign sources appeared like mushrooms after rain. People looked for them and found them. One day we even came into possession of a secret report of the Central Committee of the Communist Party which gave rather an objective account of the situation and a not very flattering characterization of Nasser. There was nothing mysterious in this. There just happened to be a good Jew in the information service of the Central Committee, and the Six-Day War meant something for him also.

It is difficult to describe how Jewish backs had straightened after the War. Exit visas had not yet been given, diplomatic relations with Israel had been broken off, but Jews were in high spirits. They began to hope. And the more anti-Israel articles appeared in the Soviet press, the surer we were that Israel and we were right.

There was no time for idleness. The work had to be continued. Young people had so many questions that had to be answered. And the main issue was—the War. And again we had luck. Someone brought from Moscow a picture book on the Six-Day War by General S. L. A. Marshall, which had been acquired from foreign tourists. Work began immediately. Photography is a typical Jewish profession in Russia, so we had only to look for a courageous photographer. Translation was not a problem. And soon a detailed description of the action with masses of illustrations passed from hand to hand. But this was still not enough. Time passed and the situation in the Middle East was still tense and eventful, but information still didn't come.

One day I was looking through a daily newspaper and came across an article condemning those young people who engaged in buying clothes from foreigners—socks, ties, shirts, and all such goods and chattels. There is a whole stratum of youth in the Soviet Union "seeking an easy life," according to the Soviet press. They buy goods from foreigners and then sell them to Soviet citizens for a great deal of money, making fortunes in this way. Well, God judge them, but for us it brought a new idea. We were not interested in all their trash, but perhaps they could buy for us foreign magazines in English, German, French?

One of our boys was sent to make contact and, certainly, they were ready to do anything for money. So after a time we received *Time, Life, Stern, Spiegel,* and the like. And there was always something about Israel in every issue—and every line was translated and typed.

September 1, 1968. The Jews in Riga are terribly excited. The Ministry of Interior has suddenly recommenced accepting documents and applications for exit visas. Hundreds of people rushed to post offices to send telegrams to Israeli relatives asking for immediate invitations. Not everyone knew how to compose these telegrams, but the post office girl—a Latvian—helped everyone: "Write such-and-such. I have already sent a hundred of them today."

But the joy was premature. After only a few months, the gates were closed again. But for all that the authorities had managed to create large gaps in the ranks. Most of the activists for Samizdat had left for Israel. At the same time the materials they had published had already become dated. Yet the interest of Jews, as well as the number of interested Jews, grew in geometric progression. The youth demanded information.

Therefore it became necessary that different groups existing in different cities should come together and unite their efforts in Samizdat work. The first meeting was held in Moscow, on the sixteenth of August. People from Moscow, Leningrad, Riga, Kiev, Tbilisi, Kharkov, Orel attended. There were hours of discussion in an apartment, a park, in the street, arguments and decisions, and the main principles of future activities were de-

262   *ALLA RUSINEK*

fined: unity, co-ordination, and co-operation in Samizdat work; exchange of all items both new and old; mutual help in the means of publishing. The idea of publishing a periodical collection of works was also discussed. This has been done under the name of "Iton."* There was also a discussion about exchanging information about emigration and the signing of collective letters.

The meeting proved very fruitful, and other meetings were later held in Riga and Leningrad. Delegates informed each other of activities in their cities and discussed their plans. At the Riga meeting it was decided to fix definite telephone numbers and addresses for contacts between different cities. For this purpose the names of the towns were put into codes: Riga became Roman, Moscow, Misha, Leningrad, Lyonia. The same meeting decided also on the creation of the editorial board for publishing "Iton."

We in Riga, in our turn, gathered and discussed local activities. Until that time every group had worked separately; now united activities began in full swing. Almost all of us agreed with the opinion expressed by the majority of the participants in the Moscow meeting that we should refrain from forming an organization. The Soviet Criminal Code has a special statute about participation in an anti-Soviet organization, and any kind of an organization can easily be labelled anti-Soviet. An organization would not have helped us in any way, but would have helped the KGB watch us. We could organize our work by just defining our main tasks. Those who took part in the activities were divided into two groups for the sake of more effective work. One group took part in an active open struggle, such as signing collective letters to the Government and to be sent abroad and demanding the right to leave for Israel. This group was usually called "Alef." The second group, "Beth," was engaged in preparing, duplicating, and distributing the materials of Samizdat.

The Moscow meeting had also discussed the problem of collective letters demanding the right to leave the country. We in Riga, in the summer of 1969, agreed that the time was not yet

* The Hebrew word for "newspaper."

ripe to come out with such petitions. Georgian Jews were the first to begin this heroic campaign in August 1969. With their "Letter of 18" addressed to the U.N. Committee for Human Rights.

A list of subjects about which information was needed was compiled and divided according to degree of importance. Then the information was typed, one subject after another. A number of old typewriters were acquired especially for Samizdat. But what monsters they were! Old-fashioned, terribly heavy. One of them weighed more than thirty kilograms and taking it from one house to another was an ordeal. Only one man was strong enough to do it. He walked with that monster on his back, sweating and stopping every twenty meters.

All the typewriters had to be coded. Could we say over the telephone "Bring me the Mercedes?" So this typewriter was christened "Crocodile." I wonder what the KGB thought listening to our telephone conversations about a crocodile. But the fact is that during the catastrophe of June 1970 and in later searches they didn't find the "Crocodile."

Every apartment where the materials were typed was thoroughly checked from the point of view of the neighbors: the noise of the typewriter could always betray us. The problem of typists was also a difficult one. Professional typists could work very quickly, but had little time for Samizdat. They had to earn their living. More than that they would never be willing to type on such typewriters as "Crocodile." But there were girls who could type with one or two fingers who agreed to work in any place and on any typewriter. Special attention was paid to secrecy. It was decided that each of us must know only his own typist and take the work to and from her only by himself.

In spite of numerous problems and obstacles, Samizdat materials came and went in a flood. Everyone had his own circle of readers among whom he worked. But it should be pointed out that we always thought it most important to send literature to Russia, to Jews who hadn't had it for fifty-two years, not just for twenty-five years like us Jews of Latvia. For this purpose young people would suddenly become very affectionate toward their relatives in other cities and would want to visit them. These trips were extremely dangerous and the boys and girls would spend sleepless nights on trains, keeping their eyes on their valises containing the literature. In return we received paper, carbon, tape, photo-paper, and so on.

While the means of copying and distributing material could be arranged and even planned, getting it still depended on luck. The appearance of that famous book by Mniachko, *Aggressors*, the typed translation of which is now so popular among the Jews, is a typical case of chance. A sick Jew went to a Latvian professor of medicine who had just returned from a business trip abroad. During the consultation the visitor noticed a book on a shelf with the name of Mniachko on it. He had already heard about this honest man and the book on the shelf remained in his mind after he left the professor's house. Two days later another sick Jew came to the professor for a consultation. This visitor was very strange. He couldn't really explain his illness, asked many stupid questions, and didn't leave until the professor finally left the room for something. When he returned, the visitor decided to go and did so in haste.

I don't know when the professor noticed the loss, but the same evening we middle-aged, reliable people, thieves by necessity, were standing bewitched around a table. The *Aggressors* itself had come into our hands.

Circles for studying Hebrew had existed in Riga for many years but had been of an individual character. In 1969 they began to be organized and by 1970 a whole network of these groups existed in the city. But the shortage of books prevented people from intensive studying. There were only a few copies of the primer *Elef Milim* (one thousand words) in the city, and teachers had to use old newspapers, calendars, and the Bible for lessons. Either new books had to be obtained or copies made. But then our inter-city ties helped. Our Moscow friends informed us that they had managed to make a large number of copies of *Elef Milim*, and we soon received two suitcases of wonderfully photographed copies of the book. I still remember the day those two suitcases arrived in Riga.

One of our young men, Moshe, a very quiet and effective worker, had gone to receive these books in Moscow and I was to meet him next day at the railway station to pick up the suitcases. They certainly were going to be heavy and I took along a friend, Tsvi, to help me. By the time the train was due to arrive, we were at the station. I decided to stay at the square in front of the terminal in order to be able to pick up a taxi the moment Moshe came out. The line for taxis was always terribly long and it was rather inexpedient to stand there for a long time. Tsvi went to meet Moshe at the train. A half hour passed, the train had arrived, and people came out of the terminal; then the crowd dispersed. But neither of them appeared. Ten minutes later Tsvi appeared in the door of the terminal, alone. "He didn't come by this train," he said. The next train from Moscow was due to arrive in an hour. We waited, but Moshe didn't arrive then either. There was nothing to be done and with sinking hearts we left. Had he been caught on the way, or earlier in Moscow? What else could have delayed him?

With these torturing thoughts in my head I went to a meeting that was being held in Rumbula in memory of thousands of Latvian Jews executed in this Riga suburb in 1941. I was standing in the crowd near the mass graves and heard neither the speeches nor the Kaddish. Suddenly something made me turn around and I looked into Moshe's eyes. He was standing behind me, staring at me quietly. Maybe his steady look had made me turn around.

"What happened?" I asked in a low voice, not looking at him.

"Nothing. Everything is all right." I heard his low voice behind me.

"Did you bring them?"

"Yes."

"Why didn't we meet you in the terminal?"

"I didn't see you."

"But Tsvi was there."

"Yes, I saw him. But you told me you would meet me, so I didn't go up to him. The suitcases are at my place."

I understood my mistake, and at the same time I could hardly contain the emotions I felt—joy and pride. So our young people taught us how to be exact in our dangerous activities and self-contained and cool in unexpected situations.

❈   ❈   ❈

After we had acquired the textbooks, we began to seek among older Jews those who knew Hebrew and were ready to run the risk of teaching a group. The groups were formed of people of approximately the same age, knowledge, and activity. The places where the lessons were to be given were also thoroughly checked. It was necessary that the neighbors not be too curious. All these arrangements took much time and effort, but we had enough purpose and energy because we could see the results. Masses of new young people joined in the groups studying Hebrew. The interest in Israel grew and grew, and the youth began to get together in parties, learn Israeli songs, listen to records, show each other Israeli souvenirs; and they talked and talked.

❈   ❈   ❈

And the tireless Boris was full of ideas. In 1969 he worked out and put into wide practice a wonderful thing. One of our strongest means of propaganda was Israeli picture post cards. Boris had a big collection of such postcards which was rapidly growing and which he arranged in geographical order. The post cards were photographed on slides and Boris began a series of public shows. Since he was an expert on Israeli geography and history he accompanied the shows by lectures on different themes: Jerusalem, Tel-Aviv, the Galilee, the kibbutzim, archeological excavations, agriculture in Israel, and so on.

The shows proved so successful that the idea was adopted by other cities also. Boris had to start a course for lecturers. And soon tens of shows were being held in Riga, Moscow, Leningrad. Silent, bewitched people sat in dark rooms, listening to the excited voice of their lecturer, not taking their eyes off the screen. Their hearts and minds were not in those dark rooms, but far away in the country of their dreams. Looking then at their faces

I saw that those young people were proud of belonging to their people. This meant that our task was fulfilled.

✿   ✿   ✿

Of course, my story can be continued. It is certainly not finished. But let others continue it some day. Let them add to it their own stories.

2

THE ROOTS OF THE NEW SOVIET EMPIRE

ON JANUARY 7, 1946, James Forrestal, then Secretary of the Navy, wrote a letter to Walter Lippmann in which he proposed a study 'on (1) the nature of the Russian state philosophy, both in terms of historical and dialectical materialism; (2) whether the long-term Lenin-Marxian objectives still hold; and (3) the possibility of accommodation between the democratic and communistic systems'. He commented: 'There is no place in government where such a study has been made—at least I have been unable to find one—and it seemed to me important that it be made as objectively and coldly as possible, because to me the fundamental question in respect to our relations with Russia is whether we are dealing with a nation or a religion.'[1]

It had become urgent, in Forrestal's opinion, to find an answer to this question because, in the eight months that had passed since the end of the war against Germany (and the five months since the end of the war against Japan), the international behaviour of the Soviet Union had been quite contrary to the optimistic anticipations entertained by President Roosevelt. In his editing of Forrestal's diaries, Walter Millis records that, on November 26, 1945, 'Forrestal entered in his diary a summary, compiled by an assistant, of State Department dispatches on Russian policy as they were coming in from all over the world. Everywhere, from Western Europe to Korea, they drew an unrelieved picture of Soviet high-handedness, unilateral action and aggressive pressure.'[2]

What was most alarming and bewildering in Soviet post-war behaviour was not so much the hostility and truculence displayed by Soviet officials at various levels on a number of disputed issues as the now manifest policy of using military occupation to support local Communists in territories over-run by Russian troops during the war. This was a cause of surprise to the majority of leading politicians and political commentators in the West, who had convinced themselves that Russia had given up trying to spread Communism by force. Had not Stalin been the advocate of 'socialism in one country', as against Trotsky's zeal for world revolution? Had he not formally dissolved the Comintern, the Soviet-led international organisation whose existence had always been an obstacle to normal relations between the Soviet Union and capitalist states? Yet, by the end of 1945, Soviet military backing had put Communist parties in supreme, if not exclusive, power in Poland, Rumania, Bulgaria and Hungary. These actions necessarily raised the question whether Russia was for some reason reverting to earlier practice or whether the purpose had been constant all the time and the gestures of conciliation intended merely to lull and mislead.

For Churchill, and those like him who thought of European affairs primarily in terms of an international balance of power, it made comparatively little difference whether Russia was ideologically devoted to spreading revolution or not. The fact that Churchill's own sympathies were strongly anti-Communist may have increased his desire to prevent a permanent Russian grip on Eastern and Central Europe, but this desire would have been almost as strong if Russia had been still ruled by a Tsar. Indeed, a situation similar to that of 1945 might have arisen after the First World War, if Germany had been defeated in 1916 while the Tsarist armies were still in the field and Russian power had reached far into Central Europe. It would then certainly have been British policy to restrict such a Russian expansion even if unaccompanied by an international revolutionary doctrine. But in 1945, most liberal-minded people in Britain and the United States did not see international affairs in terms of a balance of power; they simply divided nations into those that were aggressive and those that were peace-loving. Russia had been classified as peace-loving; therefore there was nothing to be feared from Russia, however powerful it might become. Hence the shock of the discovery in the months after the war (though even then there were still many people who gave the Kremlin the benefit of the doubt) that the Russians were trying to destroy the independence of several European nations by subjecting them to Communist dictatorships dependent on Russian support, and were even beginning to work in the same manner in their occupation zone of Germany.

It was, however, open to question whether Russia was installing Communist governments in nominally sovereign East European countries as a means to imperial domination, or whether its national aims were being subordinated to the purpose of extending proletarian socialist revolution wherever possible. In the words of Forrestal's letter already quoted, was the West, in regard to Russia, dealing with a nation or a religion? The form of the question implied a disjunction or even an incompatibility between the two. In fact, to this question the true answer was 'Both'. It may still be worth while to estimate the relative importance of Russian national sentiment and Marxist-Leninist ideology in the outlook of Russia's rulers; but in 1945, the two were fused. Marxism had been transformed, by amalgamation with Russian nationalism, into something that would have been unrecognisable to Marx and deplorable even to Lenin, while Russian patriotic feeling had been changed by the injection of the Communist revolutionary faith into a sense of predestined world leadership to which other nations should yield. This development had occurred the more easily in Russia since the Bolshevik Revolution because in pre-Soviet times Russian nationalism had already acquired messianic overtones, different indeed from those of Marxism, but preparing the consciousness of the Russian people for a 'politique de grandeur'.

In 1838 Michael Pogodin, a professor of history in the University of Moscow, composed for the perusal of the heir to the throne of the Tsars, the future Alexander II, a *Letter on Russian History*, in which he expounded his idea of Russia's national destiny:

> Russia—what a wonderful phenomenon on the world stage! . . . A population of 60 millions, aside from those who have not been counted, a population which increases by a million every year and will soon amount to 100 million. Let us add to this multitude 30 million more of our brothers and cousins, the Slavs. . . . We may subtract their number from Austria and Turkey and the rest of Europe and add it to our own. . . . Who can compare with us? Whom will we not force into submission? . . . It is known that our present Emperor [Nicholas I] does not think of any conquest, but I dare not fail to remark as a historian that the Russian ruler now, without any such intention, is nearer to the universal monarchy than Charles V and Napoleon ever were in their dreams.[3]

Such visions of the future were widespread early in the nineteenth century among the group of Russian writers who came to be known as Slavophiles. This trend of thought arose in response to the special cultural situation in which Russia was involved by its wholesale borrowing of institutions, customs, and ideas from Western Europe since the time of Peter the Great. The Petrine reforms had violently torn the Russians from their old traditions and sent them to school with the West. They had proved apt pupils and, in the eighteenth century, had made Russia one of the great powers of Europe, with an aristocracy— largely of German descent—which was European in its tastes and habits. But the West had not stood still; by the time Russia had learned to copy the France of the ancien régime, Western civilisation was moving forward into the age of the industrial revolution. Russians had again to go to school if they were not to be left behind. Those who were called Westerners accepted this situation; they wanted to make Russia more and more like Western Europe, and they were ready to agree that Russia's past, before the Petrine enlightenment, had been, as Chaadayev said, 'rien que néant'. They considered themselves patriotic Russians, but they felt no antagonism toward the nations of Western Europe and looked to them as sources of knowledge, wisdom and elegance for the edification of backward Russia.

For the Slavophiles, on the other hand, such an attitude was intolerably humiliating. They rebelled against the idea of the Russians as a people without a past, as clever pupils sitting at the feet of masters of superior civilisation. They could not deny that Western Europe had a lead in material and technical accomplishment, but they maintained that Russia had inherited a civilisation of its own far higher in quality than the West's. This was the heritage of the Orthodox Church, the true Christian faith, from which the Roman Catholic and Protestant religions were schismatic and heretical deviations—while the sceptical rationalism and secularism of the modern age in the West represented an even more fundamental infidelity. The Orthodox Christian faith, if taken seriously, separated the Russian nation from Western Europe but bound it by close ties of brotherhood to the other Orthodox peoples of Europe: the Greeks, the Serbs, the Bulgars and the Rumanians. This solidarity was also in part 'Slav': a word used ambiguously to denote both the family of Slav languages recognised by comparative philology and the ecclesiastical language, otherwise known as Church Slavonic, used by the Orthodox peoples other than the Greeks. In strict logic, the Slavophiles should have made up their minds whether to commit themselves to Pan-Slavism, excluding the Greeks and Rumanians, or to Pan-Orthodoxy, excluding the Poles, Czechs and Croats, who were traditionally Catholic and not Orthodox. But consistency was never the strong point of Slavophile thinking. In its vague but fervent romanticism, it combined the two bases of solidarity, so that the range of its fraternal feelings extended both southward to Athens and westward to Prague.

Many of the early Slavophiles were quite non-political; they were concerned only with religious revival, study of the folklore and folk literature of the Russians and other Slav peoples, glorification of pre-Petrine Russia (as against the Westerners' versions of Russian history), and ideological opposition to the inroads of Western influence in various spheres of Russian life. But, by the nature of its beliefs, the movement was bound to be drawn into politics. It was Russia's mission to liberate the Orthodox and the Slavs oppressed by Turkish or Austrian rule, and it would increase its own power by doing so. The project of a Russo-Greek empire went back to the time of Catherine the Great, the idea of Russia as the 'Third Rome' to the fifteenth century. The conception of Russia's imperial destiny as the heir of the Roman empire was most strikingly elaborated by the poet-diplomat Tyutchev. In his view, the rightful succession to the Roman imperial authority was located at Constantinople, the city Constantine founded to unite the universal empire and the universal church. The power established in Italy by the Papacy and the Western Empire of Charlemagne and the Ottos had been illegitimate creations, breaking the unity of the old church-empire. The shrunken Byzantine empire had preserved the Orthodox faith, but the Greeks had not been strong enough to resist the onslaught of the Turks, and Constantinople had become the capital of the infidel Ottoman. It was now Russia's historic mission to drive out the Turks, to take Constantinople (which would become, with Moscow and St Petersburg, the third capital of Russia), to join to itself the Slav peoples of Austria, to regulate the affairs of Germany and Italy (this was before the rise of Bismarck), and, by destroying the temporal power of the Papacy, to bring about the reunion of the Catholic and Orthodox communions.

Tyutchev in one of his poems indicated the territory of the future Russia as extending 'from the Neva to the Nile, from the Elbe to China, from the Volga to the Euphrates, and from the Danube to the Ganges'. Danilevksy, whose *Russia and Europe* was published in 1869, was rather more specific. In his ideal reconstruction of the political map of Europe, Russia would be the head of a confederacy of eight states comprising: Russia itself, including Poland; Bohemia and Slovakia; Hungary; Rumania; a kingdom of the Serbs, Croats and Slovenes; Bulgaria; Greece; and a territory embracing Constantinople, the Bosphorus and the Dardanelles.

To a reader in the 1960s, a century or so after Danilevsky wrote, his list of countries provokes comparison with the system of Communist-ruled satellite states organised by Stalin after the overthrow of Nazi Germany. Before the unity of the Soviet bloc was marred by the secession of Tito, the first six of the countries on Danilevsky's list were subject to supreme control from the Kremlin, with the addition of East Germany, which Danilevsky had left to an independent Prussia. His seventh and eighth units, Greece and north-western Turkey, were not included in Stalin's realm, but this had not been for the want of trying. It was the imminence of their subjection to his power which early in 1947 led the President of the United States to proclaim the Truman Doctrine for their protection.

The apocalyptic visions of the Slavophile and Pan-Slav* writers did not inspire any of the Tsars or their Foreign Ministers who directed Russian foreign policy between the Congress of Vienna in 1815 and the outbreak of the First World War in 1914. They and most of their high officials were Western in outlook; they accepted and valued Russia's position as a great power within an established European system, and felt themselves to belong to Europe. Conscious of the limitations of Russia's strength, they feared that aggressive policies would produce an anti-Russian coalition of other European powers. Nevertheless, and despite the formally autocratic power of the Tsar, Russia's leaders were susceptible in periods of international disturbance to pressure from quarters where the emotions stimulated by the Pan-Slav propaganda were strongly developed. It would be a mistake to assume that, because they never directly held political power, the Pan-Slavs can be regarded as mere cranks and visionaries whose writings may sometimes be of

---

* The term 'Slavophile' is generally used for the early, more literary, phase of the movement, and 'Pan-Slav' for the later, more directly political, development, but there is no clear line of division between the two.

interest as literature, but who did not affect the course of political history.

Although there could not be in Russia, at any rate before 1905, a public opinion in the sense which attaches to that term under a parliamentary régime, there were certainly national sentiments which the Tsardom could not ignore. Even under Nicholas I some account had to be taken of the inclinations of the nobility and higher clergy; while under Alexander II educated middle-class opinion, highly susceptible to nationalist agitation, became a factor of political significance. In 1828 Nicholas I, who had personally no predilection for the Greeks, went to war with Turkey on their behalf more in response to the passionate sympathies for their cause in Russian society than from calculations of state interest. The war brought Russia insignificant gains at great cost. Greece, once liberated, for geographical and economic reasons came more under British and French influence than Russian. Again, in 1853, Nicholas's conduct appears to have been determined more by the indignation of the Russian clergy at the success of France's intervention on behalf of the Catholics in the dispute over the custody of the Holy Places than by his concern over the issue itself. His original reluctance to embark on another war with Turkey was fully justified by the event for, in the Crimean War, confronted by the active belligerence of two of the great powers of Europe and the unfriendly neutrality of the other two, Russia suffered a military defeat on its own soil. Alexander II, with no stomach for yet another war with Turkey, was in 1877 pushed and prodded into it by an enraged public sentiment. At a later stage, this sentiment was to produce a plot for his deposition among army officers who regarded him as insufficiently devoted to the Slav cause. Thanks to a secret agreement with Austria over Bosnia, the outcome of the Russo-Turkish war was less adverse to Russia than the Crimean War had been two decades previously. Nevertheless, the Congress of Berlin in 1878 cut down Russia's gains under the Treaty of San Stephano, imposed on the defeated Turks, and left Russian patriots with a sense of frustration and failure.

In the great crisis of July 1914, when Sazonov, Russia's Foreign Minister, received news of the Austrian ultimatum to Serbia, he immediately decided that his country must go to the aid of the latter, and persuaded the Tsar to agree to this. Yet a few days later he told the Austrian ambassador that 'he had no feelings for the Balkan Slavs; they were actually a heavy burden on Russia and we [the Austrians] could hardly imagine how much trouble they had already given Russia'.[4] Thus, even Sazonov appears to have been driven on by fear of the Pan-Slav press (which in 1908 had bitterly attacked his predecessor, Izvolsky, over the Buchlau negotiations leading to complete Austrian mastery of Bosnia and Herzegovina) to adopt a policy more extreme than he would have followed on a sober calculation of Russia's vital interests. After all, Russia had no treaty obligation to go to war on Serbia's behalf, nor was Serbian territory adjacent to its own. Nevertheless, after the Austro-Serbian conflict had grown into a European war and with Turkey ranged on the side of the Central Powers, Sazonov scored a diplomatic success that would have delighted the hearts of Pogodin, Tyutchev and Danilevsky. Less than two years before the downfall of Tsardom, he obtained the consent of Britain and France to the Russian annexation of Constantinople and the Straits as part of the Allied war aims.

In Russian domestic politics, the Pan-Slavs belonged to the extreme right. Idealising as they did the Russia of the Middle Ages, they sought to preserve—or rather, to restore—a society directed spiritually by the Orthodox Church and governed autocratically by the Holy Orthodox Emperor. On the other hand, their dislike of the Tsarist bureaucracy and its many non-Russian officials (in 1880, nearly one-third of the posts in the higher civil administration were held by Baltic Germans) their denunciations of the irreligion and degeneracy of St Petersburg society, and above all their strictures on the conduct of Russian foreign policy as weak and pusillanimous, frequently brought them into collision with the authorities. Aksakov, a celebrated Pan-Slav writer, was banished from Moscow when he declared in print that the Tsar was being estranged from his people by the policy of Gorchakov, his Foreign Minister; and a number of officers were retired from the army at different times for Pan-Slav activities. At times, the Pan-Slavs sounded a note that was almost revolutionary, notably when they contended that Russia needed a fundamental social transformation if it was to carry out its messianic mission. Meanwhile, far away on the extreme left of Russian politics, in the camp of avowed revolutionaries, Pan-Slavist ideas found an echo in the doctrines of the followers of Bakunin, the anarchist leader who figured as a leading ideological opponent of Karl Marx. Bakunin's anarchism, and his hopes for a great Russian 'jacquerie' similar to the insurrection of Pugachev in the late eighteenth century, were strangely mingled with ideas and images characteristic of the Pan-Slavist mentality. In 1848, he declared:

> It is in Moscow that the slavery of the peoples subjugated by the Russian sceptre will be broken, together with the slavery of all Slav peoples; there the whole European slavery will be buried in its own ruins. Out of an ocean of blood and fire there will rise in Moscow high in the sky the star of the revolution, to become the guide of liberated mankind.[5]

Or again, writing in 1860:

> The peasant's axe will set St Petersburg right and will make possible there the national dictatorship which alone can save Russia. This dictatorship is also necessary to establish Russia's power in Europe and to turn that power to the liberation of the Slavs from Austria and Turkey.[6]

Bakunin later discarded his Pan-Slavism and became a genuine internationalist; but his earlier outlook was continued, though with less emphasis on blood and fire, by the Narodniks: a revolutionary nationalist group who saw in the Russian peasant *mir* (village community) an embryonic form of socialism, and believed that through a socialist revolution on agrarian foundations Russia could by-pass the whole capitalist and bourgeois development of Western society. Implied in this doctrine was the conclusion that Russia would thus attain world leadership—for, whereas during the age of capitalist economy, Russia lagged behind the West and had been compelled to copy it, the socialist revolution, carried out first in Russia, would put its people in the vanguard of progress, setting the example to all other nations. Where the conservative Pan-Slavs had looked back to the medieval past for their ideal, the Narodniks looked to the future and envisaged the creation of an entirely new society. But, in both cases, there was an aspiration to turn the tables on the West and affirm the superiority of Russia. As the French historian Michelet acutely observed in 1851: 'Yesterday Russia told us, "I am Christianity"; tomorrow she will tell us, "I am Socialism".'[7]

Around the beginning of the twentieth century, however, Marxism began to prevail in Russia as the creed of the socialist intelligentsia.

The rapid growth of modern industry had created for the first time a substantial urban proletariat, while the dreams of the Narodniks had been disappointed by the Russian peasantry's failure to do what was expected of it. Marxism commended itself as a doctrine appropriate to a Russia that was fast being transformed by industrialisation. It appeared to be an ideology quite incompatible with the beliefs and aspirations not only of the Christian Pan-Slavs but also of the Narodniks. The Marxists were Westerners; they idealised neither the Russia of the Middle Ages nor the contemporary Russian peasant. Since they expected the socialist revolution to be achieved first in the most advanced industrial countries, it followed that Russia, as a relatively backward country, would have to follow the lead of Western Europe in the socialist era, just as it had in the age of capitalism. The Marxists preached a social and political doctrine that had been formulated in Western Europe without any contribution from Russia, and their theoretically rigorous internationalism excluded any appeal to Russian patriotism or Pan-Slav solidarity.

When, therefore, the Russian Marxists—or rather, the Bolshevik faction of the Russian Social Democratic Party—seized power in Petrograd in November 1917, a student of political ideas might well have predicted that, if the new régime could be consolidated, it would be the end of the Russian messianic vision and the policies it promoted. Yet, by one of the great ironies of history, Marxism in Russia was destined to be combined with Russian chauvinism in an extreme form. The beginnings of the process of the russification of Marxism were discerned by Thomas Masaryk in 1921, when he wrote in *Sur le Bolshévisme*:

> The Bolsheviks have accepted Marxism and pride themselves on being its only orthodox adherents. They do not realise how much they owe to Bakunin, the adversary of Marx. From him they took over the mystic faith in the revolution, in the Russian people, in its unique socialist and communist capacity. . . . All the shortcomings which characterised the Russian state, the Russian school and the Russian church, characterise also the Bolshevik state and régime, because they come from the same people and have been formed in the same way.

40

Lenin himself was a genuine internationalist. When he carried out his coup d'état, he had not the slightest intention of building 'socialism in one country' or of extending the power of the Russian state. He regarded the Bolshevik initiative as a detonator for the revolution he believed to be imminent in Western Europe because of universal war-weariness after three years of mass slaughter in an 'imperialist' conflict. In Russia he appealed, not to patriotism and still less to a sense of national greatness, but to the craving for peace at any price, for an end to a military effort that had overtaxed Russian strength and brought on the Russian people enormous losses of men and unprecedented privations. He looked to Germany, as the homeland of Marxism, to take the lead in the second stage of the European revolution, believing Germany, with its highly developed industry, to be far riper for socialism than Russia. But the Germans did not respond to the Bolsheviks' revolutionary oratory. Far from joining hands with Russian workers and peasants to 'turn imperialist war into civil war', German soldiers, obeying their generals, advanced deep into Russia after the self-dissolution of the Russian army and imposed on the new Soviet government the Treaty of Brest-Litovsk. From the consequences of this disaster—far greater than any suffered by Russia since the time of Peter the Great—the country was delivered, not by the European revolution, but by the military defeat of Germany on the Western Front at the hands of the French, British and American armies. When revolution at last came in Germany, it was not proletarian-socialist but bourgeois-democratic in character. The hope that it might follow the Bolshevik example was dashed when a government of Social Democrats called in the unpurged German army to crush the Spartacists in Berlin.

But worse was to come. In the spring of 1920, the Russian Civil War had been decided by the Bolshevik victories over Denikin and Kolchak. The new Polish state's intervention in the Ukraine provided the opportunity for a Russian military counterattack which might not merely drive the Poles from territory regarded as Ukrainian but also pass through Poland to the borders of Germany, and thus give support to the retarded German revolution. In this enterprise, much was hoped for from the supposed sympathies with Bolshevism of Polish workers and peasants. The soldiers of the Red Army were told that they were entering Poland as liberators, not conquerors, and a Polish Revolutionary Committee—the prototype of the Soviet-controlled Lublin Committee of 1944—was set up in Russian-occupied Bialystok to welcome the invaders and take over the government of Poland when Warsaw was captured. But Warsaw was not captured; on the contrary, the Red Army was defeated and pushed far back to the east. The defeat was political as well as military. The Russians, even in their new guise of revolutionary liberators, received no help from any substantial section of the Polish population. Lenin afterwards complained bitterly to the German Communist, Clara Zetkin: 'The Polish revolution on which we counted was a failure. The Polish peasants and workers defended their class enemies, permitted our brave Red Army soldiers to die of starvation, ambushed and killed them.'

But if Western Europe and Poland rejected Communism while Russia was converted to it, this meant that Russia and Communism had, for practical purposes, become identical. By official profession of a messianic revolutionary faith whose aims, in the words of the *Communist Manifesto*, 'can only be achieved by the violent overthrow of the whole contemporary social order', Russia was separated from, and set against, the West to a degree even greater than the Slavophiles had ever imagined. Communism involved no mere change of government, or even of economic system; it was, as Sidney and Beatrice Webb called it, 'a new civilisation'. The Communists were not just another political party, but the organised following of an infallible and fiercely intolerant religion. Russia had been imagined by the Slavophiles as the chosen instrument of God's purpose in bringing about the triumph of the Orthodox Church; now it was to become the special instrument of historical necessity in bringing about the inevitable victory of the universal proletarian revolution. What the Narodniks had hoped for, and the Social Democrats declared to be impossible, had come about: Russia had bypassed the nations of the West, arriving in the age of socialism before them. Russia was in the vanguard of progress, leading the march of history. Since their faith caused the Russian Communists to regard their revolution as the most important event in history, they could not do otherwise than regard their own nation as uniquely gifted in having brought the great new society into being. For some years, their exaltation of Russia as the country of the new civilisation did not extend to the Russian past; the old Russia of the Tsars was represented in conventional Marxist terms as backward, benighted and oppressive. But it was difficult to maintain that the supremely creative genius of the Russian people dated only from 1917. Soon the past history of Russia began to glow with a lustre reflected from the glorious present; the heroes of old Russia were rehabilitated and became figures of an Old Testament preparatory to the New Testament of the Soviet régime. The Russian people had always been great and admirable; they had always been surrounded by malicious enemies, as they were now; their wars had always been just. Ivan the Terrible and Peter the Great had had to use harsh methods in order to create a strong Russian state, just as Lenin and Stalin had to do in order to establish the dictatorship of the proletariat and build socialism. There was a continuity in Russian history in which the most convinced Marxist-Leninist could find scope for the traditional emotions of national patriotism in their most extravagant form.

The revival of Russian nationalism was also significant for the relation of the Russians to the non-Russian peoples within the new 'Soviet Union'. The old Russia had been a multinational state formed by the expansion of the original Muscovite principality over several centuries. In this empire, as it stood in 1914, the Russians in the strict ethnic sense were less than a half of the total population—or nearer three-quarters, if the Ukrainians and Byelorussians were to be counted as branches of the Russian stock. The Bolsheviks in 1917 proclaimed the principle of national self-determination, with application to all the non-Russian peoples of the Tsarist empire. The Decree on Peace of November 8 denounced 'the incorporation into a large or powerful state of a small or weak nationality, without the definitely, clearly and freely expressed consent of this nationality, regardless of when this forcible incorporation took place, regardless of the degree of development or backwardness of the nation forcibly incorporated, and regardless of whether this nation is located in Europe or in distant lands beyond the seas'.

The right of national independence could not have been more uncompromisingly stated, and the principle was recognised in the constitution of the Soviet Union, which was nominally a voluntary federation of equal national states, with Russia only one among the others. But the Bolsheviks qualified the principle in a way which rendered it inoperative in practice. Communist theory subordinated the right of national self-determination to the international interests of the proletariat, and this principle was invoked to justify the intervention of Russian troops in 1918–20 to help in knocking down bourgeois nationalist governments and independence movements in the Ukraine, Transcaucasia and Central Asia. The Bolshevik methods of conducting elections meant that, once their police were in control, the peoples of these regions voted to join the new federal union with the same unanimity with which they elected nominees of the Communist Party to political office. Only in the western borderlands, in Finland, Poland and the Baltic States, were the national separatist forces strong enough, with support from Western Europe, to resist reincorporation in the new version of the Russian empire. Elsewhere, the territory that had been ruled by the Tsars was all included in the Soviet federal union and subjected to a system of government which was in practice no less unitary than that of the Tsardom, for the Communist Party of the Soviet Union (CPSU) was not organised on a federal basis, but as a single unit, and it controlled the affairs of the federation and the constituent republics alike.

It was not enough, however, merely to engineer a system of political control from Moscow over the non-Russian nationalities. To consolidate the union, an effective propaganda, including the rewriting of history, was required. Russian Marxist historians of the early Soviet period followed pre-revolution Marxism in regarding Russian expansion under the Tsars as an example of colonial imperialism. But, at Stalin's order, from about 1932 all this was revised. It was discovered that Russia had never been imperialist; it had merely extended its benevolent protection to non-Russian peoples to deliver them from alien rule or protect them against their enemies. The Russian role had always been a progressive and civilising one, and only a few reactionary troublemakers in the pay of foreign powers had ever opposed it. Shamyl, in the middle of the nineteenth century, had not led a popular resistance to the Russian conquest of the Caucasus: he had been a British agent acting against the true interest of his people. The Kazakh chiefs, celebrated in song for their struggles against the Russian settlers in Siberia, had not been patriots but merely brigands. The new propaganda of 'Soviet patriotism'—of which Communist censorship permitted no public criticism—represented the peoples of the Soviet Union as bound together by ties of traditional friendship and co-operation, in strong contrast to the violence and coercion by which other multinational states had been built up.

Outside the boundaries of the new federation, Russia again counted on people who could be, as Pogodin had imagined, subtracted from other states and added to itself. But these were no longer the Slav subjects of Turkey and Austria, all of whom were now independent nations with governments untouched by Communism. Russia's new brotherhood among men was to be far larger: nothing less than the entire world proletariat, the workers of all lands whom Marx had called on to unite—'you have nothing to lose but your chains'. Communist Russia was their country wherever they lived, and Moscow should be their Mecca. 'Leader of the Workers of the Whole World' was one of the titles bestowed on Stalin by his grateful subjects within the frontiers of the Soviet Union and echoed by devout Communists in other lands. 'Leader of Progressive Mankind' was another title of even larger scope for inclusion of all classes and political groups that might at any time or place be allied with Communists in the struggle for power—though, in the end, power must be wielded only by the proletariat and its sole legitimate representative, the Communist Party in each country. Stalin's conception of international politics was clearly summed up in his *Problems of Leninism*:

> Aim: consolidation of the dictatorship of the proletariat in one country, using it as a point of support for the overthrow of imperialism in all countries. Main force of the revolution: dictatorship of the proletariat in one country and revolutionary movement of the proletariat in all others. Main reserves: the semi-proletarian and petty peasant masses in the advanced countries and the movements for the liberation of colonies and dependent areas.[8]

The situation, however, contained possibilities not only of revolutions abroad which Russia would help to victory, but also of international wars in which Russia might be defeated. As Lenin had written: 'We are living not merely in a state but in a system of states, and it is inconceivable that the Soviet Republic should continue for a long period side by side with imperialist states. Ultimately, one or the other must conquer. Meanwhile, a number of terrible clashes between the Soviet Republic and the bourgeois states is inevitable.'[9]

The position of Communist Russia in the midst of non-Communist nations enjoined caution. The first duty of a Communist was to preserve what had already been gained and not endanger it by reckless adventures. The CPSU might aspire to lead all the workers of the world and might actually command the loyalty of organised Communists in every country, but appeals to proletarian solidarity had not stopped the German advance into Russia in 1918 or prevented the Poles from successfully counterattacking on the Vistula in 1920. The CPSU must provide leadership for the world revolution through the new Communist International, but, as wielder of power in the Soviet Union, it must conduct a foreign policy in diplomatic relations with the governments which it was its long-term purpose to overthrow. It must avoid, if possible, a war against an enemy with superior military forces or industrial capacity and, above all, avoid provoking a hostile coalition of other powerful states against which it would have to fight alone. It must keep the peace with the strong as long as it was weak and encourage conflicts between other great powers so as to take advantage of the 'contradictions of imperialism'. It was even permissible to enter into temporary alliances with capitalist states, so as to check whichever one among them appeared at any given time to be most dangerous to Russia.

From 1920 to 1933, the CPSU regarded France and Britain, the victors of the First World War, as the main enemy in Europe and sought a countervailing connection with Germany, or rather with the virtually autonomous Reichswehr within the Weimar Republic. A secret military convention brought about military co-operation between the Reichswehr and the Red Army whereby the former was enabled to some extent to evade the restrictions imposed on it by the Treaty of Versailles. The CPSU had hoped at the same time for a Communist revolution in Germany, but none appeared imminent; meanwhile, it was advantageous to have close contacts with the socially conservative German military caste, which not only had a common interest with the Soviet leaders in creating a counterpoise to the military preponderance of France in Europe, but also shared a common hatred for the new Poland that had been carved out of the pre-war territories of both Germany and Russia. A new Russo-German partition of Poland, such as was actually carried out in 1939, was the objective of General von Seeckt in his dealings with the Red Army, and the Soviet leaders on their side looked forward to reversing the military verdict of the unsuccessful campaign of 1920.

Hitler's advent to power in Germany changed all this, partly because Hitler had found it politically convenient to create a myth of himself as a 'bulwark against Bolshevism' and also—more fundamentally—

because his design for *Lebensraum* reached beyond Poland into the territory of the Soviet Union and involved an ultimate purpose of war against Russia. Hitler's hostility and the rapidly growing military strength of the new Third Reich drove Stalin to reverse Russia's pro-German policy and seek entry into the League of Nations, previously described in Communist publicity as the 'imperialist robbers' den'. Following this, military alliances were concluded with France and Czechoslovakia. Communist parties in Western democratic countries were directed to restrain their revolutionary militancy, to form alliances with other parties and groups in broadly based 'Popular Fronts' and to work for an 'anti-aggression front' in Europe. Stalin was particularly apprehensive of the project for a 'Four-Power Pact' of Britain, France, Germany and Italy, which would isolate Russia and free Hitler's hands for expansion to the east. However, it was difficult for him to be sufficiently cautious in the conduct of his foreign policy without exposing himself to charges of betraying the cause of proletarian revolution or of being over-timid in defence of the Soviet state. From his exile first in Norway and then in Mexico, Trotsky thundered his denunciations of the man who had sold the hopes of the workers of all lands in order to reach agreements with capitalist governments. Behind the scenes in Moscow, a group of generals headed by Tukhachevsky appears to have urged an 'activisation of foreign policy', which would have involved forestalling German expansion by preventive interventions in Eastern Europe. But against all his critics Stalin moved effectively in his own peculiar way. He had his principal opponents within the CPSU put to death after inducing them by special police methods to make false confessions in open court, implicating also the absent Trotsky, that they were German or Japanese agents and aimed at restoring capitalism in Russia. Tukhachevsky and his colleagues were likewise put to death after a secret court martial in which documents forged by the Nazi Gestapo and sold to the Soviet secret police were presented to the judges. The Great Purge extended from the top downwards through all grades of the party and the army; tens of thousands of party members and army officers were shot or sent to Siberia. All opposition to Stalin's personal authority was thus suppressed, his critics discredited, and his policies—both domestic and foreign—set beyond questioning.

But with the sudden British guarantee to Poland in April 1939, the international situation changed again. Hitler had now to revert to the

Seeckt policy and bid for an alliance with Russia, the price for which, as we saw in Chapter 1, was Russian occupation of part of Poland, the Baltic states and Bessarabia. This bargain enabled Russia to regain most of the western border territory held by the Russian empire before 1914 from the Gulf of Finland to the Black Sea. The anti-aggression front was now forgotten, and after Poland had been crushed by the German and Russian invasions, the Communist parties of the West were directed to agitate for French and British acceptance of the Russo-German carve-up of Eastern Europe. The expected diplomatic settlement, which would still have left France as a great power on the other side of Germany, was not, however, attained. Instead, Germany decisively crushed France in the summer of 1940, leaving Hitler free to attack Russia, which he did in the following year. Stalin, who had not expected Hitler to attack while Britain remained unsubdued, was pushed back into the camp of 'peace and democracy'. The Communist parties of the West, which had been vigorously campaigning against the 'imperialist war' carried on by Britain against Hitler (and American support for it), now discovered that any war waged in alliance with the Soviet Union was holy. The CPSU again adjusted itself to the language of liberalism; finally, the Communist International itself was formally dissolved as an indication that the aim of world revolution had been discarded.

With the defeat of Hitler, the situation again underwent a fundamental change. The Comintern was defunct, but its former leaders were very much alive, and there were Russian troops on the Vistula, the Danube and the Elbe. Now was the hour of opportunity, when the boundaries of the revolution could be extended without serious danger to what had already been achieved. Poland was prostrate, German power had been wiped out, France was impotent, Britain economically weakened, while the President of the United States was resolved to withdraw American forces from Europe as soon as possible. Stalin hastened to make hay while the sun shone. Now he could demonstrate to all Communists that he was the true heir of Lenin, that his zeal for the international victory of the proletariat was unimpaired, that he had been slandered by those who had accused him of betraying the cause of world revolution. With Communists in power, or in process of taking over power, in Warsaw and Bucharest, in Budapest and Belgrade, in Berlin and Prague, Stalin achieved an extension of the revolution that Lenin had failed to bring about and an expansion of Russian power that no Tsar had been able to accomplish. All that was lacking was Trotsky's admission that he had been wrong, but Trotsky could not make it, since he had died five years too soon, assassinated by one of Stalin's agents.

In correspondence with Tito prior to the Soviet break with Yugoslavia in 1948, Stalin—claiming that it had been the Red Army which had 'created the conditions' for the Yugoslav Communist Party to take power—remarked that 'unfortunately' it had been unable to do the same for the Communist movements of France and Italy. After his soldiers had captured Vienna, Prague and Berlin, Stalin had, however, no need to apologise because they had not also entered Paris and Rome. These were goals for the future, and his was an empire that time might yet increase.

3

THE RISE OF AMERICAN INFLUENCE
IN EUROPE

ON THE DAY after Hitler invaded Russia in 1941, Senator Harry S. Truman of Missouri declared: 'If we see that Germany is winning the war, we ought to help Russia; and if Russia is winning, we ought to help Germany, and in that way let them kill as many as possible.'[1]

The statement was no more important at the time than that of any other senator. Not even the most extravagant of political prophets would then have predicted that within four years the man who uttered these words would be in the White House. Even so, they certainly throw light on the outlook of that senator from Missouri in the days before Pearl Harbor, revealing an attitude toward Russia markedly different from President Roosevelt's. For Truman, as for a great many Americans in June 1941, Nazi Germany and Communist Russia were equally detestable; the prospect that, after combining to destroy the independence of Poland and the Baltic States, the two bloodthirsty dictatorships might now exhaust each other in mutual combat was a satisfactory one to people of Truman's way of thinking. Nor is it wholly improbable that such a view of European affairs might have prevailed in American foreign policy had a settlement with Japan averted war in the Pacific. There is no good reason to think that Congress could ever have been brought to consent to full American belligerency in the European war but for the Japanese attack on Pearl Harbor. Enthusiasm for Russia was confined to a small minority. American opinion generally had been shocked by the Hitler-Stalin Pact, and the cruelties of the mass deportations from Poland and the Baltic States had become widely known. The policy Senator Truman recommended could certainly have had strong political support on the morrow of Hitler's invasion of Russia.

But the situation was entirely transformed when the Japanese attack and Germany's declaration of war made the United States a belligerent in the war against the Axis powers. Not only was material aid extended to Russia—increasingly after the battle of Stalingrad, so that the Russian armies could advance to Vienna and Berlin—but all the resources of national wartime propaganda were employed to erase the image of two aggressive dictatorships locked in mortal conflict, and to substitute that of a humane, progressive and peace-loving Russia united with America in the pursuit of a liberal ideal. The four years from 1941 to 1945 were the golden age of pro-Soviet 'fellow-travelling' in America. Stalin became 'Uncle Joe'—a rugged, but essentially benevolent, personality: the kind of man F.D.R. might have been if he had been born in the Ozarks.

Harry Truman, however, had not completely changed his former opinion. When, by Roosevelt's unexpected demise, he suddenly became President of the United States in April 1945, Truman took a view of Soviet demands different from that of his predecessor. He shared neither the idealism nor the illusions of Roosevelt; he dreamed no dreams of the Four Freedoms, and he saw no visions of a world happy and peaceful under the supervision of the Four Policemen. Truman had come up the hard way in politics and was not inclined to optimism about human nature; he had a capacity for seeing very clearly what was in front of his nose, and he was prone neither to euphemism nor to circumlocution. Before he had been in office a fortnight, he had given a striking indication that a new hand was at the helm of American policy. On April 23, he received Molotov, who was passing through Washington on his way to San Francisco for the founding conference of the United Nations. Britain and the United States had already agreed to exclude from the conference the Polish government in exile, which they continued formally to recognise pending the 'reorganisation' of the 'Lublin Committee' government, as agreed at Yalta. But, after more than two months of negotiations had failed to produce the promised reorganisation, the Soviet government had demanded that delegates of the unreorganised Lublin group be admitted at San Francisco. The issue was not in itself of any great importance, for the new Polish government, whether reorganised or not, was in any case going to be a puppet of the Soviet Union. But the Soviet demand implied an expectation that America would yield to pressure even in flagrant disregard of the recently concluded Yalta agreement. Indeed, some of those attending a conference Truman summoned at the White House, just before Molotov's arrival, were in favour of giving way.[2] Truman, however, decided otherwise, and told Molotov so, in what Leahy (who was present) described as 'blunt language unadorned by the polite verbiage of diplomacy'.[3] According to another account, he used 'Missouri mule-driver's language'.

The alternative, however, was an indefinite yielding to Russian demands and faits accomplis. The American and British governments had already in effect signed away the independence of Poland at Yalta, and now Moscow was ignoring even the feeble conditions with which they had qualified their surrender. In making his stand against the new Russian diplomatic pressure, Truman gave warning—perhaps more roughly than was necessary—that he did not intend to permit this. He saw Soviet power expanding to south and west of Russia's pre-war frontiers, and he realised there was no other power capable of stopping its expansion unless the United States stepped into the breach. The doctrine of 'containment' was already implicit.

But Truman was not yet able to chart a new course. Henry Stimson, the Secretary of War, and George C. Marshall, the Army Chief of Staff, insisted there should be no friction with Russia while the war with Japan remained unfinished. Moreover, the new President was not only ignorant of the details of foreign affairs, of which he had had no previous experience; he was also subject to domestic political pressures that he was not yet able to over-ride. In appointing, mainly for reasons of domestic politics, James Byrnes as his Secretary of State, he entrusted the conduct of his diplomacy to a man who had a strong political standing in his own right, and ideas of his own on foreign policy. Thus, for several months after his first clash with Molotov, Truman followed a course of policy hardly distinguishable from Roosevelt's. He made no immediate response to Churchill's 'Iron Curtain' appeal, and sent Joseph Davies—of all people—to London to allay Churchill's misgivings about what was happening in Europe, while he sent Harry Hopkins to Moscow to discuss the Polish issue with Stalin. At Potsdam in July 1945, he gave only lukewarm support to Churchill's vigorous objections to Stalin's unilateral imposition of the Oder-Neisse line as Germany's eastern frontier.

It was over the capitulation of Japan that Truman again showed the spirit that had flashed out in his encounter with Molotov in April.

On this occasion, he did not personally engage in combat with Molotov or Stalin, but the American ambassador in Moscow had an unpleasant diplomatic altercation in resisting the Soviet Union's demand that the surrender of Japan should be taken, and post-war control exercised there, by coequal American and Soviet commanders. This would have meant a joint Control Council with a Soviet veto and independent zones of occupation, as in Germany. But, whereas in Germany such an arrangement corresponded to the situation produced by invasions of the enemy territory from both sides after a war in which Russia had been engaged longer than the United States, there was no similar situation in regard to Japan. The Russians, in their last-minute intervention in the Pacific war, had penetrated into Manchuria and Korea, but had not landed in Japan. There was nothing to stop the Japanese from making their surrender to America alone, as they undoubtedly would have done if Moscow had continued to refuse to accept General MacArthur as sole 'Supreme Commander for the Allied Powers'. The Soviet demand was withdrawn before Japan surrendered, but not before it had produced a major crisis in Soviet-American relations. As Truman wrote in his memoirs:

> Harriman [the American ambassador in Moscow] was, of course, expressing our set policy. . . . We wanted Japan controlled by an American Commander, acting on behalf of the Allies. . . . I was determined that the Japanese occupation should not follow in the footsteps of the German experience. I did not want divided control or separate zones.[4]

During the five months after the end of the war against Japan, conflict between the Soviet Union and the Western powers rapidly developed. It had been arranged that a Council of Foreign Ministers, initially continuing the Big Three wartime conferences of Teheran, Yalta and Potsdam, should meet in September to review the international situation; but when the Foreign Ministers met, they were deadlocked over procedural questions and parted without being able to agree about anything. Byrnes later admitted that 'nothing in his previous experience had prepared him for negotiating with Molotov'. The Western governments had now their first taste of the situation that was so frequently to confront them in the years ahead: the choice between an agreement on Russia's terms and no agreement at all. The Soviet government, strong in the conviction of its own historically invincible cause, protected by its dictatorial power from any overt criticism at home, and enabled by its domestic monopoly of press and radio to turn all news to its own advantage, never cared if a conference broke down. But the men responsible for post-war foreign policy in America and Britain could not so lightly contemplate a deadlock at a major international gathering. Byrnes was under fire from radio and newspaper commentators, most of whom maintained the favourable wartime view of the Soviet Union; while the new British Foreign Secretary, Ernest Bevin, belonged to a Labour government whose parliamentary party had been victorious at the polls in the summer of 1945 with friendship for Russia as one of the leading points in its electoral appeal. As Byrnes wrote in his memoirs:

> We were reluctant in the first instance to let the conference break down. The people were anxious for peace. We had refrained after Potsdam from publicly expressing our concern [about Russian ambitions] because of our desire to maintain friendly relations with our Russian allies. The Soviet leadership knew of our people's strong desire for peace and they thought we would not dare to let the conference fail.[5]

The Western powers did, finally, allow the September meeting of the Council of Foreign Ministers to end in deadlock rather than yield to Soviet demands, but Byrnes was very depressed by the result. He tried again in December, and this time he was willing to pay a high price in concessions—or in overlooking of Soviet faits accomplis—so as to get some sort of an agreement. He came back from Moscow, where the December meeting was held, with an agreed formula for the making of peace treaties with Germany's former allies. But the general weakness of his diplomacy now provoked public criticism in America and, what was more serious for Byrnes, a rebuke from President Truman.

Between September and December 1945, there had been a considerable movement of American opinion toward an attitude more critical of Soviet policies, particularly as more and more information became available about the behaviour of the Russian armies in occupied countries. This turn of public opinion gave Truman the opportunity to assert his authority over Byrnes; he charged his Secretary of State with having 'taken it upon himself to move the foreign policy of the United States in a direction to which I could not and would not agree'.

He told Byrnes he was 'tired of babying the Soviets' and directed him to adopt a harder line in diplomatic negotiations than he had taken at the Moscow conference. A few months later, on March 5, 1946, Truman endorsed (by his presence in the audience) a speech in which the recent actions of the Soviet Union were outspokenly denounced by Winston Churchill, no longer in a position of governmental responsibility since the defeat of his party at the polls, but retaining the attention-compelling prestige of his wartime leadership.

Another year elapsed, however, before the proclamation of the 'Truman Doctrine' definitely involved the United States in a commitment to 'contain' Soviet expansion in Europe. Until March 1947, the United States had not undertaken any obligation to sustain the resistance of any state in Europe or Asia to Soviet military aggression. There were obligations of collective security under the United Nations Charter; but, as Russia could veto any action against itself by the Security Council, no question of armed opposition to Russia by the United Nations could arise. There were American occupation forces in Germany and Austria, which would presumably oppose any attempt by Soviet troops to enter or pass through their zones, but the American public regarded their sojourn in Europe as merely temporary and had not yet begun to think of them as a cordon for the defence of Western Europe instead of simply police units in former enemy territory. In the region of the Eastern Mediterranean, the Americans had no troops at all; this was traditionally an area of British strategic interest, and, at the end of the war, there were British troops in Egypt, Palestine and Greece. But, by the beginning of 1947, it had become clear that British power was no longer sufficient to protect Greece and Turkey, the two countries under greatest pressure from the Soviet Union. The pressure on Greece was indirect; the Communist revolt, thwarted in 1944, had been renewed as a guerrilla war with support across Greece's northern borders from the newly established Communist régimes of Bulgaria, Yugoslavia and Albania. The threat to Turkey was direct; Russia had demanded the cession of the provinces of Kars and Ardahan in eastern Anatolia and a naval base in the Dardanelles, and had hinted at the use of force to obtain these objectives. Turkey had so far defied the Russian pressure, but had little hope of putting up a successful resistance by itself if Russia were to attack. In any case, if the Greek Communists were to capture Athens and turn Greece into a Soviet satellite, Turkey would be encircled and forced to capitulate. In Truman's view, Russian control of Greece and Turkey would involve domination of the whole region of the Middle East, with its vast oil reserves on which Western Europe was vitally dependent and with its central strategic position between Europe, Africa and Asia.

The situation was brought to a climax by Britain's post-war financial difficulties, which caused the British government to inform Washington on February 24, 1947, that Britain would have to withdraw its remaining troops from Greece and cease all aid to the Greek government by the end of March. At the same time, Washington was informed by its own observers on the spot that the Greek government must collapse unless assured of substantial aid, since all inland communications in northern Greece had been cut by the Communists and the towns were full of refugees for whom there was no food. It was in these circumstances that Truman decided not merely to pledge American economic and military assistance to Greece and Turkey, but to justify it as part of a general policy of containment of Communism which would be applicable to all countries threatened either with Soviet military invasion or with revolts sustained by material aid from a Communist state. In his message to Congress on March 12 asking for an appropriation of $400 million for aid to Greece and Turkey, he declared that 'it must be the policy of the United States to support free peoples who are resisting attempted subjugation by armed minorities or outside pressure'.

The proclamation of the Truman Doctrine concentrated attention on Greece and Turkey, but Truman certainly had also in mind the question of Germany, which, although less urgent, was in the long run of even greater significance. From the time of the Potsdam Conference, when it was agreed that 'so far as is practicable, there shall be uniformity of treatment of the German population throughout Germany', relations among the Allies were increasingly affected by the efforts of the Soviet occupation authority to establish Communist power in the Soviet zone and extend it to the Western zones. There were many questions at issue in Germany—reparations, dismantling, supplies between the zones, economic organisation, denazification—on which differences of interest and opinion might arise among the occupying powers, and it was to resolve these differences by negotiation that the machinery of the Control Council, and of the joint Kommandatura in Berlin, had been set up. Sharp differences on these topics arose among the Western

Allies as well as between them and the Russians. But all such issues were overshadowed by the ever more manifest intention of the Russians to bring Germany under Communist rule. There was no way in which the Western Allies could prevent the Russians from using their police forces in their own zone to give the German Communists there a monopoly of political power and suppress opposition to them. But if this was done in the Soviet zone while the Western Allies restored multiparty democracy in their zones, it followed that an end of the occupation would leave Germany divided between two incompatible political systems: a situation that would require either a decision through civil war or a permanent division into two separate states. For the Russians, however, in the months after Potsdam, the idea of putting the Communists in power only in East Germany was too modest an aspiration; they had hopes of getting a firm hold on West Germany as well before any democratic political life could be revived there. In the words of an observer at that time:

> Having insulated their own zone as far as possible against outside influences, the Russians began to interfere in the political life of the Western zones, hoping in the end to capture Western Germany for Communism under the very noses of the occupying powers. The plan was to extend the fusion of Communists and Social Democrats, already accomplished in the East, to the Western zones. In their own zone they had achieved the merger by coercion; in the West it would have to be by persuasion. . . . The very name of the new organization —the Socialist Unity Party of Germany—declared its nation-wide ambition. At the conference in the Russian zone where the new party was founded, a high proportion of representatives from the Western zones were elected to the executive. For purposes of political infiltration, if for no other, it was evident that Germany was to be treated as a whole.[6]

Although the Russians refused entry to their own zone to any anti-Communist politicians from West Germany, they expected the British and American authorities to allow a high-powered campaign in West Germany by Communist propaganda teams from the East, and in the summer of 1946 this campaign was pressed forward on a large scale. An ironical feature of it was that it was largely financed with American money. By an arrangement made before Germany's surrender, each occupying power was to print a currency for its own zone and make specific amounts of it available to the other occupying powers for inter-zonal payments. But the United States Treasury, instead of providing the Soviet authorities, as in other cases, with a recorded quantity of printed notes, handed over to them the printing plates so that they could themselves produce American zone currency without limit. Whatever the reasons for this fantastic action, its effect was to enable the Soviet Union to pay for political activities in West Germany merely by printing American zone currency with no problems of clearance or exchange.

Another feature of the campaign was Russia's overt hostility to the Western democracies and the effort to represent itself as Germany's only friend. With the behaviour of the Russian troops in their hour of victory so fresh in German memory, it was not easy to cultivate pro-Russian sentiments in the German people, but just because the Russians were so much hated, they sought to divert this unpopularity from themselves by systematic incitement against the Western powers. British and American censorship had kept all anti-Russian comment or reporting of Russian atrocities out of the German press in the Western zones, but the Russian-controlled press of East Germany became increasingly a medium for propaganda hostile to the West. For a long time, the British and American authorities ignored this propaganda; as late as February, 1947, the British Commander in Chief, General Robertson, declared with lofty disdain that 'we have no wish to compete for the role of champion of the new Germany'. But this was just what the Western powers had to do sooner or later; they had to rally the German people, unless they were to see a passive, inert and despairing Germany taken over by a small group of Russian puppets.

The American and British authorities made a late start in their endeavour to counteract the Russo-Communist political offensive, but when they did begin to give positive encouragement to democratic political forces in West Germany, the effect was remarkable. It became obvious at once that in a free political system, with other well organised parties in the field, the Communists had no chance of obtaining more than a small minority of the votes of the electorate. Even in Berlin, with the Russians in control of the eastern half of the city, elections to the city council from all the sectors in October 1946 gave the Social Democrats nearly half the votes and the Moscow-backed Socialist

Unity Party less than a fifth. But the sequel to this rout of the Communists at the polls showed that it would be impossible for the ballot-box by itself to decide the future of Germany. The meeting-place of the city council at that time was in the Soviet sector, and non-Communist members attending the meetings were intimidated and assaulted by armed Communist gangs without receiving any protection from the police. As a result, the majority of the council decided to move the seat of the city government to West Berlin: a step to which the Russians replied by setting up a purely Communist administration in East Berlin. This development revealed a new function of Western military occupation in Germany, which had not been imagined at the time of the German surrender: the protection of German democracy against Russian repression. It was not merely a police, but a military, problem. For behind the German Communist street gangs was the Russian army, and it had become clear that it was only the armies of the Western powers in West Germany and West Berlin that prevented Russia (so long, at any rate, as Russia did not desire war with the Western powers) from taking over the German capital, installing a hand-picked German central government, and extending its authority to the Rhine.

Roosevelt had told Stalin at Yalta that American troops would not remain in Europe for more than two years after the end of the war. This period would have come to an end in May 1947. But in March of that year, the Truman Doctrine had been proclaimed, and the bill for aid to Greece and Turkey became law on May 22. The United States—Congress as well as President—had rejected the isolationism that had prevailed in America between the wars, and had undertaken onerous responsibilities in the south-eastern corner of the European continent. It could hardly be less willing to contain Soviet expansion on the Elbe. Indeed, without any special discussion or debate, American opinion as a whole had come to take it for granted that United States forces would remain in Germany until a satisfactory settlement of German affairs had been reached. The conference of Foreign Ministers in Moscow in March and April 1947 left this settlement as far off as ever.

Then, on June 5, came the speech of George Marshall, now Secretary of State, at Harvard University: the speech that launched the Marshall Plan for the economic rehabilitation of Europe. The benefits of the plan were open to Russia and its satellites, but the primary intention was to stabilise Western Europe and, in Marshall's words, to achieve a 'revival of a working economy in the world so as to permit the emergence of political and social conditions in which free institutions can exist'. The main characteristic of this plan was that, instead of offering aid to particular nations on a piecemeal basis, it pledged support for the economy of Europe as a whole. When Russia and its satellites refused to have anything to do with it, this support was afforded to Western Europe, including West Germany. The American and British governments had by now ceased to think of Germany as a country apart, sealed off from its neighbours by impassable barriers. They had begun to understand that, if Western Europe were not to fall under the domination of the new Russian empire, a unified West Germany must somehow be linked with the other nations of Western Europe, and the combination supported by binding commitments from North America.

American policy was further hardened in February 1948 by a Communist revolutionary coup in Czechoslovakia, which was promoted, though not directly conducted, by the Soviet Union. Elections after the war in Czechoslovakia had returned the Communists as the strongest single party. They had had a large popular following in Bohemia even before the war, and after 1945 they were able to exploit both the traditional pro-Russian sentiments of the Czechs (dating from the days of the Habsburg domination) and the resentment felt towards the Western powers on account of the Munich 'settlement' of 1938. But the Communists did not have an absolute majority and had to enter into a coalition with other parties. Many Czechs believed that, by reason of its history, geographical position, and cultural and ethnic affinities, their nation could serve as a 'bridge' between Russia and the West. But it was Soviet policy to incorporate Czechoslovakia definitely within the Communist bloc. The Czech government at first welcomed the Marshall Plan, but it was forced by powerful Soviet diplomatic pressure to change course and reject it. This brought to a head the dissensions already manifest between Communists and non-Communists within the government. In February 1948, the Communists armed their supporters and organised mass demonstrations in Prague with the collusion of the police, who were controlled by a Communist Minister of the Interior and had been infiltrated by party members. If President Benes had called on the army to defend the democratic constitution, the troops would probably have supported him. But he was given to understand that, if there were civil war, Russian troops would march in from Poland, Hungary, East Germany and the Soviet zone of Austria. He yielded to Communist demands and gave them a position of virtually exclusive governmental power, which they soon consolidated into a permanent party dictatorship.

With a Communist Czechoslovakia now bordering on Bavaria, and with the already existing establishment of Communist power in East Germany, the question of the unification of their own zones of occupation in Germany became urgent for the three Western democracies. The British and Americans merged their zones for economic and administrative purposes early in 1947, but French intransigence—expressed in an obstinate demand for international control of the Ruhr—held up agreement on fusion of the three zones until the middle of 1948. Meanwhile, seeing that the prospects of an early Communist ascendancy in West Germany had disappeared, the Russians began to concentrate on Berlin. General Lucius Clay, the American commander in Germany, had a sense of impending crisis during the early months of 1948.

> Somehow I felt instinctively that a definite change in the attitude of the Russians in Berlin had occurred and that something was about to happen. From Sokolovsky down, there was a new attitude, faintly contemptuous, slightly arrogant and certainly assured.... In making my report to General Bradley I pointed out that I had no confirming intelligence of a positive nature, but that I did sense a change in the Soviet action in Germany.[7]

On March 20, the Russian delegates walked out of the Control Council and declined to attend any further meetings. Eleven days later, the Russian and East German blockade of West Berlin began. Had it not been for the 'miracle' of the Berlin airlift, the ground blockade would certainly have achieved its purpose of forcing the Allied garrisons out of West Berlin and bringing its two million inhabitants under Communist control. Stalin was probably convinced that he was taking only a slight risk of war, since it was unlikely that the Allies, with inferior military forces available for immediate action, would take the initiative in an attempt to force a way through the Soviet zone to Berlin. But when, to the surprise of the Western governments almost as much as of the Kremlin, it was found that air transport could keep West Berlin supplied even when all ground communication with West Germany

61

had been cut, the boot was on the other foot. It was now Stalin who had to take the initiative in belligerency. To stop the airlift he would have to shoot down Allied planes. His nerve was not so strong; in the end, he admitted defeat and called off the blockade. West Berlin remained unsubdued. But there could now be no reversion to the state of affairs that had existed before the Russians left the Control Council. It was impossible any longer even to pretend that Germany was being governed or supervised jointly by the victors of the Second World War. There were now unambiguously two separate German political régimes sponsored respectively by the three Western Allies and the Soviet Union, with West Berlin as an Allied enclave deep within the Soviet zone.

In the Berlin blockade Russia had stopped short of war, but it was impossible to count on a similar restraint in future. The experience of the Berlin crisis had left a deep impression of Russian ruthlessness and malevolence. The three Western powers had been driven by Russian pressure to co-ordinate their policies and had stood together in resistance to the blockade. It was now recognised that some more formal and organised commitment would be needed for the future, especially as the military governments in Germany would soon have to be brought to an end, and some other basis found for maintaining Western forces east of the Rhine—if it was desired to keep them there. Memories of the years before 1939, when isolationism and neutrality had contributed so much to Hitler's successful aggressions, added force to the impulse to build a strong defensive alliance against the new power of Soviet Russia. Britain, France and the Low Countries had already formed a 'Western Union' alliance; and, on April 4, 1949—even before the Berlin blockade had been lifted—twelve nations signed the agreement setting up the North Atlantic Treaty Organisation (NATO). This treaty involved both the United States and Canada in defined military commitments in defence of any one of the ten European signatory states. The American Senate ratified the treaty by a majority of 82 to 13.

Strategically, the new structure of power created to oppose the expansion of the Soviet empire confronted the latter on a front extending from the extreme north to the extreme south of Europe, from the North Cape to Malta. Its core consisted of the two great powers that had gone to war with Germany in 1939; with them were Holland and Belgium, countries that, after their recent experience, were no longer inclined to rely on their traditional neutrality for safety in a grim world. To the north, the alliance included Denmark, Norway and Iceland, likewise disillusioned over policies of neutrality by experience in the Second World War; still profoundly pacific and with very modest armed forces of their own, they were nevertheless convinced that a maritime war involving Britain, Russia and the United States would not leave them unscathed as neutrals. To the south, the alliance reached out to include Portugal and Italy. Portugal was remote from 'the front' in Central Europe, yet was important for a strategy that allowed for the possibility of initial defeat in the event of a general war, for, if ever a victorious Russian offensive should sweep through to the Bay of Biscay, an allied Portugal would still provide the United States with a bridgehead on the European continent, as it had done for Britain in the Napoleonic wars. Spain could not be brought into the alliance because General Franco, installed in power with the backing of Hitler and Mussolini after three years of civil war, was still unacceptable to very many people in the Western democracies. Even so, it could be taken for granted that Franco would not be on the side of Russia. Further east, a post-Fascist democratic Italy, with a large and menacing internal Communist party, confronted on its north-eastern border and across the Adriatic the Communist states of Yugoslavia and Albania. When the North Atlantic Treaty was signed, Yugoslavia had already been expelled from the brotherhood of Communist states for its defiance of Moscow; but it could not be taken as certain that the breach would be permanent. Indeed, the idea of neutralism as a political principle was only gradually evolved by Tito.

The participation of the United States, Canada and Britain in NATO involved all three in unprecedented peacetime defence commitments. The two North American powers had never before assumed advance obligations of military action in Europe, while Britain, though bound in the period between the wars by the terms of the Locarno Treaty and subsequently by the guarantee to Poland, had not previously undertaken to keep armed forces on the European continent in time of peace. For the three powers outside continental Europe, the new alliance required a fundamental repudiation of isolationist traditions, a political change such as could hardly have been brought about but for the blockade of Berlin and the memory of what had occurred through disunity and unpreparedness in facing Hitler.

It remained to bring three other countries into the alliance: Greece, Turkey and West Germany. The inclusion of Greece and Turkey was a natural extension of the West European combination, even though the designation of 'Atlantic' hardly covered them. They had been taken under American protection through the Truman Doctrine, and could be linked with Italy in a strategic zone extending eastward along the north side of the Mediterranean. The case of West Germany involved a greater modification of the original conception. It had been assumed from the beginning that the alliance would defend the American, British and French occupation zones in Germany—and thus also the new German Federal Republic—as well as the territories of the member states. But it soon came to be regarded as desirable that West Germany should itself be associated as an ally, both to give it equal status in accordance with the restoration of German sovereignty, and to obtain from it a contribution to the military forces available to the alliance. It was, indeed, ironic that, so soon after a war that had had as one of its aims the total and permanent disarmament of Germany, the Western powers should want to create a new German army. Certainly, the West had not taken the initiative in arming Germans after 1945; German rearmament had begun in the Soviet zone with the formation of the Communist Volkspolizei, equipped with artillery and tanks. But the reappearance of German soldiers west of the Elbe could not fail to arouse misgiving and alarm in all countries that had suffered from the trampling oppression of Hitler's armies.

There were qualms even in Britain and the United States, while in Poland, Czechoslovakia and Russia, Communist propaganda acquired a theme it could exploit to great effect both domestically and abroad. Wide sections of the population, indifferent to Marxist-Leninist slogans and sceptical of other charges against the Western powers, could be roused by reports of a revival of German militarism and national ambitions. The record of world history since 1945 does not sustain the thesis that Communist policies have been motivated solely by the quest for security against a revival of German power, but fears of such a revival have been real enough among the masses. Russians imagine the Herrenvolk back once again in Kharkov and Sebastopol; Poles see no saviour but Russia as long as West Germany and the NATO powers decline to recognise the Oder–Neisse line as the western frontier of Poland. How to bring West Germany as a willing partner into the new society of Western nations and persuade it to contribute to its own defence without at the same time rallying Russians, Poles and Czechs in the opposite camp—this is a problem that has taxed Western statesmanship to the utmost. It is not a problem that has grown any easier with the passage of time.

4

FAR EASTERN TRANSFORMATION

WHEN JAPAN'S SURRENDER ended the Pacific war, the American army had not yet set foot on the soil of the Japanese homeland. By the terms of the surrender, American troops were to occupy Japan, but it was with great caution and considerable misgiving that they approached the shores of the volcanic islands that had never before submitted to a foreign yoke. They remembered the suicide attacks of the Kamikaze pilots on American ships off Okinawa and the desperate, fanatical resistance of the doomed Japanese garrisons on Saipan and Iwojima. Was it possible that this warlike nation, which had fought a losing war with such bitter obstinacy, would yield to an alien conquerer in its own territory without some kind of guerrilla resistance from last-ditch patriots? When the American troops sailed into Yokohama and saw a large banner on the quay inscribed 'Welcome to the American Army', weapons were brought to the ready. Surely there must be a hidden ambush in those piles of rubble behind the docks!

But there was no resistance, either in Yokohama or anywhere else in Japan. Whether in the ruins of their bombed cities or in the green, unravaged countryside, the Japanese were orderly, disciplined, docile and obedient to the orders of the occupation authorities. In spite of the confusion due to the wandering of millions of homeless people, there was everywhere a civil administration able to translate directives into terms of day-to-day government. The Imperial Japanese Army gave up its weapons and disbanded itself without even a show of hostility. The Japanese did not seem to be the same people as those whom the Americans had encountered in battle only a month before. In fact, they had simply accepted their defeat with a national unanimity produced by long years of submission to the state. They had lost the war, and that was that. It could not be helped; the Emperor himself had told them to surrender. The Americans were clearly more powerful than they were, and it would be prudent to defer to them; perhaps, also, one might learn something from them.

By the time a peace treaty was concluded between the United States and Japan, the main international alignments of the Pacific war had been completely reversed. America had fought against Japan with China as an ally; but by 1952, when the San Francisco Treaty ended the military occupation of Japan and the authority of the Supreme Commander for the Allied Powers over the Japanese government, a disarmed and democratised Japan was willing to sign a security pact with the United States, while China—or at least the Chinese government that controlled all the territory of China with the exception of the island of Formosa—had been virtually at war with the United States since the entry of the 'Chinese People's Volunteers' into Korea in the autumn of 1950. Just as the sequel to the war against Hitler in Europe was the inclusion of the Federal Republic of Germany in the North Atlantic Alliance, while Poland and Czechoslovakia became satellites of the Soviet Union, so, in the Far East, the sequel to the war that began with the bombing of Pearl Harbor was a military alliance between the United States and Japan, and another between the Soviet Union and Communist China. There was, however, one outstanding difference. Whereas in Europe the tensions of the Cold War between the Soviet Union and the West involved no more belligerent conflict than the Berlin blockade, the clash of policies in the Far East led to three years of hard fighting in the Korean peninsula: the one major war in the world, so far, since 1945.

A further difference between Europe and the Far East after the Second World War was Japan's avoidance of the partition that was Germany's fate. President Truman's insistence on an American supreme command in the occupation of Japan prevented a repetition there of the co-ordinate zoning that rendered possible the emergence of a Communist régime under Russian military protection in a part of Germany. That a zonal occupation system in Japan would have had the same result as in Germany was strongly indicated by the outcome in Korea.

Japan survived defeat and military occupation as a single national state. Nor did it suffer losses of Japanese-inhabited territories comparable to the amputation from Germany of the lands east of the Oder–Neisse line. Japan lost its colonial territories of Korea and Formosa, as well as all the countries of Asia brought under Japanese domination after 1931; but the only areas of solid Japanese population taken from national control were South Sakhalin (Karafuto) and the Kuriles (Chishima), which were annexed by the Soviet Union, and the Ryukyu islands (including Okinawa), which were temporarily detached under American administration for strategic reasons. The number of Japanese repatriated from overseas colonial or conquered territories, or driven from their homes in Sakhalin and the Kuriles, was an appreciable addition to the population of a country as impoverished as Japan in the immediate post-war period; but it was small in comparison with the host of 'expellees' in Germany. Indeed, Japan in defeat fared much better than Germany.

The surrender, nevertheless, left the Japanese people in a miserable plight. Three quarters of all the urban dwellings in Japan had been destroyed by bombing; a great part of the nation's industrial equipment had been wrecked, or worn out by wartime use without repair or replacement; most of the merchant marine had been sunk and foreign trade virtually eliminated. The occupation authority, as in Germany, was not at first disposed to do anything to restore economic life beyond the minimum necessary to avert widespread starvation. The domestic political situation, with the army abolished and the old system of government discredited, was favourable to the growth of Communism if the occupational authority would tolerate it. At first, it seemed that this might be so. Imprisoned Communist leaders were released as soon as the Americans arrived, and there was no interference with tumultuous Communist-organised demonstrations which the bewildered Japanese police—told that, in the new era of democracy, they must no longer deal with crowds in the traditional manner—were unable or unwilling to control. But General MacArthur took the view that he had not become the Supreme Commander for the Allied Powers in order to preside over the communisation of Japan, and his position was strong enough for his view to prevail in Washington. With the development of the Cold War and the waning of America's enragement with Japan, it became an object of United States policy not merely to disarm and punish the beaten enemy but to prepare the way for a reconciliation with the Japanese people, and give them hope for the future by promoting their economic revival.

Since there was not only an undivided state but also continuity of administration in Japan after the surrender, the adoption of a new democratic constitution took place earlier there than in West Germany. In the new constitution, the inspiration of the political experts at General MacArthur's headquarters brought about the insertion of a clause whereby Japan renounced all armed forces and the right to belligerency in any circumstances. This wonderful gesture of unilateral pacifism was regarded at the time as a triumph of American policy, and it gave the Japanese themselves the consolatory feeling that, if they had failed to win the war, they were at any rate leading the world in the formal renunciation of arms. But, before long, this constitutional prohibition was to be found highly inconvenient when the United States desired a limited rearmament of Japan as part of a system for the containment of Communist power in the Far East, and when the Japanese government itself, with the conclusion of the peace treaty in 1952 and the withdrawal of American occupation forces, wished to guard against the possibility of the country's being taken over by a single airborne division from the mainland of Asia. Because of the provisions of the new constitution, the rearmament of Japan could be carried out only by a set of legal subterfuges. The new army could not be recognised as such but was called, first, a Special Police Reserve, and, later, a Self-Defence Force; new equivalents had to be found for the old, abolished military ranks. Japan thus regained a military capability, but the successor to the old Imperial Army was numerically inferior to the military establishment of either North or South Korea, and its constitutionally dubious character had an adverse effect on its own morale and on its standing in public esteem.

The 'MacArthur Constitution' eliminated the Emperor's prerogatives, preserved by the former Meiji Constitution of 1889, and made him simply a 'symbol of the state', deprived even of the function that constitutional monarchs in Europe fulfil in receiving the credentials of foreign ambassadors. There had been in the United States some support for the idea of abolishing the Japanese monarchy completely, in view of the use which had been made of it by the military party before and during the war, but it was finally decided to retain it under the control of the Allied occupation authority. If the Emperor *had* been deposed, it would certainly have reduced the prospects of national unity and stability in post-war Japan, and increased the risk of revolutionary upheaval and civil war after the end of the occupation. As it was, despite much political effervescence (particularly of youth organisations) of a kind very shocking to conservative Japanese, the new democratic parliamentary system worked reasonably well, without either a paralysis of government or a resort to dictatorial measures. Japan's emergence as a genuine political democracy was closely linked to the degree of industrialisation that set the Japanese apart from all other nations of Asia except the Soviet Union, and ranked them with the peoples of Western Europe in capital formation, technology and standards of living. The revival of Japanese industry after 1948 was comparable to the similar revival in West Germany. In both cases, the economic expansion helped to take the sting out of defeat in war and to reduce the attraction of revolutionary politics.

In one way, however, the American occupation changed the social structure of Japan, not by economic assistance or even by constitutional reforms, but by direct intervention in Japanese domestic affairs. The American government insisted on a radical agrarian reform, which would probably not otherwise have come about without a revolution. In pre-war Japan, the social tensions of the countryside and the impoverishment of large sections of the peasantry had been a main factor in the political unrest that was then for the most part channelled into rightwing nationalist agitation. After the war, the Communists effectively exploited agrarian discontent elsewhere in Asia; but in Japan, legislation enacted under American pressure drastically restricted the size of property holdings, and many former tenants were transformed into peasant proprietors. The extension of peasant ownership had a stabilising effect on Japanese society, and created a strong vested interest in support of the new democracy. Japanese landlords suffered heavy losses, but at least they could console themselves with the reflection that they had escaped the worse fate that befell the land-owning gentry of China.

The political life of post-war Japan, as of West Germany, showed a predominance of the moderate right, standing for a capitalist economy and international alignment with the West, and a strong socialist party in opposition. There was, however, the difference that, whereas the German Social Democrats, faced with the Soviet-sponsored tyranny of Ulbricht in East Germany, supported a policy of membership of the North Atlantic Alliance and resistance to Russian ascendancy in Central Europe, the Japanese Socialists, with no local Ulbricht to provoke them, were neutralist and opposed to any strategic commitment to the United States. The Japanese-American Security Pact, concluded in 1952 at the same time as the San Francisco Peace Treaty, thus depended on the retention of political power in Japan by the right; there was no bipartisan foreign policy. The Japanese Communists remained a small minority, but there was a widespread mood combining emotional pacifism, anti-Americanism, obsession with national sovereignty, and sentiments of solidarity with People's China. This mood was particularly strong among the intelligentsia, and it introduced serious difficulties into relations with America, as was shown by the riots of 1960 that caused President Eisenhower to cancel a projected visit to Japan.

The Japanese democratic constitution and the agrarian reforms were imposed by the American occupation authorities, which, by the terms of the surrender, had an unlimited right to issue orders to the Japanese government. That these two political changes survived the occupation was due to their being sustained by strong political forces within Japan. But the seven years of tutelage under the Supreme Commander for the Allied Powers were essential to the process of orderly change in Japanese society.

There could scarcely be a more vivid contrast than that between the destinies of Japan and China in the post-war period. In China, the Americans had no such legal authority as they had in Japan; but they hoped to use their influence to promote the same kind of political and social evolution that they were able to enforce in Japan. That they failed —disastrously so for themselves—was due to their inability to recognise both the extent of the disintegration of Chinese society under the stress of eight years of foreign invasion, and also the depth of the political divisions that made civil war unavoidable after the end of the struggle against Japan. The American government believed that it could avert the civil war by mediation and, by using the dependence of the Chinese 'National' government on American aid, compel it to desist from military operations against the Chinese Communists at a time when it had the upper hand. However, the only result was a renewal of the civil war, after a year's armistice, under conditions much more favourable for the Communists and leading to their eventual conquest of China in late 1949.

The Chinese government—which, during the war had had its temporary capital at Chungking in western China, but which moved back to Nanking soon after Japan's surrender—was headed by Chiang Kai-shek and controlled by the Kuomintang: the 'bourgeois nationalist' party created by Sun Yat-sen a generation earlier. Sun's programme envisaged the Kuomintang governing China under single-party rule until the country had been fully unified after the years of 'warlord' anarchy and made ready for the institutions of parliamentary democracy. The Kuomintang, however, was opposed by the Chinese Communist Party. With their own army and territorial administration in north-west China, the Communists were able, by guerrilla action, to extend their sway eastward during the war as far as the coast of the Yellow Sea, after the Chinese government's authority there had been eliminated by the Japanese invasion. Since two armed parties thus contended for power, and since no genuine democratic elections had ever been held to create a representative national parliament to give legitimacy to either of them, the conflict could only be decided by force, unless the opponents could be persuaded to join together in a coalition government with amalgamation of the armies. The Kuomintang, on the face of it, seemed to be in the stronger position. It had the great advantage of international recognition as the legal government of China; its *de jure* authority was accepted not only by the United States and Britain but also by the Soviet Union. The United States, as the country that had given the Chinese government more economic and military assistance than any other during the war against Japan, would therefore have been well within its rights in continuing such assistance after the war to enable it to put down an internal revolt. However, instead of doing so, America decided that its responsibility was to prevent the recognised Chinese government from taking action to crush the revolt.

There is still some mystery about the motives and calculations governing this policy of the United States, but three distinct factors can be identified as converging to produce the general state of mind in Washington towards China during the eighteen months after Japan's surrender. The first was sheer idealism: it was held to be right for America to do everything possible to prevent civil war in an allied country, and wrong to help an established government to assert its domestic authority by force of arms. This outlook was shared by many

72

Americans who certainly had no sympathy for Communism, but it helps to explain the strength of the second factor, namely, the positively favourable attitude of not a few Americans towards Chinese Communism. This attitude also derived from American idealism, being a manifestation of the urge to reform and improve China. In the nineteenth century, it had taken the form of Christian evangelism, but in the twentieth century, it became more and more secular, with strong overtones of social radicalism. Serious-minded Americans living in China were shocked at the poverty and destitution they saw around them, at the indifference of the wealthy classes to the sufferings of the poor, and at the inefficiency and corruption of governmental administration. Neither the republican revolution of 1911, nor the Kuomintang conquest of China in 1927, had fundamentally changed the old ways of Chinese society. By contrast, the Chinese Communist Party seemed genuinely concerned about the welfare of the people. Its leaders practised an austere simplicity that made a favourable impression on the spiritual heirs of American puritanism. Moreover, it was all the easier for Americans in China to become enthusiastic over the Chinese Communists because of the widespread belief that they were not really Communists at all. Defeated in their bid for power in the cities, the Chinese Communists had built up their power in the countryside with peasant support; this was taken to mean that they were not convinced Marxist-Leninists, but simply 'agragrian reformers'. Indeed, an official memorandum, written by Byrnes when Secretary of State, referred to them as the 'so-called Communists'.[1] They were also believed to be good democrats, with no desire to create a single-party state on the Soviet model.

A third factor influencing American policy was the fear that, if there were prolonged civil war in China between the Kuomintang and the Communists, and if the United States gave strong support to the Chinese government, the Soviet Union would assist the other side, with the danger of a serious conflict between the two great powers growing out of the strife of their protégés in China. The situation was complicated by the concessions at the expense of China made by President Roosevelt at Yalta, as part of Russia's price for entering the war against Japan. The vesting in the Soviet Union—by an agreement in which the Chinese government was not consulted, but which it was later compelled to accept—of rights over Port Arthur, Dairen and the

Manchurian trunk railways meant in effect that the United States recognised Manchuria as a Russian sphere of influence. The record of American policy with regard to Manchuria in the autumn of 1945 indicates that the Yalta agreement was so understood by Byrnes and Acheson. China, in fact, was treated at Yalta as a country which was not fully sovereign. The consequences of this act were more far-reaching than Roosevelt may have realised at the time, for what was at stake in China was not merely a matter of local economic and strategic interests but a question of the political alignment of nearly a quarter of the human race.

After Japan's surrender early in August 1945, the situation in China developed rapidly. The Japanese were still in occupation of the principal cities of China—including Nanking, Shanghai, Tientsin and Peking— the Russians were interpenetrating Manchuria, the Communists were astride the trunk railways of north China, and the main military strength of the Chinese government was south of the Yangtse. General MacArthur, as Supreme Commander for the Allied powers, ordered the Japanese forces in Manchuria to surrender to the Russians and those south of the Great Wall to surrender to officers designated by Chiang Kai-shek, the recognised commander-in-chief in the Chinese theatre of operations. This meant that the Chinese Communists were given no right to receive the surrender of Japanese troops or to take their arms and munitions and the places they occupied. But Chinese government forces could not exercise their exclusive right to take over from the Japanese unless they could move quickly to the places held by the Japanese army, and this they could not do by themselves, except in south China, because of lack of transport and Communist obstruction of overland communications. This difficulty was resolved by the provision of American air and sea transport to move Chinese government troops to their objectives. In this way, Nanking, Shanghai, Tientsin and Peking were recovered, and the Kuomintang was indirectly assisted against the Communists, who otherwise might have captured these places. However, the advantage thus gained by the Chinese government with American support was countered by Communist acquisitions due to Russian collusion. A part of the Communist forces in north China were sent into Manchuria, then under Russian military occupation, and they were not only allowed to help themselves from the Japanese arms dumps captured by the Russians—thus equipping themselves for the first time with a sufficiency of weapons—but were permitted to occupy Manchurian ports other than Dairen (which the Russians held as their own) in order to prevent Chinese government forces from entering Manchuria from the sea to take over from the Russians, as promised in the Russo-Chinese treaty concluded in August on the basis of the Yalta agreement. When American ships carrying Chinese government troops approached Dairen, they were refused permission to land, although nothing in the treaty entitled the Soviet Union to refuse passage to Chinese regular forces. Unable to land at Dairen, the ships tried the ports of Yingkow and Hulutao, but found both of them held in force by the Communists. That the Russians were conniving at this opposition was shown by the fact that at Yingkow Soviet troops were still in town but had handed over the dock area to the Communists. As the American naval commander escorting the troopships had orders not to force a landing at any place held by 'dissident' Chinese forces, he could only turn back and put the government troops ashore at Chingwangtao, south of the Great Wall, which had already been taken over from the Japanese.[2] From here, it was possible to march into Manchuria by land along the coast through the narrow defile at Shanhaikwan where the mountain range which forms the northern boundary of the North China Plain comes down to the sea. The Russians had captured Shanhaikwan, but turned it over to the Communists, and if the latter had been able to hold this strong position, Chiang Kai-shek's forces would never have been able to get into Manchuria at all; Manchuria would then have been effectively detached from the rest of China as a Soviet 'Manchukuo'. The circumstantial evidence indicates that this was Stalin's aim, that he intended to control Mongolia and Manchuria as Russia's sphere in China and was ready to leave the rest of the country to the Americans.

If this was the plan, however, it miscarried. Chinese government troops advanced from Chingwangtao and captured Shanhaikwan, thus breaking into Manchuria overland. After this fiasco, Stalin appears to have regarded the Chinese Communists as a broken reed; a little over two years later, in February 1948, he told Kardelj, the Yugoslav Foreign Minister, that he had advised the Chinese Communists that their armed insurrection 'had no prospect' and that it would be better for them to disband their army and confine themselves to political action. Stalin then admitted that he had been wrong—the only known occasion on which he conceded that his judgement had been in error. But it was not an unreasonable conclusion from the military record of the Chinese Communists up to November of 1945. Stalin took a hard, unsentimental view of foreign Communist parties and judged them according to their actual performance; if the Chinese Communists could not hold a position such at Shanhaikwan after it had been given to them, they were obviously incompetent. Since he was not willing to use Russian troops against Chinese government forces and thus risk a serious conflict with the United States, the advice he gave to the Chinese comrades was simply good sense from his own point of view. Mao Tse-tung might have accepted it after a brief delay, for the Communists during November and December 1945, were suffering defeats in north China as well as in Manchuria at the hands of the government forces. But their fortunes were soon to change.

If a Kuomintang army had succeeded in forcing its way into Manchuria in spite of the facilities the Soviet occupation army had given the Communists for keeping it out, this was no thanks to any diplomatic action of the United States on China's behalf. Since the August treaty had been concluded between China and the Soviet Union on the basis of the Yalta agreement, to which America was a party, the Chinese government urged the United States to protest at the Soviet behaviour in Manchuria, which involved a serious violation of that treaty, but the American government declined to do so. Yet, even with the separation of Manchuria (which had been in any case lost to China since 1931 as a result of Japanese action), Chiang Kai-shek's government might have survived if it had been allowed to complete the clearing of railway communications through north China which it had successfully begun. The cessation of the offensive directed to this end was due, not to the strength of the Communists, but to the American government's insistence that it could not assist Chiang Kai-shek beyond helping him to build up thirty-nine divisions (he had wanted ninety), and then only on condition that the forces—as President Truman told T. V. Soong—be not 'diverted for use in fratricidal warfare or to support undemocratic administration'.[3] General Wedemeyer, whose own sympathies were with Chiang Kai-shek, had to inform him that 'no assistance could be furnished for the Central Government's actions against the rebellious military elements within Chinese territory', and that 'the degree to which China has obtained political stability and security under a unified government completely representative of the people will be regarded as a fundamental condition governing the United States' economic, military and other forms of assistance'.[4] This stability under unified government was to be obtained, in the State Department's view, not by crushing revolts, but by a peaceful reconciliation of the contending factions.

The American policy was not only a matter of words. Large stocks of Lend Lease munitions, assembled in India for delivery to China in the final stages of the war against Japan, were destroyed or dumped in the sea on orders from Washington. Later, after General Marshall had been sent to China by President Truman to impose his mediation on irreconcilable enemies, a total embargo on arms for China was applied by the United States and Britain; hence, the Chinese government was precluded even from buying arms abroad with such foreign exchange as it could acquire. This embargo remained in force from July 1946 to May 1947. It was hoped by American officials that 'such a move might assist their efforts to bring peace in China'.

Marshall arrived in China on December 20, 1945, and succeeded in arranging a cease-fire agreement effective from January 10, 1946. Politically, he succeeded in getting the government and the Communists to agree on a settlement in general terms; but, as soon as it came to applying it in detail, deadlock ensued. Fighting broke out again in Manchuria in the spring, and in north China in July. Marshall arranged further truces, but he could not assuage the bitter hostility and distrust with which the two parties regarded each other, and at last he requested Truman to recall him. He left China in January 1947, and was immediately appointed Secretary of State in succession to Byrnes. Full-scale civil war was now resumed in China, but the situation had changed greatly to the advantage of the Communists during the year of Marshall's mediation. They had gained a year in which to consolidate their hold on the territories into which they had spread at the end of the Pacific war and to raise new armies from them, while the morale of the Kuomintang forces, which had been good at the end of 1945, had declined with the frustration of the American-imposed truces, and shortages of ammunition now precluded them from prolonged offensive operations. The American arms embargo was continued for four months after Marshall left China, and even when it was formally lifted, Washington showed no inclination to sustain the Chinese government with the supplies it required. The Truman Doctrine, which provided for American military assistance to the Greek government in a civil war against Communists, gave American advocates of support for the Chinese government an opportunity to press for similar action in China; but the plea was rejected on the ground that there was no analogy with the situation in Greece. As Acheson declared in justifying his policy: 'The Chinese Government is not at the present time in the position that the Greek Government is in. It is not approaching collapse. It is not threatened with defeat by the Communists. The war with the Communists is going on much as it has been for the last twenty years.'[5]

In 1947, the Truman administration thus refused help to the Chinese government on the ground that it was not needed. Later on, when the Kuomintang forces had suffered a series of serious defeats, help was refused on the ground that it would be in vain. In March 1948, Congress—against the will of the State Department—voted $125 million in military aid to China, but the delivery of arms was subject to mysterious delays and no shipment was made until November, when the Kuomintang armies had already been routed both in Manchuria and in Shantung. In the summer and autumn of 1948, the Communists went over to the offensive, and the military position and morale of the government forces rapidly deteriorated. In April 1949, the Communists captured Nanking, the seat of the Kuomintang government, and during the next six months the whole mainland of China fell to their armies. On October 1 they proclaimed the Chinese People's Republic with Peking as its capital and called for international recognition of their new régime as the *de jure* government of China. The Kuomintang government meanwhile had withdrawn to Formosa where the hundred miles of sea separating it from the mainland gave it a secure refuge for the time being.

As the Communists swept on to final victory in China, there was increasing criticism in the United States of the policy followed by the Truman administration in regard to Chinese affairs since the end of the Pacific war. To meet these recriminations, Acheson published in August 1949 a White Paper of selected documents with a Letter of Transmittal in which he declared:

The unfortunate but inescapable fact is that the ominous result of the civil war in China was beyond the control of the Government of the United States. Nothing that this country did or could have done within the reasonable limits of its capabilities could have changed that result; nothing that was left undone by this country has contributed to it.

In describing the outcome of the Chinese civil war as 'ominous', Acheson showed that no trace remained of the idea that Chinese Communists were mere 'agrarian reformers'. On July 1, Mao Tse-tung had issued a pronouncement on foreign policy in which he had made it quite clear that China under Communist rule would be aligned with the Soviet Union against 'imperialism', identified particularly with the United States. He declared that 'the Chinese people must lean either to the side of imperialism or to that of socialism', and that 'a third road does not exist'. After this, the makers of Far Eastern policy in the American government could no longer conceal from themselves or from the American public the fact that a friendly China had been replaced by a hostile one. Their apologia therefore could only take the form of a claim that they had done everything possible short of direct intervention with American troops to support the Kuomintang government; but this claim was so much at variance with the facts of the record that the Truman administration was forced more and more on to the defensive, with the Republican Party exploiting in domestic politics the 'loss' of China. Acheson, as Secretary of State, however, still sought to disengage America completely from China. On January 12, 1950, he made a speech to the National Press Club in which he drew an American 'defence perimeter' in the western Pacific through the Aleutians, Japan, Okinawa, and the Philippines; by implication, he abandoned both Formosa and South Korea as areas outside this perimeter which the Communists might take if they could without American interference. Yet when, on June 25 of the same year, the army of North Korea crossed the parallel which was the boundary between the Communist and anti-Communist régimes in the Korean peninsula, President Truman, with Acheson's concurrence, decided not only to give armed support to South Korea but also to use the American navy to prevent a seaborne invasion of Formosa by Chinese Communist forces.

This decision involved a reversal of American policy as sharp as that made by the Chamberlain cabinet in Britain when, in March 1939, it reversed its policy of 'appeasement' by the guarantee to Poland. In both cases, a tidal movement of public opinion was the main reason for the change of course, though second thoughts within the government itself about the wisdom of the policy previously pursued also contributed to the reversal. In the United States of June 1950, with Congressional elections only five months away, it had become politically impossible for Truman and Acheson to sit back and do nothing while South Korea and Formosa were over-run. It was no longer possible to persuade the American people that it was essential to contain Communism in Europe, but not essential in Asia. Truman had received endorsement from the Congress and the American public for military aid to Greece and Turkey, for resistance to a Communist subjugation of West Berlin, and finally for the North Atlantic Alliance. It made no sense at the same time to abandon totally to Communist conquest the nation that American insistence had made one of the five permanent members of the United Nations Security Council or the state that had been set up under American auspices in the southern half of Korea.

American troops had occupied Korea south of the 38th Parallel by agreement with the Soviet Union, which occupied Korea north of that line, after the end of the Pacific war. This was not intended as an occupation of an enemy country, though Korea was territory then under Japanese sovereignty, but was for the purpose of disarming and sending back to Japan the Japanese troops there and liberating the Korean people from Japanese rule. The occupation forces were also to maintain law and order while the Koreans established their own national state; the demarcation line between the Soviet and American zones was not thought of on the American side as a political division but only as a matter of military convenience between two allied armies entering the country from opposite directions. What happened, however, was almost exactly the same as what happened in Germany. The Korean Communists—whose leader, Kim Il Sung, had served in the Soviet army— took over power in the north with the backing of the Russian occupation authority, and their political opponents were persuaded to collaborate or were forcibly suppressed by arrests and executions. The Communists tried to take over in the south as well, but were prevented from doing so by the American authorities, so that, as in Germany, two rival governments emerged in the two occupation zones. Unable to reach any agreement with the Soviet Union for the unification of Korea, the American government in 1947 turned over the problem to the United Nations, which, by a majority in the Assembly, voted to send a commission to Korea to supervise elections throughout the country. The commission was refused entry into Communist-ruled North Korea but carried out its mission in the south, and the South Korean government which emerged from the elections was therefore declared legitimate by the United Nations and recognised diplomatically by the Western powers, while the nations of the Soviet bloc recognised the Communist régime in the north. The two Korean governments, each claiming to be the only lawful government of the whole country, regarded each other with bitter hatred, but as long as the American and Soviet military forces remained, they were unable to fight each other because hostilities would have at once involved the occupying troops, and Washington and Moscow were not ready to go to war over Korea. But the two great powers agreed to withdraw their troops from Korea —a withdrawal desired by the American Defense Department because of manpower shortage—and the two Koreas were left confronting each other across an artificial frontier that both aspired to obliterate. In the circumstances, it was inevitable that whichever side might be confident of superior strength would try to reunite Korea by force. It was American policy to make sure that the army of South Korea was decisively weaker than its rival, in order that the South Korean government might not be tempted to embarrass Washington by a march northwards. It was denied 'offensive weapons'—heavy artillery and tanks—which were liberally supplied to the army of North Korea by the Soviet Union. In October 1949, Congress voted a sum for military aid to South Korea, but it was held up by the same obstruction that delayed the supplies for China in March 1948. By June 25, 1950, when the North Koreans attacked, nothing but some signal wire had been delivered. 'To prevent them from attacking', explained General Roberts in charge of the training of the South Korean army, 'we gave them no combat air force or tanks or heavy artillery'.[6] Hence, starved of necessary weapons, the South Korean army naturally collapsed when attacked by heavily armed North Korean forces, and in order to avert the consequences of its own idiotic policy, the American government then committed American troops to turn the scales in a war that was to cost the United States more than 140,000 casualties.

It is not easy to explain the disparity between the European and Far Eastern policies of the United States between the end of the Second

World War and the outbreak of the war in Korea. In Europe, the foreign policy pursued by the Truman administration was increasingly one of opposition to the spread of Communist revolution and of strong support for governments that were resisting it; in the Far East, the continuing unwillingness of the same administration to provide arms for anti-Communist governments appeared to serve quite opposite political ends. Probably the most important single factor in this incoherence of American foreign policy was the state of mind of General Marshall, who shaped American Far Eastern policy more than anyone else over the crucial three years from the end of 1945 to the end of 1948. Marshall went to China with an unconsciously patronising attitude towards the Chinese; he had been sent to compose their domestic quarrels, and it never occurred to him that the Chinese might not appreciate the idea of a foreigner meddling their affairs. They wasted a year of his life in strenuous diplomatic activity ending in utter frustration, and he left China with a conviction that the Chinese were impossible to deal with. As Secretary of State, he did not want to have anything to do with them. Europe faced him with relatively simple problems. As a professional soldier, he could understand the threat of a Russian army on the Elbe; and, as the great wartime organiser of American power, he was accustomed to negotiating with European representatives who proceeded from political and economic conceptions similar to his own. But the Chinese baffled him; they seemed to belong to another world. In August 1948, he is said to have declared: 'I wash my hands of the problem [of China] which has passed altogether beyond my comprehension and my power to make judgements.'[7] His over-riding wish was to disengage from continental Asia and be quit of responsibility for what happened there, and he seems to have consoled himself with the thought that, even if the Communists took over China, they could not be, like the Russians, a serious danger to American interests. But if he washed his hands of China, they would not stay washed, and America was to suffer from the hostility of the new China sooner than Marshall could have imagined. Less than two years after he vacated the office of Secretary of State, an American army was in full retreat under attack by numerically superior Chinese Communist forces in Korea.

5

THE KOREAN WAR: EXPERIMENT IN LIMITED CONFLICT

T HE KOREAN WAR, fought from 1950 to 1953, has been—up to the time of writing, and not excluding the war in Vietnam, which has not so far involved a direct collision of great powers—the only major armed struggle in the world since 1945. It was in many ways a conflict unique in military history. It involved in actual hostilities four out of the five recognised great powers, yet none of them declared war. On the one side, it was held by America, Britain and France that they were merely supplying contingents for a police action of the United Nations; on the other, China maintained the fiction that only a body of 'People's Volunteers', not its regular forces, were fighting in Korea. In so far as the United Nations Security Council called for the intervention to repel the North Korean aggression, and appointed a commander-in-chief, it was the first (and has been so far the only) occasion on which an international security organisation has conducted a major military campaign against an aggressor. Yet, although a majority of the members of the United Nations condemned both North Korea and Communist China as aggressors, and sixteen nations took part in some degree in the UN expeditionary force, the territory of the Chinese aggressor remained by tacit agreement immune from attack throughout the war. It was a hard-fought and sanguinary struggle, but the fear of its escalation into a third world war kept it strictly limited to the Korean peninsula. It was extraordinary also in its termination, for two-thirds of its duration consisted of armistice negotiations that developed into a kind of political duel parallel with the armed combat in the field; the truce that at last terminated hostilities was only achieved at the 159th session of the armistice conference. Last, but not least, it led neither to a treaty of peace nor to the minimum of normal political relations usual after even the worst of wars. The final battle line in Korea became, after the armistice, a fortified frontier which no human being could

83

cross in either direction, and the continued American protection of the Kuomintang in Formosa precluded any diplomatic relations between Washington and Peking.

As has already been pointed out, the American decision to intervene in Korea, taken in the last week of June 1950, entailed a reversal of the policy of disengagement from continental Asia that was being pursued by the Truman administration at the beginning of the year and that had been proclaimed in Acheson's speech to the National Press Club on January 12, 1950. This declaration by the Secretary of State, disclaiming any American intention of protecting either South Korea or Formosa, gave the green light to the Communists in Korea and China respectively for assaults to gain these two territories. Kim Il Sung's decision to invade South Korea was thus presumably taken in the belief that American intervention could be ruled out; and if either Stalin or Mao Tse-tung were consulted about it, they must have been of the same opinion. The poorly equipped South Korean army was unable to stand up to the Russian-built tanks which swarmed across the 38th Parallel at dawn on June 25. Without American action, Korea would have been effectively unified under Communist rule by the end of July. A seaborne invasion of Formosa was, apparently, planned to follow soon afterwards, for there was a great increase in the concentration of Chinese Communist troops on the mainland opposite during the month just before the outbreak of war in Korea. The conquest of Formosa was a more hazardous undertaking than the subjugation of South Korea because of the difficulty of amphibious operations across a hundred miles of open sea, but in the absence of any material support from the United States, and with the collapse of South Korea before their eyes, the morale of the defenders might well have failed, as it had so often failed in the last stages of the civil war on the mainland. If Formosa had been taken, both China and Korea would then have been completely subjected to Communist rule, and Communist power would have directly confronted Acheson's famous perimeter.

But the decisions taken by President Truman, in conference with his advisers during the five days following the North Korean attack, caused the armed forces of the United States to be moved forward from the perimeter to protect Formosa and assist South Korea. General Mac-Arthur, who was in command of all American forces in the Far East as well as Supreme Commander for the Allied Powers in the military occupation of Japan, was ordered to provide air and naval forces in support of South Korea and to send the Seventh Fleet to the Formosa Strait to prevent Chinese Communist operations that might enlarge the area of conflict. Strategically, it was the latter move which was the easy one, for the Chinese Communists, with virtually no navy, could not challenge the Seventh Fleet. But it was doubtful whether air and naval support would by itself be sufficient to rescue South Korea, which was being attacked overland by a more powerful army. On June 29, after Seoul, the South Korean capital, had fallen to the invaders, MacArthur flew to the front from Tokyo, and reported that the South Koreans could not hold out unless American ground forces were committed to action. On the following day he was authorised to send to Korea combat units drawn from the American army of occupation in Japan.

Meanwhile, the Security Council of the United Nations had taken steps that were to turn the American intervention in Korea into a United Nations war. The day after the North Korean attack,* the Security Council passed by nine votes to nil, with one abstention (Yugoslavia), a resolution calling for a cease-fire in Korea and the withdrawal of the North Korean forces behind the 38th Parallel. This resolution only escaped a Soviet veto because the Soviet delegation, in protest at the Security Council's unwillingness to transfer China's seat to a representative of the People's Republic, was boycotting the proceedings of the Council. In the Soviet view no valid resolution could be adopted by the Council in the absence of the Soviet Union, but the other members claimed that the right of veto could only be exercised through attendance. By its first resolution on the war, the Council thus took up a stand politically against North Korea; but it did not yet recommend any action. Only on June 27, when North Korea had ignored the previous resolution, did the Security Council call on members of the United Nations 'to furnish such assistance to the Republic of Korea as may be necessary to repel the armed attack'. The voting on this resolution differed significantly from that on the earlier one, which did not require anybody to do anything; the seven votes of the United States, Britain, France, Nationalist China, Cuba, Norway and Ecuador provided a sufficient majority; but Yugoslavia, which had

* Formally the same day, but the North Korean attack of June 25, 1950 began while it was still June 24 in New York.

abstained on the previous resolution, now voted against, and India and Egypt, which had supported the resolution of June 25, now abstained. Yugoslavia's loyalty to the international cause of Communism proved stronger than its attachment to the United Nations Charter, and India and Egypt interpreted their neutrality in the Cold War as precluding any approval of action to repel aggression by a Communist state.

The United Nations could not be said to have initiated the intervention in Korea, for the American government's committal of naval and air forces to the defence of South Korea preceded the Security Council resolution of June 27, 1950. Nor did the Security Council cover the American move to protect Formosa, which remained a solitary undertaking of the United States, without endorsement even from America's NATO allies. But the Security Council's vote on aid to South Korea did accomplish something without precedent in the history of mankind, for the League of Nations had never reached the point of authorising the use of force, and this the United Nations was now doing for the first time. Fifteen nations in addition to the United States sent contingents of some kind to serve in Korea, and the international character of the army assembled there was emphasised by the creation of a United Nations Command (the UNC), vested in General MacArthur. Yet the driving force of the intervention was always American, and throughout the war the United States provided the great bulk of the United Nations non-Korean forces and suffered most of the casualties (142,000 American as compared with 17,000 for all other non-Korean contingents).

The North Koreans were not deterred from their swift advance by the United Nations resolution or by the arrival in South Korea of small American combat formations. Since no preparations had been made by the United States for a campaign in Korea, and reinforcements from America were not immediately available, the North Koreans could hope to overcome all resistance and be in possession of all the ports of Korea before a substantial American or United Nations army could be assembled. The UNC, however, succeeded by hard fighting in holding an area round Pusan in the south-east corner of Korea, the port nearest to Japan. Then, in the middle of September, a counterstroke planned by General MacArthur took the North Korean army in the rear by a landing at Inchon, the port of Seoul, on the west coast of the peninsula. The North Koreans fled back to their home territory after suffering very heavy losses. The UNC, the American government and the delegates at the United Nations were now faced with the question whether to halt at the 38th Parallel, where the war had started, or to follow the retreating enemy into North Korea. Militarily, it was plainly prudent to pursue the North Koreans and prevent them from rallying their forces after their defeat; politically, it could be held that, by their aggression, they had forfeited their own right to immunity from attack, and that their military collapse provided an opportunity to carry out the already declared policy of the United Nations, which was to bring about the reunification of Korea through nation-wide free elections under United Nations supervision. The UNC, therefore, was authorised to cross the 38th Parallel and advance into North Korea. But Communist China, faced with the imminent prospect of the elimination of the North Korean régime and the establishment of an unfriendly power on the frontier of Manchuria, decided to intervene in turn with regular forces thinly disguised as 'Chinese People's Volunteers'. Although warnings were conveyed to Washington through Delhi of the Chinese determination to enter the war if the UNC forces moved towards the Yalu, the threat was regarded as a bluff, and even after a Chinese military presence had been identified south of the Yalu, American intelligence reports estimated the numbers of the new enemy at only a quarter of what they actually were. When on November 24, 1950, General MacArthur launched a final offensive which was to reach the Yalu, end the war, and 'bring the boys home by Christmas', a crushing Chinese counter-offensive enveloped his right flank and forced a headlong retreat.

With victory thus suddenly transformed into defeat, MacArthur declared that 'we face an entirely new war', and began to press for direct action to be taken by sea and air against Chinese territory. But the unexpected disaster caused the Truman administration to abandon the objective of subduing North Korea rather than extend the war geographically beyond Korea. The main reason was the fear that direct operations against China would bring in the Soviet Union, which was already a formidable 'non-belligerent' on the side of the enemy. According to the former Polish military attaché in Pyongyang, who later defected to the West, there were already in 1951 about 5,000 Soviet citizens serving in North Korea and Manchuria as military engineers, jet pilots and anti-aircraft gunners.[1] An extension of the war might cause the Soviet Union to commit major military and naval forces in the Far East, or alternatively move forward in Europe, taking full advantage of the American involvement in a war with China. The British government was even more alarmed than the American at the prospect of complications in Europe, and in addition was extremely reluctant to get into a conflict with the Chinese People's Republic, which Britain had recognised as the *de jure* government of China before the outbreak of the Korean War, and which in any case held a hostage for British good behaviour in the shape of the all too vulnerable colony of Hong Kong. Britain had willingly joined with the United States in what had seemed a limited international police action in Korea, but began to back down as soon as there was a question of full-scale war against Communist China.

President Truman now found himself in an extremely difficult situation. On the one hand, General MacArthur was demanding, with widespread support from American public opinion, an extension of the war in order to force the withdrawal of Chinese forces from Korea; and on the other, the British government was urging a settlement with Peking at almost any price. An incautious admission by the President at a press conference that the use of the atomic bomb in Korea had been considered brought Attlee, the British Prime Minister, in haste to Washington to restrain the supposed recklessness of the American government. At the same time, MacArthur in Tokyo was proposing measures that would in his view 'inflict such a destructive blow upon Red China's capacity to wage aggressive war that it would remove her as a further threat to peace in Asia for generations to come'. The Republican opposition in American domestic politics, reinforced by significant victories in the mid-term Congressional elections, was now exploiting the theme that President Truman had involved America in a war in Asia, but refused to do anything effective to win it. A historian of the Korean war has thus summed up Truman's dilemma: 'The necessity of keeping NATO and the Allied front in the UN intact only emphasised that, while any Administration concession to the Taft–MacArthur alliance could destroy America's international coalition, too complete an alignment with the British attitude towards Peking could only mean the disintegration of the Administration's precarious support in Congress.'[2]

Truman was delivered from this painful predicament by two developments. In the first place, the intransigence of Peking thwarted British efforts to come to some accommodation with Communist China; and in the second, the defeat of a Communist offensive in January by the UNC, now under the inspiring command of General Ridgeway as MacArthur's immediate subordinate, rendered a holding war, limited to Korea, a practical strategic proposition. In the United Nations, flexible American tactics encouraged the Chinese Communists to over-reach themselves. Although not in possession of China's seat there, Peking was invited in November 1950 to send a representative to put its case to the Security Council. But in his speech on November 8, delivered after receiving news of the Chinese victory on the Chongchon, Peking's representative took such an uncompromising attitude as to leave no room for negotiation—except on the basis of complete capitulation by the United Nations on all the issues involved. Even so, further moves were made in the Council and the Assembly for bringing about an armistice in Korea, to be followed by a peace conference. But Peking demanded that, before any cease-fire, there must be agreement on the withdrawal of the United Nations forces from Korea, the cancellation of American protection for Formosa, and the transfer to Peking of China's UN seat. Not even the British government was willing to concede these demands, and it finally voted for a resolution of the Assembly, on February 1, 1951, condemning Communist China as an aggressor. With this evidence of substantial, if tardy, British support, Truman was able to face the critics who were alleging that he was sustaining Britain's cause in Europe while Britain was letting down America in the Far East. All the same, he could hardly have maintained, politically, his policy of limited war if the United Nations forces, with their massive American component, had been driven from the Korean peninsula. However, the Chinese Communist attempt to push on south of the 38th Parallel was checked, and Seoul was for a second time recaptured from the Communists. It was now possible to hold that the original objective of the war—the preservation of South Korea from Communist conquest—had been attained, and that there was no need to take the risks of extending the war in order to fulfil a wider political aim.

General MacArthur, nevertheless, continued to object and to make his objections public. His insubordination became intolerable for the President of the United States, and in March 1951 Truman dismissed him from his command. He received an immense popular ovation on returning to America, his reception on Broadway, as measured by the quantity of paper thrown down from office windows, breaking all previous records. It seemed for a moment as if the dismissal was recoiling on the President, and indeed, if Truman had been removable by a parliamentary vote of censure, he might have fallen from power there and then. But he had another year and a half of his administration to run, and when the first emotion had subsided the vast majority of Americans, whatever their opinions on the issues that divided the President and the General, concluded that the whole Constitution would be overturned if a military commander were to be sustained in defiance of the supreme civil authority. MacArthur himself, moreover, despite his flair for publicity, had none of the skills necessary for entry into democratic politics. It was not he, but another and more homely military figure, who was destined to capture the White House from the Democratic Party in the presidential election of 1952.

Truman's position was strengthened in the late spring of 1951 by the failure of two great offensives launched by the Chinese and the North Koreans (now reduced to mere auxiliaries of their allies), the first in April on the western, and the second in May on the eastern, sector of the Korean front. These were the greatest battles of the Korean war, and their outcome was a great defensive victory for the UNC. Confronted by a continuous line of defence across the Korean peninsula, the Chinese were no longer able to infiltrate and outflank the United Nations forces; they had to break through by frontal attack. This they tried to do by a reckless expenditure of manpower, but they were driven back with very heavy casualties. A military stalemate having now been reached and the Chinese forces being in bad shape after their defeats, Peking decided that the time had come for armistice negotiations, and a hint to that effect was duly given by the Soviet delegate to the Security Council, who had resumed his functions there when it had become apparent that the policy of boycott was ineffective. Truce talks were begun, and it was assumed in Washington that an armistice would be arranged within a month. The Americans soon discovered, however, that with the relaxation of the military pressure, the Communist side was in no hurry to terminate hostilities. Peking and its sympathisers regarded the armistice negotiations as an opportunity for prolonged haggling over details to the accompaniment of a world-wide propaganda campaign against imperialism, in which the ordinary charges of instigating war and enslaving the peoples of Asia were soon augmented by accusations that the Americans were trying to spread epidemic disease in North Korea and Manchuria by means of bacteria dropped from aircraft.

Even so, the armistice would probably have been concluded by the end of 1951 but for a dispute over prisoners of war to which no solution could be found. The nature of this dispute was symptomatic of the ideological character of the war as a struggle against Communism over and above a normal conflict of state interests. In established international law and traditional military theory, prisoners were automatically set outside the war in which they had been engaged; they were no longer involved in it and it was the duty of the captor nation to hold them under reasonably good conditions of captivity (to be verified by the International Red Cross), and return them to their own country after the end of the war. But in an ideological war, the political beliefs of soldiers are no less relevant than their military potential, and the former do not cease to be relevant after they have been taken prisoner. The enemy's troops in captivity can be made objects of propaganda for conversion; and, if converted, they can be made instruments of propaganda for the subversion of their fellow countrymen. During the Second World War, the Soviet Union recruited anti-Nazis from prison camps and used them for broadcasting to Germany; the Western Allies were reluctant to embark on this kind of political warfare, but they encouraged anti-Nazi prisoners to declare themselves and provided them with opportunities for political re-education with a view to the part they might play in post-war Germany. These variants of political selection among prisoners were repeated in Korea. American and other United Nations prisoners were subjected to prolonged indoctrination designed to make them endorse the Communist version of the war as an aggression of 'Wall Street imperialism' against the people of Korea, and pressures of all kinds were applied to break down resistance to conversion. The initial conditions of captivity were intolerably harsh, and large numbers of prisoners died from hunger, disease and ill-treatment; afterwards, those who showed themselves responsive to the propaganda of their captors got better treatment, while defiant 'reactionaries' continued to suffer. There was no possibility of protest or appeal, since no supervision by the International Red Cross was permitted; the only visitors admitted to the camps were European or American Communists who supported the propaganda of the camp authorities.

Turning to their own advantage the conception of war guilt as applied by the Allies to Germany and Japan after the Second World War, the Chinese and North Korean Communists told their prisoners that, since they had taken part in an aggressive war, they were all war criminals deserving death, but that they would be treated leniently if they showed proof of a sincere repentance. As a result of this combination of persuasion and menace, a considerable proportion of the prisoners became 'progressives'. In most cases the conversion did not last beyond release from captivity, but in some it inspired a permanent, and often fanatical, Communist conviction.

A special treatment was applied to a group of American air force officers who were required to confess to having taken part in waging bacterial warfare against the peoples of China and Korea. According to a report by Dr Charles Mayo submitted to the United Nations Political Committee after the end of the war, these officers were subjected to 'extreme and prolonged physical and mental torture' to make them confess to participation in acts which, in the light of all the evidence available, never took place. Of 107 who were charged with taking part in germ warfare, 36 signed confessions, 40 refused to sign and survived, and 31 perished under the treatment.[3]

On the other side of the firing line, there were no similar drives for ideological conversion or the production of useful confessions. The UN prisoners' camps were open to inspection by the International Red Cross. Prisoners with anti-Communist sentiments were, however, encouraged to declare themselves and they proved to be very numerous. But their fellow prisoners who remained loyal to the Communist cause were not disposed to tolerate this defection, and the extremely lax conditions under which prisoners were held under American guard on the island of Koje, whither most of them had been sent, rendered possible an extraordinary exercise of Communist power within the prison camps. A Communist organisation directed by radio from Pyongyang set up tribunals which passed death sentences on anti-Communist prisoners and finally kidnapped the American commandant, compelling him to sign a propaganda statement about conditions in the camps as the price of his life. The Communist control in the camps was finally broken by bringing in strong units of American troops; but the rioting and violence gave the Communists an opportunity to claim that the Americans were using force to intimidate Chinese and North Korean prisoners and compel them to declare that they did not wish to be repatriated after the war.

The battle was now joined on the issue of prisoner repatriation. The Communists had no wish to prevent the repatriation of the prisoners whom they had converted to 'progressive' views, but on the contrary wished them to go back to their own countries as preachers of the gospel. Communist parties were lawful in the United States and Britain, and ex-prisoners would not be liable to any legal penalty for having changed their political opinions while in captivity. For anti-Communist Chinese or North Korean prisoners, on the other hand, return to their homes after the war would mean imprisonment or death; their defection was counter-revolution and treason. They were desperately afraid of being sent back and claimed the protection of those who had encouraged them to declare their sympathies. But the Communist states concerned could not admit that any large number of their citizens might genuinely prefer exile to repatriation, for they claimed virtually unanimous support of their peoples. If, therefore, any of their soldiers said they did not wish to return, it must be the result of American intimidation, and it was an obvious imperative of policy to insist on their repatriation. The insistence was all the more emphatic because of the statistical claims of the UNC: a large minority of the North Korean prisoners and a clear majority of the Chinese prisoners were alleged not to desire repatriation.

On this question, the armistice negotiations reached a deadlock that went on and on. The Communist side demanded that all prisoners should be repatriated, if necessary against their will; the UNC stood firm on the principle of voluntary repatriation. It now became a test of endurance, for the UNC had no way of compelling the Chinese to accept a cease-fire as long as the war was confined to Korea. The Communist forces now held a deeply fortified line across the peninsula; it could be pierced, if at all, only at the cost of extremely heavy casualties, and even then there could be no certainty that an end to hostilities would have been brought any nearer. Intensified bombing of North Korea might make Kim Il Sung more disposed to end the war, but it could not coerce China, which would remain untouched by it. Peking appeared to be ready to go on with the war for another ten years rather than yield on the question of prisoner repatriation. The war was no longer an affair of big battles, but of local, tactical encounters. These, which were usually for possession of some commanding height, were often hard-fought and bloody, so that there was never a time when the prolongation of hostilities could be ignored. American casualties, which were nearly 80,000 for the first year of the Korean war, still ran to some 30,000 for each of the two years which were taken up by the armistice negotiations.

In the United States there was an ever more exasperated demand that the government should somehow bring the war to an end. The inability of the Truman administration to terminate it was a major factor in bringing about the defeat of the Democratic Party in the presidential election of 1952, which Eisenhower won largely on the strength of a pledge to go to Korea if he were elected, and review the situation on the spot. The electorate was moved by the hope that the soldier who had held supreme command in Western Europe from D-day to the surrender of Germany would find the solution that had eluded his civilian predecessor. But Eisenhower was faced with the same dilemma that had baffled Truman. He duly went to Korea within a month of his election, but he could only confirm the fact of a military stalemate in the peninsula. At Panmunjon, the armistice negotiations dragged on in a weary routine with no sign of producing any result. Eisenhower and his new Secretary of State, John Foster Dulles, now came back to reconsider the policy of a direct attack on China—the policy for persisting in which MacArthur had been deprived of his command. The risks appeared no less formidable than two years previously, and British disapproval was as strong as ever. But in March 1953, an event occurred which profoundly modified the configuration of world affairs. Stalin died, and the Soviet Union, with a disputed succession and uncertainty of policy at home, no longer cast over the world as menacing a shadow as it had done during the lifetime of the great despot. The risks of bombing China, no longer to evict the Chinese army from Korea but simply to persuade Peking to agree to an armistice without forcible repatriation of all Chinese prisoners, could now be marked down. In May, while nuclear weapons were not too secretly sent to Okinawa, Dulles went to Delhi and told Indian officials for the information of Peking that, if there was no armistice in Korea in the very near future, the United States would extend the war. Early in June, the Communist delegates at the armistice conference accepted the principle of voluntary repatriation. After some further haggling, an armistice was finally concluded on

The Korean War: Experiment in Limited Conflict

July 27, 1953, three years and a month after the North Korean tanks had rumbled across the 38th Parallel in the early hours of June 25, 1950.

There was no political settlement of the Korean question after the termination of hostilities. The fighting had not been preceded by any declarations of war and it was not followed by any peace treaty. The armistice itself, drawing a new line of demarcation between North and South Korea, different from the 38th Parallel but almost equivalent to it, has remained the only agreed regulator of Korean affairs; it has continued to divide a single nation by a heavily fortified frontier that no one can cross in either direction. The political conference that was to have produced a settlement after the armistice was deadlocked on the same issue which had thwarted all endeavours to unite Korea before the war; the Communists had to have, as in Germany, either the whole or a half of the country, but they would not accept a unified national state with democratic elections in which they might be defeated. President Syngman Rhee of South Korea, who had never agreed to Truman's renunciation of the conquest of North Korea as a war aim, had done his best to prevent the conclusion of the armistice by threatening that South Korea would fight on alone. It was obviously incapable of doing so, and eventually Rhee abandoned his opposition, though not before he had obtained a definite military commitment of the United States for the future defence of South Korea in addition to the more precarious protection of the United Nations. Two American divisions remained permanently in South Korea after the armistice together with the formal organisation of the United Nations Command, ready to be 'reactivated' at any time if Communist forces should again drive south. But thirteen years have passed, at the time of writing, without violation of the armistice line, and the no-man's-land between the fortifications on each side has become an uninhabited wilderness.

If Korea remained divided by a *de facto* frontier without an agreed partition, so also did China. The United States continued to protect Formosa as well as South Korea, so that the two anti-Communist territories which had been left outside the Acheson Line at the beginning of 1950 were now both guaranteed against Communist conquest by American power. But this was a situation that caused serious complications on a world scale. If the armed Communist avalanche in East Asia had been allowed to overwhelm South Korea and Formosa, both Korea and China would have been unified under Communist rule and would have qualified for American diplomatic recognition no less than Rumania, Hungary or Czechoslovakia. They would also probably very soon have entered the United Nations, a Communist delegate taking over the seat already belonging to China, and a representative of a Communist Korea getting in as part of some package deal. But as far as the United States was concerned, continued recognition of anti-Communist governments in both countries excluded diplomatic relations with their Communist authorities. For the United Nations, which had sponsored the government elected under its auspices as the only legitimate authority in Korea, North Korean membership was out of the question as long as the South Korean régime survived; but so also was South Korean membership because of the Soviet veto. Korea therefore had no prospect of entering the United Nations at all. China, on the other hand, was already a member and it was only a question of which Chinese government was entitled to nominate the Chinese delegates. Until the organs of the United Nations themselves decided to transfer the Chinese seat to delegates of the People's Republic, the Kuomintang government would continue to hold it. Yet the United Nations had no special commitment to the Kuomintang régime, as it had to South Korea, and it could be argued that the Communists, having brought under their effective authority the whole of China except Formosa, were entitled to represent the Chinese nation internationally. This was the view held by Trygve Lie as Secretary-General of the United Nations, and it was strongly supported by the British government which, even during the early period of the Korean War, was trying hard to bring about the seating of delegates from Peking. But Communist representation of China in the United Nations was incompatible with American armed protection of Formosa (turned into a formal defensive military alliance by the Eisenhower administration), for the Peking government, once recognised as representative of China by the United Nations, would be able to appeal against American policy as aiding rebels in defiance of China's international rights.

The protection of Formosa, therefore, necessarily involved the United States in a permanent political struggle within the United Nations to prevent the seating of delegates of Communist China. In support of their position, the Americans could argue (and convincingly for many) that Communist China, having fought against a United Nations army and been condemned as an aggressor by the United Nations Assembly, should not be allowed to take its place in the international security organisation without some expression of repentance—which was obviously quite incompatible with the Communist version of the nature and origins of the Korean War. Yet this argument, however logical if the function of the United Nations as a security organisation were to be taken seriously, was open to the criticism that it involved the exclusion of Communist China indefinitely from the world society. There was certainly no good ground for supposing, as was widely imagined in Britain, that the admission of Communist China to the United Nations would automatically bring about a détente in the Far East. The Soviet Union's foundation membership of the United Nations had not, after all, prevented the Cold War. But the American protection of Formosa and refusal of diplomatic recognition, and the denial (in so far as it lay within the power of American diplomacy) of United Nations representation to the new régime in China, meant that there was an antagonism between Washington and Peking sharper and more intractable than any which existed between Washington and Moscow. In this conflict, America could not count on the co-operation with Britain that had been established in European affairs. After 1952 Britain—fearful of a mortal quarrel with America—refrained from trying to get the United Nations seat for Peking, but remained (and the attitude was shared by both the main political parties) fundamentally unsympathetic to America's China policy, indifferent to the fate of Formosa, and apprehensive of being dragged into a new Far Eastern war by American bellicosity in the China Seas. Britain's frontier might now be on the Elbe, but it was certainly nowhere near Quemoy.

6

THE NEW WEAPONRY: PROSPECT OF
TOTAL CONFLICT

AMONG THOSE WHO waited in the darkness before dawn for the testing of the first atomic bomb in the desert of New Mexico, there was no certainty that the experiment would succeed at all. As one of them has recorded: 'The scientists felt that their figuring must be right and that the bomb had to go off, but there was in everyone's mind a strong measure of doubt.'[1] Everyone had made guesses as to the force of the bomb if it did go off, but the highest fell far short of the actual figure, and most guessed an amount that was less than a quarter of the destructive force released by the explosion when it took place. After so much work had been done and such a vast expenditure incurred, the men whose professional reputations were bound up with the project had a sickening fear of anti-climax. But their apprehension proved to have been unfounded.

The President of the United States had already arrived in Potsdam for his conference with the heads of the British and Soviet governments when the bomb was tested in Alamogordo. He received a cable announcing the success of the test on July 16, 1945; five days later came a full report from General Groves, who had been in charge of the project. His subordinate, General Farrell, who had observed the explosion from a control shelter, told the story with lyrical enthusiasm. 'No man-made phenomenon of such tremendous power had ever occurred before', he wrote. 'The lighting effects beggared description. The whole country was lighted by a searing light with an intensity many times that of the midday sun. It was golden, purple, violet, gray and blue. It lighted every peak, crevasse, and ridge of the nearby mountain range with a clarity and beauty that cannot be described but must be seen to be imagined. It was that beauty the great poets dream about but describe most poorly and inadequately.'[2]

President Truman, however, could only enjoy at second hand the aesthetic experience of the light that men had never seen before. His own task in relation to it was severely practical: the bomb had been made as a weapon of war, to burn and destroy the bodies of human beings. The President had, therefore, in consultation with his military advisers, to decide if and against what targets it should be used. But of even greater urgency was the need to give some account of the impending public detonation to his Russian ally. The British Prime Minister knew of the bomb, for British scientists had contributed to its inception. Stalin, on the other hand, as far as Truman and Churchill were aware, had no knowledge of what was going on. It was obviously desirable that he should be informed before an atomic explosion over Japan divulged the secret to the whole world; even so, it would be somewhat embarrassing if he were to ask why he had not been told of it already. After discussing the matter with Churchill and Byrnes, Truman decided to mention it to Stalin in a quite informal way during a break between sessions of the conference. On July 24, he 'casually mentioned', to use his own words, 'that we had a new weapon of unusual destructive force'.[3] Stalin showed no special interest or surprise but said he was glad to hear of it and hoped effective use would be made of it against the Japanese. In memoirs written much later, Truman, Churchill and Byrnes all expressed their conviction that Stalin had not grasped the significance of what he had been told. However, the sum total of evidence since the war about Soviet espionage operations in the United States during this period leaves no reasonable doubt that Stalin already knew about the atomic bomb and that his strange lack of response to the divulging of the secret by Truman was due to the fact that he had been fully prepared for it. It would, perhaps, have been more prudent for him to have feigned a surprise he did not feel, but the Western statesmen had too blind a faith in the security measures of their own governments for his indifference to arouse in them the suspicion that he already knew their secret. It may be that he did not attach to the development of the atomic bomb the full significance which in retrospect we see it to have had; he could hardly at that time have had a higher estimate of its potency than the scientists who produced it. But the 'Manhattan Project' had been of sufficient importance to attract the close attention of the Soviet spy network which had penetrated into many parts of the American federal administration.

Having, as he supposed, imparted to Stalin knowledge of a previously unknown fact, Truman proceeded to give his approval to a directive for the use of the bomb against Japan. The so-called Interim Committee in Washington, set up to advise on what was to be done with the bomb when it was made, had turned down a suggestion that Japan might be driven to surrender if the power of the bomb were to be demonstrated in an uninhabited place; it was held that only the destruction of a city or cities would have the desired effect. But the doomed targets had to be selected, and the air force generals informed Stimson that they wanted to put 'your pet city' first on the list. This was Kyoto, which Stimson wished to spare, not because he had ever been there, but because someone had told him it contained important cultural monuments. Stimson persisted in his refusal to consent to the obliteration of Kyoto, and was supported by the President.[1] Finally, a target list was endorsed, comprising Hiroshima, Kokura, Niigata and Nagasaki—in that order of priority. Hiroshima was bombed on August 6, 1945. Kokura should have met its fate on August 9, but there was such thick cloud over the city that the pilot flew across it three times without being able to find it. Fuel was running low; since Niigata was too far for it to reach, the aircraft went on to Nagasaki and the second bomb was dropped there.

The devastation of Hiroshima was announced to the world from Washington in a statement that declared: 'It is an atomic bomb. It is a harnessing of the basic power of the universe. The force from which the sun draws its power has been loosed against those who brought war to the Far East.'

But what was to be done with the basic power of the universe when it was no longer needed for putting an end to the war against Japan? What if others also acquired the same fearful capacity for mass destruction? The future then would promise no serene security, but only a road darkened by shadows of utter annihilation. The rejoicings of victory were soon chilled by forebodings that had already begun to trouble high American officials even before the bomb was used. The problem that urgently called for answer was whether or not to divulge to the Russians the secrets, such as they were, of how the bomb was manufactured. If they were not told, they would be able in time to find them out for themselves, but there would be an interval during which

America would have a lead. During this period of time, it might be possible to reach an international agreement that would prevent a race in the production of nuclear weapons and render it impossible for any nation to make them secretly. This was (and is) the crux of the matter. Looking back after more than two decades, we can see how, from the beginning, the issue was one of a fear reaching down to the most fundamental instincts of men living in a system of sovereign states. These were secrets too terrible to be shared with anyone who might become an enemy; this was a weapon too frightful to be renounced by treaty without absolute guarantees against bad faith. Even among nations accustomed to frank and friendly diplomatic dealing with one another, the conclusion of an agreement for nuclear disarmament must involve painful demonstrations of mutual suspicion and distrust. Such suspicion and distrust were bound to be multiplied many times over when it came to dealing with a dictatorial régime whose political philosophy was one of universal violent revolution, whose recent record was one of cruel repression at home and armed expansion abroad, and whose system of government precluded the freedom of observation required for a credible pact of nuclear renunciation.

From the time the two atomic bombs were dropped on Japan, the scientists were saying that they would soon be able to make much more powerful ones as well as multiply their number indefinitely. To this prospect was shortly added an awareness of another aspect of nuclear weapons that, on the day of the bombing of Hiroshima, had been concealed, not only from the public, but also from the men who had made the bomb. It was, indeed, known to atomic scientists that radioactivity was dangerous to organic life, and it was anticipated that lethal rays would be released by an atomic explosion. But, after the test in New Mexico, it was believed that their range would be too short to kill anyone who had escaped death by fire and blast. It was only when the American forces arrived in Japan to take over control of the country after the surrender that it was realised in the West that large numbers of people in the atom-bombed cities who had been only injured, or even unhurt, by the explosion of the bombs had later died or become seriously ill, either from the discharge of gamma rays at the moment of the burst or from the radio-active contamination of the ground in the affected areas. Doctors in Hiroshima and Nagasaki had been unable to diagnose the strange illnesses with which so many survivors of the bombing were afflicted, and the rumour spread in Japan that the bombs had contained a poison gas. But, in Tokyo, there lived one of the world's most eminent radiologists, Masao Tsuzuki, who some years before the war had published in an American medical journal an important paper entitled "Experimental Studies on the Biological Action of Hard Roentgen Rays". The effects of radio-activity he had studied in rabbits he now observed on a large scale in human beings. By the time the American occupation forces arrived in Japan, he and a few colleagues had acquired an extensive scientific knowledge of the new man-made disease of radiation sickness.

For the world at large, the realisation that an atomic bomb could kill not only by its terrific heat and blast but also by invisible and imperceptible rays, or by a lingering radio-active contamination, added enormously to the horror the weapon inspired. This was to be further increased when the development of the hydrogen bomb brought with it the new danger of radio-active 'fall-out' drifting with the wind for long distances from the place of an explosion. Fall-out, as an extension of the effects of nuclear weapons, introduced an element of the uncontrollable into the prospect of a nuclear war and even of peacetime testing. By a strange historical coincidence, Japan, after being the first recipient of an atomic bomb in war, provided also the first victims of accidental fall-out in time of peace, for in March 1954 a Japanese fishing boat was enveloped in a cloud of radio-active dust from the testing of an American hydrogen bomb in the Marshall Islands, nearly a hundred miles away. In war, there could be no doubt that neutrals as well as belligerents would suffer from the effects of fall-out, and mere peacetime testing, even though carried out in remote and uninhabited areas, was found to affect the whole surface of the globe. Radio-active dust carried into the stratosphere would descend and settle, in accordance with the prevailing winds, around the world, adding appreciably to natural levels of radio-activity (hitherto too low to be harmful). Nor was the harm likely to be confined to those whose lives or health were directly involved: radiation could cause serious genetic damage to human beings whom it did not kill, and part of the consequences, whether on a small or large scale, would be passed on to future generations.

In the years that followed the atomic bombing of Hiroshima, no sentiment was so universal as fear of a war between nuclear powers, and no thought so often expressed as the opinion that mankind must put an end to war before war destroyed mankind. Time was short if an agreement for the abolition or international control of nuclear weapons was to be achieved before there was more than one nuclear power in the world. The American monopoly in these weapons could not be expected to last more than a few years. The initiative lay with the Americans as the first producers of the bomb; it was for them to propose conditions on which they would renounce national possession of it. They had to make proposals in the knowledge that other nations would also be able to make atomic bombs if the conditions were unacceptable to them. On the other hand, they had to seek safeguards lest a potentially hostile power might by stealth acquire the monopoly they would abandon. The outcome of the American government's prolonged study of the problem was the Baruch Plan, released in June 1946, less than a year after the first testing of the bomb in Alamogordo. The Soviet Union refused to consider this plan even as a basis for negotiation, and thus condemned the world to the nuclear arms race that has gone on ever since and to the vast accumulation of nuclear weapons that hourly threatens mankind with slaughter and destruction on a scale never before imagined.

There are some, even outside the Communist camp, who maintain that the Baruch Plan was unfair to the Soviet Union and that its government could not have been expected to agree to the American proposal. But the Russian propaganda offensive against the plan—including virulent personal attacks on Baruch—was no mere criticism of particular provisions, which might have led to constructive negotiations; it was an uncompromising rejection of the whole principle of international control or inspection to provide guarantees against violation of a treaty for the renunciation of nuclear weapons. The Soviet Union's own counter-proposals simply required governments to agree not to produce or use atomic bombs, and to destroy all existing bombs (i.e. the American stock pile) within three months of ratification of such a treaty. Thereafter, there would be no safeguard against illicit production of such weapons except the good faith of the signatories. The Soviet Union took the position it has maintained ever since, that any unimpeded international inspection of possible nuclear arms in Soviet territory is equivalent to espionage, even though other nations are prepared to give exactly the same facilities for observation that they require from Russia.

Since Russia would not agree to a system of international inspection or control of atomic energy, and since the United States would not discard its atomic armoury without it, a competitive striving for ever more efficient nuclear weapons necessarily ensued. In this race, Russia, in spite of its late start, had certain advantages. In a land of secret government, policy on nuclear arms development became the closest of all secrets. There was never any public discussion of the issue or public announcement of the government's intentions; the same absolute silence enveloped Moscow's nuclear plans in time of peace as had enfolded the Manhattan Project in time of war, and progress was revealed only by the successful tests of completed weapons. As long as Russia lacked atomic arms, the Russian people were hardly informed of their existence. The surrender of Japan was officially attributed, not to the dropping of the atomic bombs, but to the intervention of Russia in the war. It was not until 1954 that the Soviet public was allowed to see for the first time a picture of the sinister mushroom cloud that had long been so familiar in the West. But the reticence that spared peoples under Communist rule an awareness of the new form of armed power in which the capitalist world was still superior was not a feature of Communist propaganda in countries outside the 'socialist camp'. Every device in the vast panoply of political warfare was used to intensify in Western and uncommitted nations the sentiments of fear and horror aroused by nuclear weapons, to accentuate the sense of guilt widespread among those who had been concerned with their genesis, and to concentrate attention on appeals to outlaw the weapons without mention of safeguards against clandestine production. Even without this propaganda, there were bound to be profound misgivings and diversities of opinion in the Western democracies as to what should be done. There were some who were ready to trust Russia without strict guarantees; there were others who believed that America must retain nuclear arms but that somehow a halt could be called in their further development.

A crisis came in 1949. In September of that year, it was announced that the Russians had exploded an atomic bomb. Russia had thus also become a nuclear power, though it was reasonable to suppose that America would for some time to come have the larger stockpile. The question now, however, was whether to proceed to the production of a new and far more powerful type of nuclear weapon, the hydrogen bomb, which the advance of atomic technology had rendered possible. All but one of the members of the United States Atomic Energy Commission were against a programme for development of the hydrogen bomb. They relied largely on the testimony of Robert Oppenheimer, the eminent physicist who had been director of the Los Alamos Laboratory where the first atomic bombs were made, during the war. An idealist of leftwing views, and a man of high moral principles who had suffered torments of conscience on account of the dreadful thing he had helped to bring into the world, Oppenheimer expressed the view that Russia would not make the hydrogen bomb if America did not. His scientific genius in the realm of physics did not prevent him from being ready to believe that Stalin would never wish to surpass, but only to match, American power. To support this essentially political judgement, however, Oppenheimer adduced technical arguments, which he would probably not have taken seriously if he had not been opposed to making the bomb on other grounds. The only member of the Commission who was not convinced by his case was the chairman, Lewis Strauss, who relied on the advice of Edward Teller, a rival scientist, and believed that Russia would go into the lead with the new weapon if America did nothing about it. In spite of the contrary opinion of his colleagues, Strauss succeeded in persuading President Truman to order work to proceed on the hydrogen bomb in February 1950. In the outcome, Russia produced it as soon as America did. Because of the complete secrecy of such policy decisions in Moscow, there is even now no way of knowing whether Stalin ordered H-bombs to be made before or after Truman did; but, given the fact that the H-bomb was technically feasible, and given the general character of Stalin's policy, there is good ground for endorsing the conclusion reached by a British reviewer of Lewis Strauss' memoirs (*Men and Decisions*) that, if Strauss had failed to persuade Truman to go ahead with the H-bomb when he did, 'the Soviet Union would certainly have overtaken America in the nuclear arms race, with consequences to the West more disastrous than any previous military defeat in history'.*

* Peregrine Worsthorne in the *Sunday Telegraph*, April 7, 1963. The bitter controversy over Oppenheimer's disqualification as a 'security risk' is really quite irrelevant to this issue. Oppenheimer might have done his country infinitely more harm by his honest, but perverse, opinion than if he had given a technical secret to a Soviet agent, which there was never any good reason to believe that he would do.

With the advent of the H-bomb, a situation arose that had been inherent in nuclear weaponry since 1945 but only became manifest with the great increases in explosive force registered by the new hydrogen weapons. Before, it had been possible to regard the atomic bomb as an additional military arm which, however terrific its single explosions, could not by itself decide the issue of a war against a great power, except against one as weakened as Japan was in August 1945. (And even then the leaders of the Japanese army had been in favour of continuing the war on the ground that the Americans could not have many of the bombs and that they could not be used effectively to cover a seaborne invasion.) But with the indefinite multiplication of the bombs and their enormously increased explosive power, and with the wide range of lethal fall-out produced by the larger types, it became clear that an enemy country could be completely devastated and its population almost exterminated by a long-range bombardment bypassing military forces in the field or naval fleets in intervening seas. There could be no adequate defence against such bombardments. If the nuclear weapons were bombs dropped from manned aircraft, their explosive force was such that terrible damage could be inflicted even if the majority of the bombers were to be shot down before reaching their targets. As for the ballistic missiles developed from the German V2 rocket of 1945: these could not be kept off at all, since there was no known way of intercepting them once they had been fired. Casualties and damage might be reduced by a well-organised system of civil defence, 'hardening' of buildings, and evacuation of people from large cities to the countryside in an emergency; but it was no longer open to doubt after 1952 that a nation well armed with nuclear weapons and the means of delivering them possessed a power unprecedented in history for achieving the physical destruction of another people.

It followed from this that the only real defence against nuclear attack lay in counter-attack. A power without nuclear weapons must be overcome in war by one which possessed them and used them, even if it had a superiority in what came to be known as 'conventional forces', since it would be subjected to continuous nuclear bombardment without the possibility of retaliation. If, on the other hand, two powers, each possessing nuclear weapons, were to be at war with one another, neither would be able to prevent a rain of nuclear bombs and missiles on its territory. But this very capacity for mutual devastation meant that a country under attack could make it too costly for the attacker to continue the war after the initial onset, or, better still, that it could deter attack altogether by the mere threat of an irresistible retaliation. Thus, the most violently offensive of all arms acquired the theoretical status of an instrument of strict self-defence and by a curious semantic development nuclear forces came to be called simply 'the deterrent'.

Further consequences followed from the conception of the hydrogen bomb as the 'absolute weapon'. It was held that, if it could be used to deter or counter an attack with nuclear weapons, it could also be used to deter or counter an attack with conventional forces. There was therefore no need for a nuclear power to match the conventional forces of a potential enemy. It could even be argued that all non-nuclear arms had become superfluous and might be discarded. Since nuclear arms were extremely expensive, it was naturally an attractive idea for politicians and finance ministry officials that such arms might be made a substitute for, instead of a supplement to, the conventional forces on which states had been accustomed to spend their defence budgets. In relation to foreign policy, the possibility of using nuclear power to stop local aggressions in remote places seemed to provide opportunities to protect other countries at a distance without the usual problems of military assembly and logistics. This was the origin of John Foster Dulles's famous doctrine of 'massive retaliation'. It was subsequently adopted in Britain by a government which was anxious, for domestic political reasons, to abolish military conscription and, for financial reasons, to relieve the burden of armaments on the British economy. Duncan Sandys, the Defence Minister in 1957, was carried away by the notion of the absolute weapon, and sponsored the belief—for some time prevalent—that if Britain acquired a nuclear armoury of its own, the army and navy could be run down, even to the extent of going back on obligations already undertaken for collective defence in Europe under the North Atlantic Treaty.

But all such calculations for the use or threatened use of nuclear weapons against conventional military attack ran up against the objection that they involved 'escalation': the initiation of nuclear warfare to decide a non-nuclear armed conflict. Even if this meant only an action against a non-nuclear state with no risk of nuclear reprisal, it was not a straightforward matter because of the very strong moral inhibitions that had grown up in the democracies and in the world at large against the use of such a means of mass destruction on a people who could not hit back—inhibitions that might be defied by a ruthless dictatorship, but could hardly be ignored by a government holding power in a liberal society. There was a widespread feeling that the responsibility for initiating nuclear hostilities in the age of the H-bomb was a more serious matter than the responsibility for starting a war at the level of conventional arms. But if this was so in relation to a non-nuclear state, the inhibition was likely to be far greater if resort to nuclear warfare were to involve receiving nuclear blows as well as dealing them, through engaging another nuclear power or one of its allies. It was all very well to say that, by having nuclear weapons, one could deter an aggressive nation from making any forward move, but if the consequences of resistance or intervention were to be so appalling, for oneself also, whatever might be the rights and wrongs of the question at issue, the deterrent could be cancelled out by the counter-deterrent of the opposing nuclear power.

What interest or principle could be of such magnitude for any nation as to make resort to nuclear warfare worth while? People who were not outright pacifists were inclined to agree that it would be necessary to strike back in kind if an enemy actually attacked with nuclear weapons, but in that case the responsibility for first use would be his. A nation might declare that it would use nuclear weapons to repel a nuclear assault, but not otherwise; their purpose would then be strictly defined and it would be reasonable to expect that they would be used as stated. If, on the other hand, a nation relied on its nuclear armaments for victory in any kind of armed conflict, there would be a large element of doubt in the matter; either a government might use them recklessly when the other side was not expecting it—and thus bring on a great catastrophe out of all proportion to the *casus belli*—or, on the contrary, it might be paralysed by fear of the consequences of resorting to nuclear war, even on a most serious issue, and thus be driven to make major concessions to a bold enemy. The agonising choice between nuclear war and political surrender would indeed always confront a power which was strong in nuclear arms, but lacked adequate conventional forces. This situation also raised the question of the 'credibility of the deterrent', for the mere possession of nuclear weapons could not deter an enemy if the latter did not believe they would really be used in a crisis.

After a period in which conventional forces were widely regarded as being obsolescent and superfluous, they began to come back into their own to meet the world condition of 'nuclear stalemate', in which it was recognised that opposed nuclear powers had the capacity virtually to annihilate each other, and that their nuclear armaments therefore tended to cancel out, so that a great superiority in old-fashioned military strength might still be decisive. The concept of balanced forces gradually came to prevail over that of the nuclear deterrent as the solution for all problems of defence—though not, as far as Britain was concerned, until after national service conscription had been abolished and it had become extremely difficult, if not impossible, to maintain adequate conventional forces without conscription. The need to have both strong nuclear and strong conventional forces in order to keep up the position of a great power imposed a crushing burden of armaments on the principal nations of the world in the absence of any international pact for controlled disarmament. But none of them refused to take part in the race or relied simply on international good will for the protection of its national sovereignty and interest.

Apart from the unprecedented destructiveness of nuclear bombs, the hitherto unheard-of speeds of their instruments of delivery created entirely new strategic problems through the possibility of sudden overwhelming attack without previous declaration of war. The surprise attack on Pearl Harbor by bombers operating from Japanese aircraft-carriers in December 1941—itself a more deadly repetition of the torpedo-boat attack on the Russian fleet in the roadstead of Port Arthur in February 1904—was fresh in the memory of all Americans. But now long-range supersonic bombers and ballistic missiles passing through the stratosphere at prodigious speeds vastly increased the danger of a decisive surprise attack at the outset of a war. Surprise had always been an important element in war, but never before had there been even a theoretical possibility of knocking out a nation by a single unexpected blow, for never before had it been possible to reach all parts of an enemy country simultaneously and with a capacity for wholesale destruction. It was the new weaponry that now gave a fresh significance to the old adage:

> Right blest is he who has his quarrel just,
> But thrice blest he who gets his blow in fust.

If one nuclear power, by a sudden attack, could destroy most of the bombers and missiles of another on the ground before they could be used, it would thereafter hold the enemy country at its mercy while reducing retaliation on its own territory to a minimum. In the initial period after the introduction of the H-bomb, only two forms of defence were considered possible against such a contingency. One was a high degree of alert, whereby all missiles would be ready for firing at a few minutes' notice and all bombers would be ready to take off or be already airborne. The other was a 'spoiling' or pre-emptive attack, forestalling the enemy by getting the blow in first. Both forms of defence depended on previous information or indications of enemy attack, but with the difference that, whereas the period of high alert could do no harm if the enemy did not, in fact, attack, the pre-emptive attack might precipitate a war that had not really been intended by the other side. The high alert, therefore, was the preferable form of defence against surprise attack. Yet it was of doubtful efficacy. Full preparedness to meet sudden attack cannot be kept up over a long period; it is too costly and too much of a strain on serving officers and men. Most planning for measures to be taken in the emergency of a sudden outbreak of war assumes several days' warning, but the climax, in spite of all precautionary measures, might well come quite unexpectedly. The 'bolt from the blue', the surprise attack without any preliminary tension, is generally, and rightly, discounted by strategists; but a prolonged, or chronic, state of tension can provide the conditions for surprise, particularly if there have already been several false alarms. In the classic case of Pearl Harbor, there had been too much warning rather than too little; after previous alerts in which nothing had happened, the warnings issued in the days preceding the actual Japanese attack failed to revive the vigilance of the local commanders, and signals sent out after the attack had begun had to be accompanied by the explanation: 'This is not drill.'

Because of the difficulties of ensuring maximum alert at the critical moment, some American military theorists were inclined to the belief that pre-emptive attack was the only solution to the problem. But pre-emption not only involved the risk of starting through a misapprehension a war not intended by the enemy; it was also subject to the risk that the enemy, learning in time of preparations to pre-empt, would himself pre-empt, thus achieving the decisive first blow after all, whether or not he had previously decided to go to war. Fortunately for mankind, the period during which high alert and pre-emption were the only alternatives for defence against a 'nuclear Pearl Harbor' did not last long. It was found that a high degree of invulnerability could be provided for ballistic missiles by siting them deep underground in 'hardened sites'. At the same time, the invention of a submarine able to fire missiles while submerged created a mobile source of nuclear bombardment which could not be pin-pointed as a target before the outbreak of hostilities. These developments decisively reduced the danger that a nation's nuclear strength, contained in bombers on air-fields and missiles standing in the open, might be almost entirely destroyed on the ground by a single unheralded blow. The new tech-niques of hardening and concealment meant that, whatever devastation an aggressor might achieve by a surprise attack, he could not win a war outright by such action, for his foe would retain the capacity for strategic nuclear counter-attack. The dangers of surprise attack and pre-emption have thus receded during the last few years; no state is now tempted suddenly to attack a rival nuclear power in the belief that it could by so doing achieve the mastery of the world with negligible damage to itself; nor is any state urged to pre-empt on the ground that it dare not take the risk of losing all its strategic striking power if the enemy attacks first. A 'nuclear stalemate', a 'balance of terror', has been created, and the world can breathe more freely in the knowledge that, at present, any government contemplating resort to strategic nuclear war against another nuclear power has to reckon on incurring appalling consequences for its own territory and population.

Indeed, so far has the 'invulnerability of the deterrent' now been achieved that there is even a disposition to be thankful for nuclear weapons: a feeling that the nuclear stalemate provides the world with a better guarantee against a major war than would have been possible if we still had nothing but conventional weapons. The nuclear armouries inspire less horror than they did a few years ago; their existence now brings comfort to those who believe that they are so terrible that human beings will never dare to make use of them. As a factor of international stability, however, the nuclear stalemate is hardly convincing. The lower the probability that nuclear powers will exchange salvoes of hydrogen bombs, the less the restraint either on nuclear action against a non-nuclear power or on conventional warfare which does not involve invasion of the actual territory of a nuclear power. It is the doubt as to whether the full strategic capacity of a nuclear power would be used in war against another nuclear power to save a non-nuclear ally that was to afford President de Gaulle his most cogent argument for building up an independent nuclear force in France, even though America was committed by its NATO obligations to defend Western Europe, including France. India has so far had no alliance with any nuclear power but, now that Communist China has a nuclear capability, India would be at China's mercy in a crisis unless it either produced nuclear weapons of its own or got a definite and convincing guarantee of protection by one or more nuclear powers against a Chinese nuclear attack. The very improbability of a nuclear power's using its full strength except in defence of its own homeland thus increases the tendency towards proliferation of nuclear weapons, as countries with a sense of insecurity seek their own 'independent deterrents'. In itself, proliferation is not such a dreadful thing as is often supposed; it can even be argued that, in a world where some states possess nuclear weapons, the best thing would be for everyone to have them, so that all states would be able to deter attack on themselves. But, in practice, the majority of states would not be able to afford to build up a nuclear capability that would be strategically significant. Proliferation would merely divide the world between one group of states with a great or small ability for nuclear self-defence, and another group with no such ability. Even if it is assumed that a number of states possess a nuclear capability sufficient to deter any attack on their home territories, the rest of the world would still lie open to aggressions, nuclear or conventional, and there would still be the possibility of opposed nuclear powers being drawn into conflicts outside the zone of nuclear self-defence, so that a war might after all escalate into a full-scale nuclear exchange even though this was not originally intended by either side. What makes for uncertainty and perplexity in this situation is that nobody can really predict whether and to what degree a nation might use nuclear power outside its own borders on behalf of an ally. It may be held that this dubiety has by itself a deterrent effect, but it can also encourage an aggressively inclined government to go too far in the belief that it incurs no real danger of retaliation.

There is, finally, the anti-missile. It has not yet, as far as is publicly known, reached a stage at which it can alter the proposition that in a nuclear war the great majority of missiles fired would explode some-where near their targets. If and when the anti-missile does reach the stage of providing an effective defence against nuclear bombardment, it will no longer be suicidal for a nuclear power strong in anti-missiles to attack another, and there would be a very strong temptation for a power which first obtained a lead in anti-missiles to go to war while it still had such a decisive advantage. The anti-missile can only destabilise the nuclear stalemate. Our present safety, such as it is, lies in the 'balance of terror': in the knowledge that, because ballistic missiles cannot be intercepted after they have been fired, any war against a nuclear power must involve immense losses. If one state acquires, or thinks it has acquired, a superiority in anti-missiles, it may consider itself able to inflict nuclear blows with impunity or only 'acceptable' losses. In this case, a nuclear armoury will in itself no longer deter.

PART TWO

THE DECLINE OF THE COLONIAL POWERS, AND HOPES FOR A NEW INTERNATIONAL ORDER

7

DECOLONISATION IN SOUTH AND
SOUTH-EAST ASIA

ONE DAY EARLY in 1945, a circular to the staff of the British South-east Asia Command informed them that 'as from today the BTA (Burmese Traitor Army) will be known as the BPF (Burmese Patriotic Forces)'. The reference was to a Burmese force under Aung San which had collaborated with the Japanese against the British in return for Japanese recognition of the independence of Burma, but which changed sides by a timely negotiation with the British when it became clear that Japan was losing the war. It was, of course, only from a British point of view that the conduct of Aung San's followers changed from treason to patriotism; in their own eyes, they were at all times patriotic, since their varying alignments were dictated simply by tactical expediency in the cause of Burmese national independence.

When the Pacific war began in December 1941, the whole of South and South-east Asia from the Khyber Pass east to Luzon, with the exception of Siam, was under the control of Western colonial powers, with no prospect of an early termination of their rule save in the Philippines, to which the United States had pledged itself to grant independence by 1946. Four Western nations, of which three were great powers, divided between them this vast region containing nearly a quarter of the population of the globe. Britain held India, Ceylon, Burma, Malaya, and a territory in northern Borneo whose neighbour, the state of Sarawak, might in effect, if not juridically, be regarded as part of the British empire in the East since it was ruled by European rajahs of the Brooke family. France controlled the combination of the former states of Annam (Vietnam), Cambodia and Laos which went by the name of Indochina. The United States had sovereignty over the Philippines, annexed after the Spanish-American war of 1898. Holland possessed the extensive insular territory of the Netherlands East

Indies, on which European geographers had bestowed the name of Indonesia. South of the frontiers of China, Siam alone survived as an independent Asian state, and even Siam was greatly subject to the influence of its imperial neighbours, British and French advisers being neatly balanced in its administration.

The political map of the area had remained unaffected by the First World War. Since then, as already mentioned, the United States had given the Philippines a promise of independence, with a large measure of interim self-government, but national sovereignty was still five years away when the bombs fell on Pearl Harbor and Clark Field. In India, a substantial measure of self-government had been conceded under the Government of India Act of 1935, but full independence was not yet in sight. In French Indochina and the Dutch East Indies, the elements of national autonomy were still very small. In all the European-governed territories at the time the war broke out in Europe in 1939, the authorities regarded the situation with complacency; their military and police forces were quite sufficient to deal with any local disturbances, and there were no signs of large-scale upheavals. All the four imperial powers were democracies and did not deny in principle the ultimate right of their colonial subjects to self-government, but they considered that the latter were not yet ready to make use of democratic rights, which were not in their own ethnic traditions, and that to restore power to their former dynastic rulers would be merely retrograde. A continuation of European rule, or at least ultimate supervision, would therefore be in the best interests of the Asian dependencies for a long time to come. The Americans had a somewhat different attitude. They had had disturbing qualms of conscience about taking the Philippines in the first place, and they were more susceptible than European colonial powers to the appeals of an emerging independence movement. The United States achieved the distinction of conceding independence on a set time-table to a subject Asian people. The example did not, however, have quite so much effect in Asia as might have been supposed. The Filipinos, as a predominantly Catholic people, heavily influenced by three centuries of Spanish rule and with little native Asian culture of their own, seemed somehow to be outside Asia and largely irrelevant to its problems.

Hitler's victories in Western Europe in 1940 meant that both French Indochina and the Dutch East Indies became separated from their metropolitan countries, now under German control. But, while the French authorities in Indochina continued to give their allegiance to the Vichy government of France, the Dutch administration in Batavia (now Djakarta) took orders from the Netherlands government in exile in London. In neither case did the collapse of the metropolitan power produce a revolt in its South-east Asian colonial territories. The French, however, under heavy Japanese pressure, conceded military bases in Indochina to Japan, and it was from these bases that the Japanese launched their invasions of Malaya and (through Siam) of Burma. Since the French did not resist the Japanese, they were able until the spring of 1945 to keep their own civil and military administration intact; but Japan, at war with the United States, Britain and the Netherlands, sought to exploit a native nationalist movement hostile to each of these three Western powers in its South-east Asian territory.

This endeavour was least successful in the Philippines, for the Filipinos had in any case only five years to wait for independence, and the Americans, after the Philippines had fallen to the Japanese, advanced the date to give sovereign status to the Filipino government in exile formed by President Quezon, leader of the nationalist movement. Even so, Japanese anti-American propaganda had some effect, and a Filipino politician named Laurel (who had a secret understanding with Quezon) proclaimed a Japanese-sponsored independence and set up a collaborationist government, so that national sovereignty might be preserved whichever side won the war.

At the other end of South-east Asia, the Japanese proclaimed the independence of Burma, and received military co-operation from the Burmese rebel nationalist force under Aung San (who later, as already mentioned, changed sides after the tide of war had turned). While they were in Burma, the Japanese paid considerable attention to the encouragement of Burmese nationalism, for a British army remained on the Indo-Burmese frontier and it was important for the Japanese to obtain strong local support. A certain Ba Maw was installed as President of Burma and built up by propaganda as a great national figure. This endeavour to win over the Burmese people was not altogether successful, for the rough ways of the Japanese army and its need to live off the country marred the image of Japan as the liberator of Asian peoples. Nevertheless, the restoration of Burma's lost independence, even if only in form, was a gesture the effect of which could not easily be undone when a victorious British army returned to Rangoon.

Further south, the Japanese were less anxious to promote local nationalism because, after the collapse of the British in Malaya and of the Dutch in Java, there seemed little danger of a counter-attack and therefore much less need of political support from the native inhabitants. The Japanese left the Malay sultans as they were, under Japanese, instead of British, protection; Singapore they kept under their own direct control, intending to make it a great strategic base and the centre for their future ascendancy in South-east Asia. The Dutch East Indies were at first divided into three separate administrative zones; there was no idea of creating an Indonesian national state. But, when the war began to go against Japan, the Japanese authorities encouraged a nationalist political organisation headed by Sukarno and raised an Indonesian militia to help them repel possible British landings on the coasts of Java or Sumatra. With local Japanese army backing, Sukarno proclaimed the independence of Indonesia on August 17, 1945—after Japan had surrendered but more than a month before the first British troops arrived in Java to round up and disarm the still undefeated Japanese forces there.

In Indochina, the French administrators, left isolated by the elimination of the Vichy régime in France, secretly sought contacts with the government of General de Gaulle, which wanted to take part in the war against Japan as an ally of Britain and the United States. Having discovered what was afoot, the Japanese suddenly attacked the French, disarmed their troops and interned their officials; they then recognised Vietnam as an independent state under its hereditary 'emperor', Bao Dai, who still reigned in Hué though he had been shorn of all real power by the French. But the old Vietnamese monarchy was unable to assume the leadership of the nationalist movement; it could not compete for popular support with the powerful underground organisation of the revolutionary Vietminh, which had its base across the border in China and was both anti-French and anti-Japanese. Unlike the extreme nationalist groups in Burma and Indonesia, which collaborated with the Japanese, the Vietminh was Communist-led; this was known to Chiang Kai-shek, but he nevertheless gave it material support since it was the only group of Vietnamese exiles capable of fighting effectively against the Japanese. Chiang Kai-shek had not forgotten the Franco-

Chinese war of 1884, and hoped to prevent a restoration of French rule in Indochina after the defeat of Japan. He therefore reached an agreement with the Americans whereby a Chinese army was to receive the surrender of the Japanese forces in the northern half of the country. The Chinese marched in and, after disarming the Japanese, allowed the Vietminh to take over the administration. Bao Dai abdicated, and a government led by the Vietminh leader, Ho Chi Minh, was set up in Hanoi, claiming authority over the whole of Vietnam.

In India, the effect of the Japanese conquests could only be indirect, for the Japanese never penetrated India except in a small border area, and British authority was never displaced by a Japanese military occupation. But British prestige was seriously damaged by the catastrophic defeats in Burma and Malaya, and especially by the fall of Singapore, where occurred the surrender of the largest British army ever to give itself up to a victorious enemy. Even Britain's successes in the final campaign in Burma could not efface the memory of these disasters. The spectacle of an Asian power's extinguishing European rule from Amboyna to Rangoon had made an indelible impression on Indian minds. Subhas Bose, the leader of a pro-Japanese section of the Indian Congress Party, was broadcasting incitements to revolt over the Japanese radio, and a phantom 'Indian Provisional Government' was issuing orders from Japanese-occupied Singapore. Very few Indians wanted to see the Japanese in Calcutta, but strong emotions were stirred by the symbolic heralding of Indian independence. When the war ended, there was a new sense of movement, change and instability; nothing could be again as it had been before.

For the moment, however, British power in India was not only intact but moving forward. Burma had been recovered before the end of the Pacific war; Mandalay was retaken in March 1945, and Rangoon at the beginning of May. There was no recognition of Burmese independence. 'I have not become the King's First Minister', Churchill had declared, 'in order to preside over the dissolution of the British Empire.' He believed that British authority could and should be maintained for an indefinite time to come in Delhi, Rangoon and Singapore. But in July 1945, he was replaced in office by a Labour Prime Minister, and the direction of policy passed into the hands of a party committed by its principles to making large concessions to colonial nationalism. This did not make any immediate difference, for the plans to take over from the Japanese in Malaya and North Borneo went forward as arranged after Japan's surrender, and Attlee was just as insistent as Churchill would have been that Hong Kong be taken over by British, and not by Chinese, troops—as Chiang Kai-shek, with American support, had proposed. However, in the course of the next two years, the effect of the new outlook in London slowly became apparent.

The demand for independence in India was becoming more and more vehement, and there were rumours of impending insurrection. Even if the British government had wished to hold on to India, it could not be sure of having the means to suppress a revolt. For the first time since the Mutiny of 1857, the sentiments of the Indian army gave grounds for concern. Nor could even the British army in India be entirely relied on. 'The enthusiasm against Empire had spread in the British army among both private soldiers and officers. Most of the troops had one chief wish: to return home and be demobilised as quickly as possible. Only a tactful visit to India by the Labour Secretary of State for War prevented some of the troops from mutinying.'[1] In the fight against Germany and Japan, British soldiers had been continually told that they were contending for the liberties of nations against aggressive tyrants; it would be difficult now to use them against forces struggling for national independence. Moreover, there was a long tradition in British political thought sustaining the belief that independence would be, not the demise, but the fulfilment of British rule in India. As Macaulay had said in his oft-quoted speech on the India Bill in 1833:

> It may be that the public mind of India will expand under our system till it has outgrown that system; that by good government we may educate our subjects into a capacity for better government; that, having become instructed in European knowledge, they may in some future age demand European institutions. Whether such a day will ever come, I know not. But never will I attempt to avert or retard it. Whenever it comes, it will be the proudest day in English history.

That day had now come, and it was Attlee's great merit that he saw it clearly. But it was not simply a question of giving up authority; this had to be handed over to an Indian government able to exercise it. To plunge India into anarchy by withdrawing certainly would not be a fulfilment of British rule in India, and those who had wished to prevent or postpone the transfer of power into Indian hands had always warned that this would be the consequence of a British abdication. The British achievement in India had been primarily one of unification—or rather of reunification: they had restored the country's political unity after the Mogul empire had dissolved in chaos in the eighteenth century. Might it not again dissolve if there were no longer the British Raj to hold it together? The nationalists of the Congress Party claimed that such fears were groundless, that the Indian people as a single national entity from the Khyber to the borders of Burma would elect a government whose authority would be everywhere accepted. This claim was challenged, however, by the Muslim League, which demanded a separate state for the parts of India where Muslims were a majority of the population. In India, the diversity of spoken languages—which in Europe would have been a ground for a number of national states—was not a fatal impediment to unity, but the cleavage between Hindu and Muslim went too deep. This was no mere difference of religious belief but a division between communities, each with its own social customs and laws. Muslims had been masters on the Indus and Ganges rivers for centuries before the British ruled, but, as a minority, they would be overwhelmed in a unified, democratic India. Nehru and other Congress leaders were secularists, and maintained that there would be no religious discrimination in the new India; but such assurances counted for little in the middle and lower levels of Indian society. For the ordinary Muslim, a Congress government meant a Hindu Raj.

The British had no desire to see a partition of India. Although they had in the past sometimes taken political advantage of Hindu–Muslim antagonism, that antagonism was not of their making, and the idea that the realm they had administered as a single whole might be split in two was generally repugnant to them. There was, nevertheless, no other way out, for it became evident that a simple transfer of power to a Congress government would mean a revolt of the Muslim areas and the adhesion of the large Muslim component of the Indian army to its insurgent co-religionists. India was therefore divided on British initiative into two states, the larger of which continued to be called India, while the smaller—the separate state demanded by the Muslim League—assumed the name of Pakistan: a designation invented for a country that had never existed before, though its raison d'être went far back into history.*

The Congress Party leaders reluctantly agreed to partition as the only alternative to a devastating civil war. In the rank and file of the party, however, there were some who would have been ready to fight it out. 'The British', complained one of them, 'are stopping us from having a civil war. Why shouldn't we have a civil war? The Americans had one to preserve the unity of their country and are now the strongest power in the world.'[2] Such logic has not lost its appeal in India, and the idea that Pakistan may one day be forcibly reincorporated in an India made one from Peshawar to Chittagong has never ceased to fascinate some Indian minds. The separation was marked by violence, and bitter animosity has characterised Indo-Pakistani relations ever since. In 1947-48, there were massacres in the Punjab on each side of the new frontier, with tens of thousands of dead and millions of refugees to perpetuate hatred. Since then, the question of Kashmir has been a constant source of hostility between the two states, leading in 1965 to open warfare.

One reason why a verdict of arms was not sought in 1945 was the extremely pacific and civilian character of the Congress Party. Gandhi, with his immense influence over the masses, was a pacifist on religious grounds; other leaders, who did not share his convictions, had grown up under the Pax Britannica and had never touched weapons. The Indian army was an instrument of British imperialism and for that reason an object of censure; Congress nationalists continually complained that too much money from India's revenue was being spent on it. Yet, since the British left India, military expenditure has risen steeply, and for a less extensive territory. The British did not, in fact, maintain large forces in India in proportion to the size of the country, for, once they had extended their power to the Himalayas and the Khyber Pass, they had strong natural frontiers, easy to defend. Russia was on the other side of the Hindu Kush, and China in those days was a negligible military factor. But, after 1945, two strong armies confronted each other in the plains of the Punjab; and after the Chinese conquest

* Paradoxically, Pakistan contains in its territory the most ancient remains of Hindu civilisation, and most of the notable monuments of Muslim architecture are in the new state of India. The historic architecture of Delhi, capital of India, is all Muslim; the traveller who wishes to see old Hindu temples must go elsewhere.

of Tibet in 1950, a formidable military power was established in the Himalayas. The desire for military security, intensified by defeat at the hands of the Chinese in the border war of 1962, was the cause of a new expansion of the Indian army and great increases in the military budget. If India today is not a warlike nation, it is certainly no longer an unmilitary one. Indian patriots certainly are not strangers to the thought of violence to the extent they were in 1947. India and Pakistan have now already fought a war against each other and they may do so again.

The issue between Hindu and Muslim in 1947 was complicated by the problem of the future of the numerous large and small Indian-ruled monarchical states within the boundaries of the 'subcontinent'. These 'princely states' were the remnants of the 'country powers' of eighteenth-century India whose territories had not been annexed. They were bound to the British Raj by specific treaties, but were also subject to a supreme control known as paramountcy. Their rulers had been promised that paramountcy would not be transferred to an independent Indian government, and the Attlee cabinet felt bound by this pledge. The princes were therefore legally entitled to accede either to India or to Pakistan, or to declare themselves independent. Only one princely state, Hyderabad, chose independence. (It was later incorporated by force into India.) Another state, Junagadh, opted for Pakistan but was compelled to accede to India. In Kashmir, on the other hand, where a Hindu dynasty ruled over a predominantly Muslim population, India accepted the accession of the Maharaja and sent troops to enforce it against a Muslim revolt supported from Pakistan. After more than a year of desultory fighting, an armistice left a large part of Kashmir to the rebels but kept the capital, Srinagar, in Indian hands. Since then, the dispute between India and Pakistan over Kashmir has proved one of the most intractable of all international problems. The United Nations has repeatedly failed to find a solution acceptable to both sides, and no agreement had emerged from direct Indo-Pakistani negotiations by 1965, the year when open hostilities broke out on the truce-line dividing Kashmir and spread to the Punjab.

The British Raj in India came to an end on August 27, 1947—196 years after Clive's capture of Arcot first made the British a power in Indian affairs. The British left India voluntarily and peacefully, and the transfer of official functions to the successor states was accomplished without a hitch. A number of British officials stayed on in the service of either India or Pakistan, although their retention was not essential; both the civil service and the army were already so 'Indianised' that men of Indian birth who were professionally qualified for the highest posts were at once forthcoming. Britain's withdrawal was unconditional. In March 1946, the British government had announced that India and Pakistan would be free to leave the Commonwealth, and no attempt was made to bind the successor states in advance by treaties safeguarding British interests or retaining military or naval bases. India and Pakistan, however, voluntarily decided to remain in the Commonwealth, their membership of this new form of association being facilitated by London's acceptance of the principle that republicanism need not be a bar to entry. Nehru himself affirmed that the period of British rule in India was a part of Indian history and that its monuments should not be removed or defaced; as a result, there were still statues of British viceroys and roads named after them in Delhi more than a decade after liberation from the British yoke.

When power had once been transferred in the Indian subcontinent, independence could not long be denied to Ceylon or Burma. Both received it within a year of the withdrawal from India. Ceylon remained in the Commonwealth and granted Britain a naval base at Trincomalee; later on, with a change of government in Colombo, Britain was asked to give up the base, and did so. In Burma, the transition was not quite so smooth because of the background of events during the war against Japan. Burma decided to leave the Commonwealth, but Britain made no attempt to prevent it from doing so, and friendly diplomatic relations were established after a peaceful transfer of power.

France and Holland had no such success in relinquishing their colonial empires in Asia after the defeat of Japan. Both were involved in prolonged and bloody wars against nationalist revolutions, and both were in the end compelled to renounce their authority in circumstances which precluded friendly relations with the successor-states for a long time to come. This outcome is not to be attributed solely to the pursuit of wiser policies in London than in Paris or The Hague. The British had had the advantage of being able to make concessions from strength; they had held India throughout the war and returned to Burma with massive forces, suppressing the Japanese-sponsored independence of that country and only giving a new independence three years later. The French and Dutch were no less eager to go back and regain control of their former dependencies that had been over-run by the Japanese before entering into negotiations with nationalist leaders; but, unlike the British, they had no substantial forces available on the spot when Japan surrendered. It was to the British South-east Asia Command that an Anglo-American agreement assigned the task of accepting the Japanese surrender in the Dutch East Indies and southern Indochina (the Chinese, as already mentioned, being entitled to take it in northern Indochina). In Java, the British, who had no zeal for helping the Dutch, recognised Sukarno as the *de facto* ruler, and thus gave him a degree of legitimacy of which he could not afterwards be deprived. In Saigon, they did not recognise the Vietminh as the *de facto* authority, for France was after all a great power, even though somewhat diminished for the time being, and one could not act towards the French as one could towards the Dutch. In the north, however, the Vietminh was under Chinese protection and could not be dislodged until the French had obtained the withdrawal of the Chinese forces by a treaty with China in February 1946, renouncing in return various French rights such as the French concession in Shanghai and the leased territory of Kwangchow. After the departure of the Chinese, the French were able to send troops to the north, though extending a limited recognition to Ho Chi Minh's régime. Hostilities between the French and the Vietminh broke out before the end of 1946, developing into a war that continued until it ended with the defeat of the French in 1954.

In Indonesia, the process of eviction was more rapid, though the Dutch were never decisively defeated by the Indonesians. Indeed, they virtually won the war in December 1948 by a brilliant paratroop action at Jogjakarta in which they captured Sukarno and other principal leaders of the Indonesian Republic. However, they were compelled to withdraw by the United Nations, which, at the instance of the United States, had imposed on them a Committee of Good Offices and severely censured them for their 'police action' in what was still juridically their own territory. Anti-colonialism was now a growing force in world affairs, powerfully reinforced by India as soon as it gained its own independence and could raise its voice in the United Nations. Holland, as a small nation with a large empire, was the first target for the anti-colonial crusade, and had to yield to it. The Dutch finally signed away their East Indian empire in 1949, two years after the end of British rule in India.

The French were in a stronger international position. Their right of veto in the United Nations Security Council enabled them to prevent adverse resolutions such as had been passed against the Dutch, and they treated the anti-colonial clamour with disdain. It was easier, however, to defy the tides of world opinion than to destroy the Vietminh bands which, under the leadership of Vo Nguyên Giap, had adopted the methods of guerrilla warfare developed by the Chinese Communists. The Vietminh were still holding out in the mountains and jungles when the end of the civil war in China in 1949 brought Chinese Communist power to the northern border of Vietnam. Henceforth, the Vietminh received substantial material aid from China and were also able to send their cadres across the frontier for military training.

If this course of events made the strategic problem more serious for the French, it also obtained for them, from the time of the outbreak of the Korean War, the moral and material support of the United States for their campaign in Indochina. The American government no longer regarded the war against the Communist-led and Chinese-supported Vietminh as the suppression of a national movement by a colonial power, but as one of the fronts against Communism. Within Vietnam itself, the Communist character of the Vietminh set many Vietnamese against it. To rally the anti-Communist forces, the French brought back the ex-emperor Bao Dai from the Riviera, whither he had emigrated, to be head of state of a Vietnamese Republic. Nevertheless, all plans for victory came to nothing when the Vietminh cut off and killed or captured the main striking force of the French army at Dienbienphu, and Chinese anti-aircraft guns shot down the transport planes with which General Navarre, the French commander-in-chief, had hoped to keep it supplied. The French then decided to cut their losses and come to terms with the Vietminh. They still held South Vietnam, but, at the Geneva conference in 1954, it was agreed that elections should be held throughout Vietnam in 1956. This implied that the Vietminh would dominate the whole country, since the population was greater in the North, where the Vietminh could obtain a virtually unanimous vote by rigging the elections, and so gain a national majority whatever the result in the South. The American government, however, refused to endorse this settlement and used its financial support of Bao Dai's régime to persuade him to appoint as Prime Minister a certain Ngo Dinh Diem, an inflexible anti-Communist who was determined to oppose a Vietminh take-over in the South. In the transitional phase before the final withdrawal of their forces, the French military authorities vainly endeavoured to prevent the consolidation of Diem's power, and French and American officers were hard put to it to refrain from shooting one another in the streets of Saigon.

Diem's government (which soon got rid of Bao Dai as head of state) refused, when the time came, to participate in nation-wide elections on the valid ground that their freedom in the North could not be guaranteed. Vietnam thus remained, like Korea, divided by an armistice line between a Communist North and an anti-Communist South. Local conditions, however, rendered the division less stable and enduring than in Korea. The boundary between the two Vietnamese states along the 18th Parallel was short and fairly easy to hold against Communist infiltration; but to the west, South Vietnam shared long frontiers with Laos and Cambodia, and these became pervious to the passage of armed Vietminh groups and military supplies, moving through tracts of mountain and jungle. To prevent this infiltration was inherently difficult, and political collusion made it impossible. Laos had its own armed Communist forces, the Pathet Lao, who were supported by the Vietminh. The Geneva Agreement of 1954 laid down that they were to be integrated into the Laotian national army, but all attempts to do so on conditions that would end their existence as a distinct party formation inevitably ended in failure. American support for anti-Communist forces in Laos prevented the Pathet Lao from taking over the whole country and led to a complicated international diplomatic game of arranging coalition governments in the capital. Even so, Pathet Lao control was gradually extended southward through the thinly inhabited and mountainous eastern part of Laos, providing access to South Vietnam for Communist infiltration. Cambodia, to the south of Laos, did not have a separate zone of Communist armed power, but its effective ruler, the royal demagogue Prince Sihanouk, entered into close relations with Communist China, partly because of his belief that Peking was destined in time to gain control of the whole region, and partly in order to assure Cambodia's future survival as a small state between two more powerful neighbours, Vietnam and Thailand. This pro-Chinese and anti-American orientation led the Cambodian government to turn a blind eye to the use of its territory for Vietminh operations against South Vietnam, which was thus exposed to Communist infiltration on its Cambodian, as well as its Laotian, frontiers.

The Vietnam Communist Party in power in the North decided in 1959 to organise a guerrilla insurrection in the South, and cadres originally from the South were sent back there after courses of training in the North. The revolt they brought about gained enough local support to be able to claim the character of an internal rising in South Vietnam, but it still depended on the North for political direction, strategic leadership and supplies of arms.

The United States, having committed itself to the support of South Vietnam, continued to give economic and military aid to Diem's government, including a large team of military advisers; but the revolt of the Vietcong (the name given to the Vietminh in its new incarnation) continued to spread in the rural areas, while South Vietnam's power of resistance was increasingly undermined by conflict of a different kind: the antagonism between Roman Catholics and Buddhists which was a legacy of the French colonial period. The French, who had originally gone into Vietnam in the nineteenth century to protect Catholic converts, had given Catholicism a privileged position. Hence it became a symbol of alien ascendancy, while Buddhism was able to identify itself closely with nationalist sentiment. The end of French rule did not eliminate this cleavage, for Ngo Dinh Diem was a Catholic and had an archbishop among his brothers. Acts of discrimination against the Buddhists caused the latter to organise a campaign of protest demonstrations, including spectacular suicides by fire, against the government. Violent methods of suppression failed to subdue the Buddhists. The Americans, embarrassed at being involved in a religious conflict, withdrew support from Diem; when the army turned against him, he was overthrown by a coup d'état in November 1963 and murdered. But it proved easier to get rid of Diem than to find a new government of equal authority to succeed him. Saigon became a city of chronic rioting and disturbances to which the Vietcong contributed through secret agents. South Vietnam's instability (which well-meant American endeavours to substitute civilian for military rule served only to aggravate) threatened to open the way for a Communist take-over. The Vietcong intensified their guerrilla attacks, and from the beginning of 1965 began to direct them, not only against the South Vietnamese army, but also against its American 'advisory' component. The United States government retaliated by ordering air raids against Vietcong bases and communications in North Vietnam. By 1965, the war in Indochina had become the most serious open conflict between Communist and Western forces since the Korean War. America became more and more deeply involved. The danger of a collapse of the régime in South Vietnam caused President Johnson to send massive reinforcements of American combat troops to fight the Vietcong, while the Soviet Union sent ground-to-air missiles for the defence of North Vietnam against American air raids.

While the war in the former French territory in south-east Asia thus increased in scope from 1959, another war, though less sanguinary, was engendered by the decolonisation of the last dependencies of a Western power in the area: the group of British-governed territories in the Malay peninsula and North Borneo. These had had various historical origins in the nineteenth century: the old 'Straits Settlements'; the nine 'Malay States'; the protected Sultanate of Brunei; Sarawak, ruled for a century by a dynasty of English rajahs; and British North Borneo, which was administered by a chartered company until after the Second World War. Since none of these territories had formed part of the Dutch East Indies, the new state of Indonesia—the successor-state to the former Dutch sovereignty—could have no legal claim to them, and it was British policy, in terminating colonial rule in the area, to combine them in a federation that would form a single viable state. This federation was formally established in September 1963, Malaya itself having achieved independence in 1957.

Indonesia, however, declared its opposition to the new Federation of Malaysia and, when interference from Djakarta was rejected, began to exert pressure by armed raids—first in Borneo (now called Sabah) and later also in Malaya—in the name of 'confrontation'. This procedure, which would have been regarded as war before the age of decolonisation, was justified by Indonesia on the ground that Malaysia was a tool of 'neocolonialism', and Sukarno's aggression received the moral and political support of the Soviet Union, China and other Communist countries. Thus, a policy that was in its original inspiration one of national expansion, corresponding to the Pan-Malayan ethnic doctrine and aspirations to restore the medieval Javanese empire of Madjapahit, provided yet another front of 'national liberation', with Moscow and Peking in rivalry for influence at the court of Indonesia's dictator. The United States, which had hoped to build up Sukarno's régime as a bulwark against Communism, had to withdraw from the competition for his favour when it became clear that it would involve support for acts of war against Britain—British forces being committed to help to defend Malaysia by a treaty of alliance concluded when the Malaysian Federation was set up.

The long delay in decolonisation in Malaya had been due primarily to the absence there of a degree of ethnic cohesion from which a nationalist movement could naturally arise. Malaya was essentially a plural society in which the Malays, the original inhabitants of the country, had come to be outnumbered by Chinese immigrants, most of them of recent arrival. Hence the Malays' enthusiasm for independence was dampened by the fear that departure of the British would mean a Chinese ascendancy. The peninsula's ethnic division had also been a main cause of the failure of the Communist guerrilla revolt which began there in 1947, creating the 'Emergency' that lasted until 1960. Support for the Communist armed rising was virtually confined to the Chinese, and the hostility of the Malays toward what seemed to them a Chinese attempt to gain power helped the British authorities, after a long and arduous campaign, to crush the insurrection. But Malaya could not go on indefinitely as a British colony in the midst of independent Asian states, and at length a coalition party of Malays and Chinese was formed to take over, in 1957, the power that Britain was ready to relinquish. Even so, the Malays insisted on the separation of Singapore, whose almost entirely Chinese population would tip the balance of numbers in favour of the Chinese if included in Malaya. Some form of union between Malaya and its financial and commercial metropolis was clearly essential, however, and this would be facilitated from the Malay point of view if both Malaya and Singapore were to be federated with the Borneo territories in which Malays predominated. This motive provided the driving force for federation in Kuala Lumpur. In British Borneo, where the only practical alternative was union with Indonesia, it was naturally more attractive for the majority to join up with a country of flourishing economy, as Malaya was, rather than with a state whose economic incompetence and maladministration were notorious.

Malaya and Singapore, with their massive Chinese population—the highest in percentage of the total among the countries of south-east Asia—nevertheless remained potentially a zone of Chinese political ascendancy through which China itself could exert a controlling influence over the whole region. This was probably one of the main considerations, though it was not the only one, that impelled Peking to take up a stand on the side of Indonesia in the confrontation with Malaysia. Superficially, an Indonesian absorption of Malaya could not be to the advantage of the 'Overseas Chinese', for the Chinese in Indonesia, a small minority of the total population, were subject to adverse discrimination of a kind far more serious than any restrictions affecting the Chinese in Malaysia. But it may well have been reckoned in Peking that, while Indonesia might be strong enough to 'chew' Malaysia, it would not—in view of the Djakarta government's manifest inability properly to administer its own territories—be strong enough to govern it, so that the collapse of the structure left behind by the British would enable the Chinese to dominate the whole area. This was certainly not the objective of Sukarno or even of the Indonesian Communists, but it was inherent in the situation of instability ensuing on the liquidation of the old colonial system in south-east Asia.

The Soviet Union supplied the Indonesian armed forces with modern weapons and encouraged Sukarno in his 'confrontation' policy; but the Indonesian Communist Party, the strongest in Asia outside the Communist states there, was more attracted by the revolutionary militancy of the Chinese version of Marxist-Leninist doctrine than by Soviet 'revisionism'. The party was favoured up to a point by Sukarno, who tried to base his personal power on a balanced coalition of the Nationalists (his own party), the Communists and a Muslim religious faction. Since the Communists were the most disciplined and determined of the three, the coalition gave them an increasing political ascendancy; but strong opposition was concentrated against them in the army, whose leaders were prepared to resist by force an expected Communist seizure of power on the demise of Sukarno. In October 1965, a premature coup d'état by an element in the army sympathetic to the Communists gave the generals who survived it a pretext for a massive proscription of the Communists, accompanied by popular violence against the Chinese, regarded in Java as the backers of Communism. By the end of 1965, it seemed that Indonesia had moved into the anti-Communist camp, though Sukarno still remained as titular head of government and the 'confrontation' with Malaysia continued.

Meanwhile, Singapore, with its predominantly Chinese population, had seceded from the Malaysian Federation and declared itself independent. A complicated situation was thus created in which the conflict between Djakarta and Kuala Lumpur cut across the lines drawn by the anti-Chinese Malay nationalism common to both Malaya and Indonesia. Malay nationalism was a force which in the long run must be antagonistic to the existence of Singapore as an independent state, but the time might come when Peking would take an active interest in this great Chinese city far to the south of the frontiers of China.

8

DECOLONISATION IN THE MIDDLE EAST AND AFRICA

THE BRITISH relinquished India in August 1947; they evacuated Palestine in May 1948. In both cases, they left behind division and not unity, but in Palestine their departure also precipitated a war. In India there were massacres and migrations of refugees, but the two successor-states recognised their new frontier and refrained from armed hostilities with each other. In Palestine, however, Arabs and Jews were already fighting even as the British troops withdrew to their ships, and the outcome of their war was the starting point of a new era in the history of the Middle East.

At the time of Germany's surrender in 1945, Britain's position in the Middle East seemed to be stronger than it had ever been. There had been no recession of British power there during the war comparable with the loss of Malaya and Burma to the Japanese. British troops had repelled the Italian and German invasions of Egypt and had taken Libya from Italy; they had crushed the German-instigated revolt of Rashid Ali in Iraq and had (in concert with Gaullist French units) overthrown the Vichy French administration of Syria (exercised under a League of Nations Mandate) when the latter permitted the German use of Syrian airfields. When the war ended, there were more than 250,000 British troops in Egypt, Libya, Palestine, Jordan, Syria and Iraq.

There were two factors, however, working to undermine this position of apparently impregnable power. The first, somewhat paradoxically, was the elimination of the French from Syria. In order to obtain local Arab support for the overturn of the Vichy authorities in Syria, General de Gaulle had consented to a promise of independence for Syria and Lebanon. This need not in itself have put these countries in a more favourable position than Egypt or Iraq, which were formally independent but had conceded military bases to Britain; the French assumed that similar bases could be obtained from Syria and Lebanon. But

French prestige had been so reduced by the events of the war that neither state would concede a base, and the British wartime occupation was used to thwart the French. In May 1945, after fighting had broken out between French and Syrian forces in Damascus, the French were virtually forced to withdraw from the city by British intervention. France was thus unable to retain any strategic foothold in the Levant. Superficially, this was for Britain a favourable outcome of a century-and-a-half of Anglo-French jealousy and rivalry in the Middle East. But the departure of the French did not add to the strength of the British position; on the contrary, the example set by Syria in success-fully refusing a military base to a former European overlord encouraged Egypt to do likewise when the treaty for British tenure of the Suez Canal base came up for renewal.

The second factor adverse to Britain was even more serious. It arose from the British Mandate for Palestine and the responsibility for a National Home for the Jews which it included. With the growth of Arab nationalism, the need to conciliate Arab states had become more and more important for British foreign policy. This made the respon-sibility for protecting the Jews increasingly irksome to the British government and the Mandate administrators in Palestine. To placate the Arabs, Jewish immigration into Palestine was restricted. But Hitler's genocide of European Jewry increased the pressure for it, and after 1945 desperate efforts were made by Jewish refugees to enter Palestine illegally with the help of Jews already settled there. The measures taken by the British authorities to stop the immigration led to armed clashes with a secret Jewish paramilitary organisation and then to terrorist acts against British officials; these had the effect of making the latter even more anti-Jewish and pro-Arab than they were already. The administration of Palestine was rendered more and more costly and difficult, and in April 1947, the British government turned over the problem to the United Nations. In November, the United Nations Assembly voted for a partition of Palestine into Arab and Jewish states and asked Britain to stay for two years to prepare it. Britain, however, declined to have anything to do with the scheme and announced its intention of giving up the Mandate on May 14, 1948. Theoretically, the British retained responsibility for law and order until that date, but from January onward, with rare exceptions, they ceased to do anything to protect Jewish settlements from attacks by Arab irregulars, and allowed an 'Arab Liberation Army' of volunteers recruited in Syria to enter Palestine and take part in the fighting.

After the official termination of the Mandate, a sovereign state of Israel was formally proclaimed, but it had to contend not only with irregulars but also with the regular armies of Syria, Transjordan and Egypt. It seemed that the infant republic would be overwhelmed, particularly since its defence force, the Haganah, had been almost unarmed at the beginning of the year. The arms embargo for the Middle East declared by the United Nations was naturally to the disadvantage of Israel as compared with the Arab states, which already possessed stocks of their own. Czechoslovakia, however, provided Israel with arms after an Israeli emissary had obtained Soviet permission for the Czechs to do so.* With these supplies, the Jews succeeded in beating off the invasions. They were fighting for their lives and for the land on which they had settled, under an efficient central command, while the Arabs had no co-ordinated strategy and each of the three Arab states was in rivalry with the others for the future control of Palestine. When the war was at last ended by an armistice, the Jews had not merely held their own but occupied a larger area than had been assigned to them in the United Nations partition scheme—a scheme that in detail had been unpractical since the boundaries it laid out for the proposed Jewish state were strategically indefensible.

The humiliating defeat of the Arab armies in Palestine had a profound effect throughout all Arabic-speaking countries. It created an obsession with Palestine, a deep sense of frustration, and a demand for pan-ethnic unity and regeneration. In the words of an Arab writer, Musa Alami: 'Palestine and the self-respect of the Arabs must be recovered. Without Palestine there is no life for them. . . . This is the first phase of a long war.'[1] Many other Arab writers followed him in contending that Palestine could be recovered only through 'a total political and social renaissance' in the Arab world. Since the corruption, incompetence and disunity of the governing classes in the Arab countries were blamed for the disaster, the defeat also stimulated all the forces of political and social revolution in the Arab world. Arab indignation was also turned against Britain for having created the Jewish

* The Czechs kept the account straight by selling arms also to the Arabs. Some arms were also obtained by Israel in Britain and the United States by use of faked export licences for South America.

National Home in the first place, and for not having turned over Palestine to the Arabs before giving up the Mandate. The Jews found it easier to forgive the unsuccessful British collusion with their enemies than the Arabs the British failure to give them more active support.

> The outcome of the war in Palestine was in effect more of a defeat for imperial Britain than for the Arab countries. . . . The British Government assumed that an empire could abdicate at will and start or stop the process as you start and stop a bus. . . . The main issue which was involved in Palestine . . . was not the clash of Jew and Arab, but the inability of Mr Attlee's Government to maintain the Pax Britannica on which the Middle East order had been built.[2]

In Egypt, a revolution in 1952 overthrew the monarchy and a coup soon after brought to power a man who, as an army officer, had witnessed the rout of the Egyptians in the Negev. Abdul Nasser pursued with resolute purpose, great skill and complete lack of moral inhibitions, two closely linked aims: the destruction of Israel, and the unity of all Arabs from Muscat to Morocco under his own leadership. The two aims were interdependent, for only by a combined effort of the Arab states could Israel be conquered, and only through a common hatred of Israel could the centrifugal forces of the Arab world be overcome. Talk of Arab unity was not new, but such unity had not existed as a political fact since the days of the Ommayad Caliphate in the eighth century, and no modern Arab leader before Nasser had had any idea of how in practice to unite the Arab peoples.

Nasser, however, was a man of the modern age, and in radio broadcasting he found the instrument he needed for reaching every corner of the Arab lands. Radio Cairo became an institution of world significance. No funds were spared to make it technically of the highest efficiency, and Germans who had formerly worked for Goebbels were recruited, glad to serve in a new phase of their Nazi war against the Jews. The broadcast word reached not only the cities—Damascus, Baghdad, Beirut, Tunis, Algiers, Marrakesh—where there was already an intelligentsia responsive to Pan-arabism, but also thousands of villages and desert encampments that had previously been unaffected by the new politics. Much of the Arab world, enfolded in deserts, had remained extremely primitive far into the twentieth century. But now, cheap radio sets enabled Arabs everywhere to listen to the voices of

Cairo. And stirring voices they were, full of romantic idealism, of burning hatred against enemies and traitors, and of glorification of the leader who had dedicated himself to the sacred cause.

Second only to the incitement against Israel, anti-imperialism was the theme of Radio Cairo, and it was preached, not only in Arabic, but also in Swahili and other African languages. Concretely, Egypt had made the decisive move against imperialism in the Middle East by refusing to renew the treaty that provided for the great British military base on the Suez Canal. This base was the pivot of British power in the Middle East. Britain had maintained military forces in Egypt since 1882, and had used Egypt as an operational base in both world wars. Formerly, Egypt's strategic importance had been as the key country on the short route to India; with the end of British rule in India, it was still deemed important in London to secure maritime communications through the Suez Canal to Aden and the Persian Gulf in order to protect British oil interests in Iraq and Kuwait. But Egyptian nationalism was set against the continuation of a British base on Egyptian soil. To the example of the Syrian refusal to concede a base to France there was added, after 1947, the greater example of India, which had gained independence without conceding any bases to Britain, and had demonstratively adopted an attitude of non-alignment in the conflict between the Western and Soviet power blocs. In London, where a Conservative government had replaced a Labour one in 1951, some politicians of the extreme right—the so-called Suez Group—had urged that Britain remain in Egypt, with or without Egyptian consent, arguing that a tough line would in the end compel Cairo to come to terms. But Eden, as Foreign Secretary, believed that it would be unwise for Britain thus to over-ride the rights of a sovereign state, especially as the American government—with the idea of winning Egyptian support in the Cold War—was urging Britain to yield. In 1954, Britain gave up the Canal base and handed over its massive installations to Egypt. The sequel was not an improvement in Anglo-Egyptian relations but an intensification of Cairo's anti-British propaganda. In Nasser's eyes, Britain's withdrawal was merely proof of the declining power of the British. Eden incurred severe criticism from the Suez Group; this, and the uncompromising hostility of Nasser, made him highly sensitive to the Egyptian problem. When, in July 1956, Nasser nationalised the Suez Canal Company, Eden began to think of using force, not merely to obtain an international administration of the Canal, but to upset Nasser's dictatorship in Egypt and replace him with someone less hostile to Britain. As a British official explained it at the time, 'What we want is a nicer Nasser.'

In the intention of deposing the messiah of the Arab world, French policy was now converging with British, mainly on account of the war that had broken out in Algeria. When, in 1954, France had ended by capitulation the eight years of war in Indochina, it had hoped there would be a respite from fighting overseas and that its resources could be devoted to the restoration of French military power in Europe. But no sooner were the guns silent in Indochina than an embittered and exhausting struggle began in North Africa. The nationalist and Pan-Arab ferment in the Middle East had spread westward to Tunisia, Algeria and Morocco. The first and third of these countries were French protectorates, retaining their native governments even though under French control. After difficult negotiations and not a little bloodshed, agreements were reached by which Tunisia and Morocco became independent. But Algeria was another matter. It was under direct French administration and constitutionally formed part of France; moreover, it contained a large minority population of French settlers, the 'colons' (though many of them, in fact, were of Italian or Spanish descent), and these were strongly represented in French politics. 'Algérie française' became a slogan to which every Paris cabinet had to bow. But, for the Arabs, Algeria was an Islamic country, as much entitled to independence as Tunisia and Morocco. When the more extreme Algerian nationalists began an armed rising against French rule, Nasser naturally gave it his blessing. His support was not confined to the sympathy expressed by Radio Cairo; when, after September 1955, Egypt received supplies of arms from Czechoslovakia, some of them were diverted to Algeria. The French came to the conclusion that the best place for seeking a decision of the Algerian war was in Cairo. To this motive was added the interest that France shared with Britain in access to supplies of Middle Eastern oil.

In their desire to take action against Nasser, however, the two governments were confronted by the difficulty that they had no good ground in international law for invading Egypt to prevent nationalisation of the Suez Canal Company, for nationalistion was well within Egypt's sovereign rights. However, information of an impending anti-Egyptian action by Israel seemed to give the opportunity for an intervention that could be represented as being for the protection of international Canal traffic against interruption by Egypto-Israeli hostilities. Israel's grievances against Egypt had nothing to do with the nationalisation of the Canal, with the lost British base there, or with Egyptian support for the revolt in Algeria. Yet the Israelis did have a grievance of their own in regard to the Canal, for the Egyptians, holding that they were permanently at war with Israel (the armistice of 1949 never having been followed by a peace treaty), had closed the Canal to all shipping bound for Israeli ports—in this ignoring a UN Security Council resolution that they should allow free passage. Moreover, Egypt had, by means of coastal batteries, closed the Straits of Tiran to all Red Sea shipping bound for Eilat, the Israeli port on the Gulf of Aqaba, thus cutting off Israel from all maritime trade except through the Mediterranean. Finally, taking advantage of the long, narrow territorial shape of Israel, Nasser had organised raids across the frontier by guerrilla bands of *fedayeen* who operated from camps in Egypt and were paid and equipped by the Egyptian War Ministry. This was, in fact, aggressive war against Israel, even though regular armed forces were not engaged; but the Israelis could not hope for any redress because the international situation was against them. The United States and the Soviet Union were competing for Egypt's friendship; and Britain and France, though desiring the overthrow of Nasser, did not wish to offend other Arab and Islamic states by openly taking Israel's side. The Israelis decided, therefore, to take independent action by wiping out the *fedayeen* bases and occupying the Egyptian coast of the Straits of Tiran. When this intention became known in London and Paris, it seemed to provide a pretext for seizing the Suez Canal in order to 'separate the combatants'.

As in 1948–49, the Israelis decisively defeated the Egyptian army and there was nothing to stop them from advancing to the Canal. But the action taken by Britain and France in intervening in the war was a blunder of the first magnitude. By invading Egypt themselves, they lost their position of political advantage as third parties to the conflict. Their ability to crush Egypt militarily—after the Israelis had already done it —availed them nothing against an almost unanimous condemnation by the United Nations and the hostile attitudes of both the United States and the Soviet Union. Their pleas of justification fell on deaf ears, the Anglo-French action appearing to world opinion as aggression in the worst tradition of old-style imperialism. The Suez crisis and its aftermath were a disastrous setback for Britain and France. Instead of obtaining safeguards for traffic through the Canal, they lost the use of it for months and suffered an oil famine which reduced them to pleading with oil interests in the United States for a relaxation of restrictions on American oil production. Far from regaining full possession of the Canal Zone, Britain lost even its residual right (retained in 1954) to use the base in time of war. British investments and assets in Egypt were seized by the Cairo government. Nasser, instead of becoming a figure of shame, the military leader whose troops had been ingloriously chased out of Sinai by the Israelis, emerged as the Arab world's mighty hero, the leader who had successfully defied two great powers and finally liberated Egypt from the fetters of imperialism.

The Suez crisis was the turning point for the Arab world both east and west of Egypt. In Arab Asia, Nasser's prestige as a Pan-Arab leader was vastly increased—though the traditional claims of Damascus and Baghdad to primacy in the Arab world continued to be substantial obstacles to Egyptian hegemony—and the Soviet Union exerted new influence as the power that allegedly had saved Egypt by the threat to use rockets against France and Britain.

The American government, having helped by diplomatic and financial pressure to bring about the failure of the Anglo-French expedition, now became alarmed lest the Soviet Union fill the Middle East power vacuum created by the decline of British power. John Foster Dulles, the Secretary of State, therefore formulated a policy, subsequently known as the Eisenhower Doctrine, which sought to extend to the Middle East the protection already given by the Truman Doctrine to Greece and Turkey. A declaration that the United States would assist any nation in the area in 'the development of economic strength dedicated to the maintenance of national independence', and would use armed force to assist any nation 'requesting assistance against armed aggression from any country controlled by international Communism', was approved by Congress and signed by the President in March 1957. The Eisenhower Doctrine was calculated to reinforce the defensive alliance of Britain, Turkey, Iraq, Iran and Pakistan (the Baghdad Pact) that had been formed to prevent a feared southward expansion of the Soviet Union. Of the Asian members of the Baghdad Pact, only Turkey and Iran had a common frontier with the USSR, and their adherence to the alliance was primarily dictated by the desire for security against possible Russian aggression. Turkey had been guaranteed by the Truman Doctrine since 1947 and had been a member of NATO since 1951. Iran, which had had an unpleasant experience of Soviet behaviour in 1946, when the Russians had tried to set up a separate state in the north-west of the country, had sought American arms and advisers, and had joined the Baghdad Pact in 1953. Pakistan and Iraq, on the other hand, having no common frontiers with the USSR and no historical experience of Russian invasions, were less conscious of the Soviet danger and valued the Pact mainly as a means of strengthening themselves against non-Communist rivals. Pakistan considered that the alliance brought an increase of strength in its relations with India; Iraq, under the leadership of Nuri es-Said, regarded a British alliance as support against Egypt and Syria.

But, in July 1958, a military revolution, led by General Kassem, overthrew the government of Nuri es-Said and the Hashemite dynasty in Iraq, and took that country out of the Baghdad Pact. At the same time, there was a revolt in the Lebanon against a government headed by President Chamoun, who had endorsed the Eisenhower Doctrine. The situation appeared to call for an application of the Doctrine, since Communists played a prominent part in Kassem's revolution and were also extremely active in Syria. The American government, therefore, landed a force of marines in Beirut to defend the Lebanon: an action that drew a vehement protest from the Soviet Union and a demand for a summit conference on Middle Eastern affairs between Western and Soviet leaders. The US intervention was anti-climactic, however, because it soon became evident that the revolt in the Lebanon was almost entirely a domestic affair. A United Nations commission, sent to the Syrian border, reported that there had been only a small passage of arms across the frontier and 'no proven case of persons coming in to fight'. American policy was now modified to allow for neutralism in Arab countries, and to avoid any suggestion of the United States' claiming a right of intervention in Arab affairs.

Nasser, in spite of his acceptance of arms from the Soviet bloc and refusal to align himself in any way with the West, was sufficiently anti-Communist in his domestic policy to convince Washington that he could be trusted to oppose an expansion of Communism in the Middle East. The United States reverted to the policy of support for Nasser which had been interrupted by his recognition of Communist China and by Dulles' withdrawal of American aid for the construction of the Aswan Dam. But, whatever his attitude towards Communism, Nasser had not departed from his resolve to eliminate all traces of British or French imperial control within the Arab world. In 1962, he sent an Egyptian army across the Red Sea into the Yemen to support a republican revolution against the monarchy of the Imam, who had been until then the autocratic ruler of this archaic Arabian kingdom. The revolution was only partially successful for, although the republicans held the capital, the followers of the Imam maintained a guerrilla war in the mountains with supplies of arms from Saudi Arabia, whose king was alarmed at the threat of Nasserite republicanism to his own throne. The Yemenis showed a strong dislike for the Egyptian intruders, and, two years after the fighting began, it was estimated that one-third of Egypt's military forces were tied down in the Yemen. But this war did not only involve Arabs: the Yemen had always laid claim to the British territory of Aden and protectorate over a number of local rulers to the north of it. As the sponsor of the new régime in the Yemen, Egypt was now in effect on the border of the British-controlled area of southern Arabia, and although Britain refrained from any intervention in the Yemen war, the Egyptian intelligence service directed a revolutionary organisation in Aden which carried out terrorist attacks on British civil and military personnel and their families. The British were ready to divest themselves of their colonial authority in Aden, but were not willing to cede it to Egypt or the Yemen; instead, they proposed to build up a South Arabian Federation which would become a sovereign state after British withdrawal. The construction of such a state, however, involving as it did the union of a modern city with a primitive 'feudal' hinterland, was no simple matter, and it remained to be seen whether it would prove politically or strategically viable if Egypt once succeeded in unifying the Yemen under its hegemony.

To the west of Egypt, 'Algérie française' survived by five years the failure of the French action against Egypt, but French arms were unable to crush a revolt which now received moral and material support from all the independent states of the Arab world. In September 1958, the headquarters of the insurgents in Cairo proclaimed a Provisional Government of the Algerian Republic and it was at once recognised by Egypt, Iraq and Libya. Morocco and Tunisia, recognised by France as fully independent states in the spring of 1956, provided bases for the Algerian rebels and passage for supplies of arms. The French government—or rather governments, for one succeeded another in the traditional style of French parliamentary democracy—hesitated to spread the war by retaliation against Algeria's neighbours. With 400,000 French troops engaged, France was still unable to terminate the insurrection, which numbered among its organisers former soldiers of the French African forces who, as prisoners of war in Indochina, had been turned against France and instructed in the art of guerrilla warfare by the Vietminh. Paris sought to negotiate with the rebels, but the prospect of accepting defeat produced violent protests from the 'colons' and a section of the French army. The latter, in May 1958, staged a counter-revolt in Algiers and forced the Pflimlin cabinet out of office. Faced with civil war in France, President Coty recalled to power General de Gaulle, who assumed leadership of the nation without making any commitment as to what his policy would be. In fact, his mind was already made up. Giving an absolute priority to the strategic position of France in Europe, he believed that an overseas colony that needed half a million French troops for its retention was not worth keeping. He moved slowly and cautiously towards a settlement with the Algerian nationalists; in November 1960, he spoke for the first time in public of an 'Algerian Republic'. For this, he naturally incurred the bitter hatred of the French 'ultras' whose insurgency had given him power; but, unlike his predecessors, he was not to be intimidated by them, even when they went to the length of attempting to assassinate him. The independence of Algeria was at last recognised in 1961, the majority of the 'colons' being resettled in France, where a booming economy provided them with employment.

With the liberation of Algeria, the whole Arab world now consisted of independent states, except for Aden and the British protectorates in southern and eastern Arabia. It was, however, far from any kind of political unity. A formal union in 1963 of Egypt and Syria, under the title of the United Arab Republic, proved short-lived—though Egypt hopefully went on using the name after Syria had broken away. The difficulty was that, although Nasser personally was admired throughout the Arab world, there was such a general dislike of Egyptians that a political integration with them—which would mean, in effect, an Egyptian hegemony—was everywhere resisted. The Arab states went their own ways. There were seven of them in Asia: Lebanon, Syria, Iraq, Jordan, Saudi Arabia, Yemen and Kuwait; and seven in Africa: Egypt, Sudan, Libya, Tunisia, Algeria, Morocco and Mauritania. They were united only in hostility to Israel and in a general spirit of anti-colonialism. This anti-colonialist spirit was, however, compatible with wide variations of attitude among the Arab states, in accordance with their special interests, towards the imperial powers formerly predominant in the Middle Eastern and North African areas.

South of the Sahara, nationalism came later than in the Arab world; but, when it came, it was no less explosive. At the end of the Second World War, there were still only two native African independent states south of the zone of Arabic speech: Ethiopia, the ancient Christian kingdom that had been conquered by the Italians in 1936, but liberated by the British during the war; and Liberia, founded early in the nineteenth century as a settlement for freed Negro slaves from America. The rest of Africa south of the Sahara consisted of the colonies, protectorates and League of Nations mandates of five European nations—Britain, France, Belgium, Portugal and Spain—and the independent white settler state of South Africa, at this time a Dominion within the British Commonwealth. A second white settler state existed *de facto* in Southern Rhodesia, where internal self-government on a limited franchise had been granted by Britain, albeit ultimate sovereignty remained vested in the British Crown. Except for Ethiopia and Somaliland, whose ethnic and cultural affinities were with North Africa, the continent south of the Sahara was 'black Africa', distinguished by the predominance of the negroid racial type and by a quality which some French African writers described as 'négritude'.

Before the coming of the European conquerors, the whole of the area had been one of primitive economy and culture in comparison with the lands of southern Asia and the Mediterranean littoral of Africa. It was generally assumed that, even if independence had to be conceded by the imperial powers to Asian and Arab peoples, it would be a long time before black Africa could be 'ready' for self-government. In 1945, there was virtually no native bourgeoisie anywhere south of the Sahara; major enterprises were owned and operated by Europeans, and local trade was mainly in the hands of Indian or Arab immigrants. But there now existed everywhere a small class of men who had received an education in a European language and had qualified as lawyers, doctors, school-teachers, journalists or minor civil servants. For members of this class, it was intolerable that black Africans should be denied political independence when it was granted to Indians and Arabs; the idea that they might be less capable of facing life as sovereign states in the modern world was regarded as grossly insulting and a mere pretext of imperialism for denying them their rights. Nationalist agitation began immediately after the war in British and French West Africa, and soon afterwards spread to Central and East Africa. In 1946, three substantial political parties were formed: the United Gold Coast Convention in what was to become Ghana; the Kenya African Union in British East Africa; and the Rassemblement Démocratique Africain in French West Africa. The news of the transfer of power in India greatly stimulated the political activity of these and other parties, the granting of independence to Tunisia and Morocco gave an even greater impetus, and the political defeat of Britain and France in the Suez crisis of 1956 was taken as decisive confirmation of the collapse of imperialism. Decolonisation now swept over Africa like a tidal wave.

Ghana was the first country to achieve full independence. Following riots in Accra in 1948, the British government decided to introduce parliamentary democracy with universal suffrage in what was then still called the Gold Coast. A general election, held in 1951, returned a large majority for the Convention People's Party, whose leader, Dr Nkrumah, was then in prison; he was released and made Prime Minister. The nationalist victory was followed by a transitional period of six years, during which certain reserve powers were still held by the British Governor, and then full sovereignty was transferred to the new régime in March 1957. No sooner had Nkrumah established himself as the leader of a fully independent nation than he aspired to become the leader of all Africa. In April 1958, he convened in Accra a meeting of independent African states, of which there were still so far only eight: Ghana itself, Egypt, Sudan, Libya, Tunisia, Morocco, Ethiopia and Liberia. At the end of the year, a much larger and more challenging conference was held in Accra; this was the All-African Peoples' Conference, which was attended by delegates of sixty-two African nationalist organisations from all over the continent. Among those who attended it were Tom Mboya from Kenya and Patrice Lumumba from the Belgian Congo.

Had Britain and France been in a mood forcibly to maintain their rule in their remaining African territories, they might have regarded Ghana's promotion of this revolutionary gathering as an international provocation. But both of them were by now committed to concessions to African nationalism which could hardly stop short of complete independence everywhere. Britain was already applying in Nigeria, in Uganda and in Kenya the procedures which had brought independence to Ghana. France, deeply involved in a war to hold Algeria, could not afford revolts in its West and Central African territories as well. French Africa south of the Sahara comprised an area eight times the size of France with a population of over 45 millions. Up to 1956, there had been no serious intention in Paris of relaxing control over French Africa, but in that year the Mollet cabinet produced a legislative proposal providing for elected African governments with limited powers. This was extended in 1958 by de Gaulle, who toured French Africa in company with the Ivory Coast politician Houphouët-Boigny and offered the inhabitants of its twelve provinces the choice between complete independence (without further French aid) or autonomy within a French Community. Eleven of the provinces chose the latter alternative, but Guinea opted for total independence. Guinea was duly cut off from any form of further economic or administrative aid from France, but the new state succeeded in carrying on thanks to financial assistance from the Soviet Union and Ghana. The example caused the other eleven to regret their acceptance of an inferior status, and France was finally forced to recognise their full sovereignty. In addition to the twelve states formed out of former French West and Equatorial Africa (Mauritania, Senegal, Mali, Guinea, Ivory Coast, Upper Volta, Dahomey, Niger, Chad, Gabon, Congo (Brazzaville) and the Central African Republic) and two adjacent United Nations trusteeship territories of Cameroon and Togo, France also conceded independence to Madagascar, the great island to the south-east of the continent whose ethnic affinities were not African, but Malay.

The rapid transitions towards independence in British and French Africa gave a sudden jolt to the colonial policy of Belgium, whose administration of an empire in the Congo, more than seventy times the size of the Belgian homeland, had been excessively paternal ever since the Belgian state took it over from the discredited régime of the 'Congo

Free State' under Leopold II in 1908. Until 1958, the Belgian government paid virtually no heed either to the rather feeble nationalist
agitation within the Congo or to what was going on elsewhere in Africa.
But in that year there came the impact of two dramatic events: in August,
General de Gaulle in a speech in Brazzaville, just across the river from
the capital of the Belgian Congo, offered the French Congo its choice
between autonomy and independence; and in December, Patrice
Lumumba, leader of the Mouvement National Congolais, figured
prominently at the All-African Peoples' Conference in Accra, which
demanded immediate independence for all African countries. In
January 1959, there were riots in Leopoldville.

Belgium now suddenly swung round from ultra-authoritarian rule to
the profession of the most extreme liberal principles, and announced
that full sovereignty would be conferred on the Congo in July 1960.
No preparation had been made for the transition, and when the time
came only 5 per cent of the civil servants were Congolese, while there
was not a single Congolese officer in the state's army, the Force Publique. The Belgians assumed that the dependence of a nominally
independent Congolese government on Belgian army officers and civil
administrators would ensure them a controlling influence in the new
state. But a few weeks after the formal transfer of power, the Force
Publique mutinied and drove out its Belgian officers. Belgians and their
families all over the country were attacked by mutinous soldiers and
mobs; to protect them, 5,000 troops were flown out from Belgium. To
avert a Belgian military occupation, Lumumba, the Prime Minister
of the new Congolese government, invoked the assistance of the United
Nations. The consequences of this appeal as an episode in the history
of the United Nations do not concern us here;* its consequence in
Central Africa was that the successor-state to the former Belgian
Congo was held together for four years not by its own cohesion or
military forces, but by an international army acting under the authority
of the Secretary-General of the United Nations in New York.

The Belgian Congo had had no ethnic or historic unity. There had
once been, it is true, a kingdom of Bakongo on the lower reaches of the
great river, but the up-river peoples had been its enemies, and the
colonial administrative entity inherited by the new state was an artificial
creation that could hardly be preserved except by compulsive force.

* See Chapter 9, pp. 156-171

When the mutiny of the Force Publique deprived the central government of any effective means of coercion, the way was clear for the Conakat party in the province of Katanga, led by Moise Tshombe, to bring about the secession which was its declared policy. Katanga, the province of the copper mines, provided two-thirds of the total revenue of the Congo, and the Conakat aimed at employing its wealth for the benefit of its own inhabitants instead of having it drained away to sustain the central government at Leopoldville and subsidise the poverty-stricken provinces of the north and east. The Belgians had opposed Katangan separation before the transfer of power in the Congo, wishing to keep in being the highly centralised administration they had created and expected to continue to control. When the army mutiny upset all these calculations, Katanga was the only part of the Congo where Belgians were protected by the native authorities. Tshombe used the Katanga provincial gendarmerie to disarm the Force Publique mutineers, and kept order locally on his own authority, with the result that he obtained the support of the Belgians, which he had not had before. This was to his advantage, but it earned him the reputation among zealous anti-colonialists all over Africa of being a colonial puppet and collaborator, for African opinion, ignoring the atrocities which had provoked the Belgians' intervention after the Force Publique mutiny, regarded it merely as an attempt to reimpose colonial rule. Tshombe's reputation suffered still more from his presumed complicity in the killing of Lumumba. Deposed by President Kasavubu in 1961 from the office of Prime Minister in the central government, Lumumba had been arrested and handed over to Tshombe for safe-keeping, the anarchic conditions in Leopoldville making it too dangerous to keep him in detention there. Lumumba succeeded in escaping from his prison in Katanga, but only to be killed by villagers who found him in hiding. There was never any direct evidence that Tshombe had ordered him to be put to death, but Communist propaganda throughout the world asserted that he had, and it was generally believed all over Africa. The intervention of the United Nations had prevented a direct clash between East and West in the Congo, but there was a fierce struggle for political influence between the United States and the Soviet Union who supported, respectively, the Kasavubu and the Lumumba factions. At the same time, certain financial interests in the West gave support to Tshombe's claims for Katangese autonomy. In these circumstances,

Lumumba, a great spell-binding orator who had distinguished himself when in power by the bitterness of his hatred for the former colonial masters of his country, became a world hero for anti-imperialists and Communists alike. His murder led immediately to his being canonised as the great saint and martyr of the Pan-African cause; a quasi-religious cult of his departed spirit was promoted in the eastern Congo by the political enemies of Kasavubu and Tshombe; and the Soviet Union ostentatiously established a Patrice Lumumba University in Moscow for African, Asian and Latin American students.

As the opponent of the glorious Lumumba, Tshombe was the devil incarnate. Yet it proved impossible to get rid of him. He was, indeed, in 1963, driven out of Katanga by the United Nations which, while disclaiming any intention of interfering in the domestic affairs of the Congo, declared that it had a responsibility to prevent the secession of any part of it. Katanga was restored by the UN troops to the Congolese central government, and the Congolese National Army—the inefficient and undisciplined successor of the Force Publique—was allowed to occupy it. But the UN military presence came to an end in the middle of 1964 and, even before the last soldiers of the international force were flown out, it was clear that, without UN troops, the Congolese central government would be unable to hold Katanga unless the leader of the province were in power in Leopoldville. So, in 1964, Tshombe came back to the Congo, this time no longer as President of a seceding Katanga, but as Prime Minister of the whole country. Faced with the outbreak of a formidable revolt of the Lumumbist faction in Kivu province, he recruited a force of European mercenaries to act as the vanguard of his government's army in operations against the rebels —an action which inflamed still further the hatred he inspired among the Pan-African zealots. The attempt of the Lumumbist rebels to use European civilians as hostages to stop the advance of Tshombe's forces led to a rescue operation in two places by Belgian paratroopers carried in American aircraft; this in turn provoked a tremendous explosion of wrath throughout Africa, and several African governments, with the support of the Soviet Union, vehemently protested to the United Nations.

By this time, the independent African states had come together in a loose association called the Organisation of African Unity (OAU), in which Egypt, Algeria and Ghana formed a dominant group. These states openly sent arms to the Congolese rebels, and the Sudan, Congo-Brazzaville, Tanganyika and Uganda co-operated in their delivery. The new significance of Communist China in African affairs was at the same time exemplified by the aid and guerrilla training it gave to the Kivu insurgents. The revolt, nevertheless, collapsed after a series of defeats at the hands of the white mercenaries. By the beginning of March 1965, Tshombe's position had been so far consolidated that, among the foreign ministers of thirty-five African governments—to which figure the number of African states had by then risen—a proposal to bring representatives of the Congolese rebels into the session was defeated, despite intense lobbying by Egypt. African political unity remained even less of a reality than Arab unity, yet the Lumumba myth, with its counterpart in hatred of Tshombe, continued to be a great irrational motive force in African affairs, capable of being exploited by ambitious politicians seeking to build a federal union of black Africa.

Even so, when Tshombe came to grief as Prime Minister of the Congo in 1965, it was not as a result of the revolt of the Lumumbists or of any action by the OAU, but because of a quarrel with President Kasavubu, who displaced him and tried to govern without him. But General Mobutu, the commander-in-chief of the army, drove out Kasavubu with the support of Tshombe, and set himself up as a military dictator. He continued to rely on white mercenaries as the indispensable means of holding the country together. Kasavubu had promised Nkrumah to get rid of them, but Mobutu declared that the government could not do without them, and this was one of his reasons for deposing Kasavubu. Thus, the largest black state of Africa was propped up by white soldiers recruited mainly from the strongholds of white supremacy in South Africa and Rhodesia.

South of the Congo were the African lands where European ascendancy remained: the colonial rule of Portugal in Angola and Mozambique, and the white settler rule in South Africa and Southern Rhodesia. Portugal had refused to join with Britain, France and Belgium on the path of decolonisation; and, although a native revolt in Angola in 1962–63 had caused the Portuguese authorities a great deal of trouble, it had failed to eject them. In South Africa, the principle of Apartheid had been adopted, separating the white minority from the black majority, and depriving the latter of any right to a common political franchise with the whites. Apartheid was universally condemned abroad, and opposition to it within the British Commonwealth led to South Africa's leaving that association and to declaring itself a republic in 1961. But the world's detestation made no impression on South African policy—other than, perhaps, to strengthen the 'white laager' mentality of the government and its supporters—and the flourishing condition of the country's economy enabled them to go their own way without regard to international opinion.

Southern Rhodesia was in a different position. It remained constitutionally a British crown colony, though enjoying internal self-government with a limited franchise which kept power in the hands of the white settlers. The settler government had control of the local armed forces, which included a small, but highly efficient, air force. It was, therefore, difficult if not impossible for Britain to impose a new and liberal constitution on the white settlers without their consent. Yet, as long as the British government retained nominal sovereignty in Southern Rhodesia, it was exposed to denunciation and abuse by the independent African states for not enfranchising the negro majority. In practice, the most that any British government could do was to threaten economic reprisals if the government in Salisbury were to make a unilateral declaration of independence. But there was no prospect of submission by the white settlers to the constitutional changes desired in London. Negotiations by the Conservative government and by its Labour successor, elected in October 1964, failed to reach agreement with the government of Ian Smith. Despite warnings of the consequences, Southern Rhodesia (now calling itself simply Rhodesia after Northern Rhodesia, on becoming independent, had taken the name of Zambia) unilaterally declared its independence from Britain in November 1965. The British government thereupon embarked on a policy of economic sanctions (under pressure from African states to use force) in the hope of persuading the rebels to mend their ways.

As a result of decolonisation in Africa during the twenty years between 1945 and 1965, the continent came to be divided into two major zones: one in the north and centre, comprising independent African states; the other in the south, consisting of the Portuguese colonies and the settler-governed territories of South Africa and Rhodesia. Between these zones there was a deep and embittered conflict, and the most prominent leaders of the former colonial countries declared their intention of liberating by force the indigenous peoples of the southern zone.

The countries of the ex-colonial bloc, however, were much divided among themselves. There was the important cleavage between Arab and non-Arab—particularly significant in relation to Israel, for non-Arab Africans took no interest in the Arab vendetta against the Israelis; and there was a sharp conflict between a radical Pan-African and anti-Western group of states, with Egypt and Ghana competing for its leadership, and a more conservative group—including such countries as Senegal, the Ivory Coast, Nigeria and Tshombe's Congo—which sought to maintain good relations with America and Europe and avoid Pan-African armed adventures. These divisions prevented Africa from speaking with the single voice that the promoters of continental political unity hoped to create. The Organisation of African Unity was an impressive body as long as it was a matter of passing resolutions in general terms against imperialism, but it showed itself impotent when confronted with the defiance of a Tshombe. The new nations remained for the most part poverty-stricken, underdeveloped and largely dependent on foreign economic and technical aid for such progress as they were able to make. There was no great power in Africa, though both South Africa and Egypt, at opposite ends of the continent, had become states of considerable military strength. The general desire of the newly independent African states was to be neutral in the Cold War, to keep clear of the quarrels of Europe and Asia, and confine themselves to purely African affairs.

It might be, therefore, that from the point of view of the West, there was a possibility of insulating Africa from the major conflicts of world affairs, of leaving the emancipated peoples of the former European empires to their own devices, with enough economic assistance to provide conditions for a continuing development of their natural resources. A realistic survey of the African scene at the end of 1965 did not, however, confirm the hope that Africa might go its own way without the prospect of events that could endanger the peace of the world. There was no reconciliation in sight between the revival of native Africa and the unliquidated strongholds of white supremacy remaining in the south of the continent. The Pan-African forays against Portugal had so far come to nothing, but bigger and more challenging armed enterprises of the same kind were to be expected. An Arab attack on Israel might come at any time, and a revolutionary war against Rhodesia and South Africa was a high, if not the first, priority in foreign policy for several African states. It was not reasonable to suppose that Africa could thus erupt without drawing in interventions and counter-interventions of the Western and Communist powers. The politics of Cairo, Accra and Dar-es-Salaam could not, in a time of crisis, be irrelevant to those of Washington, London and Moscow.

9

THE UNITED AND DISUNITED NATIONS

'THE PARLIAMENT OF MAN, the federation of the world' was in the vision of Tennyson's *Locksley Hall*; it came after the sight of 'the nations' airy navies grappling in the central blue', and only when 'the war drums throbbed no longer and the battle-flags were furled'. But in our age, an institution which can be described as the parliament of man, if not the federation of the world, has coexisted with the war-drums and the battle-flags still in the possession of armed sovereign states. The idea of such an institution became politically potent during the First World War, the 'war to end war'; after four years of unprecedented slaughter, the victors created the League of Nations to ensure that it did not happen again.

The League was designed to fulfil two main purposes: to provide procedures for the settlement of disputes between nations, and to afford security against armed attack. In the first of these functions, it continued the practices of traditional diplomacy which had sought to deal with serious international difficulties through conferences of ambassadors or occasional congresses attended by heads of governments. The Covenant of the League, however, required meetings of the representatives of its member states at regular intervals, provided them with a permanent secretarial organisation, and gave the smaller nations a voice in the new system such as they had not had in the old. The proceedings of the League, moreover, were to be conducted in public instead of by means of the old secret diplomacy. They were, in fact, to have a parliamentary character, the delegates of governments addressing themselves to the public opinion of the world and not merely to a small group of diplomatists behind closed doors. In practice, of course, secret diplomacy continued, largely nullifying Woodrow Wilson's idea of 'open covenants openly arrived at'. But, for better or worse, the habit of making public speeches to the world in an international forum became an essential part of the conduct of relations between sovereign states.

It was, however, primarily as a security system that the League of Nations was judged. The all-important Article 16 of the Covenant laid down that if any member state resorted to war contrary to its obligations under the Covenant, it would be deemed to have committed an act of war against all other members of the League, and that they were bound to apply economic embargoes and blockade measures against it.* Direct military action was not required, but blockading involved the use of force at sea. The article was, indeed, framed so as to be acceptable to public sentiment in Britain and the United States, which was more willing to contemplate fighting at sea than the dispatch of expeditionary armies. The main point of Article 16, however, was that the obligation it enjoined to give assistance to the victim of an aggression was independent of any decision or direction by any organ of the League. The form of the undertaking was similar to that of alliance treaties of the old style, in which the contracting parties pledged aid to each other without reference to any international authority to tell them whether the *casus foederis* had arisen or not. Strictly speaking, the members of the League should all have applied sanctions against Japan in 1931 as soon as it became obvious that the Japanese army in Manchuria was taking control of the country and not merely dealing with a local incident. Similarly, they should have applied them in full against Italy in 1935 as soon as the Italian army crossed the frontier of Abyssinia. But, because the other great powers of the League did not wish, in either case, to take action, and because there were organs of the League charged with settlement of disputes, the convention was adopted—contrary to the plain language of Article 16—that there should be no automatic sanctions, and that it was for the Council and Assembly of the League to decide whether there had been an aggression, and if so, what should be done about it. After the League had failed to take any effective action to stop either Japan or Italy in their courses of conquest, no nation could have faith in the League as its protector, nor was any would-be aggressor likely to be frightened by Article 16. In the language of a later time, the League as a deterrent had ceased to be credible.

When the Covenant of the League was replaced by the Charter of the United Nations, automatic sanctions were ruled out legally as well as in the practice of the great powers. No longer did states bind themselves,

* Article 17 bound members of the League to take similar action against an aggressor state which was not a member of the League.

157

even if only on paper, to take action to stop an aggression which they could see for themselves had been committed. The safeguarding of member states was now the responsibility of the Security Council, and no state was under any obligation to help another except as directed by the Security Council. Since, however, the five permanent members of the Security Council had the right to veto any action against themselves, it followed that no member of the United Nations could expect protection against an aggression by one of the Big Five, except in so far as one or more of the other great powers might come to its help without authority from the Security Council. The task of the Security Council was not to deal with possible aggressions by the Big Five, but with the misdemeanours of lesser powers. It was against the wickedness of small nations—or of the defeated and disarmed ex-enemy states—that it was intended to protect mankind. The basic idea of the United Nations was Roosevelt's notion of the Four Policemen, who became five when the French prodigal son was received back into the company of the elect. It was Roosevelt's assumption that these 'World Policemen' would agree among themselves, and that none of them could be guilty of an act of aggression. Wilson, who in this matter was a man of hard-headed common sense compared with Roosevelt, never made any such assumption about the great powers who were on the winning side in the First World War; Article 16 of the Covenant was applicable to any one of them. The fact that members of the League defaulted on their legal obligations in 1931 and 1935 does not alter the clear intention of the Covenant that no state should be immune from the penalties for aggression. The United Nations Charter created such immunities by making the Security Council exclusively responsible for enforcement of its provisions and then giving the five great powers rights of veto. Yet in Europe, after 1945, it was precisely aggression by one of the Big Five that was most to be feared, and nations that could not hope for any protection from the veto-bound Security Council fell back on old-fashioned defensive alliances to insure themselves against the danger from an over-mighty power.

Even so, in spite of a constitution which was so adverse to the concept of collective security, the United Nations has achieved what the League of Nations never did; it has initiated and conducted military operations, and this not once, but four times. In 1950, it launched a war for the preservation of the Republic of Korea in which sixteen nations fought under a United Nations command. In 1956, it sent an international military force to Egypt to stand between the Egyptians and the Israelis, and though this force did not have to do any fighting, its presence was essential for the uneasy *modus vivendi* that was arranged to terminate the Egyptian-Israeli war. In 1960, the United Nations sent another international force to the Congo to deal with the situation created by the mutiny of the Force Publique after the transfer of power by Belgium, and in this case United Nations troops conducted minor operations against a seceding province, which, whatever may be thought of their moral and political implications, were at any rate militarily successful. In 1964, following the British 'police' intervention in Cyprus to forestall a Turkish invasion after the Christmas massacres of Turkish Cypriots by Greek Cypriots, a United Nations force was sent to the island to prevent fighting between the two communities and in the hope of persuading them to arrive at a political settlement. These four cases of armed intervention were, indeed, different in scale and political setting. The war in Korea was carried on by three great powers and developed into a major military struggle; the interventions in Egypt, the Congo and Cyprus, on the other hand, were effected with forces drawn only from 'small power' nations, and even the fighting in the Congo was insignificant compared with the Korean War. Further, the war in Korea was contrary to the will of one of the Big Five, and the action of the Security Council was only rendered possible by the fact that Russia was boycotting its meetings at the time and was therefore not present to veto the resolutions that were passed. The interventions in Egypt, the Congo and Cyprus were based on resolutions in which Russia had concurred, though Russia took exception to the way in which the Egyptian and Congo operations were carried out and refused to contribute financially to their support.

There have been two main developments in the United Nations since its foundation: first, the growth in the power and activity of the Assembly; and secondly, the growth in the power and activity of the Secretary-General. Both have been indirectly due to the recurring paralysis of the Security Council by the Soviet Union's use of the veto. In the original conception of the United Nations, it was certainly intended that the Security Council should play the leading part and that its directing nucleus should be the Big Three of the wartime Teheran and Yalta conferences. But, as the Cold War replaced the Allied co-operation against Hitler, it became more and more difficult to take clear-cut decisions in the Security Council because of Russia's use of the veto. The Assembly, however, was not restricted by any veto. Although it could only make 'recommendations' and lacked the legal powers of the Security Council, it could pass valid resolutions un-impeded, and thus express what might legitimately be regarded as world opinion. The Assembly, moreover, became the forum for the smaller or weaker nations of the world in their collective opposition to domination by the great powers.

The tendency for the small nations to get together in the Assembly, and increase its weight in relation to the more select conciliar body, had already been apparent in the League, but it became still more marked in the United Nations. In the old diplomacy, the small nations had played very little part collectively; the great powers, who alone were supposed to have world-wide interests, might meet in conferences or congresses, but the small nations had no opportunities to gather together, and were consulted, if at all, by the mighty only when their interests as individual states were directly affected. But in the Assemblies of the League and the United Nations the lesser nations could raise their voices and combine with one another to make their views heeded by the great powers. Further, since they were countries of inferior military strength, they tended to rely more on public debate and appeals to world opinion, so that the Assembly became a forum for oratory and increasingly like a parliament—in contrast to the Council, where the tendency rather was to make set speeches and leave the real decision-making to talks behind the scenes.

The United Nations Assembly also became more parliamentary with the increase in the number of nations represented in it. When this passed the hundred mark in 1963, the delegations became so numerous that harassed foreign ministers occasionally attending sessions had some difficulty in remembering the names of all the constituent countries. With the growth in numbers, the Assembly tended to become somewhat confused and tumultuous, creating difficulties for the President in ensuring everyone's right to be heard. It was theoretically impossible to let parties put up speakers, as in normal parliamentary debate, because there were not supposed to be any parties. In fact, of course, there were from the beginning, both in the League and the United Nations, logrolling blocs and factions, with much intriguing on the backstairs. Yet, what is remarkable in the history of both the League and the United Nations Assemblies is not the extent of the factional politics, but the degree of unanimity with which the conscience of mankind has been manifested on several occasions of international crisis. The votes of the League Assembly in condemnation of Japan and Italy in the Manchurian and Abyssinian crises were nearly unanimous, and if nothing was done in either case to give effect to these condemnations, this cannot be blamed on the blindness or pusillanimity of the small nations. After the failure to stop Italy, however, the small nations became more wary, and if the League Assembly had been asked to condemn Germany in 1939—as it was not—many of its members would have been more concerned about German reprisals than the merits of the case. The United Nations Assembly has on occasions shown no less a capacity than the League Assembly for making up its mind decisively on evidence of aggression; its votes during the Suez crisis were nearly unanimous, and those on Korea in 1950 and on Hungary in 1956 were impressively decisive—though in all questions involving Russian or Communist satellite aggression, Moscow has been able to rally not only all the votes of the Communist bloc, but a number of 'neutrals' whose conception of neutrality in the Cold War is that they must never vote against Russia.

Even so, the greatest international crisis since 1945—the confrontation in 1962 of Russia and America over Cuba—never reached the Assembly at all, and it can only be imagined what might have been its attitude had war, possibly nuclear war, broken out between the two antagonists. One of the outstanding features of the contemporary international situation is the extreme contrast between the great diffusion of peacetime political power among all nations of the world, and the unprecedented concentration of military power in the hands of a very few, with two nations in a class by themselves. Certainly, the development of the United Nations has led to a considerable shift of political influence from the great powers to the collectivity of small states, and the shift has been geographical as well as political, for nearly all the new states since 1945 have been Asian and African and these are now more than half of the members. Yet, in terms of power politics in the nuclear age, only the United States and the Soviet Union really count, with Britain, France and China a good way behind. As long as international tension is low, or as long as there is a stable nuclear stalemate, the voices of the weak can carry weight, and the public opinion of the world can be brought to bear on international issues. But, when the world comes close to nuclear war, it no longer matters much whether the votes of Lebanon and Upper Volta are added to those of Costa Rica and Paraguay.

The activity of the United Nations Assembly was given a great impetus after 1950 by the policy of the United States, when Washington foresaw that the return of the Soviet delegate to the Security Council would render impossible in future the kind of response to an act of Communist aggression that the Security Council had given to the invasion of South Korea. Under the formula of 'uniting for peace', the Assembly was encouraged to discuss matters of peace and war which were supposed to have been reserved by the Charter for the Security Council. The enlargement of its sphere was not in the long run entirely to the advantage of American diplomacy, for the influx of new Asian and African states increased the 'neutralist' element in the Assembly, and reduced the importance of the Latin American bloc on which Washington greatly relied in the early years of the United Nations for support of its policies. But the Assembly, if unwilling to be guided by the United States, was not disposed to submit to the will of Moscow either. This was clearly manifest in its resistance to Soviet proposals in 1960 for a 'Troika' of representatives of the two power blocs and the uncommitted countries, each with a veto right, to perform the functions of the Secretary-General. The suggestion of bringing in a separate representative of the neutrals was a bait for the Assembly majority, but it would have nothing to do with it. It was fully aware that the Soviet aim was to paralyse by use of the veto the actions of the United Nations Secretariat no less than those of the Security Council. For the Assembly, the elected Secretary-General embodied more than anyone else the authority of the United Nations in world affairs, being, so to speak, ideally the Prime Minister of the world.

The Secretary-General of the United Nations was from the beginning a more important person than the Secretary-General of the League, because he was empowered on his own initiative to call the attention of the Security Council to any matter involving a danger to the peace of the world instead of merely summoning the Council at the request of a member, as under the old League Covenant. Sir Eric Drummond, the first Secretary-General of the League, had had considerable influence, but principally as a mediator behind the scenes; his background was that of a professional civil servant and he conceived his task to be administrative rather than political. Trygve Lie, the first Secretary-General of the United Nations, was more of a politician and a man of strong and rugged character; fortified by the greater power of initiative conferred on him by the Charter, he was not afraid to give a lead in moments of crisis. When war broke out in Korea in June 1950, he opened the meeting of the Security Council with the words: 'I consider it the clear duty of the Security Council to take steps necessary to re-establish peace in that area.' By the initiative he then took, he associated, in the words of a historian of the United Nations, 'himself and his office with the most determined effort the world has yet seen to give reality to the principles of collective security'.[1] For this he incurred the undying enmity of Russia, which vetoed his nomination for re-appointment in the Security Council when his term of office expired in late 1950. Constitutionally, the Assembly elects the Secretary-General on nomination by the Security Council; but the Russian veto prevented Lie's renomination from going forward from the Security Council. The American delegate then announced that he would use his veto against any candidate but Lie, declaring that 'the use of the veto to punish the Secretary-General for his efforts to resist aggression in Korea . . . made it impossible to consider new nominations on their merits'. The Security Council was thus unable to nominate at all, but the Assembly extended Lie's term of office for three years.

The appointment in spring 1953 of his successor, Dag Hammarskjöld of Sweden, was to mark an important new phase in the development of the office. Lie had played a part in organising the military intervention in Korea in 1950 by urging the fifty member states approving the intervention to furnish contingents for the war. The military command was given to General MacArthur, and thenceforward the Secretary-General had little say in the conduct of the war. The bulk of the forces engaged were American, and the heavy cost of what proved to be a three-year struggle on a large scale was borne directly or indirectly by the United States. Very different were the military interventions carried out while Hammarskjöld was Secretary-General. He envisaged operations with forces from countries other than the great powers, financed directly by the United Nations on its own budget, and controlled by himself. In the first of these operations (in 1956), Hammarskjöld obtained the consent of the Egyptians for the stationing of United Nations troops on their territory to save them from being routed again by the Israelis in the event of a renewal of fighting. He insisted on the unconditional withdrawal of the Israelis from the Egyptian territory they had over-run. So uncompromising was he that his name was taken to signify 'the Hammer of Israel and the Shield of the Arabs'. Nevertheless, in the event, the Israelis received a remedy of the two main grievances for which they had launched the offensive against Egypt: the *fedayeen* raids and the blocking of the Tiran Straits. The United Nations forces occupying the Egyptian frontier area prevented the Egyptians from using it for further raids, and a detachment on the shore of the Tiran Straits kept the passage open for ships going to Eilat. The operation was a notable success in that it prevented a renewal of fighting and remedied a situation which had inevitably led to a serious clash of arms. All the same, the arrangement made had the defect that it in no way resolved the basic conflict between Arabs and Israelis; and since the presence of the United Nations military units on Egyptian soil was by consent of Egypt, they could be sent away whenever the Egyptians might feel confident that they were strong enough not to have to fear another armed contest with Israel.

The United Nations intervention in the Egyptian–Israeli war was a relatively straightforward matter; it consisted in interposing a neutral international force between two belligerents. The subsequent intervention in the Congo in 1960 was a much more complicated affair, and led by an almost imperceptible change of objective into a campaign on behalf of the Congolese central government against a seceding province. There was no regular war between Belgium and the newly emancipated Congolese republic, but there were operations by Belgian troops for the protection of Belgian nationals following the mutiny of the Belgian-officered Congolese army, the dissolution of the state into a condition of anarchy, and numerous atrocities against Belgians and their families who had remained in the Congo after independence. In the circumstances, the action taken by Belgium was quite justifiable in international law. But, in the eyes of the Congolese government and of anti-colonialists throughout the world, it looked like a reimposition of Belgian rule on what had been a few months previously a Belgian colonial territory. The original purpose, therefore, of the United Nations expedition sent at the invitation of the Congolese government was to restore order in the Congo, protecting Europeans from outrage or murder, while at the same time rebuilding the civil and military organisation of the Congolese Republic so that it could again function as a responsible sovereign state. Yet the question soon arose: if the task of the United Nations troops was to restore order while not abrogating the rights of the Congolese government over its citizens, did not this task also include the suppression of revolts against its authority and, in particular, the thwarting of the separatist movement in the province of Katanga, whose copper mines provided the main part of the Congo's wealth and revenue? The view prevailed that the UN commitment in the Congo implied the forcible preservation of the unity of the Congolese state as the Belgians had built it up by a series of annexations towards the end of the nineteenth century and as it had been handed over to Lumumba, complete with the Force Publique and a central bureaucracy in Leopoldville.

Yet this idea not only involved a transformation of the original purpose of the intervention, but also the emergence of a policy which was hardly compatible with the United Nations Charter. It was no part of the constitutional theory of the United Nations that it should interfere in any country to assist the government of that country in suppressing a revolt of its own citizens, whether that revolt was for the purpose of seizing power at the centre or creating a new state by the secession of part of its territory. There was plenty of evidence that the Katangan secession was a genuine national movement, but with the difference that, as compared with other African national movements, it was directed against Negro rulers and not against a European colonial administration. The principal tribe of Katanga, the Lunda, until the arrival of the Belgians, had never had any political unity with the down-river tribes; on the contrary, it had long traditions of warfare with them. When the native inhabitants of the Congo were suddenly informed that they were about to become independent through termination of the Belgian authority, the Lunda and their tribal allies came to the conclusion that they would be better off if they had the revenues of the local copper mines for themselves instead of sending them to Leopoldville. In the elections held by the Belgians just before the transfer of power, parties standing for secession obtained a majority of the votes in

Katanga.* The Belgians strongly opposed this trend; they wished to preserve the unity of the Congo, expecting to maintain their influence there after independence in more or less the same way as the French had maintained theirs in West Africa. It was only after all their hopes had been dashed by the behaviour of Lumumba and the mutiny of the Force Publique that they became reconciled to the idea of Katangan separation, for Katanga was the one province in the whole of the Congo where order was maintained and Belgians protected. But this revision of the Belgian attitude towards Katanga was fatal to the prospects of Tshombe's separatist régime in relation to the United Nations. It was represented as a mere puppet of Belgian imperialism, a device for maintaining the profits of the Union Minière and denying rich natural resources to a new African nation. The Afro-Asian states almost unanimously condemned Katangan separatism; the Soviet bloc backed them, and the American government considered it wise to go along with the Afro-Asians. Britain and France objected, but their opposition only increased the conviction among all anti-colonialists that Katangan nationalism was nothing but an invention of the Union Minière. The issue also got mixed up in the Cold War, for the Soviet Union had shown a disposition to exploit the factional strife in the Congo, and there was alarm in Washington lest the territory might become an arena of civil war with Western and Soviet interventions on opposite sides. Since the Congolese central government would not recognise the secession of Katanga, but was by itself incapable of ending it, someone had to help them suppress the revolt, and the American government greatly preferred that the United Nations should do this work so as to avert the danger of a direct American-Soviet rivalry in a war-torn Congo.

So the United Nations came to be committed to the use of its armed forces for the extinction of Katangan independence. The UN operations received great publicity and enabled Conor Cruise O'Brien to write his name in history with the most famous of Irish exploits since the Cattle Raid of Cooley. In the end, the United Nations army broke Katanga and put it under the rule of the Congolese central government, which promptly proceeded to violate various promises it had given for the purpose of inducing the Katangans to submit. It was, after

* The Baluba of northern Katanga were enemies of the Lunda and supported the central government, whereas in the neighbouring province of Kasai, the Baluba were against the central government because it was supported by the Lulua, who were their enemies.

all, a sovereign government which could do as it liked in its own
territory.

The United Nations in the Congo performed, in a sense, the functions
of a colonial power in its work of military conquest, but it did not assume
the responsibilities of one; it could only turn over the people it subdued
to an administration over which it had no control. The UN command
tried to restrain the excesses of the Congolese national army, but it
could do nothing to punish them since the United Nations had no
criminal jurisdiction in the Congo. Nor, indeed, was there any such
jurisdiction over the contingents of the UN force itself. Each national
component of the international force was responsible for its own discipline, and if any one of them committed atrocious acts against
prisoners or the civilian population, there were no United Nations
courts before which offenders could be brought to trial. There was
substantial evidence of barbarous behaviour in Katanga by certain
United Nations units, particularly the Ethiopians. It was not to be
expected, perhaps, that Ethiopian soldiers would be more humane and
law-abiding in the conduct of a police operation for the United Nations
in another country than they habitually were in suppressing disorders
in their own. But what was most deplorable and ominous for the future
in this context was not so much the fact of the excesses as the attitude
of high United Nations officials towards them. For a long time, they
flatly denied that there had been any atrocities and then, when the
accumulation of evidence was too strong for complete denial, tried to
explain them away as isolated incidents that did not reflect any discredit
on the forces involved. The persistent effort to conceal the truth
indicated the nature of the difficulty in which the United Nations was
caught by its commitment for waging what was, in effect, a prolonged
colonial war in tropical Africa.

Not only had the United Nations no jurisdiction in this matter over
the citizens of member states; it could not even seriously reprimand
member states for the misconduct of the troops they had voluntarily
contributed to a United Nations expedition, for any unpleasantness
about such matters would make it much harder to get states to provide
contingents the next time an international force was required. One can
have sympathy for the officials of the United Nations in this embarrassing situation. Nevertheless, the moral damage done to it by the
Katanga operation was very serious, and the episode raised in an acute

form the question of the future of the use of force under United Nations direction. Many people have seen in international policing operations controlled by a world authority a great hope for the future, believing that if such operations were successfully conducted and clearly stopped wars or prevented their enlargement, mankind would come to rely more and more on this method of keeping the peace until, in the end, even the great powers would allow their quarrels to be thus composed. But those who cherished such hopes expected that any military operations carried out by the United Nations would be strictly in accordance with the Charter, and that the behaviour of the troops engaged would conform to the Geneva Convention. They did not expect to see a campaign undertaken without justification under the Charter and acts of savage cruelty unrebuked by the United Nations authorities.

The United Nations action in Cyprus has not, up to the time of writing, involved any fighting. Like the occupation in Sinai and the Gaza Strip, it has been essentially a military presence to prevent fighting between two mutually hostile forces, and not an operation to crush one of them. But, as in the Congo, it has involved a degree of interference in the domestic affairs of a sovereign state because the armed struggle which it has stopped by its presence was one between two ethnic groups within Cyprus, and it was impossible to intervene without some kind of assumption with regard to their respective rights. The international conflict was an indirect one. It arose out of the agreements between Britain, Greece and Turkey for the protection of the Turkish minority that were concluded in 1960, when Cyprus was made an independent state after the long guerrilla insurrection of the Greek Cypriot terrorist organisation EOKA against British rule. This insurrection originally aimed, not at independence, but at *enosis*, or union with Greece. Turkey opposed *enosis* on the ground that the cession of Cyprus to Greece would radically alter the existing balance of power in the eastern Mediterranean. In the end, Cyprus became independent with a constitution which gave certain special rights to the Turkish minority, guaranteed by Britain, Greece and Turkey.

The Cypriot government, headed by Archbishop Makarios, made no secret of its intention to get rid of this constitution, and tension between the two communities in the island exploded in December 1963. The Turkish Cypriots were in danger of being overwhelmed by Greek

Cypriot irregulars recruited by the Ministry of the Interior, and Turkey prepared to intervene in accordance with its treaty rights. Makarios, in fear of a Turkish invasion, appealed to Britain to restore order, British forces being available on the island in the two bases retained when British rule over Cyprus was brought to an end. Britain accepted the invitation, but did not make it conditional on any undertaking by Makarios to observe the constitution. Duncan Sandys, the British Minister for Commonwealth Relations, flew to Cyprus and handled the situation as if Greece and Turkey did not exist; his main concern was to conciliate Makarios so as to check agitation among the Greek Cypriots against the continuation of the British bases. Obtaining security against a Turkish invasion without having to give any undertakings in return, the Archbishop behaved as might have been expected. He proceeded to violate the constitution in every respect, proclaiming that he was not bound by the agreements of 1960. The position of the British forces soon became extremely uncomfortable, for they were denounced by the Greek Cypriots for interfering with the suppression of rebels, while Turkey still threatened to intervene if the Turkish minority was not protected. Plans for a NATO force in Cyprus having been rejected by Makarios, the responsibility was passed to the United Nations.

Following the British example, the United Nations also committed itself to keeping the peace in Cyprus without obtaining any undertaking from Makarios to respect the constitution, and without deciding the question whether the armed Turkish Cypriots were merely domestic insurgents or people whose internationally guaranteed rights had been over-ridden. Turkey held that the agreements of 1960 remained fully valid and that its right of intervention was undiminished, while Greece threatened to go to war if the Turks landed in Cyprus, and unofficially sent a number of officers and men of the Greek army to serve in the Greek Cypriot National Guard. The situation inevitably involved the great powers. The United States and Britain were anxious to avert a war between two members of NATO with all its possible consequences; while the Soviet Union, if not actually desiring to promote such a war, was glad to see Greece and Turkey at odds, and had an interest both in preventing the union of Cyprus with Greece and in eliminating the British bases. In these circumstances, all the United Nations could do to resolve the conflict politically was to appoint a mediator. But by the end of 1965, mediation had led nowhere, and it seemed that the peace-keeping force would have to remain indefinitely if fighting were not to start again as soon as it withdrew.

This was indeed what had already happened in the Congo, where the United Nations forces were pulled out in the summer of 1964 after nearly four years of duty there. Civil war began again almost immediately. This time, however, it was not civil war between the central government and a seceding Katanga (the leader of the Katanga secession, Moise Tshombe, having himself become the head of the central government), but conflict between the central government supported by Katanga, on the one hand, and a left wing 'Lumumbist' revolt in the northern and eastern provinces, on the other. This struggle and its international repercussions have already been described in Chapter 8, in connection with decolonisation in Africa. Their main relevance for the prospects of the United Nations lay in their demonstration, added to the examples of Sinai and Cyprus, that temporary peace-keeping by the United Nations does not necessarily bring any permanent pacification, so that UN peace-keeping must either be continued indefinitely or produce a fresh crisis when it is brought to an end.

Wars, after all, produce results if only because one side wins or else both sides fight to exhaustion and the contest is terminated by some kind of settlement. But if a high authority merely imposes a truce without having the ability to bring about a political settlement, the hounds of war are merely held on leash for a while and their energies increased rather than reduced by the frustrating delay. In none of the conflicts in which the United Nations intervened were the contending forces any more disposed to come to a settlement because the United Nations army had been preventing, for a few months or even years, bitter enemies from flying at each others' throats.

It would appear that, in some cases, UN peace-keeping in an area of unresolved tension should involve a more or less permanent stationing of troops. But whether their sojourn is to be short or long, they must be paid for; and it was over the finances of peace-keeping that the United Nations reached its most serious crisis in the autumn of 1964. The refusal of the Soviet Union and France to contribute to the expenses of peace-keeping operations of which they had not approved, and the refusal of the United States to agree to any relaxation of the clause of the Charter that deprives defaulting members of their votes, led to a deadlock so serious that the disruption of the United Nations was avoided only by the procedure of not taking any formal votes during the meetings of the Assembly.

The issue was fundamentally the same as that which had been haunting the organisation since 1950: the question as to whether the Assembly has the right to take decisions on matters of international security, or to inititiate peace-keeping operations. The Soviet Union has always maintained that the Assembly has no such right, and that the Security Council (subject to the vetoes of the five great powers) is alone competent in such matters. The withholding of financial contributions from peace-keeping operations authorised by the Assembly was, however, only a consequence of the Soviet Union's basic attitude towards any important activity of the United Nations that it cannot control through exercise of its Security Council veto. Operations can, of course, be financed by states approving of or taking part in them; but, if they are not carried on the budget of the organisation, they are no longer actions of the United Nations as such.

The dispute over finance was, in the end, settled by a compromise agreement reached in 1965; but the effect of the prolonged deadlock was to make it unlikely that any further peace-keeping operations would be launched by the Assembly without the authority of the veto-bound Security Council.

IO

DISARMAMENT

AMONG THE TASKS assigned to the United Nations after the
Second World War was that of arranging for disarmament
among its members. Germany and Japan having been subject
to total disarmament and demilitarisation, it was widely hoped that the
victors would be able to agree to discard at least a large part of their
armed forces and military establishments. The precedents of the disarmament negotiations after the First World War were not, indeed, encouraging, but in that period the Washington and London naval treaties had, for
a time at any rate, limited the arms race at sea. The generation which
saw the establishment of the United Nations at San Francisco in the
spring of 1945 expected its statesmen to do better, not worse, than their
predecessors.

The basic theory of international disarmament is a simple one. Nations,
the theory argues, should discard their weapons so that, if and when
their wills are in conflict, they will lack the means to do serious harm
to each other. Against this idea of total disarmament, however, it has
always been contended that it is not elaborate and sophisticated armaments of themselves that enable men to fight; that primitive tribes
battle with knives and clubs; and that Alexander the Great, Chingiz
Khan and the like conquered their worlds long before there were tanks,
bomber aircraft or intercontinental missiles. Moreover, even advocates
of 'total' disarmament—unless they are absolute non-resisters, rejecting
the use of force in any circumstances—grant that society must have
the means for the preservation of internal order, for the restraint of
violent crime or political disturbance. But a national organisation which
possesses arms and has men trained to use them, whether a professional
police force or a militia, is capable of conducting operations across a
frontier, and even a state without armed forces capable of waging a
regular war can encourage, or fail to prevent, filibustering activities by
a group of its citizens on the territory of another country.

Nevertheless, it can be argued that, even if acts of violence and elementary forms of warfare were still to persist under conditions of what may be called minimum armaments, mankind would, by disarming to this low level, render armed conflicts less ruinous and destructive, and would also save the vast sums of money which nations in proportion to their means, and often beyond their means, spend on maintaining high levels of military power in competition with one another. If all nations would agree to disarm down to the minimum level required for internal order, none, it is argued, would retain an effective striking power against its neighbours, and the hopes and fears arising out of a nation's capacities for decisive military action would be very greatly reduced. Moreover, the investing of money, otherwise devoted to defence expenditure, in economic growth, increased social services or aid to underdeveloped countries would of itself, so runs the argument, be an important factor in reducing international tensions. Such schemes of general disarmament are usually accompanied by projects for a world government with an international police force to enforce its universal authority; but a case can be made for the view that general disarmament would be conducive to peace, or at least render warfare less catastrophic, even without a supranational peace-keeping power.

The enormous practical difficulty encountered in all negotiations for international disarmament is not due primarily either to the inherent bellicosity of states or to the vested interests of existing armed forces or manufacturers of armaments. It is due, in the first place, to the unequal effects on various nations of any set of principles for cutting down armaments; and, secondly, to the possibilities of cheating after a disarmament pact has been concluded. As between these two kinds of difficulty in the way of disarming, there is a striking contrast between the efforts that were made to achieve it after the First World War and those that have been made since the Second. In disarmament diplomacy between 1919 and 1935, the fear of secret violation of agreements that might be reached appears to have played little part in the thinking of statesmen and their specialist advisers on the subject. There was a general assumption that states would observe disarmament treaties once they had signed them, and that if they did not, no major violation could escape detection—which would free non-offending nations from their obligations in time for them to take balancing counter-measures. The controversies of that period were about the principles on which the permitted sizes of armies and navies were to be calculated, and about the definitions of offensive and defensive weapons.

Since 1945, however, the emphasis in all discussion of disarmament, as well as in actual negotiations, has been less on what would be fair ratios of armed strength for each nation to retain under the terms of a disarmament treaty, than on what measures are required to ensure that no signatory to a treaty secretly violates its provisions. This change of preoccupation in the approach to the problems of disarmament has been due partly to the deep distrust engendered in international relations by the experience of the age of Hitler and Stalin, but even more to the nature of the most formidable of the weapons of the modern age—weapons giving a decisive strategic advantage to any government that secretly violated an agreement for their abolition. In this context, it must be noted that a small quantity of weapons of high capacity that would be insignificant in a balance of heavily armed powers might become decisive if nations were disarmed to low or minimum levels. One recalls that, at the end of the nineteenth century, a fire-power which might be trivial in a clash of European armies could be overwhelming in a colonial campaign in Africa. As Hilaire Belloc put it:

> Whatever happens, we have got
> The Gatling gun and they have not.

In our time, disarmament has to be considered in relation to two categories of arms so different in their capacity for destruction as to be of separate orders of magnitude. Disarmament can be nuclear or conventional, and it would be possible to retain fairly strong conventional forces after abolition of nuclear weapons. Whereas at least a minimum level of conventional forces would still be needed for internal order purposes, there would be no need at all for nuclear weapons if nations agreed on their abolition and on effective measures to detect clandestine violations of the agreement. It makes sense, therefore, to consider nuclear arms separately, not only because they are so much more terrible and dangerous than any other weapons, but because it is possible to aim at their total abolition, whereas conventional forces cannot be reduced beyond a certain point, and there is room for endless controversy as to just where that point should be. If a satisfactory agreement could be reached for the abolition of nuclear weapons, the principal danger of catastrophe for mankind would be removed, and it would then be possible to go on to tackle the lesser, but more complex, problems of disarmament in conventional weapons.

There are those, however, who take the opposite view, holding that the world as it is now is safer with nuclear weapons than without them. They point out that two world wars have been fought in the present century before nuclear armaments existed, and argue that we might well have had a third after 1945 but for the nuclear stalemate and its balance of terror. The very frightfulness of these weapons and the inability of even the most heavily armed state, so far, to shield its territory from missiles carrying megaton warheads constitute, according to this view, the best safeguard against resort to war between nuclear powers. Unfortunately, neither experience nor a reasonable estimate of probable future trends supports the belief that nuclear arms are their own cure. In 1962, the United States was prepared to wage nuclear war rather than tolerate the stationing of Russian ballistic missiles in Cuba, and nuclear war would have resulted if the Soviet government had not backed down. It cannot, therefore, be held that it is impossible for a nuclear war to take place simply because nobody will have the nerve to face it. The future prospect is even less reassuring, for progress in anti-missile technology could destabilise the nuclear stalemate without diminishing the destructive force of missiles which are not intercepted.

If, then, there is no good ground for believing that peace can be guaranteed by the mere abundance of nuclear weapons, there can be no way of ensuring that mankind will escape nuclear war except by getting rid of such weapons—that is to say, by stopping their production and by destroying those which already exist. The powers that possess and produce these weapons have only to agree to get rid of them, for all of them to be in an equal position of deprivation, while states that chafe at being still outside the nuclear club will no longer be able to complain that they are underprivileged. But there is one essential condition for a general renunciation of nuclear weapons: those who renounce them must be certain that, if they honour their signatures to a treaty of abolition, no other state can evade it either by clandestine production or by failure to declare the whole of its existing stocks. The consequences of such an evasion would be terrific. A state that accumulated even only a small quantity of hydrogen bombs when no other nation had any would indeed 'have the Gatling gun' and an absolute superiority over all its rivals. Nor would it avail for other ex-nuclear powers to resume production if and when they discovered that the treaty was being violated, for the violator would presumably have been evading his obligations in order to obtain a strategic advantage, and would therefore be impelled to use his lead to knock out his rivals before they could restore their nuclear capability. The idea that a government inclined to act thus—particularly if it were a totalitarian government—would be deterred simply by the moral censure of neutral countries can hardly be convincing to any student of *Realpolitik*. Such censure has power only in a humane, liberal and law-abiding world; yet it would be the effect of a nuclear hegemony to wipe out such a world, and under a *Pax Megatonica*, the tyrant would receive not rebuke, but flattery. As Hitler said: 'If we win the war, nobody will ask whether we were justified or not.'

Unless, therefore, the statesmen of a government possessing nuclear weapons are either ridiculously trustful or grossly negligent of the national interest for which they are responsible, they will not agree to a treaty for the abolition of nuclear armaments unless it includes knave-proof provisions for detection of fraud. Such provisions must be of a very sweeping and comprehensive character because the possibilities of secret activity in this field are considerable. In fact, the only terms adequate for the purpose—and even then some element of risk would remain—are that inspectors appointed to check on the fulfilment of the provisions of such a treaty should have unimpeded rights of access, without previous notice, to any place where they may suspect that nuclear arms are being stored, tested or produced. Clearly, such a right of inspection involves a most formidable inroad into a nation's terri-torial sovereignty, and would mean the end of military secrecy as hitherto understood, for, if rights of entry are to be entirely unrestricted, there can be no way of ensuring that the inspectors do not discover non-nuclear as well as nuclear secrets. Yet nothing less than an unlimited right of inspection could provide proper safeguards. Any scheme that enabled an offending government to limit, obstruct or delay investiga-tion would be worse than useless, since it would merely induce a false sense of security among the innocent parties to the treaty.

Inspection to verify nuclear disarmament would have to be carried out by an international Control Authority with the responsibility both of supervising all known nuclear plants and of investigating all reports of clandestine production or undeclared stocks. But the initiative would not, and should not, be left entirely to this international body. The governments most concerned to prevent any infringement of the treaty by their rivals would maintain their own intelligence services, and would pass on to the Control Authority any information they obtained. If the Control Authority failed to investigate immediately on receipt of such information, the informing government would be released from its obligations under the treaty. In connection with the sources of information, it would be necessary to include in the treaty a provision that no citizen of any signatory country reporting violations of the treaty by his own government should be liable for trial for espionage. In view of the ease with which, in a totalitarian state, a person who incurs the displeasure of the authorities can be convicted of a crime which he has not committed,* such a person should be under the special protection of the Control Authority, and should not be liable to any kind of criminal prosecution except in a special court. Since the tracing of clandestine production or stocks would certainly require the disclosure of secret information by someone, it would be essential to be able to protect an informer against the vengeance of his own state.

With such restrictions on national sovereignty as would be involved in any adequate treaty for the abolition of nuclear armaments, each signatory nation would need protection against possible disclosures of industrial secrets through operations of the inspectorate. To meet this need, a comprehensive agreement on patents would be required as a concomitant of the disarmament treaty. A more difficult problem would be set by the probability that non-nuclear military secrets would be revealed by the investigations of suspected nuclear law-breaking. This would be a risk inherent in nuclear disarmament with inspection, but the risk would be equal for all nations adhering to the treaty, and it is unlikely that any of them would be militarily hamstrung by such discoveries.

The great obstacle to nuclear disarmament with inspection lies, not in any inherent impracticability of an inspection system, but in the objection of the Soviet Union to any kind of foreign or international

---

* An example was the case of Mme Ivinskaya, the friend of Pasternak, whose real offence to the Soviet authorities lay in her influence over the writer, but who was indicted, after his death, on a framed-up currency charge and given a long prison sentence.

activity on its own soil that is not under the ultimate control of the Soviet authorities. Again and again the Russians have contended that inspections on Soviet territory would be espionage, regardless of the fact that any inspection to be imposed on the Soviet Union in connection with disarmament would be equally applicable to other powers. The Soviet Union, it seems, has so many more secrets than anyone else that it has much more to lose than any other country from a universal surveillance. To some extent this is true. The Soviet political system, with its curbs on freedom of speech, its total control over the population, and its extreme secrecy of administration has been able to conceal from the outside world facts of a kind ascertainable in other countries, and this has proved to be of definite military value. In the 'thirties, the locations of new factories, railways and roads were state secrets and so were even items of physical geography. (A professor of Kiev University was shot during the Great Purge of 1936–38 for having disclosed in a lecture to students the depth of the river Dnieper at various points in its course.) As a result of such restrictions on publicity, the Germans were greatly handicapped in their invasion of Russia in 1941 by the lack of up-to-date and adequate maps, and by their defective knowledge of the terrain; everything had to be found out by aerial reconnaissance. With this experience, it is natural that the Soviet régime should cling to secretiveness as one of its greatest assets and be most reluctant to give it up. There is, however, another—though not unrelated—reason for the Soviet fear of an unconditional right of movement and access for international inspectors on Soviet territory. The Soviet citizen is conditioned not only to unquestioning obedience in his relations with the Soviet state, but also to the idea that its authority has a legitimacy that cannot be shared by any non-Communist state. If, therefore, international inspectors representing the Western powers and the uncommitted countries, as well as the Communist bloc, were to have legal rights within the Soviet Union, if they were free to go where they pleased and make enquiries without anyone being able to stop them, this could not fail to have a most damaging effect on the prestige of Soviet officialdom and its still greatly feared security police. An international inspectorate that would be easily acceptable in a liberal democracy could be a very subversive and disruptive factor in a totalitarian state that cannot allow the authority of its own officials to be less than absolute.

The Russian Communists thus have reasons for disliking international inspectors, even if they have no intention of cheating on any disarmament treaty they may sign. But recognition of these reasons should not make the Western powers less insistent on adequate inspection as a condition of disarmament. The nature of the Communist régime is not only, by its secretiveness and exclusiveness, adverse to international inspectors; it is also unpropitious for the voluntary keeping of a disarmament treaty, since it is inspired by an ideology which makes advancement of the cause of Communism the supreme criterion of moral value. Lenin has provided his disciples with a whole armoury of justification for the use of any expedient means in the service of the revolution. Even if the old revolutionary fanaticism has dwindled in the Soviet Union, the doctrine that identifies Soviet state interests with the forward march of human history remains intact, and gives ethical sanction to the most disreputable devices that hard-bitten politicians may be inclined to adopt in the contests of international power politics.

The Russian attitude towards international inspection and control became manifest during the discussions in the United Nations following the presentation of the Baruch Plan in 1946. In this plan, the Americans proposed the creation of an international atomic energy control authority, to which the United States would hand over its still unique nuclear armament. The Russian delegation rejected entirely the idea of such an international authority; its own counterproposal was for an agreement to renounce atomic weapons and to destroy existing stocks—that is, the American, the only stocks existing at that time—within three months of the signing of the agreement. But the Soviet proposal contained no safeguards against clandestine production. The United Nations, however, set up a twelve-nation Atomic Energy Commission, and it soon became apparent that all the members of this Commission, except the Soviet Union and its satellite, Poland, were in favour of some form of international control. The Soviet government, driven on to the defensive, then regained the initiative by presenting the Assembly with a grandiose scheme for total disarmament, conventional as well as nuclear. This scheme provided for controls, but they were to come into force only after disarmament had been accomplished and were to be operated by the Security Council subject to the great power veto—qualifications which left no safeguard at all against the surreptitious retention of arms or the subsequent secret production of them. The zeal of Molotov for universal disarmament nevertheless had its effect on the Assembly, and a Soviet commentator gleefully declared that 'the Soviet delegation's consistent policy knocks the cards from the hands of its opponents'. Gromyko, who took over from Molotov the representation of the Soviet Union in the battle against international inspection, derided the idea that there might be a danger of clandestine production of atomic arms, for, as he declared with a winning childlike innocence, 'each nation would report faithfully a complete list of its factories'.

Ever since the controversy over the Baruch Plan, the Russians have maintained their basic opposition to inspection in all disarmament negotiations, though with a certain tactical flexibility that has enabled them to avoid commitment to an absolute negation. The popular desire for disarmament in the Western democracies and in the world at large has been so strong, and such an important political factor in international affairs, that Soviet propaganda has always endeavoured to exploit it by projecting visions of a weaponless era. It is this, its leaders claim, that the Soviet Union is trying to bring about. Western governments, whose suspicions have been intensified by the evident Soviet determination never to accept adequate inspection, have been hard put to it to justify their insistence on it before an uninformed public opinion.

In the United Nations, there has been a prolonged struggle over the composition of committees for the discussion of disarmament, with the Soviet Union striving to escape from its minority position and present a picture of an equal division of opinion. In 1952, the United Nations Assembly set up a Disarmament Commission, and in 1954 directed this Commission to set up a subcommittee of 'the powers principally involved which should seek in private an acceptable solution' to the problem of disarmament. The members of the subcommittee were the Soviet Union, the United States, Britain, France and Canada. After prolonged negotiations, the Western powers produced in August 1957 a draft resolution for which they thought a basis of agreement had been found, but it was rejected by the Soviet delegate. When it was endorsed by the Assembly with a vote of 57 against 9 (3 Soviet plus 6 satellite votes), the Soviet Union proposed that the

Disarmament Commission be enlarged to include all eighty-two (the number at that time) member states of the United Nations. This proposal was defeated by 46 votes to 9. After further negotiations and Soviet threats to boycott both the Disarmament Commission and its subcommittee, in 1958 a new subcommittee was created on a basis of parity between the two power blocs; the United States, Britain, France, Italy and Canada represented NATO, and the Soviet Union, Poland, Czechoslovakia, Rumania and Bulgaria represented the Communist camp. This ten-nation subcommittee made no more progress than its predecessor, and the Soviet Union finally withdrew from its deliberations. Then, in September 1961, the Conference of Heads of Non-aligned States in Belgrade recommended that representatives of uncommitted nations should take part in disarmament. After four months of haggling between the Soviet Union and the United States, it was finally agreed to invite to the ten-nation subcommittee eight additional members: one European (Sweden), two Latin American (Brazil and Mexico), two Asian (India and Burma), and three African (the United Arab Republic, Ethiopia and Nigeria). The United Nations Assembly endorsed this eighteen-member disarmament body in December 1961.

The eight new arrivals infused new life into the disarmament talks, for they had a sceptical and critical attitude towards the proposals of the two blocs, and were not committed to any particular formula. The delegate of Brazil in his initial address to the committee declared:

> We are sure that the best way for us [to contribute to disarmament] is to preserve our independence of judgement and the authority of our voice in order to lend them to everything calculated to promote effective and immediate disarmament, and to refuse them to everything that merely aggravates polemics, emphasises antagonisms, impresses public opinion or delays settlement.[1]

The pressure of the Eight has compelled both the power blocs to redefine their positions and offer concessions. If there were any prospect of basic agreement, the mediatory activities of the Eight would be very valuable. In the actual situation, however, it may be doubted whether they are beneficial, for inevitably they aim at arranging a compromise settlement, and the principle of inspection in disarmament is one on which no real compromise is possible. It is as if there were to be a demand for an area of two square miles into which the police should never be allowed to enter in search of stolen goods; some people might consider it a fair compromise if the two square miles were to be reduced to one, but there would be no real difference in the effect, because it would be precisely in the one remaining square mile that the thieves would deposit their booty.

In the absence of any substantial progress towards either nuclear or conventional disarmament during all the negotiations since 1946, popular hopes have been concentrated to an inordinate extent on a treaty for the banning of nuclear tests. A partial test-ban treaty (for atmospheric, though not for underground, testing) was, in fact, concluded in 1963 by the United States, Russia and Britain. This has certainly had great value, both as a measure to slow down the arms race, and also as a means of preventing the global contamination of the atmosphere by fall-out from major explosions, such as that of the 52-megaton bomb detonated by the Soviet Union in a series of tests in 1961.

The implications of the test-ban treaty and the politico-military prospects for disarmament are discussed more fully in Chapter 16. It is, however, relevant to point out here that the importance attached to the test-ban reflects an emotional urge to escape from reality rather than a rational approach to the problem of disarmament. Tests in the atmosphere receive the widest publicity; they are terrifying reminders to all mankind of the existence of nuclear weapons and of their frightful destructive power. But mankind does not want to be reminded; it would rather forget. If there are no more publicised tests, it will be possible to brush all the disquieting dirt under the carpet. The making of nuclear weapons can still go on, as can experiments for their improvement in other ways than by explosion in the atmosphere; but attention will no longer dramatically be drawn to the ugly reality. If there were to be a complete cessation of atmospheric tests, it is probable that the nuclear problem, with all its fearful implications, would make much less impact on ordinary human consciousness. So far, however, there has not been a cessation of atmospheric tests, despite the three-power treaty, for France and China, being still at an early stage of nuclear weaponry, declined to adhere to the test-ban agreement. The effect has been unfairly to concentrate on these two countries the odium for continuing production of nuclear weapons, and to divert popular attention from the real obstacle in the way of the general abolition of such weapons.

It has, of course, been hoped that the test-ban treaty would open the way to wider measures of disarmament, and that a system of inspection devised for checking on tests could be extended to other fields of weaponry. But the continued resistance of the Soviet Union to on-site investigations of underground disturbances recorded by seismographs gives no ground for optimism about the prospects of reaching an agreement allowing for foreign inspectors to search for clandestine nuclear plants or hidden stockpiles. After all, there has never been any difficulty about detecting atmospheric tests, for these cannot be concealed. The day when Russia will declare its willingness to open the whole of its territory to international scrutiny remains as far off as ever.

PART THREE

FROM THE KOREAN WAR TO THE TASHKENT CONFERENCE

II

THE SOVIET UNION AFTER STALIN

'HE IS THE BEST that humanity possesses. For Stalin is hope, he is expectation; he is the beacon that guides all progressive mankind. Stalin is our Banner! Stalin is our will! Stalin is our victory!'

Thus Nikita Khrushchev in 1937. Stalin was then the master of Russia; there was advancement in his smile and death in his frown. Nineteen years later, the same Khrushchev spoke a different language; Stalin was dead and his corpse could neither punish nor reward. It would be a mistake, however, to see in Khrushchev's denunciation of his late master in his speech to a secret session of the Twentieth Congress of the CPSU in 1956 merely an act of vindictiveness against a tyrant who could no longer kill (or compel Khrushchev, as he once did, to dance the *gopak* for the amusement of the Communist Tsar and his friends), or an expression of moral revulsion from the crimes in which Khrushchev, and in some degree all those who listened to him, had been involved as instruments of Stalin's despotic power. The speech against Stalin was a political act which, in condemning the past, laid down a course for the future, and it was an act of the party rather than of Khrushchev himself. Khrushchev denounced Stalin's despotism over the party and promised a return to the practice of Lenin because the barons of the party oligarchy insisted that he should, as the price of their acceptance of his leadership.*

When, on March 2, 1953, Stalin became unconscious as a result of a cerebral haemorrhage, the men close to the throne began to confer together on the arrangements for the succession to his power. They were apparently not yet agreed when he actually died, for the announcement of his death was delayed for six hours. When at last the news was

---

* The view taken here of Khrushchev's secret speech is substantially that of G. Paloczi-Horvath in his book *Khrushchev: The Road to Power*. His arguments in support of his interpretation seem to me to be irrefutable.

given to the world, the note struck by the official declaration was one not so much of grief at the passing of a beloved leader as of alarm at what the event might bring with it. 'Our task', it stated, 'is to guard the steel-like and monolithic unity of the Party . . . to educate all Communists and toiling people in high political vigilance, irreconcilability and firmness in the struggle against inner and outer foes . . . to ensure the greatest unity of leadership and the prevention of any kind of disorder and panic.'

The Communist leaders who awaited the death of Stalin in those days of March 1953 were possessed by two great fears: fear of the Russian people, and fear of one another. There was the danger of popular uprisings, perhaps with support from the army, when the terrible dictator drew his last breath. To guard as far as possible against such a peril, Moscow was sealed off and occupied by special troops of the MVD. But who was to take over the reins of power that slipped from the fingers of the dying man? The heir-designate was Georgi Malenkov, who had delivered the report of the Central Committee at the Nineteenth Congress of the CPSU, less than five months before Stalin's death. He now became Prime Minister in succession to Stalin and also First Secretary of the Central Committee Secretariat, which controlled the 'apparatus'—the permanent officials of the Communist Party organisation. But only a fortnight after these appointments were announced, the Soviet public was informed that Malenkov wished to devote all his time to his work as head of the government and had therefore given up his post as First Secretary of the party. This function was taken over by Nikita Khrushchev, though he was not given the formal title until September. The jealousy of Malenkov's colleagues, and their fear that he would continue Stalin's purging methods, had compelled him to renounce the combination of offices on which Stalin's power had been based.

Beria, suspected—rightly or wrongly—of plotting to seize supreme power by a coup d'état with his security forces, was arrested in June 1953 and executed by a decision of the party Presidium; he was posthumously tried by a secret tribunal and duly found guilty. There have been widely different versions of what happened, and even now, such is the secrecy of the Soviet system of government, it is impossible to verify them. In its political setting this episode still belongs to the Stalin era; and, in consonance with Stalin's practice of representing domestic opponents as agents of foreign powers, the executed Beria was denounced as an imperialist spy. His fall, however, was followed by a weakening and curbing of the secret police power which greatly lightened the atmosphere of Russian life. Soon after Stalin's death, the new leadership, in an attempt to win popularity, had declared an amnesty that set free about half the inmates of the prison camps, while the 'Doctors' Plot', through which Stalin in the last months of his life seems to have been planning to destroy Beria and probably other members of the Presidium, was declared a fabrication.

After Beria's execution, the secret police and security forces were reorganised and placed under the control of a party committee, which was meant to make it more difficult for any one individual to use them as instruments of personal power. The MVD of 1953 was the heir—through the intermediate stages of the GPU and the NKVD—of the Cheka of Lenin's day, which had operated with great ruthlessness and a minimum of legality in the period of the civil war of 1918–20. It had been the general population outside the ranks of the Communist Party, and especially members of the former propertied classes, who had had cause to fear the Cheka, for members of the party in the early period of the Soviet régime were protected from its terrorism by an elaborate system of rules applied by party committees that made it virtually impossible for them to be arrested without solid evidence of guilt on a specific charge. By 1934, however, this immunity of party members had disappeared. On the ground of the alleged treason of the Trotskyite and Bukharinite factions, party members were suddenly arrested on orders from Stalin or secret police officials and forced by third-degree interrogations to confess to crimes they had not committed, and were shot or sentenced to long terms of forced labour without any kind of legal trial. Liability to these terrible proscriptions, against which there was no defence or redress, had for two decades cast a dark shadow over the lives of party members, from the lowest to the highest, and had gone far to cancel the attraction of the many privileges which they enjoyed. At the height of the Great Purge in 1938, applications for membership had almost ceased because it was considered safer to be outside the party than in it.

After Stalin's death, party members hoped once again to have security for themselves and their families against administrative murder. They had no intention of relaxing the party's monopoly of political power in the Soviet Union or even, despite the talk of 'collective leadership', of dispensing with a strong personal authority at the head of the party to prevent it from disintegrating through factional strife. But they sought to ensure that such a leader would in future be restrained from the arbitrary tyranny that had been characteristic of the later years of Stalin's rule. This involved the question of Stalin's image, for, as long as he remained in the status of quasi-divinity accorded to him over many years by Communist propaganda, his methods of government would be sacrosanct and could be invoked as valid precedents by a successor inclined to follow his example in destroying all who incurred his suspicion or displeasure. If Stalin's practice was to be condemned, he himself must be demoted from his godlike eminence.

The twenty months, from the arrest of Beria in June 1953 to the resignation of Malenkov as Prime Minister in February 1955, are often known as the 'Malenkov era', for during this period Malenkov had a primacy of power, though he was being gradually undermined by Khrushchev and the party apparatus. Malenkov exalted the state in relation to the party; he regularly put the party's Central Committee after the government in references to these institutions in his speeches: an order of words which in the Soviet Union was highly significant. In economic policy, he charted a 'new course' by declaring the production of consumer goods to be of equal importance with heavy industry. This was highly popular with the masses of the people, who for so many years had suffered from shortages of essential commodities, and it also stimulated general economic development by providing for greater incentives. Outwardly, Malenkov's position appeared to be a strong one, and he may himself have believed that he could build up the organs of the state administration to be more powerful than the party apparatus. But such a hope was ultimately incompatible with the system of single-party rule. Malenkov was neither the minister of a hereditary monarch nor the head of a government produced by democratic elections. His office was in the gift of the party which controlled the state; the party could depose him and it did. The attack on Malenkov was launched in the party journal, *Pravda*, on January 24, 1955, and on the following day Khrushchev, in a speech to the Central Committee, denounced the policy of equal status for light and heavy industry as 'a belching up of the rightist deviation, a regurgitation of views hostile to

Leninism, views which Rykov, Bukharin and their like once preached'. On February 8, Malenkov resigned and was replaced as Prime Minister by Bulganin on the nomination of Khrushchev, who recommended him as a 'worthy disciple of the great Lenin and one of the closest comrades-in-arms of the continuer of Lenin's cause—Josip Vissarionovitch Stalin'.

In December 1953, in the heyday of the Malenkov era and only nine months after Stalin's death, Stalin's birthday had gone almost unnoticed in the Soviet press. But a year later it was the occasion for eulogies of him. The cult of Stalin was being cautiously revived, and in references to Khrushchev there appeared something of the language of adulation previously directed towards Stalin. This trend increased greatly during 1955 after Malenkov's resignation, and with the approach of the Twentieth Congress of the party, scheduled for February 1956, the publicity build-up of Khrushchev as Stalin's heir was extravaagntly promoted by his henchmen. It was met, however, by a counter-move ment demanding a condemnation of Stalin's blood-purges and guarantees against their recurrence. The anti-Stalinists were led by Mikoyan, a man with a special standing in the party, for he had been eminent since the days of Lenin, but had never sought supreme power for himself and had always managed to avoid either opposition to Stalin or close implication in his 'cases' against other party leaders.

What happened just before and during the Congress is still obscure, but it seems that a draft was prepared of a speech denouncing Stalin to be delivered to a closed session of the Congress, and that a majority of the Presidium called on Khrushchev to be the speaker. He was most unwilling and in his opening, public speech to the Congress spoke of Stalin in moderate, but respectful, terms. In opposition to the Presidium majority, Khrushchev had the support of two of the most important foreign Communist leaders: Maurice Thorez of France and Mao Tse-tung of China—the former present at the Congress as a fraternal delegate, and the latter sending greetings by telegram. Both bracketed Stalin with Lenin, and Mao also referred to 'the correct leadership of the well-tried Central Committee of the CPSU headed by Comrade Khrushchev'.* But Mikoyan in *his* public speech not only attacked the memory of Stalin, but referred by name to two leading men of the party

* Constitutionally, neither the Central Committee nor the Presidium had any permanent 'head', but Stalin, as the *Vozhd* of the party, had in effect been recognised as holding such a position.

who had been put to death under Stalin, although innocent of the crimes they were alleged to have committed. These were Ovseyenko and Kossior. The mention of Kossior had a special significance, for Kossior, as First Secretary of the party in the Ukraine, had been purged by a commission consisting of Yezhov, Molotov and Khrushchev, and the last-named had succeeded him in his office. The reference to the administrative murder of Kossior was a warning that Khrushchev himself would be denounced to the Congress if he refused to conform to the decision of the Presidium. Even so, there seems to have been a last-minute hitch, for the closed session of the Congress was scheduled for six o'clock on the evening of February 24, but did not begin until after midnight. When at last it did start its business, it heard from Khrushchev the speech which, although delivered in formally secret session, was soon to become so famous throughout the world.

In denouncing the crimes of Stalin, Khrushchev was careful indirectly to clear himself of the responsibility for the death of Kossior and other victims of the purge in the Ukraine. Stalin, he declared, had 'decided everything'. But the question of responsibility for past acts was of secondary importance; what was vital was that Khrushchev had to accept constitutional limitations on his own power. 'We must abolish', he told the delegates, 'the cult of personality decisively, once and for all; we must draw the proper conclusions concerning both ideological-theoretical and practical work. It is necessary for this purpose . . . to fight the wilfulness of individuals abusing their power. The evil caused by acts violating revolutionary legality . . . has to be completely corrected.'[1]

This imposition of checks on personal power was represented as a return to Leninism, and so in a sense it was, for Lenin had exhorted his followers never to let their political quarrels within the party lead to homicide. It was precisely Stalin's breach of this principle that had given the later period of his political ascendancy its 'Stalinist' character. 'Destalinisation' meant simply that Communists were to stop murdering one another. Since the party had survived in power for nineteen years after the October Revolution without executions of dissident members or of critics of the current leadership, it could not be claimed that such drastic measures were essential to the discipline of the party; and since the accusation of treason and espionage on which so many leading Communists had been put to death had now been admitted to have been fabricated, it would be difficult in future to obtain credence for such charges. The repudiation of Stalin's methods of government at the Twentieth Congress meant a real restoration of constitutional limits on personal authority within the Communist Party.

But the new régime's avowal of its 'return to Lenin' made nonsense of the view held by some Western political commentators that destalinisation meant a development in the direction of general political liberty in the Soviet Union. Lenin it was who had established the absolute dictatorship of the Communist Party in Russia and had suppressed every form of organised opposition to its rule. Rejection of the 'cult of personality' did not imply any relaxation of the dictatorship of the party over the peoples of the Soviet Union. Indirectly, indeed, the people at large also gained from the curbing of the secret police. They were less liable to arbitrary arrest, and a great reduction of forced-labour undertakings—found to be uneconomic in relation to the new economic growth of the post-Stalin era—cut down the demand for convicts which had caused the MVD always to be discovering new 'enemies of the people' or 'socially dangerous elements'. But the secret police were still there to pounce on anyone who questioned the right of the Communist Party to govern, or claimed national independence for a non-Russian people of the Soviet Union, or criticised official policies or versions of news. The new emphasis on 'socialist legality' might diminish the dangers of penal sentence without due process of law; but, since a man could legally receive severe punishment for being in possession of 'anti-Soviet literature'—which could include any foreign book or newspaper containing passages critical of Soviet policies—an increased respect for law on the part of the authorities was not necessarily much of a protection for anyone who took an interest in ideas or questions of fact independently of the current party line. The party retained a total control of press, radio and all forms of publicity on current affairs; it also kept its rights of censorship over literature and the arts. The Soviet régime was still a dictatorship, though a less brutal one than in the days when Stalin was its head.

If destalinisation meant a real, though strictly limited, change in the internal politics of the Soviet Union, its significance for foreign affairs was slight because there was really no such thing as Stalinism in the conduct of external affairs. Whereas Stalin's career in the acquisition and exercise of political power within Russia shows a continuity of specific character from Lenin's lifetime to his own death, in foreign affairs Stalin veered to and fro in accordance with changes in the international situation. In domestic politics, a return from Stalin to Lenin meant the abolition of blood-purges in the party and of arbitrary personal rule. In foreign policy, it should have meant—if anything— a return to the rhetoric of world revolution. Stalin in the mid-1920s identified himself with the idea of 'socialism in one country', and thus gained for himself in the West the reputation of being a realist and a moderate in contrast with the fanatical Lenin. But, around 1930, he instigated political warfare against the non-Communist left in Europe, denounced as 'social fascists', and fostered contacts with the German Reichswehr. Then, a few years later, he went in for Popular Fronts, alliances with the Western democracies and an 'anti-aggression front'. His line soon changed again, however, and he joined with Hitler in a territorial partition of Eastern Europe. This alliance with Hitler did not last long, and he became the partner of Churchill and Roosevelt. Finally, in the aftermath of the war, he imposed revolutions from above on half-a-dozen European countries, and became the sworn foe of 'American imperialism'. From all these changes of line, it is impossible to form a notion of a specifically Stalinist foreign policy.

Even so, since the last stage of his foreign policy was one of great rigidity and intransigence, any turn towards greater flexibility and willingness to negotiate was bound to appear as destalinisation. More-over, in one way, Stalin's methods of government affected the conduct of foreign relations. The paranoid suspicion with which he and his secret police regarded any Soviet citizen who had close contact with foreigners reduced to a minimum Russian diplomatic and cultural intercourse with the outer world, with consequent international isolation and loss of the capacity to exert influence beyond the boundaries of Communist power. One of the first effects of Stalin's death was to lighten the weight of fear on the Russian whose dealings with foreigners, however innocent, exposed him to being made the subject of a possible 'case' by the MVD.

The international situation at the moment of Stalin's death was one of great tension. While in Europe Soviet power was now confronted with the North Atlantic Alliance, in the Far East the Korean War— prolonged by interminable arguments over the terms for an armistice—

still held possibilities of an extension that might involve Russia as a belligerent. The heirs of Stalin, who on the morrow of his death expressed their fear of 'disorder and panic' in the Soviet Union, could not afford in addition to run the risk of a major international crisis, and they hastened to lower the tension. In Korea, within three weeks of Stalin's demise, the truce talks began to make progress, and an armistice was finally concluded on July 27, 1953. Although Russia was not directly involved in these negotiations, it was generally believed that Moscow's influence had been exerted on Peking in favour of compromise over the intractable issue of prisoner repatriation. In January 1954, the Council of Foreign Ministers met for the first time in five years to discuss the problem of Germany, and although no agreement was reached, it was something that the governments were again on speaking terms. There followed the negotiations at Geneva for ending the war in Indochina, and there was a considerable degree of diplomatic co-operation between the Soviet, British and French governments to this end. The fact that the American government refused to endorse the agreement reached was, of course, to the advantage of the Soviet Union as driving a wedge between the United States and its European allies. But the behaviour of the Russians at the conference, being in the manner of normal, traditional diplomacy, was widely regarded in the West as opening a new phase in relations with Russia, in welcome contrast to the stonewalling obstruction and doctrinaire vituperation that had been characteristic of the Russian attitude in all international dealings during the last six years of Stalin's lifetime.

The part played by the Soviet Union at the Geneva Conference in the summer of 1954 was the principal achievement of the Malenkov era in the field of Soviet–Western relations. It is reasonable to attribute it largely to Malenkov himself, because, although Molotov remained in charge of foreign policy and represented the Soviet government at Geneva, it was a milder and more flexible Molotov than had previously been encountered.* There is no evidence that during this period Khrushchev had much to do with the making of policy towards the

* Trotsky used to call him 'Stalin's Molotov', as if he were some kind of machine. After Stalin's death, he became Malenkov's Molotov, and might have been Khrushchev's Molotov, but Khrushchev got rid of him as a gesture to Tito.

Western powers. The First Secretary of the CPSU was, however, extremely active in the sphere of relations with other Communist parties, especially those which were in control of state governments, so that he was gradually moving into the field of international diplomacy. He attended the Polish Communist Party Congress in March 1954, and the Czech Congress in June. In October of the same year he went to China, accompanied by Bulganin as Defence Minister, and made himself *persona grata* for the time being with Mao Tse-tung. After he had succeeded in deposing Malenkov from the office of Prime Minister, he undertook a more ambitious operation. In the hope of composing the Soviet quarrel with Tito and thus restoring the unity of the international Communist movement, he flew to Belgrade in May 1955, accompanied by Bulganin (now Prime Minister) and Mikoyan. This enterprise, however, was only a partial success, for Tito, while accepting Khrushchev's apologies for past Soviet behaviour as amends due to him, stoutly declined to repudiate the ideological heresy into which he had deviated since the break with Stalin. Failure on this occasion to re-establish ideological uniformity had far-reaching consequences for Khrushchev. His condoning of the Titoist heresy made it difficult for him to condemn similar tendencies in other Communist countries, and he thus exposed himself—though the penalty was not to be visited on him for another four years—to attack from China for betrayal of Marxist-Leninist orthodoxy.

Less than two months after his journey to Belgrade, Khruschev emerged on to the international stage beyond the boundaries of the Communist world by attending the 1955 Summit Conference at Geneva. His presence there was in itself an important innovation in international affairs. Stalin had never gone abroad or attended international governmental conferences when he was merely General Secretary of the CPSU (as Khrushchev now was); it was as Prime Minister of the Soviet Union that Stalin had gone to Teheran, Yalta and Potsdam. But Khrushchev, without holding a state office, expected for himself the formal honours due to the head of a state or government, thereby claiming a kind of diplomatic recognition for the Soviet Communist Party as such. This was in accordance with his reversal of the attitude of Malenkov, who had sought to give the Soviet government precedence over the party. Khruschev, as head of the party apparatus, reaffirmed the supremacy of the party over the state, and demanded that this be also accepted internationally. Western statesmen, recognising that, in fact, Khrushchev was now the most powerful of the Soviet leaders, were ready to overlook the breach of protocol involved in treating him as at least Bulganin's equal at meetings of heads of governments, and henceforth 'K & B' were partners on state visits. It was not until March 1958 that Khrushchev acquired the proper official status by making himself Prime Minister, as well as First Secretary of the CPSU.

Whether Prime Minister or not, Khrushchev may be regarded as having been in supreme control of Soviet policies, foreign as well as domestic, after February 1955. His conduct of foreign affairs from that time, until his deposition in October 1964, displayed certain special characteristics. The manner of it was, indeed, very different from Stalin's, although this appears to have been the outcome of a contrast of temperaments rather than of calculation. Khrushchev's famous 'ebullience' made him a traveller and a talker, a globe-trotter and a lover of crowds, a folksy 'good fellow' with a salesman's patter and a dash of the clown: a personality altogether unlike the aloof, reserved and immobile Stalin. Stalin never wanted to meet foreign statesmen after 1945, and even in his war-time conferences he refused to go outside the boundaries of the Soviet Union or Soviet-controlled territory. It would be impossible to imagine Stalin banging his shoe on a desk in the Assembly of the United Nations or making an impromptu speech to American journalists in his shirtsleeves from a hotel window. Stalin was always the hidden and secret man of the Kremlin, the spider at the centre of the web, while Khrushchev was the roaming busy bee. His exuberance and informality certainly gave him a capacity for wide popular appeal on visits to other countries. Yet it may be doubted whether his journeys abroad were really of great help to him in his diplomacy. He tended to antagonise the statesmen with whom he had to deal by his too obvious tactics of appealing to their peoples over their heads. He often marred initial good impressions by tactless remarks or outbursts of temper. As state visits, his progresses were lacking in dignity and often invited a disrespect which he resented—at least, when he was aware of it. At Oxford, during his visit to Britain in 1956, students greeted him by singing 'Poor Old Joe!' and 'Why were you born so beautiful? Why were you born at all?' It was disingenuously explained to him that these were traditional songs of welcome, always sung on such occasions.

The political objectives that Khrushchev pursued on these journeys abroad were not very different from those pursued in the last years of the Stalin era. The main element in the foreign policy inherited from the Stalin era was the system of satellite states, including East Germany, in which Communist governments had been imposed by 'revolution from above'. If destalinisation was to signify a basic change in foreign policy, it should have meant—subject to negotiation of agreements with former wartime allies on future security in Europe—a restoration of political freedom to the satellite countries and a reunification of Germany on a basis of free elections. But in Khrushchev's speech against Stalin at the Twentieth Congress, there was no word of condemnation of the dictator's acts in imposing the rule of Bierut, Rakosi and Ulbricht on their respective peoples, any more than there was of the annexation of the Baltic states or the Katyn massacre. The Soviet empire built by Stalin was a possession his heirs were determined to keep, and nothing that he had done for the sake of its construction was counted among his crimes.

But this was in 1956. There is some reason to believe that in the Malenkov era an alternative policy was at least considered. Khrushchev was to assert in 1960, as an additional charge against the 'anti-party group' and in defence of his own record of Communist zeal (questioned by the Chinese), that, after Stalin's death, Malenkov was prepared to abandon the Communist régime in East Germany. If Malenkov did entertain such an idea, it would have been in line with the Russian attitude towards France and Britain during the negotiations for the ending of the war in Indochina. A continued development in the spirit of the diplomacy of the summer of 1954 could have opened up the possibility of a European settlement with a unified, democratic, but neutralised, Germany—given a willingness on the Russian side to sacrifice Ulbricht and on the side of Britain and France to consent to German neutrality. It is sometimes argued that it was Western insistence that a reunified Germany must be free to join NATO that rendered any agreement with the Soviet Union on Germany impossible. But a process of diplomatic bargaining might, in the end, have produced strategic disengagement and the neutralisation of Germany in return for German unity on the basis of free elections. It was the Russian determination to preserve their 'Vopoland' that was the insuperable obstacle to any such settlement, for a disengagement which left the German nation divided into two mutually hostile states, whether separate or nominally combined in a 'confederation', would simply have maximised instability and the danger of war in Central Europe. Certainly, after Khrushchev deposed Malenkov, there was no sign of any disposition to allow free elections in East Germany on any conditions whatsoever. The Summit conference of July 1955 adopted the formula that 'the settlement of the German question and the reunification of Germany by means of free elections shall be carried out in conformity with the national interests of the German people and the interests of European security'. But this soon turned out to mean, in the Russian view, that there could not be any free elections in Ulbricht's domain.

Those who hold the opinion that Moscow's policies in Europe since 1945 have been dictated solely by a desire for national security are hard put to it to explain why the preservation of the Communist régime in East Germany was such a vital interest for the Soviet Union, for in strategic terms its elimination would have been a small price to pay for an agreed peace treaty imposing arms limitations and neutrality on Germany, and providing for the withdrawal of American forces from Europe. The 'national security' argument, though important, does not of itself explain Soviet foreign policy; in particular, it neglects to take account of the imperatives of the party's role in policy and of Communist theory. Khrushchev was First Secretary of the CPSU and his power was based on the party apparatus, for which the maintenance of Communist power, wherever it has once been established, is the paramount interest. It is essential to the party that the dogma of an irresistible and irreversible historical process leading to Communism should be confirmed. If, for a while, it is not practical politics to advance, it is at any rate vitally important not to give up any ground that has been gained. The overthrow of a Communist régime in any one country would be a reversal of the historical process, and might produce a chain reaction involving other countries, and in the end the Soviet Union itself.

The Russian intervention in Hungary in the autumn of 1956, for example, was dictated by the interests of the party in preventing any break-away from the established international Communist system. It is difficult to believe that the secession of Hungary from the Warsaw Pact and its withdrawal into the neutrality already professed by Austria and Yugoslavia could have been a serious threat to Soviet security, since the two other neutral states already interposed a buffer between the power blocs in the Danubian area. But when, on October 30, 1956, Imre Nagy in Budapest proclaimed the abolition of the one-party system, this spelled in effect the end of Communist rule in Hungary, for nobody could expect the Hungarian Communists in free elections to obtain more than a small fraction of the votes cast. At that time, the Russian troops had already begun to withdraw from Hungary, but after Nagy's proclamation they were reinforced and began the attack which ended in the sanguinary suppression of the revolt. Khrushchev subsequently made it clear that any Communist-governed state, in which the rule of the party was endangered by internal insurrection, would be liable to similar Soviet intervention. The satellite countries of Eastern Europe have taken the warning to heart; they understand that, although their Communist leaders may now be allowed a considerable measure of freedom in policy-making within the framework of the international Communist system, such national rights are conditional on the maintenance of Communist rule and will be abrogated if this should be overthrown.

Khrushchev's political career as leader of the CPSU illustrated in a very vivid way the real nature of the Soviet political order. He rose to power as the man of the party apparatus in opposition to Malenkov who exalted state institutions at the expense of the party, and he fell from power because, having grown careless and overconfident through the long exercise of personal authority, he flouted those on whom that authority ultimately depended. He was the party's leader, and the party deposed him when he took to acting in a manner contrary to the vested interests of its professional organisers. He began to hold meetings of the Central Committee at which outsiders—managerial and technical experts of various kinds—were introduced in large numbers, thus depriving the meetings of their proper character as sessions of the controlling party organ. Even more detrimental to the authority and prestige of party functionaries was his splitting of the party organisation into industrial and agricultural sections, thus undermining the position of regional party secretaries. These changes were doubtless intended by Khrushchev to improve the economic administration of the country, but their effect was precisely that downgrading of the party and its officials which had been fatal to Malenkov. Stalin, with his ruthless use of secret police terror, could ignore the constitutional organs of the party; but Khrushchev, not possessing the ultimate means of personal despotism, had to rely on his hold over the party and could not afford to offend its bosses, even when they were men he had himself appointed.

Unlike Lenin and Stalin, he did not die in office. He was deposed in November 1964 by a political intrigue, finding himself stripped of power even before he realised what was happening to him. The coup was bloodless; there do not appear to have been even any movements of troops to provide the element of force; it was simply a consensus of feeling in the higher ranks of the party that his behaviour was becoming intolerable and that he must be removed. In the West, where the official explanations of age and infirmity as reasons for the removal were naturally not taken seriously, there were manifold speculations as to the real causes of it. The growing crisis in Sino-Soviet relations; Khrushchev's proposed visit to Bonn; loss of prestige due to the failure to control the East European satellites; the fiasco of the 'virgin lands' scheme and other difficulties in Soviet agriculture—all these, and many other failures and deficiencies for which Khrushchev could be held responsible, were assigned as the reasons for his downfall.

There were, however, no marked changes in domestic or foreign policy after Khrushchev's political demise. For the Chinese, who had expected a forthright repudiation of revisionism by Krushchev's successors, the continuity was so disappointing that they described the new era as 'Khrushchevism without Khrushchev'. The one thing that was immediately and radically altered after Khrushchev's removal was his division of the party organisation into industrial and agricultural sectors; this division was at once abolished. For this was where he had really given offence to the people who mattered. To have tried to subordinate the integrity of the party as the supreme political ruler, the bearer of the Marxist-Leninist faith, to the conveniences of economic administration—this was the crime for which there could be no forgiveness. In the Communist political system the interests of the party as such must take precedence over all other concerns. The party needs to have a personal leader, but he can never be permitted to kick away the ladder by which he ascended. The party itself is the dictator and the highest leader of the Russian people is still its servant.

12

MAO'S CHINA AND THE SINO-SOVIET
SPLIT

THE WALLS OF PEKING carried six portraits to celebrate the proclamation of the Chinese People's Republic in 1949. There were Marx and Engels, who had been the prophets of the revolution; Lenin and Stalin, who had made the revolution in Russia; Mao Tse-tung and Chu Teh, who had made the revolution in China. It was an impressive apostolic succession, even though to a patriotic Chinese it could not be altogether satisfactory that four out of the six principal figures in the iconography of the new religion should be foreigners. Times had changed since it had been assumed—only a century ago—by all educated Chinese that wisdom was to be found nowhere but in the traditional learning of the Middle Kingdom. Decades of disaster and humiliation had caused a younger generation of Chinese to discard Confucius and seek to find abroad new sources of knowledge and power. Among the Western nations from which China wanted to learn, America had for a long time held first place. But the victory of the Communists involved a switching of China's ideological and cultural alignment from America to Russia. It was from Russia that the gospel of Marxisim-Leninism had reached China. It was to fraternal Russia that the new régime looked for protection against the counter-attacks of imperialism. And it was with the help of Russian experience and, it was hoped, with Russian material help, that China would create a modern industrial economy and build socialism.

One of the most prominent institutions of the People's Republic was the Sino-Soviet Friendship Society which had branches all over China, and enjoyed the full patronage of the Chinese Communist Party. Its task was to promote the learning of the Russian language, to project a favourable image of the Soviet régime and its activities, and to exalt all things Russian at the expense of the still strongly established prestige of America. On the political plane, Mao Tse-tung went to Moscow in

February 1950 and concluded a military alliance with the Soviet Union. A Soviet loan granted to China in February 1950 seemed to portend a flow of credits that would enable the Chinese Communists to industrialise their country without either dependence on Western economic aid or such painful extremities of self-help as isolated Russia had had to resort to before the Second World War.

The value of the alliance with Russia was soon put to the test. Only a year after the proclamation of the People's Republic, Mao Tse-tung had to decide whether or not to send an army into Korea to drive back the army of the United Nations which was approaching the Yalu. Intervention in Korea meant a challenge to the sixteen nations taking part in the war against North Korea, and above all to the United States, which five years previously had brought Japan to unconditional surrender. If the full might of the United States were to be brought to bear against Communist China, if its coasts were to be blockaded and its cities and infant industries destroyed by bombing, and if Chiang Kai-shek's surviving army were to be brought back to the mainland, this time with full American support, then the newly established People's Republic might collapse and the fruit of so many years of revolutionary effort be irretrievably lost. Mao had to stake everything when he went into Korea. Had the issue been only between the United Nations and China, it would have been highly unlikely that Chinese territory could remain untouched by war. But, with the Russian alliance to cover him, Mao calculated that the Western powers, and particularly America's European allies, would be reluctant to extend the area of hostilities for fear of bringing Russia into the war. Even so, the decision was a hazardous one.

Yet the outcome justified the boldness of the resolution. In three years of war, not a single bomb fell on China. Attlee, the British Prime Minister, flew to Washington to protest when it was reported that nuclear weapons might be used in the war. General MacArthur was dismissed from his command when he insisted on action against the Manchurian 'sanctuary' on which the Chinese army and air force were based. Mao was confirmed in his faith in the intimidating effect of Russian power, and also in his view that 'imperialists are paper tigers'. The fact that the United States chose to incur 144,000 casualties in an indecisive, limited war in Korea, rather than raise the stakes by direct action against China, was to him proof that even the strongest of the

Western powers was cautious and timid if confronted by a firm and unwavering resolve on the part of the 'socialist camp'. The experience of the Korean War was to shape Mao's thinking about world affairs, and goes far to explain the confidence with which he was later on to urge a more militant policy for the international Communist movement in opposition to Khrushchev's diplomacy of détente.

When the Chinese Communists came to power in Peking twenty-two years after the first rally of guerrilla bands on Chingkanshan, many Western commentators predicted that they would soon turn out to be more Chinese than Communist. There was reason in such predictions, for it was unlikely that the rulers of the most populous nation in the world, who had made a revolution of their own with only meagre assistance from the Soviet Union and by methods altogether different from those by which the Bolsheviks had conquered Russia, would be content to accept directives from Moscow. It was even less likely that a people with such a tradition of ethnocentric pride and ancient civilisation as the Chinese would long submit to a foreign tutelage in matters of *Weltanschauung*. But most of those who correctly foresaw a self-assertion of the Chinese national ego against Russian leading-strings assumed that it would take the form of a development in the direction of liberalism, a softening of the rigours of Russian Bolshevism, and at least a partial rejection of established Marxist-Leninist doctrine. What they did not expect was that the Chinese would differ by becoming harder, not softer, than the Russians in their revolutionary will and by maintaining the purity of Marxist-Leninist orthodoxy when the Russians were backsliding from it.

During the three years following the end of the Korean war, there was little evidence to sustain the arguments of those who expected conflict between China and Russia. On the contrary, relations between the two great Communist powers appeared to be developing very harmoniously. Chinese foreign trade, which hitherto had been mainly with Western countries or Japan, was switched more and more to the Soviet Union and the East European satellites, while the Russians provided credits and technical aid on a large scale to help with the industrialisation of China. Diplomatically, the co-operation of China and Russia was in accordance with the approved notions of partnership between Communist states. At the Geneva Conference of 1954, when they had the agreeable task of gathering the fruits of victory from the war in Indochina, they presented an impressive common front. Yet the relationship was far from being that of Russia as principal and China as a mere auxiliary, for Chou En-lai, who represented the Chinese People's Republic as its Foreign Minister, made a powerful impression on European diplomats as an independent, skilful and not too intractable negotiator. In the following year, Chou was even more successful as the representative of Communist China at the Bandung conference. Although the Soviet Union was excluded from this consciously Afro-Asian gathering, there were no signs of Russian jealousy at the Chinese role; nor, on the other hand, were there any indications of Chinese objection to the four-power summit conference of July 1955, in which the participation of the Peking government was precluded by the United States' refusal to recognise it as the legal government of China. Peking seemed to be as fully in step with Moscow in world affairs as the docile claque who voted so unanimously on the Soviet side in all meetings of the United Nations. In more intimate party relations, also, China appeared sympathetic to the political trend in the Soviet Union. Peking could not fail to favour Khrushchev against Malenkov because the latter's policy of switching Soviet industry from capital to consumer goods implied a reduction in the output of capital goods available for China's industrialisation. Khrushchev's insistence on the priority of heavy industry was both better Marxism and better for China.

It was, nevertheless, over Khrushchev's exercise of his leadership within the Soviet Union that the first friction between Peking and Moscow took place—albeit this was only a slight rift compared with what was to come later. Khrushchev's secret speech against Stalin in 1956 took the Chinese by surprise. Although they had good domestic reasons, in view of Stalin's support for the Kuomintang in the 'twenties, for having reservations about his wisdom as leader of the Communist camp, the Chinese Communist leaders nevertheless saw Stalin as the great representative of 'tough' Communism during the epoch of their own rise to power. Mao referred to Stalin in terms of eulogy in his message of greeting to the Twentieth Congress on February 9, 1956. But Khrushchev, basing his domestic political tactics on the principle of 'If you can't beat 'em, join 'em', delivered his famous speech, which, even if intended only for the ears of Congress delegates, was delivered to too large an audience to be kept secret for long, and was soon published to the whole world by the American State Department.

The Chinese objected to the anti-Stalin speech for two distinct reasons. In the first place, they thought it too extreme. It failed, they argued, to bring out the 'positive role' of Stalin, and it damaged the Communist cause throughout the world, since Communist parties everywhere now had the impossible task of explaining how it was that the Soviet Communist Party, the ideologically infallible vanguard of the working class, had been for two decades led by a man who was both a knave and a fool. In the second place, and precisely because the attack on Stalin had put Communists everywhere—and not least in China—in such an embarrassing situation, Peking blamed the Soviet leadership for its failure to consult other parties. Because the demolition of the Stalin myth vitally affected the whole International Communist movement, it should not have been a matter for decision by the CPSU alone, but should have been fully discussed with at least the principal non-Soviet parties before any action was taken. The Russian failure to consult had raised the whole question of relations between Communist parties now that the Soviet party was no longer the only one controlling the government of a sovereign state. The pattern of power within the world Communist movement had changed since Stalin had exercised a virtually dictatorial authority over it. In any case, a man who so recklessly repudiated the 'cult of personality', as Khrushchev had done, could hardly expect to inherit that authority.

The events of the autumn of 1956 added to the urgency of the problem. The upheavals in Poland and Hungary threw the Communist world into disarray, and the Chinese party was at pains to define its attitude towards these rebellions. It approved of the Soviet military intervention in Hungary to avert the ending of Communist rule there, but displayed much sympathy for the autonomist aspirations of Gomulka, who continued to maintain Communist rule and to keep Poland within the Warsaw Pact alliance, but stoutly rejected the right of Moscow to interfere in Polish internal affairs. Chou En-lai was sent to Moscow and Warsaw to offer the good offices of China in mediation between the Soviet Union and Poland, and his diplomacy helped to bring about a reconciliation. This was of special significance, for it marked the first occasion on which China had ever intervened in purely European political affairs, as distinct from dealing with European powers over Far Eastern issues. To the Poles and other dissident Communists of Europe at that time, China appeared to be the champion of 'liberalism'—of 'polycentrism', as Togliatti defined it—in the international Communist movement. The impression Chou produced in Warsaw was strengthened when Cyrankiewicz and Ochab paid a return visit to Peking in the spring of 1957.

All the same, Chinese support was not for an unqualified 'polycentrism' among Communists. Mao Tse-tung, who had himself been so original in his adaptation of Leninist revolutionary theory to Chinese conditions, held that the leadership of each national party should be free to take its own decisions in relation to its own national problems. But he also held that matters of common concern to the whole international movement should be decided collectively by all the Communists of the world in conference, and that, since the Communist states had to be bound together in military alliance against the capitalist powers, the strongest among them should have a leading position for the execution of a common strategy. For this reason, Mao stood for a recognition within strict limits of the 'leadership' of the Soviet Union in the Communist camp, and tried to persuade the Poles to acknowledge it. For the same reason, he was profoundly hostile to Titoism. In his view of the world, it was outrageous that a state calling itself Communist should be neutral in the international conflict between the imperialist and socialist camps, and the fact that Yugoslavia took up such a neutral position clearly demonstrated that it was not really a Communist state at all.

More than any other contemporary Communist leader, Mao Tse-tung was a revolutionary soldier. During the twenty-two years from 1927 to 1949, the Chinese Communist Party had been engaged in armed struggle either against the Kuomintang or against the Japanese, and the three years of the war in Korea had followed almost immediately after the definitive Communist victory in the Chinese civil war. Moreover, the background of the Communist struggle for power in China had been one of chronic turmoil and violence, and this had conditioned the lives of all Chinese of Mao's generation. From the Revolution of 1911 to the consolidation of Communist power (with the possible exception of 1914), there had never been a year in which China had been entirely free from either foreign or civil war. It was from a lifetime of such experience that Mao stated his belief that 'power grows from the barrel of a gun'. This belief governed his concept of peace. 'Counter-revolutionary war', he said, 'can only be abolished by revolutionary war, unjust war by just war.'[1] In other words, peace could only be established on earth through the decisive military victory of Communism.

After 1950, the enemy for Mao's China was America, and far more exclusively the enemy than it was for Russia. Moscow had to take account, not only of America, but also of Britain and France and of a Germany with irredentist claims on the lands beyond the Oder. For China, however, there was no substantial power in the Far East save that exerted, directly or indirectly, by the United States. Japanese military power had been broken by defeat and by the political system established under Allied occupation. Though deprived of their conquests on the mainland of Asia and compelled to return to China the island of Formosa, annexed in 1895, the consequences of their defeat were not such as to give the Japanese a territorial grievance against China; no Japanese population had been expelled by China. The European colonial powers—Britain, France and the Netherlands—were waning powers in the Far East even before the Chinese Communists came to power in 1949. Weakened by the Second World War and beset with strong anti-colonial movements within their Asian colonies, they were in no position to contend with China. So untroubled were Mao and his colleagues by the European presence in the Far East that they could tolerate the continuation as colonial enclaves of British Hong Kong and Portuguese Macao. None of the new states emerging from the break-up of the Western empires could menace China, and none—save India—could even rival it in political influence. If Far Eastern affairs were to be determined simply and solely by the disposition of power among the Far Eastern states themselves, China's ascendancy throughout the area would be easier to achieve than Russian domination of Europe.

But the United States frustrated China on every front. America had a military alliance with Japan and a great fleet and air base at Okinawa; an alliance with South Korea, where two combat divisions were retained by the Americans after the end of the Korean War; an alliance with the Philippines and bases there; an alliance with Thailand, and a protective mantle over South Vietnam. Above all, American power protected the residue of the Kuomintang régime on Formosa. As long as it remained under Nationalist control, Formosa was a sharp thorn in the side of Communist China. Chiang's control of the island presented a political alternative to Communism, not as a shadow government in exile in a foreign country but as an authority actually governing some 10 million Chinese on Chinese soil.

The completion of victory by the 'liberation' of Formosa could not fail to be the most compelling objective of Chinese Communist foreign policy. But the strategic problem was a baffling one. Formosa was about a hundred miles from the mainland, and Peking could not hope in the foreseeable future to have a naval superiority in the Formosa Straits sufficient for a seaborne invasion unless the Americans withdrew from the island the protection of their Seventh Fleet, which was not only an extremely powerful conventional fighting force, but was also equipped with nuclear weapons. In addition to Formosa itself, there were also the Nationalist outposts on the small islands of Quemoy and Matsu close to the mainland. These might be taken by infantry assaults under artillery cover if the Americans would refrain from interference, but here also the Chinese Communists had good reason to believe, from the beginning of 1955, that the Seventh Fleet would scotch any offensive they might launch. In contrast to Korea, where the United States had had to commit large ground forces to hold back the North Korean and Chinese Communists from overland conquest of the peninsula, America's air and sea forces sufficed to protect Formosa, and even also the Offshore Islands, provided such forces were employed against batteries and communications on the mainland, as well as against hostile air and sea forces.

The American commitment to the defence of Formosa was a consequence of the Korean war. As pointed out earlier (Chapter 4, page 70), the American government early in 1950 had been quite ready to see Formosa fall to the Communists, but when South Korea was attacked, it extended naval protection to the island. The protection of Formosa, unlike the campaign against Korea, did not have the endorsement of the United Nations, nor did it have the support of Britain, America's principal partner in the Korean war. The British— who had given *de jure* recognition to the Communist régime in China and did not consider themselves legally at war with it on account of operations against Chinese 'People's Volunteers' in Korea—strongly objected to General MacArthur's bid to get Chinese Nationalist troops from Formosa to fight in Korea. Under the Truman administration, the American policy towards Formosa was one of 'neutralisation', which amounted simply to the sealing off of the island. But when Eisenhower won the Presidency of the United States as the Republican candidate in the election of 1952, Chiang Kai-shek was 'unleashed'— that is to say, it was announced that he would be permitted to attack the mainland. This was a marked change from the 'neutralisation' policy, yet the American government does not seem seriously to have contemplated a full-scale attack on China. The aim of the new policy was diversionary; it was hoped that a threat to the South China coast would compel the Chinese Communist high command to divert troops and supplies from Korea. The American military authorities did not consider that the Chinese Nationalists had any prospect of success in a large scale invasion of the mainland, and did not encourage them to attempt it. On the other hand, in order to make a convincing feint against Communist China from the south, they urged the Nationalists to strengthen their forces in the Offshore Islands, and this concentration remained after an armistice had been concluded in Korea.

Early in 1955, the United States concluded a formal treaty of defensive military alliance with the Nationalist government in Formosa, which Washington continued to recognise as the *de jure* government of China, and Congress gave the President authority to employ American armed forces, not only for the defence of Formosa, but also for 'the securing and protection of such related positions and territories now in friendly hands and the taking of such other measures as he judges to be required or appropriate in assuring the defence of Formosa'. This was taken to mean that American forces would join in the defence of the Offshore Islands as well as Formosa.

Confronted with the American–Formosan alliance and the threats of John Foster Dulles that any further Communist military attacks in the Far East would be met with 'massive retaliation' by nuclear weapons, the Peking government did not dare to make any move against Formosa or the Offshore Islands. But, in the autumn of 1957, Mao came to believe that the keys to success were within his reach. In August of that year, the Soviet Union announced that it had produced an intercontinental ballistic missile; and then, in October, just before the assembly in Moscow of Communists from all over the world to celebrate the fortieth anniversary of the Bolshevik revolution, the first sputnik was successfully launched. In proclaiming to the world and to the admiring comrades from other lands these triumphs of Soviet technology, the Russian Communists did not go in for understatement. The impression they created of a great Russian lead in rocketry was confirmed by the consternation caused in the United States: a consternation made all the greater by the Pentagon's 'professional' propagation of gloom in support of the defence appropriation in the budget. (In fact, the overall strategic position of the West in relation to the Soviet Union had been altered much less than was popularly supposed.) Russian boasting and American panic combined to produce in Mao Tse-tung a vision of a new era in which, to use his own words, 'the east wind prevails over the west wind'. The Communist camp, he believed, was now militarily stronger than the West. The new invincible might of nuclear-headed missiles that could be fired across oceans was, indeed, in the possession of the Soviet Union, not China. But he envisaged that, in accordance with the international solidarity and fraternity of all Communists in the struggle against imperialism, Russia's great new power would be used on behalf of the Communist camp as a whole. Now was the time to go forward, to pursue hard and vigorous policies, to take risks in the confidence of superior strength. The imperialist 'paper tigers' would probably not dare to resort to full-scale war; and if they did, they would be defeated.

There can be little doubt that the fortieth anniversary celebration in Moscow was for Mao a time of great mental exaltation, if not euphoria. The powerful state created by the great Lenin was his ally; and he, creator of the new China, was foremost among living Communists as a leader of successful revolution: a second Lenin. Now Russia and China could march forward together to new world-shaking victories: the Russians with their more advanced technology providing the long-range strategic striking power of the most modern weapons; the Chinese contributing the unlimited military manpower of the largest population in the world.

What followed, however, was a series of disappointments. The Russians under the leadership of Khrushchev seemed strangely inactive in exploiting the strategic superiority of which they boasted. When, in the summer of 1958, the revolution in Iraq and the American troop landings in the Lebanon brought about a serious international crisis, the Chinese talked about sending 'People's Volunteers' to Iraq, but Moscow's only thought seemed to be to get a summit conference. On August 23, Peking began a massive artillery bombardment of Quemoy. It was a probing operation designed to test the strength of the Nationalists on Quemoy and the will of the Americans to aid them. If these had proved inadequate, it could have been expanded into a full-scale effort to capture the island. But the Nationalists stood firm, their fighter aircraft, armed with American 'Sidewinder' air-to-air missiles, proving more than a match for the Communist air force; and Dulles on September 4 declared that Quemoy was 'increasingly related' to the defence of Formosa, hinting at American bombing of the Communist batteries if the offensive continued. Next day, the Peking government offered a renewal of ambassadorial talks with the United States. It was only then, after the tension had subsided, that Moscow clearly asserted that an attack on China would be regarded as an attack on the Soviet Union. The Soviet attitude in the earlier stages of the crisis had been very cautious and non-committal. Mao could not have derived from this episode any assurance that the Soviet Union would risk war with the United States in order to protect China from the consequences of an offensive in the Formosa Straits; indeed he may have received a specific warning that the Russians would not do so.

A hope that the Russians might be ready to use force in their own sphere of interest, if not in China's, and thus indirectly provide opportunities for Peking, dawned in November 1958, when Khrushchev threatened to turn over Russian control in Berlin to East Germany and set a time limit of six months for a negotiated settlement of the Berlin deadlock. But when the six months had passed and there was no settlement, control was not given to the East Germans, nor was there any blockade of West Berlin. Instead, there was Khrushchev's bid for a détente with the United States, leading to his conversations with Eisenhower at Camp David in September 1959.

Back from his tour of America, Khrushchev changed planes on Moscow airport and flew on to Peking. The formal reason for his visit was the celebration of the tenth anniversary of the Chinese People's Republic; its main purpose was to imbue the Chinese Communists with the Camp David spirit. He found them coldly unresponsive to his enthusiasm for an understanding with the United States. This, he could argue, might lead to Ulbricht's getting effective control of West Berlin; but he could not pretend it contained anything of advantage to China. In his approach to America, Khrushchev had had too difficult a task in trying to modify the Americans' stand on Berlin for him to risk complete failure by demanding that they change their China policy as well. However, if he had not done anything for China in his tour of the principal homeland of imperialism, he could at least give the Chinese some kindly, sensible advice. In his speech at the banquet held in his honour on September 30, he said:

> When I spoke with President Eisenhower . . . I got the impression that the President of the United States—and not a few people support him—understands the need to relax international tension. . . . There-fore, we on our part must do all we can to exclude war as a means of settling disputed questions and settle these questions by nego-tiation. . . . The socialist countries . . . have the means to defend themselves from the attacks of the imperialist aggressors if these should attempt by interference in our countries' affairs to force them to leave the socialist path and return to capitalism. . . . This, of course, does not by any means signify that, if we are so strong, then we must test by force the stability of the capitalist system. This would be wrong; the peoples would not understand and would never support those who would think of acting in this way.[2]

What was to be known as the Sino-Soviet dispute did not emerge into the open on this festive occasion, but Mao made no speech of welcome to the Soviet leader. He felt only anger at the successor of Lenin and Stalin who, instead of playing for the highest stakes with the strong hand the Chinese believed him to have, proposed a détente with the United States—and this while the Seventh Fleet still assured Chiang Kai-shek possession of Quemoy. Moreover, Khrushchev had but recently committed an even graver offence against Communist solidarity. In September, the Soviet Union had officially taken up an attitude of political neutrality with regard to the border clash between Communist China and India in Ladakh. For a Communist statesman to neglect the interests of another Communist country in pursuing those of his own was deplorable, but still within the bounds of fraternal politics. For him to fail to give even moral support to a Communist partner involved in an armed conflict with a bourgeois state—this was a betrayal beyond pardon.

The beginning of Mao Tse-tung's cold war against Khrushchev came with the speech made by K'ang Sheng as Chinese observer at a conference of Foreign Ministers of the Warsaw Pact states in February 1960. The conference was held as part of a diplomatic preparation for the summit conference of the Big Four, due to be held in Paris in May. Khrushchev issued a declaration that violently attacked the policies of West Germany, but had no unkind words for the United States. K'ang Sheng sharply dissented from its main theme, and he not only denounced the United States with great vehemence, but indulged in sarcasm at the expense of those who allowed themselves to be taken in by the wiles of American imperialism.

> While being obliged to make certain peace gestures, the US ruling circles are still pushing ahead vigorously with their arms expansion and war preparations . . . and actively trying to strengthen and patch up military blocs in an attempt to gain time to improve their inferior military position. . . . President Eisenhower's State of the Union Message recently gave the clearest indication that the new tricks of the United States are designed to gain precisely what it failed to obtain by its old tricks. The actions of the United States prove fully that its imperialist nature will not change. American imperialism still remains the arch-enemy of world peace.[3]

Two months later, in April 1960, just before the summit meeting in Paris, the Chinese Communists raised their dispute with the Soviet leadership to an ideological plane by a series of articles against 'revisionism' in the theoretical journal, *Red Flag*. The attack was specifically directed against the heretical views of Tito, but in such a way that the opinions of Khrushchev also were brought under strong criticism. The articles derided the professed Soviet faith in the prospects of a lasting peace and relaxation of tension achieved through conference diplomacy.

> If we lose our vigilance against the danger of the imperialists launching a war, if we do not work to stir the people of all countries to rise up against imperialism, but tie the hands of the people, then imperialism can prepare for war just as it pleases, and the inevitable result

will be an increase in the danger of the imperialists launching a war. . . . If the US or other imperialists . . . should dare to fly in the face of the will of all humanity by launching a war using nuclear weapons, the result will be the very speedy destruction of these monsters encircled by the peoples of the world; it will certainly not be the annihilation of mankind. . . . The Yugoslav revisionists deny the inherent class character of violence and thereby obliterate the fundamental difference between revolutionary and counter-revolutionary violence; they deny the inherent class character of war and thereby obliterate the fundamental difference between just and unjust war; they deny that imperialist war is a continuation of imperialist policy, deny the danger of the imperialists unleashing another big war, deny that it will be possible to do away with war only after doing away with the exploiting classes.[4]

Henceforth, Mao was to carry on an ideological struggle against revisionism with unmistakable reference to the policies pursued by the Soviet Union under the leadership of Khrushchev. Both Russia and China continued to be officially dedicated as party-states to the principles of Marxism-Leninism, but their interpretations of the doctrine were becoming increasingly divergent. The Chinese criticism was strongly resented in Moscow and was answered by Kuusinen in a Lenin anniversary speech on April 22, 1960:

In order to be loyal to Marxisim–Leninism today, it is not sufficient to repeat the old truth that imperialism is aggressive. The task is to make full use of the factors operating for peace in order to save humanity from the catastrophe of another war. A dogmatic position is a backward position. The correctness of our foreign policy of creative Leninism is proved best of all by the success of this policy. . . . A tangible easing of international tension has been achieved. The cold war is gradually receding. . . . The most burning questions of the international situation have at long last become the subject of serious East–West negotiations.[5]

Unfortunately for this attempt to show that the Soviet policy was correct because it worked in practice, the break-up of the Paris summit conference less than a month later showed that it was not working at all. Khrushchev put the blame on Eisenhower for the failure of the conference, but this, in Communist eyes, was to admit that his optimism had been unfounded. What he had meant by the Camp David spirit was that he was going to get something for nothing: he had thought he could win Berlin by blarney. The discovery that he could not found him still unwilling to challenge America to mortal combat by taking Berlin with force of arms. He now had to contend openly with the unpersuaded dogmatists of Peking in abstract theoretical controversy about the inevitability of imperialist war.

The verbal struggle between Moscow and Peking became extremely violent. It was carried on at a meeting in the Chinese capital of the General Council of the Communist-controlled World Federation of Trade Unions, early in June 1960, and, later in the same month, at the congress of the Rumanian Communist Party, attended by fraternal delegates from other parties in the 'socialist camp'. The trade union conference revealed for the first time that the Chinese Communists were not alone in their discontent with Khrushchev's policies, and it marked the beginning of a split within the world Communist movement along continental lines. All the European delegations, and also the Indian representatives, supported the Soviet policy line, but China received some degree of support from the delegates of Indonesia, Japan, Burma, North Vietnam, Ceylon, Zanzibar, Sudan, Somalia and Argentina.[6]

The disarray at this conference, where, according to an Italian correspondent, the European delegates were 'amazed' at the violence of the Chinese attack, stung Khrushchev into a counter-offensive. He went to Bucharest for the Rumanian party congress in person. The Chinese party was represented there by P'eng Chen, a member of its Politburo. According to leaked reports of the proceedings in a closed session, Khrushchev made a bitter personal attack on Mao Tse-tung, comparing him to Stalin. P'eng Chen replied with an uncompromising denunciation of Khrushchev for confusing basic issues of Marxism-Leninism. In his public speech, in order to prove his toughness in the face of imperialism, Khrushchev claimed to have stopped both the Anglo-French attack on Egypt in 1956 and an intended Anglo-American intervention in Iraq in 1958 by warning that the Soviet Union would 'deal a devastating blow unless aggression were stopped'. But he did not explain why threats of nuclear war, alleged to have been effective in these cases, could not be used in other cases because of the paramount need to avoid a nuclear war. If Khrushchev had hoped to force a Chinese retreat at Bucharest, he was disappointed, for P'eng Chen did not yield an inch. Moscow then applied sanctions of a more material kind against China. Technical specialists, who had been sent to China to assist in the process of industrialisation, were suddenly withdrawn. But this did not bring the Chinese to their knees either.

By the end of the summer of 1960, the press polemics between the two countries had become so embittered that a complete rupture between them appeared probable. But neither in Moscow nor Peking was such a final split, involving a cleavage also of the whole international Communist movement, contemplated without grave misgiving. A strenuous attempt was therefore made to find some formula of compromise through a world conference of eighty-one Communist parties, held in Moscow in November and December 1960. After prolonged debates behind closed doors, the conference finally produced a declaration which a historian of the Sino-Soviet conflict has describes as 'a maste piece of ambiguity'. A majority of the parties represented at the conference was on the Soviet side, and the text of the declaration— while allowing scope for divergent interpretations, of which the Chinese later made full use—was, on the whole, favourable to the Soviet thesis. Khrushchev was, however, reported to have been subjected to biting invective from the Chinese delegate and, in particular, derided for having made definite threats over Berlin that he failed to carry out. Chinese scorn and anger were to be even sharper after the Cuban missile crisis in 1962.

An indirect effect of the Sino-Soviet controversy was to give greater independence to all Communist parties, including those that took the Soviet side in the dispute. Since there were now two rival centres of leadership in the Communist world, each of the other parties was being canvassed for its support, and was in a position to change sides if displeased with the leader initially preferred. Khrushchev after 1962 wanted to hold a new conference of all the parties, seeking thereby to rally the Soviet Union's supporters and to compel the Chinese to choose between submission to the Moscow line and excommunication. But he came up against a strong reluctance, even among parties adhering to the Soviet side in the dispute, to accept the idea of such a conference. This was not only because of the fear among Communists throughout the world of the scandal of a formal schism in the international Communist movement—the Russians were prepared to face that—but also because of the perception in many of the other parties that such a split would lose for them the bargaining power accruing to them from the existing situation.

The most notable example of trimming between Moscow and Peking was provided by Rumania. Deep currents of anti-Russian nationalism in that country enabled the Rumanian Communist Party to obtain strong popular backing for a policy of recalcitrance towards Moscow, particularly with regard to Soviet plans for a division of economic functions among Communist states that the Rumanians saw as a new kind of colonialism. By skilful tactical manoeuvres for mediating in the Sino-Soviet dispute, the Rumanian Communist leaders were able to exact concessions from Moscow which they could not have hoped to get if they had not been in a position to hold an auction for their political support. There continued to be an international Communist movement, but the days were over when there was only one Marxist pope whom a believer might acknowledge.

13

CONFRONTATIONS OVER BERLIN
AND CUBA, 1958–62

KHRUSHCHEV IN MARCH 1958 became Prime Minister of the
Soviet Union, in addition to being First Secretary of the Soviet
Communist Party. He thus held the combination of offices that
Stalin held during the last years of his life, and could feel that he had
attained full personal command of the party-state as the third leader in
the succession after Lenin and Stalin. It was, however, no easy matter
to live up to the standards of achievement set by his predecessors. Lenin
had created the Soviet Union; Stalin had enlarged its territory and
established the system of Communist satellite states in Eastern Europe.
Khrushchev had to prove himself worthy of his inheritance. The
apparatchiks were well-disciplined, but they expected their commander
to win victories. He could make a name for himself in domestic politics
by ploughing up virgin lands and talking about the transition from
socialism to communism, but success in foreign policy was also required.
Here, the most convincing demonstration of his calibre—in an international situation that did not afford prospects of sweeping gains at an
early date—would be to succeed where Stalin had failed. Stalin's great
political successes at the end of the Second World War and in its
immediate aftermath had ended with two failures: the failure to suppress the defiance of Tito, and the failure to get control of West Berlin
by blockade. Khrushchev set himself to remedy both these frustations.

Tito was to be tamed by kindness; the prodigal son was to be brought
back into the fold from which the paternal harshness of Stalin had
driven him. Khrushchev flew to Belgrade in May 1955 and there was a
reconciliation, though it looked more like an apology of the Soviet
Union to Yugoslavia than a forgiving of the prodigal. Tito was, in fact,
rehabilitated without abjuring his heresies.

Berlin was the more difficult problem, resisting even a semblance of a successful solution. Garrisons of the three Western powers remained in the city, and the air corridors which had saved the Western sectors from strangulation in 1948 could not be violated without a challenge to war. At the same time, the unsubdued territorial enclave of West Berlin was becoming more and more a 'bone in the throat' (Khrushchev's own phrase) both for the Ulbricht régime in East Germany and for the Soviet Union as its sponsor and protector. Since 1949, American and West German money had been poured into it to revive its economic life and overcome the effects of its separation from the territory surrounding it. West Berlin had become a thriving, prosperous urban area, and an impressive shopwindow for the West and for capitalism in striking contrast to the bleak austerity of East Germany under Communist rule. Moreover, it was the 'escape hatch' through which hundreds of thousands of East Germans, discontented for one reason or another with the conditions of life in their zone, emigrated to West Germany, making their way from one district of Berlin into another and then being flown out through the air corridor. As long as West and East Berlin were not physically separated, the Vopos (Volkpolizei, the oppressive security police of the Ulbricht régime) could not stop the flow. The emigration was a scandal and a humiliation for a party that claimed broad popular support; it was also a threat to the economic viability of East Germany, for a large proportion of those who escaped were young men and women with valuable professional qualifications. Until the 'Wall of Shame' was built in 1961, the drain of manpower to the West continued. No less threatening to East Germany, and indeed to the Eastern bloc as a whole, was the very existence of West Berlin as a free society. With its free municipal elections and press, its new university independent of governmental control, and its flourishing political parties outlawed in East Germany, West Berlin had a most disturbing effect on the political life of the territory around it.

To put an end to this state of affairs, two things were essential. In the first place, the Western military garrisons in West Berlin would have to be eliminated, so that they could no longer protect the German civilian population from the use or threat of force from East Berlin. Secondly, the East German Communist authorities would have to acquire enough control over air communications from West Berlin to enable them to stop individuals from entering or leaving the city.

It was in November 1958 that Khrushchev began his drive to get the Western powers out of Berlin. In a speech in Poland on November 10, he declared that the Soviet Union would soon hand over its rights in Berlin to East Germany, with which thereafter the Western powers would have to negotiate rights of access to their sectors of the city. Any armed violation of East German sovereignty by them would be considered an attack on the Soviet Union. A fortnight later, he followed up this warning shot with a proposal to make West Berlin a 'free city', from which Western military garrisons would have to be withdrawn. Finally, in January 1959, he proposed that a German peace treaty be concluded, with both German states represented at a peace conference together with all states that had been at war with Germany. He added the warning that, if the Western powers did not fall in with this, the Soviet Union and other Communist countries would unilaterally conclude a peace treaty with East Germany, giving the latter full sovereignty over its own territory and air space, so that the Western powers would have no rights of access to Berlin except by consent of the East German government.

The bargaining position thus taken up by Khrushchev was essentially one of blackmail by threat of war, although the peculiar circumstances of the Western presence in Berlin meant that he could represent this as only a warning against a use of force by the other side. If matters developed to the final stage in which East Germany, claiming sovereignty by land, water and air over the area between West Germany and West Berlin, were to obstruct Western access in all three elements, the Western powers would then either have to accept East German terms for an agreement or use force to reopen communications. In the latter case, the Soviet Union would claim that East Germany was the victim of aggression and would come to its assistance as an ally. As Khrushchev was later to tell Harriman: 'If you want war you can have it, but remember it will be your war.'

The Western answer to Russia's claim of defensive rights in the approaches to Berlin was that, whatever the Russians might do in divesting themselves of their own rights in Berlin in favour of East Germany, they could not legally transfer the rights of the other occupying powers without their consent. Western rights of access to Berlin could not be unilaterally abrogated by the signature of a peace treaty between East Germany and the Soviet Union. But the juridical arguments about responsibility for a war which had not yet broken out were of secondary importance compared with the fact that the Soviet Union was indeed threatening war if the Western powers would not accept terms which would subject West Berlin, by degrees if not all at once, to Communist control. Diplomatically, the threat was not too crude, because the 'free city' idea was put forward as a proposal that the Western powers could accept by agreement with the Soviet Union. Only if they rejected it would they be left to talk to Ulbricht, with the armed power of the Soviet Union ready to protect him if he took action to enforce his demands. In contrast to Stalin's Berlin blockade of 1948, the Russians would not this time do the blockading; they would merely be the guarantors of East Germany's sovereign rights. On the other hand, the new blockade that was being threatened would apply, not only to the surface of the land, as in the earlier blockade, but also to the air corridors that Stalin had not dared to touch. The strangling fingers would choke the windpipe through which, in 1948, West Berlin had still been able to breathe.

Khrushchev demanded negotiations on Berlin, but these, as defined by him, would only be to determine the form and extent of Western concessions; he was not offering anything in return for getting his way on Berlin. The only *quid pro quo* for acceptance of his demands was to be 'relaxation of international tension'. Having created an international crisis by demanding with menaces a new status for West Berlin, he was determined to make the relaxation of tension conditional on his obtaining what he wanted—just as a gunman in a bank seeks to relax the tension arising from his request to the cashier to hand over the bank's money. In Soviet propaganda confected for mass consumption, however, this desire for reducing tension was invested with an aura of saintly virtue. The Soviet Union was depicted as basing its whole policy on the principle of peaceful coexistence among countries with different social systems, as deploring all wars, cold or hot, and as seeking, above all, to save mankind from the peril of thermonuclear devastation by negotiated settlements of disputed issues. By refusing to negotiate, the West was held to be standing in the way of peaceful solutions.

It was quite true that the Western powers were unwilling to negotiate about Berlin. They had no 'safety-margin' for such negotiations. The existing conditions in the former German capital were the minimum required to afford the West Berliners freedom from Communist control; there were no concessions of any importance that could be made without involving a total surrender of the Western position. Negotiations imply give and take, but Khrushchev was not giving anything, and he could not take anything without taking everything. Negotiations on Berlin could only end either in deadlock or in a decisive capitulation by the West: a capitulation whose consequences would not be confined to Berlin. Even so, the West could not continue to refuse negotiations on Berlin, because, as the sense of crisis grew and as the spectre of war loomed on the horizon, there was an increasing popular demand for talks to save the peace.

Negotiations therefore began in May 1959 between the three Western powers and the Soviet Union. They continued until July without resulting in any agreement. But Khrushchev did not expect to get anywhere through this kind of diplomatic process. From the beginning of the year, he had been bidding for direct top-level talks with the President of the United States. In January 1959, Mikoyan had been sent on a goodwill mission to the United States, where he produced a most favourable impression of reasonableness and moderation, especially on the businessmen present at meetings addressed by him. The mortal illness and consequent resignation of John Foster Dulles from the office of Secretary of State in April also favoured a trend towards appeasement, for it removed from the American administration the inflexible opponent of Communist expansion to whom Eisenhower had been content to leave the direction of his government's foreign policy. The President was now more open to the influences urging him to spare no effort to avert war. At last, on August 3, it was announced that Khrushchev had been invited to visit the United States and that Eisenhower would go on a return visit to the Soviet Union.

In his tour of America in September 1959, Khrushchev did his best to meet the people and project an image of himself as the apostle of peace. But his real business was with Eisenhower. He had already met him at the Geneva 'exploratory' summit conference four years previously. From his observation at that time of Eisenhower's kindly, generous nature and defective knowledge of international political issues, Khrushchev, it would seem, had come to the conclusion that the President would be vulnerable to a 'soft sell'. For the same reason, the State Department was very apprehensive of the consequences of the President's being left alone with Khrushchev for any length of time; they could not be sure what American interests he might not give away from sheer goodness of heart. Indeed, the Camp David meeting was to prove a victory for Khrushchev, though it was one whose fruits he was never able to gather. He believed that he had received from Eisenhower assurances of American concessions on Berlin that would give the Soviet Union substantially what it wanted. Eisenhower was probably not aware of having made any commitment, mainly because he did not understand the full implications of the problem of Berlin. Since he no longer had Dulles to do his thinking for him, he had been all at sea on foreign policy. Certainly, he did not mean to deceive Khrushchev by encouraging him to expect concessions which he had no intention of making. But he was anxious to please his guest and to show himself accommodating. The force of Khrushchev's personality also doubtless made its impact. At his press conference afterwards, the President referred to the 'abnormal situation' in Berlin, but without any suggestion that the situation in East Germany might also be abnormal. He thereby appeared to commit himself to the view that the existing order in West Berlin was an anomaly which must be put right. He added that 'we agreed that these negotiations should not be prolonged indefinitely but there could be no fixed time limit on them'.

After Khrushchev's departure, the State Department set to work to mend the broken fences and prepare a strong American position for the summit conference to be held in the spring of 1960. (It was originally fixed for April, but was postponed until the middle of May.) The State Department's efforts were reinforced by the arrival from Europe of Adenauer and de Gaulle: personalities as forceful as Khrushchev but operating in the opposite direction. Adenauer came to Washington in March 1960 and de Gaulle in April. Both were strongly opposed to any substantial concessions on Berlin. Adenauer talked of the fatal damage to West Germany's morale and its confidence in NATO if the West Berliners were to be abandoned after their long struggle against Communist pressure and intimidation. De Gaulle did not think that the Soviet Union would go to war over Berlin; in any case, the West's position was not of such strategic inferiority as to compel it to yield to Soviet demands without getting anything in return.

A distinct hardening of the American attitude was revealed in a speech on April 4 by Christian Herter, successor to Dulles as Secretary of State. Khrushchev replied, on April 25 at Baku, with an angry speech delivered with a strong note of menace. It was now certain that the summit conference, due to open in Paris on May 16, was going to be a stormy one, and there was the danger that, if Khrushchev came away from it empty-handed, he might have to restore his prestige by some action over Berlin that would bring the world close to a major war.

On May 1, however, an event occurred which was to sidetrack the conference on to an issue which had nothing to do with Berlin. A high-flying American U-2 reconnaissance aircraft was shot down near Sverdlovsk, more than a thousand miles within the borders of the Soviet Union. In reporting this to a session of the Supreme Soviet on May 5, Khrushchev called the flight 'aggressive provocation aimed at wrecking the summit conference'. He expressed the view that the President of the United States sincerely desired peace, but that he was being thwarted by people in Washington who wished to maintain tension. In giving dramatic publicity to the shooting-down of the U-2 five days after it occurred, Khrushchev was making a calculated move on the international chessboard. There could not be in the Soviet Union any reporting of such an incident unless the government wanted it, and for the purposes of Soviet counterespionage, it would have been better to leave American intelligence aware that a U-2 had been lost, but not knowing what had happened to it or its pilot.

What then was Khrushchev's motive for announcing the news eleven days before the conference was due to begin? It may be taken as certain that he did not know the most important fact behind the incident, namely, that Eisenhower had himself personally authorised the flight. He probably assumed that the President, who was so ready to leave foreign affairs to others, was equally ready to delegate authority in military matters; hence, flights over Soviet territory might be ordered by subordinates without Eisenhower's knowledge. Khrushchev does not seem to have realised that Eisenhower, a professional soldier, continued as President to take an active interest in all decisions related to defence and strategic planning. Foreign affairs may not have been his métier: military affairs were. Eisenhower held the view that observation flights over Soviet territory were a necessary part of America's security, an essential precaution against surprise attack in an age of nuclear-headed intercontinental missiles. But he insisted that all such flights needed specific approval from a committee of which he himself was chairman. If Khrushchev had known this, he would have realised that Eisenhower could not repudiate an act which he had himself authorised, and that to demand an apology from the President and 'punishment of the culprits' would be merely to wreck the conference. It is just possible that this was Khrushchev's aim. It is much more likely, however, that he really believed that the U-2 flights had been undertaken without Eisenhower's knowledge, and that by denouncing them he would compel the President to disown his provocative subordinates, break with the 'cold war warriors', and come to Paris an embarrassed and crestfallen man, anxious to make amends in negotiation for the outrage done by his fellow countrymen.

It did not, however, turn out like this. Since Eisenhower was personally responsible for the flights, he could not disown his subordinates, and he could not himself apologise without repudiating a course of action he had thought right in the interests of his country. So, instead of an admission of guilt, attributed to persons as far away as possible from the top of the government, the Secretary of State publicly justified the U-2 flights on the ground that the secrecy of Soviet military preparations made them necessary. Eisenhower came to Paris hoping that Khrushchev would forgo an apology and be content with an undertaking not to make any further U-2 flights. But Khrushchev remained firm in his demand for an apology, and then, when the summit conference broke down on Eisenhower's refusal to give it, achieved one of the great theatrical triumphs of his career in his address to the world's journalists assembled to cover the conference. Although he had made no diplomatic gain at a conference that had never reached its proper agenda, Khrushchev saved his personal prestige by standing before the world as the uncompromisingly indignant leader of a great nation whose sovereignty had been violated.

It was the world's good fortune that all attention was focused on the U-2, Berlin being for the moment quite forgotten. His prestige preserved by a public verbal chastisement of the American President and his country, there was no need for Khrushchev to do anything spectacular about the dispute that was to have been the main subject for decision at the conference. He now appeared to be no longer in a hurry over Berlin; he made no move to conclude the threatened separate peace treaty with East Germany. Instead, he talked about resuming negotiations with the next American President, who was not due to take office for another eight months.

Although the lucky diversion provided by the U-2 incident had saved Khrushchev from an agonising dilemma between risky action over Berlin and the humiliation of a diplomatic defeat at the summit conference, he still had to face the consequences of the refutation by events of his confidence in the prospects of a policy of détente. Within the Soviet Union, his position was now strong enough to render him virtually immune to criticism of the 'I-told-you-so' type. But the Chinese Communists, having mounted their ideological offensive against his principles in April 1960, before the opening of the summit conference, now pressed their advantage. They claimed that the fiasco in Paris proved how futile it was to suppose that imperialism could change its nature, or that one could gain anything by conciliating it. This was the point, as has been shown in Chapter 12, at which the Sino-Soviet differences widened into a definite breach.

It is impossible to estimate how much effect Chinese goading had on Khrushchev's resolution to try again to take West Berlin. In any case, he was by now deeply committed, in the eyes of all Communists, to getting his way over Berlin somehow or other. Prolonged failure to do so would lower both his own prestige and that of the Soviet Union to a serious degree. But how was it to be done? Cajolery with Eisenhower had failed; would his successor be any easier to talk round? The replacement of Eisenhower by Kennedy was no help from Khrushchev's point of view. The new President was a young man, but one who had all his wits about him, and the meeting of the two leaders in Vienna in early June 1961 did not encourage Khrushchev to expect that he was going to be given West Berlin on a plate through either absence of mind or a craving for appeasement in the White House.

There remained only the possibility of a stronger pressure than had yet been used. The Americans had not been intimidated by Khrushchev's threats of making a separate peace treaty with East Germany and then daring the West to break an East German blockade. But perhaps this was because the Americans took the prospect of nuclear war too lightly. Since their initial response of alarm and despondency over the Russians' production of the intercontinental missile in 1957, they had regained confidence in their own nuclear strength. They had installed intermediate and medium range missiles in NATO countries in Europe; they had still a great superiority in long-range manned bombers; and they had now a most formidable new means of delivery for nuclear weapons in the Polaris submarine, which could bombard the Soviet Union from the Mediterranean, the Baltic or the Arctic Ocean. How then was the Soviet Union to attain a position of convincing superior strength, or at least one of such particular menace to the United States that the American will to stand firm in Europe would be weakened? In the absence of any spectacular technological breakthrough that would shatter American self-confidence, there was only one means of pressure likely to be effective: the establishment of a Soviet forward strategic base in the Western hemisphere, a nuclear launching-pad that would end the American immunity from local attack. As long as the Americans had bases in Britain, Spain, Turkey and Okinawa, while the Soviet Union had no base on the far side of the Atlantic or Pacific Oceans, the United States still possessed an immense geopolitical advantage in the global confrontation of the two super-powers.

Before 1959, the Soviet Union had no possibility of being able to deploy bombers or rockets in the Western hemisphere. But in that year Fidel Castro came to power in Cuba in close concert with the Cuban Communists and dedicated to a strongly anti-Yanqui form of national and social revolution. In January 1961, there was a rupture of diplomatic relations between Cuba and the United States. For the first time, a Latin American country was looking to the Soviet Union for economic and military assistance against the great northern neighbour. Castro's Cuba was one of the two Latin American countries geographically closest to that neighbour. For Khruschev, opportunity was now knocking at the door.

Meanwhile, in Berlin there was the Wall. The building of this barrier to seal off all contact between the people of East and West Berlin began on August 31, 1961. The Western powers protested with all possible vigour, but were hamstrung by the fact that the Wall was being built by the acknowledged civil power in East Berlin on its own side of the line dividing the Western and Russian sectors. A good many people at the time, particularly in West Germany, angrily asked why the Western powers did not 'stop' the Wall-building. The reason was that to stop the building of the barrier on the Eastern side of the sector-line would of necessity have required the use of force against the East German para-military police, with incalculably perilous consequences, for this would have been a direct attack by the West on the accepted division of political control in Berlin. Khrushchev and Ulbricht exploited to the full this basic weakness in the Western position.

For Khrushchev, the Wall was only a stopgap, but it was better than nothing; it stopped, or almost stopped, the drain of manpower from East Germany. But the Wall was a bad advertisement for Communism. It was extremely embarrassing to have to spend so much money and effort before the eyes of the whole world in order to prevent ordinary people from running away from Ulbricht's socialist paradise. Nor was the Communist image, which Khrushchevite propaganda had been trying to render more acceptable in Western liberal eyes, improved by such brutalities as the incident in which a boy, shot while trying to escape across the Wall, was left to bleed to death by Vopos who prevented medical aid from reaching him. Even so, all this unpleasant publicity was not too high a price to pay for the capacity to stop East Germans savouring freedom and prosperity in West Berlin or migrating permanently from their homes. It was a partial solution, averting the worst consequences to Communism of West Berlin's independent existence until such time as that independence might be brought to an end. Khrushchev could hope that the time was now not far off.

During 1961, a Russian military mission in Cuba was followed by the arrival of complete combat units of Russian mechanised troops, and these were followed in the spring of 1962 by anti-aircraft batteries equipped with the most up-to-date ground-to-air rockets, capable of bringing down trespassing reconnaissance aircraft, including U-2s. Then, in September 1962, in conditions of the utmost secrecy, launching equipment for medium and intermediate range ballistic missiles arrived, together with some of the missiles themselves.

Castro's agreement to the stationing of Soviet ballistic missiles in Cuba was defensive in intention. He was haunted by the fear that the United States might one day take direct military action against him. The 'Bay of Pigs' attack by anti-Castro Cuban exiles in April 1961 had proved a fiasco, despite official American collusion with the exiles; but the Cuban leader had no illusions about the capacity of his régime to withstand a real American invasion. The Russian purpose in putting missiles there, on the other hand, was not simply to defend Cuba. Weapons that could hit Washington or New York from the Caribbean could play an important part as components in a blackmailing threat the next time Khrushchev pressed his demands on Berlin. As compared with intercontinental missiles based on the Soviet Union, Cuban-based medium- and intermediate-range missiles would be cheaper, more accurate and capable of being delivered within a fraction of the radar warning-time of the intercontinentals. Once the missiles in Cuba were operational, the United States could not interfere with them without the great risk that some of them would be fired. But it was very important that the work on the installations should be concealed until they were ready. For this, reliance was placed on the anti-aircraft batteries to prevent observation from the air, while Castro's formidable secret police ensured security on the ground. At the same time, efforts were made to lull American suspicions that something unusual was going on in Cuba. On September 11, 1962, Khrushchev declared at a press conference that Soviet rockets were so powerful that they could hit any target in the world from Soviet territory, and that there was therefore no need to site them in any other country—'for example, in Cuba'. He also sent a private assurance to Kennedy through a Soviet embassy intermediary that only anti-aircraft missiles were being sent to Cuba.

Intelligence reports reaching Washington nevertheless caused so much alarm that it was decided to send a U-2 over Cuba to investigate. Since May 1960 there had been no further U-2 flights over the Soviet Union, but they had been continued over China (with Chinese Nationalist pilots), and from January 1961, when diplomatic relations with Havana were severed, they had also been carried out over Cuba. On September 9, 1962, however, a U-2 was shot down over China, and it was decided to suspend all flights for the time being, so that during the next few weeks, precisely at the time when work was being begun on ballistic missile installations in Cuba, there was no American aerial reconnaissance of the country. But the decision to suspend flights was reversed because of the reports coming in from Cuba, and a U-2 flew the whole length of the island at a height of fourteen miles, apparently undetected, on October 14. Its photographs, when analysed, showed several MRBM and IRBM sites under construction. There followed urgent top-level discussions in Washington as to the course of action to be taken. Expert advice was that the sites would become operational early in November, and that measures must be taken to eliminate them before then or it would be too late.

The purpose of the Cuban installations was revealed to President Kennedy on October 18, when Gromyko, the Soviet Foreign Minister, called on him and informed him that the Soviet Union would conclude a separate peace treaty with East Germany, immediately after the American mid-term Congressional elections on November 6, 1962. This was approximately the date by which the Cuban missile bases would become operational. At a critical point in urgent negotiations on Berlin, Khrushchev would then be able to disclose that he now had a formidable fire-power deployed on America's very doorstep.

It was decided in Washington to do four things. First, to prepare forces for an air attack on the missile sites and for an invasion of Cuba not later than the end of the month. Secondly, to declare on October 22 a naval blockade of Cuba in order to intercept missile reinforcements believed to be on their way there by sea. Thirdly, on the same day to put all American nuclear forces throughout the world in a state of instant readiness for war. Fourthly, also on the same day, to address a note to the Soviet Union demanding removal of all ballistic missiles from Cuba. President Kennedy and his advisers were fully aware of the gravity of these decisions. There was to be no definite time-limit to what was virtually an ultimatum from one nuclear power to another, but it was to be made clear to the Russians, without telling them the zero hour for the attack on Cuba, that they had not much time in which to make up their minds. The dawn of Tuesday, October 30, was in fact the hour when, if the Soviet Union had not by then agreed to withdraw its missiles from Cuba, American bombers were to go in to demolish the uncompleted installations (with conventional, not nuclear bombs), and American assault troops were to land on the Cuban coast.

The world learned with dread the full gravity of the crisis when Kennedy broadcast on October 22 his government's counterchallenge to the Soviet Union. The two great powers, for so long in hostile confrontation, were now poised on the brink of war. The onus of decision swung back to Russia. If the American ultimatum were ignored and the United States attacked Cuba, Khrushchev would have to take counteraction of some kind. There were by this time some

14,000 Russian troops in Cuba, and they would bear the brunt of the fighting there, the Cuban forces being suitable only for guerrilla warfare. It would be impossible for the Soviet Union to remain inactive while a Russian expeditionary force was overwhelmed by superior numbers. Yet nothing could be done directly to relieve the force in Cuba because Russia did not have command of the sea. The alternative for Khrushchev was either to launch a strategic nuclear attack on the United States, or to seek a compensatory gain in Europe by the seizure of West Berlin. But any hope of being able to seize West Berlin without a nuclear war was ruled out by Kennedy's solemn words in his broadcast.

We will not prematurely or unnecessarily risk the costs of world-wide nuclear war in which even the fruits of victory would be ashes in our mouth, but neither will we shrink from that risk at any time it must be faced. Any hostile move anywhere in the world against the safety and freedom of peoples to whom we are committed—including in particular the brave people of West Berlin—will be met by whatever action is needed.

Khrushchev had no reason to believe that Kennedy was bluffing. His intelligence services must have told him that American war preparations were serious.

But a face-saving way out was offered to him. If he would agree to take his missiles out of Cuba, the American government would pledge itself not to invade Cuba—which it had had no intention of doing until the missile sites were discovered there. Thus Khrushchev could say that he had achieved his purpose in putting the missiles into Cuba and had only withdrawn them when the security of Cuba was assured. This has, in fact, been ever since the official Soviet version of what happened in Cuba. Khrushchev took the way out offered and agreed to remove the missiles on October 28, two days before the American invasion of Cuba was to have been launched. He declared that, with Kennedy's assurances, 'the motives which induced us to render assistance of such a kind to Cuba disappear'. There was no peace treaty with East Germany and, so far as West Berlin was concerned, Khrushchev was back exactly where he had started five years previously.

So yet another of his experiments in the deft use of 'peaceful coexistence' had failed. All his efforts to 'relax international tension' and get hold of

West Berlin without having to fight for it had been in vain. In his own country the truth could be concealed. But the Chinese, who watched all his moves with an implacable malevolence, did not fail to point out that he had flinched from the challenge of war after having provoked it. He had put missiles into Cuba and had then taken them out again when the Americans dared him to fight.

However, whatever the Chinese might say, the world at large was profoundly thankful that war had been averted. When it was all over, there were indeed many who thought the situation had not been so dangerous after all. But the Cuban missile crisis was, in fact, one of mortal danger. Mankind was only two days away from a war that would have been the most catastrophic in all history if it had once begun. If Khrushchev had not climbed down when he did, nothing could have stopped the escalation after the first bombs on Cuba. 'Now it can go either way', were Kennedy's words after making his final offer to Moscow. It went the way of peace, but it could have gone the way of war.

14

NEUTRALISM AND THE NEW POWER BALANCE

IN FORMER TIMES, neutrality was a condition that existed only in relation to actual war; a neutral was a nation which took no part in a war waged by other states and had certain rights and duties recognised in international law. The term was not applied to nations that remained outside major alliances of powers in time of peace. Nobody in 1900 would have called Britain a neutral because it did not belong to either of the alliances then linking together the other five great powers of Europe—although it was customary to speak of Britain's 'isolation'. But, since 1945, the development of the metaphorical Cold War has produced its metaphorical neutrals, and 'neutralism' has come to be the name for national policies that aspire after inclusion in the category of states also called 'nonaligned' or 'uncommitted'.

The neutral countries today fall into two groups: those of Europe, and those of Asia, Africa and Latin America. The European neutrals are very much a minority in Europe. Not counting Spain—which, although for special political reasons not a member of NATO, is closely aligned with it—they are six in number, and five of them form two buffer zones between NATO and the Warsaw Pact powers. To the north, in the Baltic area, are Finland and Sweden; and to the south are Switzerland, Austria and Yugoslavia; on the western margin of Europe there is Ireland, which since 1922 has enjoyed an idyllic seclusion from the politics of the twentieth century. But it is only outside Europe, and away from the main confrontation of the two great military camps, that neutrals are really thick on the ground. They comprise more than half of the non-Communist states of Asia and nearly all the states of Africa. Since these countries belong also to the category of the 'under-developed' and have in the past been in a colonial or semi-colonial relation to Europe, they have much in common despite their diversity, and form a recognisable group in international affairs which has been called the 'Third World'. It extends to the south of the NATO and Soviet blocs from Morocco to Indonesia.

In time of open war, a weak neutral state in proximity to a powerful belligerent is in a dangerous situation, for the belligerent, seeking to make strategic use of its territory or utilise its economic resources for carrying on the war, may invade and over-run it. In time of peace, however, when there is a strong political rivalry between groups of nations but the direct use of armed force is in abeyance, the neutral position can be a very advantageous one. The non-aligned state will be courted by both sides, and can hold an auction for its favours without ever fully committing itself to either camp.

Since 1945 two nations in particular—India and Egypt—have successfully carried on foreign policies based on non-alignment between the Western and Soviet power blocs. In both cases, the competitive wooing of a neutral government by rival powers has been carried to such lengths that the suitors have been ready to sacrifice the interests of their own allies and supporters in pursuit of the graces of the uncommitted. Thus, for the sake of influence in Delhi, the Soviet Union failed to support its Communist partner China in the latter's quarrel with India, while Britain and the United States have strengthened India at the expense of Pakistan, their ally in the CENTO and SEATO military pacts. Similarly, in its quest for good relations with Nasser and Arab nationalism, American policy has repeatedly clashed with British and French interests, while the Soviet Union has been willing to turn a blind eye to drastic repressions of Arab Communists.

In the years after India's attainment of independence, Nehru, the Prime Minister of the new state, became the prophet of non-alignment for the peoples of Asia and Africa. India was economically poor and militarily weak, but imposing by reason of its huge population—the second largest in the world—and with a very influential position in world affairs as the natural leader of the new nations which had emerged, or were emerging, from colonial dependency, but had not undergone a Communist revolution. Nehru spoke to these nations from Indian experience, and what he said had a powerful appeal for the ex-colonial peoples. He told them that they must be independent in their foreign as well as their domestic policies, that they must no longer allow their destinies to be decided in other continents, and that they should not be 'dragged in the wake of conflicts in Europe'. Nehru also asserted the principle of 'aid without strings' as a right of under-developed countries. 'If', he declared in 1948 to a session of the United Nations Economic Commission for Asia and the Far East, 'it is considered right in the larger interest of the world that a country like India should be industrialised, and should increase and modernise its agricultural production, it is in the interest of those countries which can help to help, with capital, equipment and their special experience. But no Asian country will welcome such assistance if there are conditions attached to it which lead to any kind of economic domination. We would rather delay our development.'

In accordance with this principle, India accepted economic aid, and later also supplies of arms, from both the Western powers and the Soviet Union without considering itself to be under any political obligation to either side. Non-alignment, however, can be slanted to one side rather than the other, and over the years Indian foreign policy tended to have a definite bias in favour of the Soviet bloc. The recoil from British tutelage and the desire to show independence of judgement; the strength of the pro-Communist fellow-travelling element in the left wing of the Congress Party; sympathy for Communist China as another Asian country struggling against Western imperialism; and, after 1955, hostility to Pakistan's association with the Western powers in the Baghdad and SEATO pacts—all these factors combined to produce a trend in favour of the Communist camp on major international issues. This was demonstrated in 1950 and again in 1956. On the outbreak of the war in Korea, the Indian delegate to the Security Council voted with the majority in condemning the North Korean attack and calling on North Korea to withdraw its troops across the 38th Parallel. But this participation in an enterprise that soon came to have the appearance of a new Western intervention in Asian affairs produced a lively agitation in Delhi for nullification of the effect of India's own vote. In consequence, India contributed no combat unit to the United Nations forces in Korea, and proposed a cease-fire at a moment when the North Koreans had over-run almost the whole territory of South Korea: a peace move that, had it been accepted by the United Nations, would have secured to the North Koreans the fruits of their temporary victory. During the Suez crisis of 1956, India was unsparing in condemnation of the Anglo-French action against Egypt, but declined to take part in condemnation of the simultaneous Soviet military inter-vention in Hungary. In Nehru's view, apparently, it was morally wrong for Britain and France to use force to seize the Suez Canal, but quite permissible for Russia to use it to overthrow the government of Imre Nagy. This strange inconsistency of attitude was attributed mainly, and not without reason, to the influence of India's most notable fellow-traveller, Krishna Menon, whose close personal friendship with Nehru often enabled him to steer Indian policy into courses which Nehru, left to himself, would hardly have followed.

At the time when the Chinese Communists established their rule over China, they were extremely hostile to Nehru and the Congress régime in India. An article in a Communist magazine in September 1949 attacked Nehru in terms to which the Chinese were to revert at at a later date:

> The India of Nehru attained 'dominion status' only two years ago, and is not even formally independent in the full sense of the word. But Nehru, riding behind the imperialists whose stooge he is, considers himself the leader of the Asian peoples. Into his slavish and bourgeois reactionary character has now been instilled the beastly ambition for aggression, and he thinks that his role as a hireling of imperialism makes him an imperialist himself. He has announced that Bhutan is an Indian protectorate and now declares that Tibet has never acknowledged China's suzerainty in order to carry out his plot to create incidents in Tibet. Under the long-standing influence of British imperialism, the bourgeoisie of India, of whom Nehru is the representative, have learned the ways of the imperialists and are harbouring designs against Tibet and Sikkim as well as Bhutan. . . . As a rebel against the movement for national independence, as a blackguard who undermines the progress of the people's liberation movement, and as a loyal slave of imperialism, Nehru has already been made the substitute for Chiang Kai-shek by the imperialists.[1]

The Indian government did, indeed, aspire in 1949 to preserve the protective relations with the Himalayan states of Sikkim and Bhutan which had been established by the British Raj, and to maintain Tibet as the friendly, independent buffer state it had been since the expulsion of the Chinese garrisons in 1912. When Chinese Communist troops invaded Tibet in the summer of 1950, Nehru protested to Peking. But in the autumn he suddenly changed his policy, abandoned the cause of Tibetan independence, and blocked Tibet's appeal to the United Nations.

This reversal of India's stand on Tibet, together with the corresponding reversal of India's original support for the United Nations' action in Korea, caused Peking to take a more favourable view of Nehru and the Indian government. As the going got harder for the Chinese People's Republic, and as the shadow of Dullesian 'massive retaliation' lengthened across the China Seas, the diplomatic support of New Delhi became a very valuable asset to Peking. Scurrilous invective against Nehru was replaced by 'the Bandung spirit' and by 'Panch Sheela': the Five Principles of Peaceful Coexistence. Nehru was well pleased with this development. At the small sacrifice of the independence of Tibet, he had obtained the firm friendship of mighty and populous China. The Indian Communists and fellow-travellers were overjoyed at the growth of the concord between New Delhi and Peking, so obnoxious to America.

Yet, even during the period of blossoming goodwill, it was to be noted that the enthusiasm for the relationship on the Indian side was hardly matched in China. Indian writers and journalists, with official approval, glorified the real or alleged social and economic achievements of Communist China—and did so to an extent that proved extremely embarrassing for a country, like India, which was trying to make progress under a different system. But the Chinese public was never permitted to know of any Indian achievements, and an Indian traveller in China found that people he met declined to believe that India had a single steel plant, except for one that had been provided by Russia. The Chinese Communists accepted Indian admiration as confirming their own high opinion of themselves; their attitude to India, however, was one of pitying disdain for a country which, not having undergone a real people's revolution, must still be riddled with social contradictions and could only develop at a snail's pace. This attitude was natural enough in the middle 'fifties, for China's economic plans were far more ambitious than India's and seemed well on their way to fulfilment; China's own self-confidence and reputation abroad for economic miracles reached a climax in 1958, the first year of the Great Leap Forward, when sensational figures of progress in both industry and agriculture were published. But soon it had to be admitted that the figures for the grain harvest had been miscalculated, and then a disastrous failure in agriculture was revealed to the world by the irrefutable evidence of China's emergency purchases of wheat in Canada and Australia. The deflation of China's prestige now made comparison with India damaging for Peking. The tortoise was catching up with the hare, and it was no longer self-evident that a Communist dictatorship was better than a liberal democracy for speeding the economic advance of an underdeveloped country. Moreover, if India could rival China's economic growth, it would compete with China for political leadership of the Afro-Asian world and set itself up as another great power of Asia. This situation would have been enough to revive the earlier Chinese Communist enmity for India even if there had been no more direct and immediate conflict between the two countries. But already, even before China's stumbling in the Great Leap Forward had compelled Peking to take India seriously as an international rival, the latent dispute over territorial claims in the Himalayan borderland had broken out in an open quarrel that soon pricked the glittering bubble of Panch Sheela.

When Nehru, yielding to pro-Chinese influences in his entourage, abandoned his diplomatic opposition to the Chinese reconquest of Tibet, certain persons in the Indian bureaucracy, without his knowledge, engaged in a collusion with China that was to have far-reaching consequences.* Indian Communists, fellow-travellers within the Congress Party, extreme nationalists hostile to Pakistan, and the pro-Indian faction in Kashmir were united in hoping for at least the benevolent neutrality of China in the event of a renewal of warfare in Kashmir. Hence, the Chinese in the winter of 1950–51 were able, without arousing public awareness in India, to send a column of troops from the province of Sinkiang into western Tibet across the north-east salient of Kashmir territory known as the Aksai Chin, and in 1956–57 to construct a military road along the same route. The Aksai Chin, an area of high plateau between the Karakoram and Kunlun mountain ranges, was uninhabited save for herdsmen in summer, but it was marked as Indian territory on Indian official maps. It was not until

---

* That some Indian officials must have been aware of what was going on in north-east Ladakh is indicated by the evidence of Indian police patrols in the area in the Report of the Joint Chinese–Indian Boundary Commission, published in Delhi in 1961.

October 1958 that Nehru heard about the road. He then sent to Peking a Note protesting at China's action in building a road across a stretch of 'indisputably Indian territory' without asking permission from the Indian government. Peking replied with the claim that the Aksai Chin was Chinese territory. Subsequent diplomatic correspondence brought out the fact that China did not consider any part of the Sino-Indian frontier to have been properly demarcated, and claimed not only the Aksai Chin, but also 40,000 square miles of tribal territory to the north of Assam included in the Indian North East Frontier Agency (NEFA). Nehru was alarmed to learn that the frontier was in dispute, and complained that the Chinese had told him nothing about their claims when, in 1954, he had concluded a treaty recognising Chinese sovereignty in Tibet and renouncing the special rights there that India had inherited from the British Raj. To this, Peking replied that the frontier issue had not been raised in 1954 because 'conditions were not yet ripe for its settlement and the Chinese side had had no time to study the question'.

Still clinging to Panch Sheela, and unwilling to lose the friendship of China for the sake of a desert plateau, Nehru sought a compromise and at the same time endeavoured to retain his freedom in negotiation by minimising in speeches to the Indian parliament the importance of the Aksai Chin. He made members from Madras and Bengal shiver in their seats by telling them how terribly cold it was in that high altitude, and deployed all his powers of eloquence to emphasise the worthlessness and remoteness of the area. But it was too late. Indian public opinion was aroused and was not prepared to allow an inch of Indian national territory to be surrendered. Nor was a policy of conciliation made any easier for Nehru by the insolent tone of the Chinese diplomatic Notes, so different from the political billing and cooing of 1955, or by a vituperative anti-Indian propaganda in the Chinese press.

The dispute over the frontier was complicated and aggravated by a revolt in Tibet. This reached its climax in the spring of 1959, when the Dalai Lama fled from Lhasa and sought political asylum in India to escape arrest by the Chinese authorities. The Indian government had done nothing to help the rebels, and up to the time of the flight of the Dalai Lama had denied that there was any trouble in Tibet, even threatening to deport a British correspondent who transmitted detailed reports of it to his newspaper. This did not prevent the Chinese government from declaring that 'American imperialists and the Chiang Kai-shek clique' had engineered the revolt, using Kalimpong in India as their base with the connivance of the Indian government. The accusations against India were multiplied when Nehru, acting under strong pressure from public opinion which was strongly moved by sympathy for the Tibetans, granted asylum to the Dalai Lama and allowed him to hold press conferences that gave world-wide publicity to what had happened in Tibet. Feeling against China was already running high in India when, in October 1959, the verbal dispute over the frontier turned into actual conflict. An Indian military patrol in Ladakh, within what was claimed in Delhi as Indian territory, was attacked by Chinese troops, some of the men being killed and the rest captured. Nehru refused to be provoked into armed reprisals, but it became harder than ever for him to make concessions in negotiation with China.

It was at this point that the Soviet Union became involved in the Sino-Indian conflict. In the early 'fifties, there had been less goodwill in India for Russia than for China. Russia was regarded as a European, and not as an Asian, power, and official Indian opinion considered that non-alignment in the Cold War required a restraint in dealings with Russia as well as with the United States. However, after the state visit of Khrushchev and Bulganin to India in November 1955, Indian national sentiment warmed towards Moscow. Russia now began to exert a powerful influence in Delhi, partly because of the economic aid that it was now able to provide in competition with the West, but mainly because Moscow had come out unequivocally on the side of India in the dispute with Pakistan over Kashmir. Pakistan had been persuaded to join with Britain, Iraq, Turkey and Iran in the Baghdad Pact, an alliance formed with the backing, though not with the formal participation, of the United States as part of the defensive system for the 'containment' of the Soviet Union. Pakistan had no common frontier with the Soviet Union, and was not under any immediate threat of Soviet aggression. In joining a combination of states intended to restrain Soviet expansion, the Pakistani government undoubtedly had in mind primarily the strengthening of its position vis-à-vis India. Although the Baghdad Pact was not formally applicable to its quarrel with India, Pakistan hoped, as an ally of Britain and virtually also of the United States, to enjoy both a priority over non-aligned India in economic and military aid from the West, and also Western diplomatic support in its struggle for Kashmir. In fact, Britain and the United States avoided any active intervention on the side of Pakistan in the Kashmir dispute, but at least they were precluded by their alliance from coming out on the side of India. Now, support for India was just what Russia, regarding the Baghdad Pact states as a hostile confederacy, was only too willing to give. The forthright Soviet declaration in 1955 that Kashmir—the whole of Kashmir and not only the part actually in Indian control—rightly belonged to India was naturally much appreciated in Delhi, and it created the conviction among many Indians, far from sympathetic to Communism, that India's case against Pakistan was better understood by Russia than by the Western powers.

Even though Sino-Indian relations were still friendly at the time of the Russian declaration over Kashmir, and the tension over the frontier had not yet arisen, Communist China avoided endorsement of the Soviet support for the Indian case against Pakistan. Moscow could give such support without reservations because Russia had no common frontier with India and no potential disputes with it over territorial jurisdiction. Peking, on the other hand, was always aware that, because of the extent of its claims in the Himalayan borderland, conflicts with India must arise sooner or later; the Chinese therefore considered it expedient to leave the way open for an understanding with Pakistan, even though the latter had become a member of the SEATO alliance directed against China, as well as of the Baghdad Pact alliance directed against Russia.

As a result of Russia's backing up India's case on Kashmir, Moscow's diplomatic position in Delhi had, by 1959, become an extremely favourable one. The Soviet government was most reluctant to spoil it by any undue partiality for China in the Sino-Indian frontier dispute. For as long as they could, the Russians refrained from any involvement in the dispute. But when military clashes took place on the frontier—first at Lonju in August 1959, and then in Ladakh two months later—and extended hostilities between India and China became a serious possibility, Moscow issued the declaration of neutrality which the Chinese Communists were subsequently to represent as an unpardonable betrayal of one Communist country by another. On September 9,

1959, the TASS news agency called the Sino-Indian conflict 'deplorable'. In calling on the two countries to settle it, the statement made no suggestion that China was in the right and India in the wrong. Khrushchev at a press conference on November 8 affirmed that he would do all he could to help find a solution to the problem, but his statement contained no condemnation of India or any expression of support for the Chinese contention that Nehru was being egged on by American imperialists to encroach on Chinese territory. In taking up the attitude he did, Khrushchev undoubtedly offended against the principle of the solidarity of Communist states in all dealings with the capitalist world, and repudiated a most important part of Communist doctrine: the claim that all wars are necessarily of capitalist origin and that no socialist country can ever be guilty of aggression. Although he did not actually take the Indian side over the border incidents, he implied that the Chinese were just as likely as the Indians to have been to blame for them.

It was a further Chinese grievance that so much Soviet economic aid was going to India at a time when China was badly in need of it. China had derived great benefit from Soviet aid; but, after the upheavals in Eastern Europe in the autumn of 1956, the priority in large-scale Russian economic support was given to the European Communist satellites to enable their governments to allay popular discontent. At the same time, substantial aid was extended to India, Egypt and other uncommitted countries which were also receiving economic assistance from the West. These charges on Soviet bounty meant so much the less for China, and Peking watched with growing indignation Nehru's gracious acceptance of gifts from India's competing suitors. Although it could be argued that Soviet influence in Delhi was to the advantage of the Communist bloc as a whole, the Chinese held that Communist countries should come first in the distributing of economic aid, especially since they were precluded from obtaining aid from the West. The grievance was greatly aggravated in the summer of 1960 when the Soviet Union, exasperated by the Chinese ideological opposition to its policies, abruptly withdrew Russian technicians from China and cancelled a number of industrial contracts. It appeared that, though aid to India might be without strings, aid to China was certainly conditional on subservience to the will of Moscow. Nor was Khrushchev content merely to strengthen India's economic position, while leaving the Chinese to sink or swim as best they could: he was ready to help in building up India's armed power as well. In spite of British protests, Krishna Menon, as Indian Defence Minister, accepted a Russian offer to supply India with MIG fighter aircraft, and also to set up a factory in India for making them.

When warfare broke out between India and China in the Assam Himalaya in October and November 1962, the Indian army was badly beaten. Britain and the United States rushed arms and munitions to India, and Krishna Menon was forced out of office by public indignation at the disaster. For a moment, it seemed that India would be drawn into the Western orbit. But Nehru was determined not to lose his uncommitted position. He showed the minimum appreciation of British and American help, sang the praises of the Russian MIG fighters even before any had actually been delivered, and attributed the withdrawal of the Chinese forces after their victory to Russian pressure on Peking (there has never been any evidence to support this). Thus he contrived to remain non-aligned, morally elevated above the senseless quarrels of the Cold War, courted as before by both the Soviet Union and the West, and respected as the friend of all nations—except his two principal neighbours.

It was not only China that had felt aggrieved by the competition between the Soviet Union and the Western powers for the good graces of Nehru. Just as Moscow had ignored the interests and sentiments of China, so London and Washington ignored the interests and sentiments of Pakistan. The massive military aid to India from Britain and the United States (accompanied internally in India by a doubling of the numbers of the Indian army) was intended only to strengthen India against a renewed attack by China; but it could not fail also to strengthen India against Pakistan. This aroused lively resentment among Pakistanis. They pointed out that India would not have been so weak on the China border if it had not kept the bulk of its armed forces concentrated against Pakistan in the Punjab. After years of non-alignment and refusal to co-operate with Pakistan in a system of joint defence of the subcontinent, India was now being given priority for Western military aid. Yet there could be no guarantee that India would not reach a settlement with China and turn its newly increased power against Pakistan. Such was the grievance of the Pakistani government. It suggested that Britain and the United States should at least make their military aid to India conditional on Indian concessions to Pakistan over Kashmir. London and Washington were unwilling to do this, but they managed to persuade Nehru in 1963 to reopen negotiations with Pakistan. The Indian position, however, remained as uncompromising as before; after several months of unfruitful discussion, the negotiations ended in deadlock.

Meanwhile, unable to get support from any of India's friends, Pakistan had turned to India's enemy. The Chinese amicably settled some unresolved border disputes they had with Pakistan, just as they had also settled similar disputes with Burma and Nepal. The way was clear for an entente between the two countries. In July 1963, the Pakistani Foreign Minister declared that, in the event of aggression by India, Pakistan would have the support of 'the largest Asian state'. It was possible to infer from his words the existence of a secret military understanding between Rawalpindi and Peking. If there was indeed such a bond, it meant that, while America was arming neutralist India against China, America's ally Pakistan was in league with China against India. But, whatever they might suspect, neither the Americans nor the British could afford to repudiate their obligations to Pakistan. Since the revolution in Iraq in 1958, Pakistan had been the indispensable prop of CENTO, the successor-alliance to the Baghdad Pact, and the disruption of this alliance would mean the surrender of Iran to Soviet ascendancy and the extension of Soviet power to the Persian Gulf.

In the autumn of 1965, the smouldering antagonism between India and Pakistan over Kashmir burst out into open warfare. While the two armies fought each other in Kashmir and in the plains of the Punjab, China massed troops on India's Himalayan frontier and made gestures of menace, accusing India—for want of any more serious grievance—of thefts of yaks and sheep from Chinese territory. Whether or not China actually had the intention of launching a military offensive, its troop-concentrations compelled India to keep a large part of its army facing China, and thus they indirectly helped Pakistan, which would have been in a hopelessly weak position if the bulk of the Indian army could have been massed in the Punjab.

With China and Pakistan combining, in effect, against India, both the United States and the Soviet Union moved swiftly to stop the war and avert an Indian collapse beneath the feared Chinese aggression. For the first time since the founding of the United Nations, the two great antagonists of the Cold War acted in concert over a major issue in the Security Council. A resolution that called for a cease-fire was passed, and the backing of the two super-powers was sufficient to ensure that it was observed. In the sequel, the Soviet Union provided its good offices as mediator between the belligerents. An interim settlement was reached at a conference in Tashkent in January 1966: the place of meeting itself representing a triumph for Soviet policy since it symbolised the Soviet Union's status as an Asian power, a status rejected by the Chinese. The United States was prepared to acquiesce in Russia's assumption of the mediator's role in the affairs of the Indian sub-continent, since at any rate this impeded China; but America strove by fresh economic aid, especially for the relief of famine conditions in India, to preserve its influence in Delhi. Pakistan, thwarted in Kashmir and deeply resentful towards the two super-powers, yet not daring openly to defy them, continued sullenly to nurse its grievances and to cherish the alignment between Rawalpindi and Peking. Liu Shao-chi, President of the Chinese People's Republic, paid a visit to Pakistan in March 1966, and publicly reaffirmed China's 'unswerving support' over Kashmir.

The complications that arose in south Asia from the competitive courting of non-aligned India by the Western powers and the Soviet Union had an analogy in events ensuing from the rivalries for influence over uncommitted Egypt from 1955 onwards. The Western powers, after the conclusion of the war between the Arab states and Israel by the 1949 armistice, had tried to preserve peace in the Middle East by restricting supplies of arms both to Israel and to its Arab neighbours so that neither side would be able to resume hostilities. However, in the autumn of 1955, large supplies of arms from the Soviet bloc were offered to Egypt. This not only established the Soviet Union as a rival influence to the Western powers in Cairo, but encouraged the Egyptians to look forward to undertaking a fresh assault on Israel, this time with Soviet support. Russian policy had been favourable to Israel in 1948, when Zionism had been in acute conflict with Britain; but since then it had veered round to an anti-Israeli course because of the attraction the new Jewish state had for Jews in the Soviet Union and the Communist countries of Eastern Europe. Russia now posed as the champion of Arab nationalism against the imperialism of Britain and the United

States, and against their obnoxious creation on Arab soil: the state of Israel.

Nasser took the fullest advantage of this Russian bidding. Britain and America were required to show themselves not less anti-Israeli than the Russians if they were to retain any place in Egyptian favour. They tried hard to stay in the auction by condoning the *fedayeen* raids and other hostile Egyptian actions against Israel. After the nationalisation of the Suez Canal, the American, British and French governments were united for a short time in putting pressure on Egypt to accept an international authority over the Canal. When Nasser proved obdurate, however, the American government took the line that it was essential to recover influence in Cairo, and that therefore the Canal must be left under full Egyptian control. The Anglo-French military intervention in Egypt in 1956 found the United States in opposition and therefore lined up with the Soviet Union on the issue in the United Nations. Britain and France used their vetoes to bar a resolution for a cease-fire, introduced into the Security Council by the United States. When a similar resolution was carried in the Assembly by 64 votes to 5, the American and Russian delegations voted together with the majority. The Soviet Union, at that time busily suppressing the rising in Hungary, exploited the rift in the Western alliance to embarrass the American government and to represent itself as the protector of the Arab world. A Soviet Note to Washington called on the United States to join with the Soviet Union in waging war against Britain and France to compel them to withdraw from Egypt. President Eisenhower was not prepared to go quite so far, even to prove to Nasser that he was a better friend to him than Khrushchev. Indeed, he at once issued a statement to the effect that the United States would oppose Russian military intervention in the Middle East. But the Soviet government's declaration that it was 'fully determined to crush the aggressors and restore peace in the Middle East through the use of force' had an intimidating effect on London and Paris, and enabled Moscow to proclaim to the Arab world that the cease-fire which was finally brought about had been entirely due to Soviet threats.

For a while, the Russian star was in the ascendant, not only in Cairo, but in all Arab lands; while Nasser emerged from his catastrophic military defeat at the hands of the Israelis as a triumphant hero with nearly all the world on his side. Nevertheless, Nasser's gratitude to

Moscow did not extend to willingness to tolerate Arab Communists, either in Egypt or anywhere else in the Arab world. Nasser's ideal was one of pure Arab nationalism under his own predominance: there was no room in it for a Communist party either as a sharer of power or as a legal opposition. Hence the warm associate of Soviet Russia in general international affairs was to be found suppressing the Communists in Egypt and helping to crush them in Syria, where they had built up a strong position. The linking in 1963 of Syria with Egypt in the United Arab Republic was primarily due to the willingness of conservative elements in Syria to accept Nasser's rule for the time being as the alternative to a further growth of Communist power. Nasser's anti-Communism, however, while winning him golden opinions in Washington, did not deter the Soviet Union from continuing to seek his favour by subsidising the construction of the Aswan Dam and by supplying large quantities of modern weapons for the Egyptian armed forces.

The bidding for influence in Cairo between the United States and the Soviet Union continued, and in 1962 it led the former to promote Egyptian interests at the expense of its British ally. The coup that overthrew the Imam of the Yemen in that year was supported by a strong Egyptian expeditionary force sent across the Red Sea. This, the first step in Nasser's design for a Pan-Arab unification of Arabia, was a serious threat to the British position in Aden: the last stronghold for the protection of the threatened British oil interests in Kuwait, and a vital base of operations for the military aid promised, if needed, to Iran as a member of CENTO. The United States, none the less, hastened to recognise the new régime in the Yemen without waiting for the outcome of the civil war there between royalists and republicans, and without obtaining any effective guarantees for the withdrawal of Egyptian troops. It seemed that, in the eyes of the State Department, the opportunity to do a good turn to the dictator of Egypt outweighed every other consideration.

The most serious aspect of Egypt's political auction, however, was the evident intention of Nasser to use it to obtain active support for, or at least acquiescence in, his projected war against Israel. In this bidding, the Soviet Union had a basic advantage for it had no scruples about aiding and abetting a state engaging in aggressive war in the name of anti-imperialism—as was shown by its vote on behalf of Indonesia in the Security Council in September 1964, after the Indonesian paratroop landings in Malaya. The Western powers were hardly likely to go so far in the effort to please Nasser; yet, in their attempts to keep up with the Soviet bidding, they might well in effect connive at Arab aggression against Israel, particularly as the countries of Western Europe were vulnerable to an oil embargo by the Arab states. The Secretary-General of the Arab League declared in 1965 that oil should be employed by the Arabs as a weapon in support of causes in which they were interested, especially the Palestine question. Probably the only way in which war between Arabs and Israelis could be averted would be by a clear declaration by the United States that it would not be tolerated. If Washington were to prove too susceptible to Arab resentment to make such a declaration, events would be likely to take their course until the day when a war of the most extreme ferocity would convulse the Middle East: a war in which the Israelis, faced with the annihilation promised them by the Arabs, would certainly use all the resources of modern science to defend themselves.

The examples of the uncommitted role, as played by India and Egypt in the period of world-wide hostility between the Western and the Soviet camps, show how diplomatically strong the non-aligned position can be even when sustained only by a weak economy and very inferior military strength. The more equally balanced the great power blocs, the keener the rivalry for the support of the uncommitted, or at least for influence to prevent them from joining the other side. A skilful political leader can use the posture of non-alignment to get more and more economic aid and armaments from both sides and, on occasion, endorsement for provocative or aggressive policies.

Moreover, the psychological effect of competitive bidding for the favour of the uncommitted is such that the great powers which engage in this auction tend to sacrifice the interests of their own allies, whose loyalty has come to be taken for granted, in order to win states that are bound by no alliances but incline this way or that according to the offers made to them. The good fortune of the Third World in time of peace—but its peril in a time of general war—is for it to be disputed between the two major power blocs.

PART FOUR

PATTERNS OF THE FUTURE

15

THE LOOSENING OF THE ALLIANCES

ALL THE FIVE STATES recognised as great powers by permanent membership of the Security Council of the United Nations were, by the middle of 1950, ranged by treaties of military alliance in one or other of two opposed camps. The United States, Britain and France were bound together by the North Atlantic Treaty, while the Soviet Union was linked by a military pact with the government which had *de facto* control of nearly the whole of China. These were blocs of ideology as well as of national interests. The democracies of the West stood opposed to the countries of Communist party dictatorship—or, as the Communists themselves called it, of 'socialism'. To the Big Five were soon attached on one side or the other the two major defeated powers of the Second World War: the larger part of Germany and the whole of Japan were linked to the West, while East Germany went with Russia. Various treaties also joined a number of lesser states to one or other of the two blocs.

However, these combinations, although giving a certain definiteness of structure to the political landscape of the world, were not altogether stable. Stresses and strains of two kinds affected them. One danger to their permanence arose from the existence in each country of a political opposition to the established foreign policy, or even to the form of the state: an opposition which might change the government either through elections or through revolution, and swing the country from its existing alliances into neutrality or into the opposite camp.

All the Western democracies, and also Japan, tolerated the activity of Communist parties and the advocacy of neutralism and pacifism. These factors often added up to a powerful political force. When France signed the North Atlantic Treaty, the French Communist Party, though it had declined from the position of strength it had in 1945, still commanded the votes of the greater part of the industrial working class. In Britain in the late 1950s, the Campaign for Nuclear Disarmament came to exert considerable influence in favour, not only of unilateral renunciation of nuclear weapons, but also of neutrality in the Cold War. In America, where the tradition of isolationism died hard, policies advocating strategic involvement in Europe and Asia and the containment of Communism, even though supported by the leaders of both of the main political parties, were subjected to pungent criticism by a number of influential public personalities. Perhaps the most notable of such critics has been Senator Fulbright, who has sought to promote American disengagement from Asia. In Germany, where revulsion from the Nazi régime often produced pure pacifism or a cynical detachment from all politics, the *Ohne Mich* attitude was widespread. And in Japan, where the threat of Soviet domination was less obvious than in the case of Germany, neutralist agitation against the Security Pact with the United States became so violent in the summer of 1960 that President Eisenhower had to cancel his intended visit to Tokyo. Yet in none of the countries mentioned were the main foreign policy alignments, once adopted, deflected by the internal political opposition. Even in Japan, the Security Pact was ratified, and a general election showed a clear majority for the party supporting it. The only case of a state's definitely breaking away from the Western alliance system was Iraq, where the coup d'état of 1958 put an end to that country's adherence to the Baghdad Pact.

In Communist countries, there could be no open opposition to official foreign policies. Unless the Communist régime in a given country turned sour towards Moscow, popular discontent with the alliances could only exist underground. Yet such discontent did exist. It burst forth in 1956 in Hungary, whose departure from the Warsaw Pact coalition would have been as complete as Iraq's from the Baghdad Pact had not the revolution been crushed by Russian military intervention. Among Communists it had been taken for granted before 1948 that, even without any formal treaties of alliance, Communist parties in power would stand together as military allies against the capitalist world. But after Yugoslavia had proclaimed a policy of neutrality between the power blocs, it was clearly shown to be possible for a state to profess Communist principles without belonging to the Soviet system of military alliances. In so far as the Yugoslav League of Communists was eventually accepted during Khrushchev's period of rule as a 'fraternal' party by the Communists of the Soviet Union, its right to neutrality came to be admitted by them. It must be remembered, however, that in certain circumstances one country can be more helpful as a neutral than as an ally. Germany would have been better off if Italy had remained neutral throughout the Second World War; and a friendly Yugoslavia can contribute more to Soviet policy as a channel of political influence on the uncommitted countries than it can by its relatively small military strength.

Even so, neither in the Western nor the Soviet bloc has the principal danger of disruption come from internal opposition to the alignments adopted by governments. The main danger has come from conflicts among the allied states within the framework of the alliances, and without any formal repudiation of them. Even de Gaulle, in withdrawing France from NATO as a military organisation, has not repudiated his political alliances. Indeed, in the controversies that have arisen, the main charges have been that a partner in a particular alliance has failed to live up to its spirit or to show the consideration due to an equal fellow-member of an international coalition. The conflicts of General de Gaulle with Washington, and of Mao Tse-tung with Moscow, have both been essentially revolts of junior against senior partners, and have been inspired by resentment at what was considered to be overbearing and detrimental behaviour on the part of the stronger ally. Alliances may be based on national interest, or on a common ideology, or on a combination of both; but in all cases they require great diplomatic skill and tact if they are to be kept in good working order. Allies remain sovereign states with special interests, which may conflict, and with peculiarities of outlook due to differences of national experience and tradition. The discrepancies require adjustment. This is easier if the allies are either approximately equal in power so that they are conscious of dealing *inter pares,* or if there is a very great disparity of strength, so that the weaker state is ready to accept a subordinate role. The greatest difficulty arises when, given a considerable disparity of power but not so great a disparity as to be different in kind, the weaker state is not ready to be treated as less than equal. The weaker state may be particularly intractable either because it is in decline as a great power and clings to a grandeur that it can no longer properly sustain, or because it is on the upgrade and measures its rights in accordance with a future greatness to which it confidently looks forward. Britain and France have been examples of the first type in the contemporary world, and China of the second type.

Britain and France were the greatest powers of yesterday: the pioneers of the industrial revolution and the creators of vast colonial empires. They had long been dwindling relatively to the rising power of America, Germany and Russia before the Second World War, but it was only after 1945 that their decline to the second rank became fully manifest with the dissolution of their colonial empires and the emergence of America and Russia as powers of a higher category. They still, indeed, had assets that made them internationally important: highly developed industries and eminent capacities in science and technology; great experience in diplomacy; and world-wide financial and trading contacts. But their pretensions in the age after Hitler arose, at least in part, from a refusal to admit how much they had come down in the world. Like impoverished noble families, they tried to keep up a standard and style of living which they could no longer afford, and scorned the 'nouveaux riches' of the world community even when reduced to begging favours from them.

The case of China was different. China also had a great history and proud traditions of imperial splendour; but the more recent past had been one of disaster and humiliation in the field of international politics, and of intolerable backwardness in that of economic and scientific affairs. Far from having been in the vanguard of modern industrial progress, China had been its most conspicuous laggard. But China had a vast territory and the largest population of any country in the world. The Chinese looked to the future with the consciousness of being a rising and not a declining people, however weak they might be at the moment. They might nourish their national pride on the faded glories of imperial Peking, but their thoughts were without nostalgia. The Communist revolution in China had been a drastic and bloody break with the past, and the Chinese aimed at a day when their standing in the world should be worthy of their numbers and their great economic and military potential. Meanwhile they would resist any attempt by nations that might be jealous of their rising power to direct their development or impose fetters on their freedom of action.

The states of mind generated in the British and French as nations by their efforts to resist their relative diminution, and in the Chinese by their struggle to attain the great power status to which they deemed themselves entitled, brought each of them into conflict with the super-powers to which they were respectively allied.

In the West, both Britain and France, though dependent on the United States for the maintenance of a balance of power in Europe by which alone they could remain independent, were frequently at loggerheads with Washington. But there were fundamental reasons why this was more serious in the case of France than of Britain.

Britain claimed to have—and really did have, in spite of all tiffs and altercations—a 'special relationship' with the United States. The stress on common language and historic origins, which is the central theme of Churchill's *History of the English-speaking Peoples*, is politically valid even though it can easily be reduced to absurdity by sentimental exaggeration. However, what has been historically more important than the mere fact of a predominantly 'Anglo-Saxon' settlement in America north of the Rio Grande has been the persistent effort of British diplomacy over a long period to avoid dangerous crises in Anglo-American relations, and to build up a permanent entente (though this word was never used) between London and Washington. This has been too much taken for granted by historians. The effort, in fact, was remarkable for it could so easily have been otherwise. Lord Strang, in his interesting study of British diplomatic history, *Britain in World Affairs*, has shown how, on several occasions during the nineteenth century, the two countries could have drifted into war if British policy had been less restrained than it was. Until Canada became independent, Britain had direct responsibility for a long land frontier with the United States, while in Latin America right up to the beginning of the present century there were points of serious conflict between the two countries. The Americans had not forgotten Yorktown (or the burning of the White House in 1812) even if the British had, and there were always those in the United States who were ready for another go at the mercenaries of King George III, his heirs and successors. In Britain, there long persisted an attitude that refused to take the United States seriously as a stable political entity or as an emerging great power. But a sure political instinct, rather than any formulated theory of foreign policy, told British statesmen at the height of their country's power that friendship with the United States was essential for an island nation that lay outside the continent of Europe but could always be endangered from it.

The wisdom of this conviction was demonstrated in two great wars, in both of which the British came near to disaster, and again in 1949 when the United States signed—and ratified—the North Atlantic Treaty. During the Second World War, the co-operation and joint planning of British and American military staffs and economic agencies was so close as to resemble the workings of a federation rather than a normal wartime alliance. This experience of common activities laid the foundation for joint commands and staff work when NATO was brought into being. All this was not incompatible, as so many war memoirs reveal, with arduous—and sometimes ferocious—wrangles and disputes. Yet it added up to a degree of habitual collaboration quite exceptional among sovereign states.

The British tendency to look across the Atlantic rather than across the Channel for the closest international understanding did not diminish even when America began to remind Britain that it was a European country and should participate in some kind of European union. The British, generally speaking, simply did not feel themselves to be part of Europe. The European ideal flourished only among a small minority, and even those (like Churchill) who professed an enthusiasm for it were singularly inactive when it came to doing anything about it. In Washington, it appeared self-evident that Western Europe would be stronger and more prosperous if its constituent states came together in a form of federal union, and would, moreover, be able to relieve the United States of part of the burden of world-wide strategic responsibilities it had assumed as a result of its foreign policy from 1947 onwards. But in Britain the prospect of being merged in a federation with Frenchmen, Germans and Italians—peoples who were foreign in a way the Americans were not*—was profoundly distasteful. When the Conservative government in 1962, after having refused to have anything to do with the European Common Market at its inception, finally resolved to take the plunge and apply for membership, political attitudes among the two major parties ranged from formal

* A woman who kept a boarding-house, when admonished by a policeman for not having registered American guests as foreigners, replied: 'But Americans aren't foreigners; they speak English just like we do.' This was not a sophisticated view, but it was more representative of ordinary English sentiment than might be supposed.

opposition by the Labour Party to resigned indifference, mingled with disquiet, among most of the government's own supporters. Probably no nation was ever so relieved at not getting what it wanted as Britain was when the negotiations for entry broke down in January 1963. Even though it was recognised that Britain, like America, must keep an army on the Rhine and that the days of 'splendid isolation' could not return, the British people as a whole still clung to the twin ideals of detachment from continental Europe and a special relationship with the United States.

This is not to say that there were not deep currents of feeling critical of, and indeed hostile to, the United States. Anti-Americanism flourished both on the extreme left and on the extreme right of British politics. But it counted for little between these extremes. On the left, the Communists, fellow-travellers and unilateralist nuclear disarmers inveighed against the alliance with the 'war-mongering capitalists' of Wall Street and the 'aggressive militarists' of the Pentagon; they demanded friendship with Russia, withdrawal from NATO, and the removal of American bombers from British airfields. At the opposite end of the political spectrum were those who regarded the United States as the wrecker of the British Empire, always ready to curry favour with Asians and Africans at Britain's expense.[1] It was, indeed, true that American policy was hostile to the old European colonial system, partly from an anti-colonial ideology—which was not, however, as strong in Truman or Eisenhower as in Roosevelt—and partly because, as the Cold War with the Soviet Union developed, it seemed in Washington essential to conciliate nationalist sentiments and aspirations in Asia and Africa. If Britain had resolutely tried to maintain its colonial empire after 1945, the conflict with America on this issue might have become acute. But it soon became evident that British governments—and not even the change back from Attlee to Churchill reversed the process—were of their own accord dismantling the Empire as fast as they could.

As it was, the one major crisis in Anglo-American relations arose out of an old imperial interest of Britain's. At the end of October 1956, the Anglo-French ultimatum to Egypt brought relations between London and Washington to a point of extreme tension. For the 'Suez Group' Conservatives, the American attitude at that time confirmed their worst fears and suspicions. But it was the sequel to Suez rather than the bitter feelings aroused at the time that was significant. The British national attitude after it was all over was superficially a rather inconsistent one, yet characteristic of a fundamental political outlook. In spite of moral thunders from the left at an aggression violating the United Nations Charter, there was no 'national repentance' over Suez. The British people in general wished the venture had succeeded and forgave the Conservative government for its failure, so that the Labour Party found it impossible to make it a good campaign issue in the general election of 1959. On the other hand, the British people also forgave America for having thwarted the venture, and a year after the débâcle there was astonishingly little resentment against America harboured among them. Once more, a deep political instinct was prevailing over an unpleasantness arising from an issue that was seen to have no permanent relevance in Anglo American relations, since what had happened in Egypt was now irrevocable. In short, no crying over spilt milk. The important thing was to restore the special relationship. For a brief period during the Suez crisis, when Khrushchev threatened with his rockets, Britain had perceived what it would mean to face war with Russia without the American alliance. The momentary glimpse had been enough to make that alliance seem far more important than anything else.

In the field that has come to have the greatest significance for strategic power in the new era, the special relationship worked well, though not without some friction. Britain had participated during the war in the early stages of the scientific work for the development of the American atomic bomb. Later on, when the question arose of the independent production of the bomb by Britain, this experience rendered it relatively easy for the British to make it. Legislation by Congress prohibited disclosure of atomic secrets to any other nation, and subsequent spy scandals in Britain did not dispose senators to revise the law in favour of Britain. But there was initially no American objection to Britain's becoming a nuclear power on its own, as there was to be later to the French nuclear programme. The American Strategic Air Command co-operated very closely with the Royal Air Force Bomber Command, which was responsible for the deployment of British nuclear weapons when they were produced. The American outlook came to be modified when more emphasis was laid in the Pentagon on conventional military forces for the defence of Western

Europe, and it was then held that Britain would do better to leave the nuclear deterrent to the United States and concentrate its defence budget on its too small and inadequately equipped army. Yet British opposition to such a division of functions did not cause excessive irritation in Washington, and when the Skybolt missile, on trial in the United States for the Royal Air Force, had to be scrapped owing to poor performance in testing, President Kennedy was quite willing for Britain to have the Polaris submarine missile instead. Criticism of the arrangement in Britain on the ground that it would mean a permanent dependence on the United States for supplies of nuclear weapons, so that Britain would not have a really 'independent deterrent', had no great effect because there was confidence that America would carry out the agreement and would not try to force Britain to renounce nuclear power.

The French endeavour to develop nuclear power, on the other hand, was differently regarded in Washington because it was undertaken in a political context of antagonism to America. The Suez crisis, coming after the bitter Franco-American disagreements over Indochina, convinced French official circles that France would not be treated with proper respect by America unless it had an independent nuclear capacity of its own. The decision to go ahead with the production of nuclear weapons, and make France a fourth nuclear power, was taken before the return of General de Gaulle to political leadership in 1958. But it was his leadership that sought to make the 'force de frappe' a symbol of France's revival as a great power. He initiated a grandiose policy of building up a Western European 'third force', based on Paris, as a new political combination independent of both Washington and Moscow. In de Gaulle's view, the situation in Europe was favourable to this policy if France would rise to its opportunities, for Germany was no longer a rival and stronger power challenging France. After 1945, Germany was not only disarmed and partitioned, but so oppressed by the new power of Russia that its western part was wholly dependent on its association with America, Britain and France. Not less vital to West Germany than the American military presence in Europe was friendship with France. Far from seeing Germany as a threat, de Gaulle perceived in this situation the opportunity for a close Franco-German entente that would make him the leader of a united Western Europe.

There were no other rivals challenging France. Britain had excluded itself from European political and economic union for too long to be an effective obstacle to de Gaulle's policy. Italy was no longer the jealous rival of France that it had been under Mussolini; the latter's disastrous military campaigns that had brought the nation to utter defeat in the Second World War had left the Italians with little stomach for ambitious ventures and with a relatively modest view of their place in the world. The way was therefore open for France to organise Western Europe under its own leadership.

The Common Market was to provide the economic framework for this political combination. A union of Western Europe need not in itself mean any weakening of NATO; indeed, it could strengthen it by providing a greater unity among NATO's European members. The United States was fully in favour of the Common Market, on the understanding that it included Britain, whose presence therein would prevent a French domination of it and ensure that it was not given an anti-American twist. But it was precisely these considerations that made British entry unacceptable to de Gaulle. His vetoing further negotiations between Britain and the Common Market countries was as much a defiance of America as a rebuff to Britain.

The French had been on the 'right side' at Yorktown, but they never had, or tried to have, the special relationship with America that Britain had so long cultivated. The French felt that they belonged wholly to Europe and that the Americans were people of another continent. When de Gaulle spoke of Europe as extending from the Atlantic to the Urals, he meant exactly what he said, and it was in accordance with the normal French outlook, for the French have been much less ready than Germans and Poles to accept the idea that the Russians are really Asiatics.* For de Gaulle, the ideal organisation of Europe would be the unification under French hegemony that was so nearly achieved by Napoleon; but, as this had been recognised to be unobtainable since Waterloo, the second best would be a European balance of power such as existed between 1815 and 1870, with France one of the main elements in the balance. The upsetting of the balance by Germany had twice

* The Urals are not, of course, a real boundary but only a convenient geographer's line to distinguish the bunch of peninsulas that is Europe from the great land mass of Asia. Nevertheless, the Soviet Union remains primarily a European power in the geographical sense, with its capital half-way between the Urals and the Baltic.

required the military intervention of the United States in Europe, and the excessive might of Russia since 1945 had rendered necessary an American strategic presence on the Elbe. But the French did not see this as meaning that Western Europe must be swallowed up within an American-controlled NATO. If Western Europe were properly integrated, they argued, it could provide by itself an equipoise to Russia, with American power in reserve to be invoked only in the last resort.

Most observers took the view that de Gaulle's project, if indeed it represented the real aims of French policy, was too ambitious and indeed beyond the economic capacity of France to pursue. France could not attain a strategic nuclear capacity that would enable it to stand up to Russia on equal terms as a guardian of Europe. De Gaulle's policy carried with it a risk of isolating France and of weakening Western Europe. Even if France, after withdrawing from NATO—as de Gaulle formally announced his decision to do on February 21, 1966—were to participate as an ally in the defence of Western Europe in an emergency, the lack of concerted pre-conflict planning, and the absence of installations on French territory that American forces could immediately use for the reinforcement of West Germany, would make it extremely difficult for effective resistance to be offered to a westward advance of Russian and other Warsaw Pact forces. The speed of initial movement possible in modern war renders it futile for allied nations to start co-ordinating their strategy after war has actually broken out. Even as long ago as 1914, the British Expeditionary Force was only of value in France because the logistics of its deployment had been worked out in Anglo-French military staff conversations some ten years previously. De Gaulle has nursed resentment against the NATO system of planning and command because it has seemed to him to vest too much authority in America as the strongest single power in the organisation. But, unless he can agree with his allies on some alternative method of peace-time strategic co-ordination, he may make continental Western Europe virtually indefensible against an attack by conventional forces—and this can hardly be in the interests of France.

Moreover, the recklessness with which the French President has rocked the NATO boat for political ends is all the more dangerous in view of the levity of the current British attitude towards European security. While British attention has been devoted to the problem of mixed nuclear forces (which is a political question and strategically irrelevant since there is already more than enough nuclear power in the Atlantic alliance) and to exercises of power 'east of Suez', Britain's reduced military manpower is quite inadequate to maintain its Army of the Rhine in a state of efficient preparedness or to reinforce it substantially in a crisis. The decline of Western military manpower, furthermore, is now to be accentuated by the withdrawal of American units for service in Vietnam.

Apart from these disagreements arising between France and the United States over the organisation of the NATO alliance, their conflicts since 1945 have mainly been on colonial issues. The French were far more reluctant than the British after the Second World War to liquidate their empire. They fought two large-scale wars—one in Indochina and the other in Algeria—to preserve it. In relation both to Indochina and Algeria, the behaviour of the United States was the cause of great resentment in France, and there developed a fixed idea in Paris that the American government was always ready to propitiate Afro-Asians at the expense of France. But this, as the French discovered, was a game at which two could play. Having been pushed out of Indochina in 1954, the French could feel that they no longer had anything to lose in the area. The Americans, on the other hand, by taking responsibility for the preservation of the anti-Communist régime in South Vietnam, had put themselves in the position of a colonial power, even though, formally, their presence there was at the request of an independent sovereign state. In this area, therefore, the French were able, by the early 1960s, to take advantage of local anti-imperialist sentiments. From the time of de Gaulle's return to power in 1958, France became the advocate of the neutralisation of south-east Asia.

It is difficult to see in this policy anything more than a will to upset the American apple-cart and settle accounts with Washington for the help it gave the Vietminh in 1945 and Ngo Dinh Diem in 1954, at the expense of the French. President de Gaulle can hardly believe that neutralisation could be genuine if it were the outcome of an American defeat, or that international guarantees of such a solution would have any force if American power were to be removed from south-east Asia. Neutralisation under these circumstances could only be a formula to cover a transition towards the establishment of Communist rule over the whole of Vietnam and elsewhere on the south-east Asian mainland. But de Gaulle does not view the spread of Communism in Asia, where there is no longer a French presence, as a threat to France. Rather than see the United States victorious where France has failed, he prefers to join with Russia and China in pressing for the withdrawal of American forces. At the time of writing, Vietnam is the most acute issue between the great powers, and the anti-American alignment of France on this question has put a most formidable strain on the Franco-American alliance: a strain made all the more severe by de Gaulle's decision to withdraw all French forces from NATO.

De Gaulle's rebellion against American leadership of the Western power bloc is, nevertheless, intended to stop short of a final dissolution of the bond of alliance with the United States. He believes that American protection for Western Europe is ultimately not a matter of reward for deferential French behaviour, but of American unwillingness to see the whole economic and strategic potential of Europe fall under the supremacy of Moscow. He therefore calculates that he can make a thorough nuisance of himself without causing Washington, in exasperation, to throw him to the Russian bear. The reasoning is fundamentally valid, yet it is a dangerous game to play, for an alliance cannot function properly when such strains are placed on it. A sudden crisis in Europe might find it too greatly disarrayed for the performance of its essential political and strategic tasks.

The rebellion of Mao Tse-tung against Moscow has a close analogy with that of de Gaulle against Washington. China, like France, believes its interests have been disregarded and its aims flouted by the senior partner. Russia's courting of India at the expense of China resembles America's courting of Arabs and Vietnamese at the expense of France; and America's unwillingness to help France to become a nuclear power has found a parallel in Russia's unwillingness to do likewise for China. However, there are important differences between the two cases. The Sino-Soviet dispute, given the character of Communism, inevitably developed into an ideological controversy. No such altercation over political theory has taken place between Paris and Washington; the French have not claimed to be better democrats than the Americans. But even more striking is the contrast between the attitudes of the two senior partners. The Americans have been irritated by French intransigence, but not to the extent of taking punitive measures against their recalcitrant ally, as the Russians have tried to do against China. This difference in the attitudes of the United States and the Soviet Union to the problem of dissidence in their respective alliances reflects the different potential of the two dissenters. The Americans have regarded France, perhaps too readily, as a 'has been', and the French have been concerned to show that they are not so powerless after all. Yet there are clear limits to the possibilities of French revival; nobody thinks there can be another Napoleon. But China, though still weak, inspires fear of what it may become; to what dimensions will the dragon grow? Undoubtedly, Moscow's willingness to aid in the industrialisation and military development of China was tempered from the start by caution lest China's progress should go too fast and too far. In the course of the polemics between Peking and Moscow, the Chinese have shown that they are well aware of the existence of such a motive in Russian behaviour. They have, however, in spite of the unhelpfulness of their major ally, taken the first steps towards making themselves a power of the first rank; and though they still have far to go, their vast manpower and material resources assure them a future of development on a grand scale.

The embittered polemics of the Sino-Soviet dispute and the deep personal antagonism between Khrushchev and Mao Tse-tung—the personalities have been less antipathetic since Khrushchev's fall, though the clash of policies has continued—have certainly strained the Communist alliance, and it is doubted in some quarters if it can be said to exist any longer. But it has not been destroyed by China's revolt, any more than the Western alliance has been destroyed by de Gaulle's intransigence. Just as America still cannot afford to see Western Europe pass into the Russian orbit, so the Soviet Union cannot afford to see a collapse of the Communist régime in China. The downfall of the existing Communist leadership in China would be more likely to be followed by a military dictatorship that would turn to America for aid and support than by the installation of comrades more amenable to direction from Moscow. The Sino-Soviet alliance, like the Franco-American, has been loosened, but not finally broken.

Indeed, in the current phase of international relations, the loosening of alliances has been less serious on the side of the Communists than on that of the West. Vietnam has tended to bring Russia and China together again in spite of Chinese doubts about Russia's firmness of purpose. The two Communist powers are agreed, at any rate, that the

United States is an aggressor against the people of Vietnam, and must be eliminated from that country's affairs; whereas the aims of the United States in Vietnam are flatly opposed by France, and receive from Britain only an uneasy official support which is repudiated by a strong group in the Labour government's own party and by a powerful section of the national press. At the time of writing, the Vietcong have produced greater dissensions in the Western camp than between Moscow and Peking.

16

THE CRATER'S EDGE

THE FIRST ATOMIC BOMB had an explosive force of 20,000 tons of TNT. Today, the total explosive potential of the world's nuclear weapons is estimated at well over 50,000 million tons. The central problem of our time is to get rid of this terrible store of destructive power, for if it is not eliminated in time, it will almost certainly sooner or later be used.

Confidence that men will never fight with these weapons, even though they possess them, depends on a very high estimate of human rationality. But if men are so rational that enlightened self-interest will be sufficient to prevent them from using arms of such monstrous destructive power, why is their rationality unequal to the task of agreeing to dismantle nuclear weapons and set up an international system of inspection to see that it is done? Of the test-ban treaty initialled on July 25, 1963, *The Times* commented in an editorial: 'Genuine disarmament, to which the treaty looks hopefully forward, requires a system of inspection, verification and control that no party can evade. A partial test ban calls a halt where inspection and verification are unnecessary, for all but underground tests have been readily detectable for years.'

Certainly, even a ban on nuclear tests other than those carried out under ground is better than nothing, but the significant fact is that the exception was made because Russia would not accept any serious scheme of inspection for earth tremors that could not be identified without it. Thus, no progress was made towards an inspected nuclear disarmament. Although it is true that, as the British Foreign Secretary at the time claimed, the test-ban treaty was 'the first agreement of any substance which the West has been able to make with the Russians since the Austrian Treaty of 1955', it hardly justified that mood of optimism about future Soviet-Western relations which began to spread after its conclusion. This mood was largely the outcome of a special kind of wishful thinking that sought to compensate for the frustration over real nuclear disarmament by the hope that the two super-powers would come to such a sincere understanding with one another that their armouries would no longer be a danger. But a more serious derivation from this mood was a reasoned interpretation of Soviet policy as having been fundamentally modified during the last few years. Among British specialists on Soviet affairs, Edward Crankshaw has been the most firm advocate of this view. In July 1963, he wrote: 'Fifteen years ago the Western world deployed itself to meet a very real menace. This was the menace of Russia under Stalin, but it was called, confusingly, the Communist challenge. When Stalin died in 1953, that menace died with him—but it has taken ten years for that fact to be brought home to us.'[1]

Such a view, at any rate, holds that there *was* a menace from Russia under Stalin. But even this is denied by those who argue that the Cold War had no ground in Soviet policy, but only in the folly or knavery of the Truman administration.[2] However, the difference between the two interpretations is merely a question of past history, for by the Crankshaw thesis, the 'Russian menace'—even if it did once exist—exists no longer, and Western policies that assume it still does are anachronistic. With the death of Stalin, it is argued, Russia 'lost the will and the strength to conduct itself imperially'. What, then, can the Cold War now be about and what reason can there be for alliances to assure a security that is not endangered?

In order to attempt an answer to this question, it is first of all necessary to draw up some sort of balance sheet of the Cold War. Who, in fact, has been winning it or has there been simply a stalemate? It may be held that, since none of the East European satellites of Russia has been liberated, since the Communist régime in China has not been overthrown, and since the majority of the nations of the world prefer to be unaligned in the struggle of the two great blocs, the policies of the West, or more particularly of the United States, since 1947 have suffered defeat. But if the record is judged by the standard of 'containment', the outstanding fact is that the main forward moves of Communist power have been repelled. The blockade of Berlin in 1948–49 was broken; the attempt to get Berlin in 1962 by the supplementary threat of missiles in Cuba was likewise thwarted. The Greek Communists failed to take over Greece, and Russian threats to Turkey were discontinued after the Truman Doctrine was proclaimed. The Korean

War had its setbacks, but the conquest of South Korea was prevented; in Vietnam, Communism won the north, but has so far been foiled in its hope of taking the south as well; the Communist insurrections in the Philippines, Indonesia, Malaya, Burma and central India from 1947 onwards were all failures. Whatever may be thought of the wisdom of America's China policy since 1950, it has in fact stopped the Chinese Communists from taking Formosa or even Matsu and Quemoy. Indeed, since the Geneva Conference of 1954 confirmed the Vietminh in control of North Vietnam, Communism has not been able to achieve a single important territorial gain with the one exception of Cuba, and even that was a revolution which was not originally made under overt Communist leadership, but was taken over from within after its initial success.

If the purpose of the Cold War from the Western point of view was to bar the military-political expansion of Russia and China, and frustrate new Communist seizures of power, the policy must be reckoned on the evidence of results up to now to have been very successful in accomplishing its task. More cannot be expected of a purely defensive political combination than that it should have beaten off a number of serious assaults delivered against it. Containment has been an essentially defensive policy; a more aggressive note was indeed sounded in America in the Republican Party campaign slogans of 1952 and in some of the speeches of John Foster Dulles, but it was never translated into real policy decisions. The Western powers combined, in so far as they did so, to oppose an expansion of revolutionary Communism in conjunction with the military power of the Soviet Union, which had been left unchecked in Europe and the Far East by the strategic elimination of Germany and Japan. So effective has been the opposition, so stable over a period the new balance of power, that it can now plausibly be claimed that opposition has ceased to be necessary. If this is so, the problem for Western statesmen is to be sure that the dismantling of the fortifications does not revive the danger they were built to meet.

It must first of all be kept in mind—in view of the thesis of the exclusive responsibility of Stalin for Soviet truculence after the defeat of Nazi Germany—that the most serious international crisis since 1945, the one which came nearest to starting a Third World War, occurred nine years after the death of Stalin and cannot be attributed to his action. Despite the supposed radical change in Soviet policies since 1953, Khrushchev tried as hard as Stalin did to get control of West Berlin, and his attempt to attain his end by blackmailing the United States with nuclear missiles in Cuba was in the circumstances more of a challenge to war than Stalin's blockade. In both cases, war was averted when Russia backed down, but a comparison of them provides no ground for contrasting an aggressive, imperial Stalin with a pacific and prudent Khrushchev.

On the other hand, there has certainly been a change in the CPSU's formulation of Marxist-Leninist theory since Stalin's death. This was marked by doctrinal innovations at the Twentieth and succeeding congresses of the Party, and was expressed in an important official publication, *The Fundamentals of Marxism-Leninism*, printed in 1959 and designed to supersede works of the Stalin era which had previously been in use as Communist textbooks both within and outside the Soviet Union. The reformulation of Communist doctrine was a response to three basic conditions of the period after Stalin's death. There was, first of all, the rapid growth in the potency of nuclear weapons, which, despite Russia's possession of such weapons, rendered war a much more alarming prospect for theorists of Communism than it had been when it meant fighting with conventional armaments only. There was, secondly, the stabilisation of the Western world and the absence of any prospect of a Communist seizure of power in any Western country. As against these two factors that checked the spread of Communism and rendered provocative policies more hazardous than ever before, there was to be set, as a third condition for policy-making, the high rate of growth attained by Soviet industry after the Second World War. In this situation, the traditional Marxist dogma that the replacement of capitalism by socialism was historically in-evitable could be presented in a somewhat less cataclysmic way than had been customary. It could be predicted that, with a period of peace, Russia and other Communist bloc countries would soon outstrip the capitalist world in economic production, and that this would make their social system at once so powerful and so attractive to the peoples of the world that the capitalist order would disintegrate without the risk of a nuclear war, and even, in Western countries at least, without violent revolutions. Such an easy and almost painless accomplishment of the great social transformation prophesied by Marx and Lenin was an idea not without charm for the generation of Russians who remembered the privations of the industrial effort under Stalin and the slaughter and devastation of the war against Germany. To enjoy years of peace with a steadily rising standard of living, to be followed at the end by the automatic triumph of the good cause, was a conception more welcome, even to many party cadres, than the dark and bloodstained way ahead that the older version of the doctrine had indicated. It was also a conception much more presentable to socialist and radical liberal circles of the Western world; by means of it a new amiable image of Communism could be projected to replace the unpopular visage of the Stalin era.

It would be a great mistake to regard this new teaching as mere humbug designed to put the West off guard. The new ideas have been propounded in publications intended for Communists themselves and have been bitterly attacked by the Chinese, so that it must be recognised that there is a reality of intention in the revision of the doctrine. But the alluring picture of the 'inevitability of gradualness' bringing about a sort of euthanasia of capitalism requires some qualification. We are still dealing with Marxist-Leninists, and a little attention to the nuances of the new doctrine shows that the ideal is not so much an avoidance of the use of force, as the possession of a force so overwhelming that the enemy will not try to resist. It has been explained in Russia that 'the peaceful path of revolution' means that the bourgeoisie in a given country may prefer to yield power peacefully to the proletariat, i.e. to the Communist Party, because the relation of power on the international scale will become increasingly favourable to the proletariat. In other words, an outside intervention of irresistible power will be available to tip the scales whenever a Communist party is ready to take over, and non-Communists will recognise opposition to be hopeless. That this is the real significance of the 'peaceful path' was confirmed by Khrushchev when, in a speech to the Twentieth Congress, he cited Poland and Czechoslovakia as examples of transition without civil war. But the transfer of power to the Polish Communists was 'peaceful' only because Russian troops were occupying Poland in such overwhelming force that resistance was impossible. In Czechoslovakia, there was no Russian army of occupation at the time of the coup of February 1948, but the failure of President Benes to call on the Czech army—which would almost certainly have followed him—to act in defence of the constitution against the armed demonstrators and Communist-infiltrated police of Prague was due to a plain threat of Soviet military intervention if civil war were to be the outcome of his action. For Communist future plans, the Czech model is clearly to be preferred, for it does not require an actual occupation by Russian or other Communist troops, but only a threat of intervention, with any counterintervention from outside being deterred by the decisively superior military strength of the Communist bloc.

Communists naturally expect such a preponderance in military strength to be a consequence of the all-round economic superiority they hope to have after a period of one or two decades. As Khrushchev declared in addressing the Twenty-first Congress of the CPSU in 1959:

> When all the socialist countries together will be producing more than half the world's industrial output, the international situation will change radically. . . . The new balance of forces will be so evident that even the most die-hard imperialists will clearly see the futility of any attempt to unleash war against the socialist camp. Relying on the might of the socialist camp the peace-loving nations will then be able to compel the militant circles of imperialism to abandon plans for a new world war. [3]

Translating the jargon of Communist speech-making into plain English, this means that the Communist bloc will become so strong that the West will no longer dare to fight for such positions as West Berlin or to counter Soviet assistance for revolutions in particular countries. The world will thus be transformed little by little, until the bourgeoisie has everywhere surrendered, without risk of a major war. Meanwhile, it will be prudent to pursue relatively 'soft' policies, to avoid tensions that might lead to a nuclear war while the imperialists are still powerful, and to keep the peace while the Soviet Union goes ahead overtaking and outstripping the West in economic production. On the international plane this means a diplomacy of détente and propaganda for 'relaxation of tension' and disarmament à la russe. For individual Communist parties outside the bloc, it means popular fronts, manœuvres for combination with non-Communist leftwing parties, and programmes which will put neutralism and anti-war slogans before more narrowly Communist objectives. It will be enough if the Communists during the interim period can dissolve the Western alliances and perhaps even bring about measures of uninspected disarmament; they can await their day of total power when the might of the Soviet Union has duly matured.

From the point of view of those who have no desire for Communist rule, it can be argued that a Soviet policy of postponing the struggle with the West should be in any case a cause for satisfaction, since it will give the world a respite from the threat of nuclear war, and there is no good ground for supposing that the Soviet Union will in the outcome be successful in obtaining that decisive economic and strategic lead over the West that the theory requires. If the Soviet Union fails to win the economic and strategic race in the manner predicted, yet affords further rises in standards of living to the Soviet people and bureaucracy, it can be expected that there will be a further 'embourgeoisement' in Russian life and a further decline in revolutionary conviction, rendering serious clashes between Russia and the West less and less likely. The optimists foresee a decade of continual thawing and softening in Russia, with steady progress towards political democracy and freedom broadening down from precedent to precedent. If the Communists are convinced that the world will soon go their way without war, liberal idealists are equally convinced that the world will soon go *their* way no less peacefully.

A political observer, called on to estimate the probable trends of world history in the next twenty years, might well come to the conclusion that the development of strong pressures for political liberty within the Soviet Union is much more probable than Communist-led revolutions in Western Europe or North America. But it is just in this probability that the danger to the peace of the world principally lies. If the Khrushchevite dream were ever to come true, and the Soviet Union by the sheer superiority of its economic system were to become irresistibly powerful, this might be a depressing prospect for those who value freedom, but at least the world would be spared a general war, since nobody would dare to oppose the new order. But if in a world in which no state was irresistibly powerful, the Communist Party of the Soviet Union were to embark on an adventurous foreign policy in order to stave off threats to its domestic monopoly of power, a Third World War fought with nuclear weapons could be the result. The world is more in danger of war from the breakdown of Communism than from its triumphal forward march: from its instability than from its certainty of the future.

The Khrushchevite theory assumes that the CPSU will have no difficulty in preserving its political monopoly in the Soviet Union throughout the period needed for the attainment of a clear economic lead over the West. But no such assumption is justified, for the reforms carried out by Khrushchev and his successors have not resolved the contradictions of the régime. They have merely eased its dilemma for the time being. Communist rule is a dictatorship dedicated to an idea; apart from the idea it cannot have the legitimacy which belongs either to a hereditary monarchy or to a genuinely elective democratic government. The Communist title to govern is inseparable from the ideology. Without it, the party—and this means primarily the apparatchiks, the professional organisers and propagandists of the party—cannot justify its retention of an exclusive, total and permanent control over society. The monopoly of political power is both demanded by the theory and defended by the collective vested interest of the corps of party functionaries who exercise it. This is the fundamental character of the régime and nothing that has been done in the way of destalinisation has altered it. On the contrary, Khrushchev reasserted the primacy of the party and its functionaries where Malenkov attempted to make the state bureaucracy independent of them. All kinds of developments are possible in Russia, but the one thing that can be predicted with certainty is that the party will resist by all means any political changes that would destroy its monopoly of power and allow a real opposition to emerge. If the time comes when there is a serious pressure from the Russian people for genuine democratic liberties, when there is an extensive agitation for something more than a curbing of police terror or permission to publish a story about one of Stalin's forced labour camps, then the party will no longer be able to afford the gestures of indulgent toleration which fill liberal optimists in the West with such glowing hopes of complete democratisation. It will begin to fight to retain the absolute power over the state which it can at present take for granted. This fight will necessarily in part take the form of internal repression, but it cannot be expected to stop there. The party will also invoke the threat from the external enemy, re-emphasise the machinations of imperialism against both the cause of socialism and the security of the Soviet land, and convict domestic rebels as traitorous agents of foreign powers. For the policies of international détente, of peaceful coexistence and reduced tension, which may seem advantageous for the current period on the assumption that the régime remains free from internal trouble, would become highly dangerous if the CPSU were to be faced at home with a growing demand for political democracy. If imperialism is no longer a threat, there can no longer be a patriotic appeal to the Russian people to rally round the party in defence of the homeland; if the West is no longer hostile and evil, then there can be no harm in being receptive to its influence; if the non-Communist world is not simply an abode of snakes and scorpions, then its ideas may not perhaps be so poisonous after all. International détente for a prolonged period may be quite genuinely intended as a policy by the existing Soviet leadership, but it is likely, if pursued for any length of time, to produce just those political consequences within the Soviet Union that must lead to its reversal.

That Khrushchev himself was not unaware of the dilemma in which his foreign policy involved him was indicated by a speech he made to the Central Committee of the CPSU on June 21, 1963, in which he said:

> Hatred of class enemies is necessary, because it is not possible to become a good fighter for your people or for Communism if one does not know how to hate enemies. Yes, comrades, a harsh class struggle is now in progress throughout the world. Enemies are attacking our Marxist-Leninist ideology and are attempting to corrupt the spirit and consciousness of the people.

These words were spoken, not to delegates of a foreign Communist party coming to the Soviet Union from a country groaning under the yoke of landlords and capitalists, but to members of the second highest party organ in a country that had been under Communist rule for forty-five years: a country where private property in the means of production had long since been abolished, and where propertied classes therefore no longer existed. It can hardly be maintained that the hatred to which Soviet Communists were exhorted by their leader was to be directed merely against those illegal speculators who were making profits by providing Soviet citizens with the commodities they were unable to obtain from the economic enterprises of the state. The hatred clearly was meant to be international in its scope. Russians, even though themselves exempt from the oppression of the bourgeoisie, must join in the hatred appropriate to the class struggle 'now in progress throughout the world'. But why did Khrushchev try to stir up this hatred in

Russian hearts at the same time that he preached to the Chinese the virtues of peaceful coexistence? The answer to this question is that he could not do otherwise. He desired to avoid war with the West, but he could not allow hatred to die, because if genuine peace and goodwill were to prevail in the world, Communist parties would lose their raison d'être. Of course, the Communists can, and do, justify the simultaneous preaching of peace and incitement to hatred by claiming that peaceful coexistence between states does not involve ideological coexistence. But can even peace between states be preserved for long on a basis of hatred deliberately cultivated by those who are simultaneously talking about the need to spare mankind the horrors of war?

The détente diplomacy of Khrushchev and his successors holds out no prospect of the kind of international co-operation to which Western liberals aspire. The minimum condition for a peaceful coexistence that is to be something more than an armed truce is that conflicts of interest arising among the most powerful sovereign states shall not be aggravated by a permanent will on one side to bring about the destruction of the other, even if this destruction is to be deferred for a period of time. The famous words of Khrushchev, 'We will bury you!' cannot, unfortunately, be dismissed as mere idle chatter; they represent the basic attitude of the rulers of one of the two most powerful states on earth.

The outlook for mankind in the years ahead would thus be a sombre one if the only guarantees of peace were to be a resolve of the Soviet Union not to try again to disturb the status quo and a willingness of the United States to tolerate fresh Cubas. Whatever may be the immediate intentions of governments—or of personalities for the time being in control of governments—they can be altered by tides of circumstance that cannot be foreseen, and there can be no ultimate stability in relations between armed sovereign states that are deeply antagonistic to one another, even if they desire to avoid war. This is not in itself a new situation. It is the old 'international anarchy' that has always been with us. What is new is the frightfulness of the weapons which are now in the hands of organised human societies divided by such deep conflicts. Nobody can doubt that a Third World War would be infinitely more dreadful and destructive than the two which we have already experienced in this century. But this knowledge provides no assurance that it will not take place.

Is there any action that men can take to reduce the danger that affords a reasonable prospect of success? Something can, no doubt, be achieved by diplomacy directed towards settlement of particular issues; it may be possible to lighten the atmosphere for a while by agreements of limited scope, like the test-ban treaty of 1963. But this sort of détente will not affect the underlying antagonism, and it can even be a cause of disaster in so far as it nourishes the belief that nuclear war can be indefinitely averted even though nuclear armaments remain. The real problem is how to rid the world of nuclear armaments. But this is something that cannot be expected to emerge from governmental disarmament conferences, where every proposal will sooner or later come to grief on the stubborn refusal of the Soviet Union to accept an adequate system of international inspection. There is only one possible way ahead past this obstacle, and that is through a political offensive designed to carry the argument directly into the Communist camp. If the Western powers are serious in the desire for nuclear disarmament, if they are aware that it is the supreme issue transcending every other in importance, then by concentrating all their means of publicity on the demand for inspection they would have some prospect of imposing it. The first premise for any such campaign would have to be the conviction that the abolition of nuclear arms is universally desired by the peoples of the world, and not least by those under Communist rule, so that no political appeal can be stronger than that of a determined effort to bring it about. The second premise would be that the case for an international inspection, applicable to all countries alike, is irresistible if properly and persistently made, and that the Russians really cannot argue that it is espionage if foreign inspectors search for hidden atomic plants or stores in the Soviet Union, but not espionage if they do the same in the United States. If the Soviet Union continued to reject the principle of unrestricted inspection, the resources of modern broadcasting are now, in fact, so superior to 'jamming' techniques that the Western case could be presented directly to the peoples of the Communist world on a question that is one of life and death for all mankind. In such a concentrated appeal to the peoples of Communist and uncommitted countries, it would be essential not to attack Communism as such, but to confine the offensive to the one issue of disarmament inspection, and in emphasising that there can be no valid reason for refusing inspection unless a government has something to hide, to avoid suggesting that a Communist régime is inherently uninspectable. For the issue is not whether states are capitalist or socialist, nor even whether they are democratically or dictatorially governed. In relation to the most important question which confronts humanity, there are only two significant categories of nations: those which are willing to submit to unrestricted verification of a disarmament treaty and those which are not.

There are, nevertheless, quite apart from the inertia and timidity that obstruct any bold initiative in politics, two reasons why such a campaign as that outlined above might be opposed within the Western democracies themselves. There is, in the first place, the vested interest of defence planners in nuclear weapons as compensation for an inferiority in conventional forces on the ground in continental Europe. If nuclear arms were to be abolished, the countries of Western Europe would need to augment their conventional forces in order to provide a strength matching that of the Warsaw Pact countries. In Britain, for example, this would involve a restoration of national military service, which it has been the traditional privilege of the British people to dispense with. But if it is worth while making a supreme effort to get rid of nuclear armaments—and nothing else is so much worth while— then responsible statesmen must be ready to face whatever adjustments in national or alliance defence measures may be involved—at any rate until a general reduction of conventional armaments can be agreed on.

The second, and even more formidable, objection to a political offensive on the issue of inspection would be likely to come from quarters which pin their hopes of peace on a détente in East–West relations and regard any form of pressure on the Soviet Union, even if only a struggle of verbal argument, as an intensification of the Cold War. The Soviet government would, of course, do its best to represent a direct appeal to its own people as a hostile act undoing all the work already done for the lessening of international tension; the initial effect would certainly be to heighten tensions and provoke the most vituperative counterattacks from Moscow. How much easier to avoid the issue and rely on prudence and goodwill to keep the peace between nuclear powers, allaying our fears with the sight of Foreign Ministers smiling in front of cameras. Surely if we continue on the path of détente, we can even have as many non-aggression pacts as those which Stalin violated in 1939! The mirage is bound to attract many. If it dominates Western public opinion, nothing can be done to challenge the Soviet Union over disarmament inspection. It will only be possible to remind those who are so much comforted by Communist zeal for an ending of the Cold War that the smile they see on a Soviet leader's face can change overnight to a frown, but that the megaton bombs which they do not see will remain unchanged until they are either dismantled or fired.

It will also be objected, no doubt, that the abolition of nuclear armaments would not in itself abolish war, and that, as the know-how of nuclear weapons would remain in the countries that had previously possessed them, these countries could start making them again if they were to go to war. But there would still be a vast difference between starting a war with thousands of nuclear bombs and resuming production of nuclear weapons in the course of a war fought at the outset conventionally. The belligerents would begin by being subject to the nuclear disarmament inspectorate, and in order to manufacture nuclear weapons they would have to obstruct or drive out the inspectors. The first of the belligerents to do so would brand itself as the treaty-breaker while justifying its enemy in following suit immediately. While such a development could not be ruled out in an international conflict subsequent to nuclear disarmament, it does not appear to be a danger sufficient to nullify the value of such disarmament as an objective of policy.

It may be that the objective cannot in any case be achieved, that the Soviet government, despite all the West can do to mobilise the public opinion of the world and carry the argument through the Iron Curtain, will remain unmoved. Yet it is worth trying, because it is the only form of action that holds out any prospect of success at all. If it fails, or if it is not tried, the odds are against the prevention of nuclear war in the coming period of human history. It is all very well to talk of 'living with the bomb', but mankind cannot live with the bomb. As long as the great nuclear armouries exist, they are part of the system of international power politics. If they are not dismantled in time, the day will come when the game of threat and counterthreat will be played once too often, and then it will happen: the day when the world

> Will rock in the shock of the mad machines
> And the house will come down.

I7

THE PRESENT AND THE FUTURE

THE YEAR 1965 saw the twentieth anniversaries of the death of Hitler and of the surrenders of Germany and Japan that ended the Second World War. The close of that year is therefore a suitable time for stocktaking and for an effort to estimate the broad significance of what has happened in the world over the last two decades. The outstanding historical fact of this epoch in international relations has been the Cold War: the conflict, not developing into general armed struggle but more than once coming near to it, between the Soviet Union and the three major powers of North America and Western Europe. The great question at this time is whether the trend of events is towards a relaxation and dwindling of the Cold War, or whether it remains unresolved and threatens new tensions and crises in the near future.

As has been noted in Chapter 16, the belief is now widespread in America, and even more so in Britain, that the Cold War as we knew it in the days of Stalin is already over, that there has been a real and lasting détente, and that the prospect of war between the principal powers has become so remote that it can virtually be ignored. It is admitted that the Third World has produced new and very intractable international problems, but it is held that the Soviet commitment to the doctrine of peaceful coexistence renders it extremely unlikely that local disturbances in Asia, Africa or Latin America can threaten strife between the Soviet Union and the West. On the other hand, there are, as we have seen, strong reasons for expecting renewals of Soviet policies hostile to the West if the Communist régime in the Soviet Union feels itself in the future threatened by domestic discontent; and, as long as Communist China holds to a more militant form of Marxist-Leninist ideology, the Soviet leadership will be under pressure to demonstrate, in rebuttal of Chinese accusations, that its zeal for revolutionary causes is beyond reproach. In these political factors there is the danger of a return to Cold War conditions, especially if the Western nations, misled by a false sense of security, relax their precautions and dissipate their political cohesion by quarrels among themselves.

Occasions for serious conflict between the Western and Communist worlds during the next decade are most likely to arise from the commotions of the Third World: the zone of former colonial and semicolonial countries in Asia, Africa and Latin America. It is in these areas, rather than in the lands of advanced industrial economy and established political democracy, that those who have a vested ideological interest in revolutionary upheaval can now see their brightest prospects. It is in the Third World that violent uprisings may be expected to occur in the coming years, whether or not they get help from Russia and China.

Whether or not to assist revolutions is a merely theoretical question as long as there are no revolutions to assist. In the old days of the Comintern, there was plenty of revolutionary talk but very little successful revolutionary action, because the world consisted in the main of stable capitalist states and of strongly controlled colonial empires. What has now opened the way for a new epoch of revolutions is the disappearance of the colonial system and the creation in its stead of vast zones of weakness, confusion and instability. The actual achievement of sovereign independence, in most cases without armed insurrection, has not meant an end but rather a beginning of violent troubles for the new countries, especially in Africa. Several of the new states have achieved internal cohesion only by the adoption of aggressive and interventionist foreign policies. These troubles might not threaten peace on a world scale if the zones of post-colonial upheaval could be kept insulated from the rivalries of the great powers. This, of course, is what the Afro-Asians themselves seek. They declare their non-alignment in the Cold War and their indifference to the conflict between Communism and the West. But they cannot in practice remain outside this conflict because of their dependence on aid from the Western or the Communist powers for their economic development, and still more for their military capabilities. Ideally, the great powers might agree among themselves to keep out of these turmoils, but recent experience suggests that such agreements, even if reached, will be no more effective in holding the ring than was 'non-intervention' in the Spanish Civil War from 1936 to 1939.

The Present and the Future

The men of the Kremlin might lack zeal for interventions in the struggles of the Third World were it not for the great factor that makes for the revival of the original world-revolutionary impetus of Leninism: the competitive revolutionary appeal of Peking. A party dedicated to the idea of a universal transformation of human society becomes vulnerable to attack by zealots when it begins to go in for moderation and adaptation to the existing order of things. When Stalin, in the circumstances of the 1930s, switched the Communist party line to the League of Nations and to Popular Fronts, he was denounced by Trotsky for betraying the revolution. His answer was to arrest the Trotskyites (or ex-Trotskyites) in Russia and induce them by suitable methods to confess in court that they were agents of foreign powers whose only purpose was to restore capitalism in Russia. Having thus discredited Trostkyism, Stalin completed his refutation by having Trotsky himself assassinated. But Khrushchev and his successors have not been able to bring Mao Tse-tung into a court to confess that he has been all the time working for the CIA; nor has it been a practical proposition to have him assassinated. The Soviet leaders of the post-Stalin era cannot silence the Chinese criticism of them as revisionists. They have had to cope with it partly by polemics, but partly also by trying to compete with the Chinese in those parts of the world where the propaganda of Chinese militancy makes the strongest appeal. They must seek to avoid the defection of Asian and African Communist parties and radical nationalists to the Chinese camp by showing that Moscow is a more effective champion against imperialism than Peking. This inevitably leads them into active support of anti-Western political movements and revolutions, even though the causes of these are far removed in character from the proletarian revolutions of Marxist theory. In the words of a discerning analyst of Chinese policy in Africa:

> Step by step Peking has come to count on the colonial revolutions, first for weakening the imperialist enemy by an ubiquitous war of attrition, then for disturbing any attempt at a Russo-American dialogue by a series of crises, and finally for proving its superior revolutionary zeal in the factional struggle for control of the world Communist movement. . . . [In the Chinese Communist view] the working classes of the advanced industrial nations are reduced to the role of mere auxiliaries of the liberation struggle of the coloured

races; the historic mission that Marx assigned to what Arnold Toynbee has called the 'internal proletariat' of Western civilization has been transferred by Mao to Toynbee's 'external proletariat'. Such a transfer goes far beyond Lenin; in fact, it reverses the roles envisaged by Lenin when he first conceived the alliance between the industrial workers and the colonial peoples—for Lenin never doubted that the colonial peoples would be the auxiliaries of the workers. But the persistent failure of the industrial proletariat of the advanced nations to seize power under the Communist banner on one side, and the Communist victory in underdeveloped China and the revolutionary ferment among colonial peoples on the other, have brought about a situation in which the would-be follower of Lenin has to choose between his belief in the Marxian proletariat and his unconditional devotion to revolutionary struggle.¹

The contemporary world has indeed put asunder the two things that Marx joined together: the industrial proletariat and the violent social revolution it was destined to carry out. Today the unheeding American worker drives to work in his car while the authentic fighting revolutionary emerges from the forests of the Congo wearing a monkeyskin hood. Many a Russian is no doubt better pleased with the former than with the latter. But can the heirs of Lenin fail to help the revolution of the dead Lumumba, especially when they have named in his memory a university for African students in Moscow? Can they forsake entirely the cause of those who are actually killing imperialists when the Chinese are on the watch to charge them with revisionism if they do? The answer is that they cannot.

It may, nevertheless, be held that all this does not matter very much on a world scale because the conflicts thus arising can be kept localised. If the Soviet Union supports Indonesia in waging war on Britain as protector of Malaysia, or the Congolese 'lions' in murdering American missionaries in the Congo, this need not, it is argued, spoil the détente between Moscow and the Western powers, much less create the danger of a major war. Sarawak and Stanleyville are far away; the peace of the world is not really threatened as long as there is no crisis in Berlin. Unfortunately for this view of world affairs, any serious conflict between the Soviet Union and the West arising over issues in Asia, Africa or Latin America is likely to reopen the wounds of Europe, and any war between the Soviet Union and the West would have to be fought primarily in Europe. There is no good reason for believing that clashes between Soviet and Western policies over the Third World can permanently be kept separate from the main area of their confrontation. If Soviet backing for revolutions and 'wars of national liberation' in the Third World clashes to a serious degree with the interests of the Western powers, such conflicts must affect Soviet–Western relations in Europe as well as elsewhere. Moreover, if they become acute, they must call in question the sincerity of the Soviet Union's professed desire for peaceful coexistence. On New Year's Day 1965, after the Russian denunciation in the United Nations of the American-Belgian action in rescuing hostages threatened by death—and many of the hostages were indeed killed—by Lumumbist rebels in the Congo, *The Times* commented in a leading article on 'the contradiction between Russia's prating about the peaceful settlement of disputes while encouraging rebellions all over the place', and declared that 'the real answer to the Russians is that if they send arms to inflame disputes in the Third World, then they cannot expect their talk of peaceful coexistence between the main world camps to be convincing'.

In the opening days of 1966, a 'Three Continents Conference' was held in Havana, with the Cuban Communist Party acting as hosts. The conference set up a permanent organisation to represent the 'peoples' of Asia, Africa and Latin America. An organisation of a similar type, the Asian and African Peoples' Solidarity Organisation (AAPSO), had already existed for several years with its headquarters in Cairo, and the Havana conference extended this to Latin America. It was, nevertheless, a highly provocative gathering for, although these 'peoples' solidarity organisations' do not formally represent governments and most of their delegates are sent by obscure 'national liberation fronts' in their countries of origin, the delegations of the Soviet Union and China are, in fact, appointed by the ruling Communist parties of those states and are the exponents of official policies. The Three Continents Conference set up a special bureau, on which both Russia and China were represented, to give 'moral, political and material aid' to 'national liberation movements', especially to those engaged in 'armed struggle'. Three subcommittees were created to support such struggles in Vietnam, Oman and Zimbabwe (Rhodesia). The Soviet delegates appear to have been carried away by the atmosphere of militant revolutionary enthusiasm prevailing at the conference; at any rate, they gave no indication at this meeting, held close to the shores of the United States, that they regarded material aid for armed revolts in Western spheres of influence as in any way incompatible with peaceful co-existence.

The only reassuring feature of the demonstration was the absence, in spite of a stirring speech by Castro calling on the Latin American peoples to engage in 'a most violent struggle' against the United States, of any subcommittee that would have pledged the Soviet Union to give material support to a revolutionary uprising in a Latin American country. A declaration of support for the Vietcong was inevitable since the Soviet Union was already involved in Vietnam. Open backing for armed actions in Arabia and Rhodesia entailed no risk, since the power challenged in these areas was not the United States but Britain; and it is considered in Moscow that the tail of the enfeebled British lion can be twisted with impunity. But to have assured similar support to the rebel guerrilla forces in Venezuela would have been decidedly imprudent. Ever since 1962, the Russian leaders have recognised that their intervention in the affairs of the Western hemisphere can be a very dangerous proceeding. That they should be to this extent so cautious was a sign that they wished to set a limit to their participation in the new international revolutionary militancy. Nevertheless, the fact remained that representatives of the CPSU played a part at Havana hardly to be distinguished from that of the Soviet delegates to the Comintern in the days of Lenin and Stalin.

The United Nations cannot be expected in the foreseeable future to be capable of maintaining the peace of the world by more than moral suasion, much less to perform the functions of a world government. Peace continues to depend ultimately on diplomacy between sovereign states, and this diplomacy requires for its effective conduct a certain minimum of agreement on what is permissible in international politics. It is difficult enough to keep the peace even if there are recognised rules of the game; it becomes almost impossible if there are to be no rules at all. It is unlikely that peace can long be preserved in our time if it is considered normal for states to promote and assist armed revolts in the territories of their neighbours. If it is claimed on principle that one state has the right in the name of 'liberation' to direct armed subversion against another state, there is no longer any clear line between peace and war, and there can be no logical objection to counter-intervention save on the basis that one side is ideologically right and the other ideologically wrong: a line of argument that the other side naturally does not accept. Peaceful coexistence in a system of sovereign states must imply that each side recognises the established spheres of influence of the other and does not encroach on them either by direct military aggression or by promoting and assisting armed revolts. Unfortunately, the Soviet Union—in spite of all its talk about peaceful coexistence—has never made up its mind definitely to renounce armed subversion as an instrument of policy; and the need to outbid the Chinese Communists has caused it to revert, as at the Havana conference, to the language and methods of the Comintern. It is a situation full of danger for the future, since there are today so many possibilities of violent upheaval in various parts of the Third World. It is from rival interventions and counter-interventions in domestic revolts and civil wars, rather than from direct attacks of nations against one another, that the peace of the world is likely to be threatened in the coming years.

The twentieth century, with its two world wars and many revolutions, has so far been an age of violence on an unprecedented scale. It is now a question whether mankind can avoid a third world war before the century is out. If such a war were to be fought with the full use of strategic nuclear weapons, it would be a catastrophe of vast extent and the casualties would be numbered in hundreds of millions. It would not be the end of mankind, or even of civilisation, for modern science and technology have spread too widely to be extinguished by anything short of the total extermination of the human race. But the unprecedented slaughter would certainly tend to remove all inhibitions on the use of power. The most drastic coercion and discipline would be needed to restore even a minimum of order in the world, and an age of grim violence and tyranny would follow the fiery cataclysm. If one power were to gain a decisive victory in such a war, it would establish a world empire, forcing all other states to disarm and dictating to them with overwhelming prepotence. It would be more probable, however, than an all-out nuclear war would end indecisively. The great nuclear powers would be left with their territories devastated, but still in possession of quantities of nuclear weapons; with these they would terrorise non-nuclear countries and compel them to supply the food-stuffs and commodities for which the ruined belligerents would no longer be able to pay.

There is also the possibility of a major war in which conventional arms and tactical nuclear weapons would be used, but in which escalation would be stopped short of the full use of strategic nuclear weapons. Such a war would be far less devastating (except in certain localities) than an all-out nuclear struggle. It would very probably be confined geographically within certain limits, for it can be assumed that a super-power would use its full nuclear capacity rather than submit to outright conquest by an enemy. Thus, although super-powers took part in a war of this kind, operations would be virtually limited to intermediate zones: a large-scale repetition of the war in Korea. As has been pointed out in Chapter 6, a nuclear stalemate combined with a marked inferiority of one side in conventional forces offers to the conventionally stronger side a temptation to attack, in the belief that the final escalation of the war to full nuclear exchanges can be prevented. In such a conflict, the Soviet Union might over-run Western Europe without bringing on a mortal nuclear duel with America. The outcome could be a division of the world that, internationally—though not necessarily as regards internal politics—would fulfil George Orwell's prediction in *Nineteen Eighty-Four* of a threefold partition of the globe into Oceania, Eurasia and Eastasia. This would be a disunited and warlike world, but there would still be a balance of power within it.

If a general war can be averted, mankind can look forward to an age of economic progress in which standards of living could everywhere be raised, and conditions of famine at any rate could be eliminated by the end of the century. The problems set by the great increase of the world population are not beyond the capacity of science to solve, partly through birth-control and partly through increases of food production. Modern technology provides the possibility of assuring in a peaceful world a tolerable minimum of decent conditions of living for everyone born by the year 2000.

It goes without saying that such a goal is still remote from us, but it would be a worthy ideal for humanity to pursue during the last third of the twentieth century. The task is political no less than economic because of the great disparity of wealth that separates the Third World from the

West and increasingly also from the Soviet Union. This disparity breeds resentments and hatreds which economic aid from the richer countries does not necessarily assuage and may even aggravate. All current signs indicate much violence and turmoil in the 'under-developed' parts of the world during the years that lie ahead. The countries of more advanced economy will suffer from such troubles, but these need not involve the world in general war as long as the great powers can refrain from exploiting them in rivalry with one another to the point of irreconcilable involvements. It is just possible to hope, though with no great confidence, that in what remains of our century the countries of advanced economy, both Capitalist and Communist, may find a peaceful outlet for their energies in a co-operative economic reconstruction of the world.

CHRONOLOGY OF SIGNIFICANT EVENTS IN GREAT POWER RELATIONS FROM 1945 TO 1965

1945

February	Yalta Conference
April–May	San Francisco Conference; creation of United Nations
April 30	Suicide of Adolf Hitler
July	Potsdam Conference
August 6	Atomic bomb dropped on Hiroshima
August 14	Surrender of Japan

1946

January	General Marshall sent to China by President Truman to mediate between Kuomintang and Communists
March 5	Churchill's speech at Fulton, Missouri, denouncing the policies of the Soviet Union
July–December	Peace treaties negotiated with European wartime allies of Germany
December 30	Baruch Plan for international control of atomic energy adopted by United Nations Atomic Energy Committee

1947

March 12	Proclamation of Truman Doctrine in President's Message to Congress
June 5	Speech by Marshall, US Secretary of State, inaugurates the Marshall Plan for the economic rehabilitation of Europe
August 15	Transfer of power by Britain to India and Pakistan

1948

February	Communists seize power in Czechoslovakia
March	Beginning of Russian blockade of West Berlin
May 15	Termination of British mandate in Palestine and beginning of Israeli-Arab war
June	Rift between Soviet and Yugoslav Communist parties
November	Harry S. Truman elected President of the United States

1949

January	Armistice in Israeli-Arab war
April 4	Conclusion of North Atlantic Alliance Treaty
May 12	End of Berlin blockade

1949
August   First Soviet atomic bomb tested
October 1   Proclamation of Chinese People's Republic in Peking

1950
February 14   Conclusion of alliance treaty between Chinese People's
                Republic and Soviet Union
June 25   Invasion of South Korea by North Koreans
June 28   United Nations Security Council authorises military
                action to aid South Korea
August 17   Independence of Indonesia
November   Intervention by Communist China in the Korean War

1951
April 11   President Truman dismisses General MacArthur
July 8   Beginnings of negotiations for an armistice in Korea
October   Churchill returns to office as British Prime Minister

1952
March   Peking Radio launches 'germ-warfare' propaganda cam-
                paign against the United States
November   General Eisenhower elected President of the United
                States

1953
March 5   Death of Stalin
June 17   Rising against Communist régime in East Germany
July 27   Armistice ends war in Korea

1954
April 29   Agreement between India and Chinese People's Republic
                over Tibet
April–July   Geneva Conference on Korea and Indochina. Armistice
                between French Union and Vietminh commands on
                July ends war in Indochina
September 8   South-East Asia Alliance Treaty (SEATO) concluded at
                Manila
November 1   Algerian War of Independence begins

1955
April   Bandung Conference of Afro-Asian states. Churchill
                replaced by Eden as British Prime Minister
May 14   Warsaw Alliance Treaty (Warsaw Pact) concluded among
                European Communist states
July   Summit Conference in Paris of United States, Britain,
                France and Soviet Union

Chronology

1956

February	Twentieth Congress of Soviet Communist party; Khrushchev in secret session denounces Stalin
April	Khrushchev and Bulganin visit Britain
July 26	Egypt nationalises the Suez Canal
October 23	Revolutionary uprising in Hungary
October 29	Israel attacks Egyptian *fedayeen* camps, Israeli-Egyptian war begins. Britain and France issue ultimatum
November	Simultaneous Hungarian and Suez crises. Soviet Union crushes Budapest rising. Anglo-French troops land at Suez, withdraw and are replaced by UN detachment

1957

January 5	Eisenhower Doctrine on Middle East proclaimed in President's Address to Congress
March 25	Treaty of Rome concluded, founding of European Common Market
June–July	Soviet leadership crisis. 'Anti-party' group defeated by Khrushchev
October 4	Launching of first Soviet 'sputnik'
November	Fortieth anniversary celebrations of Bolshevik Revolution in Moscow. Declaration of the Twelve Governing Communist Parties

1958

May	General de Gaulle returns to power in France
July	Hashemite régime in Iraq overturned by General Kassem's *coup d'état*. Disturbances in Lebanon and Jordan lead, respectively, to American and British intervention
August	Bombardment of Offshore Islands by Chinese Communists. Threat of American intervention
November	Khrushchev delivers ultimatum to Western powers over West Berlin

1959

March	Khrushchev becomes Soviet Prime Minister. Flight of Dalai Lama from Tibet to India
May–July	Foreign Ministers' Conference on Berlin
August 25	Indian-Chinese border class at Longju
September 12	Soviet rocket hits the moon
September 15	Khrushchev begins visit to United States
September 25–27	Camp David talks between Eisenhower and Khrushchev

1960

May 1	American U-2 aircraft shot down at Sverdlovsk
May 14–17	Abortive Summit conference in Paris
June	Conflict between Russian and Chinese Communist delegates at Bucharest conference
July	Independence of former Belgian Congo. Mutiny of Force Publique and intervention of United Nations
November	John F. Kennedy elected President of United States
November–December	Conference of eighty-one Communist parties in Moscow tries to resolve the Sino-Soviet dispute

1961

January	Beginning of Vietcong insurgence in South Vietnam
June	Khrushchev and Kennedy meet in Vienna
August 13	Communist régime in East Germany builds Berlin Wall
October	Twenty-Second Congress of Soviet Communist party. Excommunication of Albania

1962

July 5	Independence of Algeria
October	Cuba Missile Crisis. China-India Border war in Assam

1963

January	Breakdown of negotiations for entry of Britain into European Common Market
May 25	Organisation of African Unity (OAU) founded at Addis Abba
July	Nuclear Test-Ban Treaty concluded by United States, Soviet Union and Britain. Indonesia affirms 'confrontation' policy against Malaysia
November 22	Assassination of President Kennedy. Succession of Lyndon B. Johnson
December	Outbreak of fighting between Greek and Turkish Cypriots. British 'police role' followed by UN peace-keeping forces

1964

June	Withdrawal of UN forces from the Congo
September	International crisis over airlift rescue of hostages held by rebels in Stanleyville
October	Khrushchev deposed from Soviet leadership by the Central Committee of the Soviet Communist party. Labour victory in British General Election; Harold Wilson becomes Prime Minister
November	Johnson elected President of the United States

1965

July   United States decides on increased commitment of combat forces in Vietnam

September–   War between India and Pakistan over Kashmir
December

September 30   Abortive Communist *coup* in Indonesia. Severe repression of Indonesian Communist party

November 11   Unilateral declaration of Independence by Smith régime in Rhodesia

REFERENCES

Publication details of books referred to here are given in the 'Works Cited' section of the Bibliography, p. 303 *et seq.*

CHAPTER 1: THE ENDING OF THE SECOND WORLD WAR

1. W. S. Churchill, *The Second World War*, Vol. VI, p. 352.
2. *Ibid.*, p. 498.
3. Joseph Davies, *Mission to Moscow*, p. 327.
4. R. Sherwood, *Roosevelt and Hopkins: An Intimate History*, Vol. II, p. 790.
5. *Ibid.*, Vol. II, p. 780.
6. *Ibid.*, Vol. II, p. 709.
7. J. Ciechanowski, *Defeat in Victory*, p. 410.
8. Report by Joseph Davies, quoted by H. Feis in *Churchill, Roosevelt, Stalin*, p. 651.
9. Sir Llewelyn Woodward, *British Foreign Policy in the Second World War*, p. 523.

CHAPTER 2: THE ROOTS OF THE NEW SOVIET EMPIRE

1. Walter Millis, ed., *The Forrestal Diaries: The Inner History of the Cold War*, p. 134.
2. *Ibid.*, p. 119
3. Quoted by Hans Kohn in *Panslavism: Its History and Ideology*, p. 115.
4. *Österreich-Ungarns Aussenpolitik von der Bosnischen Krise bis zum Kriegsausbruch*, VIII, 10835.
5. M. Bakunin, *Appeal of a Russian Patriot to the Slav Peoples*, 1848.
6. Bakunin, letter to Herzen from Irkutsk, 1860.
7. J. Michelet, "Légendes démocratiques du Nord", *La Sorcière*, p. 226.
8. J. V. Stalin, *Problems of Leninism*, p. 69.
9. V. I. Lenin, *Selected Works*, Vol. III, p. 33.

CHAPTER 3: THE RISE OF AMERICAN INFLUENCE IN EUROPE

1. *New York Times*, June 24, 1941.
2. *Forrestal Diaries*, pp. 48–51.
3. William D. Leahy, *I Was There*, p. 351.
4. Harry S. Truman, *Year of Decisions*, p. 363.
5. J. F. Byrnes, *Speaking Frankly*, p. 277.
6. Paul Winterton, *Inquest on an Ally*, p. 112.
7. Lucius D. Clay, *Decision in Germany*, p. 353.

CHAPTER 4: FAR EASTERN TRANSFORMATION

1. Memorandum by Byrnes, *United States Relations with China*, p. 606.
2. Herbert Feis, *The China Tangle*, p. 384.
3. *United States Relations with China*, p. 939.
4. *Hearings on Military Situation in the Far East*, Eighty-Second Congress (1951), p. 555.
5. Acheson to House of Representatives Foreign Affairs Committee, March 20, 1947.
6. General William L. Roberts, at press conference on July 14, 1950.
7. Robert Payne, *The Marshall Story*, p. 11.

CHAPTER 5: THE KOREAN WAR

1. Quoted by David Rees, *Korea: The Limited War*, p. 245.
2. *Ibid.*, p. 196.
3. Dr Charles Mayo, to United Nations Assembly Political Committee, October 26, 1953; quoted in *State Department Bulletin*, November 9, 1953.

CHAPTER 6: THE NEW WEAPONRY

1. Report by Brigadier-General Thomas F. Farrell, quoted by Herbert Feis, *Between War and Peace*, p. 168.
2. *Ibid.*, p. 169.
3. Truman, *Year of Decisions*, p. 416.
4. Herbert Feis, *Japan Subdued*, p. 73.

CHAPTER 7: DECOLONISATION IN SOUTH AND SOUTH-EAST ASIA

1. Guy Wint, *The British in Asia*, p. 145.
2. Remark made in a private conversation.

CHAPTER 8: DECOLONISATION IN THE MIDDLE EAST AND AFRICA

1. Musa Alami, *The Lesson of Palestine*; quoted in Jon and David Kimche, *Both Sides of the Hill*, p. 14.
2. J. and D. Kimche, *op. cit.*, p. 273.

CHAPTER 9: THE UNITED AND DISUNITED NATIONS

1. Stephen M. Schwebel, *The Secretary-General of the United Nations*, p. 105.

CHAPTER 10: DISARMAMENT

1. Samir Ahmed, "The Role of the Neutrals in the Geneva Negotiations", in *Disarmament and Arms Control*, Vol. I.

References

CHAPTER 11: THE SOVIET UNION AFTER STALIN

1. Bertram D. Wolfe, *Khrushchev and Stalin's Ghost*, p. 248.

CHAPTER 12: MAO'S CHINA AND THE SINO-SOVIET SPLIT

1. See Stuart R. Schram, *The Political Thought of Mao Tse-tung*, p. 267.
2. Cited in David Floyd, *Mao Against Khrushchev*, pp. 262-3.
3. *Ibid.*, p. 265.
4. *The Sino-Soviet Dispute*, published by the *China Quarterly*, 1961, p. 93.
5. Floyd, *op. cit.*, p. 273.
6. Cf. Donald S. Zagoria, *The Sino-Soviet Conflict, 1956–1961*, p. 323.

CHAPTER 14: NEUTRALISM AND THE POWER BALANCE

1. *World Culture*, September 16, 1949; quoted in Gibilal Jain, *Panch-Sheela and After*, p. 8.

CHAPTER 15: THE LOOSENING OF THE ALLIANCES

1. John Biggs-Davidson, *The Uncertain Ally*, provides a good example of criticism of American policy from a rightwing Conservative point of view.

CHAPTER 16: THE CRATER'S EDGE

1. Edward Crankshaw, "The Shattered Monolith", *Observer*, July 28, 1963.
2. See, for example, M. D. Fleming, *The History and Origins of the Cold War*.
3. *The Sino-Soviet Dispute*, published by the *China Quarterly*, 1961, p. 56.

CHAPTER 17: THE PRESENT AND THE FUTURE

1. Richard Lowenthal, in Zbigniew K. Brzezinski (ed.), *Africa and the Communist World*, p. 202.

BIBLIOGRAPHY

1. SUGGESTED READING

There is a vast literature on events in world affairs since 1945, but in the nature of things these events are too recent for much to have been done in the way of attempts at a serious general history of the period. The following works, however, can be suggested to the reader for study of one or more of the main topics dealt with in this book.

The final phase of the Second World War is covered, on the British side, in the memoirs of Churchill (*The Second World War*: Vol. VI, *Triumph and Tragedy*) and of Eden (*The Eden Memoirs: The Reckoning*) and, on the American side, by Stettinius, *Roosevelt and the Russians*, by Stimson and Bundy, *On Active Service in Peace and War*, by Admiral Leahy, *I Was There* and by *The Forrestal Diaries*, edited by Walter Millis. Two excellent studies of the wartime relations of the Big Three—one American, the other British—are Herbert Feis, *Churchill, Roosevelt, Stalin* and H. McNeil, *America, Britain and Russia, 1941–46*. Revealing personal memoirs are not to be expected from the Russian side, but *Stalin's Correspondence with Churchill, Attlee, Roosevelt and Truman, 1941–45*, published in Moscow in 1957, gives a fairly full record of official communications. A Polish point of view on the arrangements made by the Big Three at Yalta, and on the attempt to set up a Polish 'Provisional Government of National Unity', is given in the memoirs of S. Mikolajczyk, *The Pattern of Soviet Domination*.

For the immediate postwar period in Europe, there is Herbert Feis, *Between War and Peace: the Potsdam Conference*, and valuable material is to be found in James Byrnes, *Speaking Frankly* and in the memoirs of President Truman, *Year of Decisions*, and *Years of Trial and Hope*. How the Cold War appeared to a former Moscow correspondent who had been an admirer of the Soviet régime, but eventually became one of its most unsparing critics, is recorded in *Inquest on an Ally* by Paul Winterton—still worth reading as a 'tour d'horizon' of 1947.

For the background of Stalin's empire, there is L. B. Schapiro, *The Origin of the Communist Autocracy*, and for the Russian messianic tradition before Communism there is the invaluable study by Hans Kohn, *Pan-Slavism: Its History and Ideology*. For the pre-Communist background in Eastern Europe, an excellent general survey is given in C. A. Macartney and A. W. Palmer, *Independent Eastern Europe*. The beginnings of the transformation in this region are well described in John A. Lukacs, *The Great Powers and Eastern Europe*, and in Robert Lee Wolff, *The Balkans in Our Time*. The best general account of Communism as a revolutionary force up to 1952, both inside and outside Russia, is to be found in Hugh Seton-Watson, *The Pattern of Communist Revolution*; it should be read in conjunction with Franz Borkenau's *European Communism*—the work of an ex-Communist which, although hardly a balanced account, was written from direct experience of Comintern politics. Stalin's *Problems of Leninism* gives the Soviet leader's own interpretation of the Communist faith. Merle Fainsod's *How Russia is Ruled* provides a well-informed survey of the Soviet political system at the time of Stalin's death.

For the Far East, Herbert Feis, *Japan Subdued* gives an account of the ending of the war in the Pacific, including the decision to use the atomic bomb against Japan. Aspects of the post-war period in Japan are well covered by Kazuo Kawai, *Japan's American Interlude*, G. C. Allen, *Japan's Economic Recovery* and R. P. Dore, *Land Reform in Japan*. The most comprehensive work on America's policy towards China in the immediate post-war period is Tang Tsou, *America's Failure in China, 1941–50*. For studies on the rival leaders in the Chinese Civil War, there are biographies of Chiang Kai-shek by S. I. Hsiung and by Emily Hahn, and of Mao Tse-tung by Siao-yu (dealing with the early life) and by Jerome Ch'en. Books which contribute to an understanding of China's Communist revolution are: O. Edmund Clubb, *Twentieth Century China*, Robert S. Elegant, *The Centre of the World* and Tibor Mende, *China and Her Shadow*. For the foreign policy of the People's Republic of China there are Werner Levi, *Modern China's Foreign Policy* and Francis Watson, *The Frontiers of China*, which deals with China's various territorial irredentist aspirations and what has been done to give effect to them. For the special model of armed revolution provided by Communist China, the best source is *Mao Tse-tung on Guerrilla Warfare*, translated with an introduction by Brigadier General Samuel B. Griffith. Mao's general ideas are well set forth in *The Political Thought of Mao Tse-tung*, translated and edited by Stuart R. Schram.

For South Asia, a full and generally fair-minded account of the transition from British rule in India is to be found in V. P. Menon, *The Transfer of Power in India*. There are two good biographies of Nehru: Frank Moraes, *Jawaharlal Nehru* and Michael Brecher, *Nehru: A Political Biography*. (Both of these, however, were written before his death and before his foreign policy had been seriously undermined by the conflict with China.) A useful short appraisal of Nehru's role in domestic and foreign affairs is given in Geoffrey Tyson, *Nehru: The Years of Power*. Richard Symonds, *The Making of Pakistan* and Percival Spear, *India, Pakistan and the West* give an account of the effects of partition in the Indian subcontinent. The most important general work on decolonisation in South-east Asia is Russell H. Fifield, *The Diplomacy of Southeast Asia, 1945–58*. Books on Vietnam are legion; to be recommended are Donald Lancaster, *The Emancipation of French Indo-China* and Bernard B. Fall, *The Two Vietnams*.

A far-ranging survey of changes in the Islamic world during the dozen

Bibliography

years after the end of the Second World War is provided in the symposium, *The Middle East in Transition*, edited by Walter Laqueur.

For the complex and mutable affairs of the African continent, perhaps the most comprehensive view is to be obtained from the revised edition (1965) of *Africa: A Handbook to the Continent*, edited by Colin Legum. A good history of the Korean War is David Rees, *Korea: The Limited War*. Also of outstanding value for an appreciation of the nature of the conflict are: Allen S. Whiting, *China Crosses the Yalu*, General Mark Clark, *From the Danube to the Yalu* and William Vatcher, *Panmunjon*. An account of the 'brain-washing' of United Nations' prisoners by the Communists is given by Eugene Kinkead in *Why They Collaborated* (the American edition is entitled *In Every War But One*); and a highly competent analysis of the 'germ warfare' propaganda campaign is available in John C. Clews, *Communist Propaganda Techniques*.

For the Khrushchev period in the Soviet Union, three valuable books are: George Paloczi-Horvath, *Khrushchev: The Road to Power*, Bertram D. Wolfe, *Khrushchev and Stalin's Ghost* and Mark Frankland, *Khrushchev*, which carries the story to the date of his removal from office. Khrushchev's own apologia for his policies is contained in a collection of his speeches published in 1960 under the title, *For Victory in Peaceful Competition with Capitalism*. On the rift between Russia and China, the most fully documented work is David Floyd, *Mao Against Khrushchev*; other books are: Donald S. Zagoria, *The Sino-Soviet Conflict, 1956–61*, Klaus Mehnert, *Peking and Moscow* and William E. Griffith, *The Sino-Soviet Rift*.

A retrospect on the Cold War from the vantage-point of 1964 is provided by the symposium, *The Cold War*, edited by Evan Luard. For those who wish to make sure of hearing both sides of the case, there is a vigorously presented pro-Communist version of the story in Denna F. Fleming's two-volume study, *The Cold War and Its Origins, 1917–61*.

Finally, on the basic question of peace and war in the Nuclear Age, there is now a considerable specialist literature, apart from much ill-informed popular writing. Two standard works are Henry A. Kissinger, *Nuclear Weapons and Foreign Policy* and Herman Khan, *On Thermonuclear War*. Views from the other side of the hill are summarised in Raymond L. Garthoff, *Soviet Military Policy: A Historical Analysis*; with this should be read a Russian military textbook edited by Marshal Sokolovsky and translated into English under the title *Military Strategy: Soviet Doctrine and Concepts*.

2. Works Cited in Text and in Reading List

Allen, George C., *Japan's Economic Recovery*, Oxford University Press, London and New York 1958

Biggs-Davidson, John, *The Uncertain Ally*, Johnson Publications, London 1957

Borkenau, Franz, *European Communism*, Faber, London 1953; Harper Bros., New York 1953

Brecher, Michael, *Nehru: A Political Biography*, Oxford University Press, London and New York 1959

Brzezinski, Zbigniew K. (ed.), *Africa and the Communist World*, Stanford University Press, Stanford, Calif. 1963

Byrnes, James F., *Speaking Frankly*, Harper Bros., New York 1947

Ch'en, Jerome, *Mao and the Chinese Revolution*, Oxford University Press, London and New York 1965

Churchill, Sir Winston, *The Second World War*: Vol. VI, *Triumph and Tragedy*, Cassell, London 1952; Houghton Mifflin, New York 1953

Ciechanowski, J., *Defeat into Victory*, Doubleday, Garden City, N.Y. 1947

Clark, Mark, *From the Danube to the Yalu*, Harper Bros., New York, 1954; Harrap, London 1954

Clay, Lucius, *Decision in Germany*, Doubleday, New York 1950

Clews, John C., *Communist Propaganda Techniques*, Praeger, New York 1964; Methuen, London 1964

Clubb, O. Edmund, *Twentieth-Century China*, Columbia University Press, New York 1963

Davies, Joseph, *Mission to Moscow*, Simon and Schuster, New York 1941

Dore, R. P., *Land Reform in Japan*, Oxford University Press, London and New York 1959

Eden, Anthony (Earl of Avon), *The Eden Memoirs*: Vol. II, *The Reckoning*, Cassell, London 1965; Houghton Mifflin, New York 1965

Elegant, Robert S., *The Centre of the World*, Methuen, London 1963; Doubleday, New York 1964

Fainsod, Merle, *How Russia is Ruled*, Harvard University Press, Cambridge, Mass. 1953

Fall, Bernard B., *The Two Vietnams*, 2nd rev. edn, Praeger, New York 1966; Pall Mall, London 1966

Feis, Herbert, *The China Tangle*, Princeton University Press, Princeton, N.J. 1953

—— *Churchill, Roosevelt, Stalin: The War They Waged and the Peace They Fought*, Princeton University Press, Princeton, N.J. 1957

—— *Between War and Peace: The Potsdam Conference*, Princeton University Press, Princeton, N.J. 1960

—— *Japan Subdued*, Princeton University Press, Princeton, N.J. 1961

Fifield, Russell H., *The Diplomacy of Southeast Asia, 1945–58*, Harper Bros., New York 1958

Fleming, Denna F., *The Cold War and its Origins, 1917–60* (2 vols.), Doubleday, New York 1961

Floyd, David, *Mao Against Khrushchev*, Pall Mall, London 1964; Praeger, New York 1964

Frankland, Mark, *Khrushchev*, Penguin, Harmondsworth, M'sex, and Baltimore, Md. 1966

Bibliography

Garthoff, Raymond L., *Soviet Military Policy: A Historical Analysis*, Praeger, New York 1966; Faber, London 1966

Griffith, Samuel B. (ed. and trans.), *Mao Tse-tung on Guerrilla Warfare*, Praeger, New York 1961; Cassell, London 1962

Griffith, William E., *The Sino-Soviet Rift*, Allen and Unwin, London 1964; M.I.T. Press, Cambridge, Mass. 1964

Hahn, Emily, *Chiang Kai-shek*, Doubleday, New York 1955

Hsiun, S. I., *The Life of Chiang Kai-shek*, Peter Davies, London 1948

Kahn, Herman, *On Thermonuclear War*, Princeton University Press, Princeton, N.J. 1960

Kawai, Kazuo, *Japan's American Interlude*, University of Chicago Press, Chicago 1960

Khrushchev, Nikita S., *For Victory in Peaceful Competition with Capitalism*, Hutchinson, London 1960; Dutton, New York 1960

Kimche, Jon and David, *Both Sides of the Hill*, Secker and Warburg, London 1960; published in USA as *A Clash of Destinies: The Arab-Jewish War and the Founding of the State of Israel*, Praeger, New York 1960

Kinkead, Eugene, *Why They Collaborated*, Longmans, London 1960; pub. in USA as *In Every War But One*, Norton, New York 1959

Kissinger, Henry A., *Nuclear War and Foreign Policy*, Harper Bros., New York 1957

Kohn, Hans, *Pan-Slavism: Its History and Ideology*, University of Notre Dame Press, Notre Dame, Ind. 1953; rev. edn., Random House, New York 1960

Lancaster, Donald, *The Emancipation of French Indo-China*, Oxford University Press, London and New York 1961

Laqueur, Walter Z. (ed.), *The Middle East in Transition*, Routledge, London 1958; Praeger, New York 1958

Leahy, William D., *I Was There*, Gollancz, London 1950; Whittlesey House, New York 1956

Legum, Colin (ed.), *Africa: A Handbook to The Continent*, 2nd rev. edn, Blond, London 1965; Praeger, New York 1966

Levi, Werner, *Modern China's Foreign Policy*. University of Minnesota Press, Minneapolis 1953

Luard, Evan (ed.), *The Cold War*, Thames and Hudson, London 1964; Praeger, New York 1964

Lukacs, John A., *The Great Powers and Eastern Europe*, Regnery, Chicago 1954

McNeill, W. Hector, *America, Britain and Russia: Their Co-operation and Conflict*, Oxford University Press, London and New York 1953

Macartney, Carlile A. and Palmer, A. W., *Independent Eastern Europe: A History*, Macmillan, London 1962; St. Martin's Press, New York 1962

Mehnert, Klaus, *Peking and Moscow*, Putnam, New York 1963; Weidenfeld and Nicolson, London 1963

Mende, Tibor, *China and Her Shadow*, Thames and Hudson, London 1960; Coward McCann, New York 1962

Menon, V. P., *The Transfer of Power in India*, Longmans, London 1957; Princeton University Press, Princeton, N.J. 1957

Mikolajczyk, Stanislas, *The Pattern of Soviet Domination*, Sampson Low, London 1948; published in USA as *The Rape of Poland: Pattern of Soviet Aggression*, Whittlesey House, New York 1948

Millis, Walter (ed.), *The Forrestal Diaries*, Viking Press, New York 1951; Cassell, London 1951

Moraes, Frank, *Jawaharlal Nehru*, Macmillan, New York 1956

Paloczi-Horvath, George, *Khrushchev, the Road to Power*, Secker and Warburg, London 1960; published in USA as *Khrushchev: The Making of a Dictator*, Little, Brown, Boston 1960

Payne, Robert, *The Marshall Story*, Prentice-Hall, New York 1951

Rees, David, *Korea: The Limited War*, St. Martin's Press, New York 1964; Macmillan, London 1964

Schapiro, Leonard B., *The Origin of the Communist Autocracy*, Bell, London 1955; Harvard University Press, Cambridge, Mass. 1955; paperback edn, Praeger, New York and London 1965

Schram, Stuart R. (ed. and trans.), *The Political Thought of Mao Tse-tung*, Praeger, New York 1963; Pall Mall, London 1964

Schwebel, Stephen M., *The Secretary-General of the United Nations*, Harvard University Press, Cambridge, Mass. 1952

Sherwood, Robert E., *Roosevelt and Hopkins: An Intimate History*, rev. edn, Harper Bros., New York 1950

Seton Watson, Hugh, *The Pattern of Communist Revolution*, Methuen, London 1953

Siao-yu, *Mao Tse-tung and I Were Beggars*, Syracuse University Press, Syracuse, N.Y. 1959; Hutchinson, London 1961

Sokolovsky, V. D. (ed.), *Military Strategy: Soviet Doctrine and Concepts*, Praeger, New York 1963; Pall Mall, London 1963

Spear, Percival, *India, Pakistan and the West*, Oxford University Press, London and New York, 3rd edn 1958

Stalin, J. V., *Problems of Leninism*, Foreign Languages Publishing House, Moscow 1947

—— *Stalin's Correspondence with Churchill, Attlee, Roosevelt and Truman, 1941–45*, Foreign Languages Publishing House, Moscow 1957

Stettinius, Edward R., Jr., *Roosevelt and the Russians: The Yalta Conference*, Doubleday, New York 1949

Stimson, Henry L. and Bundy, McGeorge, *On Active Service in Peace and War*, Harper Bros., New York 1948

Symonds, Richard, *The Making of Pakistan*, Faber, London, 3rd edn 1951

Truman, Harry S., *Memoirs of Harry S. Truman*: Vol. I, *Years of Decisions*, Vol. II, *Years of Trial and Hope*, Doubleday, New York 1958; published in Britain as *Year of Decisions, 1945*, and *Years of Trial and*

Hope, 1946–53, Hodder and Stoughton, London 1954 and 1955

Tsou, Tang, *America's Failure in China, 1941–50,* University of Chicago Press, Chicago 1963

Tyson, Geoffrey, *Nehru: The Years of Power,* Pall Mall, London 1966; Praeger, New York 1966

Vatcher, William H., Jr, *Panmunjon,* Praeger, New York 1958

Watson, Francis, *The Frontiers of China,* Chatto and Windus, London 1966; Praeger, New York 1966

Whiting, Allen S., *China Crosses the Yalu,* Macmillan, New York 1960

Winterton, Paul, *Inquest on an Ally,* Cresset, London 1948

Wolfe, Bertam D., *Khrushchev and Stalin's Ghost,* Praeger, New York 1956; Atlantic Press, London 1957

Wolff, Robert L., *The Balkans in Our Time,* Harvard University Press, Cambridge, Mass. 1956

Zagoria, Donald S., *The Sino-Soviet Conflict, 1956–61,* Princeton University Press, Princeton, N.J. 1962

INDEX

309

Index

Communism: in China, 71–9, 84–97, 202ff., 242, 270; in Czechoslovakia, 60–1, 64–5; in Indonesia, 133, 270; in Italy, 63; in Japan, 68, 71, 253; in Korea, 79–97, 270; in Middle East, 143–4; Russian concepts and organisation, 32–3, 42–7, 179, 189, 199, 201, 243, 271–7; split in, 216–17; successful opposition to, 269–70

Constantine, Emperor, 35

Constantinople, 35–6, 38

'Containment', doctrine of, 52, 55, 69, 241, 269–70

Coty, René, 145

Crankshaw, Edward, 269

Crimean War, 18, 37

Croats, 35–6

Cuba, 85, 270, 285; missile crisis, 161, 217, 228–33, 269, 271

Cyprus, 159, 168–70

Cyrankiewicz, Jozef, 207

Czechoslovakia, 20, 35, 47, 64, 96, 181; Communist coup (1948), 60–1, 67, 272–3; supplies arms to Middle East, 137, 140

DAHOMEY, 148

Dairen, 73, 75

Dalai Lama, 240–1

Damascus, 136, 138, 142

Danilevsky, Nikolai Y., 36, 38

Danube, R., 36, 48

Dardanelles, 36, 55

Davies, Joseph, 25–6, 30, 52

Decree of Peace, 43

de Gaulle, Charles, 120, 135, 224, 255, 261–5; and Common Market, 262; colonial policy, 145, 148–9; plans nuclear force, 112, 263

Denikin, Gen. A. I., 41

Denmark, 18, 63

Diem, Ngo Dinh, 129–30, 264

Dienbienphu, 128

Disarmament, 172–83, 268–9; campaigns in Britain, 254, 259, 279; international inspection for, 278–80; UN Commission on, 180–1

Djakarta, 119, 127, 131, 133–4

Doctors' Plot, 189

Drummond, Sir Eric, 162–3

Dulles, John Foster, 94, 142, 144, 210, 212, 223–5, 270; 'massive retaliation' doctrine, 107, 238

Dutch East Indies, 117–20, 127, 131

EAST Germany, 36, 57, 61, 212, 220–9, 253; escapes from, 220, 229; peace treaty proposed, 221, 231–2; Soviet policy, 198–9; Volkspolizei, 64, 220

Ecuador, 85

Eden, Sir Anthony, 27, 139

Egypt, 55, 86, 135–47, 151–2, 154; non-alignment policy, 235, 246–9; Soviet aid for, 243, 246, 248; Suez crisis, q.v.; war with Israel, 141–2, 159, 164

Eilat, 141, 164

Eisenhower, Dwight D., 71, 96, 254, 259; Allied commander, 29; elected President, 94, 210; goes to Korea, 94; relations with Khrushchev, 213, 215, 223–7, 247

Eisenhower Doctrine, 142–3

Elbe, R., 18, 30, 48, 59, 64, 82, 97, 263

Engels, Friedrich, 202

Estonia, 27

Ethiopia (Abyssinia), 146–7, 157, 161, 167, 181

European Common Market, 258, 262

FARRELL, Thomas F., 98

Finland, 20, 44, 48, 234

Index